INTRODUCTION TO BUSINESS

5TH EDITION

INTRODUCTION TO BUSINESS

5TH EDITION

HAL B. PICKLE
St. Edward's University

ROYCE L. ABRAHAMSON
Southwest Texas State University

Scott, Foresman and Company   Glenview, Illinois

Dallas, Texas   Oakland, New Jersey   Palo Alto, California
Tucker, Georgia   London, England

Acknowledgments for table, photographs, and illustrations appear on p. A-32, following the Glossary, which is an extension of the copyright page. Permission to reprint additional tables, photographs, and illustrations is acknowledged within the text.

Library of Congress Cataloging in Publication Data
Pickle, Hal B.
  Introduction to business.

  Includes bibliographical references and index.
  1. Business. I. Abrahamson, Royce L. II. Title.
HF5351.P554
     1983   650
82–17072
ISBN 0-673-16571-X

To Lucy, Debra, Karen, Eric, Lance, Sherry, Kristine, and Rachel

Preface

Our main objective in writing this text has been to provide the reader with
the basic knowledge necessary for understanding the major aspects of the
American business system and their interrelationships. A second objective
has been to provide this information in as *informative* and *concise* and *interesting* a way as possible.

The Fifth Edition of *Introduction to Business* represents a very major
revision. Each of the 23 chapters has been thoroughly revised and updated. Approximately 40 percent of the special interest features, cases,
and business profiles are new. Notable new features are the learning goals
and the summaries for each chapter. In every instance, the most recent
statistical data have been included. The glossary has been revised to include definitions of all key terms used in the text. The career information
contained in the appendix has also been brought up to date.

In keeping with users' suggestions, some parts of the text have been
reorganized. The Fifth Edition is structured as follows:

Section One:	The Foundations and Responsibilities of Business
Section Two:	Management of the Business Firm
Section Three:	Human Factors in Management
Section Four:	The Marketing Environment
Section Five:	Financing the Business Firm
Section Six:	Quantitative Aids of Business
Section Seven:	International, Legal, and Government Environment

SUPPLEMENTS TO THE FIFTH EDITION

The supplement package for *Introduction to Business* has been updated
and made more comprehensive than ever before.

The Instructor's Manual, an omnibook of resources, contains:
- expanded lecture notes for each chapter;
- answers to the text discussion questions;

- answers to the Study Guide questions;
- supplementary cases for selected chapters, with questions and answers;
- suggested films and a directory of the films' distributors.

The **Study Guide** contains:
- reviews of the major concepts in each chapter;
- approximately 40 to 50 review questions per chapter, consisting of matching, true-false, and multiple choice;
- supplementary cases;
- readings—approximately 70 percent of the readings are new to this edition.

Test Bank. For the first time, the *Introduction to Business* package includes a Test Bank, consisting of more than 2,000 questions. They are printed on perforated paper so that individual questions may be pulled from the Test Bank and assembled in any order the instructor chooses. Answers are page-referenced. Included are:
- chapter-by-chapter test questions, about 1,600 in all;
- preprinted exams for each part in the book, about 350 questions in all;
- preprinted final exams, about 200 questions in all.

Approximately 25 types of **Sample Business Documents,** provided upon adoption, give the reader "hands-on" experience with a wide variety of common business documents.

Over 200 **Transparency Masters** are available with this edition.

HAL PICKLE
ROYCE ABRAHAMSON

Acknowledgments

Finally, and most importantly, acknowledgment and thanks should be given to those who have contributed ideas to this project. The following people have given us advice and guidance on the current and/or previous editions:

James Albanese	*Rio Hondo College*
Edmond Billingsley	*Butte College*
Richard Boyd	*Mount San Antonio College*
Harvey Bronstein	*Oakland Community College*
Clara Buitenbos	*Pan American University*
Carroll Burrell	*Sam Houston State University*
Bob Buss	*Saddleback Community College*
J. Michael Cicero	*Highline Community College*
William A. Clarey	*Bradley University*
John Dier	*Mount Hood Community College*
Michael Dougherty	*Milwaukee Area Technical College*
Chester Duckhorn	*Fresno City College*
Sam Dunbar	*Delgado College*
Richard E. Esslinger	*Fayetteville Technical Institute*
Kenneth Garrett	*Catawba Technical Institute*
Helen Gilbart	*St. Petersburg Junior College*
Tom Grissom	*Pima College*
Glenn G. Grothaus	*St. Louis Community College*
Nicholas D. Grunt	*Tarrant County Junior College*
Lou Hoekstra	*Grand Rapids Junior College*
Fred Hunter	*Cerritos College*
Brian O. James	*Merritt College*
Harry Jasinski	*Northern State College*
Fran Jones	*Cypress College*
Ken Kimble	*Sinclair Community College*
George Lindall	*General College, University of Minnesota*
Brad Lutz	*Hillsborough Community College*
Jimmy McKenzie	*Tarrant County Junior College*

Sheldon A. Mador — *Los Angeles Trade and Technical College*
Edward F. Marecki — *Delaware Technical and Community College*
John Martin — *Mount San Antonio College*
Joseph W. Matthews — *Community College of Philadelphia*
Richard Lee Miller — *University of Dayton*
James O'Donovan — *Auburn Community College*
James O'Grady — *St. Louis Community College*
W. A. Parrish — *Belleville Area College*
Bill Perry — *West Valley College*
Helen Prather — *Houston Community College*
Charles Prentiss — *Phoenix College*
Edward A. Prim — *Macomb County Community College*
James J. Quinn — *Camden County College*
Gene Schneider — *Austin Community College*
Kenneth Schock — *West Valley College*
Rick Shield — *Rio Hondo College*
Bill Stitt — *Arapahoe Community College*
Larry Talton — *Central Carolina Technical Institute*
Jim TaVoularis — *Community College of Allegheny County*
Raymond Tewell — *American River College*
Harry Thiewes — *Mankato State University*
James Weglin — *North Seattle Community College*
Richard White — *Asheville-Buncombe Technical Institute*
Martin Wise — *Harrisburg Area Community College*
Bennie Woods — *Burlington County College*
Ed Yost — *Franklin University*
Richard Zahn — *Catonsville Community College*

We would also like to thank our Scott, Foresman editors—Jim Sitlington, John Nolan, Charley Schaff, and Maryann Langen—for their help in the production of the book.

H.P.
R.A.

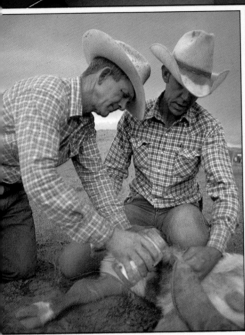

Contents

SECTION ONE
The Foundations and Responsibilities of Business

SECTION TWO
Management of the Business Firm

5 Formal and Informal Organizations 90

6 Production Management 112

CAREER OPPORTUNITIES:
Business Management and Supporting Fields 149

SECTION THREE
Human Factors in Management

8 Human Relations in Management 154

CAREER OPPORTUNITIES:

Human Resource Management and Labor Unions   226

SECTION FOUR
The Marketing Environment 229

SECTION FIVE:
Financing the Business Firm 307

17 Insurance and Risk 368

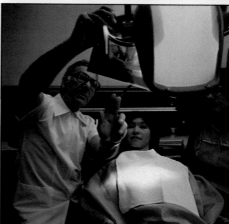

CAREER OPPORTUNITIES:
Banking, the Stock Market, and Insurance 390

SECTION SIX
Quantitative Aids of Business

18 Accounting Analysis and Budgeting 396

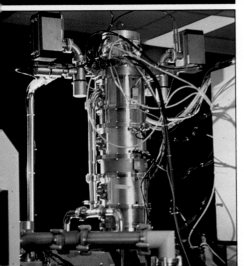

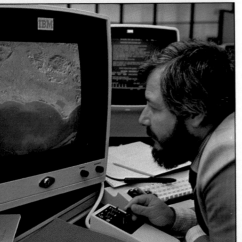

SECTION SEVEN

International, Legal, and Government Environment

CAREER OPPORTUNITIES:

Government Employment and the Legal Profession   525

APPENDIX A

Your First Job

APPENDIX B

Glossary

INDEX

The Foundations and Responsibilities of Business

SECTION ONE

1

The Economic System

LEARNING GOALS

After reading this chapter, you will understand:

1. That the ultimate goal of any economic system is production of economic goods and services to satisfy human wants and needs.

2. What the term *standard of living* means and how production and population rates affect the standards of living of different countries.

3. What the factors of production are and how a country can increase its production.

4. The real purpose of business and profit to society.

5. The comparison between privately owned businesses and government-owned businesses.

6. How individual freedom and ownership of the factors of production are related.

7. What some of the economic indicators are.

8. The differences between capitalist, communist, and socialist systems.

9. What is meant by pure competition, monopoly, monopolistic competition, and oligopoly.

KEY TERMS

Standard of living
Gross National Product
Land
Labor
Entrepreneur
Capital
Technology
Profit

Competition
Inflation
Recession
Stagflation
Centralization of
  authority
Economic indicators
Capitalism

Communism
Socialism
Pure competition
Monopoly
Monopolistic competition
Oligopoly
Genetic engineering

People all over the world would like to increase the production of goods and services to better satisfy their wants and needs. This is done by increasing the four factors of production: land, labor, capital, and technology. The economic system of each nation determines who owns these factors of production. Different economic systems have both strengths and weaknesses: the ultimate test of each system is determined by the overall effectiveness of the system in producing goods and services. In this chapter we will look at the factors of production and the advantages and disadvantages of different types of economic systems.

THE AMERICAN ECONOMIC SYSTEM

In the United States there are, and always have been, widely varying opinions as to how the output of the nation should be allocated. Expenditures for education, social programs, business investment, military, and environmental control are just a few of the areas of conflicting opinions. In one sense, it is nice that the pie is large enough to produce the problem of how to divide it.

The United States produces more goods and services than any other nation in the world (Exhibit 1–1). As a result of this output, we enjoy many benefits: work-saving appliances, rewarding leisure time, high levels of education, advanced medical services, and a reasonably comfortable way of life. This is not true in other parts of the world. In nations such as India and Nigeria, the majority of the population exists in extreme poverty, toiling long hours, living in primitive conditions, and dying from diseases that can be cured by simple medical techniques. For example, life expectancy in India is forty-seven years, and in Mali it is only thirty-five.

Why is the United States so blessed? A large part of the reason is the American economic system, which produces an abundant output of goods and services.

The choice between various economic systems is important to all nations in their attempts to increase production of goods and services. The final goal of any economic system is the production of goods and services that satisfy people. However, today conflicts exist between nations because of their different economic systems. Often, nations even attempt to force their economic systems on other nations. In addition, each country feels its economic system is the best and most efficient. But the real test of efficiency of any economic system is how well the system satisfies the wants and needs of the people; that test, in effect, is the **standard of living** of that nation.

RAISING THE STANDARD OF LIVING

Given the amount of resources available at a certain time, each nation produces only so many products and services for its people to use. Put in the most simple terms, the standard of living of a nation is the total of this production divided among the population, as shown in the following equation:

$$\text{STANDARD OF LIVING} = \frac{\text{Production}}{\text{Population}}$$

Of course, this equation ignores the quality of the production. For example, China for many years produced most of its steel in very small plants with simple equipment. As a result, the quality of the steel was very low, and products made from it were of poor quality. These products could not begin to match products made from steel produced in the United States, Germany, and Japan. In addition, items produced for people vary considerably in their value to the populations of different nations. A radio as a unit of production in an underdeveloped country could never be compared in value to a television produced in an industrial nation.

Basically, there are three possible methods of increasing a nation's standard of living, particularly in terms of food. One is for a nation to increase production while holding its population constant. A second is for a nation to reduce its population while production remains constant. Both methods are highly unlikely because birth decisions are basically determined individually. The only method that appears realistic is for a nation to increase production at a rate faster than its population increases. At the same time, to achieve needed results, a nation should attempt to slow down the rate of increase of its population by means of birth control education, which does not restrict personal freedom.

The total production of a nation is measured in terms of **Gross National Product** (GNP). Gross National Product is the total *market value* of all *final* goods and services produced by a nation during a *one-year period*. "Final goods and services" means only the end product is measured; for example, cotton sold to a textile mill would not be counted, but piece goods sold to consumers would be counted.

FACTORS OF PRODUCTION

Saying a nation should increase its production is easy; actually achieving such an increase is another matter. Each nation can produce, at maximum, a total of goods and services equal to the resources available at a specific time. The three factors of production (resources necessary for production) traditionally referred to by economists are land, labor, and capital. However, we will add a fourth—technology—because of its extreme importance in increasing production.

Food for the Future

Today, world population is over 4 billion, with more than 70 percent of the world's people living in underdeveloped nations. Experts estimate that almost 2 billion people currently exist at various levels of starvation. More than 3.5 million die each year from hunger or related diseases. The experts contend that a major crop failure in any of the world's major food-producing areas would create a massive food crisis.

After an estimated one to two million years of human existence, the world's population reached 1 billion in 1830. It took another hundred years to reach 2 billion, 30 years to reach 3 billion, and just 15 years to reach 4 billion. If current trends continue, it is estimated that the world's population will be over 6 billion by the year 2000. Food production is growing each year, but not at the rate necessary to feed 6 billion people by the turn of the century.

Some people feel the problem can be solved by the industrial nations helping the underdeveloped nations to develop their agricultural production and control their population. Others are not as optimistic. They point out that: (1) the cost of fertilizer has continually increased (petroleum is the major source of fertilizer); (2) fish harvesting from the world's oceans has been declining for several years; and (3) current environmental stress will accelerate due to increased world population and intensive farming.

It seems certain that agricultural products will become increasingly important in relations between nations in the future. For example, rising consumption, unfavorable climatic conditions, and the inefficiency of government-owned farms result each year in Russia's having to obtain huge amounts of grain from other countries. Political concessions have sometimes been part of the price Russia has paid.

Production of a nation can mean more than a particular standard of living; it may be a matter of survival for much of the population.

6

Land

In economic terms, **land** is not defined as a plot or section of ground. In the economic context, land represents any form of natural resources, such as bauxite ore, which is a natural resource (raw material) used in the production of aluminum.

Nations are not able to increase the physical wealth of their natural resources, but instead tend to deplete them over a period of time. Fortunately, technology (knowledge in science and industry) makes it possible for a nation to expand the use of raw materials in the following ways.

1. *Technology creates new techniques for discovering new sources of raw materials.* A current example of creating new techniques for discovering new sources of raw materials is the use of satellite pictures in locating mineral deposits, particularly oil.

2. *Technology makes recovery more efficient.* Some gold mines in the United States were abandoned years ago because the recovery techniques were more costly than the gold was worth. Today, improved machinery and recovery techniques, along with increased gold prices, have made reopening these mines profitable. The increase in the price of oil has also spurred the development of new techniques for recovering additional oil from old abandoned wells.

3. *Technology can turn waste products into useful natural resources.* For many years, people have used cotton for clothing, bedding, and a wide range of other products. Cottonseed, however, was considered waste and had no economic value until modern times. Today, cottonseed is valued almost as highly as cotton fiber. Manufacturers use cottonseed oil for the production of margarine, shortening, salad oil, cooking oil, soap stocks, floor covering, composition roofing, lubricants, and insulating materials. Farmers use cottonseed cake and meal for cattle, swine, and poultry feed, as well as in the manufacture of fertilizer and starch-free flour. Cottonseed hulls are used for cattle feed and chicken litter. The manufacture of explosives, cellulose acetate, rayon, plastics, ethyl cellulose, lacquers, sausage casings, and high-quality mattresses and paper all use cottonseed.

Exhibit 1–1

Gross national product of selected countries, in billions of dollars.

(SOURCE: Statistical Abstract of the United States, 1981.)

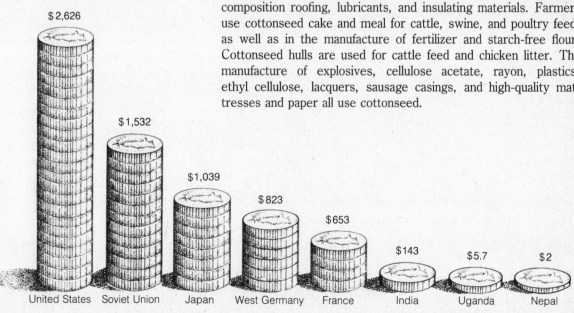

United States	Soviet Union	Japan	West Germany	France	India	Uganda	Nepal
$2,626	$1,532	$1,039	$823	$653	$143	$5.7	$2

4. *Technology develops processes that create raw materials that did not exist previously.* Bauxite ore had no value or use before the discovery of the process for making aluminum. Today, bauxite ore is a natural resource that is used extensively in the manufacture of aluminum. It is highly valued and is sought by all industrial nations.

5. *Technology creates substitutes for raw materials that are in short supply.* The United States does not have enough oil and natural gas and is rapidly using up what it does have: each year a greater part of what we use is imported from other nations. Paying for this imported oil is creating serious problems with the inflation rate and with the value of the dollar on the international market. As a result, both the government and private enterprise are pouring billions of dollars into research to develop alternate sources of energy for the future. Solar and nuclear power are two of the sources currently receiving the most attention. A number of other sources are also being researched: one scientist has developed a growing plant that can be processed to obtain oil.

Realistically, the only method available to significantly increase a nation's store of natural resources is technological advancement (Exhibit 1–2).

Labor

Labor, in the economic sense, is defined as any effort of people. However, many economists divide human effort into two parts: (1) production labor and (2) entrepreneurial and management labor.

Production Labor. This type of labor includes the actual production of goods, distribution activities, clerical tasks, professional services, and numerous other production-related works.

The most obvious method of increasing the labor supply is to increase the birthrate. This is not the most efficient method because an individual is not productive during childhood. The child, in effect, reduces the nation's standard of living, as shown in the standard-of-living formula. In reality, the only practical way to increase the labor resource is by increas-

Exhibit 1–2
Technology increases natural resources.

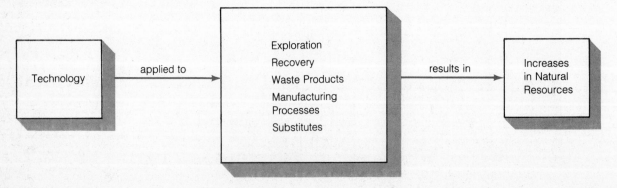

Technology → applied to → Exploration / Recovery / Waste Products / Manufacturing Processes / Substitutes → results in → Increases in Natural Resources

ing the productive output resulting from human efforts. Improved machinery and equipment and more efficient processes of production add to a worker's productivity.

Manufacturing robots, computers, and other types of electronic equipment are creating a virtual revolution in the production and distribution of products and services. They are rapidly replacing and multiplying human efforts.

Entrepreneurial and Management Labor. This type of human effort includes management and entrepreneurial activities. An **entrepreneur** is a person who creates a business for the profit.

Computers and electronic data-processing equipment and techniques have greatly increased the effectiveness of managers and entrepreneurs by providing extensive amounts of information in very short periods of time. The accuracy and quality of management and entrepreneur decisions and control have improved as a direct result of this new technology. These improved decisions have, in turn, made businesses much more efficient.

Capital

Capital is ordinarily defined as a financial concept, meaning money or investments; however, as a factor of production, it has an entirely different definition. Capital, in the economic sense, is any physical device that facilitates human efforts—tools, machinery, equipment, and other labor-saving devices. For example, the cotton farmer would use items of capital such as the tractor, the cotton picker, the fertilizer spreader, the chemical and insecticide sprayer, and the truck to haul the cotton to a collection point.

The only two ways to increase capital are (1) to have more machinery and equipment, and (2) to create more efficient machinery and equipment through technology. Improvements in capital equipment provide new uses for raw materials and increase production much more than just having more capital equipment. The production of bread is an example of the technological progress in capital equipment. Early methods of making bread used little more than pans, mixing bowls, spoons, and ovens. Today, assembly-line methods use equipment that includes giant ovens, conveyor belts, and mechanical mixing vats to improve the production of bread. Modern bakeries use completely automated, efficient processes that even improve the quality of the bread.

Technology

Technology, as a factor of production, means the advancement of knowledge. Any knowledge that affects productivity of economic goods and services by increasing quality or quantity is considered to be technology.

As previously noted, any lasting and meaningful changes or increases in the factors of land, labor, and capital can be attained only through technological innovations.

Technological innovations are the direct result of research and development programs conducted by government, industry, universities, and private foundations. During the past twenty-five years, research has expanded, and it will continue to increase in the future. Education builds the foundation for all this research and development. Therefore, improved education ultimately produces vastly improved standards of living.

Technology can be of great benefit to people, but when used improperly it can produce unwanted results, such as air and water pollution problems. However, the solutions to these pollution problems are being achieved by more technological innovations.

The problems of a society built on technology are not the fault of technology; rather, they are problems created because people did not use technology in the best ways possible. For example, atomic energy generated by safe nuclear fusion plants (current plants use nuclear fission) is a primary hope for the future generation of energy. Present sources of energy are in limited supply, and the demand for energy is growing every day. Our society will grind to a halt one day if we depend on the traditional sources of energy. Fortunately, current knowledge and future technological innovations in the field of nuclear energy will one day produce a safe and clean nuclear energy source. By contrast, nuclear energy technology has also produced weapons of war capable of mass destruction.

Human ability to create technology is the greatest resource for the betterment of society; however, people must direct this resource wisely.

THE PURPOSE OF BUSINESS

Business firms bring together the factors of production in order to produce economic goods and services. From the viewpoint of society, this is the sole justification for the existence of business. Contrary to popular opinion, the purpose of business is not to produce a profit for its owners, but rather to provide economic goods and services to satisfy people's needs (Exhibit 1–3). Profit is only a means used in private-enterprise systems for motivating individuals to achieve maximum productivity in business. Profit earned by the thousand largest firms in the United States averages between 4 and 5 percent of sales.

Business is essential to society. No modern society can exist without business. Business is the producer of the economic goods and services that allow people in any nation to survive.

OWNERSHIP OF THE FACTORS OF PRODUCTION

There are basically two systems of ownership of the factors of production, with varying degrees of ownership between, as indicated by the following diagram:

GOVERNMENT	PRIVATE
OWNERSHIP	OWNERSHIP

Complete government ownership or complete private ownership does not exist in the world today, nor would either be desirable; rather, all economic systems exist somewhere in between the two extremes. The United States is primarily a private-ownership economic system. However, some forms of business, such as the post office and the Tennessee

Exhibit 1–3
The process by which society
produces satisfaction of human
wants and needs.

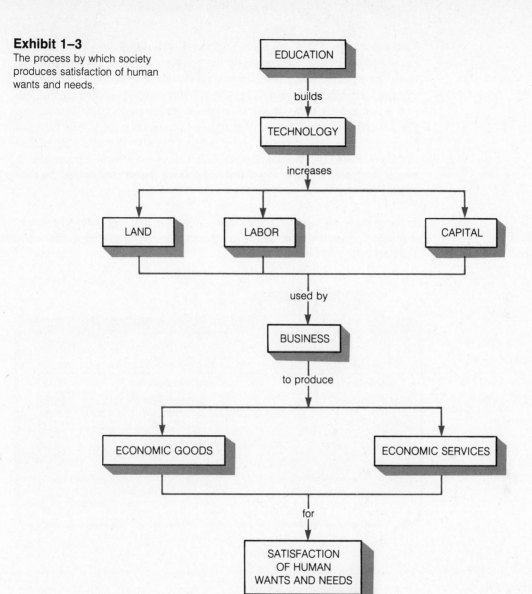

EDUCATION

builds

TECHNOLOGY

increases

LAND   LABOR   CAPITAL

used by

BUSINESS

to produce

ECONOMIC GOODS   ECONOMIC SERVICES

for

SATISFACTION
OF HUMAN
WANTS AND NEEDS

Valley Authority (TVA, an agency charged with development of the Tennessee River Basin), are owned by the government. The government also owns large amounts of undeveloped land that it leases out for timber, grazing, and oil exploration. Even the off-shore area is owned by the federal government, some of which is leased for oil exploration. In addition, the government practices varying degrees of control over a wide range of businesses, e.g., rate control in the railroad industry and safety regulation in the aviation industry. Russia, on the other hand, is primarily a government-ownership system, with only a few very small businesses owned by individuals.

PRIVATE VS. GOVERNMENT OWNERSHIP

In each basic system of ownership there are inherent advantages and problems. A comparison of these advantages and problems is shown in Exhibit 1–4.

Exhibit 1–4

Private ownership versus government ownership.

Government Ownership	Private Ownership
Advantages	*Advantages*
(1) Complete control over factors of production.	(1) Provides strong motivating force for individuals.
	(2) Dispersion of authority and responsibility.
Problems	*Problems*
(1) Little motivation of individuals.	(1) Lack of control over factors of production.
(2) Centralization of authority and responsibility.	

Advantages of the Private-Ownership System

The private-ownership system has two major advantages: it provides a strong motivating force for individuals, and it spreads authority and responsibility.

Motivation. Profit and psychological satisfaction are primary motivators in a free-enterprise system.

Profit is a reward to the business person who satisfies customers; the absence of profit eliminates the inefficient business. If a business is not doing a good job of satisfying customers, then it will not make a profit and will go out of business for lack of funds. In a government-owned system, such a business could exist forever if those in political power wished it to do so.

Business people in the private-enterprise system also gain much psychological satisfaction from their success. The pleasure of making a business a success, making it grow, meeting the challenge of everyday business and **competition,** and even the status associated with the business are powerful motivators.

Profit is absolutely essential to business firms in a private enterprise economic system. Profits are used to increase the efficiency of business firms in many ways, such as providing funds with which to buy more efficient equipment, to conduct research for new and improved products, and to replace machinery and equipment as it wears out or becomes obsolete.

The calculator industry demonstrates the advantages derived by the consumer as a result of the profit motive. Twenty years ago most colleges offered courses that taught students how to use mechanical calculators. These machines were bulky, cost several hundred dollars, and did little more than add, subtract, multiply, and divide. Companies searching for profit developed today's electronic calculator, which performs the same functions as the old calculator, costs less than ten dollars, and fits in your hand. The more advanced ones have become mini-sized computers. The companies that produce calculators today are not the ones that produced them twenty years ago. The rooms filled with large mechanical calculators have disappeared from college campuses.

The fantastic output of the private-enterprise system in the United States is certainly a monument to the motivation of individuals to succeed in business.

Dispersion of Authority and Responsibility. Millions of individual business people make their own decisions when reacting to the day-to-day demands of their customers. No central governmental planning agency controls these decisions. A vast number of local and regional markets, each having its own particular tastes, comprises the national market. The very proximity of individual businesses to these local markets allows them to adapt their operations rapidly to changing demands of the market. For example, the manufacturer of women's shoes has salespeople who are in contact with retailers who daily service customer preferences. The manufacturer is constantly seeking information as to what types of shoes are selling best in the market and adapting production to the desires of the customers in the market. By buying what pleases her, the customer is, in effect, determining what the manufacturer will produce. With a central planning agency, the style of shoes to be produced must be determined far in advance of production. A central planning agency also needs extensive lengths of time to shift production to meet consumer demands. As a result, the customer in the government-ownership system has a very limited choice of shoes that were selected by a few government bureaucrats.

To remain in business, individual business people must adapt their decisions to the demands of the market. The profit motive is the incentive

Exhibit 1–5

Worktime required by average manufacturing employee to buy selected commodities.

	U.S.	U.S.S.R
Milk (1 liter)	7 minutes	18 minutes
Hamburger meat (1 kg)	43 minutes	128 minutes
Sausage, pork (1 kg)	31 minutes	145 minutes
Potatoes (1 kg)	2 minutes	7 minutes
Apples (1 kg)	11 minutes	40 minutes
Sugar (1 kg)	5 minutes	59 minutes
White bread (1 kg)	8 minutes	18 minutes
Eggs (10)	10 minutes	99 minutes
Vodka (.5 liter)	52 minutes	380 minutes
Cigarettes (20)	9 minutes	23 minutes
Weekly food for four people	12.5 hours	42.3 hours
Soap (150 grams)	5 minutes	23 minutes
Man's leather shoes	8 hours	33 hours
Man's business suit	20 hours	68 hours
Refrigerator, small	43 hours	208 hours
Color TV set	86 hours	713 hours
Automobile (Ford)	4.1 months	35 months

SOURCE: National Federation of Independent Business.

that insures their interest in shifts in demand in the market. If the business firm does not adequately satisfy customer demands on a continuing basis, profits will rapidly decline. Continued inadequate service to customers in the market will result in the business's "going broke," that is, losing ownership over factors of production. Consequently, competition in the market will generally ensure that business people will reach decisions that maximize satisfaction of human wants and needs.

Problems of the Private-Enterprise System

As indicated before, the private-ownership system relies on decisions made by millions of independent business people reacting to market demands. Therefore, these business people determine the allocation of available resources—land, labor, capital, and technology—to the production of consumer and industrial goods.

Lack of complete control over the factors of production produces two problems—inflation and recession.

The persistent price increases of **inflation** (discussed in chapter 14) are often the result of such factors as the government spending much more than it receives in taxes, foreign nations conspiring to control production and increase prices in certain industries (OPEC and oil prices are an example), demand increasing faster than production, and wages increasing faster than productivity.

Because the private enterprise system is controlled by the market, a recurring problem has been idleness, in varying degrees, of the factors of production. Recessions occur from time to time. **Recessions** are periods in which business output and employment are dropping. Business investment and consumer buying also decline in recessions.

Historically, inflation and recession usually do not go together, but rather, represent the ups and downs of the economy. However, both have occurred together in what is called **stagflation** (**stagnation/inflation**). For example, when prices of oil and gas rose rapidly they contributed to a considerable increase in all prices because oil and gas provide most of the energy used in the production and transportation of goods. Government action to try to hold down inflation created a slump in business activity and employment. As a result, we had inflation along with a decrease in business output and employment.

Basic economic knowledge is available and is continually being refined, which allows a private-enterprise system to overcome much of the disadvantage of being unable to control idleness of the factors of production. By controlling government spending and the nation's money supply, the government can stimulate or depress the economy as needed (presented in chapter 14). Of course, we need to discover more about how and when to use these tools in order to maintain full employment of the nation's resources. Often, major disagreement occurs about which policy is best to follow at any particular time.

Since ownership of most businesses is in the hands of individuals, they make the decision as to how much they will invest in the important factors

of production—capital and technology. The profit motive is a powerful incentive; but the government can have considerable impact on private enterprise decisions by the way it taxes, its regulation policies, and how it spends its money. Investment tax credits for capital expenditures and research grants to business and colleges are two examples.

Advantages of a Government-Ownership System

The chief advantage of an economic system of governmental ownership is complete control over the factors of production. A centralized government determines entirely what economic goods and services will be produced with available resources. The government specifies what part of available resources will be used for the production of consumer goods and industrial goods, for the military, and for governmental functions such as education. Usually at the expense of the consumer, the centralized governmental agencies will pour large amounts of resources into industrial goods and education because these are the capital and technology factors of production that result in economic growth. Also, a governmental system of ownership does not allow factors of production to lie idle or unused—there is, for all practical purposes, no unemployment in the labor force.

Problems of a Government-Ownership System

As would be expected, the advantages of the private-enterprise system are disadvantages of the government-ownership system. Little motivation of individuals in business units and **centralization of authority** and responsibility create extensive bureaucracy in the government-owned system.

Motivation. In a government-ownership system, the very fact that management has no vested interest in the business (owns none of the factors of production) seriously limits motivation for improvement. Managers do not face the possibility of "going broke" if they do not make the correct decisions. The business will continue to operate, no matter how inefficient it is, as long as the central government planning body provides for its existence. Management maintains the status quo in the business. Innovation is risky and can gain a manager nothing; therefore, the manager avoids new ideas and techniques. The continued desire of the Russian government to obtain advanced computer technology from American businesses is just one example of how profit-motivated private enterprise has developed technology and government-owned business has not.

In addition, the amount of bureaucracy in a government-ownership system is so extensive that even the most energetic manager hesitates to attempt to gain approval for change. If a manager recognizes a change that would produce major benefits to the efficiency of the business unit, facing the red tape that is required to process the request is just not worth the small or nonexistent personal reward that might be obtained. *The lack of motivation in a government-ownership system is evidenced by the fact that the productivity of the Russian worker is the lowest of any industrialized nation.*

Empty supermarket shelves in Poland.

Centralization. In a government-ownership system, a highly centralized group makes the decisions. Several serious disadvantages exist in this type of system. Imagine, if you will, that a local manufacturer is forced to rely on decisions from a governmental agency in Washington to effect any changes in production or production levels. Under this centralized system of business decision making, it would be impossible for the local manufacturing unit to adapt effectively to changing market conditions and demands.

Assume that our local manufacturer recognizes that changing market conditions demand a change in the style and quantity of the product. Because all factors of production are controlled by a central planning agency, the manufacturer must process the request for change through proper governmental channels. The request, in standard form, must first be sent to an area governmental agency. If the area agency approves the request, it is sent to a regional office for evaluation. If approved, it may reach the central planning body where it may be changed, rejected, pigeonholed, or even lost. With such an involved procedure, failure of the request is likely. Also, it is impossible for any government representative at any level to have complete information on all facets of the changing local market conditions that created the initial request. Even if the request is approved in its entirety, by the time it is processed, a completely different decision may be required in a market that is constantly changing (see Exhibit 1–6).

INDIVIDUAL FREEDOM

In order for a government to regulate economic activity, it *must* limit individual freedom to some degree. The two most obvious examples of nations that use government ownership of the factors of production—Russia and the People's Republic of China—illustrate how oppressive of individual freedom a government can be as a result of rigid control of the factors of production. Within limits, it is sometimes desirable to

17

forego some less important areas of personal freedom in order to gain greater economic well-being for all. For example, all employers in the United States must participate in the workmen's compensation insurance program in order to protect the well-being of the entire work force. Sometimes even extreme measures must be instituted by the government for the common good, such as the strict wage and price controls that were in effect during World War II.

Freedom is an important goal in itself. How would you like to live in a country where you had almost no freedom of choice? You would:

work a job that was assigned to you;

not be able to determine how much education you would receive;

have a lower standard of living than in the United States because the government ownership system resulted in a less efficient production output;

have a limited choice of products and services;

pay the price set by the government, which might not have any relationship to the value of the product;

not be able to pick your own entertainment because television, movies, theater, and other forms of entertainment are selected by small groups of people;

hear only the news that a small group of people wanted you to hear;

have nothing to say about your salary or promotions;

live in a small space that was assigned to you.

It certainly does not sound like the "good life," does it? Unfortunately, it is very descriptive of life in Russia, China, and other government-ownership economic systems. One small example of economic freedom of choice is blue jeans. For years, blue jeans have been as popular with the Russian people as with Americans. Yet, for many years the central planning agencies were not responsive to consumer preference. Finally, Russian government-owned businesses began producing blue jeans, but, because of technological inefficiency, they have not been able to produce quality denim. For several years now, Russia has been importing large quantities of denim from private enterprise in the United States.

Eliminating extensive government control over people would be sufficient reason in itself to adopt a private-enterprise economic system. Fortunately, such a system also provides the most satisfaction to consumers by being the most efficient producer of economic goods and services.

ECONOMIC INDICATORS

One problem with a private enterprise economic system is lack of control over the factors of production. It is important to know where the economy is headed so actions can be initiated to lessen excessive swings in the economy. The National Bureau of Economic Research monitors many **economic indicators** in their attempts to predict economic fluctuations. The twelve most reliable indicators are:

Exhibit 1–6

Control of production decisions in government-ownership systems and private-enterprise systems.

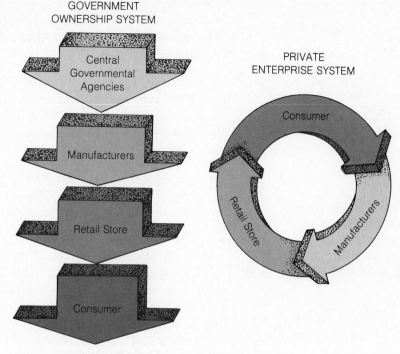

1. Average work week of production workers
2. Average weekly initial unemployment applications
3. New business formations
4. New building permits
5. New orders of durables
6. Business expenditures for new plant and equipment
7. Changes in manufacturing and trade inventories
8. Industrial raw materials prices
9. Common stock prices
10. Corporate profits
11. Price and labor cost ratio
12. Changes in consumer installment debt

CAPITALISM, COMMUNISM, AND SOCIALISM

Ownership of the factors of production of a nation usually can be classified as capitalism, communism, or socialism.

Capitalism describes an economic system in which almost all of the factors of production are privately owned. The economic activity is directed by private enterprise reacting to market demand. The United States is an example of a capitalist type of economic system.

Communism is an economic system in which virtually all of the factors of production are owned by the government. The economic activity is directed by central government planning agencies rather than by the market. Russia is an example of a nation that has a communist type of economic system.

Socialism is basically a combination of government and private ownership of the factors of production. Usually, in socialism the government owns the basic industries, such as transportation, banking, metals, and fuels. Wholesale, small manufacturing, and retail operations tend to be privately owned. The government-owned industries are controlled by government agencies and the private industries react to the marketplace. India is an example of a nation that has a socialist type of economic system.

PURE COMPETITION, MONOPOLY, MONOPOLISTIC COMPETITION, AND OLIGOPOLY

Four types of industries describe a capitalistic economic system: (1) pure competition; (2) monopoly; (3) monopolistic competition; and (4) oligopoly.

Pure competition exists when: (1) there are many sellers and each is so small relative to the market as to have no effect on the total market; and (2) there are many sellers selling identical products and the buyers don't care where they buy, so price becomes all-important. Sellers must adjust to the market price, since no seller is large enough to influence the market. Given their costs and the market price, they must determine how much they are willing to produce. Buyers determine how much they are willing to purchase, given the market price. Consequently, total market supply and demand determines the price.

Competition in this pure a form probably does not exist. Agriculture in the United States has been the historic example; however, federal government price support practices keep it from being pure competition.

Monopoly exists when (1) there is only one supplier in the market, and (2) there is no significant competition from producers of substitutes. Monopolies, except for natural monopolies (utilities, telephone companies, etc.), are illegal in the United States (natural monopolies and antitrust laws are discussed in chapter 23).

Monopolistic competition exists where there are substantial numbers of sellers of identical or closely related products that are substitutable. The producers compete on price and/or nonprice methods such as advertising. For example, the Coca Cola Company has the sole right to produce Coca Cola, but they compete in the market with Pepsi Cola and many other soft drinks. They compete primarily through advertising that attempts to convince the consumer that their product is the best, but they must keep their price in line with other producers.

Oligopoly exists when there are only a few suppliers of identical or closely substitutable products. They may or may not compete on price. Sometimes there is collaboration on pricing and output through international agreements (OPEC, for example) or the producers tend to follow the lead of one or more firms on pricing. The automobile industry in the United States is an example of oligopoly.

Genetic Engineering

Technology is able to not only increase the output of goods and services by increasing the factors of production, but it can also greatly enhance the quality of life. For example, prior to 1921, the life expectancy for people with insulin-dependent diabetes was very short; but today, with the use of insulin extracted from animals, technology allows such people to live longer, more normal lives. Nevertheless, the problems have not been completely solved: it takes 15,000 hogs and 8,500 cattle to yield 8,000 pounds of pancreas glands, which undergo complex manufacturing processes to produce 1 pound of insulin suitable for human use. Because it is not human insulin, other complications, such as nerve damage, blindness, and even death may occur. However, technology should soon have a dramatic impact on the current 34,000 deaths per year from diabetes. Recent **genetic engineering** by one team of researchers resulted in bacteria that produce insulin identical to human insulin. Another research team has designed a small pump that can be implanted in a diabetic to inject insulin on a continual basis as the body needs it.

In the future, genetic manipulation technology may be a greater boon to the world than both computer technology and laser technology. It even has the potential to eliminate world hunger. Improved plants and animals should greatly increase food production. Genetic engineering holds the promise of creating new plants and animals that do not exist today. However, many people believe it could pose a bigger threat to the world than nuclear energy technology, if not handled properly.

SUMMARY OF KEY POINTS

1. The world output of economic goods and services is not adequate. The choice between economic systems is important to all nations in their attempts to increase production.

2. The standard of living of any nation is basically its total output of goods and services divided by its population.

3. The population today is a little over 4 billion and it will exceed 6 billion by the year 2000. There are 3.6 million deaths per year from the lack of sufficient food, and the problem will get worse unless we are able to do something about it.

4. The factors of production are land, labor (production, entrepreneurial and management), capital, and technology.

5. Lasting, meaningful changes in the factors of land, labor, and capital can be attained only through technological innovations.

6. From a social viewpoint, the purpose of business is to produce economic goods and services to satisfy human wants and needs.

7. Profit is used in private enterprise systems to motivate people to achieve maximum productivity.

8. The factors of production may be privately owned, government-owned, or some combination of the two.

9. Primary advantages of the private enterprise system are motivation of people and dispersion of authority and responsibility.

10. The main problem in a private enterprise system is idleness, in varying degrees, of the factors of production.

11. The primary advantage of government-ownership systems is control over the factors of production.

12. The problems with government-ownership systems are lack of motivation of people and centralization of authority and responsibility.

13. In order for a government to control economic activity, it must limit individual freedom. Government-ownership systems severely limit individual and economic freedom.

14. Economic indicators are important in a private enterprise system because they can predict economic fluctuations.

15. Capitalism is an economic system in which the factors of production are owned privately. Communism is a system in which they are owned by the government. Socialism is a combination of capitalism and communism in which basic industries are government-owned and others are privately owned.

16. Pure competition, monopoly, monopolistic competition, and oligopoly are the types of industries in a capitalistic economic system.

DISCUSSION QUESTIONS

1. If you were head of the government of an underdeveloped country, how would you go about raising the standard of living?
2. How much of a commitment should a nation make toward education and research? Why?
3. "Business is in the business of making a profit." Evaluate this statement from the viewpoint of society.
4. If you were the head of the government of an underdeveloped country, would you use government or private ownership of the factors of production? Explain why.
5. Why is the profit motive considered by most people to be so valuable in the United States?
6. What is the difference between Russia (government ownership) and the United States (private ownership) in terms of centralization-dispersion of authority in the economic system?
7. Would you like to live in an economic system that used government ownership of the factors of production? Explain your answer.
8. How would you go about solving the world food problem before the world population reaches 6 billion in the year 2000?

STUDENT PROJECTS

1. Identify in your community:
   a. A private-enterprise business.   b. A government-owned business.
2. Select a product and identify at least one of each factor of production—land, labor, capital, and technology—used to produce the product.

CASE
A

The Oil Bonanza

Vast oil deposits have been discovered in one of the underdeveloped nations. Some national statistics of this country are compared with the United States below. The oil reserves are expected to bring an additional $4 billion per year into this country within five years. This means that per capita GNP will rise from $200 per year to $300 per year.

	Underdeveloped Nation	United States
Gross National Product (GNP)	$ 8 billion	$ 2,369 billion
Per capita GNP	$200	$10,745
Approximate GNP growth rate per year	2%	4.4%
Population	40 million	221 million
Approximate population growth rate per year	2%	.8%
Labor force	16 million	106 million
Percent of labor force in agriculture	80%	3.2%
Enrollment in higher education	0.1 million	11.6 million

They could spend all of their increased income for imported consumer goods. But the leaders of this country fear that in about twenty years the United States or some other developed nation will make a major breakthrough in energy technology. This breakthrough would vastly reduce the importance of oil and destroy the effectiveness of the international oil cartel.

You have been hired by the government of this nation as an adviser to help them plan for the future.

Questions

1. From the statistics provided, what would you conclude about this country?

2. Do you feel this country should put all of its new funds into imported consumer products? If not, what should it do with the money? Explain.

3. Tell the leaders of this nation what to do in the future in terms of standard of living and population.

4. What form of ownership of the factors of production would you suggest? Explain.

CASE

B

The Economic Debate

The Department of State is sponsoring a tour of selected American colleges for students from several underdeveloped countries. Part of the program at your school involves a discussion of the American and Russian economic systems. A member of a socialist organization in your state will present the Russian side of the discussion. You have been elected by the students in your school to present the American side of the discussion. Some of the statistics you have found are:

	U.S.	U.S.S.R.
Population (millions)	221	263
Population growth rate (annual)	.8%	.9%
Area (millions of square miles)	3.6	8.7
Gross National Product (billions)	$2,369	$1,256
Military expenditure (billions)	$108	$154
Exports (billions)	$119	$45
Telephones (millions)	162	19
Radios (millions)	416	126
Televisions (millions)	126	57

SOURCE: Statistical Abstract of the United States.

Questions

1. What do these statistics mean to you?

2. In terms of these statistics, which country seems to have the greatest concern for what the public wants? Explain.

3. Which country would appear to have the greatest amount of technology?

4. Present your argument for the American economic system.

5. Classify each of these countries as to capitalism, communism, or socialism and give your reasons for classification of each.

The Dallas Cowboys represent the ideal of American success through organization and innovation.

BUSINESS PROFILE

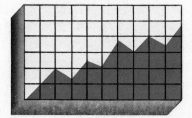

The Dallas Cowboys Football Club

Clint Murchison, Sr., built a multimillion dollar empire in what is often called the "wheeler-dealer" Texas style. He began by buying oil leases. He would buy a lease and then sell part of it for money to buy another. From buying oil leases he went to oil drilling and then to a wide range of business activities, such as ranching and chemicals.

Clint, Sr., had two sons who followed his lead in the business world. Today they have interests in more than one hundred companies. One of the sons, Clinton Murchison, Jr., obtained an expansion franchise in the National Football League in 1960, which created The Dallas Cowboys Football Club. He is the Chairman of the Board.

The Dallas Cowboys Football Club has been extremely successful. It is often referred to as "America's team" because it so represents the image of American success through organization and innovation. The team has not had a losing season since 1964. Its success is largely due to what they call "The Organization" or "The System." The Cowboys were the first to use the computer in their player selection process, and their scouting program has long been the model for all professional football teams. The "Organization" is so efficient in the player draft and in the free agent market that they never have more than one or two players who have played on other professional football teams and many teams have players who were released by the Dallas Cowboys. Another aspect that has added to the "America's Team" image is the highly publicized Dallas Cowboys Cheerleaders; the cheerleaders are also the result of a highly efficient organization.

Tom Landry is the only coach Dallas has ever had. He installed the most complex offense and defense in professional football. This, too, has added to the image.

It is probably true that among football fans, The Dallas Cowboys are the most widely loved/hated professional football team in America. It is not unusual for a team to have a low attendance one week and then fill the stadium when they play The Cowboys the next week. Organization, planning, and innovation have paid off for The Dallas football club.

2

Social Responsibility of Business

LEARNING GOALS

After reading this chapter, you will understand:

1. How and why business functions and what society expects from business.

2. The needs of the parties-at-interest in business firms and what they can do if their needs are not met.

3. What business is doing to help clean up air, water, solid waste, noise, and aesthetic pollution.

4. What business is doing to help improve the economic well-being of minority groups.

5. Why employee and product safety are so important to business and society.

6. The basic rights of consumers.

KEY TERMS

Social responsibility of business	Aesthetic pollution
Parties-at-interest	Minority
Air pollution	Employee safety
Water pollution	OSHA
Solid waste pollution	Product safety
Noise pollution	Consumer movement

> The business firm, as an organic entity intricately affected by and affecting its environment, is as appropriately adaptive . . . to demands for responsible behavior as for economic service.
>
> KENNETH R. ANDREWS

In order to identify the social responsibility of business, we must consider the ultimate goals or purposes for which business exists. People's ideas differ widely on the purpose or justification of business: the owner of a business feels the intent of the business is to provide him or her with profit and personal satisfaction; an employee may feel that the purpose or justification of the business is to provide the employee with an income.

Rather than concentrate on individual viewpoints, it is more realistic to identify the purpose of business from the viewpoint of society. From society's viewpoint, business should provide the economic goods and services that satisfy the wants and needs of the people.

Since society allows businesses to exist to provide economic goods and services, it also allows business people in the free-enterprise system a profit. If they are efficient, business people may produce a profit—their main purpose in establishing and continuing the business. Consequently, as pointed out in chapter 1, society uses profit as a motivator for business people not only to produce economic goods and services, but to help them improve their efficiency and output.

PARTIES-AT-INTEREST IN BUSINESS

People who have something to gain or lose in their relation to a business are the ones who must have their wants and needs satisfied. That is, all who have a vested interest in the business must have their wants and needs at least partially satisfied by management. Customers, owners, employees, suppliers, creditors, communities, governments, and competitors have vested interests in business firms. Of course, one person may belong to more than one group.

Management has limited resources at its disposal with which to satisfy ever-increasing human wants and needs. Consequently, it is apparent that management makes the decisions as to how to balance the satisfaction of wants and needs of these parties-at-interest with the resources it has available. Considerable argument exists over the proportion of the resources available to each party-at-interest. An example of this is the labor-management strife that occurs in some companies and industries when it is bargaining time for new contracts. All parties-at-interest constantly bring pressure to bear upon management for the satisfaction of their wants and needs (see Exhibit 2–1).

Customers

All parties-at-interest in a business firm are essential to its continued operation and well-being; however, the customers are the most important group. The business firm has as its purpose the production of economic goods and services for the satisfaction of wants and needs. The customer receives these goods and services and, in addition, provides the money for management to satisfy other parties-at-interest. Without the customer, management would be unable to satisfy any group.

Since the private-ownership economic system uses competition as a motivating device, the satisfaction of customers is a relative and ever-changing concept. The business firm must attempt to equal or exceed the efforts of its competitors to satisfy customers. In their attempts to compete, business firms continually change their offerings of goods and services. What will satisfy the customer one day will not necessarily satisfy

Exhibit 2–1

Parties-at-interest, their needs, and their recourse.

Party-at-Interest	Needs	Recourse
Customers	Desired quality of goods and services Reasonable price	Purchase from another business
Employees	Monetary rewards Job security Good working conditions	Resign Collective bargaining
Owners	Profits Security of investment Expectation of future profits Personal satisfaction	Fire the management Withdraw funds
Suppliers	Firm to be a good customer	Withdraw supplies
Creditors	Repayment of funds with interest	Refuse to lend funds
Communities	Help to enhance the community Be a good citizen	Enact legislation Withdraw support as customers
Governments	Support the government Financial support	Enact legislation Penalties under existing legislation
Competitors	Fair competition	Help enact legislation

"HOW CAN WE TELL WHO'S 'RANK' AND WHO'S 'FILE'?"

him the next day. For example, DuPont has said that 60 percent of their products were unknown ten years ago.

Some customers and employees reduce the satisfaction of all parties-at-interest by theft and shoplifting. Customer shoplifting and employee theft amount to billions of dollars of stolen goods each year. This added expense significantly reduces the resources that management has available to provide for other customers, other employees, and other parties-at-interest.

Owners

Business firms use the owners' funds to purchase the factors of production; hence, owners are essential to business firms. Owners, like other groups, have their own wants and needs, of which profit undoubtedly is the most important. In addition to profits, owners expect security of their investment, a reasonable expectation of continuing profits, and personal satisfaction.

If these wants and needs are not reasonably satisfied, management soon feels the power of the owner group. Owners may discharge managers or immediately withdraw their funds. In the past, management has had little success in bypassing the wants and needs of owners.

Employees

Business needs employees to produce economic goods and services. The employee depends on the business firm for monetary rewards, security, and good working conditions as well as for many other economic, psychological, and social satisfactions.

When employees feel their needs are not being adequately satisfied, they may take actions that are not good for the business. They may resign and go to work for someone else, possibly even the firm's competition. This hurts the business because turnover of employees is very costly. Employees may join together and form a union for collective bargaining. Unions usually take away part of management's authority and reduce its freedom in decision making. In addition, actions of labor unions sometimes restrict production and technology, thereby reducing the satisfaction of all parties-at-interest.

Suppliers

Suppliers are those businesses that provide raw materials, equipment, supplies, tools, and any other economic goods or services that the dependent firm uses in the production of economic goods and services.

Suppliers also have their own individual wants and needs that management must satisfy. The purchasing firm is a customer of the supplier and, as pointed out earlier, the customer is vital to any business; therefore, the supplier cannot exist without the buying firm.

As with other parties-at-interest, the satisfaction of suppliers is, again, largely a matter of competition. The supplier who is the only pro-

Exhibit 2–2

Average income of families by race.

(SOURCE: Statistical Abstract of the United States, 1981.)

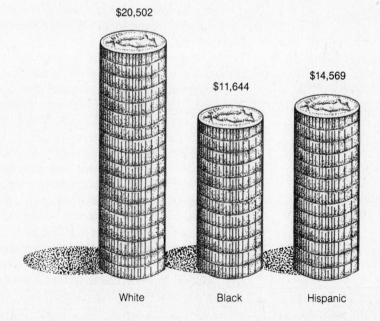

$20,502

$11,644

$14,569

White   Black   Hispanic

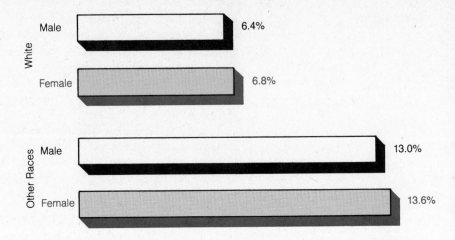

Exhibit 2–3
Unemployment by race and sex.
(SOURCE: Statistical Abstract of the United States, 1981.)

ducer in a particular field may exact a great deal of satisfaction; however, a supplier in a field where there is a high degree of competition may be forced to receive less satisfaction.

Creditors

Creditors are vital parties-at-interest in any business because when managers need funds to assemble the factors of production, they must often turn to creditors. As with other parties-at-interest, creditors have their particular wants and needs. They demand security of their funds and a payment of interest that is equal to the security of their funds.

Management must satisfy the wants and needs of creditors if it expects to obtain more funds in the future. In other words, if management does not repay monies borrowed, plus the specified interest rate, it will have a hard time borrowing. Consequently, creditors exert a strong influence on management to force satisfaction of their wants and needs.

Communities

For the most part, the community's wants and needs are not as clear as the wants and needs of other parties-at-interest. The community expects management to be an integral part of its society and to improve and enhance life within the community. Management must help the community's efforts to enhance the common environment.

Management must aid society in its attempts at solving many social problems. Industry's management is expected to clean up its contribution to air, water, noise, and trash pollution. In addition, many business firms are starting to aid in improving race relations and reducing poverty by hiring more members of minority groups. Business has developed more intensive training programs to train the people who have been unable to obtain jobs because of lack of skills.

The community is traditionally slow and indefinite in its actions if its wants and needs are not satisfied. However, after long delays and deliberation, many community laws have been passed because of the inability or unwillingness of management to satisfy the community's wants and needs. For example, to try to make the business district safe and attractive, communities have passed laws prohibiting vending on sidewalks, blocking fire lanes, or hanging outside signs. Customers and employees are also vital members of the community. If the community is not satisfied, then these groups sometimes withdraw their support of the business. The initiation of laws is traditionally slow; hence, most communities do not exert pressure on management for satisfaction of their wants and needs as immediately as some of the other parties-at-interest in a business.

Governments

Local, state, and federal governments are necessary parties-at-interest in any business. These governments provide the social structure needed for production of economic goods and services. Governments provide roadways, flood control, police and fire protection, legal systems, national defense, and many other services that are essential to the operation of any business.

In return for these services, management must support and finance these governments in their operations; consequently, governments have their own peculiar wants and needs. In order for governments to continue effective operations, business must provide approval and support of the basic concepts of the existing government. Financial support of these governments is a different matter, for governments have immediate and powerful weapons with which they are able to force management to satisfy this need. Many laws have been passed requiring management to pay part of the financial cost of supporting the operations of governments. These exist in the form of corporation taxes, income taxes, property taxes, and varying types of licenses and fees. Failure to provide financial support through these laws results in fines, imprisonment, and other forms of penalties. The government forces management to meet most of its financial obligations.

Competitors

Of all the parties-at-interest, competitors are probably of least importance to management, and thus require the least satisfaction of wants and needs. In a system that relies on competition as a major motivating force, the only form of satisfaction that management owes its competitors is fair and honest practices. Competitors have very few weapons at their command with which to force management to satisfy their wants and needs. However, competitors, like customers and employees, are also citizens in a free, democratic society and have equal voting powers. Probably the passage of various antitrust laws was partly the result of competitors joining forces with customers in pushing for legislation to outlaw unfair business practices by their competition.

Although competitors are of least importance as a party-at-interest, their actions in the marketplace are extremely important and require the constant attention of management.

ENVIRONMENTAL RESPONSIBILITY

One of the major social responsibilities is to maintain a quality environment. The majority of the people in the United States have only in the past twenty years become concerned about their environment. Before this, agriculture, industry, communities, and people in general abused the environment, knowing very little about the consequences. Once they began to understand that health and the quality of life are related to the environment, they supported passage of laws that required various segments of society to begin to clean up the environment. Although they are not the main polluters, industries spend more than half of the total amount spent for pollution in the U.S. each year. Almost all forms of pollution have decreased over the past ten years. Nature itself is a major polluter of the environment. Pollen in the air and red tides in the ocean are just two examples.

Pollution exists in the forms of air, water, waste, noise, and aesthetic pollution.

Air Pollution

The steel, chemical, petroleum, paper, coke, cement, copper-smelting, electricity-generating, and air-transportation industries are examples of industries that have traditionally polluted the air. Considerable progress has been achieved by industry in reducing its contribution to **air pollution.** Over an eight-year period, national emission of air pollutants changed as follows: particulates down 46 percent; sulfur oxides down 9 percent; nitrogen oxides up 17 percent; hydrocarbons down 2 percent; and carbon monoxide down 1 percent. Over a ten-year period, the automobile industry added equipment that resulted in the following decreases in automobile-produced air pollutants: carbon monoxide down 35 percent; hydrocarbons down 51 percent; and nitrogen oxides down 32 percent.

Methods used by industry to reduce air pollution have been expensive and time-consuming to install. Most industrial plants have reduced their air pollution with filters, after-burners, gas washing devices, and electrostatic precipitators.

The automobile probably best shows industry's problem with air pollution control. There is no practical method available at this time that will eliminate all pollution of internal combustion engines used in automobiles. In addition, if the method of eliminating the pollution of automobiles becomes too expensive, it will drastically reduce the number of automobiles sold, causing extensive unemployment. Further, attempts to reduce automobile pollution sometimes are harmful to the important national goal of reducing gasoline consumption.

Water Pollution

The largest sources of **water pollution** are agricultural runoff, storm sewer runoff, and municipal sewage. Some industrial sources are the paper, chemical, aluminum, steel, textile, metal plating, ore-smelting, strip-mining, and oil-drilling industries.

Cartoons often show industrial pollution as a small pipe pouring extremely toxic chemicals into a river. Unfortunately, eliminating water pollution is usually not as easy a task as is implied by these cartoons. For example, steel plants discharge up to 350 million gallons of water per day, which is equal to the water needs of a city of 200,000 people. Cleaning this much water every day is a difficult problem. Industrial firms use aerators, chemicals, lagoons, settling ponds, and deep wells to reduce water pollution. Needless to say, these methods are very expensive to install and operate.

While industry has made significant gains in controlling water pollution, cities and towns have not done as well. Over a four-year period, fecal coliform bacteria went up 3 percent, inadequate levels of dissolved oxygen went up 100 percent, and phosphorus stayed the same.

In eliminating water pollution, some smaller firms do not have sufficient capital to meet current water quality standards. If they do not receive some form of help, these firms will be forced out of the market, thereby reducing competition. As we saw in chapter 1, any reduction of effective competition is not desirable for society.

Solid Waste Pollution

Man's trash in modern society is rapidly becoming unmanageable. Cities like New York and Los Angeles produce tons of trash every day. Finding places to dispose of trash is a critical problem. Over an eighteen-year period, the total amount of solid waste generated in the U.S. increased by 73 percent. Each person produces about four pounds of waste per day. Products such as glass, plastic, and aluminum products become a problem

Man's trash in modern society is rapidly becoming unmanageable.

if they do not break down or decompose. Just imagine the problem of disposing of millions of old cars each year.

Business has been and can continue to be an important contributor to the solution of the **solid waste pollution** problem by developing methods of recycling and reusing what is now solid waste pollution. For example, several firms have for years maintained collection points for empty aluminum cans, which are recycled into new cans. Over the same eighteen-year period that total solid waste increased by 73 percent, resources recovered through recycling increased by 103 percent.

Noise Pollution

Aircraft, traffic, construction, various machinery, and other facets of modern civilization create **noise pollution.** This excessive noise can harm humans physically and psychologically. Decreases in hearing are a common result of noise pollution. After research confirmed that loud levels of noise reduced hearing, some cities passed laws setting the decibel level of music allowed in night clubs.

Noise pollution can be reduced by either moving the source away from people or creating quieter machines. For example, the placement of airports away from the city reduces the noise pollution of the city. Better insulation of buildings against noise can reduce noise pollution inside buildings.

Aesthetic Pollution

Anything that detracts from the beauty of nature is **aesthetic pollution.** Unsightly buildings, degraded land (such as results from strip mining), road signs, tract houses in subdivisions, junkyards, dumps, and litter on roads and streets are forms of aesthetic pollution.

Aesthetic pollution does not cause real damage in the traditional sense; however, it is a part of business's responsibility to help improve the appearance of the community.

Cost of Eliminating Pollution

Elimination of any form of pollution costs large sums of money. Protection of the quality of the environment will cost billions of dollars. The public will ultimately pay for the elimination of pollution through higher prices and taxes. As industry eliminates its pollution, the cost of its products will increase. These increases will be passed on to the consumer in the form of higher prices. Some industries may not be able to meet these costs and still compete with imports. Failure to meet costs may force industries to close, causing unemployment of its employees. The elimination of municipal wastes will increase taxes to pay for installation and operation of pollution control equipment. For example, over a twelve-year period, the federal government is providing municipalities with $24 billion to help them eliminate their water pollution. Industry has made major advances in eliminating its pollution and continues to spend billions of dollars each year for pollution control.

MINORITY RESPONSIBILITY

The term **minority** as it applies to people can be defined in many ways—race, ethnic origin, religion, occupation, etc. Some minorities in the United States have historically been economically disadvantaged in employment. Much progress has been made to correct this problem, but Exhibits 2–2 and 2–3 show that the problem has not been solved.

Many companies in the United States are devoting much energy to the elimination of discrimination. For example, for many years American Telephone and Telegraph has devoted considerable effort to increase the hiring and training of minority races. In addition, they have made major efforts to place men in what have traditionally been women's jobs, and women in what have in the past been men's jobs. As a part of this effort, they are hiring men as operators and women for service repair jobs.

Federal legislation has also established the Office of Minority Business Enterprise, which encourages the growth of minority businesses. While American Indians, blacks, and persons of Spanish-speaking ancestry comprise 14 percent of the population, they own only about 4 percent of business firms. These firms are usually small and account for less than 1 percent of the total Gross National Product of the United States.

EMPLOYEE SAFETY

Over the years, employees have worked in varying degrees of safety, depending on the type of work and the work environment provided by the company. Varying degrees of danger exist in different types of work. For example, office workers enjoy relatively comfortable and safe jobs, while test pilots and high-steel workers perform very demanding and dangerous work. In between these safety extremes exist large numbers of employees such as machine operators, construction workers, and truckers.

Many companies have developed effective safety programs because they felt a responsibility to **employee safety.** They also recognized that increases in insurance rates, increases in workmen's compensation rates, and lost time were more expensive than a comprehensive safety program.

The federal Occupational Safety and Health Act (**OSHA**) requires business firms to meet their social responsibility for the safety of employees or suffer costly penalties. The law requires that all employees must be free from any recognized hazards that might cause death or serious injury. The law requires such controls as use of personal protective equipment, control of exposure to air contaminants, and clean, orderly work areas. Such equipment as hydraulic jacks must be inspected and certified by licensed dealers on a periodic basis. The law sets up heavy penalties for violation—up to $1,000 for each violation and up to $1,000 per day unless it is corrected within a certain time. In addition, an inspector who finds a condition that could cause death or serious injury can obtain a court injunction and have the operation shut down until corrected.

The law requires the use of personal protective equipment.

Some firms have complained that a few OSHA inspectors are overly zealous to the point of requiring safety measures that border on the absurd. Also, some firms have complained that some inspectors are not sufficiently trained to perform their jobs in a realistic and effective manner. One example is a company that manufactures cat litter. They were ordered by OSHA to give *all* their employees, at company expense, a two-week mine-safety course because the company also owned a mine.

Certainly, no one would dispute the desirability of and need for reducing job-related accidents. In excess of 13,000 workers are killed on the job each year, and over 2 million sustain disabling injuries (physical impairment or loss of more than two days work).

PRODUCT SAFETY

Progress in **product safety** has come from voluntary business actions and from government. Independent companies have achieved some product safety. One example is Underwriters Laboratories, which certifies that electrical products are safe under normal use. Many electrical manufacturers have met the standards of Underwriters Laboratories and display the label on their product. They feel the label tells the consumer that theirs is a quality product.

How Much Is Your Life Worth?

Any society makes trade-offs between economic benefits and human life. For example, over 45,000 people are killed in motor vehicle accidents each year. If all motor vehicles were eliminated from our society, we could save 45,000 lives each year. In a real sense, our society has decided motor vehicles have a value in excess of 45,000 lives per year.

The value of human life is producing a vigorous argument within the federal government. About 30,000 people in the United States work in coke plants that convert coal to coke for use in the steel industry. Studies indicate that these workers have three times as many deaths from lung cancer as other steel work-

ers, and seven times more die from kidney cancer. The Occupational Health and Safety Administration (OSHA) is requiring these companies to make changes in their plants and processes that will cost about $240 million a year. It has been estimated that these changes will save about 54 lives per year—a cost of $4.5 million per life saved.

Another federal agency, the Council on Wage and Price Stability, has called these regulations inflationary because the industry would be forced to pass on this cost in the price of their product. They contend that the price is extremely high when compared with amounts spent in

other areas of health and safety. OSHA has countered that 54 lives per year cannot be measured in terms of dollars and cents. Union leaders have charged that the Council's position shows a readiness to sacrifice human lives. On the other hand, some experts are contending that life saving, in reality, is more a "consumer choice" than a moral issue.

How much is a human life worth? Imagine that by adding safety features that would double the cost of every motor vehicle in use today, we could cut the death rate and save 5,000 people each year. What would you want our society to do?

Federal and state laws have established standards of product safety. For example, federal legislation requires automobile manufacturers to increase the safety of their products by installing seat belts, shoulder harnesses, and improved bumpers. Many consumers do not want the added safety: in spite of paying the cost of this added equipment and the convincing evidence of the reduction of injuries with its use, they still do not use the seat belts and shoulder harnesses, and they disconnect the seat-belt warning system.

Federal agencies such as the Food and Drug Administration, the Department of Agriculture, and the Surgeon General's Office contribute to product safety. These agencies removed some insecticides, drugs, artificial sweeteners, chemicals, and other products from the market. An example of agency protection of the consumer relates to a certain brand of powdered milk that contained organisms that caused digestive upset. The government agency stopped production of the product and required the company to pick up every package of its product from every grocery shelf. In addition, by use of newspapers, radio, and television, it warned the nation not to use the product. The damage to the reputation of the product was so great that it has not been sold since then.

The bulk of product safety improvement has been the result of manufacturer actions. Business firms realize that selling a product that is not safe usually results in legal action that can cost them large sums in court awards and, even more important, can damage the reputation of their product. Most customers do not buy products they consider unsafe. As a result, most manufacturers perform extensive testing of their products before they produce them.

THE CONSUMER MOVEMENT

The first major **consumer movement** in the United States occurred around 1900. A group of writers who criticized some business practices during this period were given the name of "muckrakers." The writings of the "muckrakers" were instrumental in causing passage of several business control laws.

The current consumer movement began to gain momentum in the early 1960s. Many individuals and groups have been responsible for its success. In 1962, President John F. Kennedy set forth the basic rights of consumers:

1. the right to be informed;
2. the right to be safe;
3. the right to be able to choose;
4. the right to be heard.

Since then, consumer advocates have grown in number both within and outside the government. (Consumer legislation is presented in chapter 23.)

BALANCE OF RESPONSIBILITY

It is obvious from the discussion in this chapter that business has many social responsibilities. However, we should never forget that the primary responsibility of business is to produce economic goods and services for the satisfaction of human wants and needs. Both production and social responsibilities are vital to the well-being of the nation and its people. Consequently, a balance of these responsibilities is both desirable and necessary.

SUMMARY OF KEY POINTS

1. Parties-at-interest in business firms are customers, owners, employees, suppliers, creditors, communities, governments, and competitors.

2. Business has a social responsibility to help reduce air, water, solid waste, noise, and aesthetic pollution.

3. Eliminating pollution costs large sums of money that will be paid by the public through higher prices and taxes.

4. Minorities have low average incomes and high levels of unemployment. Many businesses have extensive programs designed to employ and train minority workers.

5. The federal Occupation Safety and Health Act was designed to protect the safety of workers.

6. Many firms have developed effective safety programs because they felt a responsibility to worker safety; and increases in insurance rates and lost time were more costly than the safety programs.

7. Society makes trade-offs between economic benefits and human safety.

8. Federal agencies such as the Food and Drug Administration, the Department of Agriculture, and the Surgeon General's Office contribute to product safety.

9. The bulk of product safety improvement has been the result of extensive testing of products by the manufacturers.

10. President Kennedy set forth the basic rights of consumers: the right to be informed, the right to be safe, the right to be able to choose, and the right to be heard.

11. Both the production of economic goods and services and social responsibilities of business are vital to the well-being of the nation and there must be some balance between the two.

DISCUSSION QUESTIONS

1. Laws in the United States allow individuals to own businesses. Almost all owners go into business to make a profit. Were these laws created so that individuals could make a profit? Explain your answer.

2. You are the president of a steel manufacturing company that made an operating profit of $20 million this year. How would you meet your responsibility to the various parties-at-interest in your firm?

3. What are some of the ways society can eliminate the various forms of pollution?

4. Will the nation's effort to reduce pollution cost you anything? If your answer is yes, tell the ways it will cost you.

5. What kind of responsibility do you think businesses have to minorities?

6. If you were the head of OSHA, by what amount would you try to reduce the number of workers killed or injured on the job? Explain your answer.

7. If you were the president of an automobile manufacturing company, what would you do about the safety of your product? To what extent would you go in your efforts? Explain your answers.

8. Do you think the consumer movement should be increased, decreased, or stay about the same in level of activity? Explain your answer.

STUDENT PROJECTS

1. Select a local business firm that you are familiar with and identify one of each party-at-interest.
   a. A customer
   b. An owner
   c. An employee
   d. The community
   e. A government
   f. A supplier
   g. A creditor
   h. A competitor

2. See if you can identify at least one instance each of air, water, solid waste, noise, and aesthetic pollution in your area.

3. What do you think could be done to eliminate each instance of pollution, and what do you think it would cost?

4. Identify a safety device that protects employees in a local business.

5. List two products that have been recalled or identified as unsafe in the last two years. What has the producer done to rectify the situation?

6. See if you can discover an example of business self-regulation.

Hi-Per Racing Engines

Two years ago a friend who is a leading engineer came to you with a different design concept for a racing engine. Together you formed a company, Hi-Per Racing Engines, Inc., and sold $5 million in stock to about 100 stockholders. You became the president of the company.

The engine has been well received by the racing community and has been bought by several automobile manufacturers for use as an option in their expensive sports cars.

Some of the parts for the engine are bought from other manufacturers, but many, including the engine block and head, are cast in your plant. Steel is heated in furnaces, poured in cores and molds, cooled by water from the river, and then finished by lathes and other machinery. The water is returned directly to the river, but it is hot and contains a small amount of steel particles. A giant stamping machine creates a very loud noise when it is operated.

The past year produced a very good profit (11 percent return on sales). Stock in the company is currently selling for $100 a share, and dividends are $5 per year. Last year, employee wages were about average for industry in your area, but inflation has been about 8 percent this year.

Getting the business going has been hectic and time-consuming up to this time. You want your company to be a valuable asset to society, and you are now reviewing all activities to make sure the company meets its various responsibilities.

Questions

1. Discuss each party-at-interest in the business, and tell what you feel you should do to meet your responsibility to them. What could happen if you don't?
2. What could you do to meet your environmental responsibility?
3. What could you do to meet your minority responsibility?
4. What could you do to meet your safety responsibilities with regard to your employees and your product?
5. What position would you take with regard to the consumer movement?

Industrial Waste and What to Do With It

Masterson Chemical Company manufactures chemicals for industrial users throughout the South and Southeast. The company is located in the industrial area on the outskirts of a major city in the South. The manufacturing process results in approximately 100 tons of industrial waste daily. Masterson officials have been studying several alternatives on how best to dispose of this waste. The plan that appears most feasible to them is to bury the industrial waste in 55-gallon metal barrels. As a result, Masterson has taken an option to buy a 400-acre farm, which it considers to be the best site, located in a rural area. However, the farm site is only 3.3 miles from a small "bedroom" community of 3,500. Most of the residents in the small town commute to their jobs in the city.

When residents of the small town as well as farmers in the area learned of the proposal, they immediately opposed the proposed chemical dump. A citizens' environmental committee was formed to combat the location of the chemical dump in the area. Citizens contributed funds in the amount of $100 per family to hire a lawyer to represent them.

In order to overcome the negative reaction of citizens, Masterson gave a steak dinner for the city council and property owners and presented its case for the proposal. Reaction to the proposal was hostile.

To strengthen their case, the landowners have drawn up a resolution listing their reasons for opposition to using the site for chemical waste disposal. These reasons include:

1. Burying dangerous, potentially explosive, and highly corrosive chemical and industrial wastes in metal barrels could present a danger to the health of the rural community, a direct threat to the soil and water, and therefore a threat to the 3,500 citizens of the small town.
2. Delivery of large quantities of waste materials in trucks could be hazardous to traffic on the highway system of the area.
3. Locating the waste disposal at this site would lower land values.
4. The site would produce unpleasant odors that would drift through the surrounding area.
5. The site would be used to bury biological and chemical wastes, such as tars, pitches, spent acids, spent solvents, and catalysts, some of which may contain toxic or hazardous substances.
6. The landfill would create problems for the next generation, since the metal barrels would rust, and there is the danger of the chemical contents filtering through a nearby creek system into a river that leads into the Gulf of Mexico.

The company has developed a list of arguments favoring the site. These include the following:

1. The site chosen is ideal because the soil is impermeable. Thus, there is no danger now or to future generations.
2. To prevent runoff of surface water in case of heavy rains, the company proposes to build a dike system that will withstand 24 hours of rain equal to the biggest flood recorded in the area over the past 50 years.
3. If the waste materials are not buried here, they will have to be dumped into the Gulf of Mexico.
4. Eventually, the site will be replanted with pasture grasses.

In order for the company to go ahead with its plans for the site, it must have a permit from the State Environmental Protection Commission. A hearing is scheduled, at which time both sides are to present their cases.

Questions

1. What are the "social responsibility" issues in this case?
2. If you were a member of the State Environmental Protection Commission, would you be for or against allowing Masterson to use the site? Why?

Tread temperatures are taken on this earthmover tire after a durability run on a giant test wheel at Goodyear's proving ground near San Angelo, Texas.

BUSINESS PROFILE

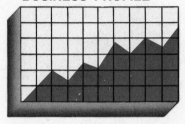

The Goodyear Tire & Rubber Company

In the winter of 1839 Charles Goodyear, who had been seeking a formula to make unstable rubber into a more useful material, found the answer. He accidentally dropped a glob of rubber and sulfur on a hot stove in his kitchen laboratory. The result was a rubber that was firm and flexible and could withstand heat and cold. The process is called *vulcanization* after Vulcan, the Roman god of fire.

Although his discovery made possible the rubber industry, the inventor died penniless in 1860. His name was remembered, however, 38 years later when Frank Seiberling borrowed $3,500 from his brother-in-law to make a down payment on a manufacturing plant in Akron, Ohio. The Goodyear Tire & Rubber Company was incorporated on August 29, 1898, and began production in November of that year with 13 employees. The first products were bicycle tires, carriage tires, and horseshoe pads. Automobile tires were added to the company's line the next year.

From this modest beginning, Goodyear grew to a position among the forty largest industrial firms in the United States. It has more than 135,000 employees worldwide, assets of nearly $5 billion and annual sales over $9 billion.

Goodyear recognizes its social responsibilities in many ways. Concern for the workplace and for the total environment has led to expenditures of millions of dollars for pollution control equipment and research. For its contributions to environmental protection, Goodyear was awarded the 1981 Enviromental Industry Award by a White House agency.

The company has undertaken projects to find constructive uses for discarded tires, including the building of artificial reefs to provide fish habitats, floating breakwaters and other shore protection devices.

3 Forms of Business Ownership

LEARNING GOALS

After reading this chapter, you will understand:

1. The characteristics, advantages, and disadvantages of the sole proprietorship, the partnership, and the corporation.

2. The difference between general partners and limited partners.

3. How the joint venture is a special type of partnership.

4. The difference between debt and ownership capital.

5. How bonds, preferred stock, and common stock are different and how they accumulate capital for corporations.

KEY TERMS

Sole proprietorship
Unlimited liability
Partnership
Articles of copartnership
General partner
Limited partner
Silent partner
Secret partner
Dormant partner
Nominal partner
Joint venture
Corporation

Stockholder
Subchapter S corporations
Debt
Ownership
Bonds
Registered bond
Bearer bond
Preferred stock
Par value
Participating preferred stock
Cumulative preferred stock
Common stock

The business of America is business.

CALVIN COOLIDGE

Sole proprietorship, partnership, and the corporation comprise the three primary forms of business ownership in the United States today. (Franchising, a special variation of any of the three basic forms of ownership, is presented in chapter 7.) Each type of business ownership has inherent advantages and disadvantages. No one form of ownership is superior to the other forms. The characteristics of each business determine which form of ownership is the most desirable for the firm. For example, the sole proprietorship form of ownership that is typical of the neighborhood drugstore would not be a desirable form of ownership for General Motors: it could never have reached its present size with the sole proprietorship form of ownership.

Several important factors need to be considered when selecting a type of business ownership: these factors are shown in Exhibit 3–1.

SOLE PROPRIETORSHIP

The sole proprietorship is clearly the most prevalent form of business ownership in the United States; it is used almost exclusively in small business firms (Exhibit 3–2). The **sole proprietorship** is a business owned by only one person and it is the least complicated of the three forms of ownership. To start a sole proprietorship, a person must acquire the necessary assets and begin business operations. Although le-

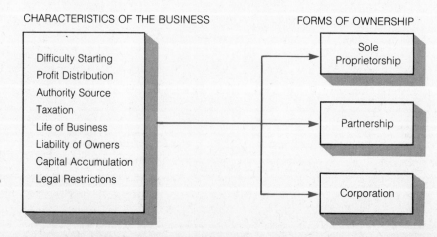

Exhibit 3–1
The characteristics of the business determine which form of ownership is best for that business.

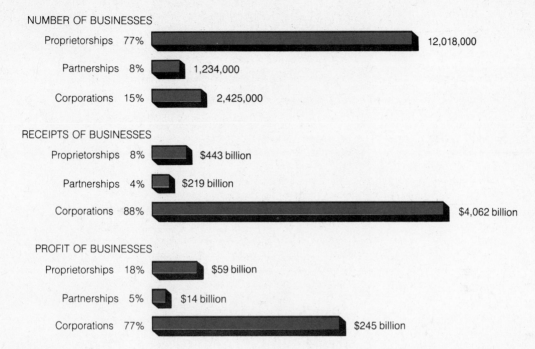

NUMBER OF BUSINESSES

Proprietorships 77% 12,018,000

Partnerships 8% 1,234,000

Corporations 15% 2,425,000

RECEIPTS OF BUSINESSES

Proprietorships 8% $443 billion

Partnerships 4% $219 billion

Corporations 88% $4,062 billion

PROFIT OF BUSINESSES

Proprietorships 18% $59 billion

Partnerships 5% $14 billion

Corporations 77% $245 billion

Exhibit 3–2

Number, receipts, and profit of proprietorships, partnerships, and corporations.

(SOURCE: Statistical Abstract of the United States, 1981.)

gal expenses of setting up a sole proprietorship are minimal, there may be other expenses, such as business licenses and tax permits.

Because ownership is vested in one person, all profits from the business go to the owner to use as he or she chooses. In addition, the owner exercises total authority over the business. Government agencies consider profit from the sole proprietorship to be a part of the owner's total income and do not tax it separately.

The length of life of the sole proprietorship is entirely dependent on the owner. The owner may terminate the business at any time; however, it does terminate automatically upon the owner's death even though the assets are still in existence. The assets simply transfer to his or her estate for distribution to heirs as specified in the will.

Sole proprietorship assigns **unlimited liability** to the owner. Debts incurred by the business firm may be collected from the business or, if not available from the business, from all other assets the owner may possess. For example, a person might invest $5,000 in starting a small hobby shop as a sole proprietorship. Suppose the operations of the business caused a death in which negligence by the firm was involved—such as an employee driving a delivery truck while drunk, which caused a fatal accident. If a large damage judgment were obtained against the business, say $100,000, the individual obtaining the judgment would be able to force sale not only of the hobby shop but of any other of the owner's assets not covered by homestead laws—for example, other business assets, stocks, bonds, and even some of the personal bank account.

The sole proprietorship is the most prevalent form of business in the United States.

The amount of capital the sole proprietorship is able to accumulate is usually rather severely limited. The extent of capital available to start or expand the business equals the total amount the owner has or can borrow. The only legal restrictions that apply to the sole proprietorship form of ownership are local and state business licenses, usually used for collecting taxes. Usually no special laws exist to control the sole proprietorship.

Most businesses are sole proprietorships primarily because of their size, their profit potential, the ease with which they are entered into, and their limited capital requirements (see Exhibit 3–3).

Exhibit 3–3

Advantages /disadvantages of the sole proprietorship.

Advantages	Disadvantages
Easy to start	Life of business is limited
All profit to one person	Unlimited liability
All authority in one person	Capital accumulation of one person
Taxed as individual income	
No special legal restriction	

PARTNERSHIP

The **partnership,** like the sole proprietorship, is a form of ownership used primarily in small business firms. Two or more owners comprise a partnership. The structure of a partnership may be established with an almost endless variation of features. The partners establish the conditions of the partnership, the contribution of each partner to the business, and the division of profits. They also decide on the amount of authority, duties, and liability each will have.

Although it is not mandatory under law, it is sound practice to have legal assistance in drawing up the contract of a partnership, which is called **articles of copartnership** (see Exhibit 3–4). This agreement establishes the exact relationship between the partners, e.g., contributions, division of profits, authority, etc. If a copartnership agreement is not drawn up between the partners, the law provides for settlement of disputes, which may or may not be the original intent of the partners.

In the partnership form of ownership, there are two basic kinds of partners: general and limited.

General Partners

Under law, each partnership must have at least one **general partner.** General partners have unlimited liability, as in the sole proprietorship form of ownership.

Exhibit 3–4
The first page of an articles of
copartnership form.

PARTNERSHIP AGREEMENT

THIS PARTNERSHIP AGREEMENT is entered into this _____ day
of _____, 19____, between the following persons whose
names and addresses are set forth below:

The above partners hereby agree that upon the commencement date of this
partnership they shall be deemed to have become partners in business. The purposes,
terms and conditions of this partnership are as follows:

1. **NAME** — The firm name of the partnership shall be

2. **PRINCIPAL PLACE OF BUSINESS** — The principal place of business of the partnership
shall be

3. **PURPOSE** — The business of the partnership is set forth below and includes any
other business related thereto.

4. **TERM** — The partnership shall commence on _____
19____, and shall continue until _____
(indefinite term or a term of years)

Limited Partners

A partnership is not required to have any **limited partners**. Limited partners are usually limited in liability to the amount of their investment. There
are four types of limited partners: silent, secret, dormant, and nominal.

Silent Partner. A **silent partner** takes no active part in the management of the business. This type of limited partner allows people to invest
in a business without having to be involved in its operation.

Secret Partner. A **secret partner** takes an active part in decision making in the business but is not known to the public. This type of partner appeals to the individual who wants a say in operation of the business, but does not want it known for some reason, such as a fear of being criticized for possible conflict of interest.

Dormant Partner. The **dormant partner** is a combination of the silent and secret partner in that the dormant partner does not take an active or public part in the management of the business. The individual who wishes to invest in a partnership strictly on a financial basis is ideally suited to be a dormant partner.

Nominal Partner. The **nominal partner** is a person who lends his or her name to the partnership but is not actually a partner in the strict sense of the word. Usually, the nominal partner is well known and allows his or her name to be associated with the business for promotional purposes. The nominal partner does not take part in the management of the business, but receives a fee for the use of his or her name.

Characteristics of a Partnership

A partnership can start its business with an agreement as to the terms of the partnership. A small legal fee for the articles of copartnership is the only cost. The partners distribute the profit according to the terms of the agreement. The division of authority among the partners is determined by the agreement, which should be set up so that conflicts and overlap of authority will be avoided. Each partner pays income taxes as an individual on his or her share of the profit, even if it is retained in the business.

A partnership may be terminated in several ways. If the partners wish the business to function for a specific period of time only, the articles of copartnership may state the time limit. In addition, withdrawal or the death of any general partner automatically dissolves the partnership, although the assets of the partnership may remain. The remaining partners may

Exhibit 3–5

Characteristics of partners.

Type of Partner	Active Part in Management	Known to Public	Ownership in the Business
General	Yes	Yes	Yes
Silent	No	Yes	Yes
Secret	Yes	No	Yes
Dormant	No	No	Yes
Nominal	No	Yes	No

establish a new partnership in any way they wish after the other's assets are settled. Any limited partner, however, may withdraw or sell his or her part of the partnership. The death of a limited partner does not terminate the partnership; the deceased partner's share goes into his or her estate.

The capital-accumulating ability of the partnership is limited by the combined total assets and borrowing power of all the partners. The only special legal restriction on the partnership is that the partners abide by their agreement.

JOINT VENTURE

A **joint venture** is a very specialized type of partnership arrangement. In the traditional partnership, two or more people join together in a *continuous business operation* for profit. In a joint venture, two or more people join together in *co-ownership for a specific limited purpose*.

For example, three people might enter into a joint venture to develop and sell a shopping center for profit. They would pool their funds, purchase the property, obtain leases, and build the shopping center. When

Exhibit 3–6

Comparison of the forms of ownership.

	Proprietorship	Partnership	Corporation
Number of owners	One	Two or more	Three or more
Method of starting form of ownership	None	Partnership agreement	State charter
Distribution of profit	Owner	Partnership agreement	Dividends to stockholders as voted
Origin of authority	Owner	Partnership agreement	Stockholders to Board of Directors
Federal income tax	Owner's personal tax	Partner's personal tax	Corporation tax and dividends to stockholders
Length of life	Life of owner or choice	Life of general partner(s) or choice	Charter
Extent of liability	Unlimited	Unlimited (general partner)	Limited to investment
Ability to accumulate capital	Assets and credit of owner	Assets and credit of partners	Ability to sell stock and bonds
Special legal restrictions	None	Partnership law	State and federal

they sell the shopping center, their joint venture ends. A joint venture is taxed as a partnership. Like traditional partnerships, joint venture agreements should be drawn up by legal counsel to avoid future problems and disputes.

Joint ventures are not as common as traditional partnerships, but they are increasing in number. They occur more often in real estate developments than in any other field of business activity.

CORPORATIONS

As interpreted by the United States Supreme Court, a **corporation** is an artificial entity that may legally own property, transact business, enter into contracts, sue and be sued, and engage in other business activities. The charters that create corporations are granted by the individual states. Each state sets its own requirements for these charters.

The owners of a corporation are called **stockholders.** They hold stock certificates for their amount of ownership in the corporation. Several large corporations, such as General Electric, General Motors, and American Telephone and Telegraph, have more than a million stockholders.

Compared to the sole proprietorship and the general partnership, the corporation requires far more effort and expense to originate the form of ownership. Legal assistance should be used to make application for the corporation charter to the proper state authority, usually the Secretary of State. Each state establishes its own charter fee. The total cost (charter fees, legal fees, etc.) of originating the corporation form of ownership for a small business is usually between $500 and $1,000.

Legally, the ultimate authority in the corporation rests with the stockholders. The stockholders elect members to the board of directors. The board protects the interests of the stockholders by setting broad policies and controlling the corporation. The board of directors appoints the president and other major officers of the corporation. The board also has the power to remove any officer of the corporation. In addition, it presents recommendations to be voted upon by the stockholders. The president and other officers of the corporation operate within the framework of the broad policies set by the board of directors.

Profit distributed to owners of the corporation (stockholders) is called *dividends.* The board of directors determines when dividends will be paid and how much will be paid. Stockholders almost never receive all the profit in the form of dividends. Usually the corporation retains part of the profit for future growth and security. The corporation has no legal obligation to pay a dividend unless the board of directors votes to do so. A few highly successful corporations have never paid a dividend but have reinvested profit for growth purposes. Their stockholders have been satisfied to increase the value of their stocks as a result of the growth.

Generally, corporations pay a federal corporation income tax. The current corporation income tax is 15 percent of the first $25,000, 18 percent of the next $25,000, 30 percent of the next $25,000, 40 percent of the next $25,000, and 46 percent of all income over $100,000. For ex-

ample, the corporation tax on a profit of $200,000 would be computed as follows:

$$
\begin{array}{rl}
15 \text{ percent of } \$\ 25{,}000 = \$ & 3{,}750 \\
18 \text{ percent of } \$\ 25{,}000 = \$ & 4{,}500 \\
30 \text{ percent of } \$\ 25{,}000 = \$ & 7{,}500 \\
40 \text{ percent of } \$\ 25{,}000 = \$ & 10{,}000 \\
46 \text{ percent of } \$100{,}000 = \underline{\$\ 46{,}000} \\
\text{Total tax} \qquad \$\ 71{,}750
\end{array}
$$

Congress can change this tax at any time by the legislative process (it has changed it several times in the past).

This tax must be paid before dividends. The dividends paid to stockholders out of the remaining profit must be reported as income to the individual in his or her own tax return. In effect, the stockholder pays a double tax through corporation and individual tax returns—one disadvantage of the corporate form of ownership. One exception is **Subchapter S corporations.** In one of its actions to help small business, the United States Congress added Subchapter S to the Internal Revenue Code. (These are regular state-chartered corporations that qualify for Subchapter S; they are not special types of corporations.) Under certain conditions, Subchapter S allows small corporations to be taxed as partnerships. In its present form it has the potential for substantial tax savings for many small firms. However, the Code is very complex and no small business should attempt to use it without the assistance of an accountant or attorney.

Many states also require corporations to pay a state corporation income tax.

A corporation's charter determines its length of life. Almost all corporation charters provide for perpetual existence of the corporation. Shares of stock (ownership) may be transferred without affecting the corporation.

The stockholder is liable to the extent of his investment in the corporation. Unlike the sole proprietor and the partner, the stockholder's personal assets cannot be sold in bankruptcy proceedings to satisfy the debts of the corporation.

Possibly the most important advantage of the corporate form of ownership is the ability to amass capital. The amount of stocks and bonds a corporation can sell is limited only by the number that people are willing to buy. There are no legal limits to the number of owners (or debtors) of a corporation.

Individuals can invest their funds in the corporation, because of the limited liability feature, without taking an active part in the management of the corporation. Without the corporate form of ownership, large corporations such as General Motors would be impossible. Imagine a business with more than a million partners.

All corporations are subject to state regulations, and many corporations are subject to federal regulations. States require that corporations make annual reports to various state agencies.

CAPITAL-ACCUMULATING INSTRUMENTS

Other than reinvesting profit, there are two main methods by which a corporation may obtain capital—**debt** and **ownership**.

Debt

Corporations may obtain short-term funds through the use of promissory notes, trade credit, etc. Long-term debt of the corporation is usually in the form of bonds issued by the corporation. **Bonds** are, in a sense, long-term promissory notes of the corporation. Bonds have a face value, which is usually in $1,000 denominations, and a maturity date, at which time the principal must be repaid. In addition, each certificate has a stated interest rate. The issuing corporation is obligated to pay the bondholder an amount of money equal to the interest percentage of the face value of the bond. For example, a bond with a face value of $1,000 and a 6 percent interest rate would require a payment of $60 a year until the bond matured.

Bonds are usually either of two types: registered or bearer. A **registered bond** is one on which the owner's name is registered with the issuer, and interest payments are automatically sent to the owner by the company. A **bearer bond** (often called a *coupon bond*) is one on which the

Exhibit 3–7
A bond certificate.

owner's name is not registered with the issuer. These bonds are the property of whoever holds them at a specific time. These bonds have coupons attached to them, and when interest is due, the holder of the bond simply clips a coupon from the bond and sends it to the source authorized to make interest payments for the issuer of the bonds. Most bonds issued today are registered bonds. (See Exhibit 3–7.)

Ownership

There are two forms of ownership: preferred stock and common stock. Corporations may issue either preferred stock or common stock or both. Both common and preferred stock may contain almost any provisions the corporation may choose. However, in most cases when corporations issue common stock and/or preferred stock, they have the following general characteristics:

Preferred Stock.   Owners of **preferred stock** usually give up some privileges in order to obtain preferential treatment in other areas. They generally forego voting rights that common stockholders usually have. On the other hand, if dividends are declared, the preferred stockholder must be paid in full before the common stockholder can be paid any dividend. When a dividend is declared, the preferred stockholders are paid a set rate that is determined by a stated percent-of-par value. **Par value** is an arbitrary amount assigned to the stock when it is issued but it has no relationship to the actual market value of the stock. For example, a share of preferred stock with par value of $100 and a stated 6 percent-of-par value would entitle the owner to a yearly $6 dividend, when declared. In rare instances, preferred stock is issued without a stated par value. Such stock is called *no-par* and must have a stated dollar dividend amount rather than a percent of par.

In some cases, in order to make the preferred stock more attractive to buyers, a corporation will issue **participating preferred stock**. This type of preferred stock has a provision that allows preferred stockholders to share with common stockholders in unusually high profits. The corporation uses a formula to determine the extent of participation of preferred and common stockholders. Preferred stock that does not have this feature is called *nonparticipating preferred stock*.

As noted earlier, preferred stockholders only receive dividends when dividends are declared. As a result, most preferred stock contains a cumulative dividend provision. This **cumulative preferred stock** accumulates dividends even in years when dividends are not declared and not paid. When dividends are declared, the cumulative preferred stockholders must receive all dividends due them, both current and past, before common stockholders can receive any dividends. If the preferred stock does not contain this provision, it is called *noncumulative preferred stock*.

Common Stock. Common stockholders usually have full voting rights. Common stockholders do not receive a stated dividend. The earnings of the corporation usually determine the dividend paid to common stockholders. Common stock may also be par or no-par. In most cases, common stock has a par value of $1 per share. (This has no relationship to the

Exhibit 3–8

Characteristics of capital-accumulating instruments of corporations.

Type of Security	Debt or Ownership	Face Falue	Dividend or Interest	Maturity	Voting Rights	Order of Payment
Corporate Bonds	Debt	Usually $1,000	Interest based on face value	Matures on date stated on bond	None	First
Preferred Stock	Ownership	Usually has par value but can be no-par	Usually fixed dividends based on percent of par	Does not mature	Usually not	Second
Common Stock	Ownership	May be par or no-par	Dividend not fixed— usually based on amount of profit	Does not mature	Almost always has voting rights	Last

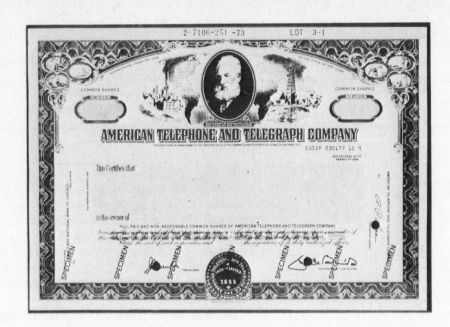

Exhibit 3–9

A common stock certificate. Over 558 million shares have been issued by AT&T.

(COURTESY: AT&T)

price it actually sells for in the market. Stock with a par value of $1 may sell for several hundred dollars per share.)

Any time a corporation liquidates its assets (usually because of bankruptcy), state laws require that creditor and owner groups be paid off in a certain order. The most common order is:

1. Accrued employee salaries;
2. Taxes owed government agencies;
3. Current creditors;
4. Bondholders;
5. Preferred stockholders;
6. Common stockholders divide remainder.

In cases of bankruptcy (when debt exceeds assets), creditors usually receive only a part of what is owed them. Consequently, those below the creditor level usually receive nothing.

Such variables as profitability of the firm, current going interest rate, prospects for sale of bonds or stocks, and the degree to which current owners are willing to spread control and ownership influence the decision to issue bonds, preferred stock, or common stock.

The vast capital-accumulating ability of corporations is best illustrated by American Telephone and Telegraph Company. They have 3.4 million stockholders holding 29 million shares of preferred stock and 686 million shares of common stock.

SUMMARY OF KEY POINTS

1. The characteristics of a business determine which form of ownership is best for that business.
2. The advantages of the sole proprietorship are that it is easy to start, the owner takes all the profit and has sole authority, profits are taxed as individual income, and there are no special legal restrictions.
3. The disadvantages of the sole proprietorship are that the life is limited, it has unlimited liability, and capital accumulation is restricted to one person.
4. A partnership should be based on an agreement that takes the form of articles of copartnership.
5. In a partnership there must be at least one general partner who has unlimited liability.
6. A partnership may have any number of limited partners (or none) who have limited liability.
7. The four types of limited partners are: silent, secret, dormant, and nominal.
8. The partnership agreement determines distribution of profit and authority.
9. A joint venture is a partnership for a limited time and purpose.
10. A corporation is an artificial entity that may own property, transact business, enter into contracts, sue and be sued, and engage in other business activities.
11. The corporation must be chartered by a state.
12. Corporations may sell stocks and bonds to accumulate capital.
13. Stock is issued in the form of preferred stock and common stock.

DISCUSSION QUESTIONS

1. Name a local sole proprietorship and explain why you think it has this form of ownership.
2. Name a local partnership and tell why you think it has this form of ownership.
3. Name a local corporation and explain why you think it is the best form of ownership for the business.
4. If you and two of your friends were going to buy some land to develop into lots for homes, what form of ownership would you use? Explain.

5. Would you rather own a bearer bond or a registered bond? Explain.

6. If you were to form a corporation to manufacture and sell some product, would you issue bonds, common stock, and/or preferred stock? Explain your selection.

STUDENT PROJECT

Give the name of one firm in your community for each of the following: (a) a sole proprietorship, (b) a partnership, (c) a corporation. Go to each business and obtain the following information.

1. Sole proprietorship—What steps did the owner take to start the business? What licenses or permits must he or she have to operate the business?

2. Partnership—Does the partnership have articles of copartnership? What type of agreement exists between the partners as to authority, profits, and work in the business? Are there any limited partners, and, if so, what type?

3. Corporation—What state issued the charter of the corporation? Where is the home office of the corporation? How many shares and what kind of stock are issued by the corporation?

Dave's Stereo Speakers

Dave Duke is an electrical engineer for a large manufacturer of industrial electronic equipment. Dave enjoys a wide range of music and has collected a large number of records and tapes. As a result, sound reproduction has become a hobby for him. To achieve the level of sound reproduction he wants, Dave has two rather large and expensive speakers. He has spent a considerable amount of his spare time investigating sound reproduction and acoustics. As a result of his study, he has been able to design a radically different speaker system. His new design creates a speaker that is one-third the size of his present speakers, costs one-half as much to produce, and has a slightly better sound reproduction quality.

Dave has been producing the new speakers in his garage in his spare time and they are selling so well to stores that he has a large number of back orders. Dave would like to resign from his present job and go into manufacturing his speakers on a full-time basis. He has designed a production line to produce the speakers and has compiled figures that indicate it will cost approximately $50,000 to get his operation started.

Dave has very little savings except for part ownership in a piece of land. Dave entered into a joint venture with three other people four years ago to buy a parcel of land for speculation purposes. The area has developed rapidly and several people have offered to buy the land for $120,000. Dave's share would be $30,000.

Dave has contacted you for advice and is willing to pay a rather nice consulting fee for your services.

Questions

1. Would you recommend (explain each answer):
   a. A sole proprietorship?
   b. A general or limited partnership?
   c. A joint venture?
   d. A corporation?

2. How could Dave obtain the additional money he needs to start the business if he used the (a) sole proprietorship, (b) general or limited partnership, or (c) corporation?

3. If he used the corporation form of ownership, would you advise him to issue bonds, common stock, or preferred stock?

Henry Dallas

Henry is a recent college graduate with a degree in business administration. He has been teaching in high school and coaching football for three years since his graduation, saving as much money as possible to fulfill his ambition of going into business for himself. One of the main reasons that he studied business administration was to obtain a good background that would be beneficial to him in business.

He lives and teaches in a city of 750,000, and this is where he plans to go into business. In fact, during his college days he and one or two of his close friends had often talked of the possibility of going into business together. They are now living in the same town, but, as is so often the case, Henry does not have sufficient capital to open the business, not even if his friends help.

He wants to open a restaurant that will specialize in steaks cooked on an open grill and served cafeteria-style. There is a favorable location away from the congested areas but on a heavily traveled street. Three large office buildings are nearby with many potential customers plus a number of other businesses.

There is no building on the available land, so the building will have to be constructed, at an estimated cost of $25,000. The land can be purchased for $7,500. Another $4,500 will be needed for fixtures (tables and chairs, air conditioning equipment, kitchen equipment, barbecue pit). An additional $5,000 will be needed to get the business in operation (initial purchases of food supplies, salary payments, etc.). Henry must make a number of decisions before he begins on his business venture.

Questions

1. Which form of ownership would be most suited to this situation (discuss the pros and cons of each):
   a. A sole proprietorship?
   b. A partnership (general or limited)?
   c. A corporation?

2. Where can Henry borrow the money for each form of ownership?

3. Explain to Henry why the selection of the form of ownership is so vital when beginning a business.

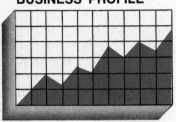

BUSINESS PROFILE

J. C. Penney Company, Inc.

The J. C. Penney Company, Inc., has evolved using two basic forms of business ownership during its history—partnerships and a corporation.

The company was started in 1902 when James Cash Penney opened his first dry goods store, called The Golden Rule, in the small mining town of Kemmerer, Wyoming. It was a partnership with total capital of $6,000. Penney was the manager-partner with one-third interest. T. M. Callahan and Guy Johnson held the other two-thirds interest. Penney's management made the store a success from the start. In 1907 Penney accepted his partners' offer to sell him their part of the Kemmerer store, and two others that had been opened, for $30,000.

Penney used the partnership plan for his chain because he wanted to give his salesmen the same opportunity to become manager-partners as he had. By 1912 there were 34 stores, all managed by partners, with Penney having either a one-third or two-thirds interest in most of them. His partnership plan enabled a store manager who had saved enough capital to buy a one-third interest in a new store that would be opened out of his store, provided he had trained a man capable of managing the store.

In 1913 the chain was incorporated as the J. C. Penney Company, Inc., in Utah in order to obtain more credit from banks for expansion. In 1914 the company headquarters were established in New York City in order to be near the place where much of the merchandise they sold was produced. In 1924 the company moved its incorporation charter to Delaware because that state's laws were more advantageous. The partnership plan was retained in the form of profit-sharing, which allowed managers and other associates to share in the earnings they helped generate.

Originally the company was basically a major retailer of clothing and a limited line of home furnishings on a cash-and-carry basis. In the late 1950s, the company (1) introduced credit selling, (2) expanded its merchandise offering to become a complete department store, and (3) introduced a catalog business. Today, the company also owns drugstores and a financial company that sells auto, home, health, and life insurance.

J. C. Penney's idea of partnership involvement and his basic philosophy of selling quality merchandise at the lowest price possible helped to build a company that now has yearly sales of over $11 billion, assets of $7 billion, operates 2,000 retail units and 1,845 catalog centers in the U.S. and 72 stores in Europe, and has over 200,000 employees and 86,000 stockholders.

Management
of the
Business Firm

SECTION TWO

4 The Management and Leadership Processes

LEARNING GOALS

After reading this chapter, you will understand:

1. The systems approach to management.

2. How managers decide on the goals and objectives for the firm.

3. The kinds of activities managers perform at various hierarchical levels in a company.

4. The functions of managers.

5. What management by objectives is.

6. The skills managers need to perform their jobs effectively.

7. The different styles of leadership used by managers.

KEY TERMS

Systems approach
Objectives
Philosophy of management
Planning
Organizing
Staffing
Actuating
Control
Management by Objectives
Leadership
Technical skills
Human relations skills

Body language
Communication process
Conceptual skills
Decision-making skills
Flextime
Autocratic leaders
Free-rein leaders
Participative leaders
Team management
Quality control circles
Participative management program
Contingency approach

> In turbulent times, an enterprise has to be managed both to withstand sudden blows and to avail itself of sudden unexpected opportunities.
>
> PETER DRUCKER

Business firms exist in a dynamic environment. The challenge of today's managers is to anticipate change and be ready to respond to it with a planned course of action. The quality of the management of a firm is a key ingredient in its ability to maintain a healthy position in the competitive environment.

Changing national and international conditions present new opportunities and new problems. Inflation, increasing domestic and international competition, changing consumer demands, new legislation, and environmental concerns are examples of the vast number of issues confronting today's managers. Managers who understand these problems and deal with them effectively have the best opportunity to achieve a strategic position among their competitors. In this dynamic environment, the task of managers is to supervise employees and coordinate their work activities as they use the financial and physical resources of the firm to insure that its goals will be achieved.

SYSTEMS APPROACH TO MANAGEMENT

The management of a firm should be viewed as a system. A system is an arrangement of interrelated parts designed to achieve objectives. By using the **systems approach** (i.e., by viewing the firm as an arrangement of interrelated parts), managers can more efficiently coordinate all of the firm's human, physical, and financial resources to accomplish the desired goals, such as greater profit or providing opportunities for employee development.

OBJECTIVES OF THE FIRM

All business organizations are established to achieve specific **objectives** or goals, and managers are responsible for making the decisions that enable the firm to achieve its objectives. Objectives in a firm are arranged in a hierarchy for each organizational level, as shown in Exhibit 4–1. The hierarchy of objectives ranges from broad company-wide objectives to specific objectives for divisions, departments, work groups, and individuals.

Exhibit 4–1
The hierarchy of objectives in an organization.

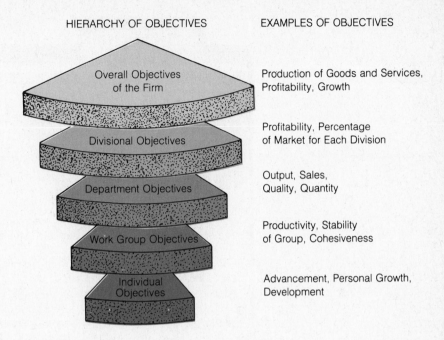

HIERARCHY OF OBJECTIVES

EXAMPLES OF OBJECTIVES

Overall Objectives of the Firm

Production of Goods and Services, Profitability, Growth

Divisional Objectives

Profitability, Percentage of Market for Each Division

Department Objectives

Output, Sales, Quality, Quantity

Work Group Objectives

Productivity, Stability of Group, Cohesiveness

Individual Objectives

Advancement, Personal Growth, Development

Philosophy of Management

The objectives of each company are based on a **philosophy of management**, which sets down the primary, long-range objectives of the organization. It provides the principles, practices, and ethical standards that guide employers in their conduct, decisions, and actions with customers, stockholders, employees, and the community.

Companies have many goals and purposes, as the statement of corporate objectives of Xerox Corporation shown in Exhibit 4–2 indicates.

LEVELS OF MANAGEMENT

A large business firm requires many managers, each with specific qualifications and specialties. It is apparent that their responsibilities and specialties differ significantly, depending upon their positions in the company. Broadly defined, the management of a company may be described as consisting of three levels: (1) top management, (2) middle management, and (3) supervisory management. Exhibit 4–3 shows these levels of management and gives typical titles of managers at each level.

Managerial Activities

What kinds of activities do managers at each level perform? A comparison of some assignments for managers illustrates some of the major activities of the three levels. Top-level managers deal with overall, long-range objectives and policies, make long-range plans, and maintain public relations contacts with the company's parties-at-interest. Middle-level managers keep closer contact with day-to-day results and make plans that will aid in achieving

Exhibit 4–2

Corporate Philosophy and Objectives of Xerox Corporation

Our corporate philosophy grew out of the personal philosophy of one man—(the late) Joe Wilson (chief executive of Xerox for 25 years)—and has been continued, and indeed expanded, through the strong convictions of his successor (C. Peter McColough, the present chairman).

Xerox believes first in innovation—in the creation of new services. . .and to market these services in a profitable way. We want to render values. We want to give men something worth getting. . .and we want the people associated with us to be proud of what they are doing.

Another stand of ours is that corporations in this society must be responsible, and that responsibility means participation and the willingness to take a position.

To put all this another way, it seems very clear to us that corporations are no different from individuals. None of us wants to go through life just taking things. We want to give something back.

The philosophy of the corporation must reflect that of the individuals who compose it. And the other side of this coin is just the trace of a thought that the kind of people we've been able to attract over the years would never have come to us if we were profit-minded only.

Courtesy: Xerox Corporation.

objectives set by top-level managers. Supervisory-level managers plan day-to-day activities and put policies in effect within objectives set down by top- and middle-level managers.

FUNCTIONS OF MANAGEMENT

The functions that managers perform as they strive to achieve company goals are planning, organizing, staffing, actuating, and controlling the task-related activities of employees. The systems approach stresses that all management functions are interrelated. Thus, managers cannot accomplish the planning function while ignoring the remaining functions: they must integrate planning with the other managerial functions to ensure that they are coordinated toward achieving company objectives. Managers at every organizational level perform these functions and they are universal in nature, since they must be executed by managers in all types of organizations—large corporations, public schools, colleges and universities, hospitals, government agencies, and small businesses. An examination of each managerial function will enable us to more clearly understand the managers' role in the organization.

Exhibit 4–3
The three levels of management.

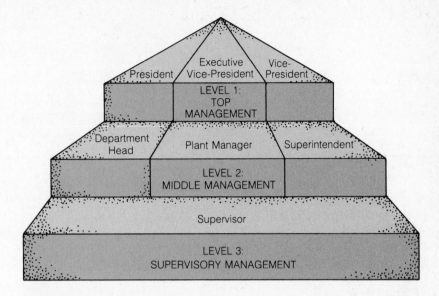

Planning

Planning, one of the oldest managerial activities, is the mental process of setting the objectives for the firm and then deciding on the courses of action that must be followed to reach the objectives. Planning includes making the decisions of who is to do a task, when it is to be done, where it is to be done, and how it is to be done. Managers must plan, regardless of their level in the company. Business firms operate in an environment that is continually changing. If firms are to remain competitive, managers need to evaluate and update plans often to keep pace with the changing conditions both inside and outside the company that affect employees and the firm's operations.

Stages in the Managerial Planning Process.   The stages of the managerial planning process, which involve determining objectives and then specifying the policies and procedures for carrying them out, are shown in Exhibit 4–4.

Identify the Objectives.   Planning requires managers to study present conditions and to decide on the objectives to be met at some future point in time. To illustrate, company executives may make a detailed intensive analysis of company sales; they may investigate the company's current sales position in relation to competitors and project sales for the future. A result of this analysis may be the establishment of a new goal: to increase total sales by 15 percent over a three-year period.

Develop Alternatives.   Once managers have the new goal, they must decide how to move from the current sales level to the projected goal. They must design alternative methods and try to anticipate any conditions that might affect progress toward the goals or objectives. What are some possible alternatives for increasing sales?

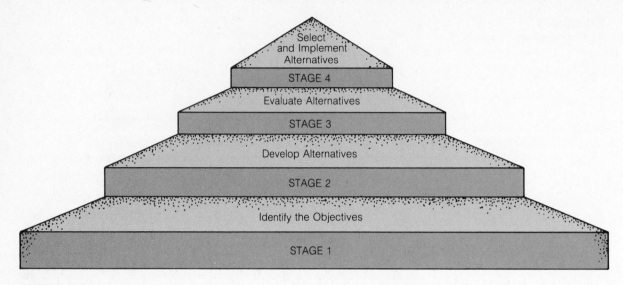

Exhibit 4–4
The management planning process.

1. Spend more funds on advertising promotions.
2. Hire additional sales personnel.
3. Build new plants in order to increase production.
4. Expand sales into new territories.
5. Develop and manufacture new products.
6. Improve existing products.

Evaluate Alternatives.   Managers must evaluate each alternative to determine its contribution to the projected goal of greater sales. This analysis may reveal that certain alternatives are not feasible. For example, investigation may show that it is not possible to build new facilities or to introduce a line of products into new geographical areas at a particular time.

Select and Implement Alternatives.   After analysis, managers select the course of action that appears most promising. This may include one or a combination of alternatives, such as increasing advertising expenditures and improving the existing product. Managers act to implement the plan for reaching the objective of increased sales.

Planning at General Electric.   An example of managerial planning in a large firm is provided by General Electric Company. Managerial planning at General Electric for the next year begins one year in advance. General Electric has 43 operating units, called strategic business units (SBUs). An SBU may be a single department or several departments. In January, each SBU begins drawing up plans for the coming year, taking into account economic and social changes. Each of the SBU plans is submitted to the sector manager at the next level. General Electric is divided into six sectors to represent the businesses in which the company is engaged: consumer products and services, industrial products and components, power systems, technical systems and materials, international operations, and Utah International, a mining company. Each sector is headed by an executive, and each of the 43 SBUs is grouped into a sector based on the nature of its operation.

The head of each sector then evaluates the plans for the SBUs under his/her direction, evaluating them in terms of the overall goals of the company. The executive then submits a master plan for all the units under his/her control to the president and the policy board. Each of the six sector executives presents plans for their sector plus summaries of the SBU plans. In November or December of each year, the policy board allocates funds to the SBUs on the basis of potential for the next year. Potential is measured according to three categories: growth, stability, or no-growth. This planning method allows the company to give the most attention to the growth areas, provide adequate funds for the units that show steady growth, and critically evaluate the no-growth areas with the possibility of disposing of these units.[1]

Organizing

The management function of **organizing** is the process of identifying and grouping tasks (activities) and establishing authority relationships between employees so that company objectives can be achieved. The organizing function consists of four related steps.

1. First, managers identify the tasks (or activities) necessary to effectively and efficiently accomplish the company's overall and specific objectives, as defined in the planning function. For example, the three essential activities for a manufacturing firm are production, sales, and finance. The production activity covers what to produce, when to produce it, and in what quantities. The sales activity focuses on finding potential customers and selling the firm's output. The finance activity refers to the methods the management of the firm uses to acquire, allocate, and expend monetary resources.

2. Second, after the activities have been identified, they must be grouped into some logical arrangement, such as departments, divisions, or sections so that the firm's limited resources can be used most efficiently. Thus, in the manufacturing firm, all similar activities are usually grouped together: all sales activities are concentrated in the sales department, all finance activities in the finance department, and all production activities in the production department. This logical grouping on the basis of similarity of activity allows managers to take advantage of task specialization.

3. Third, managers should define (preferably in writing) and delegate to the heads of each department the authority necessary to perform their tasks.

---

[1]"Mastering Diversity at GE," *Dun's Review*, December 1978, pp. 30–32.

4. Finally, authority, responsibility, and accountability relationships between employees must be established. One way to establish authority is to diagram the authority relationships (vertical and horizontal) and lines of communication between employees on an organization chart. This chart shows the organizational structure—the framework that ties together all tasks in the company into coordinated effort. Organization charts are discussed in chapter 5.

Staffing

Staffing is the function concerned with the human resources of the company. Staffing is the process of selecting qualified employees to fill the jobs identified in the organizing function. Staffing is discussed in chapter 9.

Actuating

Actuating is the complex, challenging management function that involves working with people. In performing the actuating function, the manager provides the direct, face-to-face leadership of employees as they perform their tasks. Actuating includes providing the direction for putting into action all the plans and programs necessary to achieve objectives.

Managers must communicate clearly the orders and instructions needed to guide employees toward putting plans into action. Since managers interact directly with employees in the actuating function, they have the opportunity to motivate the employees to greater achievement through their leadership style. Their ability to communicate and motivate employees is important in determining their managerial effectiveness.

Controlling

Motorists use various aids such as road maps and highway markers as check points as they travel to make sure they reach their destination. Similarly, all managers must continually use internal aids such as worker output or sales figures to determine if the company is progressing toward its objectives.

The **control** function is the process that compares the actual performance of employees with predetermined performance standards and guides their performance so that the company's objectives, defined in the planning function, are achieved. Thus, it is clear that the planning and control functions are closely interrelated.

The basic steps in the control cycle are:

1. Standards of performance must be set for measuring performance, such as an acceptable level of worker output.
2. Actual performance must be measured at regular intervals, such as hourly, daily, weekly, monthly, or annually.
3. Performance must be evaluated to determine if performance standards are being met or if there are deviations from set standards.
4. Corrective action must be taken when there are deviations from performance standards. Otherwise, the activity is allowed to continue.

Standards of performance establish how much each employee is expected to produce. Employee output is continually evaluated and compared to these standards. For example, salespersons have a performance standard of how many customers they are expected to contact in a period of a day, a week, or a month as well as how many dollars in sales they are expected to make. This standard can be compared against the number of customers actually contacted and the sales actually made to provide management with a measure of sales effectiveness. If the salesperson is calling on a sufficient number of customers but is not reaching the sales quota in dollars, it would indicate that the salesperson is probably using the wrong selling techniques. To correct the deviation from expected performance standards, the sales manager may accompany the salesperson in order to evaluate his or her selling techniques and recommend changes, or even provide additional sales training if necessary.

In order for managers to carry out their control function of checking performance against standards, they need extensive information. Managers determine the types of information they need for decision making and for the comparison of the performance of the separate units of the firm to the management-established detailed objectives of each unit. The control cycle is a dynamic process, as illustrated in Exhibit 4–5.

MANAGEMENT BY OBJECTIVES

Management by objectives (MBO) is a planning and an employee appraisal process. The term, initially coined by the distinguished management consultant Peter Drucker, allows employees to participate in defining and setting the goals they expect to accomplish.

Exhibit 4–5
The control cycle.

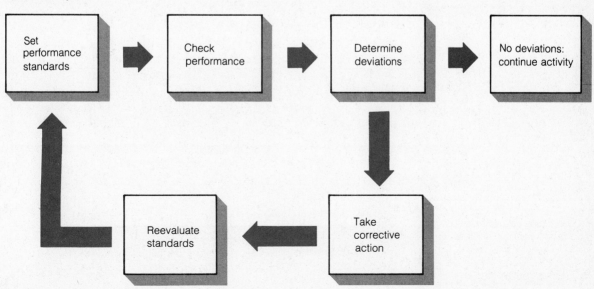

First, the supervisor and the subordinate independently set down what they expect the subordinate to accomplish during a specific time period (six months or a year). Second, the supervisor and the subordinate jointly discuss and adjust the employee's goals, which may be set too high or too low. This is an important stage because it permits employees to become mutually involved in setting their own objectives. Third, since changes may take place between the time of the initial goal setting and the end of the review cycle, there should be periodic feedback sessions planned to adjust the goals to reflect changing conditions. Fourth, the supervisor and the employee jointly evaluate how well the mutually-set objectives were met and develop ways to improve performance. In the fifth stage, the MBO goal-setting process is repeated as new goals are set for the next time period. (See Exhibit 4–6.)

THE LEADERSHIP PROCESS

Managers constantly interact with people; thus, their leadership style is an important factor in helping to build positive work relationships with employees and creating a favorable work climate within the firm. Leadership is the relationship that exists between two or more people in which one tries to influence the other toward the accomplishment of organizational goals.

Exhibit 4–6
The management by objectives process.

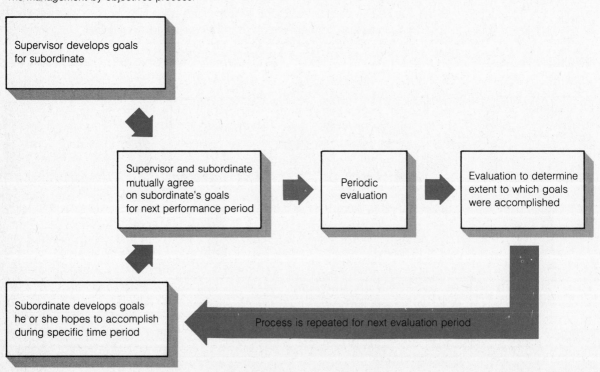

Supervisor develops goals for subordinate

Supervisor and subordinate mutually agree on subordinate's goals for next performance period

Periodic evaluation

Evaluation to determine extent to which goals were accomplished

Subordinate develops goals he or she hopes to accomplish during specific time period

Process is repeated for next evaluation period

Leadership style is an important factor in helping to build positive work relationships with employees and creating a favorable work environment.

Leadership Traits

Some researchers who have studied leadership have attempted to identify the "traits" necessary for effective leadership. Clearly, there is no universal agreement on the specific traits that distinguish effective from less effective leaders. In a survey conducted by the Gallup Organization, business leaders in large, medium, and small firms identified the traits they considered most important for advancement.[2] These traits were:

Integrity	Business knowledge
Ability to get along with others	Leadership
Industriousness	Education
Intelligence	

Managerial Skills

Managers incorporate specific skills into the process of developing an effective leadership style. These managerial skills are (1) technical, (2) human relations, (3) organizational communication, (4) conceptual, and (5) decision making. Furthermore, managers must be cognizant of the organization level at which each skill is most critical. (See Exhibit 4–7.)

Technical Skills. Technical skills are abilities for working with "things." These "things" may range from expertise in operating a complex piece of machinery (such as a lathe or a computer) to analyzing and interpreting financial records of the company. These skills are most essential for managers at the supervisory level. At this level, managers directly supervise employees who are producing goods, keeping accounting records, or typing and filing reports. Managers must understand all operations that occur in the unit that they supervise. As managers advance to higher levels, their technical skills become less important in relation to the other skills.

[2]The Wall Street Journal, November 14, 1980.

77

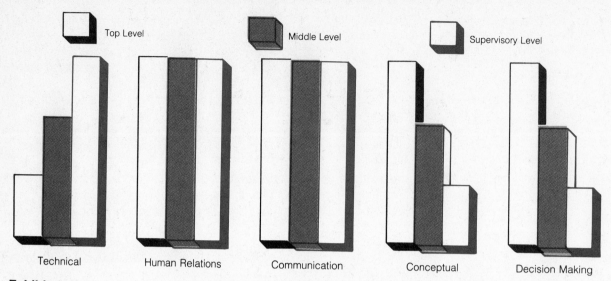

Top Level   Middle Level   Supervisory Level

Technical   Human Relations   Communication   Conceptual   Decision Making

Exhibit 4–7
The relative importance of
managerial skills at each
managerial level.

Human Relations Skills.   The ability to deal effectively with people is one
of the most essential skills managers must have. Managers find **human
relations skills** important at all levels, since they continually interact
with people at all levels. Skill in human relations is important, whether it
be the direct supervision of operating workers by first-line supervisors or
the interaction between the president and vice-presidents. Human relations is discussed in more detail in chapter 8.

Organizational Communication Skills.   The need for information to be
accurate and to flow freely through open channels of communication is
essential for all organizations. The manager who has developed skill in
organizational communication creates a climate for positive human relations
in which employees tend to be positively motivated because they have
knowledge of what is occurring in the organization. Organizational communication skills are essential for managers at all levels.

    Internal communication may flow through a number of formal vertical
channels of communication. A downward channel is used by managers to
transmit information to employees concerning task assignments, changes
in policies, and other related matters. An upward communication channel
enables employees to send information up to managers so that they are
aware of employee attitudes and concerns. In order for employees in one
department to be informed of what employees in another department are
doing, formal horizontal channels of communication must be established.
For example, personnel in the sales department and in the production
department must maintain up-to-date information about each other's activities so sales campaigns can be coordinated with production capabilities.
When it is necessary for a staff manager to communicate directly with a
line manager, then a formal diagonal channel of communication must be
established.

Much communication extends beyond company boundaries into the external environment of the company. Company representatives interact with customers, suppliers, representatives of government agencies, creditors, and stockholders in order to keep abreast of rapidly changing conditions that may affect the company.

Managers communicate in many ways to employees. Communication may be oral, either face-to-face or by telephone. Managers also communicate by means of written messages, such as by intercompany memos and staff reports. Frequently, a combination of oral and written information is communicated to aid in clarifying the message. However, managers also use nonverbal communication, called **body language**. Nonverbal communications include the signs, symbols, facial expressions, or gestures that convey information. Body language expressions such as facial expression or physical actions or movements often convey a larger part of the message a manager is communicating than what is being communicated orally. For example, looking people straight in the eye (versus looking away from them) conveys a message of self confidence.

The **communication process** consists of five basic elements, as shown in Exhibit 4–8. The basic elements are:

1. Sender—the person transmitting the information;
2. Message—the information transmitted;
3. Channel—the means chosen to transmit the information;
4. Receiver—the person or group of persons to whom the message is sent who must interpret it;
5. Feedback—the response of the receiver to the sender's message.

Barriers to Organizational Communication. In interpersonal communications, messages can easily be misinterpreted between the time they are sent and the time they are received. Some of the major communication barriers that managers should be aware of are distortion, filtering, overloading, and noise.

Distortion. Words that have one meaning for the sender may have an entirely different meaning to the recipient of the message. If the intended message is to be understood by the receiver, the sender must carefully select his or her words. Words that could possibly cause confusion should be explained clearly, especially those words that have a meaning peculiar to a company. This special language of a firm is called *company jargon*.

Filtering. The sender may screen information and transmit only what the receiver likes to hear. A subordinate may omit informing his or her supervisor of something that is unpleasant, such as not meeting a production quota. Filtered communications contain little pertinent information.

Overloading. Sometimes too much information can result in communication channels being filled with so many reports and memos that receivers cannot separate the important from the unimportant. To avoid this prob-

Exhibit 4–8
A model of the communication
process.

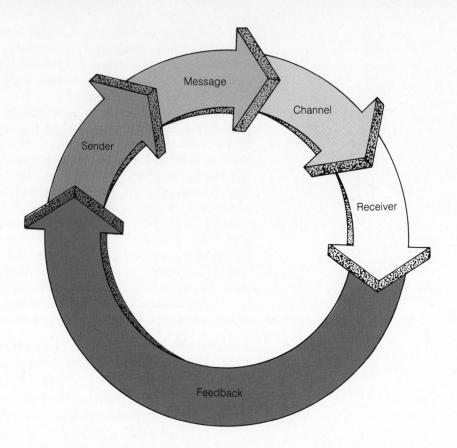

lem, the sender should give only information of the necessary quality and
quantity to make decisions.

Noise.   In interpersonal communication, noise is anything that distorts a
message. For example, trying to communicate a message in a noisy work
area interferes with message transmission and reception.

Conceptual Skills.   **Conceptual skills** refer to managers' abilities to understand the overall picture of the company and of their particular unit
within the company. A department manager's conceptual skill determines
how well he or she recognizes the department's contribution to the company's overall objectives. At the top management level, the president is
aware of how all of the various operating functions, e.g., manufacturing,
marketing, finance, fit into the company's plan of operation to make a
unified whole. Conceptual skills become increasingly important as the manager rises in the management levels, and they are particularly important
at the top level.

Decision-Making Skills.   The skill of choosing the proper course of action
to solve specific problems is the manager's **decision-making skill**. Al-

though this skill is important at all organizational levels, it is relatively more important at upper levels of management because of the nature and time dimension of the decisions involved—long range versus short range.

These management skills, like the managerial functions, are necessary in all businesses. Furthermore, these skills are transferable to other managerial positions: the skills that a manager uses in managing an industrial concern are equally applicable in school administration, hospital administration, or governmental administration.

Leadership Style

A manager's leadership style has much to do with the reactions of his/her employees. Essentially, three basic leadership styles can be identified: (1) autocratic, (2) free-rein, and (3) participative.

Autocratic. "One-man rule" best describes the autocratic leader. **Autocratic leaders** take all responsibility for decision making, actuating, communicating, motivating, and controlling subordinates. Individuals have little or no opportunity to be creative in their work since the autocratic leader outlines in detail and closely checks each employee's work. The autocratic leader ordinarily feels he or she is the only person who is qualified to make decisions. Such a manager expects obedience to his or her decisions. The manager may feel that subordinates are unable or unwilling to guide themselves and thus assumes a position of closely supervising and controlling employees.

Autocratic managers stress one-way communications that travel downward from the manager to employees. Only a minimum of upward communication exists from employees to managers. When an employee makes a mistake, the autocratic leader usually reprimands him or her.

"BUT 243 YES-MEN COULDN'T BE WRONG."

Flexible Working Hours and the Modified Work Week

Flextime is a management technique designed to reduce tardiness and turnover, raise overall job satisfaction, and increase employee participation. This system allows employees to determine, within limits, a work schedule that fits their needs. Flextime is used by some 5,000 firms of various sizes. Control Data Corporation reports that 65 percent of its employees choose the flexible work hour schedule. Employee productivity has been increased at Metropolitan Life Insurance Company's headquarters in New York since the installation of a flextime work schedule.

Companies using flextime designate a core work period when all employees must be on the job, such as from 9:30 A.M. to 4:00 P.M. Employees are permitted to select starting and quitting times during preestablished flexible bands at the beginning and end of the work day. For example, flexible bands might be from 7:30 to 9:30 A.M. and 4 to 6 P.M. Thus, employees could start as early as 7:30, with the latest starting time 9:30 A.M. The earliest leaving time is 4 P.M. and the latest leaving time is 6 P.M. The lunch period can also be flexible, from a minimum of one hour to a maximum of 2 hours. Flextime is used at Conoco Oil Company in Houston, where employees select starting times between 6:45 A.M. and 7:30 A.M. and leave work 8 ½ hours later.

Another system used by some companies since the early 1970s is the modified work week or four-day work week. At least two goals are sought by users of this system: for the company, improved employee productivity, efficiency, and morale; and for employees, more leisure time.

The modified work week (or 4/40) has received both positive and negative reactions from employees. One of the more successful companies using the four-day work week is United Services Automobile Association of San Antonio, Texas. For USAA, employee turnover has been reduced since the introduction of the 4/40 plan.

Another form of the modified work week is the compression of the work week into the two-day weekend. Hospitals use this arrangement to fill weekend shifts: nurses work two 12-hour shifts on Saturday and Sunday and are paid for 40 hours. Firestone and Goodyear pay workers wages equivalent to 36 hours for working two 12-hour shifts on the weekend: the employees are off for the rest of the week. This plan helps overcome the problems of trying to staff positions during the weekend.

Reprimands may be in the form of verbal discipline or even dismissal. Autocratic leaders tend to treat employees as individual cogs in a machine rather than as individuals who are part of effective work groups. This type of leader applies much pressure on employees as the means of getting more production. Ordinarily, pressure for increased production will increase productivity for a short time period. However, over the long run, productivity tends to be lower.

Autocratic leadership is not regarded as the leadership style that will generate positive feelings between managers and employees in today's modern business firm. Employees may react unfavorably to this style of leadership by such means as restricting their work output, sabotaging the work, increasing tardiness and absenteeism, or quitting.

Free Rein. Leaders who delegate authority for decision making to employees are **free-rein leaders**. They emphasize "the less supervision the better," believing their managerial responsibility to be one of minimal contact and supervision of employees. Free-rein leaders assign work to employees and then let them decide how they will complete the job. The only guideline is that the job be done satisfactorily. Free-rein leaders expect subordinates to assume responsibility for their own guidance, motivation, and control.

This style of leadership is used most effectively where employees are committed to the goals of the organization, are qualified to do their work on an independent basis, and prefer to work with a minimum of supervision, such as highly motivated research scientists. However, if employees are unwilling to work under this style of leadership, it will be unsatisfactory. Chaotic conditions may develop: output may decline, employees may demand more, and confusion may prevail among employees since there is no identifiable leader who is in control.

Participative. Many modern managers have built positive relationships with employees by adopting the participative or democratic management style. **Participative leaders** practice leadership by consultation. They consult with employees, seeking their comments, opinions, suggestions, and ideas. Managers involve employees actively in departmental or company matters whenever possible so that they have an important role in making decisions that affect them and their work. This leadership style is built upon the premise that individuals will give support to decisions they helped to make. Effective participative leaders seriously review the ideas of subordinates and accept their suggestions whenever possible. However, final authority on matters of importance still remains with the leader.

Communication is two-way, flowing between employees and managers. Employees are encouraged to assume greater responsibility for guiding their own efforts. People are considered the most valuable asset of the firm. When employees make a mistake, participative leaders adopt the philosophy that mistakes are an opportunity to learn to avoid similar future errors.

The participative leader takes an interest in the employees' personal life and job, which contributes significantly to building a favorable work climate. Employees usually like participative leadership. This leadership style often results in increased output, greater interest in company matters, and lower absenteeism, tardiness, and turnover. (The business profile at the end of this chapter presents an organization in which participative leadership is practiced.)

Team Management. One form of participative management practiced by some companies is **team management.** In team management, the manager works with subordinates as a team rather than on the typical one-to-one basis. The increasing complexity and rapidly changing technology in today's business world are but two factors that have made it important to have greater participation in decision making. Team management allows individuals with different specialties to contribute their expertise in making decisions. In team management, members participate in setting objectives, and they are jointly responsible for achieving them. Team management also helps to improve communication, since all members are contributing to achieving objectives.

Quality Control Circles. The **quality control circle** is an American innovation that was borrowed by the Japanese in the early 1960s and became a vital part of their successful production system. Today, American companies are "borrowing back" the concept of quality control circles. Westinghouse Electric Corporation, for example, has over 1,000 quality control circles that involve some 10,000 employees.

A major purpose of quality control circles is to encourage employee participation in decision making. A quality control circle is a small group of employees and managers who meet regularly to discuss production and other task-related problems and solutions. The purpose of quality control circles is to benefit the company through improved quality. Employees benefit through greater involvement, higher self esteem, and recognition that they are part of a team that has a vital role in the decision-making process.

Participative Management Program. Motorola, a leading electronics manufacturer, has initiated a **Participative Management Program** (PMP). In PMP, teams of employees meet frequently, sometimes daily, among themselves and with staff support personnel to discuss and deal with problems related to their work area. All team members are encouraged to define problems and recommend solutions. Management reacts by listening and taking action on the suggestions. Each team sets its own high standards and measures its progress in meeting these performance standards. Through team management, workers become more productive because they become more involved in their work; they participate in decision making; they are more informed about what is happening; and they accept more responsibility for their own job performance.

CONTINGENCY LEADERSHIP

No one leadership style is suited for all situations. A modern manager's leadership style will vary according to the situation, the type of employees supervised, and the kind of work being done. There may be isolated occasions when the autocratic, free-rein, or the participative style would be appropriate. This leadership approach is termed the **contingency approach.** Managers must be adaptable and flexible in their leadership. In our dynamic society, no two managers think exactly alike nor have the same personality; neither are two employees identical in their needs and abilities. Thus, managers must consider a multitude of factors in deciding which style of leadership is best for a specific situation. To illustrate, autocratic leadership would be more appropriate in situations where employees lack training and require close supervision. Participative leadership would be more appropriate where experienced, knowledgeable employees desire involvement in matters that affect them. Free-rein leadership is appropriate when the leader desires to delegate decision making fully to subordinates and when highly qualified subordinates are willing to accept such responsibility.

By adapting to each situation, the manager is able to provide the proper amount of attention and guidance to each person in the organization.

SUMMARY OF KEY POINTS

1. By using the systems approach to management, managers can efficiently coordinate all of the firm's human, physical, and financial resources to accomplish the firm's desired goals.

2. The objectives of the firm are arranged in a hierarchy, including overall objectives of the firm, divisional objectives, departmental objectives, work group objectives, and individual objectives.

3. The three levels of managment are top, middle, and supervisory.

4. The managerial functions are planning, organizing, staffing, actuating, and controlling.

5. The stages of the managerial planning process include identifying objectives, developing alternatives, evaluating alternatives, and selecting and implementing the proper course of action.

6. Management by objectives (MBO) is used by managers as both a planning and an appraisal process.

7. The skills a manager should possess are technical, human relations, communication, decision making, and conceptual.

8. Three leadership styles are autocratic, free-rein, and participative.

9. The contingency approach to leadership recognizes the fact that no one leadership style is appropriate for all situations.

DISCUSSION QUESTIONS

1. What is meant by the systems approach to management?
2. Explain how you would apply the four stages of the managerial planning process to a problem-solving situation.
3. What is management by objectives?
4. Outline the steps in the organizing process.
5. Why is the management function of actuating so important?
6. Describe the five managerial skills.
7. Identify the basic steps in the management function of control.
8. What are some of the problems in communication?
9. What is meant by contingency leadership?
10. Which leadership style best describes the manager you would prefer to work for?

STUDENT PROJECTS

1. Select a company that you wish to learn more about. Obtain a copy of the firm's annual report and write a short description of the firm's operations, such as the products made, the dollar sales, the number of personnel. Annual reports may be obtained by writing to the individual companies or going to your school library or public library, which usually has copies of annual reports.
2. From research in business periodicals in your school library or in interviews with business people, develop a list of leadership qualities or characteristics that are important for a manager.
3. Role play a situation in which you try to explain some activity, such as (1) how to tie a shoelace, (2) how to tie a necktie, or (3) how to change a flat tire on a car. Use only verbal communication. After the exercise is completed, identify as many communication problems that developed as possible.

New Customs for an Old Factory

Every Tuesday morning, 2,000 workers at the Quasar color-television factory here walk off the assembly line for 15 minutes. Their purpose: To let the boss know just what they think of him.

Happily, the overall boss—Matsushita Electric Corporation, a huge Japanese company—encourages this candor. In fact, management thought up the idea.

A time for change. The give-and-take program is just one of the many innovations that have been introduced since 1974, when Matsushita bought the deficit-plagued Quasar Corporation from Motorola, Inc. for 108 million dollars.

At that time, Matsushita officials realized that a series of radical changes was needed to make their new property a good investment. The plant was "a bit out of date, not modern," recalls Matsushita's president, Keiichi Takeoka.

So Japanese technicians set to work. A new TV-chassis design was introduced, reducing the number of components through the use of integrated circuits. Automatic equipment was added to insert up to 75 percent of the hundreds of electronic components on the TV chassis. Previously, 90 percent had been inserted by hand.

More money was invested to modernize all eight assembly lines. An old conveyor system that sometimes required a worker to chase a product down the line while working on it was scrapped. In its place is a "free-flow line" on which the worker presses a button to move a chassis to the work station and then presses it again after completing the job to move the set on to the next station.

Measuring gains. The changes have brought dramatic results. In 1974, each set required at least one corrective adjustment before it left the plant. Now, no more than 7 out of each 100 sets require some correction, according to company officials.

New management practices also have been adopted.

Along with the regular employee management discussions, workers say that morale has been boosted by a "Please Ask" program in which management solicits written suggestions on how to improve the working environment. The results: Absenteeism is down sharply and the labor-turnover rate is about half the average for American industry.

SOURCE: U.S. News & World Report, Sept. 14, 1981.

Questions

1. Describe the leadership style used in the Quasar factory.
2. What actions has management taken to improve communication?
3. Has the change in the work layout improved overall efficiency? Explain.

Pam's Dilemma

Albert is the head of the advertising department, which has five employees in addition to his private secretary. During the past two years, he has had four secretaries.

Inez worked for only four months. One day she walked out and didn't return. The main problem was her conflict with her boss.

Shirley replaced Inez and worked a year and quit. She would have quit sooner, but couldn't afford to because it was the best-paying job in the city, and she was working to put her husband through college. As soon as she was able, she quit. Her reason for quitting was the same—the conflict with her boss.

Judy replaced Shirley, worked three months, and quit. Her reason for quitting was the same as that of the other two secretaries.

Currently, Pam has been working in the department for four months. She is also helping to put her husband through school. On Friday, Albert was out of town attending a meeting of advertising managers. That same Friday morning, the president of the firm notified all department heads that all departments would close down at noon, giving employees an extra half-day off before the Easter weekend. Since Albert was out of town, he was unaware of the decision to give employees an extra half-day holiday. On Friday afternoon he called his office, but could get no answer. He immediately assumed that Pam had taken the afternoon off without authority while he was gone.

Without asking any questions of Pam as to why she was gone that Friday afternoon, Albert walked in Monday morning and informed her that she was fired. When Pam tried to explain why she was out of the office, even asking Albert to call the president's office to verify that they had been given the day off, he wouldn't listen. So she left.

On Tuesday, Pam came back and pleaded with Albert to let her work two more months until her husband graduated. Albert thought about it for a short time and finally agreed. However, he told Pam that he was going to watch her job performance very closely. If she was one minute late arriving or one minute early leaving, he would fire her on the spot. Furthermore, he told her she could no longer take a morning and afternoon coffee break, even though company policy stated employees were allowed one fifteen-minute break in the morning and afternoon.

Questions

1. What kind of leadership style does Albert demonstrate?
2. How effective are Albert's human relations skills?
3. Are there any communication problems evident in this case?
4. Does Pam have the right to go over Albert's head to the president?
5. What should the president do to help both Pam and Albert?

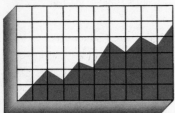

BUSINESS PROFILE

Ralston Purina Company

Ralston Purina was founded in 1894 as the Robinson-Danforth Commission Company, St. Louis, Missouri, by William H. Danforth and two associates, with a capital of $12,000. Today, the company is still a "new" company in spirit, and a fast-growing corporation. Ralston Purina is proud to be a company changing with the times and diversifying into many new fields of opportunity.

Ralston Purina is a broadly based, nutrition-oriented food and feed company that has built a solid foundation of agricultural products and services, and now is expanding rapidly in consumer industries.

Its largest single source of business volume comes from the manufacture and sale of Purina Chow animal feed for livestock, poultry, and other animals. The company is also a major manufacturer of pet food, breakfast cereals and snack crackers, seafoods (Chicken of the Sea), the owner of more than 800 restaurants (including Jack-in-the-Box restaurants), and a producer and processor of proteins in many forms designed to improve human conditions all around the world. The company also has diversified into such nonfood ventures as a four-season resort mariculture operation and a National Hockey League franchise.

Ralston Purina has always regarded its people as its main source of strength. The individual's contribution has always been recognized as the major component of corporate success. The firm stresses that personal growth of its people is a companion objective to corporate growth. This management philosophy has permitted a positive company spirit to develop in all parts of the company's worldwide organization.

The management consistently strives to build a climate throughout all organizational levels that ensures the individual a right to contribute to the company, to

Ralston Purina has always regarded its people as its main source of strength.

share in the challenge, to share in the success, and to be rewarded for it. The management also believes the reward must be fair in job satisfaction as well as in the monetary sense. The philosophy of the company toward employees is to take a human approach. Managers attempt to achieve participation among employees by pushing decision making down to the lowest possible level. To do this, they use a program called Operations Improvement: this is a job enrichment program that stresses that employees will be productive if given the opportunity. Small groups of employees from all levels (top managers down to mail clerks) meet regularly to learn better management and operation methods. Employees are encouraged to use these methods on their own jobs. The company philosophy toward individuals is spelled out in the firm's corporate objectives as follows:

> People are the ultimate source of renewal. We will bring to the corporation a steady flow of able and highly motivated individuals and then provide positive, constructive programs of management development.
>
> We must maintain an environment which fosters individual effort, rewards initiative, and encourages the free and open exchange of ideas; self-criticism and constant restudy are vital to the present health of the enterprise and are essential elements to future growth—we welcome challenging positions and opinions.
>
> Since the dynamics of an organization are related to motivation, conviction, and morale, we will endeavor to make every employee know that his optimum efforts make a difference.

Ralston Purina today employs over 60,000 employees and has annual sales in excess of $5 billion. Not content with past success, the firm is always exploring new opportunities for the company and is researching new directions in products and services.

5

Formal and Informal Organizations

LEARNING GOALS

After reading this chapter, you will understand:

1. What the formal organization is.

2. The distinction between authority, responsibility, and accountability.

3. The difference between centralization and decentralization.

4. The various types of formal organization structure: line, line-and-staff, and functional.

5. The principles of organization.

6. The role of the informal organization.

KEY TERMS

Formal organization
Organization chart
Responsibility
Authority
Accountability
Time management
Centralized authority
Decentralized authority
Line organization

Staff personnel
Line-and-staff organization
Functional organization
Matrix organization
Principles of organization
Informal organization
Grapevine
Collegial organization
Free-form organization

Most of us at one time or another have said "I must get organized." When we make this observation, we are acknowledging the fact that if we are to complete any activity in which we are engaged—work or leisure—in a satisfactory manner, we must have an organized approach to reaching our objectives. Large and small business firms have this same requirement for organization.

THE FORMAL ORGANIZATION

The formal organization is the planned structure in which people from various departments work together as a team under authority and leadership toward common objectives that mutually benefit employees and the company.

If the firm is to achieve its objectives, balanced emphasis must be given to both people and tasks. To implement the management function of organizing efficiently, tasks necessary to achieve objectives must first be identified and then grouped into departments. Then, qualified personnel must be employed to perform these tasks. It is vital that each organizational participant be given both clearly defined responsibilities and the authority necessary to complete the assigned tasks. Furthermore, authority, responsibility, and accountability relationships must be established between organizational members.

The concept of the formal organization can be illustrated by a football team, which incorporates the essential ingredients of the formal organization. The coach identifies specific assignments (tasks) for each team member, such as blocking, tackling, running with the ball, catching a pass. Players best qualified for offensive and defensive positions are then selected and given the responsibility of completing the assignment for each position. To function as a team, players must know what their specific responsibilities are and must contribute their best efforts to complete the assignment. The quarterback usually serves as the offensive team leader on the field and has authority to direct the team members as they attempt to reach their goals, such as improving this year's performance over last year's or winning a conference championship.

ORGANIZATION CHART

The formal organization structure of a company is usually diagrammed and presented as an **organization chart.** An organization chart is an outline of the lines of authority in a company. Often referred to as the "blueprint" of the company, this chart depicts the formal authority relationships between organizational members at the various hierarchical levels, as well as the formal channels of communication within the company.

The organization chart presents managers with a picture of the company, such as how many employees a manager supervises. The chart can also be an aid to identifying potential problem areas, such as one employee reporting to more than one supervisor, or a manager who is supervising too many employees.

A major benefit of organization charting is that it can enhance employee morale. The chart aids organization members in perceiving more clearly their position in the company relative to others, and in seeing how and where they fit into the overall organizational structure.

The organization chart is a "static" model of the company, since it is a picture of the company's organization structure at the time the chart is prepared. This is a major limitation of the chart, because most companies are operating in a "dynamic" environment and thus must continually adapt to changing conditions. For example, a change in company goals may require that some positions be dropped and new positions added. Therefore, to prevent the chart from becoming an obsolete representation of the formal structure, it must be revised periodically to reflect changing conditions.

"First thing we do is cut down on our executive-training program."

Companies tailor organization charts to their individual requirements. Consequently, many variations can be found in the design of these charts. The most common type of organization chart used is the pyramid chart. This chart's advantages are that it is simple, clear, and easy to understand. This chart depicts formal relationships, showing the line of authority of each manager to his or her subordinates as being single, direct, and complete. The formal channels of communication follow the lines of authority. Exhibit 5–1 shows, for three levels of management, the traditional pyramid organization chart.

RESPONSIBILITY

In the formal organization, employees in all positions have specific tasks and responsibilities assigned to them. **Responsibility** refers to the obligation that employees have to perform the assigned tasks to the best of their ability.

AUTHORITY

Employees must have sufficient authority to carry out their responsibilities. Therefore, managers delegate authority to employees. **Authority** is the right of the employee to make decisions and take action needed to carry out the assigned task. When a manager delegates authority, the manager divides authority between himself or herself and subordinates.

When managers delegate authority to employees, they expect them to fulfill their responsibility (obligation) in a manner consistent with company objectives, policies, and procedures. By accepting responsibility and authority, employees become accountable to the manager to complete the tasks assigned to them.

Exhibit 5–1
Pyramid organization chart, manufacturing firm.

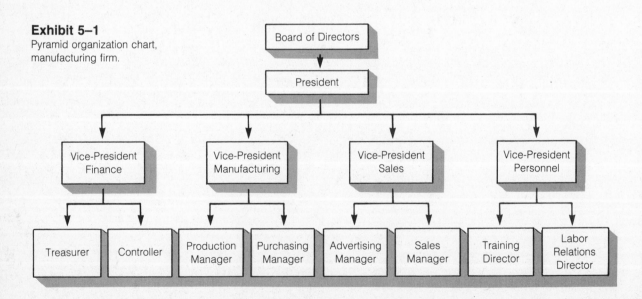

ACCOUNTABILITY

Accountability means that employees are answerable to their superiors for their performance. They accept praise or blame for the way they complete their work assignment. While managers can delegate authority and responsibility, they cannot shift ultimate accountability for results to their subordinates. Thus, managers are not only accountable for their own performance but are ultimately accountable for the actions and performance of their subordinates, as well. For example, the president of the company has final accountability for all company operations. When managers delegate authority, they should delegate it to individuals who are qualified to effectively complete their assignments.

Delegation of Authority

In the formal organization, authority is delegated downward. The board of directors delegates overall authority to run the company to the president. Since it is humanly impossible for the president to be involved in making all decisions, the president delegates a portion of his or her authority to lower-level managers. The sales manager receives authority to make decisions concerning the sales department; the production manager receives the authority to make decisions affecting the production department. Likewise, these managers delegate a portion of their authority to their employees. However, only a part of each manager's authority can be delegated. Some authority must always be reserved, meaning that certain types of authority cannot be delegated but must be retained at each level of management. For example, the top level of management cannot delegate authority to make final decisions regarding the company's long-range plans. As a practical matter, if a manager should delegate all of his or her authority, the manager actually would delegate that managerial position away, and there would be no need for that position in the company.

Time Management. All managers and employees can realize substantial increases in productivity through more efficient use of their time. **Time management** is a systematic analysis of how managers use their time. Time management analysis can reveal to managers which activities are their high-priority and low-priority tasks. Managers can then concentrate their time and energy on the high-priority items and delegate authority to their employees to complete the lower-priority tasks.

CENTRALIZATION AND DECENTRALIZATION

Managers must decide how much decision-making authority they will delegate to subordinates. Generally, authority may be centralized or decentralized. When authority is highly **centralized,** delegation is minimal and most decisions are made by a small number of high-level managers. Where decision making is highly **decentralized,** managers delegate all authority except that which must be reserved by them. Delegation of authority permits employees at lower levels to participate in making decisions relating to their work and enables higher-level managers to devote their time and energies to matters appropriate to their level. The relative strengths and weaknesses of centralization and decentralization are shown in Exhibit 5–2.

Exhibit 5–2

Strengths and weaknesses of centralized and decentralized organization structures.

Strengths	Weaknesses
Centralized Organization	
Assures uniformity of standards and policies among organizational units	Floods communication lines to a few individuals at the top of organization
Allows use of outstanding talent in managers by the whole organization rather than a single unit	Makes great demands on a few managers rather than spreading responsibility
Decisions are uniform	Personalizes decisions to the judgments of a few key decision makers
Helps eliminate duplication of effort and activity	Forces top managers to possess a broad view that may be beyond their capacity
	Gives vast amounts of power to a few individuals
	Reduces sense of participation for all but a few people
Decentralized Organization	
Reduces total responsibility to more manageable units	Lack of uniformity of standards and policies among organizational units
Helps develop more personnel in decision-making process	Capable managers are not always available or willing to participate in decision making
Shortens lines of communication	Creates problems of coordination between separate organizational units
Places decision-making close to situations affected by decisions	
Allows more people to use skills and talents in decisions	Interunit rivalry can interfere with the total organization's operations
Disperses power among many persons	Requires training programs that may be time-consuming and costly

SOURCE: Fred G. Carvell, *Human Relations in Business*, 3d ed., New York: Macmillan Co., 1980, p. 407.

TYPES OF FORMAL ORGANIZATION STRUCTURE

Earlier, we emphasized that business firms need a framework, the organization structure, within which managers can coordinate the planning, organizing, staffing, actuating, and controlling of employees' activities.

The unique requirements of individual firms result in variations of organizational structure. However, there are three main types of organization structure, which are classified by the nature of authority relationships. These are line, line-and-staff, and functional organizational structures.

Line Organization

Line organization structure, representing the oldest and the simplest type of organization patterning, is shown in Exhibit 5–3. It is a structure suitable for small business. Managers must be able to step in and make decisions on all issues that develop in their departments. Hence, they are described as generalists since they should have some knowledge of the overall operation. To cope with the added requirements associated with growth of a company, either more levels or more units at each level have to be added.

In the line organization, the authority relationships between the line managers and subordinates have three major characteristics. First, the line manager has been delegated general (or overall) authority. For example, the plant superintendent has general authority over the plant; the advertising manager has general authority over the advertising department. Because a manager has general authority, decisions can be made quickly withoug having to consult others. Second, each line manager has direct authority over his or her subordinates. Instructions and orders flow in a direct line from each manager to subordinates. Third, subordinates report to only one immediate supervisor and, likewise, receive orders from only one boss. Consequently, this type of authority is aptly defined as *unitary authority.*

Line-and-Staff Organization

As growth of the business occurs, the line manager's task becomes more complex. As a result, it is increasingly difficult, if not impossible, for a line manager to acquire the additional knowledge or have the time neces-

Exhibit 5–3
Line organization plan.

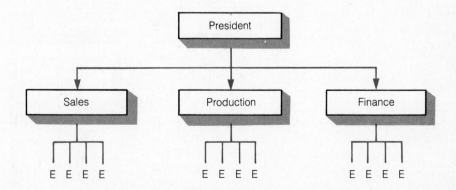

sary to give adequate attention to the enlarged managerial responsibilities. Consequently, the line manager requires the assistance of specialists, **staff personnel,** who provide this service. In the **line-and-staff organization,** a staff manager's function is to provide the line manager with the specialized advice, service, and assistance he or she needs to effectively manage.

The distinction between a line manager and a staff manager is one of authority relationships. Staff personnel facilitate the work of the line by acting as advisers. They do not have authority to make decisions or give orders except in their own departments, where they are line managers. The staff manager makes a recommendation to the line manager. The line manager, in turn, may accept or reject it. If he or she favors the recommendation, the line manager makes the decision and issues the order to implement it. (See Exhibit 5–4.)

To illustrate, when a sales department is small, the sales manager (who is a line manager) can supervise directly all phases of the sales department, such as the salespersons, the planning of advertising, and the distribution of products. However, as the company grows and sales expand, the activities within the department become more complex. As a result, the sales manager may spend more time planning, organizing, staffing, actuating, and controlling the enlarged operations of the sales department. Therefore, an advertising manager (who is a staff manager) may be added to assist the line manager in developing the advertising strategy of the company. The advertising manager is a specialist in all phases of advertising, and his or her technical assistance permits the sales manager to concentrate attention on other matters. The advertising man-

Exhibit 5–4
Line-and-staff organization.

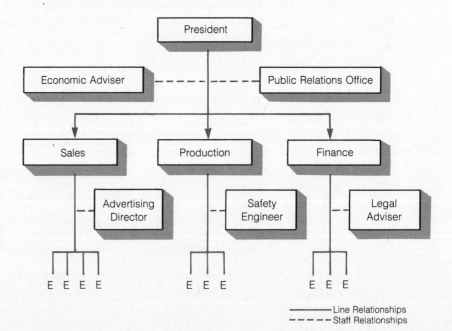

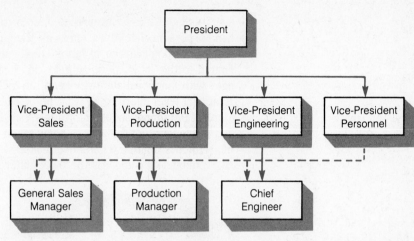

Exhibit 5–5
Flow of functional authority.

— — — — Lines of Functional Authority cut across departmental lines

ager develops an advertising program and recommends it to the sales department manager. If the line manager accepts the recommendation, he
or she will issue instructions to put it into operation.

Staff personnel can be added to the various management levels wherever they are needed to provide specialized assistance.

Functional Organization

As the line manager's work load increases, pressure begins to increase
for him or her to make decisions covering many activities. As a result, the
line manager occasionally delegates some authority to a staff manager. In
the **functional organization,** the authority the staff manager is delegated is called *functional authority.* Functional authority means that a staff
manager is delegated authority to make decisions in matters within his or
her area of specialization, such as accounting, inventory control, research, or personnel. Thus, functional authority has characteristics of both
line and staff managerial authority. Like the line manager, a manager with
functional authority can give orders and make decisions. Thus a manager
with functional authority actually has part of the line manager's authority;
however, the authority is limited to the area of specialization.

Where functional authority exists, a subordinate may sometimes receive conflicting instructions from more than one boss. Even though problems may develop, companies still use functional authority because it takes
advantage of an employee's area of specialization.

To make effective use of functional authority, it should be used only
where a real need exists, i.e., to take advantage of specialization and to
relieve the line manager of some of his or her work load. Furthermore,
the extent of functional authority normally is limited to personnel at the
next lower level in the organizational hierarchy.

Exhibit 5–5 shows that the Vice-President of Personnel has functional
authority over managers at the next lower level, who are directly supervised by another manager. In this case, the Vice-President of Personnel's
functional authority over the General Sales Manager, the Production Man-

ager, and the Chief Engineer is limited to giving them orders on how to handle personnel matters, such as the procedures to follow in handling employee complaints or in hiring employees. Thus, functional authority is limited to the "how" of doing a specific task. It is necessary that the manager with functional authority keep the other managers on the same organizational level informed of what he or she is doing. Thus, the Vice-President of Personnel should inform the Vice-Presidents of Sales, Production, and Engineering of the actions being taken at the next lower levels in their departments regarding personnel matters.

Exhibit 5–6 compares the three different organization plans.

Exhibit 5–6

A comparison of line, line-and-staff, and functional organization.

Line Organization

Advantages
1. Organizational simplicity
2. General authority of managers in their unit
3. Direct authority of manager over subordinates
4. Clear division of authority
5. Quick decisions by managers

Disadvantages
1. No provision for task specialization
2. Too much dependence on a few key personnel
3. Structure not suitable for larger organization

Line-and-Staff Organization

Advantages
1. Makes use of specialists
2. Gives line manager more time to devote to managerial responsibilities
3. Expert advice is made available to line managers

Disadvantages
1. Staff manager can only recommend to line manager
2. Line and staff may conflict if relationships are not clearly specified

Functional Organization

Advantages
1. Takes advantage of task specialization
2. Relieves line manager of a part of his work load
3. Gives manager right to make decisions, not limited to advising

Disadvantages
1. Workers may have more than one boss
2. Conflict and misunderstanding may result if relationships are not clearly defined

Matrix Organization

The **matrix** is an organization structure appropriate for companies that must respond quickly to technological change and are engaged in research and development of new and unique products or projects. The matrix structure was used when the project of landing a man on the moon was undertaken and successfully completed. Companies engaged in dynamic markets are prime users of this structure; for example, computer manufacturers and firms that design and build new systems for the government, such as for the space program.

A common description of the matrix organization is that of a product structure superimposed over a functional structure. (See Exhibit 5–7). The functional (vertical) structure is the traditional division of work activities into the departments of marketing, production, research and development, engineering, and human resources. However, when a company is confronted with initiating a project that has a specific goal and date for completion, that is complex and unique to the organization, and that requires coordinated effort and specialized skills for completion, the horizontal matrix structure may be used. This allows a project director and specialized personnel to be temporarily assigned to a project, to function as a team, and to devote their talents and concentrate their maximum efforts to completion of the project on target. When the project is completed, these personnel return to their regular departmental duties.

The functional departments have a service relationship to the project team.

There are several organizational problems with the matrix. One is that those employees assigned to the project are responsible to two bosses—the project director and the functional department manager. This violates the principle of unity of command. A second issue is that conflict may occur if the project manager and department managers do not understand the need to jointly share and supervise project team members. Thus, a high level of cooperation is required between the project director and the functional manager if the matrix structure is to work effectively.

PRINCIPLES OF ORGANIZATION

As managers fulfill their obligations, they rely on guidance and support from a variety of sources. One source is the various **principles of organization** that have been developed. These principles of organization are guides to which managers can refer for assistance. Many of these principles were developed in the early 1900s by well-known management theorists such as Frederick W. Taylor, known as the "Father of Scientific Management," and Henri Fayol, a French mining engineer. Many of these principles are still widely used today.

Successful managers have used these principles in many different work situations: in business, education, government. Some of the significant principles of organization are discussed below.

Principle of Unity of Objectives

Each part of the company must contribute to the accomplishment of the overall objectives of the firm. The sales department must concern itself with sales and also with how sales activities are integrated with all other activities in the company, such as production and finance. Each department must accomplish its own goals while at the same time working cooperatively with all other departments. Thus, the sales department should not be planning a major campaign offering easier credit terms to boost sales just at the time that the finance department is embarking on a policy of restricting credit.

Exhibit 5–7
Flow of authority of heads of functional departments.

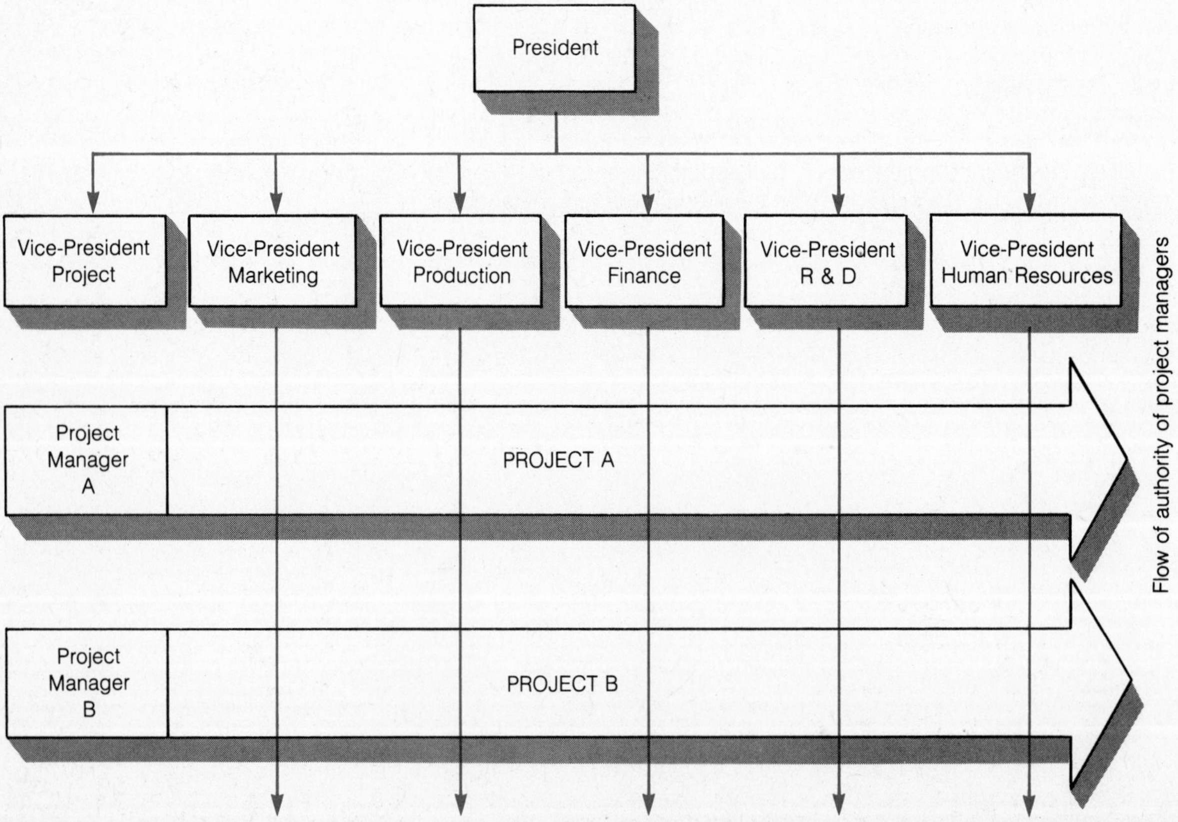

Exhibit 5–8
Bases for grouping activities.

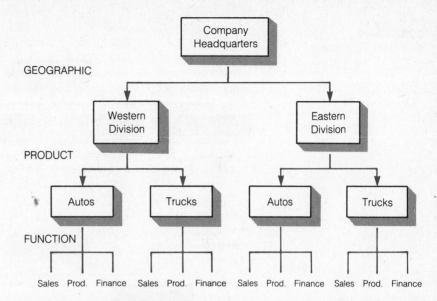

Principle of Span of Control

There is a limit to the number of workers that a manager can effectively supervise. It is impossible to specify an exact number for each situation, because that depends on such variables as (1) the type of work, (2) the manager's ability, (3) the amount of the workers' training, (4) the effectiveness of communications, and (5) the importance of time in reaching decisions.

Principle of Unity of Command

If an individual receives conflicting orders from several different people, the individual must evaluate the orders, accept one, and reject the remainder. This results in confusion and conflict between superiors and subordinates within the company. To avoid this undesirable situation, the unity-of-command principle states that an individual should receive orders from and report directly to only one supervisor.

Principle of Departmentalization

Most of the activities of a company are grouped in departments on the basis of similarity. Although there are a number of ways to departmentalize, the most common methods are by function, product, or territory. Grouping on the basis of function places all similar activities in the same department, such as locating all phases of production in the production department and all aspects of accounting in the accounting department. Product grouping signifies that all sales, production, and finance activities relating to the production of a single product are placed in one department or one plant. An example of this arrangement is General Motor's grouping of its automobiles by product, i.e., Chevrolet, Pontiac, Oldsmobile, Buick, and Cadillac. Territorial grouping refers to the clustering of activities on the basis of geographical location. All functions would be grouped according to territories, such as the Southwest region or West Coast plant (see Exhibit 5–8).

Exhibit 5–9

Flat and tall organizations.

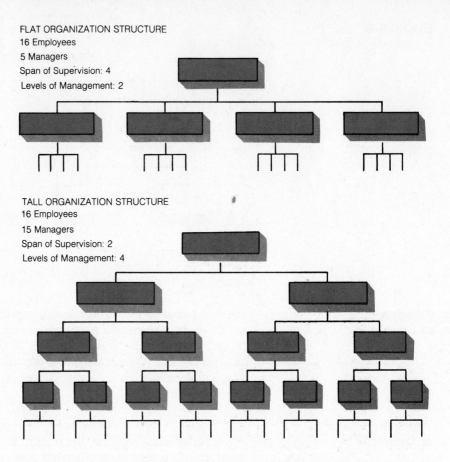

FLAT ORGANIZATION STRUCTURE
16 Employees
5 Managers
Span of Supervision: 4
Levels of Management: 2

TALL ORGANIZATION STRUCTURE
16 Employees
15 Managers
Span of Supervision: 2
Levels of Management: 4

Principle of Levels of Management

The number of levels of management in the company should be kept to a minimum. As the number of organizational levels increase, problems in communication increase, inasmuch as each message must pass through more people as it travels from point of origin to final destination. Furthermore, as each message must pass through more people, the chances increase that the message will be distorted.

An enterprise must achieve proper balance between the span of control and the number of levels of management if it is to function effectively. A company with too narrow a span of control requires many levels of management. With a wide span of control, the company needs fewer levels of management. Exhibit 5–9 shows the difference between a "tall" organization, in which managers have a narrow span of control, and a "flat" organization, in which managers have a wide span of control. The flat organization would be typical of a company where authority is decentralized while the tall organization is representative of the company where authority is centralized.

Authority Must Be Equal to Responsibility

If assigned responsibility for a task for which he or she will be accountable, an individual should have the authority necessary to complete the obligation.

Principle of Delegation of Authority

Delegation implies that authority to make decisions should be pushed down to the lowest competent level of supervision. This allows minor decisions to be made at the lower levels of management and major decisions to be made at the higher levels of management. However, delegation of authority does not relieve the delegator of any of the accountability for the actions of subordinates. A manager is always ultimately accountable for the actions of subordinates.

Principle of Flexibility

A company must be flexible so that it can adapt to changing conditions, both internally and externally. Each firm should have periodic, recurring reviews or audits to determine if it is alert to shifts in consumer demands or is aware of changing economic and social conditions. If it is not, management must initiate corrective action.

THE INFORMAL ORGANIZATION

As people work together, informal relationships develop that usually differ substantially from the authority relationships, work procedures, and channels of communication set forth in the formal organization. These informal relationships, which exist in every formal organization, are called the **informal organization.** Unlike the formal organization, the informal organization is not formally planned. Instead, it develops automatically from the interactions of employees on the job. The solid lines in

Exhibit 5–10
The informal organization.

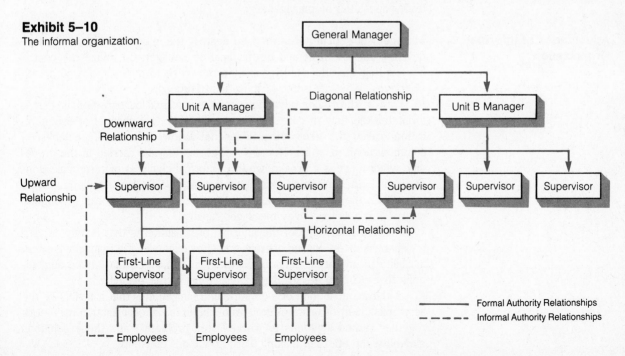

Exhibit 5–10 represent the formal relationships, and the broken lines suggest various types of informal relationships.

Informal relationships may travel in a number of directions. For example, they may pass downward from the manager to employees, such as when the manager desires to have personal contact with a particular employee, perhaps an individual with a specific expertise in computer technology. Other informal relationships traverse upward, such as when a subordinate tries to raise his or her status by having direct contact with a manager several levels removed. Informal horizontal relationships may occur if there is a need to have a quick answer to a pertinent question: the sales manager contacts the production manager about the production department's ability to meet production deadlines. The manager of sales needs these data to communicate to sales representatives the company's ability to deliver merchandise on schedule. Finally, there are diagonal relationships that develop when it becomes necessary to cut through red tape and go directly to the source that can provide urgently needed information.

The informal organization often defines how a company actually operates. Instead of authority flowing downward, as in the formal organization, authority flows upward in the informal organization. An individual is given authority by the people with whom he or she works for a variety of reasons. He or she may be the oldest employee, the most popular individual, the most intelligent, or the one with the greatest physical strength. This person becomes the informal leader and fellow workers respect that person because of some particular characteristic. As the informal leader of the work group, he or she may often have more influence than the formal leader appointed by management.

Advantages of Informal Organization

Management should not attempt to destroy the informal relationships that develop. Rather, it should be the goal of managers to utilize the contributions that the informal organization can make to help achieve corporate objectives. What are some of these contributions?

One of the major advantages of the informal organization is that it facilitates the flow of communications. The informal channel of communication, called the **grapevine,** does not follow the formally established communication network. Rumors and gossip may be carried in the grapevine when there is a breakdown in the formal channels of communication. Desirably, the informal communication network can supplement and strengthen the formal channel of communication, since it can go outside normal channels to convey messages rapidly.

Another advantage of the informal organization is that it may correct a weakness of the formal organization. For example, if a manager is weak in ability in one area, such as planning, an employee may make suggestions that will help the manager improve his or her planning.

A third contribution of the informal organization is that it facilitates the accomplishment of tasks. Members of the informal organization may work together to find solutions to work-related problems, and these solutions may have the effect of making work flow more efficiently.

The informal organization can work in a supportive relationship with the formal organization, so managers should seek the support of the informal organization to help the formal organization.

ORGANIZATIONAL DESIGN FOR FUTURE COMPANY NEEDS

The **collegial** and **free-form organization** structures seem to be compatible with changing structural demands of organizations. The collegial system, borrowed from university administration, is not so much a structure as a philosophy of management. Collegial management deemphasizes status and job titles, emphasizes self-discipline and teamwork, free flow of communications between all organization levels, and a high degree of delegation of authority.

The free-form organization structure is appropriate for firms that must respond to changing market demands, such as companies in high-technology fields. Work is accomplished by task forces made up of specialists, by participation in decision making, and by free movement of individuals within the organization. Large firms that require flexibility and are growing through merger and acquisition frequently use this organizational concept.

SUMMARY OF KEY POINTS

1. The formal organization is the planned structure in which personnel work together under authority and leadership to accomplish the goals of the organization and to benefit the employees.
2. The organization chart is a diagram of the formal organization structure that outlines the lines of authority and formal communication channels in a company.
3. Responsibility is the obligation employees have to perform their jobs to the best of their ability.
4. Authority is the right to make decisions.
5. Accountability means employees are answerable to their superior for their job performance.
6. Authority for making decisions in organizations may be centralized or decentralized.
7. The types of the formal organization structure are line, line-and-staff, and functional.
8. A number of organizational principles can be used by managers as guides for action.
9. The informal organization is the network of spontaneous relationships that develop as people work together.
10. The collegial and free-form types of organization are proposed organization systems for the future needs of companies.

DISCUSSION QUESTIONS

1. Distinguish between authority, responsibility, and accountability.
2. Explain the difference between the formal organization and the informal organization.
3. What is the difference between the principle of unity of objectives and the principle of unity of command?
4. What are some problems involved in an organization with many levels of management?
5. What is the principle of departmentalization?
6. What are some reasons for using an organization chart? What are some disadvantages of the organization chart?
7. Distinguish between the various types of formal organization plans.
8. Explain the difference between centralization and decentralization of authority.

STUDENT PROJECT

Select a company that you are interested in and obtain a copy of its organization chart. Determine whether the firm is organized on the basis of function, product, or territory.

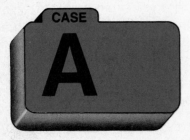

Oak City Florist Shop

Danny was attending college, working on a BBA degree in management. During the summers, he worked full-time to help pay for his expenses. Last summer he was employed by Oak City Florist, one of the larger florists in the city. Fifty people worked for Oak City Florist. The organization of the company included sales, office administration, flower designers, and delivery. The firm made deliveries throughout the city.

Danny worked in the delivery department. There were six full-time delivery personnel: Helen, two older men (in their 50s), two high school senior students, and Danny (a college sophomore). The delivery department was located in a separate building from the other departments. With the exception of a morning and afternoon inspection by the assistant manager, there was no manager to make assignments. As long as the flowers were delivered without complication, the delivery department had a free rein in getting the job done.

Danny soon learned that Helen was the informal leader of the department, due to her seniority and age. She, along with the two older men, made up one group, the two high-school students, the other. Danny could not relate to either group, and as a result he worked alone.

For the first week, everyone seemed to get along fairly well. Danny would arrive at work, load his delivery van, and make deliveries to houses, businesses, or hospitals. Each delivery run lasted about two and one-half hours.

After the first week, Helen (the informal leader) accused Danny of working too hard. She accused him of making the other five appear slow and unmotivated, and wanted to know why Danny was in such a hurry and worked so hard all the time. Danny said he thought he was only doing his job as it was supposed to be done, not trying to show up the others. Helen then told Danny that if he didn't take twenty minutes longer on each delivery run, she could and would have him fired.

The next morning, Danny talked to the assistant manager about the situation. He told Danny not to worry but to continue his delivery runs as usual. Another week went by without further direct encounters, but it was obvious that relations were strained in the department between Danny and Helen.

On Monday morning of the third week of Danny's employment, he was called to the assistant manager's office and told he was being transferred to the office administration department for the remainder of the summer, with a $1.00 an hour pay increase. Danny worked in that department the remainder of the summer and had no further contact with the delivery personnel. The other five members in the delivery department continued to operate as usual.

Questions

1. What type of leadership style was used by the assistant manager in the delivery department?
2. What effect did the informal organization have on how the department operated?
3. In your opinion, why was Helen the informal leader in the delivery department?
4. Why do you think Danny was transferred?
5. What would you have done if you were the assistant manager?

Morris Electronics

After graduating from Central City Junior College with an Associate of Science degree in electronics, Raymond Morris opened his own small business—an electronics manufacturing firm, organized as a single proprietorship. His technical skills in electronics as well as the long hours he spent at work enabled his firm to make a reasonable profit. After fifteen years, the firm had grown to 220 employees, had sales of $7 million, and was incorporated. The firm now has four major departments: engineering, production, sales, and finance. Exhibit 5–11 shows the organization for the firm. One of the major accomplishments of the firm was designing an electronic guidance system that was used in the rockets in America's space program. This achievement was a source of pride for all employees. Although the business has grown, Mr. Morris retains tight management control over the company in much the same way as when the firm was smaller. Mr. Morris still makes all the decisions.

Tom Watson is the manager in charge of the sales department, which has 12 employees. Lately, Watson has complained to Morris that his workload is too heavy. As a result, Morris hired Albert Brown to help Watson. Instead of appointing him as Watson's assistant, Brown was given the title of co-manager of the sales department. Now Watson and Brown have equal authority and responsibility for the department's operations. Sales personnel report to whichever co-manager is available. And both managers give orders to sales personnel.

Roland Allen is the manager in charge of the engineering department, which has 16 employees. He attended electronics school, and he has a high level of

Exhibit 5–11
Organization of Morris Electronics.

```
                        ┌─────────────────┐
                        │  Raymond Morris │
                        │    President    │
                        └─────────────────┘
     ┌──────────────┬──────────────┬──────────────┐
┌───────────┐ ┌───────────┐ ┌───────────┐ ┌───────────┐
│ Tom Watson│ │Roland Allen│ │Phil Simmons│ │Henry Adams│
│    and    │ │Engineering │ │ Production │ │ Financial │
│Albert Brown│ │ Department │ │  Manager   │ │  Manager  │
│Co-managers│ │  Manager   │ │            │ │           │
│Sales Dept │ │            │ │            │ │           │
└───────────┘ └───────────┘ └───────────┘ └───────────┘
┌───────────┐ ┌───────────┐ ┌───────────┐ ┌───────────┐
│12 employees│ │16 employees│ │10 supervisors│ │8 employees│
└───────────┘ └───────────┘ └───────────┘ └───────────┘
                             ┌───────────┐
                             │168 employees│
                             └───────────┘
```

technical skills, as does Mr. Morris. However, Allen has been upset lately because Mr. Morris continues to go directly to the employees in the engineering department and give them instructions that are often in conflict with Allen's instructions. Employees in the engineering department are becoming frustrated because they never know whose orders to follow. When Allen complained to Morris, Morris simply replied, "You should be glad I take time from my busy schedule to help you."

Phil Simmons heads the production department, which has 10 foremen and 168 employees. He has five years experience as production manager prior to joining Morris Electronics. Simmons has become so sure of himself in his job that he has delegated nearly all his authority to the 10 foremen in the production department. As a result, Simmons is left with very little authority and control over his department. The foremen have been delegated so much authority that they now, in effect, run the department and make most of the decisions.

Henry Adams is manager of the finance department, which has eight accountants. Mark Ferguson is the only member of the finance department who has a college degree in accounting. All the others, including Adams, either learned accounting on the job or attended business college. Consequently, whenever Henry Adams has a problem in accounting or needs specialized advice in accounting procedures, he goes directly to Ferguson. Likewise, all other employees in the finance department go to Ferguson rather than to Adams with their problems. All members of the department respect Ferguson.

Questions

1. On what basis are company activities grouped into departments?
2. What principles of organization are being violated in each department?
3. What is the role of the informal organization in the finance department?
4. Discuss the informal relations in the finance department.

A selection of Pillsbury pizza products.

BUSINESS PROFILE

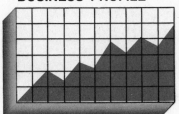

The Pillsbury Company

From a decrepit flour mill in 1869, located on the outskirts of what is today Minneapolis, Minnesota, The Pillsbury Company has grown into an international food company. In its first year of operation, The Pillsbury Company had a $6,000 profit. Today, the firm has more than $3 billion in sales and 60,000 employees.

In 1872, Pillsbury's BEST trademark, the famous XXXX, was adopted. In 1935, the company was incorporated as Pillsbury Flour Mills. In 1949, the first Pillsbury BAKE-OFF was held. By 1959, the character of the corporation had changed so dramatically from its early years that Pillsbury Flour Mills Company became The Pillsbury Company. Pillsbury expanded into international markets in 1960 and continues to be active in these markets today.

A major objective of The Pillsbury Company is to be exclusively a food company. In order to accomplish this goal, the company has been restructured, selling off their businesses engaged in poultry farming, publishing, wine making, and flower farming. In addition, the company has attempted to strengthen its top management team both by internal promotions and by bringing in personnel from the outside.

The company is organized into thee major groups: Consumer Products, Restaurants, and Agri-Products. The Consumer Products Group makes and sells branded food products through grocery stores. The Agri-Products Group mills flour for sale to bakeries, restaurants, hotels, and institutions. Through the Restaurant Group, Burger King operates and franchises Burger King fast-food restaurants. The company currently operates 15 percent of its 3,022 restaurants. The company also manufactures and sells consumer food products through subsidiaries in foreign countries.

Some of the businesses that make up Pillsbury are Steak and Ale, a restaurant chain; Burger King; Totino's Finer Foods, Inc., a processor of frozen pizza; American Beauty Macaroni Company; Poppin Fresh Pie Shops, selling quality pies, sandwiches, and salads and Green Giant, selling canned and frozen vegetables and entrees.

In 1978, the company began to expand its research and marketing into vended foods with products for microwave ovens. Among those products are pancakes, popcorn, and pizza. From an old, dilapidated flour mill, The Pillsbury Company has become a leading diversified food company.

6 Production Management

LEARNING GOALS

After reading this chapter, you will understand:

1. How important production management and technology are to the wealth of our nation.

2. How and why people decide to locate plants in certain towns and cities.

3. The production control process that allows a product to be produced with a minimum cost in materials, time, and labor.

4. The importance of quality control and the use of humans and machines in the inspection process.

5. How a company buys raw materials and parts to use in production.

6. How a company maintains enough material to make products yet keeps the amount down to save carrying costs.

7. That many companies use computers to help perform their production control, quality control, purchasing, and inventory control functions.

8. How production robots are rapidly replacing humans in the actual production process.

KEY TERMS

Production management	Dispatching	Value analysis
Cybernetics	Follow-up	Inventory control
Production control	PERT	Perpetual inventory
Planning	CPM	Microcomputers
Routing	Quality control	Perpetual inventory card
Scheduling	Purchasing	Production robots

> Success in most industries today requires an organizational commitment to compete in the marketplace on technological grounds—that is, to compete over the long run by offering superior products.
>
> ROBERT H. HAYES & WILLIAM J. ABERNATHY

Production management involves the management of manufacturing firms. Much of the management process of the manufacturing operation is the same as that of any other business and involves most of the material included in this book. However, production management has some areas that apply only to manufacturing firms. These areas are plant location, production control, quality control, raw material purchasing, and inventory control.

Over the years, increases in production technology and efficiency have resulted in gigantic steps in productivity. The resulting output of economic goods has greatly increased the standard of living for the people of the United States. In addition, many other nations have adopted our production techniques, increasing their own national output. Exhibit 6–1 shows the rapid expansion of productivity in the United States, which is attributable primarily to the advances in production technology. Eli Whitney's development of interchangeable parts in production; Henry Ford's introduction of specialization of labor, assembly lines, and mass production techniques; and the more recent production robots using computer control are some of the highlights of the revolution in production that has occurred in the United States.

PLANT LOCATION

For some firms, the location of their manufacturing plant has little effect on their success; however, the location of most firms can mean the difference between success and failure. Many variables enter into plant location decisions, and these variables are of different degrees of importance to different types of firms. The more common considerations are the market, raw materials, transportation, community opinions, labor supply, taxes, availability of land, land prices, and climate.

Firms that produce perishable products or products that are relatively expensive to ship must usually locate near their markets. For example, a bakery must locate its manufacturing plant near its market in order to deliver fresh bread. Also, the ready-mixed concrete plant must locate near its market because of the high cost of delivering heavy and bulky concrete.

Manufacturing companies that produce a product using raw material that is more expensive to ship than the finished product usually locate their plants near their source of supply of raw materials. For instance, the smelting plant that extracts refined gold from gold ore must locate as close to the mine as possible, since ore is bulky and extremely heavy, and refined gold is very small relative to its worth. The perishability of raw materials may force a firm to locate its production facilities near the source of raw material; firms that can food products must locate fairly close to the fields of the products that they process.

Weight, size, and price of product generally determine the importance of transportation in the plant location decision. Products such as bricks, which are heavy yet have a relatively low price, cost a good deal to ship, and the transportation cost is large relative to the unit price of the product. As a consequence, manufacturers of this type of product compete only in a limited area. On the other hand, automobiles are both heavy and bulky, yet manufacturers of automobiles ship over large areas. The transportation charge is expensive but at the same time is not a significant part of the total cost. Manufacturers of automobiles have such large volume that they are able to save on transportation charges by establishing branch assembly plants. Watches, on the other hand, weigh little and are relatively high in value per unit. As a result, manufacturers of watches compete over long distances, and transportation costs are an unimportant factor in their plant location decisions. Industries that rely heavily on rail or water transportation must choose locations that supply these facilities.

During the process of selecting a plant location site, it is important to consider community attitudes, taxes, and services. Many communities like

Exhibit 6–1

Gross National Product 1870–1980.

(SOURCE: Historical Statistics of the U.S., Colonial Times to 1970, and Statistical Abstract of the U.S., 1981.)

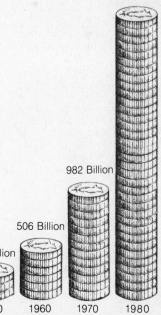

| 7 Billion | 11 Billion | 13 Billion | 19 Billion | 35 Billion | 92 Billion | 91 Billion | 100 Billion | 286 Billion | 506 Billion | 982 Billion | 2,626 Billion |
| 1870 | 1880 | 1890 | 1900 | 1910 | 1920 | 1930 | 1940 | 1950 | 1960 | 1970 | 1980 |

to exclude certain types of industry, and a few communities resent any new industry. Plants that produce offensive smells or other forms of pollution are having increasing difficulty finding communities that welcome them, in spite of the increased employment they provide. It is difficult for a manufacturing plant to operate in a hostile environment.

Taxes can sometimes become an important factor in plant location, since taxes vary from state to state and community to community. A production firm that operates on a narrow margin of profit may find that extra-heavy tax levies eliminate their profit.

Industries searching for plant locations should always look at the services offered by different communities. For example, a firm may want to locate on the edge of the community, and find that one community is willing to bring city utilities to them at no cost to the business. Another

Exhibit 6–2

The importance of plant location factors to different types of firms.

Plant Location Factors	Particularly Important to Firms	Examples
Market	Who produce perishable products	Bakeries
	Who produce finished products expensive to ship	Ready-mix concrete plants
Raw materials	Whose raw materials are more expensive to ship than their finished products	Ore-smelting plants
	Whose raw materials are perishable	Food-canning plants
Transportation	Whose product is large in weight and/or size relative to price	Brick-manufacturing plants
Labor supply	Who require a highly skilled or trained work force	Aerospace-engineering firms
Taxes	Who have a high investment in the plant facilities	Petroleum plants
Community opinions	Who produce pollution or dangerous products	Soap factories Explosive plants
Availability of land	Who have need of large amounts of land for storage, production facilities, or growing raw materials	Paper mills
Land prices	Who need large amounts of land	Steel mills
Climate	Who require certain temperature or clear days	Aircraft firms

community may require the extension of city water and sewerage over a long distance to the plant at the expense of the business. Other community services are important to prospective firms: the quality of the educational system is important to the firm's workers; plants whose facilities extend high off the ground may find their insurance premiums excessively expensive if the local fire department does not have the correct equipment; and plants that use excessive amounts of electricity in their production process will want to find a community that has adequate power available.

An adequate labor supply is often one of the more important considerations in plant location. The more technical and skilled the labor supply needed, the more important it becomes to the plant location decision. Unskilled labor exists in almost any locale, and the business firm that uses only this type of labor may consider local wage rates and unionization the most important factors in their labor considerations. Conversely, a lack of technical and highly skilled workers may limit a firm's selection because they must locate where a pool of these workers exists.

Sometimes, other factors become so important that a firm must locate in a particular locale that does not contain the required pool of skilled workers. In this situation, the firm must attract the needed personnel into the area. Most people hesitate to relocate, and the firm usually must increase the pay scale to attract employees. Increasing the pay scale may cause a significant increase in the operating expenses.

Since most manufacturing plants require considerable amounts of land, the price of land is important to them. This is why most manufacturing firms locate on the fringes of towns and cities.

In some instances climate is an important consideration in determining plant location. Aircraft manufacturers performing considerable testing usually locate in parts of the country that maintain clear climates for a major part of the year.

PRODUCTION CONTROL

Production control is one of the most important functions related to the production process in most plants. In order to hold its production costs down and maintain a satisfactory level of production, a factory must keep its machines and employees producing as much of the time as possible. Idle or wasted time rapidly consumes company profits.

Production control must maintain an orderly flow of work at all work stations in the plant. Imagine the problems an automobile assembly plant would face without good production control. In the automobile assembly line, the frame of the auto moves along a main assembly line with parts to be assembled to the frame moving in from both sides of the line as it moves from work station to work station. Each auto produced by the assembly line usually is different from any other auto in the line because of wide choices customers have in color, body style, and accessories.

If a station wagon frame is to move on the line, the correct motor and body must arrive at installation points at the same time. If a sedan body arrived, the entire assembly line would shut down while the sedan body was moved out of the way and another body put in its place. When one

The Cybernetic Revolution

The Industrial Revolution created an enormous change in most of the world: It brought about the modern miracles of science and industry. A wealth of products and services has been produced in the industrial nations of the world to increase the well being of their people.

Many authorities say that we are now entering a new revolution that will, by comparison, make the Industrial Revolution look insignificant. Some have termed it the cybernetic revolution. In dictionary terms, **cybernetics** is the area of knowledge that compares the way electronic computers function to the function of the human nervous system. These authorities maintain that electronic computers and other electronic devices will vastly increase in capabilities while decreasing in size. Electronic computers will program other computers that will program and control production machinery and equipment. These experts predict that all production in the future will be completely automated, virtually without human input. In addition, the time required for development of new technology will be reduced by the use of electronic equipment. They envision electronic devices taking over not only all production, but much of the service industry. For example, a physician will be able to connect an electronically controlled device to a patient which would then feed body function information to a central medical computer. The computer would then notify the physician of additional tests that were needed or would immediately give a diagnosis and suggest a treatment.

Unfortunately, the cybernetic revolution will create problems for people, just as the Industrial Revolution did. For example, many people in such an advanced technological society may not be employable. Hopefully, rapidly evolving knowledge will produce solutions not only to today's problems, but to those of the future.

In order to maintain a satisfactory level of production, a factory must keep its machines and employees producing as much of the time as possible.

multiplies all possible combinations of equipment available with the body style and correct motor, it is clear that an automobile assembly plant could not function without adequate production control techniques.

The production-control process consists of five basic functions or steps: planning, routing, scheduling, dispatching, and follow-up. To illustrate each of the five functions, assume we are going to make 100 simple tree-swing seats consisting of a painted wooden board containing rope holes.

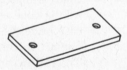

Planning

The **planning** function of production control is the process that determines what resources are needed—machines, employees, raw materials, supplies, etc.—to manufacture the product. If some of the items needed to manufacture the order are not in stock, the production-control department must then tell the stores department to order them.

The planning function in our example would involve determining that the production of the swing seats would require sawing, drilling, sanding, and painting wooden boards. We must also check to see if we have the required amount of boards in the correct width and the correct color of paint.

Routing

Routing is the process of identifying the correct order in which the production operations must be performed. The swing seats would be routed to the saw first, the drill second, the sanding station third, and the paint station last.

Scheduling

Scheduling operations involve determining when operations will start and stop at each phase of the production process. Scheduling the swing seats might result in the following schedule:

Oct. 3	1 P.M.	Saw station	Start sawing boards
Oct. 3	3 P.M.	Drill station	Start drilling holes in boards
Oct. 4	8 A.M.	Sanding station	Start sanding on seats
Oct. 4	11 A.M.	Paint station	Start painting seats
Oct. 4	4 P.M.		Painting of seats is finished

Dispatching

The function of **dispatching** in the production control process consists of issuing instructions to various departments detailing the work with specific starting times for each machine (determined in the scheduling step) involved in the customer orders. The dispatching function is performed in the production of the swing seats by sending an order to each station to start production at the assigned time. For example, the saw station is notified that it should start sawing boards to specifications at 1 P.M. on October 3 and that they should be finished at 3 P.M.

Follow-up

Sending orders for production activity at specific times to specific work stations does not automatically guarantee that the work will be finished at the designated times. Machine breakdown, a new machine operator who has not reached peak efficiency, and many other factors can cause delays. Production control must be aware of these delays, or it will not be able to schedule and coordinate production adequately in the plant. Consequently, controls must be established to assure production control that the work will be done as planned. Notification to production control by foremen in case of delays, and daily progress reports on all work stations, allow the production control department to compare progress with the schedule. The **follow-up** function in our example would be performed by each station reporting the time spent on each order during the day. For example, the saw station might report that it started production at 1:15 P.M. and finished at 3:05 P.M.

Most large firms have turned to the use of computers for performance of the five production control functions. These computer operations have the ability to handle functions such as scheduling, dispatching, and follow-up faster and with more dependability than human-controlled operations.

PERT and CPM

Two important techniques for planning and controlling large, complex, and nonrecurrent projects are Program Evaluation and Review Technique (**PERT**) and Critical Path Method (**CPM**). PERT was developed to speed the Polaris submarine program and CPM was developed by E. I. DuPont to schedule and control activities in building chemical plants. PERT determines the sequence and estimated times of events that must occur to complete the project. As a simple example, suppose you are contracting to build the foundation of a building. The sequence of events is:

Clear and Level Land → Build Forms → Fill Forms → Lay Foundation Plumbing → Pour Concrete → Remove Forms

If each event requires one day of work, it appears it would take only six days to complete the foundation. However, other events must occur for this critical path to be achieved, such as: contract for earth-moving equipment, order form lumber, contract with cement workers, contract with plumbers, order fill material, and order concrete. If it takes six days to contract and get the plumbers on the job, it is obvious that the job will take more than six days.

CPM is less involved in that it determines the critical path (such as the example above) to the completion of the project. It establishes what activities can be done at the same time in order to determine which is the shortest and least expensive path to complete the project.

QUALITY CONTROL

Quality control is very important to the manufacturing concern because it is directly related to customer satisfaction. If a customer buys a product that does not work or one that is below quality, he or she is not likely to purchase that brand of product again. In addition, that customer may influence other people's purchases of the product by telling them of the problem with the product.

Quality control is performed by humans, machines, or both. Human inspection in quality control is not 100 percent effective because of human error caused by monotony, fatigue, and other job-related factors. For example, one company, in an attempt to check on its quality control, mixed fifty defective parts with a group of good parts. Their inspectors caught only thirty-nine the first time through, nine the second time, and one the third time. The final defective part was not found by the inspectors—a customer found it.

As technology advances, manufacturing firms turn more and more to machine inspection for quality control. The computer makes highly accurate inspection possible in automated manufacturing processes. For example, machines that make wire are often attached to gauges that measure the thickness of the wire as it comes out of the machine. When the wire is too thick or too thin, this information is electronically relayed to the computer, which makes adjustments in the machine through electronically controlled devices. This process makes possible a consistent size of wire, which would be impossible to obtain under human control.

Some types of inspection are not feasible except by human inspection. Time, cost, human fatigue, and other factors often result in human inspection being performed on a sample basis. The thinking behind sample inspection is that if one item is defective in the manufacturing process, then the cause of the defect would probably cause other items manufactured at the same time to be defective. For example, a machine may be out of alignment or a batch of raw material may be bad. Sample inspection is usually achieved through statistical methods. One manufacturer of very exclusive automobiles is an excellent example of sample inspection. In their quality control procedures for their automobile motors, they broke down every twenty-fifth motor and inspected every part (most were X-rayed). If any part was defective, all twenty-five motors in the group were

"LET'S FACE IT — WE HAVE NO QUALITY
AND WE HAVE NO CONTROL."

torn down and inspected. This type of quality control was so effective that the manufacturer boasts that the only sound the driver can hear is the rush of air past the car and the swish of the tires.

PURCHASING AND INVENTORY CONTROL

Purchasing and inventory control in the industrial concern are essential functions, for they provide for the orderly flow of raw materials and supplies into the production process.

Purchasing

The **purchasing** department's responsibility in the industrial firm is to purchase the *right* quality, the optimum quantity, at the best price, and at the right time. The purchasing department's personnel are experts in where and how to buy and not in what to buy. They must rely on engineers and production people to tell them what to buy.

The purchasing department should always attempt to buy the quality that is *right* for for its purpose. For example, a purchasing agent in an automobile manufacturing firm may have to buy bolts for two different purposes, head bolts that must withstand 200 foot-pounds of torque, and ashtray bolts that must withstand 10 foot-pounds of torque. Consequently, the purchasing agent must buy high-quality steel bolts with strength specifications for the head bolts. Bolts of lesser quality would cause the motor to function incorrectly. Conversely, almost any type of bolt of the correct size will suffice for attaching ashtrays. If the purchasing department buys a higher-quality bolt, the cost becomes too high. The purchasing department must obtain information from production and engineering sources to determine the right quality of product to purchase. Anything less may cause failure of the product, and anything more is a waste of money.

Many purchasing departments, in conjunction with their firm's engineering department, perform an operation called **value analysis.** In conference, they analyze the regularly used items to determine if the least expensive item that satisfies the purpose is being used in production. For example, one large firm bought approximately 125 different types of bolts each year. Many of these bolts were nonstandard sizes (which are more expensive) and were often made of expensive metals. The purchasing department, in conference with the design engineers, carefully considered every bolt in their products. The purchasing department had information on the cost of various bolts, and the engineers had information concerning stress and metal requirements. They found that many of the off-size bolts could be replaced with slightly larger common-size bolts without any effect on the product. In addition, they found that bolts made of less expensive metal could be substituted for some of the more expensive bolts with no reduction in performance or life of the product. They reduced the number of types of bolts needed to 24, and they saved in excess of $100,000 per year without reducing the quality of the product.

Savings by the purchasing department are particularly important to the business firm since any dollar saved in costs without affecting quality means an increase of a dollar in profits to the firm.

The purchasing procedure begins when some unit in the firm—usually the stores department—places a requisition for some material or supply. A purchasing agent processes the requisition, since he or she is familiar with the specific type of product ordered. In the process of selecting a vendor, the purchasing agent considers price, quantity discounts, vendor services and dependability, cash terms or credit terms, shipping time, and quality of product. It is often a good idea to patronize more than one vendor of a specific product. If one vendor is unable to deliver, for some reason—such as a strike or fire—the company will have another vendor to turn to for its purchase of the product.

If the purchase is large, the purchasing agent will send out notices to several vendors asking for bids on the order. The company sends a purchase order to the vendor they have selected. Based on previous experience, the company sets up a reasonable estimate of expected delivery date and they place a copy of the order in a filing system under the date of expected arrival. At the end of the day the shipment is due to arrive, purchasing compares receipts received from the stores department with the expected purchases for that day. If the shipment has not arrived, they send a tracer to the vendor to determine when the shipment will arrive. When receiving sends a shipment receipt to purchasing, they put one copy in purchasing's permanent files and send receipt records to accounting.

Inventory Control

Inventory control must balance two needs of the firm, (1) a need to maintain adequate materials and supplies on hand in order to meet customer delivery dates and not delay production, and (2) a need to minimize the amount of inventory carried on hand in order to lower carrying costs.

Inventory control must always maintain a sufficient amount of material and supplies on hand to meet the demands of the production unit. Being out of stock on an item may cause idle time and necessitate extensive production rescheduling. In addition, waiting for materials to arrive may so delay deliveries that the company loses business because customers feel they cannot depend on the company to meet delivery dates.

Exhibit 6–3

Perpetual inventory card.

Name _Steel Rods 2" x 6'_		Location _Section 5 Shelf 10_	
Source _Acme Steel Company_		Reorder Point _100_	

Received		Withdrawn		Balance
Date	Amount	Date	Amount	Amount
3/15	200			200
		3/1	50	150
		3/14	60	90
3/20	200			290

At the same time, because of cost, a firm does not want to carry more inventory than it needs. Spoilage, obsolescence, insurance, added storage space, money tied up in inventory, and interest paid on working capital loans are excess costs a firm may suffer if it maintains too large an inventory.

The two needs must be balanced by careful study of past and future turnover of inventory, amount of quantity discounts relative to carrying costs, time required to obtain the merchandise, and other factors such as impending strikes in the supplier industry.

Perpetual Inventory.　A **perpetual inventory** system records all receipts and withdrawals of material from the storeroom. A simple perpetual inventory system is a record-filing system of cards such as the one illustrated in Exhibit 6–3. When the company receives any materials or supplies, they record the date and the amount of materials, and they adjust the balance. By the same process, when they use items in the production process, they make an entry in the withdrawal column, recording the date and the amount, and they adjust the balance. In this way, a look at the card will tell how much of this type of material is on hand at any given time. In addition, optimum reorder points may be calculated by the purchasing department and the amount placed on the card. When they withdraw materials to bring the balance below this amount, they automatically send a requisition to purchasing for replacement of stock.

Computer Control.　Many business firms use computers to run their perpetual inventory systems. In the past only large companies could afford to maintain computer control of the inventory, but the rapid development of low-cost **microcomputers** now makes it possible for almost any size business to maintain its inventory on a computer. These microcomputers also perform many other functions, such as accounting and production control. The process is basically the same as with the card system that is operated by hand, but it is achieved by the computer with fantastic speed and accuracy. Considerable additional analysis of the inventory is also possible with the computer.

A building-materials chain with many stores located around the nation feeds all purchases and sales into their central computer. The computer keeps an up-to-date inventory on every store. Within a matter of minutes the firm can obtain a printout of the complete inventory of all stores. Through the use of the computer, they purchase merchandise for their stores in very large volume. They often buy carload lots of merchandise and divide it up between several of their stores by having the railroad car stopped at each store for unloading. This system has allowed them to carry only about 40 percent of the inventory they would have to carry if they did not use a computer. This reduced inventory means considerable savings in costs to the firm. Of course, they also obtain other services from the computer system, such as customer billing, payroll, etc.

Physical Inventory Count.   At least once a year, the business firm should take inventory, that is, count the physical inventory on hand and compare it to the perpetual inventory records for validation. If they do not agree, the perpetual inventory card should be corrected and an attempt made to determine why it deviates, to prevent a recurrence. Several factors may cause deviation of recorded amounts from physical counts such as theft, incorrect entries, and materials lost in the plant.

PRODUCTION ROBOTS

Manufacturing companies are currently buying **production robots** at an increasingly accelerated rate. Production robots promise to change the very face of production in the U.S. and other nations. These computer-controlled machines will soon replace most humans in the actual production process and provide low-cost, high-quality products.

Robots are used at a GM plant in Germany. Eight bumper beams are carried automatically by electromagnets from an indexing conveyor to a basket container. This robot eliminates cumbersome manual work, reduces noise, and improves container capacity utilization.

One example of how these robots function can be seen in the welding of automobile bodies at General Motors. Four robots spot-weld *continuously moving* automobile bodies. Electronic sensors track the bodies as they move down the assembly line and feed the information into the robot's computer. The robots then follow the bodies down the assembly line, placing spot welds where they are needed. The four robots can put 200 spot welds on 48 automobile bodies per hour.

The development of microcomputers has led to computer-assisted design systems, which, in turn, make computer-assisted manufacturing more efficient. Engineers and designers are able to use a video screen to design parts and products. The computer then has valuable information that makes it possible to computerize production planning, order raw materials, and schedule production runs. The computerized geometric design information is also used to program production robots to make the parts and put them together. One simple example is the drilling of boards for integrated circuits. The designer plans the size and location of holes on a video screen: this information is then sent to a robot, which drills the holes in the exact location and of the exact size. The computer-controlled machine even automatically changes drill bits.

SUMMARY OF KEY POINTS

1. Plant location variables are: the market, raw materials, transportation, community opinions, labor supply, taxes, availability of land, land prices, and climate.

2. Many authorities contend we are now entering a cybernetic revolution that will result in vast changes in our society.

3. Production control consists of five functions: planning, routing, scheduling, dispatching, and follow-up.

4. Quality control inspection may be performed by humans or by electronically controlled machinery. Human inspection is usually performed on a statistical sample basis.

5. The purchasing department's responsibility is to purchase the right quality, in the optimum quantity, at the best price, and at the right time.

6. Inventory control must maintain adequate supplies on hand while keeping inventory as low as possible to reduce carrying costs.

7. Computers are often used to perform production control, quality control, purchasing, and inventory control functions.

8. Production robots will soon replace most humans in the production process while providing low-cost, high-quality products.

DISCUSSION QUESTIONS

1. What factors would you consider when planning for the location of an oil-refining plant?
2. If you were going to build a plant to produce custom-built wooden kitchen and bathroom cabinets, where would you locate? Explain.
3. You are working for a company that custom builds wooden bookcases. It has five production departments—staining and varnishing, sanding, crating and shipping, assembly, and sawing. Tell how you would perform the five production control functions to produce an order.
4. If you were manufacturing a product, would you use machine or human inspectors for quality control?
5. What is the basic responsibility of the purchasing department?
6. If you were working in the purchasing department of the firm described in question 3, how might you perform value analysis?
7. What is the basic function of inventory control in this company?
8. Do you need a physical inventory count if the company uses a perpetual inventory system? Explain.
9. What are some uses of the computer in the manufacturing firm?

STUDENT PROJECTS

1. Select some simple product you would like to manufacture and decide where you would locate your plant.
2. Perform the planning and routing functions in production control:
   a. Determine the men, materials, and machines you would need.
   b. Estimate the standard for each work station or process.
   c. Route the product through the work stations or processes.
3. Determine quality control for your production.
4. Set up a perpetual inventory card for each raw material you would need to produce the product. Estimate your first purchase of the raw material and how much you would issue for the first week's production. Enter these amounts on the card in the proper place.

Casey's HomRun Specials

Jack Jones just retired from major league baseball after fifteen years as one of its outstanding players with a lifetime batting average of 301. Naturally, the press gave him the nickname "Casey." He wants to start a business, and manufacturing baseball bats seems a natural. He plans to name them "Casey's HomRun Specials." Jack is sure he can sell them, and he has the money to set up a plant in any part of the country. His only problem is that he does not know anything about production management.

You and Jack have been close friends since college. Since you majored in business, he offers you part of the business. He will put up all the money and market the bats. Jack wants you to locate the plant, set up the production operations, and manage the plant.

In the production process, hardwood must be sawed, lathed, sanded, stamped with the name, covered with a protective coating, and packaged.

Jack says that in manufacturing a bat, you must (1) be sure to get a good piece of wood that will not split, (2) lathe it to the correct shape and balance, (3) be sure the weight is correct, and (4) give the bat a good appearance.

Questions

1. In general, where would you locate the plant? Explain your answer.
2. If one of the major league teams orders 100 bats from you, describe how the five production control functions will be performed.
3. What quality control steps would you install? Explain where they would be performed and how.
4. Explain how the purchasing of the protective coating would be established.
5. Set up a perpetual inventory card for the protective coating if it is bought in 55-gallon drums.
6. Establish the steps in purchasing additional amounts of the coating after the plant is in operation.

Protect-All Railings Company

Kelly O'Brien started producing steel railings on a night and weekend basis several years ago. The railings were used primarily in commercial buildings such as apartments. He bid on the jobs and did all the production work himself in his garage, in addition to his regular job. Kelly found he was getting more work than he could handle on a part-time basis, and two years ago he quit his regular job and devoted full time to producing the steel railings. He now finds he is unable to do all the work and he is planning to hire a part-time salesperson, who will also do the bidding, and two full-time production workers.

The work stations in the new plant will be: sandblasting, to clean the steel; welding, to assemble the steel; and painting, for appearance and protection. The railings will also have to be inspected and shipped.

Kelly is very knowledgeable about building steel railings, but he knows almost nothing about production management. He has hired you to help select a plant site and set up his production management systems.

Questions

1. In general, where should he locate his plant? He is now located in a city that is growing rapidly and he feels it is the best market for his product.
2. Describe the five production control functions he would perform.
3. What quality control steps would you install? Explain where they should be performed and how.
4. Explain how the purchasing of steel and paint should be established.
5. Set up a perpetual inventory control system for the paint.
6. Do you think Kelly should use production robots? Explain your answer.

One of the first applications of the moving assembly line was this magneto assembly operation at the Ford Motor Company Highland Park Plant in 1913. Magnetos were pushed from one workman to the next, reducing production time by about one-half.

BUSINESS PROFILE

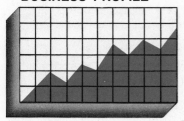

Ford Motor Company

Henry Ford ushered in the modern assembly line and the mass-production era. He is an excellent example of a man who saw the potential of a product, innovated new production techniques, and became an industrial giant as a result of his efforts.

Henry Ford was born in 1863 on a farm near Dearborn, Michigan, which is the home of the Ford Motor Company. Ford was a man of outstanding mechanical ability and a natural to take interest in the newly emerging automobile. The Ford Motor Company began in 1903 with $28,000 in capital.

Most people viewed the automobile at this time as a rich man's toy that would be produced on a limited custom-built production process. Ford did not share this view; rather, he saw its mass-production–mass-marketing potential. His philosophy was to reduce price, increase sales, and improve production efficiency to further reduce price. To improve production efficiency, he (1) established a standardized production process and product, (2) produced many of the parts that went into the automobile, (3) built assembly-line plants around the country to decrease transportation charges, and (4) established his production process on a continuous assembly-line–to–assembly-line flow. He achieved immediate success. By 1927, the Ford Motor Company had produced 15 million Model T automobiles and had a surplus balance of $700 million.

While his production-related innovations made him an instant success, his failure to keep pace with a changing market caused Ford to slip to second place in production of automobiles. He maintained mechanical brakes instead of hydraulic brakes, the four-cylinder engine instead of the six, and produced only black cars. When he realized that he'd made an error in marketing, he immediately retooled and introduced the eight-cylinder engine. Henry Ford died in 1947, but the company he founded now has more than $23 billion in assets, provides employment for 494,600 people with a yearly payroll of $10.1 billion, and is currently producing about 3.6 million vehicles per year.

7

Small Business Management and Franchising

LEARNING GOALS

After reading this chapter, you will understand:

1. That small business firms make substantial contributions to the U.S. economy by providing jobs and producing goods and services.

2. The purposes of the Small Business Administration.

3. The criteria established by the Committee on Economic Development and the Small Business Administration for classifying a business as small.

4. The advantages and disadvantages of owning your own business.

5. The major causes of business failure.

6. Many of the factors that should be considered before deciding to go into business for yourself.

7. What franchising is, as well as some of the advantages of franchising.

8. Some of the legal issues of franchising.

KEY TERMS

Small Business Administration
SCORE
ACE
Minority Enterprise Program
Small business
Committee for Economic Development
Retail firm

Service firm
Wholesale firm
Manufacturing firm
Franchising
Franchiser
Franchisee
Franchise agreement

> These people have a need for control. They just have to be in charge of what they're doing. It's not a need for power. It's a need for freedom.
>
> JOHN WELSH
> Director, Caruth Institute of Owner Managed Business
> Southern Methodist University

As many as 500,000 new businesses are started each year in this country. Thousands of people elect self-employment as the avenue for fulfilling personal goals. Individuals who start a small business are motivated by a desire for personal and financial independence and regard it as a means of expressing their unique creativity in the work life.

Thousands of small business success stories abound. One such success is John Haretakis, who in 1965 took $6,000 of his own money and $10,000 in borrowed funds and opened a family-style restaurant called Spires in California. Today, there are 21 restaurants and the number is still growing. Sales now exceed $25 million annually.[1]

SMALL BUSINESS IN OUR ECONOMY

Of the 11 million businesses in the United States (excluding farms), nearly 97 percent are classed as "small" by the Small Business Administration. Small business makes a real contribution to our economy, including the following:[2]

1. Small business provides employment for about 58 percent of the American workforce.
2. Small firms account for approximately 43 percent of the gross national output.
3. Small firms account for nearly $8 out of every $10 made by construction firms.
4. Small firms account for nearly $7 out of every $10 made by retailers and wholesalers.
5. Members of minority groups own 4.4 percent of all U.S. businesses. Most minority-owned businesses are small. Women own 4.6 percent of all U.S. businesses and 5.7 percent of all U.S. small businesses. Nearly all women-owned firms are small.
6. The livelihood of more than 100 million Americans is provided directly or indirectly by small businesses.
7. The small business sector creates more jobs than any other sector.

---

[1]*Nation's Business,* February, 1981, p. 18.

[2]"Small Facts," *Enterprise,* March, 1980, p. 15.

CHARACTERISTICS OF SMALL BUSINESS MANAGERS

Small business ownership is an effective outlet for individuals to express their creativity and initiative. A person considering a career in small business should be aware of the characteristics of successful small business managers. For example, one study found that small business managers who are successful possess the following characteristics:

1. Drive—comprised of responsibility, vigor, initiative, persistence, and health.
2. Thinking ability—comprised of original thinking, creative thinking, critical thinking, and analytical thinking.
3. Human relations ability—comprised of ascendancy, emotional stability, sociability, cautiousness, personal relations, consideration, cheerfulness, cooperation, and tactfulness.
4. Communications ability—comprised of verbal and written communications.
5. Technical knowledge—all-encompassing know-how related to the business.[3]

SMALL BUSINESS ADMINISTRATION

The **Small Business Administration** (SBA) is an independent agency of the federal government that was created by Congress when it passed the Small Business Act in 1953. The purpose of the SBA is to encourage, counsel, protect, and assist small businesses, which are the backbone of America's competitive, free-enterprise economy.

The SBA also seeks to increase the opportunities for small businesses to get started and compete with other business firms on an equitable basis in a number of different ways.

For example, the SBA tries to ensure that small businesses get a fair share of government contracts. The agency also provides management training to prospective, new, and established small business owners. Management training is provided through special courses, one-day conferences, problem-solving clinics, and workshops. Management counseling offered by the Small Business Administration is intended to help the small business owner with management problems and to provide prospective owners of small businesses with management information about specific types of business.

Small Business Administration Loans

Under certain conditions, small businesses may borrow from the SBA to construct, expand, or convert facilities, to purchase machinery, equipment, buildings, supplies, or materials, or to obtain working capital. The SBA may (1) provide direct loans to a business for the entire amount, if funds are available, (2) participate in loans with lending institutions, (3)

---

[3]Hal. B. Pickle, *Personality and Success: An Evaluation of Personal Characteristics of Successful Small Business Managers* (Washington, D.C.: Small Business Administration, 1964), p. 34.

guarantee loans (up to 90 percent) which a bank or other lender agrees to make.

The SBA tries first to guarantee loans from lending institutions. Next it tries to participate in loans if the business can obtain funds from other sources. Finally, it tries to make direct loans in an effort to spread its available funds as far as possible. Usually the demand for the direct loans exceeds the SBA's supply of money for this purpose. As a result, most SBA loans are made in cooperation with banks.

To avoid competing with private enterprise, the SBA will not grant or participate in a loan if the business can obtain funds from a private financial institution such as a bank.

The SBA also makes a variety of specialized loans. One example is an economic opportunity loan designed to help persons who are socially or economically disadvantaged own their business. Another type of assistance is the loan to handicapped small business owners. Disaster loans are made to help businesses damaged by such natural disasters as fire, hurricane, or flood. Another source of assistance is provided by volunteer groups. One group is **SCORE,** the Service Corps of Retired Executives, retired executives who volunteer their service to aid small business owners. Another volunteer group, **ACE** (Active Corps of Executives), is composed of managers still active in business who provide counseling to small business owners. Many national professional associations also provide counseling services.

As noted in chapter 2, the SBA has combined its efforts with private industry, bankers, local communities, and other federal government agencies to increase the number of minority-owned, operated, and managed businesses under the **Minority Enterprise Program**.

WHAT IS A SMALL BUSINESS?

Although small businesses make significant contributions to our economy, there is no clear understanding of what a small business is. To some, a **small business** is a company with no more than a specific number of employees, such as four to eight. Others consider a business small if it serves only a local market. To others, businesses are small if they are in a certain line of business, such as clothing stores, jewelry stores, or barber shops.

The **Committee for Economic Development (CED)** has established guidelines for classifying small businesses. The CED states that a business is small if it meets two or more of the following criteria:[4]

1. Management is independent. Usually the managers are also the owners.

2. An individual or small group supplies capital and holds the ownership.

---

[4]*Meeting the Special Problems of Small Business* (New York: Committee for Economic Development, 1947), p. 14.

3. The area of operations is mainly local. Workers and owners are in one home community. Markets need not be local.

4. The business is small when compared to the biggest units in its field. The size of the top bracket varies greatly, so that what might seem large in one field would definitely be small in another.

The SBA defines a business as small if (1) it is independently owned and operated, (2) it is not dominant in its field of operation, (3) it meets particular size standards for its industry or area, which are based on the number of employees or the dollar volume of sales or receipts of the firm, and (4) it is operated for a profit. For purposes of deciding who is eligible for a Small Business Administration loan, the SBA classifies the following types of businesses as small if they meet the criteria listed below.

1. A **retail firm** is small if its annual sales are not over $2 to $7.5 million, depending on the industry. A retail business is one that buys goods from suppliers and sells them to customers. Typical kinds of retail firms are food, clothing, and drugstores.

2. A **service firm** with annual receipts not exceeding $2 million to $8 million, depending on the industry, is classed as small. A service firm provides services for customers, and types of service firms include hotels, barber and beauty shops, and repair shops.

3. A **wholesale firm** with annual receipts of not over $9.5 to $22 million, depending on the industry, is classed as small. Wholesalers buy and resell merchandise, primarily to retailers and commercial and industrial users, and do not sell in significant amounts to final consumers.

4. A **manufacturing firm** is classified as small if its number of employees does not exceed 250 persons and large if its number of employees exceeds 1,500 persons. If employment is between 250 and 1,500, a size that is standard for the industry is used. Some 96 percent of all manufacturing firms have 250 employees or less. A manufacturer takes raw materials and converts them into finished goods for sale.

The Small Business Administration is currently reevaluating these size classification standards.

ADVANTAGES OF SMALL BUSINESS OWNERSHIP

The advantages of small business ownership include independence, profit expectation, ease of starting the business, personalized customer service, and direct contact with employees. Each of these advantages is discussed below.

Independence

By owning your own business, you can achieve the goal of being independent. Many people have a strong need to make it on their own, to make their own decisions, to use their own ideas. Since you are your own boss as the owner of the small business, you make the decisions that affect your customers, creditors, suppliers, competitors, employees, and the community. The independence gained through small business ownership is a valuable source of personal pride and satisfaction to the entrepreneur.

Profit Expectation

Since small business owner-managers are self-employed, the profits earned in their firms are their salaries. The amount of profit earned is related directly to the kind of management decisions made by the small business owner and the time and effort devoted to the business.

Ease of Starting the Business

Going into business for oneself is relatively easy, especially for the single proprietorship form of ownership. As noted earlier, all that is necessary to open the business is a location, the special licenses required by city, county, state, and federal government agencies (such as a retail store license, liquor license, individual and business health certificates for food places and restaurants, Internal Revenue requirements), and the funds necessary for the business. Usually no other restrictions are placed on starting small business operations.

Personalized Customer Service

Many small business owners have the opportunity to get to know customers on a personal basis. In many cases, the personalized service that the small business owner can give customers is the major reason they continue to patronize the small business.

Direct Contact with Employees

In the small business, there is ordinarily only one level of management. It is not uncommon for the owner-manager to work side by side with employees in the daily operations of the firm. Consequently, the owner-

In many cases, personalized service is the major reason customers continue to patronize the small business.

manager has the opportunity to build positive relationships with employees. He or she can better understand the needs of employees, and in turn employees are able to more clearly understand the small business owner's position. This close relationship allows many problems to be handled on a more personal basis, resulting in greater harmony between employees and the owner-manager.

DISADVANTAGES OF SMALL BUSINESS OWNERSHIP

Several disadvantages of small business ownership should also be evaluated: these include risk of funds, the need for the owner to be a generalist, and long hours of work.

Risk and Limitation of Funds

Individuals who accept the challenges and opportunities of small business ownership usually invest all or a substantial portion of their own funds. Often additional funds must be borrowed for start-up and expansion purposes. Since the small business owner has limited collateral, he or she may have difficulty in raising the extra funds.

If the business does not succeed, the owner-manager faces not only the loss of his or her own funds, but, if it is a single proprietorship, the owner will be personally liable for all debts of the firm.

When starting a new business, a useful guideline is that an owner-manager should set aside enough money for living and business expenses for three months or longer and use this money only for these purposes. This will allow the owner-manager to concentrate his or her energies on building the business and not be unduly concerned about the financial status of the business.

Small Business Owners Must Be Generalists, Not Specialists

Large corporations hire specialists to perform such activities as accounting, selling, and hiring. However, the small business owner has limited resources and he or she must perform most or all of the required activities in the firm. Consequently, small business owners must be generalists. Since much of their time is spent handling everyday business problems, they have little time left to devote to developing long-range plans for the business. Small business managers will definitely benefit from time management analysis, since efficient utilization of time can be a major factor in the small business owner's success.

Long Hours of Work

The owner-manager must devote long hours to the business. Usually the owner-manager is the first to arrive in the morning and the last to leave in the evening. It is not uncommon for small business owners to spend sixty or more hours a week in their business. Many businesses are open seven days a week.

PROBLEMS OF SMALL BUSINESS

If you desire to own your own business, you should be aware of some of the causes of business failure before you open your business.

Dun & Bradstreet reports annually on the causes of business failures. While there are causes for failures in all sizes of business, you, the small business owner, should be aware of these problem areas and analyze them as they relate to your firm. In this way, you will be better prepared to prevent such occurrences. The causes of business failure are shown in Exhibit 7–1.

Inadequate Management

By far the major cause of all business failure is inadequate management. As the Dun & Bradstreet data show, nearly 92 percent of all business failures are attributed to this one cause. What contributes to inadequate management? Again referring to Exhibit 7–1, we see that causes of inadequate management include a lack of experience in the line of business, a lack of managerial experience, unbalanced business experience, and incompetence.

An owner shows poor management by making wrong decisions that can prove costly to the firm or by delaying decisions or putting them off indefinitely. Managers reveal incompetence in such problems as inadequate sales, poor location, carrying the wrong kind of merchandise in inventory, carrying too much inventory, carrying outdated merchandise, being reluctant to change in order to meet the needs of customers, being unable to meet competitors' prices, ignorance of business practices and principles, lack of proper record-keeping procedures, and insufficient promotion and advertising.

**Other Causes
of Business Failure**

While inadequate management is the chief cause of all business failures, the Dun & Bradstreet report lists other causes of business failure: neglect, fraud, and disaster. Although they account for less than 3 percent of all failures, the small business owner cannot ignore these causes. Some causes of failure could not be identified.

Exhibit 7–1

Causes of business failure.

Underlying Causes	Percent of Total Failures
Major Cause	
Inadequate management	91.9
Lack of experience in the line	14.9
Lack of managerial experience	16.8
Unbalanced experience	15.8
Incompetence	44.4
Other Causes	
Neglect	1.1
Fraud	0.6
Disaster	0.6
Reason unknown	5.8

SOURCE: The Business Failure Record, Dun and Bradstreet, Inc.

Neglect.   Some small businesses fail because the owner neglects to devote the time and energy necessary to sustain the vitality of the firm. The more common reasons given for this neglect include bad habits, marital problems, and health problems.

Fraud.   Intentionally misrepresenting the truth for the purpose of deceiving another is fraud. Fraud in the small business commonly appears as the use of a misleading firm name, supplying false financial reports, or improperly disposing of the assets of the firm to satisfy personal debts.

Disaster.   Fires, earthquakes, storms, employee fraud and theft, burglary, and labor strikes are types of disasters that may hurt the small business. Small business owners can protect themselves against total loss from such disasters by carrying insurance. (Insurance is discussed in detail in chapter 17.)

FRANCHISING

Franchising has provided many people who want to own and operate a small business with a greater chance of being successful. **Franchising** is the arrangement made by one firm (**franchiser**) to license another firm (**franchisee**) with exclusive rights to sell its product or service in a specified territory. The franchisee owns the business and is responsible for its operation. The franchising boom started just after World War II. Franchise operations offer owners the opportunity to sell a variety of products and services, such as fast food restaurants and auto repair shops. Franchised retail outlets now account for more than 30 percent of all retail sales. Economic growth in many international markets is opening expansion opportunities for franchising.

The Franchise Agreement

The **franchise agreement** is the contract that details the relationship between the franchiser and franchisee. These items are typically included in the franchise agreement:

1. Franchisee fee;
2. Description of the conditions under which the franchise agreement may be terminated by either party;
3. Selling and renewal of the franchise;
4. Advertising and promotion;
5. Patent and liability protection;
6. Franchiser services;
7. Commissions and royalties;
8. Training;
9. Financing;
10. Territory;
11. Exclusive vs. nonexclusive;
12. Site selection.

Checklist for Going into Business for Yourself

Before starting your own business, you should complete the following checklist. It will help you consider many of the important matters regarding business ownership under the three main headings: before you start your business, getting your business started, and making a go of your business.

BEFORE YOU START
How About You?
Are you the kind of person who can get a business started and make it go?

Think about *why* you want to own your own business. Do you want to badly enough to keep working long hours without knowing how much money you'll end up with?

Have you worked in a business like the one you want to start?

Have you worked for someone else as a foreman or manager?

Have you had any business training in school?

Have you saved any money?

How About the Money?
Do you know how much money you will need to get your business started?

Have you counted up how much of your own money you can put into the business?

Do you know how much credit you can get from your suppliers?

Do you know where you can borrow the rest of the money you need to start your business?

Have you figured out what net income per year you expect to

get from your business? Count your salary and your profit on the money you put into the business.

Can you live on less than this so that you can use some of it to help your business grow?

Have you talked to a banker about your plans?

How About a Partner?
If you need a partner with money or know-how that you don't have, do you know someone who will fit—someone you can get along with?

Do you know the good and bad points about going it alone, having a partner, and incorporating your business?

Have you talked to a lawyer?

How About Your Customers?
Do most businesses in your community seem to be doing well?

Have you tried to find out whether stores like the one you want to open are doing well in your community and the rest of the country?

Do you know what kind of people will want to buy what you plan to sell?

Do people like that live in the area where you want to open your store?

Do they need a store like yours?

If not, have you thought about opening a different kind of store or going to another neighborhood?

GETTING STARTED
Your Building
Have you found a good building for your store?

Will you have enough room when your business gets bigger?

Can you fix the building the way you want it without spending too much money?

Can people get to it easily from parking spaces, bus stops, or their homes?

Have you had a lawyer check the lease and zoning?

Equipment and Supplies
Do you know just what equipment and supplies you need and how much they will cost?

Can you save some money by buying secondhand equipment?

Your Merchandise
Have you decided what things you will sell?

Do you know how much or how many of each you will buy to open your store with?

Have you found suppliers who will sell you what you need at a good price?

Have you compared the prices and credit terms of suppliers?

Your Records
Have you planned a system of records that will keep track of your income and expenses, what you owe other people, and what other people owe you?

Have you worked out a way to keep track of your inventory so that you will always have enough on hand for your customers but not more than you can sell?

Have you figured out how to keep payroll records and make tax reports and payments?

Do you know what financial statements you should prepare?

Do you know how to use these financial statements?

Do you know an accountant who will help you with your records and financial statements?

Your Store and the Law

Do you know what licenses and permits you need?

Do you know what business laws you have to obey?

Do you know a lawyer you can go to for advice and for help with legal papers?

Protecting Your Store

Have you made plans for protecting your store against thefts of all kinds—shoplifting, robbery, burglary, employee stealing?

Have you talked with an insurance agent about what kinds of insurance you need?

Buying a Business Someone Else Has Started

Have you made a list of what you like and don't like about buying a business someone else has started?

Are your sure you know the real reason why the owner wants to sell the business?

Have you compared the cost of buying the business with the cost of starting a new business?

Is the stock up to date and in good condition?

Is the building in good condition?

Will the owner of the building transfer the lease to you?

Have you talked with other business owners in the area to see what they think of the business?

Have you talked with the company's suppliers?

Have you talked with a lawyer?

MAKING IT GO
Advertising

Have you decided how you will advertise? (Newspapers—posters—handbills—radio—by mail?)

Do you know where to get help with your ads?

Have you watched what other stores do to get people to buy?

The Prices You Charge

Do you know how to figure what you should charge for each item you sell?

Do you know what other stores like yours charge?

Buying

Do you have a plan for finding out what your customers want?

Will your plan for keeping track of your inventory tell you when it is time to order more and how much to order?

Do you plan to buy most of your stock from a few suppliers rather than a little from many, so that those you buy from will want to help you succeed?

Selling

Have you decided whether you will have salesclerks or self-service?

Do you know how to get customers to buy?

Have you thought about why you like to buy from some salespeople while others turn you off?

Your Employees

If you need to hire someone to help you, do you know where to look?

Do you know what kind of person you need?

Do you know how much to pay?

Do you have a plan for training your employees?

Credit for Your Customers

Have you decided whether to let your customers buy on credit?

Do you know the good and bad points about joining a credit-card plan?

Can you tell a deadbeat from a good credit customer?

A FEW EXTRA QUESTIONS

Have you figured out whether you could make more money working for someone else?

Does your family go along with your plan to start a business of your own?

Do you know where to find out about new ideas and new products?

Do you have a work plan for yourself and your employees?

Have you gone to the nearest Small Business Administration office for help with your plans?

If you have answered all these questions carefully, you've done some hard work, and serious thinking. That's good. But you probably found some things you still need to know more about or do something about.

Do all you can for yourself, but don't hesitate to ask for help from people who can tell you what you need to know. Remember, running a business takes guts! You've got to be able to decide what you need and then go after it.

Good luck!

SOURCE: *Small Marketer's Aid*, No. 71. Washington, D.C.: Small Business Administration, 1975.

Franchiser Services

The franchiser provides many types of assistance to the franchisee, such as standard operating procedures, professional help and training, supplies and products at wholesale, financial assistance, and a proven brand-name product.

Standard Operating Procedures.   The franchiser often provides plans for standard facilities and a standard method of operating the business. For example, Shakey's Pizza Parlors provides franchisees with standard building plans for a building that matches the market area. Shakey's also provides a detailed operations manual that provides specifications on:

1. Pizza construction and ingredient specifications;
2. Other food products (salad, chicken, and potatoes);
3. Personnel management;
4. Customer service;
5. Parlor maintenance and sanitation;
6. Equipment;
7. Management and cost controls;
8. Trademarks and service marks.

Many franchised operations also receive standardized forms and procedures for various types of control, such as daily cash records, payroll forms, tax bulletins, operating manuals, inventory records, and purchase records.

Professional Assistance and Training.   Many franchisers have established "universities" where new franchise operators are given training in the standardized methods of operating the franchise. Production training focuses on the product and the process, quality control, standards, and repairs and maintenance of equipment. Profit training stresses sales development and forecasting, cost controls, cash controls, security, personnel administration, financial planning, employee scheduling, basic bookkeeping and accounting systems, purchasing, inventory control, advertising, and time management. For example, Dunkin' Donuts requires franchise owners to complete the company's five-week training program at Dunkin' Donuts University, which covers all phases of franchise operations.

Professional assistance continues after the initial training. The franchiser's representatives regularly visit franchise owners who can then discuss problems and opportunities of the business and learn new skills and techniques in sales, production, and finance. These visits allow the franchiser's representative to insure that the franchisee maintains the high standards of the franchiser.

Supplies and Products at Wholesale.   Franchisers often purchase products in huge lots from manufacturers and sell at wholesale to their franchised stores. Muffler or brake repair franchises usually have contractual agreements with manufacturers to produce repair parts for them in very large quantities. Franchisers then sell these repair parts to the franchised stores at wholesale prices. They also furnish supplies at wholesale prices. A motel franchise operation will usually buy soap, towels, letterhead stationery, and other items in large amounts from manufacturers and supply them to their franchised operations at relatively low prices.

Financial Assistance. The franchisee may receive financial assistance in one or more of three ways. First, the franchiser usually requires a specific investment to construct the building, buy equipment, and finance opening promotions. Often, the franchiser will finance as much as half the original investment, with the franchisee paying the remainder over several years. Second, the franchiser will often finance the store's inventory, on a 60- to 90-day basis. Third, a few franchisers offer an option to enter into a joint venture agreement. By this method the franchiser finances part of the original investment and is part owner in the franchised operation, although the franchiser usually takes no part in the management.

Proven Brand-name Product. Most franchise operations owe much of their success to a product with proven customer acceptance. The parent company supplies or instructs the franchisee to produce a product or service that has been developed over several years in many stores. In addition, the franchiser can build a brand-name identification on a national basis by having a nationwide (or international) system of stores and national advertising.

Franchiser's Fees

In return for the franchise and the benefits provided by the franchiser, each franchisee pays the parent company fees as specified in the franchise agreement. Fees may be based on a percentage of gross sales; or there may be a fixed fee per month or year, or a combination of the two. When the percentage of gross sales method is used, the franchisee pays a percentage of sales: Dunkin' Donuts, for example, receives a weekly fee of 4.9 percent of gross sales from franchisees. The standard fixed fee agreement requires the franchisee to pay a set fee on a periodic basis: franchisees might be required to pay $400 per month to the parent company, regardless of sales. In some cases, the size of the market determines the fixed fee. The combination method requires the payment of a fixed monthly fee plus a stated percentage of weekly or monthly sales.

LEGAL ISSUES IN FRANCHISING

The franchising system of distributing goods and providing services to consumers has provided opportunities for success to both franchiser and franchisee. However, some problems have resulted.

Some franchisers have misrepresented the sales income or profits of the franchise, unfairly attempted to terminate the franchise agreement, or illegally tried to force the franchisee to buy supplies from the franchiser. To protect franchisees from such abuses, the Federal Trade Commission has issued a regulation requiring franchisers to provide detailed substanti-

"IT'S DELICIOUS— JUST THE THING FOR OUR NATIONWIDE FRANCHISE OPERATION."

ation to franchisees of their earnings claims. The regulation carries the force of law and violators are subject to fines up to $10,000 for each violation.

Under the regulation, franchisers have to provide prospective buyers of a franchise with a full-disclosure statement at least ten days before a contract is signed or any money changes hands. The rule also forbids making statements about actual or potential profits of the franchise unless the statements can be shown to be accurate by documented records.

The FTC initiated its first enforcement action against Singer, a Chicago-based franchiser of frozen pizza distributorships. Singer was alleged to have sold franchises without providing disclosure information and to have made undocumented earnings claims. The Commission obtained a restraining order freezing the firm's assets and accounts, and further requested the court to begin contempt hearings against the firm for failing to provide an inventory of assets.[5]

THE FUTURE OF FRANCHISING

Franchising will continue to be a dominant force in the economy of the 1980s, especially in the retail and service sectors. Retail firms that feature technological items such as home computers will be strong growth areas; service franchises that concentrate on convenience and specialization will also be strong performers.

The Department of Commerce expects the 1980s to be a period when foreign franchisors, mainly from Canada, but also from England, Europe,

---

[5]*Restaurant Business Magazine*, March 15, 1981, p. 68.

and Japan, will make significant inroads into the U.S. market. The foreign franchisors will specialize in restaurants, clothing, furniture, and auto products and services.

It is anticipated that larger corporations will step up their efforts to take over independent franchise chains.

SUMMARY OF KEY POINTS

1. Small business firms make significant contributions to the economy of the United States by providing employment opportunities and by accounting for a sizeable share of the GNP.

2. Successful small business managers possess the following characteristics: drive, thinking ability, human relations ability, communications ability, and technical knowledge.

3. The purpose of the Small Business Administration is to encourage, counsel, protect, and assist small business owners by providing counseling and training services and by making loans.

4. A small business, as defined by the SBA, has independent ownership and operation, is not dominant in the field of operation, meets particular size standards, and is operated for a profit.

5. Among the advantages of small business ownership are independence, profit expectation, ease of starting, personalized customer service, and direct contact with employees.

6. Some disadvantages of small business ownership are that it requires the risking of funds; it requires owners to be generalists; and it requires long hours of work.

7. The major cause of business failure is inadequate management: neglect, fraud, and disaster are also contributors.

8. Franchising is the arrangement whereby the franchiser licenses the franchisee with exclusive rights to sell a product or service in a specific territory.

9. Some legal issues have arisen in conjunction with some of the actions of a limited number of franchisers.

DISCUSSION QUESTIONS

1. What contributions do small businesses make to our economy in providing jobs and producing goods and services?

2. How does the Committee on Economic Development define a small business?

3. What is the Small Business Administration?

4. Under the Small Business Administration guidelines, when would you classify a retail firm as a small firm?

5. What are the advantages and disadvantages of owning your own business?

6. Identify the causes of business failures.

7. How do franchisers ensure that the franchisee sells a proven product?

8. What are some of the financial arrangements by which franchisers help franchised operations?

9. What are some of the methods by which a franchisee pays the franchiser?

STUDENT PROJECTS

1. Assume that you wish to go into business for yourself. Select the type of business you would like to own (such as retailing, service, manufacturing, construction) and write a short report (one or two pages) stating the reasons you selected this type of business.

2. Identify as many pros and cons as you can (in addition to those in the text) for going into business for yourself.

3. Select a franchise and make a preliminary inquiry into a franchise agreement. Near the end of the school term, report on the main points of the agreement.

4. From the classified section of your daily paper, *The Wall Street Journal,* or other publication, such as a magazine, make a list of three or four franchise opportunities shown. Include the requirements listed for each franchise.

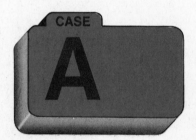

CASE

A

Jim's Career

Jim Huntly is a successful 28-year-old insurance salesperson for a national insurance organization, specializing in selling insurance to business clients—fire, worker compensation, health programs. Jim has been with the firm for five years and has shown steady progress in building his commercial accounts. He has considerable flexibility in his job as far as hours of work are concerned, and his earnings are based on sales commission. Prior to this position, Jim held two other sales positions in insurance, one for a period of two years and the other for one. Jim graduated from college eight years ago with a BBA degree; he majored in marketing. He paid for his college expenses by doing contract painting of residential homes in the university city.

Jim is aggressive and is motivated by a high achievement motive. Although he is making a very comfortable living for himself and his wife, Jim is not entirely satisfied with his progress toward a management position. Promotions are based on seniority, and the management positions above him are filled with managers whose ages range from only slightly older than Jim to those who have as much as twenty-five years of service with the company.

Feeling "boxed in" as far as future progression into a management position is concerned, Jim is evaluating other alternatives that will enable him to use his initiative and energy and enjoy greater personal fulfillment. He feels that the experience gained from painting houses while in college demonstrated his ability to work on his own.

Jim has discussed his career dilemma with his wife. He is strongly inclined toward the alternative of leaving the sales position and going it alone as an independent businessperson.

Jim has considered two main options: one is to start an independent business of his own; the other alternative is to purchase a franchise business. Jim scans the classified ads in the Sunday newspaper and reads some of the following franchise opportunities.

1. A franchise for repairing, reconditioning, and rebuilding transmissions for all cars. Franchisees do not need to have a technical background but should have a strong business background.
2. A fast food restaurant of a nationwide chain that serves a moderately priced menu of hamburgers, cheeseburgers, french fries, shakes, and assorted beverages.

Questions

1. What factors should Jim consider with regard to opening an independent small business?
2. What factors should he consider in buying a franchised operation?
3. Check the classified ads in a newspaper and identify other franchise opportunities available to Jim.
4. If you were Jim, what would you do?

Wilbur and Richard

Wilbur is a store manager of a supermarket for a major grocery chain. He has been with the same company for twenty-four years. His work week is fifty-five to sixty hours long. In return for his strong job performance the company provides Wilbur with a very good salary and many benefits, including five weeks of vacation annually.

Richard owns his own business, a small combination tavern-restaurant. He is his own boss. No one tells Richard what products to buy and sell, He can decide what food he wishes to list on his menu, and it can be prepared the way he wishes it to be prepared.

No one pays Richard for his vacation except himself. The only vacation he has had was a four-day vacation six years ago. Richard's business is open from about 10 A.M. until 2 A.M. the next morning, six days a week. Each working day is sixteen hours, ninety-six hours a week. Richard has owned his business for twenty-five years, and it has provided him and his family with a comfortable living.

Question

Analyze why Richard chooses to own his own business instead of working as a manager for a large firm.

The small restaurant started by Colonel Harland Sanders as a sole proprietorship has grown into a world-wide franchise operation with some 6,400 outlets in fifty countries.

BUSINESS PROFILE

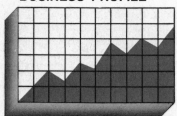

Kentucky Fried Chicken Corporation (KFC Corporation)

Kentucky Fried Chicken Corporation (now KFC Corporation) is the success story of a business that began as a sole proprietorship selling customers a product they liked, then incorporated, and began franchising its product on a world-wide basis.

Colonel Harland Sanders started doing much of the family cooking at age 6 because his father died and his mother had to go to work. He held various jobs but returned to cooking when he was 40 years old. He operated a service station in Kentucky and began selling meals in his home next door. When customers began to patronize the food operation heavily, he dispensed with the gas pumps, expanded the size of the food operation to accommodate 142 people, and concentrated on the food retailing operation.

Colonel Sanders (an honorary title bestowed on him by the governor of Kentucky) suffered business setbacks as a result of World War II and the rerouting of a highway that left his business off the major thoroughfare. Consequently, he began his chicken franchising business by traveling from restaurant to restaurant cooking his special recipe chicken for the owners and seeking their help. If they liked his chicken, he would enter into a handshake agreement that the restaurant owner would pay him a nickel for each chicken sold that was cooked according to his secret recipe. By 1963, he had more than 600 franchised outlets in the United States and Canada. In 1963, he sold his interest in the U.S. market for $2 million to John Y. Brown and his partner. In 1971, Hueblein Corporation purchased Kentucky Fried Chicken for $280 million. Colonel Sanders remained active in promoting KFC Corporation until his death in 1980 at the age of 90.

The number of competing fast-food restaurants that specialize in fried chicken has increased dramatically. In addition, other franchises, such as Burger King, Wendy's, McDonald's, and Long John Silver's, have added chicken to their line of food products to bolster sales. KFC Corporation has experimented with other food items, such as beef ribs; however, they now concentrate their sales efforts on Colonel Sanders' Original Recipe and Extra-Crispy fried chicken and chicken sandwiches, and "Kentucky Fries" have been added to the menu.

KFC Corporation has some 6,400 outlets in fifty countries and some 4,400 of these outlets are in the United States. Sales are over $2.2 billion annually. Franchisees pay the KFC Corporation a $4,000 franchise fee and 4 percent of gross sales annually. The franchise stresses quality, service, cleanliness, and value in their advertising.

Business Management and Supporting Fields

Many career opportunities are available in the various fields of management as well as office administration. These positions exist at both entry-level and high-level occupations. A sample of career opportunities and their expected growth to 1990 and a representative listing of job titles and descriptions is shown below. The appendix contains additional career information.

Occupation	Number Currently Employed	Number of Openings for Each Year to 1990
Administrative:		
City managers	3,300	350
Hotel managers	168,000	8,900
Public relations workers	131,000	7,500
Health administrators	180,000	8,900
Purchasing agents	185,000	13,400
Urban planners	17,000	8,000
Office:		
Cashiers	1,400,000	119,000
File clerks	273,000	16,500
Library assistants	172,000	7,700
Medical-records clerks	50,000	4,900
Office-machine operators	160,000	9,700
Receptionists	588,000	40,000
Shipping clerks	461,000	22,000
Secretaries, stenographers	3,684,000	305,000
Stock clerks	507,000	23,000
Typists	1,044,000	59,000

SOURCE: U.S. Department of Labor, *Occupational Outlook Handbook*, 1980–81.

MANAGER OF INDUSTRIAL ORGANIZATION (any industry) May have the title general manager, director. Manages industrial organizations, including coordination of activities of departments; reviews programs in purchasing, accounting, research, etc.; determines and implements company policies through subordinates.

OFFICE MANAGER   Supervises and coordinates activities of office personnel. Activities include directing office staff, planning office layout, coordination of activities with other departments, standardizing office procedures.

SUPERVISOR (any industry)   Supervises and coordinates workers who perform one type of work.

CITY MANAGER   Directs and coordinates administration of city government according to policies set by city council. Plans for future city development, appoints department heads, supervises activities of departments.

HOSPITAL ADMINISTRATOR   Supervises hospital operations and all related activities. Supervises and coordinates administrative activities of the hospital with the medical services.

FRANCHISE PROMOTION   Plans the location of franchised retail stores, arranges details of the lease, and gives assistance to store operators, such as planning store location and training store personnel.

ADMINISTRATIVE ASSISTANT   Acts in staff capacity, aiding managers by preparing the budget, conducting special studies of work methods to make them more efficient, and analyzing operations of the firm.

HOTEL MANAGER   Has overall responsibility for profitable hotel operation, including supervision of personnel, publicity of the hotel, and finances of hotel operations.

MANAGEMENT TRAINEE (any industry)   Performs and observes a variety of activities in many or all departments. Gets a broad picture of the organization as well as training and experience for promotion to management position.

INDUSTRIAL DESIGNER   Combines technical knowledge of materials, machines, and production with artistic talent in order to improve the appearance and function of machine-made products.

MANAGER, SERVICE ESTABLISHMENT (any type of establishment)   Provides a service to the public, such as a business service, repair service, or a personal service.

STOCK CLERK   Controls flow of goods received, stored, and issued.

INVENTORY CLERK   Takes periodic counts of items on hand and makes reports showing stock balances.

PROCUREMENT CLERK   Works in factories and prepares orders for purchase of new equipment.

STOCK SUPERVISOR   Supervises and coordinates workers engaged in handling merchandise in storeroom or warehouses.

STOCK-CONTROL CLERK   Compiles records concerned with ordering, receiving, storing, or issuing goods.

PURCHASING AGENT   Buys machinery, equipment, other materials necessary for operation of an organization.

PRODUCTION-CONTROL CLERK   Keeps records of parts being worked on and completed and distributes material and parts to workers.

SHIPPING AND RECEIVING CLERK   Receives incoming merchandise shipments, prepares merchandise for shipment, and keeps related records.

STENOGRAPHER   Takes routine dictation and does other general office activities, such as typing, filing, operating office machines.

SECRETARY   Relieves employer of routine duties and performs special duties. A legal secretary does legal research and helps prepare briefs. A medical secretary prepares case histories and medical reports.

CLERK TYPIST   Combines typing with filing, sorting mail, answering the telephone, and other general office work.

RECEPTIONIST   Greets customers and visitors, and determines their needs; refers them to persons who can help them. May perform a variety of clerical activities.

GENERAL OFFICE CLERK   Writes or types bills, statements, receipts, or other tasks not requiring knowledge of systems or procedures.

ADMINISTRATIVE CLERK   Copies data and compiles records and reports using knowledge of systems and procedures.

FILE CLERK   Handles office information by classifying, storing, updating, and retrieving on request. In smaller offices, may operate several different types of office equipment.

CAREER PROFILES

Sam Reeves received his BBA degree from Georgia Southern University. He joined the Southland Corporation after working for two other companies.

Since joining Southland, Sam has developed definite career goals. He was promoted from management trainee to auditor to supervisor to division personnel manager in just six years. He was then moved up to district manager, responsible for the operation of twenty-one 7-Eleven convenience stores. His responsibilities included management of line operations, accounting functions, and personnel activities related to the twenty-one stores under his direction.

A most rewarding part of Sam's district manager job is having a part in the hiring and placement of employees and helping them to succeed and advance in the corporation. One of the most difficult parts of his job is getting things done through other people.

Sam's new position will be in the personnel field in Southland's special operations division. His career goal in this new position is to become an expert in personnel administration. This new position will enable Sam to get a better picture of Southland's total business operation. With the knowledge and experience gained from this position Sam is confident that he will be able to advance further within the Southland Corporation.

Lysbeth Hasegawa's initial employment was as a sales clerk in a gift shop while a senior in high school. While studying for a degree in merchandising and sales at Chabot College, she continued to work part-time in the gift shop. After graduation, she accepted full-time employment as a salesperson. Since she desired to advance more rapidly, she returned to college and completed all requirements for a legal secretary certificate. During this time, she worked part-time in a department store.

Lysbeth felt a job as a secretary was too confining, so she went to work as a manager trainee in a department store, where she was later promoted to a department manager position. Since she preferred a small store environment, she left the department store to accept employment with a small retail clothing store, where she has become a store manager. Her responsibilities include personnel, staffing and training, merchandise handling, display, customer service, cash handling, daily store operations, store security, store maintenance and aesthetics, and staff- and self-development.

Association with a smaller business has provided Lysbeth with many opportunities. She was given the opportunity to open a new store, and she feels her future opportunities are endless. She says, "I enjoy accepting challenges. The accomplishments generate self-satisfaction, which is most gratifying."

Lysbeth's Introduction to Business instructor was Donald Green of Chabot College.

Human Factors in Management

8

Human Relations in Management

LEARNING GOALS

After reading this chapter, you will understand:

1. That motivation and job satisfaction are the results of a person's value system, abilities, expectation of rewards, rewards, and perception of how equitable these rewards are.

2. Basic human needs and how they can be satisfied.

3. That what a manager assumes about the nature of people determines how he or she manages people.

4. Why some workers have excellent morale and others have poor morale.

5. The indicators of poor morale.

KEY TERMS

Motivation	Recognition needs	Theory Y
Job performance	Esteem needs	Theory Z
Physiological needs	Self-realization needs	Morale
Safety needs	Theory X	

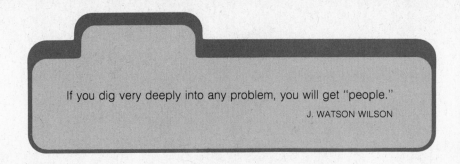

If you dig very deeply into any problem, you will get "people."

J. WATSON WILSON

Human resources, both worker and management, are the most important resources in any business firm. Machines and all other resources of the business will produce nothing without the human element to plan and control them. In fact, the efficiency of the business firm depends more on the human being than on any other resource.

In addition to being the most important resource, the human is by far the most complex resource in the business firm. More than 18,000 words in the English language refer to personal qualities or personal conduct. Moreover, a person is not just the sum total of all his or her personality traits; rather, a person is the product of the total interaction of all his or her personality traits. For example, assume a person has only two personality traits, ambition and honesty. If the person has a high degree of ambition and a low degree of honesty, ambition may entirely negate the honesty trait in certain situations. Since the human being has several hundred personality traits, it is easy to understand why the human is the most complex of all resources, and why no two persons are alike.

MOTIVATION AND JOB PERFORMANCE

Motivation of individuals is important to business firms because it determines job performance. An individual's job performance is primarily the result of (1) the person's value system, (2) the person's abilities, (3) expectation of rewards, (4) rewards/punishment, and (5) the person's perception of how equitable these rewards are. (See Exhibit 8–1.)

Value System

All people are not motivated by the same things. In general, people have value systems that place different values on various factors. For example, person A may value authority, be willing to accept responsibility, and value money: person B may have little value for authority, dislike responsibility, but value money. Other things being equal, person A would probably exert considerably more effort than person B toward obtaining a promotion. The value system of an individual is determined primarily by the environment he or she existed in during the formative years. Parental values contribute significantly to the individual's value system. Differing value systems produce different amounts of job satisfaction or dissatisfac-

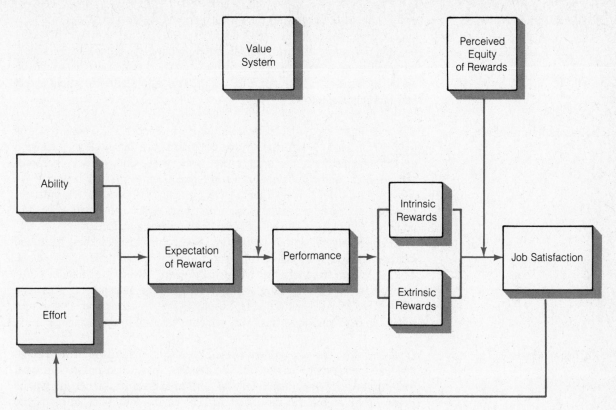

Exhibit 8–1
The process and factors that
determine job satisfaction.

tion. In fact, one research project indicates that a particular job factor that
may result in job satisfaction for one person may cause job dissatisfaction
for another.[1] In a job that is very challenging, one person might feel satisfaction from achieving the task while another might feel frustration from
the effort required or from lack of ability to perform the job.

Abilities

It is quite obvious that individuals must have the ability to perform assigned tasks. The perception of the individual as to whether or not he or
she has the ability to perform the task is also important. The individual
must expect to be able to perform the task and receive the reward. If the
individual feels the task is too difficult or too easy, he or she often will
exert less energy to accomplish the task. It is extremely important to staff
jobs with people who are able to perform them but who are not significantly overqualified.

---

[1]R. J. House and L. A. Wigdor, "Herzberg's Dual Factor-Theory of Job Satisfaction
and Motivation: A Review of the Evidence and a Criticism," *Personnel Psychology* 20
(Winter, 1967).

Expectation of Reward

For people to be motivated they must expect that certain actions will produce certain rewards. In our example above, person A would probably exert more effort toward obtaining a promotion. However, if person A thought he or she could not obtain the promotion because it would be given to person C, a relative of the president, person A would exert considerably less effort.

Rewards/Punishment

Rewards must be available for a person to be motivated. These rewards may be intrinsic or extrinsic. Intrinsic rewards are the positive feelings a person obtains from performing the work well. Competency, personal achievement, and self-esteem are some examples of intrinsic rewards. An individual who feels a task is too easy usually will receive few intrinsic rewards. Extrinsic rewards come from outside the individual. Pay, promotions, and praise are some examples of extrinsic rewards.

Punishment is another motivating force: the threat of being fired and losing income may motivate a person to exert considerable effort on the job. However, the individual will usually exert only the amount of effort he or she perceives as being sufficient to avoid the punishment. This type of negative reinforcement usually results in job dissatisfaction; this in turn results in high employee turnover, which is harmful to the business.

Equity of Rewards

How equitable the person *perceives* rewards to be is important to that individual's motivation. A worker who receives pay, recognition, etc. that the worker feels is equitable for the performance of his or her job will be more willing to expend the effort to achieve the task than an employee who does not feel he or she is being rewarded fairly.

The worker's evaluation of his or her reward in relation to rewards received by other persons is also important. For example, a person who thinks the pay for his or her job is reasonable may be satisfied; but if the same person found that someone else, doing the same job, at the same level of proficiency, was receiving a higher level of pay, he or she probably would become dissatisfied.

Notice that we have used the words *perceive, perception,* and *feel* often in our discussion. Usually when dealing with people, their *perception* of reality is much more important than what *is* reality.

THE HAWTHORNE STUDIES

The early "Hawthorne Studies," which have become a classic in human relations literature, amply illustrate the relationship between worker attitudes and productivity. In 1927, Elton Mayo (often called the father of the human relations movement) and F. J. Roethlisberger headed a group of researchers studying the Hawthorne plant of Western Electric Company. One of their studies consisted of determining the relationship between lighting and employee productivity in a manufacturing process. They set up a test group that experienced increases in lighting, and a control group that did not experience any increases in

Exhibit 8–2

Hierarchy of human needs.

(SOURCE: A. H. Maslow, *Motivation and Personality*. New York: Harper and Row, Publishers, 1954.)

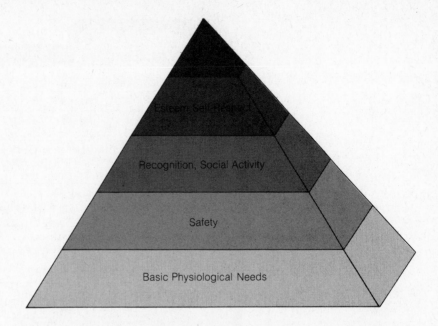

Esteem, Self-Respect

Recognition, Social Activity

Safety

Basic Physiological Needs

lighting. Lighting for the test group was increased by stages from 24 to 70 foot-candles of power (70 foot-candles of power produces unpleasant glare). When the lighting was increased for the test group, production went up. However, production also went up by about the same amount for the control group. Even when the lighting was later reduced by stages, production stayed up. Not until the lighting of the test group was lowered to .06 foot-candles (equal to moonlight) did production decrease for the test group. The researchers concluded that the workers' productivity increased simply because the attention they received by being involved in the experiment made them more motivated to perform. Psychological factors were more important to the workers than physical job factors. This change in motivation due to psychological factors related to experimental conditions became known as the *Hawthorne Effect*.

HIERARCHY OF HUMAN NEEDS

A. H. Maslow, a noted psychologist, maintains that there are five levels of priority in human needs, as represented by Exhibits 8–2 and 8–3.

Basic Physiological Needs

Everyone has **physiological needs;** that is, needs of the body. Food, air, drink, clothing, and shelter satisfy these needs.

Safety Needs

The individual's need for **safety** includes not only safety from danger, but also safety in a financial sense. Job security, safe working conditions, and various types of insurance are some of the factors that satisfy these needs.

Exhibit 8–3

Human needs are varied.

Need Level	Needs	Satisfied By
Physiological Needs	Needs of the body	Food, shelter, clothing, etc.
Safety Needs	Safety from danger and financial safety	Job security, safe working conditions, and insurance
Recognition and Social Activity Needs	Acceptance and recognition by other people	Awards, promotions, level of pay, publicity, etc.
Esteem or Self-Respect Needs	Self-respect as a worthwhile individual	Successfully meeting challenges and accomplishing difficult tasks
Self-Realization Needs	Belief that some concept or philosophy is all-important	Living by some concept or belief

Recognition and Social Activity Needs

A person needs acceptance and **recognition** as a worthwhile individual by other people. Status and status symbols are closely related to this need. Awards, promotions, and the level of pay the individual receives are some of the factors that satisfy these needs.

Esteem or Self-Respect Needs

The person who accomplishes an outstanding feat and feels a strong sense of accomplishment, even though no one else may know of it, is achieving satisfaction of an **esteem need.** For example, the athlete who sets a new world record would feel social-activity need satisfaction from the crowd's acclaim; however, he would also feel esteem satisfaction in knowing he had achieved something no other person in the world had been able to do. Meeting challenges and accomplishing difficult tasks satisfy these needs.

Self-Realization Needs

Self-realization needs come into prominence only when the other needs have been relatively satisfied. These needs exist when a concept or philosophy becomes more important than anything else to the individual. Very few people ever reach the point at which they function primarily in this need level. Albert Schweitzer is an example of an individual who attained this level of need satisfaction: he believed in the brotherhood of human beings and spent his life helping other human beings.

Basically, a person functions at one level of human needs at a time, although there is considerable overlap. Starting at the lowest level, basic physiological needs, each need level must be generally satisfied before the individual begins to function in the next highest level of needs. In other words, as a person satisfies each level of needs, the individual moves up a step to the next level of needs. However, once the person moves up to any higher level, if any lower level of needs is threatened, the individual will revert and begin to function in the threatened level of needs.

To illustrate this concept, try to imagine the following rather improbable situation:

1. You live on the fourth floor of a dormitory.
2. You are taking a shower when a fire starts.
3. The fire blocks all ways of exit except one: If you run past a wall of flame and crash headfirst through a window, you can get out.
4. You cannot reach your clothing.
5. The heat from the fire causes you pain.
6. The dense smoke from the fire prevents you from breathing.
7. A crowd of several hundred gathers to watch the fire.

The reactions of almost anyone would be fairly easy to predict. The inability to breathe and the pain from the heat would become so unbearable that you would crash through the window with little thought of the result-

Safety from danger is a basic physiological need.

ing fall. Clearly, you would be functioning in the first level of needs, basic physiological needs. However, once you are clear of the window, able to breathe, not suffering pain from the heat, and falling, physical discomfort would no longer be foremost in your mind. At this moment the thought of hitting the ground would become all-consuming. You would now have moved from the first level, basic physiological needs, to the second level, safety needs. Next, imagine that you land in a fireman's net and are not harmed in any way. By this time, the physiological needs of breathing and escaping pain and the safety need of falling without injury have been satisfied; however, a new problem now becomes all-important: appearing before a large crowd without clothes. At this point, the first two levels of needs have been satisfied and forgotten, and you have moved into the third level, where you were probably functioning before the fire incident.

Although not realistic, our example illustrates that a person existing in any of the higher levels of needs would revert to any lower level of needs and then progress up the hierarchy of needs as each successive level is satisfied. Even a person who has progressed to the very top level of self-realization would react in much the same manner.

Less than 1 percent of the population of the United States functions mainly in the top two levels—self-respect and self-realization—while approximately 20 percent of the population functions basically in the first two levels—basic physiological needs and safety needs. The remainder, or nearly 80 percent, operate in the third level—social activity.

Basic physiological needs are satisfied with items that money can buy—such as food, shelter, and clothing. Safety needs are, to a degree, satisfied with purchased items such as insurance and savings for emergencies. People who operate in these two levels are primarily interested in the size of their income from their employment.

The social activity and recognition level of human needs is satisfied by a wide range of factors such as job title, authority, status, job achievement, educational level, and relativeness of pay (i.e., level of pay relative to others in the same company, or others in the community). These items often are obtained by means other than money. Certainly, factors such as recognition for efficient work have no relationship to money. Persons operating basically in the level of social activity are interested in other factors in addition to income, and often the relation of the income to that of other persons becomes more important than the size of the income as a purchasing instrument.

THEORIES X, Y, AND Z

A noted social scientist, Douglas McGregor, contends that there are two extreme assumptions management makes about people, and that the assumptions a manager adopts between these extremes determine how he or she manages. McGregor called these assumptions "Theory X" and "Theory Y."[2]

---

[2]Douglas McGregor, *The Human Side of Enterprise* (New York: McGraw-Hill Book Company, 1960).

Exhibit 8–4
Theory X–Theory Y assumptions
result in leadership styles.

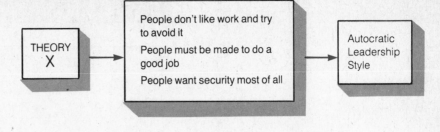

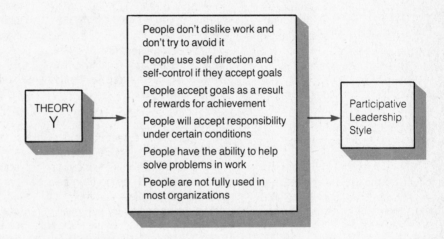

Theory X

According to McGregor, **Theory X** assumes:

1. People do not like work and try to avoid it.
2. People must be "coerced, controlled, directed, and threatened with punishment" to get them to do a good job.
3. People want security more than anything else. They have no ambition, like to be told what to do, and dislike responsibility.

Theory X implies that people are primarily motivated to work for money to satisfy their basic physiological and safety needs (see Hierarchy of Human Needs). The manager who adopts Theory X will tend to have a highly autocratic leadership style. He or she will tend to view the worker as a resource the manager must manipulate to achieve company goals.

Theory Y

According to McGregor, **Theory Y** assumes:

1. People do not inherently dislike work and do not try to avoid it. It is as natural as play and rest to them.
2. People will exercise self-direction and self-control if they accept and believe in the goals of their work.
3. People's commitment to the goals of their work is determined by the rewards associated with the achievement of these goals.
4. Under certain conditions, people will not avoid responsibility but will accept and seek it.

Making Jobs More Interesting

Early developers of mass-production techniques did not take into full consideration the human element in their labor forces. Giving an employee one relatively simple task to do over and over meant the worker could learn the task quickly, and that workers with few skills could become expert at performing the task in a short period of time.

But humans do not function the same as machines, and these highly repetitive tasks become dull, monotonous, and fatiguing to the worker. Just imagine putting the front and rear wheels on the right side of automobiles in an assembly-line operation, eight hours a day, five days a week, fifty weeks a year.

Imagine sitting at a table for the same time period, threading strands of wire through eyelets in paper tags and then twisting the wire.

Many companies have tried various methods of making a repetitive job more attractive for the worker. One method used is called job enlargement. One automobile maker enlarged the work to such an extent that it dropped its factory-wide assembly line and divided its workers into groups. Each group then assembled a complete automobile.

Some companies try to make work more attractive by allowing workers to set their own starting time. Many of these companies allow their workers to start work any time between 7 A.M. and 9 A.M. Their work day is over when their eight hours have been completed. One of these companies even allows their employees to go home when they have completed their assigned tasks. They are paid for eight hours regardless of whether or not they have worked eight hours.

The company that had workers wiring the paper tags described above changed from small tables to one long table with workers sitting anywhere they pleased on both sides of the table. The workers formed into groups along the table based on common interests and friends. Wiring the tags was so simple and repetitive that the workers could perform their work without thinking about or looking at the work. Their day became a continued visit with their friends. Output increased and days absent from work decreased drastically.

5. Most people have the ability to use a high degree of imagination, ingenuity, and creativity in the solution of problems in an organization.

6. The talents and potentials of people are not fully used in most organizations.

Theory Y is a more realistic view of most people. It implies that most people are motivated by recognition, self-respect, and self-realization (see Hierarchy of Human Needs). Theory Y also implies that the job of management is "creating opportunities, releasing potential, removing obstacles, encouraging growth, providing guidance."[3] The manager who adopts Theory Y will tend to use the participative style of leadership.

Theory Z

McGregor implied that Theory X is not good and Theory Y is good. A later theory, **Theory Z,** holds that efficiency might be increased by either, depending on the situation. Theory X and Theory Y imply that there are only two variables, work and the basic nature of people. Theory Z assumes that there are many variables that interact within the organization, such as the size of the organization, the personality of the people, and the goals of the employees. For example, a temporary work group with few of the required skills would probably perform best with very specific instructions, frequent checking on work performed, and little participation in the decision-making process.

THE JAPANESE MANAGEMENT STYLE

Japanese manufacturers have been very successful in the world markets and it is generally accepted that this is largely the result of their management style. The main characteristics of their management style are decision making by consensus and lifetime employment. Japanese management involves a collective group orientation of workers both in decision making and in their approach toward the work environment. Employees are usually hired directly after they finish their schooling and continue to work for the same firm until they retire.

Japanese manufacturers make use of quality control circles, which are informal problem-solving groups made up of workers and managers. Their purpose is to improve quality control and solve production problems. Their success is shown by the fact that Japanese companies in the electronics industry tolerate only one faulty part out of every 10,000, while their American counterparts tolerate one faulty part out of every 100.

The Japanese management style is reflected in their motto: "Make everyone a manager." It should be noted that the Japanese management style is very close to McGregor's Theory Y and is a form of the participative management concept that has been taught in American universities for at least thirty years.

---

[3]Ibid.

MORALE

Morale is the mental attitude of the employee toward the work environment. A major contributor to morale is the degree of satisfaction the worker derives from the work environment. There are many different opinions as to what constitutes morale. One outstanding testing device attempts to measure the following relatively comprehensive factors of morale:

1. Satisfaction with working conditions
   a. Adequacy of working conditions
   b. Effects of these conditions on work efficiency
   c. Adequacy of equipment
   d. Reasonable hours of work
   e. Absence of physical and mental pressures
2. Satisfaction with financial reward
   a. Adequacy of pay
   b. Effectiveness of personnel policies with respect to pay
   c. Benefit programs and pay in comparison with other companies
3. Confidence in management
   a. Management's organizing ability
   b. Employee benefit policies
   c. Adequacy of two-way communications
   d. Interest in employees
4. Opinion about immediate supervisor
   a. How well the supervisor organizes his or her work
   b. Knowledge of the job
   c. Ability to get things done on time
   d. Supplying adequate equipment
   e. Letting employees know what is expected
   f. Emphasizing proper training
   g. Making employees work together
   h. Treating employees fairly
   i.. Keeping promises
   j. Giving encouragement
   k. Interest in employee welfare
5. Satisfaction with self-development
   a. Feeling of belonging
   b. Feeling of participation
   c. Pride in the company
   d. Pride in doing something worthwhile
   e. Growth on the job[4]

Morale in the well-managed firm should mean providing an atmosphere in which the employee may derive satisfaction from the job and be motivated to perform well in assigned tasks. The degree to which the em-

---

[4]Zile S. Dabas, "The Dimensions of Morale: An Item Factorization of the SRA Employee Inventory," *Personnel Psychology* 11 (1958), pp. 217–34.

"I FIND THIS WORK TRULY FULFILLING IN MANY WAYS — THERE'S THE EXERCISE, THE SENSE OF ACCOMPLISHMENT, AND, MOST IMPORTANT, THE OPPORTUNITY TO MAKE LOTS OF NOISE."

ployee derives satisfaction and motivation from the employment is dependent, to a large extent, on the actions of management. However, the employee's reaction to the type of job itself contributes to his or her level of satisfaction and motivation. It is hard for management to create very high levels of motivation and job satisfaction for most people who perform highly routine and monotonous types of work. It is much easier for management to create job satisfaction and motivation for the highly skilled cabinet maker than for the worker who does nothing all day but attach the right front wheel in an automobile assembly line. Of course, this does not mean that the employee in monotonous work will have bad morale. It means that employee will not attain as high a level of good morale as the other worker when both are in environments of good human relations practices. Many companies are now attempting to broaden the activities of some jobs (called job enlargement) and to rotate jobs in order to relieve job monotony.

Probably the best way to see the benefits of good morale is to look at the indicators of bad morale. The business firm that suffers from poor morale will usually sustain:

1. A high rate of turnover of employees;
2. Low levels of production;
3. High levels of wasted materials;

4. A high number of product rejects;

5. Higher incidence of accidents;

6. More absenteeism;

7. More tardiness;

8. Frequent complaints;

9. Work slowdowns;

10. Strikes, if unionized.

Firms that suffer from low morale almost always sustain a high employee turnover rate. People who are forced to work in an environment of low morale have a tendency to move to other companies in their early years of employment or become so dissatisfied with the work situation that they engage in activities that result in their dismissal. Hiring and training employees is a high-cost task that often runs into thousands of dollars when replacing highly specialized personnel. As a result, high rates of employee turnover can be very expensive to the low-morale firm.

The degree of turnover in the firm suffering from bad morale is dependent on the mobility of the workers used in the jobs. Bad morale in a company that employs highly-skilled workers who are in high demand in the employment market will cause high turnover, while another company with the same degree of bad morale that employs only low-skilled workers will maintain a much lower turnover rate. The employee with little mobility working in an atmosphere of low morale will tend to stay on the job, but will evidence his or her dissatisfaction in many other ways that are equally expensive for the firm.

Often the firm that has low morale will suffer from lower levels of production than the firm that creates good morale. It stands to reason that the employee who derives satisfaction from his or her job will be more motivated to perform the job well than will the employee who is dissatisfied with the work situation. Again, the definition of good morale is job satisfaction and motivation, and not just happiness. The employee who works in an environment of low morale may produce at high levels of output because of excessive negative motivation, threats of firing, etc. However, the same worker will exhibit dissatisfaction in other ways and will not work to improve the job by making suggestions for improvement. In addition, the worker will be more likely to join a union, and the resulting union will rapidly reduce the ability of the firm to engage in negative motivation.

Employees in conditions of poor morale usually lose interest in their jobs and pay less attention to them. Poor morale causes daydreaming, slipshod work, and a lax attitude. The employee who perceives his or her job in this way will find many excuses for not going to work. There are even some cases of psychologically induced illness that occur during the work week (but never on the weekend) due to extreme dislike of a job

Exhibit 8–5
Morale indicators warn management
of low morale.

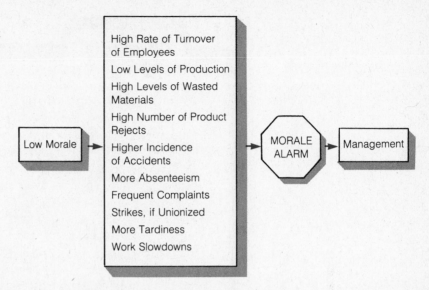

High Rate of Turnover
of Employees

Low Levels of Production

High Levels of Wasted
Materials

High Number of Product
Rejects

Low Morale → Higher Incidence
of Accidents

More Absenteeism

Frequent Complaints

Strikes, if Unionized

More Tardiness

Work Slowdowns

→ MORALE ALARM → Management

situation. In addition, there is usually more tardiness among workers in low-morale situations than among employees operating under high-morale conditions.

The worker suffering from bad morale will certainly complain more than will the worker with good morale. Not only will the low-morale worker complain more frequently, but the complaints will be of greater intensity. These complaints, when not properly dealt with, have a tendency to increase in intensity and cause other complaints. The continued growth in number and intensity of complaints of employees will finally cause severe group reactions such as acts of sabotage, work slowdowns, and strikes.

Poor morale can cause so many undesirable problems that it is easy to see why it is very expensive. The level of morale of employees often makes or breaks a firm. Why is it, then, that all firms do not maintain high levels of morale? Usually upper levels of management don't even know when their firm is suffering from low morale. The very complexity and diversity of the human personality make it difficult to create job satisfaction and motivation. Management must understand psychological concepts and be able to practice empathy (the ability to look at an issue from the viewpoint of the other person). There are people who are unable to practice good human relations because their own peculiar psychological needs do not allow action on their part that will create good morale. For example, some people have such an intense need for authority that, when they become supervisors, they attempt to force an almost master-servant relationship with employees to satisfy their own needs. Action of this nature is sure to lower morale.

SUMMARY OF KEY POINTS

1. Human resources are the most important and most complex resource in any business firm.

2. Motivation and job performance are primarily the result of a person's value system, abilities, expectation of rewards, rewards, and perception of how equitable these rewards are.

3. The Hawthorne Studies laid the groundwork for the human relations approach to employee motivation.

4. The priority of human needs is: (1) basic physiological needs, (2) safety needs, (3) recognition and social activity needs, (4) esteem and self-respect needs, and (5) self-realization needs.

5. The assumptions a manager makes about people determine how he or she manages: Theory X assumes people do not like work and try to avoid it; Theory Y assumes work is as natural as play to people.

6. Theory Z assumes there are many variables that interact on the organization, and either Theory X or Theory Y may increase efficiency, depending on the situation.

7. Japanese management stresses decision making by consensus and lifetime employment.

8. Morale in the well-managed firm should mean providing an atmosphere in which the employee feels satisfied in his or her job and motivated to work efficiently.

9. Some indicators of poor morale are high employee turnover, low production, waste, product rejects, accidents, absenteeism, tardiness, frequency of complaints, work slowdowns, and strikes.

DISCUSSION QUESTIONS

1. If you were a microcomputer salesperson, how would you relate the section on motivation and job performance to yourself?

2. Give an example of how you function in each of Maslow's human needs, in their correct order.

3. Do you agree with Theory X or Theory Y? Explain your reasons.

4. What is good morale?

5. Would you want good morale in your business? Explain why you would or would not want it.

STUDENT PROJECTS

1. Interview someone with a full-time job: try to estimate the person's morale level by discussing the factors of morale listed in the textbook.
   a. Satisfaction with working conditions
   b. Satisfaction with financial reward
   c. Confidence in management
   d. Opinion about immediate supervisor
   e. Satisfaction with self-development
2. Interview someone who supervises people. By asking questions about the person's assumptions concerning people, try to determine if the person believes more in Theory X or Theory Y.

Sam West

Sam West was employed by the Tinker Tire Company as an auditor shortly after his graduation from a noted southern university. Sam has worked for Tinker Tire for three years, has always received the highest rankings possible in the company's rating system, has been awarded four large pay increases, and receives $2,200 per month. Sam is very happy with his job and hopes to be promoted into a management position in the near future. Sam was particularly happy about his salary when he first came to Tinker, for it was well above the salary amount received by his friends who graduated at the same time.

Betty Best graduated from a rather small southern college two months ago and joined Tinker Tire as an auditor. Betty was considered a valuable employee. She was competent in her work and the company was trying to hire more female employees in case of any future problems with the Civil Rights Act of 1964. Betty had several good job offers, and the company had to go well above its normal starting salary to employ her.

Sam and Betty were auditing one of the firm's plants when Betty casually mentioned during a coffee break that she felt fortunate indeed to find a job that paid her $2,400 per month in starting salary. Sam had little else to say for the remainder of the audit. As soon as Sam returned to the main office, he went to the chief accountant's office and in a very harsh tone informed the chief accountant that he was tired of "working for peanuts" and felt the company "should do something about it." The chief accountant tried to explain to Sam that his salary was already high in relation to most of the accountants in the office and that he could not justify a higher pay scale. Sam retorted, "Well, if that is all the company thinks of me, they can jump in the lake," and stormed out of the office.

Questions

1. Is Sam unhappy because he is not able to purchase as many things as he wishes due to the size of his salary?
2. Why was Sam at first happy with his salary and now unhappy with it?
3. In which level of the hierarchy of needs does Sam operate? Explain.
4. What actions would you possibly expect from Sam in the near future?
5. How would you solve this problem without creating any additional problems in the accounting department?

Harry Sage—Good or Bad?

Tom Rose owns a small electric-motor-rewinding plant that employs forty-eight people. Tom directly supervises a sales representative, two office workers, and four foremen. One of these foremen is Richard Tiner, who has been in his job for about one year.

Recently, Tom was in Tiner's section of the plant and noticed that Tiner had put up an "employee of the month" board in a place where it could easily be seen. Tom was somewhat surprised to see Harry Sage's name on it as the employee of the month for Tiner's rewind section. The previous foreman had complained about Harry's being lazy and was on the verge of firing him before the foreman left the plant for other employment.

Tom had noticed a considerable difference in the two foremen. When the previous foreman would come to Tom's office to discuss something, he would often hurry off saying, "I had better get back and put my people back to work—they probably quit working the minute I got out of sight." Tom also noticed that the previous foreman was very demanding and would really "chew out" an employee if the employee made a mistake.

The new foreman seems to be just the opposite. Tiner seems more easy-going and often compliments an employee on doing a good job when it is deserved. He calmly discusses mistakes with employees, making sure they understand why they are mistakes and how to avoid them in the future.

Questions

1. Does Tiner use positive motivation? Give two examples.
2. In what level of Maslow's Hierarchy of Human Needs do you feel Harry functions?
3. Which foreman believed more in Theory X than the other? Explain your choice.
4. What should have changed in the section after Tiner took over?

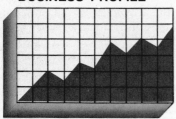

BUSINESS PROFILE

Lincoln Electric Company

The Lincoln Electric Company has long been considered a pioneer in morale and incentive programs. The company serves as an excellent example of the benefits that can be derived from positive motivation and good morale.

Lincoln Electric, with manufacturing plants in the U.S., Canada, Australia, and France, is the world's largest manufacturer of electric arc-welding products and a leading manufacturer of industrial electric motors. As head of the company, James F. Lincoln was a man who believed in people. Lincoln established a system in the company in which (1) an advisory board of elected employees meets regularly with management to discuss all aspects of the company, (2) promotions are made almost entirely from within the company and strictly on merit rather than seniority, (3) employees are paid according to their productivity, (4) all employees are encouraged to suggest improvements in manufacturing operations and, (5) employment is guaranteed.

James F. Lincoln, former board
chairman and chief executive officer
of the Lincoln Electric Company,
was responsible for its many
innovative management techniques.

The present company's management feels that employees must have an attitude of confidence and trust in management for their system to work. They feel that it takes considerable work and effort to maintain this attitude.

The success of Lincoln Electric's program is shown by the results: (1) there has been virtually no foreign competition in this country, (2) customers have received a fair price, (3) stockholders have received a fair dividend, and (4) the amount the employees have earned in salary and bonuses has been almost twice the amount earned by employees in comparable companies. In addition, no time is lost due to labor disputes.

Sales of the U.S. company exceed $450 million per year and it employs 2,650 people.

9

Personnel:
The Management of
Human Resources

LEARNING GOALS

After reading this chapter, you will understand:

1. The importance of human resource selection for the business firm.

2. The sources used by human resource personnel in recruiting employees.

3. The purposes of job analysis, job description, and job specification.

4. How the Civil Rights Act affects employment practices.

5. The types of tests used to select employees as well as the different types of programs companies use to train employees.

6. The purposes of orientation, induction, and counseling in human resource management.

7. The compensation and benefit plans companies use to reward employees.

KEY TERMS

Human resources	Induction	Apprenticeship
Job analysis	Counseling	training
Job description	Performance appraisal	Management
Job specification	Promotion	development
Application form	Transfers	Exit interview
Bona fide occupational	Demotion	Job evaluation
qualification	Termination	Bonus plan
Human resource	On-the-job-training	Profit-sharing plans
orientation	Vestibule training	Merit raise
		Fringe benefits

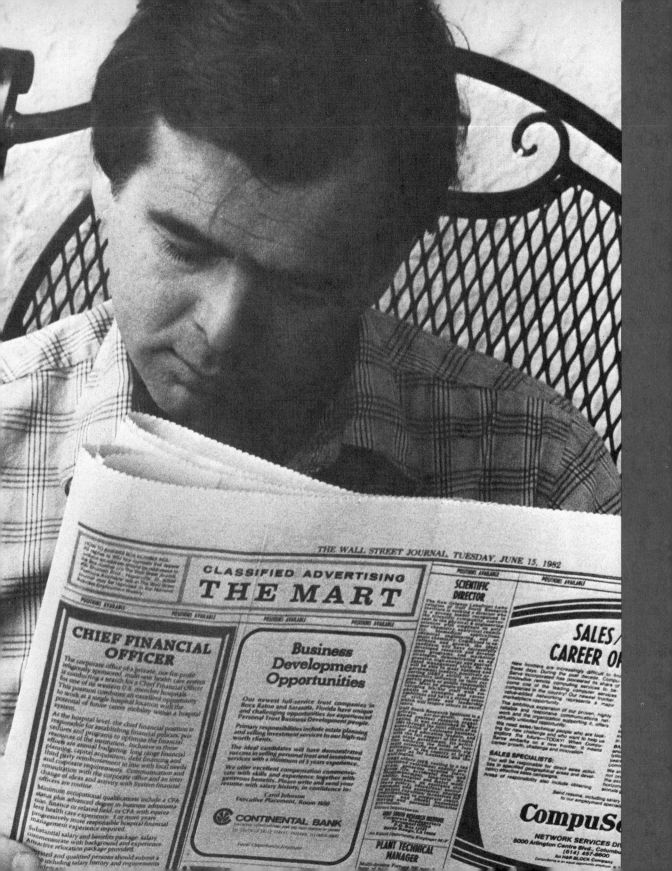

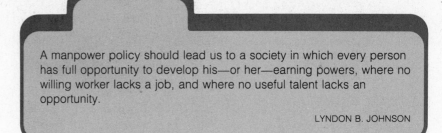

A manpower policy should lead us to a society in which every person has full opportunity to develop his—or her—earning powers, where no willing worker lacks a job, and where no useful talent lacks an opportunity.

LYNDON B. JOHNSON

Human resources, the people who staff the positions in the company, are its major asset. Human resource managers, or personnel managers, are actively involved in all aspects of human resource management. Since personnel managers have staff authority relationships with line managers, they offer advice and assistance to line managers in the critical human

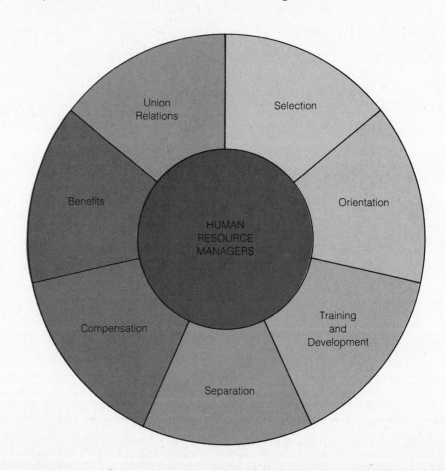

Exhibit 9–1
Functions of human resource managers.

"THIS RESUMÉ IS ONE OF THE MOST BOASTFUL, DECEPTIVE PIECES OF FRAUD I'VE EVER SEEN. YOU'RE HIRED."

resource activities of selection, orientation, training, separation, and compensation and benefits. Another important activity, union relations, is discussed separately in chapter 10. Exhibit 9–1 presents the human resource activities in which personnel managers are engaged.

HUMAN RESOURCE SELECTION PROCESS

Human resource managers assist line managers in selecting and placing people in positions for which they are most qualified, in which they are interested, and which offer opportunity for individual development and advancement. When employee abilities are matched with position requirements, employees tend to be positively motivated toward their colleagues, the job, and the company, and tend to be more productive. Conversely, an improper match between abilities and position requirements will most likely result in employee frustration, low morale, lower productivity, and high turnover of employees.

The process of human resource selection is more efficient in organizations that make a concerted effort to identify the task and human requirements. Specific tools used by managers in the human resource selection process are job analysis, job description, job specification, recruitment, the application form, personal interviews, and employment tests.

Job Analysis, Job Description, and Job Specification

Job analysis involves the systematic collection of all information about a job to determine its requirements. This information should be obtained from a number of sources, such as the person performing the task, the immediate supervisor, observation by work-study specialists, and labor union representatives, in unionized companies. From the job analysis, a job description is prepared. The **job description** identifies the authority of the task, its location in the company, and the activities and major responsibilities of the job. Whereas the job description describes the task, the **job specification** focuses on people. It outlines the personal qualifi-

EXHIBIT 9–2

Example of job description and specification.

Nonsupervisory Job Description

Job number: 2-202

Job classification: Transportation Agent—General or ATO

Summary of Duties: Perform any combination of the following duties: Sell tickets; check in passengers and baggage; furnish air transportation information to passengers; make reservations and perform related airport ticket counter services; meet and dispatch flights from ramp; announce arrivals and departures; assist in loading and unloading passengers; coordinate ramp and service functions; in some locations may assist in loading and unloading baggage, mail, express, and other cargo; function as coordinator between TWA Weight Control Office and AMF, REA, and Air Freight Office, keeping all concerned informed of loads available; list for shipment available mail and express loads; prepare or check required forms; prepare waybills; determine routings and fares. As required by nonroutine operations, explain delays to passengers, arrange alternate transportation, prepare or make refunds, etc., to give best possible service and retain passenger good will. Perform miscellaneous office detail related to any of above duties.

Job Specifications

Factors	Minimum Requirements
Education	4 years high school.
Experience	Sales, cargo handling, or related office clerical work.
Complexity	Semi-routine duties requiring a general knowledge of ticketing, station operations, air mail forms, etc. A high degree of judgment and memory required.
Work of Others	None.
Contacts	Individual responsibility for specialized or frequent contacts with the public requiring a high degree of tact in servicing and selling customers.
Confidential Data and Records	None.
Assets	Individual responsibility for considerable daily cash receipts and/or some responsibility for equipment and control of costs through check of records.
Physical Requirements	Some physical effort lifting and carrying baggage for short distances. Sustained standing and walking.
Working Conditions	Frequent exposure to some disagreeable elements. No traveling.

Effective _____   Labor Grade _____

cations essential for completing the task, such as education, experience, mental and visual abilities; the supervisory responsibility for the position; the physical requirements of the task; accountability; the complexity of duties; working conditions; and work relations expected with others. This information is critical for human resource managers as they assist line managers in completing the staffing process. Exhibit 9–2 shows a sample job description and job specification.

The U.S. Department of Labor lists some 20,000 job titles and descriptions in the *Dictionary of Occupational Titles*. In order to conform with civil rights legislation, some 3,500 of these titles have been changed. Some examples of changes in job titles are shown in Exhibit 9–3.

Recruitment

A major activity in the human resource selection process is to maintain a current file of prospective applicants who possess the skills and knowledge necessary to perform the tasks in the company. To accomplish this objective, members of the human resource department should regularly analyze the sources of potential employees, such as the sources described in the following paragraphs.

Advertising.   The "help-wanted" ads of the daily newspaper, radio, television, and various trade and professional magazines advertise open positions. Many applicants may respond to these ads; however, a disadvantage of this type of recruitment is that it does not provide a means for screening out the unqualified applicants.

Public Employment Agencies.   Both federal and state employment agencies maintain employment offices. Public employment agencies help place skilled, semiskilled, unskilled, professional, and technical personnel. These services are provided at no cost to employee or employer.

Exhibit 9–3

Changes in job titles.

From	To
Salesman	Sales Associate, Sales Representative, Sales Agent
Foreman	Supervisor
Junior Executive	Executive Trainee
Repairman	Repairer
Bus Boy	Dining Room Attendant
Airplane Stewardess	Airplane Flight Attendant
Twenty-six Girl	Dice Game Attendant
Public Relations Man	Public Relations Practitioner
Host	Host/Hostess

Private Employment Agencies.   A private agency charges a fee for its placement service. Either the job applicant or the employer pays the fee, which may be either a large percentage of the first month's gross salary or a small percentage of the first year's salary. Normally these agencies are important sources for filling specific types of jobs, such as clerical, manual, or technical jobs.

Executive-Search Firms.   Private agencies, called executive-search firms, assist in locating managerial talent for high-level managerial positions. Companies usually initiate the request to the executive-recruitment firm to assist them; consequently, the company normally pays the placement fees.

Colleges and Universities.   Educational institutions are a prime source of quality employees. Company representatives visit campuses across the nation to interview applicants. Qualified candidates may then be invited to the company, at the company's expense, for additional interviews.

Vocational Schools.   Vocational high schools, trade schools, and vocational programs in junior colleges are a vital source of employees. These schools produce personnel with varying degrees of skills in diverse fields.

Labor Unions.   Union hiring halls are important sources of employees in certain types of occupations, such as longshoremen, musicians, and carpenters. The unions provide a ready source of employees in industries characterized by sharp fluctuations in demand for employees.

Friends or Relatives of Workers.   Many firms encourage their present employees to recommend friends or relatives as potential employees. Where there is a critical labor shortage, such as a scarcity of qualified secretaries, a firm may offer a financial reward to an employee for recommending a person who is hired.

Former Military Personnel.   Today's military services require that their members have specific job skills. Consequently, when a person leaves the service, the training received there may be put to effective use in civilian life, as when airlines hire former military pilots.

Application Forms

When a prospective employee is recruited, an initial source of information about the potential employee is provided on the application form. The **application form** (shown in Exhibit 9–4) provides a written summary of the individual's background. Typical application forms generally request such biographical information as full name, address, telephone number, type of work desired, previous work experience, educational background, and personal and professional references. Since the candidate must complete this information, the application form also demonstrates his or her ability to organize and present personal data in a concise manner. The interviewer uses the application form as a guide for discussion during the personal interview of the prospective employee.

Personal Interviews

The personal interview provides face-to-face contact between the company representative and the job applicant so that the interviewer can evaluate the candidate relative to the requirements of the job. During the personal interview, the interviewer should try to establish rapport with the interviewee. By putting the interviewee at ease, effective two-way communication is possible and the applicant should offer information and ask questions more openly.

The screening interview enables the interviewer to make a preliminary evaluation of an applicant. The interviewer can assess the applicant's personal appearance and ability to communicate. The purpose of the screening interview is to decide which candidate will be recommended for further consideration for employment. Recommended applicants then undergo more intensive, in-depth interviews. Generally, specialists from the personnel department conduct the in-depth interviews. A skillful interviewer can accumulate much data about an individual during the in-depth interview: insight into the individual's motivational level, goals (long- as well as short-range), attitudes toward others and himself or herself, and an indication of behavior. The interviewer may also check personal and business references. The manager for whom the prospective employee would work should also interview the candidate. This procedure gives the immediate supervisor the opportunity to participate in evaluating the applicant. A positive employment practice is for the immediate supervisor to have the final say in whether the applicant should be hired, since he or she will be working directly with the new employee.

Employment Testing

Employment tests may be used as an aid in the selection process. The purpose of testing is to assist in making human resource selection more efficient. The following are representative types of tests that can be used in the human resource selection process.

Intelligence Tests. Sometimes called IQ tests, these tests are designed to measure an applicant's general capacity for learning and problem solving. Types of mental abilities measured by intelligence tests are verbal, quantitative, reasoning, spatial, memory, and perception.

Aptitude Tests. While intelligence tests may be considered a kind of general aptitude test, aptitude tests are designed to measure a person's ability to learn a specific job requiring special skills or abilities. Example of specific abilities measured are mechanical, clerical, manual dexterity, and eye-hand coordination.

Exhibit 9–4
Example of employee application form.

Application for Employment

Name: _____ Date: _____

Address: _____
(Street)   (City)   (State)   (Zip)

Phone: _____ Soc. Sec. No.: _____ Date available for employment: _____ Salary required: _____

Employment Status Desired: Permanent Full Time _____ Permanent Part Time _____ Temporary _____ Summer _____

Positions for which you are applying: 1.) _____ 2.) _____ 3.) _____

WORK EXPERIENCE   (List your most recent experience first): <u>Please include military service</u>. If you have had teaching experience, list under duties—grade level and subjects taught (including practice teaching).

Type of Business: _____

Firm Name: _____ Full Time __ Part Time __ Hrs. worked per week __

Address: _____ Dates of employment: _____

_____ Job title: _____

Beginning   Ending

Telephone: _____ Salary _____ Salary _____

Supervisor: _____ May we check this reference? _____

Nature of your duties: _____

SPECIAL SKILLS AND/OR ABILITIES

Typewriter _____ wpm   Dictaphone _____   Shorthand _____

Other Office Machines _____

What special interests or abilities have you? _____

Reasons for your interest in XYZ Company: _____

If applying for Sales or Consultant Position
Territory preferred: _____

Territories acceptable: _____

Who referred you to XYZ Company? _____

( ) Reply to Advertisement   ( ) Employee Referral   ( ) State Employment Office

( ) Walk-in   ( ) Private Placement Agency   ( ) College Placement Service

Have you previously worked for XYZ Company? _____ If yes, where? _____

Dates worked: _____ Reason for leaving: _____

MILITARY SERVICE* Yes _____   No _____

Branch of Armed Forces _____ From _____ To _____

* The Vietnam Era Veterans Readjustment Assistance Act requires government contractors to take Affirmative Action to employ disabled veterans and veterans of the Vietnam Era.

REFERENCES

List two professional-work related references (do not include relatives):

Name: _____   Name: _____

Address: _____   Address: _____

_____   _____

Telephone: _____   Telephone: _____

Occupation: _____   Occupation: _____

EDUCATION

Please list name and location of each school attended.	Circle Last Year Completed And Give Dates Attended		Major Field	Minor Field	Degree Received	Average Grades
High School	9 10 11 12 From To					
College	1 2 3 4 From To					
Graduate school or other (specify)	From To					

To determine my qualifications for employment, I authorize XYZ Company to conduct an investigation of my application. I understand that any false or misleading information furnished by me on this application form or in connection with my application for employment may result in rejection of the application, or if employed by XYZ Company, in the termination of employment. I also understand that should I become employed by XYZ as a Permanent Full Time employee, I agree to submit to a physical examination.

_____   _____

Date   Signature of applicant

XYZ Company is an equal employment opportunity employer and shall be non-discriminatory in its employment practices with respect to race, color, religion, sex, national origin, veteran status, age, or disability.

Achievement Tests. Achievement tests are sometimes referred to as performance tests or proficiency tests. They attempt to measure a person's skill or proficiency at a particular task. Such a test may require the applicant to demonstrate a particular skill. Common types of achievement tests measure proficiency in typewriting, shorthand, or operating office equipment such as calculators or adding machines.

Trade tests are another type of achievement test. They are designed to measure the learning one has gained from specific occupational training or experience; for instance, they may measure a worker's proficiency at the skills of an electrician or machinist.

Interest Tests.   These tests measure an applicant's interests, to determine such things as whether the employee prefers to work with people or things. In addition to their help in placing an employee in a suitable job, the tests can also be used as an aid in helping to determine the job for which a person should be trained.

Personality Tests.   For certain types of jobs (managers and salespersons, for example) skills in interpersonal relations may be more important than job knowledge or skill. These tests are used in selection and placement to measure such personality traits as ambition, motivation, patience, stability, self-confidence, and decisiveness. However, these tests are among the most difficult to evaluate.

Polygraph Tests.   Some firms administer polygraph tests (or lie detectors or truth verifiers) to employees and/or job applicants. For example, a company may administer the test to employees when investigating a specific theft of money or materials from the firm. Polygraph tests may be substituted for the extensive background checks of employees. Questions asked usually relate to matters considered important by the company, such as the applicant's employment record.

The polygraph instrument is attached to an applicant's hand and/or arm; it registers physiological changes in breathing, pulse, or blood pressure in the person being tested and records these changes on paper.

The use of polygraph testing is controversial. Critics object to its use on the grounds that it invades privacy, that it may require self-incrimination, that it is an insult to human dignity, and that the test results are questionable.

A number of states have passed laws prohibiting employers from requiring such tests as a condition of employment. Laws have also been passed to regulate professional polygraph examiners.

Employment Tests and Equal Opportunity.   The human resource manager in today's firm must be aware that the use of employment tests has come under strong criticism on the basis that they tend to discriminate against minorities. The Civil Rights Acts of 1964 and 1972 specify that firms can administer professional ability employment tests provided that they do not discriminate because of color, race, religion, sex, or national origin. For example, the law provides that specific tests of job ability, such as typing tests for typists or arithmetic and change-making tests for cashiers, can be given. As a result of these nondiscrimination requirements, many firms have greatly reduced or even done away with using tests as a selection device rather than go to the expense and difficulty of having professional employment tests developed.

Physical Examination

Many companies require applicants to have a physical examination to determine if they can meet the physical requirements of the job detailed in the job specification. This examination will reveal any physical limitations,

Exhibit 9–5
Sequence of steps in human
resource selection process.

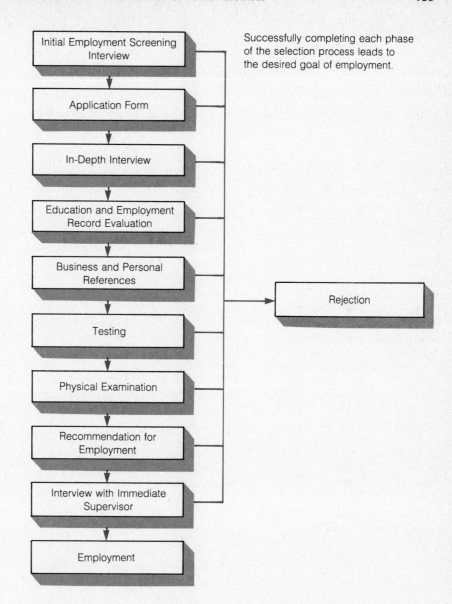

Successfully completing each phase
of the selection process leads to
the desired goal of employment.

Initial Employment Screening
Interview

Application Form

In-Depth Interview

Education and Employment
Record Evaluation

Business and Personal
References

Testing

Physical Examination

Recommendation for
Employment

Interview with Immediate
Supervisor

Employment

Rejection

such as being unable to lift heavy objects, that would limit the prospective
employee's job performance.

Physical examinations also enable the employer to comply with state
worker compensation laws. These exams serve to protect the company
against future physical disability claims on injuries or accidents incurred in
previous employment.

**THE HUMAN RESOURCE
ORIENTATION PROCESS**

Human resource orientation is made up of two major activities: induction and counseling. Induction is designed to acquaint new employees with their fellow employees, task environment, and company pol-

Equal Employment Opportunity and Affirmative Action

Human resource managers must be aware of the influence that state and federal governments have in human resource selection. For example, federal legislation such as the Civil Rights Acts of 1964 and 1972 are designed to prevent discrimination in hiring practices. Thus, much of the information usually requested on the application forms has been altered or omitted. Examples of unacceptable questions prior to employment are given below.

The Civil Rights Acts of 1964 and 1972 cover firms that have fifteen or more employees if they are in a business engaged in interstate commerce. The laws prohibit discrimination except where there is a **bona fide occupational qualification,** (BFOQ). Race and color can never be a BFOQ; neither can religion, sex, or national origin except in rare instances. Women cannot be refused employment on the bases that they are less able to do certain kinds of work or that separate facilities would be required for them.

To make certain that they comply with the provisions of the laws, firms have had to develop affirmative action plans. Affirmative action means that firms must analyze the distribution of jobs by sex, race, and color; if there are inequities, then the firm must develop a plan outlining the steps and the time needed to correct the imbalance. Many firms have appointed an Affirmative Action Officer, who has the responsibility to oversee the affirmative action plans of the firm.

Employers should not ask job applicants the following questions prior to employment.
1. Are you over 21?
2. How long have you been a resident of the United States?
3. What holidays do you observe?
4. How did you acquire your foreign language skills?
5. Do you own your home?
6. Have you ever been arrested?
7. Do you have an established credit rating?
8. How long do you intend to work?
9. What type of military discharge do you have?
10. List the clubs, societies, lodges, or professional organizations of which you are a member.
11. List the names and ages of minor children and dependents.

The following types of questions are also unacceptable.
1. Questions regarding marital status, maiden name, age, date or place of birth, social security number, religious preference (unless job-related), sexual preference, height, weight, hair color, eye color, or complexion color.
2. Requests for photographs.
3. Questions about the applicant's spouse, such as, "Would your spouse object to your traveling?"
4. Questions about physical or mental handicaps, if not job-related.

icies. Counseling is an on-going program to keep apprised of each employee's progress after employment.

Induction.   Once an employee is hired, it is vital that he or she be given a thorough orientation into the company, called **induction.** The personnel department has the initial responsibility for conducting the induction program. An induction program should provide a comprehensive overview of the new employee's position and role in the company. This information can relieve much of the initial insecurity that most new employees experience. When an employee is given a below-par orientation, he or she may develop negative attitudes toward the company or perhaps may not even return to work the second day.

The Employee Handbook.   All employees should be given a copy of the firm's employee handbook (or organization manual). The handbook not only provides employees with a broad perspective of the total organization but helps them to view their specific responsibilities and contributions to the company. As part of the induction process, each employee should be given an explanation of any special policies or procedures in the handbook.

The handbook usually discusses a variety of topics that directly affect each employee, such as those shown in Exhibit 9–6.

Another step in the induction process is for each new employee to be taken to his or her work area and be personally introduced by the supervisor to the members of the group with which he or she will be working. The new employee should be shown the work area in more detail, and informed of the functions of the department and his or her role in the department. Any other special information helpful to the employee should be furnished at this time. The supervisor should encourage the new employee to ask questions and to feel free to ask questions later if he or she is unsure of the new assignment.

Counseling

Employee orientation needs to be extended beyond induction, however. It is necessary to collect up-to-date data and follow up on each employee's progress. Much of this information can be gathered, and guidance can be offered, through an employee counseling program. **Counseling** is a face-to-face, private interview between a counselor and an employee. Sometimes counseling may take the form of helping an individual solve personal problems, such as family or financial matters.

Counselors may use a directive or nondirective approach when interviewing employees. In the directive method, a counselor asks for specific information. The replies are usually very short, perhaps only a *yes* or a *no,* and the individual can usually tell the desired answer by the way the counselor phrases the question. The nondirective approach uses broad, open-end questions that require a narrative answer. The counselor uses such statements as: "Tell me about it," or "What was it like?" Since the

Exhibit 9–6

Topics Covered in Employee Handbook

1. Introduction to employees from the firm's president
2. Purpose of the handbook
3. Basic company philosophy
4. History of the firm
5. Organization chart of company
6. Locations of company plants from coast to coast
7. Employee information
   a. Selection of employees
   b. Pay
   c. Medical services
   d. Hours of work
   e. Working conditions
   f. Supervision and you
   g. Job instruction
   h. Safety
   i. Recognition of service
   j. Holidays
   k. Military service
   l. Jury duty
8. Opportunities in the company
   a. Stability of employment
   b. Tuition refund program
   c. Promotion and advancement
   d. Improved work methods
9. Employee benefits and services
   a. Life insurance
   b. Group accident and health insurance
   c. Vacation
   d. Blue Cross-Blue Shield Hospital and Surgical Plan
   e. Service and recognition awards
   f. Pension and retirement plan
10. Personal appearance and work habits
11. Pay policies
12. The future of the company

person being interviewed has no idea of what the desired answer is, the responses usually reveal much about an individual's attitudes or problems.

Performance Appraisals

Another form of counseling is the **performance appraisal**. Performance appraisals are evaluations of an individual's job performance by the immediate supervisor. A typical appraisal form is shown in Exhibit 9–7. Appraisal interviews provide individuals with the guidance needed to improve their work. Performance appraisals are also useful in determining who should be promoted, transferred, laid off, demoted, or terminated.

Exhibit 9–7
Performance appraisal form.

Employee's Name _____ Job Title _____

Department _____ Evaluation Period From _____ To _____

Instructions for evaluating: Evaluate all factors. Place a check mark in the box that most closely indicates your judgment on each factor. Consider the factors only as they are defined. Evaluate the employee on the job he or she now holds. Comments should be made on each factor evaluated.

Factors to be rated

1. **Quality of work**—Thorough, neat, and accurate work that meets acceptable standards set for job.
   ☐ Exceptionally high   ☐ Substandard   **Comments**
   ☐ High type of work   ☐ Unacceptable
   ☐ Satisfactory

2. **Quantity of work**—Produces acceptable volume of work.
   ☐ Exceptionally high   ☐ Low   **Comments**
   ☐ Above normal   ☐ Very low
   ☐ Normal

3. **Knowledge of job**—Clear understanding of all factors relating to job.
   ☐ Excellent   ☐ Fair   **Comments**
   ☐ Good   ☐ Unsatisfactory
   ☐ Satisfactory

4. **Contact with others**—How well did employee work with and for others in company?
   ☐ Exceptionally successful   ☐ Had some difficulty   **Comments**
   ☐ Very successful   ☐ Ineffective
   ☐ Generally successful

5. **Dependability**—Conscientious, thorough, reliable, able to perform with minimum of supervision.
   ☐ Exceptionally reliable   ☐ Required considerable   **Comments**
   ☐ Very reliable   supervision
   ☐ Reliable   ☐ Unreliable

6. **Initiative**—Seeks increased responsibilities.
   ☐ Never had to be told   ☐ Frequently had to be told   **Comments**
   ☐ Rarely had to be told   ☐ Always had to be told
   ☐ Occasionally had to be told

7. **Development**—How has employee developed on job?
   ☐ Very rapidly   ☐ Slowly   **Comments**
   ☐ Rapidly   ☐ Very slowly
   ☐ Normally

8. **Judgment**—Decisions based on sound knowledge.
   ☐ Exceptionally sound and   ☐ Frequent errors   **Comments**
       logical   ☐ Poor
   ☐ Well above average
   ☐ Usually sound

Promotions.   A **promotion** is an upward movement in an organization to a position of more authority, responsibility, accountability, and monetary reward. Performance should be the main criteria for promotions. However, companies can promote on the basis of seniority. Performance appraisals are guides for determining who deserves promotion. Only when two employees are equally qualified should seniority be the deciding factor in promotion.

Transfers.   The horizontal movements of personnel in a company are called **transfers.** A transfer may or may not involve more money, responsibility, or accountability.

Layoffs.   During times of business slowdowns, some employees may have to be let go for a period of time. When business picks up, these people should be the first to be rehired. Seniority often serves as the basis in determining which employees should be laid off.

Demotions.   Changes in technology may cause elimination of some jobs. Employees may be promoted beyond their level of capability. In such cases, **demotion,** a downward movement to a job of lesser responsibility and less pay, is necessary. Performance appraisals can also serve as an index of those people who are not performing well.

Terminations.   A permanent separation from the firm is a **termination,** or discharge. Discharge of employees today is limited to specific causes, such as repeated inability to perform the work, serious violation of work rules, elimination of a job, or closing down of a plant.

HUMAN RESOURCE TRAINING AND DEVELOPMENT

Constant changes in today's business environment demand that job skills be continually upgraded. Formal education requirements have risen for many positions. Therefore, companies have instituted various types of programs designed to provide employees with training in required skills. Effective training can help reduce accidents, turnover, and absenteeism; boost morale; improve employees' communication; increase productivity; and reduce the need for close supervision.

A major question is who should do the training. Various approaches are followed by individual companies. A company may use outside consultants to conduct their training. Some companies have training specialists or set up a separate training department. In other companies, line managers do the training. Sometimes, training duties are divided. Training specialists conduct classes away from the work floor and also train line supervisors to be better trainers. Line supervisors then do the training in the work area.

Companies may use several types of training and development programs. Some provide training for a particular task, some are aimed at improving an individual's educational background, and some are designed to develop prospective managers or to improve management skills.

A typical training class.

Job Training

Programs for job training include (1) on-the-job training, (2) vestibule training, and (3) apprenticeship training.

On-the-Job Training. Commonly called OJT, the **on-the-job training** method involves showing a trainee how to do a job under real working conditions and then having the trainee try it. Learning takes place by doing. The trainee is given corrections, suggestions, explanations, and encouragement for improving job performance.

Once OJT is given on an individual basis by a supervisor or experienced employee, the trainers must devote time to properly instructing each trainee. On-the-job training is an easy and inexpensive method of training and requires no special equipment. A disadvantage is that the inexperienced worker may cause some waste of time or materials or interference with work routine while being trained.

Vestibule Training. The main feature of **vestibule training** is that it is given in a reproduction of the work area that is set up away from the actual job. The advantages of this type of training are that the person who conducts it is qualified and recognized for his or her ability to teach, and that the learner can learn without being subjected to the pressure for production. There is no danger that the inexperienced worker will destroy or ruin an expensive piece of machinery while learning how to operate it. Consequently, training can proceed more efficiently. Disadvantages of vestibule training are the cost of setting up the separate facility and failure to prepare the worker for the pressure or noise of the actual job.

Apprenticeship Training. The learning of a skilled trade (plumber, electrician, meat cutter, tool and die maker) is **apprenticeship training**. Both formal classroom instruction in the principles and theory of the trade and on-the-job training are included in apprenticeship training. The training is extensive and may vary from two to five years, depending on the specific trade. Upon completing the apprenticeship, the worker becomes a journeyman, which indicates that he or she has acquired the necessary skills to perform the job.

Formal Training

In addition to providing training for specific jobs, many companies offer employees the opportunity to broaden their general educational background in such areas of study as mathematics, English, consumer economics, or history. Instructors teach the courses at the company site after working hours, and the courses are usually provided at no cost to participants.

In another type of formal training program, the company sends selected employees to college, on either a full-time or part-time basis. This program is designed to help those without a college degree to work toward a degree and to aid those who have a degree to pursue a higher degree. As an incentive to employees, the company will usually pay for all, or a major portion of, the expenses incurred.

This training program can be used to advantage in recruiting new employees and retaining qualified ones. In addition, it allows the individual to expand his or her education beyond the task assignment. The company benefits from the program because these employees can contribute significantly more to the company with their additional knowledge.

Management Development

Management development includes many types of training. The basic purposes of all management development are to provide opportunities for present managers to improve their managerial skills, to broaden their managerial knowledge, and to provide training for employees who demonstrate potential for promotion to management positions.

Management development programs may be offered either on the company premises or away from the company. They may be conducted by company personnel or by training specialists (such as college professors or management consultants).

HUMAN RESOURCE SEPARATION FROM THE FIRM

Employee turnover results from a variety of causes: some employees leave for better paying positions or positions of more authority; some retire. A certain amount of employee turnover is desirable because new employees bring fresh ideas into the company. However. turnover should be kept low, since considerable costs are involved in placing workers on the payroll, in training them, and then in having to train replacements. If the company experiences a high turnover rate, it may be a symptom of a serious problem, as noted in the previous chapter. Some conditions that contribute to high employee turnover are low wages, unequal or unfair treatment of employees on the job by the supervisor, poor working conditions, or improper job placement.

A sound company policy is to attempt to determine the reasons why employees are leaving. Specialists from the personnel department seek this information in the employees' **exit interviews.** An employee who is leaving tends to be willing to disclose the real reasons behind the decision to quit. Analysis of the data gathered in these interviews may indicate an overall pattern in the reasons why employees are quitting. If the personnel department can isolate the cause, then a positive course of corrective action can be taken to remove the cause. In turn, this should lead to a lower turnover rate. For example, if low wages are the cause, the company should investigate the wages being paid in the community and compare them with its own wage structure. If necessary, upward adjustments in the wage structure should be made to bring wages into line with those of competitors.

HUMAN RESOURCE COMPENSATION

Human resource compensation includes both direct financial rewards and indirect fringe benefits (discussed later in this chapter). Direct financial rewards are made available to employees in the form of wages, salaries, and bonuses. Wages are payments made to workers on an hourly rated basis while salaries are payments made on a weekly, biweekly, or monthly basis. A bonus is a method of rewarding employees for extra performance.

A fair employee compensation system is necessary for all employees in order to prevent many labor-management problems from developing, to provide an incentive for employees to produce more, to help retain valuable employees, and to aid in recruiting new employees. A technique used by many firms to establish an equitable monetary reward system is job evaluation. **Job evaluation** is the systematic process of determining the correct rate of pay for each job in relation to other jobs being performed in the company. The human resource manager and his or her staff play key roles in establishing an equitable compensation plan.

Types of Compensation Plans

The fundamental criterion of a compensation plan is that it should provide equitable distribution of rewards for all employees. Payment plans that a company may adopt include piece rate, hourly rate, straight salary, and bonus plans. The first two are wage payments, the third is a salary payment, and the fourth is an incentive plan.

Piece Rate. A piece-rate plan rewards employees on the basis of productivity. Piece-rate payments are made on either an individual or group basis, according to a specified amount for each acceptable unit produced. For this system to be used, the output of the individual employee or the group must be measurable. For example, employees assembling toys are paid 75¢ for each acceptable unit produced. An employee who assembled 100 toys in a day would earn $75. If output were increased to 110 acceptable units, the daily rate would increase to $82.50. Payment on a group basis would be calculated the same way.

Hourly Rate. In situations where the amount of output is difficult to measure or cannot be controlled by the worker, employees may be paid at an hourly rate. For example, if the hourly rate is $5 and an employee works eight hours, the rate is $40 daily. Employees can increase their income under this wage plan only by working longer hours. In industries where the federal wage and hour law is applicable, overtime (the hours worked in excess of 40 hours per week) is paid for at the rate of time and one-half, and on Sundays and holidays at double the hourly rate.

Straight Salary.   Employees who are paid on a salary basis are usually clerical, secretarial, supervisory, and managerial personnel—white collar workers. Under this payment system, employees receive a fixed amount per year. Managers and supervisors usually are not eligible to receive overtime pay. In some firms, production workers receive a straight salary under a guaranteed annual wage plan (GAW). Employees are paid a wage based on a guaranteed number of hours of work per year.

Bonus Plan.   A **bonus plan** is used as an incentive for greater output. Under this system, the company establishes a production quota for either individual or group output. An individual who produces more than the established quota receives a bonus for his or her additional production. This incentive plan can be used with the piece-rate payment plan. In the toy example, suppose the production quota established is 80 toys per day, and a rate of 75¢ is paid for each toy assembled. An employee who produces 80 acceptable units would receive $60 daily. If a 50¢ bonus is paid for each acceptable unit in excess of 80, a worker can increase his or her daily earnings. If 90 toys were assembled, the daily rate would be calculated as follows:

$$
\begin{array}{ll}
80 \text{ units } \times \ 75\text{¢ per unit} & = \$60.00 \\
10 \text{ units } \times \ \$1.25 \text{ per unit} & = \underline{\$12.50} \\
\text{Total earnings} & = \$72.50
\end{array}
$$

Under the straight piece rate plan, earnings would be $67.50. The bonus plan attempts to motivate employees by rewarding them for higher productivity.

Other Incentive Plans.   Other incentive plans are in common use today. For example, many companies now have **profit-sharing plans** in which a percentage of the company's annual profits are shared with employees. The purpose of a profit-sharing plan is to encourage employees to produce more and to use their knowledge and skills to help increase the profits of the firm. In turn, their earnings are increased.

A **merit raise** is an incentive plan that rewards good performance. This plan is designed to increase worker motivation by giving the employee a permanent addition to his or her wage or salary as well as recognition for strong work performance.

HUMAN RESOURCE BENEFITS

Wages and salaries paid to employees for work are called *direct payments*. However, many manufacturing and nonmanufacturing firms make additional payments available to employees in the form of indirect or extra payments called **fringe benefits** (see Exhibit 9–8).

Exhibit 9–8

Types of fringe benefits.

Insurance (life, hospital, surgical, medical)
Pensions (nongovernment)
Old-age, survivors, disability, and health insurance taxes
Paid vacations
Paid rest periods, coffee breaks, lunch periods
Paid holidays
Unemployment compensation taxes
Workers' compensation
Paid sick leave
Profit-sharing payments
Christmas or other special bonuses, suggestion awards
Thrift plans
Salary continuation or long-term disability
Employee meals furnished free
Dental insurance
Discounts on goods and services purchased from the company by employees
Employee education expenditures
Paid personal holidays
Paid automobile insurance
Paid homeowner and legal insurance
Financial counseling services
Day-care centers

The annual cost to employers of providing fringe benefits amounts to some 37 percent of total payroll dollars. Firms in petroleum, chemicals, transportation equipment, primary metals, public utilities, and banks, finance, and trust companies average the highest benefit payments. Major fringe benefits are medical, life, hospital and surgical insurance. Other benefits being offered are dental care, paid legal services, career counseling, annual physical exams, professional and financial counseling, and group auto insurance.

Some companies offer employees a "cafeteria" compensation plan. This plan usually provides a standard base salary plus fringe benefits. For example, the base salary may be $14,000 and the fringe benefit package $3,000. The cafeteria plan allows employees to choose how they wish to receive their salary and benefits. The younger worker may choose to take the total compensation of $17,000 as salary while older employees with fewer financial obligations may opt for a larger share of their compensation in the form of fringe benefits. Mobil Corporation has a cafeteria insurance plan that is designed to meet the needs of different lifestyles.

SUMMARY OF KEY POINTS

1. Human resources are the major asset of the firm.

2. Selection of the firm's human resources is made more efficient by the use of job analysis, job descriptions, and job specifications.

3. Sources of locating potential human resources are advertising, public and private employment agencies, colleges and universities, vocational schools, labor unions, friends and relatives of workers, and former military personnel.

4. The application form provides a written summary of the individual's background.

5. Personal interviews permit face-to-face contact between interviewer and interviewee so that the interviewer can evaluate the candidate's qualifications for the job.

6. Various types of tests can be used to aid in the staffing process.

7. The Civil Rights Act prohibits discrimination in employment practices.

8. Employees should be given proper orientation into the company and counseled on a continuous basis after employment.

9. Performance appraisal is used as an aid in making decisions about personnel.

10. Various types of training programs are used by modern companies, including OJT, vestibule, apprenticeship, formal training, and management development.

11. It is important to determine the employees' reasons for leaving the firm.

12. A compensation plan must provide for equitable distribution of rewards.

13. Types of compensation plans are piece rate, salary, bonus, and hourly.

14. Fringe benefits are indirect payments made to employees.

DISCUSSION QUESTIONS

1. Explain the difference between a job description and a job specification.

2. Identify various sources for locating potential employees. Can you think of additional sources not included in the text?

3. What are the differences between aptitude, intelligence, achievement, personality, and interest tests?

4. What effect has the Civil Rights Act of 1964 had on employee testing?
5. What are some purposes of counseling?
6. What are the various types of training programs used by business firms?
7. What is an exit interview? What is its significance to a company?
8. Distinguish between piece-rate and hourly-rate wage systems.

STUDENT PROJECTS

1. Prepare a list of questions that you would ask an employer about a job you are interested in.
2. From the newspaper, read the ads for employment and select several that you might be interested in and report on them to the class.
3. Visit the school placement office and have a representative explain the factors they consider to be most important in a job interview with a potential employee.
4. Prepare a personal resumé using the outline suggested in the appendix to the text.

The Auditors

The Audit Division in a state agency consists of field auditors who travel throughout the state, and the supervisory and clerical personnel who remain at the home office. Auditors are classified as follows: Auditor I, the entry level position; Auditor II, a one-step promotion, referred to as a "junior" auditor; and Auditor III, senior auditor. The Auditor III is the leader of the team of auditors when they are out conducting audits in various state agencies. A team usually consists of a senior auditor and two or three Auditor I's and/or II's.

The ten Auditor III's are all between 35 and 40 years of age, have ten or more years experience with the division, have college degrees, and are adjusted to the extensive travel required of auditors. There has been no employee turnover in Auditor III positions in four years.

David Page has been with the division six years and has been promoted to Auditor II. Since promotions are based solely on seniority, David realizes that promotions are extremely slow.

David has worked very hard. He is often given assignments to lead the audit teams as if he were an Auditor III. He welcomes these additional assignments because he feels upper management has confidence in him.

Because promotions are limited, David has applied for other positions in the state agency, but with no success. When a vacancy occurred in the Finance Division, David was interviewed for the position.

About a month later, the head of the Finance Division contacted David and told him he had been selected for the position. All that remained was to obtain a formal recommendation from Martin Stone, David's supervisor. At the time, Mr. Stone was away on vacation.

When Mr. Stone returned from vacation and learned of David's possible promotion into another division, he complained to the head of the state agency that the Finance Division was raiding the Audit Division of its best employees. This complaint kept David from getting the promotion.

Questions

1. What effect will David's not getting the promotion have on his future job performance in the Audit Division?
2. In your opinion, why do you think Mr. Stone blocked the promotion?
3. What effect will blocking a promotion likely have on an employee who is well qualified for promotion?
4. What should David do now?
5. Is a promotion system based solely on seniority a good policy?

Cuddly Toys, Inc.

The Cuddly Toy Company will open a new manufacturing facility in 60 days. The new plant will produce stuffed animal toys of various sizes to be sold in a ten-state region. Plans call for 500 toys to be produced daily. To achieve this level of production, the company will require the following number of people for each job.

Job Title	Number of Employees Required
President	1
Production Manager	1
Office Manager	1
Human Resource Manager	1
Cutters	4
Sewers	12
Stuffers	4
Shipping Clerk	2
Sales Manager	1
Salespersons	4
Accountant	2
Office Clerk	3
Secretary	1

You have been hired as the human resource manager of the company. Since this is a new company, you must design a human resource system for selecting, orienting, training, and compensating the new employees.

Questions

1. Suggest the process by which you would hire employees for the company.
2. What type of orientation plan should be used for the new employees?
3. Describe the type of training program that would be feasible for the Cuddly Toy Company.
4. What fringe benefits would you provide for employees?
5. Discuss the type of compensation plan you would recommend for this company.

BUSINESS PROFILE

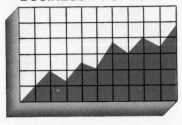

Snelling and Snelling

Snelling and Snelling is the world's largest private employment service, with more than 500 offices coast to coast and overseas.

The company was founded in 1951. In 1955 it began franchising its services, and in 1969 it went public. The formula for success in Snelling and Snelling is that new offices are constantly being franchised and added to its international network. Internally, the company has developed a training program for all franchisee personnel that is the model for the profession.

As a private employment service, Snelling and Snelling specializes in placing people in secretarial, office, clerical, administrative, technical, and sales positions. To do this, the company services the personnel needs of client companies on a regular basis and maintains contact with prospective employers to obtain listings for job openings.

There is no charge for the many services that Snelling and Snelling performs for a job applicant—such as interviewing, evaluating, counseling, calling employers, and arranging interviews—until the applicant has accepted a position that is satisfactory.

Community involvement is of prime consideration in every Snelling and Snelling office. Among its many corporate citizenship commitments, the company initiated and vigorously supports Back-to-School Programs for youth.

As a leader in the field, Snelling and Snelling has been an imaginative innovator. It has created and established some of the basic standards, ethics, and procedures that are accepted by many as the criteria for the employment service profession.

Snelling and Snelling recommends the following points as guidelines when making contact with a private employment service:

Mr. and Mrs. Robert O. Snelling. Mr. Snelling is Chairman of the Board and President, Mrs. Snelling is Vice President.

1. Be honest with the service. When completing your application, make the information clear and complete.

2. Make your specific job desires known. The counselor will give you pertinent details regarding job openings and will furnish you with information about prospective employers.

3. Have a realistic target. Do not underestimate or overestimate yourself and your abilities. The counselor will give you a professional appraisal of your strengths and weaknesses.

4. Read the Employment Service Agreement carefully, and fully understand this contract.

5. Let the counselor know the results of your interview immediately. The counselor may be able to tell you the company's reaction and possibly offer advice based on that impression.

6. The service charge may be paid by either the job seeker or the hiring firm. Ask in advance and look for a 100-day guarantee, which is usually offerred.

7. Be particular when it comes to selecting your employment service. Check with your Chamber of Commerce or Better Business Bureau to find reliable, capable private employment services.

10 Union and Management Relations

KEY WORDS

American Federation of Labor
Craft union
Industrial union
Congress of Industrial
  Organizations
Local union
International union
Coalition of Labor Union Women
Quality of work life

Collective bargaining
Open shop
Agency shop
Closed shop
Union shop
"Yellow-dog"
  contract
Featherbedding
"Right-to-work" law

Conciliation
Mediation
Arbitration
Picketing
Boycotting
Strike
Injunction
Lockout

> It is one of the characteristics of a free and democratic nation that it have free and independent labor unions.
>
> FRANKLIN D. ROOSEVELT

Of the workforce in America, approximately 20 percent are members of labor unions. This fact has a profound impact on management in terms of its relationships with employees. Union membership enables people to strive to achieve their goals collectively rather than through individual effort. There is no single reason for union membership. People are motivated to join unions for a variety of reasons, which include:

1. To achieve better working conditions;
2. To gain higher wages or a better fringe benefit package;
3. To strengthen job security;
4. To improve communication between management and employees;
5. To satisfy a job requirement (some jobs require a person to join a union within a certain period of time after employment).

HISTORY OF LABOR UNIONS

The labor union movement as we know it today in the United States is actually of recent origin, dating back only to the mid-1930s. Labor unions in the early periods of our country's history were organized on a local basis. Many of these unions were organized to achieve a specific goal, such as a wage increase or shorter working hours. When these goals were achieved, many of the unions disbanded. Some unions used the strike to reach their goals. Some unions were tried in court and ultimately dissolved. Early union activity is highlighted by the following events:

1786　The earliest authenticated strike of workers in the United States in a single trade occurred when Philadelphia printers gained a minimum wage of $6 a week.

1792　Philadelphia shoemakers organized the first local craft union formed for collective bargaining. It disbanded in less than a year.

1825　The United Tailoresses of New York, a trade union organization for women only, was formed in New York City.

1834　The National Trades' Union was formed in New York City. The first attempt at founding a national labor federation in the United States, it failed to survive the financial panic of 1837.

1852 The Typographical Union, the first national organization of workers to continue to the present day, was formed.

1863 The present-day Brotherhood of Locomotive Engineers was founded.[1]

The Noble Order of the Knights of Labor was organized in 1869 in Philadelphia and was the first important national union. This union gained many followers through its successful strikes against the railroad and promotion of the cause of the eight-hour work day. By 1886, it numbered over 700,000 members, but internal strife caused it to lose much of its early strength.

The rise of the **American Federation of Labor (AFL)** hastened this loss of strength. Under the dynamic leadership of its first president, Samuel Gompers, the AFL enjoyed remarkable growth. By 1920, approximately 75 percent of all organized workers were members of the AFL.

Skilled workers make up the membership of the AFL; thus, the AFL is a craft union. **Craft unions** are dominant in construction, printing, and publishing. Membership consists of individuals who have mastered a trade, such as electricians and plumbers.

The Committee for Industrial Organization began in 1935 within the AFL. Its purpose was to provide a union for industrial workers, those who were not eligible for membership in the craft union. These unions are called **industrial unions** and are predominant in manufacturing, transportation, finance, and mining. Membership consists of production and maintenance workers.

Members of the AFL feared that they would lose both status and security because of their affiliation with the industrial union. As a result, the Committee for Industrial Organization (which changed its name to the current **Congress of Industrial Organizations—CIO)** was expelled from the AFL in 1938.

After its expulsion, there were confrontations in organizing campaigns between the AFL and CIO. This struggle ended in 1955 when the two unions merged and formed the AFL-CIO.

Although the union movement has been rather turbulent, it has also been dynamic and important in changing the character of many management-labor relationships.

Growth of Labor Unions

As the history of unions indicates, the labor movement in the United States has experienced difficult periods. Gradually, however, changes took place that gave impetus to the union movement. One significant change was the increased acceptance of labor unions by the public. Another substantial factor encouraging union growth was the emergence of more positive attitudes of state and local governments toward unions, as

---

[1]Bureau of Labor Statistics, *Brief History of the American Labor Movement*, Bulletin No. 1000 (Washington, D.C.: U.S. Government Printing Office, 1976), pp. 78–79.

evidenced by passage of legislation favorable to the union movement. Still another supportive factor was that court decisions began to recognize rights of unions to organize for collective purposes.

UNION STRUCTURE

The primary organizational unit for labor groups is the local union. Local unions engage in a number of activities, including electing officers, admitting and recruiting members, educating workers, and working in political activities.

National or International Unions

Most local unions affiliate with a national or international union. An international union is the same as a national union except that it has locals and membership in Canada, Central America, or Mexico. The international union provides a number of services to the local unions, such as organization or contract negotiations. The internationals have power to issue or withdraw the charters of the locals. As a result, they have authority to control the locals. Some of the more familiar international unions are the Teamsters, Steelworkers, and United Auto Workers.

Some 62 percent of the international unions are affiliated with the AFL-CIO on a voluntary basis, and it acts as a general trade union organization. The AFL-CIO provides key services to the national and international unions affiliated with it. For example, the AFL-CIO's Committee on Political Education (COPE) works for passage of legislation favorable to organized labor at local, state, and federal levels and to get candidates supportive of organized labor elected to political office. George Meany, who served as president of the AFL-CIO for almost 30 years, was instrumental in the growth of the union. The profile in this chapter is focused on the AFL-CIO.

Union Membership

Approximately 21.7 million members now belong to international unions, including about 1.7 million members employed outside the United States (mainly in Canada). Of these, about 85 percent hold membership in unions affiliated with the AFL-CIO. Exhibit 10–1 shows the ten national and international unions with the largest membership.

Independent Unions

Some well-known unions, such as the United Mine Workers (UMW), the Teamsters, and the United Automobile Workers, are independents (not affiliated with the AFL-CIO). The UMW was at various times affiliated with both the AFL and the CIO but John L. Lewis, then president of the UMW, withdrew the membership from the AFL for the last time in 1948, and it became an independent union. The Teamsters were expelled from the AFL-CIO in 1957 on charges of being dominated by corrupt influences. In 1968, the UAW withdrew from the AFL-CIO and joined the Teamsters and UMW District 50, forming the Alliance for Labor Action (ALA). The ALA's purposes were to coordinate bargaining, facilitate communication, and work for political goals. The ALA was disbanded in 1971. In 1981, the UAW was once more affiliated with the AFL-CIO.

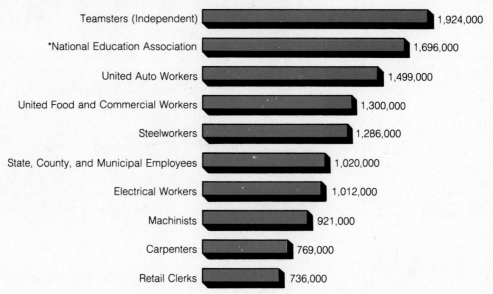

Teamsters (Independent)	1,924,000
*National Education Association	1,696,000
United Auto Workers	1,499,000
United Food and Commercial Workers	1,300,000
Steelworkers	1,286,000
State, County, and Municipal Employees	1,020,000
Electrical Workers	1,012,000
Machinists	921,000
Carpenters	769,000
Retail Clerks	736,000

*The NEA is technically an employee association but performs the functions of a union for its members.

Exhibit 10–1
The ten largest national unions. (SOURCE: U.S. Department of Labor.)

WOMEN IN UNIONS

Women comprise approximately 25 percent of total union membership. In 1974, the Coalition of Labor Union Women (CLUW) was formed. Its purposes are to more aggressively organize women workers; increase women's participation in union activities; combat sex discrimination in hiring and promotion; and improve day-care programs, minimum wages, maternity and pension benefits, and health and safety laws. Unions that account for about half of all women union members are the Teamsters; the American Federation of State, County, and Municipal Employees (AFSCME); Retail Clerks; Clothing and Textile Workers; Service Employees; Electrical Workers; and Automobile Workers.

ORGANIZING A LABOR UNION

A series of steps must be followed in order for a union to be recognized by management as the collective bargaining agent for employees:

1. A petition calling for a union election must be signed by at least 30 percent of the employees.
2. The National Labor Relations Board (NLRB) obtains a list of all employees of a particular unit or company to determine if union organizers have enough signatures from the specific group to order an election.

Members of Service Employees International Union picketing in Boston.

3. The NLRB calls a hearing with management and union representatives.

4. An election to vote on whether employees want union membership is held within three weeks of the hearing.

5. For the union to win approval as the bargaining unit for employees, more than 50 percent of the employees must vote in favor of having the union represent them. If less than a majority vote in favor, the union loses the election.

6. After an election, the NLRB issues a certificate showing which union is the official bargaining agent for the employees. If a majority of the employees voted that no union be designated to represent them, the certificate contains this information. The certificate covers a 12-month period and another election cannot be held until that time period has elapsed.

COLLECTIVE BARGAINING

Employees join unions to strengthen their chances for getting management to grant their demands. When management and union negotiators sit down at the bargaining table to discuss grievances, the negotiation process is called collective bargaining. For example, inflation is of concern for everyone, including union members. Through collective bargaining, many unions have negotiated to have an escalator clause incorporated into the union contract. This clause provides for a cost-of-living adjustment (COLA), which automatically increases as the cost-of-living index rises during the term of the union agreement.

The Union Contract

The union-management contract is a result of collective bargaining. This agreement contains numerous clauses that cover a variety of topics governing management and union activities for the duration of the contract. The topics contained in a typical union contract include:

Parties to the contract	Incentive wage plans
Union recognition	Transfers, promotions, demotions
Union representation	Regular hours of work
Grievance procedures	Overtime
Strikes and lockout	Holidays
Union security	Absences and leaves
Union activities and rights	Vacations
Management rights	Working conditions
Wages	Insurance and benefit plans
Differentials in pay	Special employees

Some trends have occurred in collective bargaining agreements. Contracts have increased in number, coverage, breadth, and complexity. The scope of collective bargaining has been expanded, and contracts have become more detailed to leave as little as possible open to dispute. Contracts are becoming more complex and lengthy, with some extending to several hundred pages.

UNION SECURITY

A major objective of the union is to ensure security for its members and for the union itself. Specific shop agreements provide different types of recognition of the union within a company.

Open Shop

An **open shop** gives employees the right to decide whether or not they desire to join a union. Management does not attempt to influence the employee's decision on union membership. Generally, companies with an open shop are prime targets of union organizing attempts.

Agency Shop

The **agency shop** requires both union and nonunion employees to pay union dues. However, an individual does not have to join the union as a condition of employment. This type of shop agreement counteracts the objection that some employers have to force all workers to join a union. Union members feel that since all workers share in the benefits the labor union wins through collective bargaining, all should pay union dues. Thus, union members look upon the agency shop as a fair agreement. Nonunion members do not participate in union activities such as voting for union officers or voting on a new union contract.

Closed Shop

To be hired and retained in a **closed shop,** an employee must be a union member in good standing. Labor unions favor this type of security agreement. In a closed shop, managers have little choice in employee selection since the union refers prospective employees to the company.

Union Shop

In the **union shop** employees hired do not have to be union members. However, within a stipulated time period (30 days in most industries) a new employee must join the union and remain a member as a condition of employment. This type of union security is the most widely recognized security agreement.

Quality of Work Life

Increasing concern for humaniza-
tion of work and raising the level
of job satisfaction has resulted in
the development of the concept
of **Quality of work life** (QWL).
Quality of work life is best considered as an approach to managing that is designed to improve
the total workplace for employees.

Some labor union leaders have
reacted quite positively to QWL,
believing that it will enhance the
workers' life through greater participation in decision making, better and safer working conditions,
and more equitable sharing of rewards and resources. Other
union leaders feel that QWL may
be a way of manipulating employees to produce more without
having to pay higher wages.

The aspects included in QWL
demonstrate the extensiveness of
the concept. Factors considered
in QWL are shown in Exhibit
10–2.

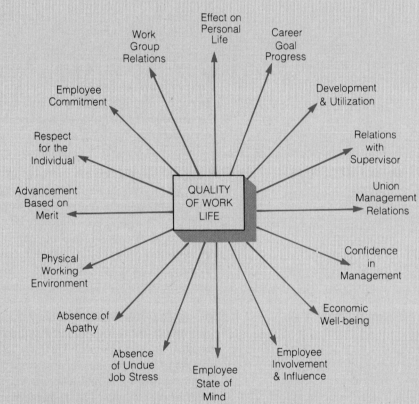

Exhibit 10–2
Factors considered in quality of
work life.

Exhibit 10–3

Characteristics of basic shop agreements.

	Previous to Employment	**During Duration of Employment**
Open Shop	May or may not be a union member	May or may not be a union member
Agency Shop	May or may not be a union member	May or may not be a union member
Closed Shop	Must be a union member	Must be a union member
Union Shop ·	May or may not be a union member	Must be a union member

The benefit for management in the union shop is that managers can select and hire the employees. The advantage for employees is that if they decide to quit before the 30-day grace period expires, they have not paid any union membership fees.

A union-shop contract clause in a United Automobile Workers' contract reads: "Each employee shall, on or after the thirtieth day following the first day of employment in a bargaining unit, be required as a condition of employment in that bargaining unit to be and remain a member of the Union."

Union membership in the four basic shop agreements is shown in Exhibit 10–3.

LABOR LEGISLATION

Attitudes of society and government toward organized labor have changed significantly with the rise of industrial development in our country. The passage of labor legislation pertaining to the union movement underscores these changes.

Railway Labor Act of 1926

Although the Railway Labor Act applied only to employees in the railroad industry, portions of this legislation were later incorporated and expanded into legislation that applied to employees other than railroad employees.

A main feature of the Act was that employers had to bargain collectively with employees. Formerly, employers could require their employees to sign a pledge in which they agreed not to join a union or attempt to form a union as a condition for their employment. This agreement was called a "yellow-dog" contract. The Railway Labor Act declared that it was illegal for the railroads to require employees to sign this type of agreement in order to be employed. In addition, the Act provided means to settle disputes between management and labor.

Norris-La Guardia Act of 1932 (Anti-Injunction Act)

Certain provisions of the Railway Labor Act were expanded to include all workers. The Norris-La Guardia Act extended the outlawing of the "yellow-dog" contracts to all industries. An additional provision prohibited an employer from using an injunction to prevent a work stoppage by employees except in specific instances.

National Labor Relations Act of 1935

The National Labor Relations Act, more commonly identified as the Wagner Act, established a national labor policy. This Act made important contributions to the cause of organized labor by defining the rights of employees and specifying unfair labor practices of employers.

Specifically, the rights of employees were defined in Section 7 of the law thusly: "Employees shall have the right to self-organization, to form, join, or assist labor organizations, to bargain collectively through representatives of their own choosing, and to engage in concerted activities, for the purpose of collective bargaining or other mutual aid or protection."[2]

Unfair labor practices of the employer were identified in Section 8 of the Act as follows:

It shall be an unfair labor practice for an employer

1. To interfere with, restrain, or coerce employees in the exercise of the rights guaranteed in Section 7.
2. To dominate or interfere with the formation or administration of any labor organization or contribute financial or other support to it.
3. By discrimination in regard to hire or tenure of employment or any term or condition of employment to encourage or discourage membership in any labor organization.
4. To discharge or other otherwise discriminate against an employee because he has filed charges or given testimony under this act.[3]

The Wagner Act also created the National Labor Relations Board (NLRB). This Board, consisting of three members, was given the power to decide the appropriate unit for collective bargaining, to conduct elections for union representation by secret ballot, and to prevent an employer from engaging in unfair (antiunion) labor practices as defined above. In addition, the Board has the power to appoint arbitrators to settle labor disputes when the parties to the dispute submit it to arbitration.

Labor Management Relations Act of 1947

Also known as the Taft-Hartley Act, the Labor Management Relations Act of 1947 was an amendment to the Wagner Act. In the years following the passage of the Wagner Act, organized labor's membership grew rapidly and its power increased. As a result, there was concern that there was too great an imbalance between unions and management. The Taft-Hartley

---

[2]*Congressional Record Proceedings and Debates,* vol. 79, part 3, 74th Congress, 1st Session, February 21, 1935, to March 12, 1935 (Washington, D.C.: Government Printing Office, 1935), p. 2369.

[3]*Ibid.*

Act attempted to balance the power between management and the unions. This Act retained the basic provisions of the Wagner Act outlined above, but it designated unfair labor practices of unions. One of these unfair practices stated that the union could not restrain or coerce an employer in the choice of the parties to bargain in the employer's behalf. Also, the union would be guilty of an unfair labor practice if it persuaded an employer to discriminate against any employees or if it refused to bargain collectively with an employer in good faith. Both management and union officials are required to bargain in good faith. In collective bargaining, good faith bargaining requires that both sides make every reasonable attempt to reach an agreement. Further unfair labor practices prohibited were participation in secondary boycotts, charging excessive initiation fees, and paying employees for work not done, a practice termed featherbedding.

This Act also provided that a court injunction can be obtained by the president of the United States to postpone a strike for a period of eighty days if this strike threatens the health and welfare of the nation. During the first sixty days of this period, further negotiations are to be continued. If an agreement is not reached during the sixty days, the remaining twenty days are used to determine, by secret ballot, whether the employees will accept the employer's last and final offer. If the final offer is not accepted, employees may continue the strike. For example, President Carter invoked the Taft-Hartley Act in March 1978 in an effort to get striking coal miners back to work and negotiators back to the bargaining table. The justification for invoking the Act was the harmful effect the strike was having on the American economy.

One controversial section of the Taft-Hartley Act is Section 14-b, the "right-to-work" section. Section 14-b permits individual states to pass legislation which provides that a person does not have to belong to a union in order to be employed or to continue employment. Labor unions have tried, so far unsuccessfully, to have Section 14-b repealed. Those favoring the "right-to-work" provision feel it offers individuals freedom to choose whether or not to join a union. Some twenty states now have a "right-to-work" law (see Exhibit 10–4).

Other major provisions of the Act included: (1) the closed shop was declared illegal, (2) union officers were required to file anticommunist affidavits, (3) the checkoff, or the practice of deducting union dues by the employer, was prohibited unless agreed to in writing by the employee, and (4) freedom-of-speech restrictions on the employer were relaxed.

The Act also created the Federal Mediation and Conciliation Service (FMCS) as an independent agency. The FMCS may offer to assist in settling labor disputes between management and unions that threaten to cause a major interruption of business. The FMCS may provide mediation and conciliation services voluntarily or at the request of one or both parties (management or union). The functions of the FMCS are to aid management and unions to reach collective bargaining agreements and avoid work stoppages, and to assist in settling grievances that occur under the administration of collective bargaining agreements.

Exhibit 10–4

The twenty states that have a "right-to-work" law (shaded).

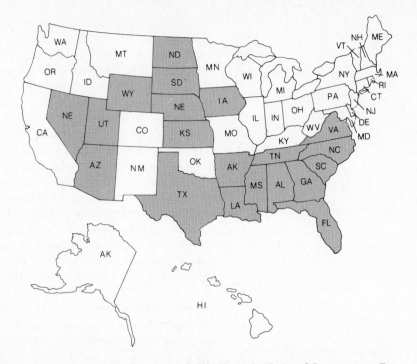

The Labor-Management Reporting and Disclosure Act of 1959

Otherwise known as the Landrum-Griffin Act, the Labor-Management Reporting and Disclosure Act of 1959 is aimed primarily at establishing guidelines for eliminating improper activities by either labor or management. One provision of the Act provides protection for the rights of union members. All union members may nominate candidates for union leadership, vote in union elections, attend union meetings, and vote on union matters. The Act also provides for filing reports that describe the organization, financial dealings, and business practices of the union and its officers and certain employees. Guidelines were established for handling union funds. The filing of the anticommunist affidavit required under the Taft-Hartley Act was repealed.

While the closed shop was declared illegal under the Taft-Hartley Act, the Landrum-Griffin Act exempted the construction industry by substituting a seven-day probationary period instead of the usual thirty-day period. As a practical matter, employers prefer to hire union members rather than nonunion members who would have to be replaced in seven days.

RESOLVING UNION AND MANAGEMENT CONFLICTS

There are instances in which the union has grievances against some management practices, such as alleged unfair treatment of employees or unsafe working conditions. The union contract establishes the procedures to be followed in settling the grievance (Exhibit 10–5). When neither labor nor management is able to agree on an acceptable solution, conflict develops. If they are not willing to compromise on the issues, a deadlock results. What avenues are available that will allow these management-labor disputes to be settled? Basically, there are three techniques that can be used to promote settlement of management-labor disagreements.

Conciliation

In a labor-management dispute, **conciliation** means the effort to get the parties to the dispute together to discuss in more detail the issues surrounding the disagreement. The third party involved, the conciliator, has no authority to require that management and union continue their discussion. The conciliator's role is to encourage labor and management representatives to reevaluate their thinking and work constructively toward a solution of the problem.

Mediation

Mediation differs from conciliation in that the mediator, the third party, can make specific recommendations for the solution to the dispute. Recommendations are usually in addition to those suggestions already offered by management and labor representatives. The mediator's strength centers in the influence he or she is able to exert on management and labor representatives in getting them to reach a settlement acceptable to both parties.

Arbitration

The final stage in settling labor-management disputes is **arbitration.** Unlike the preceding two methods, arbitration means that an impartial third party renders a decision that is binding on both labor and management. The arbitrator acts in the capacity of a judge. Arbitration is undertaken when all possible attempts at solving the disagreement have collapsed. When the parties cannot agree on one arbitrator, a panel of arbitrators

---

Exhibit 10–5

Steps in grievance procedure.

Step Number	Union Representative		Company Representative
1	Employee alone or Shop Committee Representative alone or Employee and Shop Committee Representative	Presents Grievance to →	Employee's Supervisor
2	Local Grievance Committee (composed of up to three employees)	Presents Grievance to →	Superintendent or Department Head
3	International Representatives and/or Local Grievance Committee	Presents Grievance to →	Director of Industrial Relations
4	Arbitration		

may be used. Three members compose this panel—one selected by the company, one by the union, and the third, an unbiased individual.

Arbitration may be of three types. In voluntary arbitration both management and labor agree to submit their cases to arbitration as a last resort after they have failed to negotiate an agreement. Both parties agree to abide by the arbitration panel's decision. Compulsory arbitration requires labor and management (usually by federal law) to submit their disputes to arbitration. Automatic arbitration occurs when labor and management have an agreement in their contract to submit to arbitration those work disputes or contract interpretations that cannot be settled by the normal grievance procedures.

UNION METHODS FOR ACHIEVING GOALS

How does the union make its demands known to management? What actions can the union take and what pressures can the union exert in order to get safer working conditions, for example? In actual practice, a number of methods are effective in getting management to listen to the union's demands.

Picketing

Unions can effectively exert pressure on management to meet their demands by picketing. **Picketing** is the practice of workers marching at the entrances to an employer's place of business. There are various purposes that picketing may serve:

1. Economic picketing: picketing by striking employees to place economic pressure on a struck employer to win a strike.
2. Informational or publicity picketing: picketing to advise the public that an employer fails to meet union labor standards.
3. Recognition picketing: picketing to force an employer to recognize the picketing union.
4. Organizational picketing: picketing to induce an employer's workers to join the picketing union.[4]

While picketing, workers usually carry signs identifying complaints against the employer. Picketing may keep other employees, both union and nonunion, away from the job if they honor the picket line and refuse to cross it to go to work. For example, union employees from other companies, such as union truck drivers, will usually refuse to cross a picket line to deliver supplies to a business.

Boycott

A **boycott** is a technique union members use to prevent an employer from selling goods or services. There are two kinds of boycotts, primary and secondary. A primary boycott exists when union members are told not to

---

[4]"Personnel Management-Labor-Relations," Prentice-Hall Loose Leaf Reports, *Labor Relations Guide*, vol. 1 (Englewood Cliffs, N.J.: Prentice-Hall), p. 3334.

Exhibit 10–6

Main issues in strikes.

(SOURCE: Bureau of Labor Statistics.)

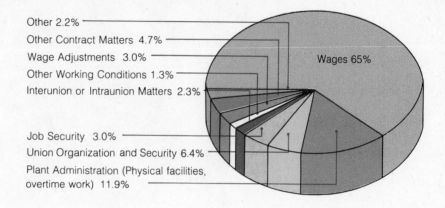

Other 2.2%

Other Contract Matters 4.7%

Wage Adjustments 3.0%

Other Working Conditions 1.3%

Interunion or Intraunion Matters 2.3%

Job Security 3.0%

Union Organization and Security 6.4%

Plant Administration (Physical facilities, overtime work) 11.9%

Wages 65%

buy the products of the company. A secondary boycott exists when a third party who is not directly involved in the dispute is influenced or coerced to bring pressure on the company by discontinuing business with the company. For example, the union may attempt to increase pressure on the company by threatening to strike a customer firm unless the second firm ceases to purchase products from the company during the duration of the strike. Most secondary boycotts, such as our example, are illegal under the provisions of the Taft-Hartley and Landrum-Griffin Acts.

Strike

The most effective weapon of the union is the **strike,** when employees stay off the job, stopping work, in an attempt to gain their demands. Exhibit 10–6 shows the main issues involved in strikes during a one-year period. A number of issues may be involved in a strike. For example, a strike may be over economic issues related to wages, fringe benefits, or other money matters. Some strikes are called to protest alleged unfair labor practices by management. In a jurisdictional dispute between unions, one union may strike to try to force an employer to recognize or assign work to one union instead of another.

Strikes may be of long or short duration. For example, the longest strike in the steel industry began on July 15, 1958; new labor-management contracts were not signed until early January, 1960. A strike against the Kohler Company of Wisconsin lasted ten years.

One type of strike, the wildcat strike, is not authorized by unions. It is an unofficial strike. Local unions may strike over local grievances even though there may be a no-strike clause in the labor contract agreement. In a wildcat strike, union leaders attempt to get workers to return to work. Management may go to federal court to enforce the no-strike provision.

No one really wins in a strike, regardless of its outcome. Employees lose their income for the period of the strike. Even though they are given aid from the union during the strike, the amount is much less than their

The most effective weapon of the union is the strike.

normal take-home pay. If they receive a wage hike, they still cannot make up for their lost income. Employers also lose because when their goods are unavailable, potential customers begin buying competitors' products.

MANAGEMENT METHODS FOR ACHIEVING GOALS

What steps can management take to apply pressure to the union? To counteract the techniques employed by the union, management also has effective measures that can be followed. These measures include injunctions, lockouts, and employer associations.

Injunction

Management may get a court order to prohibit the union from picketing or performing some other act. This legal maneuver is called an **injunction**. If the union violates the injunction, it may then be held in contempt of court; it may be fined, and its leadership may be imprisoned.

Lockout

The strike is the most potent weapon for a union while the **lockout** is the most powerful weapon of management. When management uses this method, they literally lock employees out of the company until the settlement is reached. In these situations, the management of the firm may attempt to keep the company operating by having the managers perform vital jobs until the issue is settled. The lockout is, in effect, a management strike.

Employer Associations

Just as employees attempt to strengthen their demands by joining together for collective efforts, so may employers join together in associations to counteract this force. This management technique, employer associations, makes it possible for employers to present a united front in dealing with the demands of organized labor. There is increasing demand by unions for industry-wide bargaining (bargaining for union contracts to which all or most employers in an industry, such as coal, railroad, or steel, or in a geographical area, are parties). Hence, employer associations, acting as representatives of individual employers, bargain with the unions to reach agreement.

There are local and state employer associations. The National Association of Manufacturers and the United States Chamber of Commerce are national associations. Although they do not negotiate contracts, they do express views of their members on major issues.

COMPOSITION OF THE LABOR FORCE

The *labor force* is defined as the number of people sixteen years of age or older who are classified as employed or unemployed. Noticeable changes have taken place in the growth and composition of the American labor force, which will continue to impact the unions in the future.

Participation Rate

The labor force *participation rate* is the percentage of eligible workers in a specific category (such as male, female, age group) who are employed. The participation rate for males is currently 77 percent and is expected to remain at this level. For females, it is 50 percent and is projected to increase to 60 percent by 1990. For black and other minority men, the participation rate is 72 percent and for black and other minority women, the rate is 54 percent. One trend has been the increase in the number of women in the labor force. Females now account for about 42 percent of the workforce and males approximately 58 percent.

Education Level

The level of education achieved by members of the workforce has risen. Exhibit 10–7 shows the percentage of workers by age groups who have completed high school. For all workers, almost 73 percent have completed twelve years of formal schooling. This is expected to increase to about 80 percent in 1990. In addition, about 16 percent of the labor force has completed four or more years of college, and this is projected to increase to about 22 percent by 1990. These changes, plus other changes discussed below, will have a tremendous impact on labor unions in the future.

THE FUTURE OF LABOR UNIONS

Unions have traditionally recruited members from the ranks of the blue-collar workers in manufacturing. However, the number of blue-collar workers has declined so that they account for only about a third of the total labor force and this decline is expected to continue. White-collar workers now number over 50 percent of the workforce.

Exhibit 10–7
Percentage of workers by age groups who have completed high school.
(SOURCE: U.S. Department of Labor.)

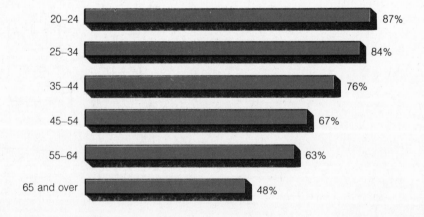

Age	Percentage
20–24	87%
25–34	84%
35–44	76%
45–54	67%
55–64	63%
65 and over	48%

Exhibit 10–8

Projected percentage growth of employment in major occupational groups by 1990.

Occupational Group	Projected Percentage Growth to 1990
White-collar workers	**24.0**
Professional and technical	19.0
Managers and administrators, except farm	21.0
Sales	27.0
Clerical	28.0
Blue-collar workers	**16.0**
Craft	20.0
Operatives	15.0
Nonfarm laborers	9.0
Service workers	**35.0**
Farm workers	**−14.0**

SOURCE: U.S. Department of Labor.

If unions are to expand, growth will depend on the success of unions in organizing workers in different sectors of the economy: government employees, office workers, educators, agricultural workers, and professional athletes (see Exhibit 10–8).

Federal Government Employees

Employees in federal government service are a potential source for union growth. Prior to 1962, federal employees were prohibited by law from membership in unions. However, President Kennedy issued an executive order in 1962, which was reaffirmed in 1968 by President Nixon, giving federal employees the right to hold union membership. Some 1.4 million federal employees are now unionized. Unions representing government employees may bargain for better working conditions and for grievance and arbitration procedures. However, federal employees are prohibited from striking under provisions of the Taft-Hartley Act. A violation of the strike prohibition calls for violators to be discharged. For example, in 1981 when the Air Traffic Controllers went on strike, some 11,000 were terminated.

Educators

Unions have made inroads in organizing public school teachers. The American Federation of Teachers (AFT), affiliated with the AFL-CIO, has a membership of some 500,000 classroom teachers. However, many teachers belong to employee associations. Employee associations function in the same way as labor unions. They differ in that membership is made up almost entirely of groups of professional and state and local government employees (i.e., white-collar workers).

The largest employee association is the National Education Association, with approximately 1.7 million members, most of whom are classroom teachers. Both the AFT and the NEA bargain collectively and their members have gone out on strike to enforce their demands. The NEA and the AFT also act as bargaining agents for a number of two-year and four-year college faculties. Other large employee associations are the New York State Employees Association, American Nurses Association, Fraternal Order of Police, and the California State Employees Association.

Office Workers

Another focal point of union organizing is office workers. Unions are focusing organizing efforts on secretaries, typists, cashiers, and other clerical employees. The Department of Labor projects that the number of office workers will increase to 22 million by 1990. Currently, only about 2.5 million of these workers belong to a union.

State and Local Government Employees

Unions have made some progress in organizing state and local government employees. Some 4.5 million state and local government employees belong to trade unions or employee associations. They comprise some 19 percent of all union members. Fire fighters, police officers, city transportation drivers, sanitation workers, and other municipal employees are organized for collective action in many cities. These employees are also bound by the no-strike provision for public employees, but there are strikes each year, nevertheless.

Agricultural Workers

Union recognition for agricultural workers has been achieved on a limited scale. The most notable case is the organization of agricultural workers in California. Union membership in the agricultural and fishing sector is small, accounting for less than 1 percent of total union membership.

Professional Athletes

Professional athletes now are members of unions. For example, baseball players are represented by the Major League Baseball Players' Association, football players by the National Football League Players' Association, basketball players by the National Basketball Players' Association, hockey players by the National Hockey League Players' Association, and soccer players by the North American Soccer League Players' Association. Players bargain collectively for increased benefits or more pay through their elected representative, an Executive Director or General Counsel. When demands are not met by the owners of the teams, the players may use the strike to attempt to get their demands satisfied. The most notable strike was the strike by professional baseball players in the middle of the 1981 season. About one-third of the season was cancelled before the strike was settled.

SUMMARY OF KEY POINTS

1. Workers join unions to satisfy a number of goals.

2. The study of the history of labor unions reveals that the union movement as we know it today dates back to the mid-1930s.

3. Many local unions are affiliated with national or international unions.

4. Women now comprise about a fourth of all union members.

5. Union organizing must progress through a sequence of steps.

6. Collective bargaining is the negotiating process by which management and unions attempt to resolve their differences.

7. The types of union security are open shop, agency shop, closed shop, and union shop.

8. Legislation aids in determining the rights and responsibilities of management and unions.

9. Conciliation, mediation, and arbitration are means for settling disputes between the union and management.

10. The union may use picketing, a boycott, or a strike to exert pressure on management.

11. Management may use an injunction, a lockout, or membership in an employer association to achieve its goals.

12. The future composition of union membership will change to include more white-collar workers and fewer blue-collar workers.

DISCUSSION QUESTIONS

1. Identify several reasons why people join unions.

2. What inroads have women made into union membership?

3. Explain the difference between a craft and an industrial union and give examples of each.

4. Distinguish between the various types of union security agreements.

5. What was the major contribution of the Norris-La Guardia Act of 1932 to the union movement?

6. What is an unfair labor practice of an employer? Of a union?

7. What is the National Labor Relations Board? What are its functions?

8. Discuss the major features of the Taft-Hartley Act.

9. Identify the three techniques for settling labor-management conflict.

10. Explain the chief means that a labor union uses to achieve its demands.

STUDENT PROJECTS

1. Read several articles from current business magazines in the library on the topic of labor unions. Prepare a list of the pros and cons of labor unions.

2. A group of from four to eight members of the class should be selected. Half the members of the group are assigned the role of presenting management's arguments against unions; the remaining members are assigned the role of presenting arguments favoring unionism.

3. The class should be divided into groups of four to eight members each. Half the group members are assigned the role of management representation and half are assigned the role of labor representatives. These labor-management members are to serve as a collective bargaining team to resolve the issue of labor's demand for a $10-a-week wage increase and management's unwillingness to grant the increase. Each labor-management group is assigned the task of working out a satisfactory agreement to both sides and reporting their findings.

4. Obtain a copy of a labor contract. Copies may be available in your library in the following reference: Bureau of National Affairs, *Collective Bargaining: Negotiations and Contracts* (Washington, D.C.: Bureau of National Affairs, Inc.).

5. From the daily newspaper, report to the class on some event reported about labor-management negotiations, strikes, boycotts, etc.

Gaston Electronics

Gaston Electronics has recently opened a new plant that manufactures and assembles specialized electronic measuring instruments. The plant was built in a geographical area where there are no labor unions. Since the firm was a new industry in the community, people were eager to go to work for them. For the first year, operations ran smoothly, with no signs of worker dissatisfaction. However, some signs of labor unrest have begun to appear. Employees have expressed their dissatisfaction on a number of matters. Specifically, these are their complaints:

1. Poor working conditions (dirty work area, no air conditioning).

2. Long hours of work, including some Saturdays and Sundays. While employees are paid overtime, they dislike being told they have to work overtime and do not have a choice in whether they desire to work overtime.

3. Hourly wages are lower at Gaston than at other firms in the area.

4. While the company has a health insurance plan, it does not have a pension or disability plan.

5. Workers were originally paid for fifteen-minute break periods twice daily, but in a move to save money, the company no longer pays the employees while they are on break.

6. There is no place for employees to eat lunch except in the work area.

7. The parking lot is not paved: it is graveled. Cars become caked with mud in rainy weather or covered with gravel dust in dry weather.

Each time employee representatives have tried to tell management of these grievances, management has ignored them. In fact, three employee representatives were fired, and management has announced that anyone else who talks about union membership for employees will be fired also. Instead of reducing employee unrest, employees are now actively campaigning to organize.

Questions

1. What are the causes of the union organizing attempt in this company?
2. Does management have to allow employees the opportunity to vote on union representation? If so, what federal laws are involved?
3. How would you encourage members to vote for the union?
4. What action can (or could) management take to counteract this organizing attempt?
5. Is there any evidence of unfair labor practices in this situation?
6. What type of union security currently exists in this company? What type of security does the union prefer? What type of security agreement will be allowed if a union is voted in to represent employees?
7. Are there any arguments management can use against unionization?

Harry's Workers on Strike

Union members carry signs in front of all of Harry's fast-food restaurants urging people to boycott Harry's. The conflict between Harry's and the union involves worker rights, including the right to union representation. The employees of Harry's are on strike to force the company to live up to the terms of the union contract and to win back-pay as well as proper wages. The union's position is that Harry's tried to break their contract with the union. However, the National Labor Relations Board ruled that Harry's was bound by the contract. The union claims that Harry's continues to ignore the NLRB decision and as a result this has had the following effects on the workers:

1. General harassment and intimidation;
2. Low wages below present union scale;
3. No raises for two and a half years;
4. No seniority rights;
5. Possible loss of all health, welfare, and pension benefits.

Questions

1. What is the purpose of the boycott?
2. Would you boycott Harry's?
3. How should the conflict be resolved?

Biennial meeting of the AFL-CIO.

BUSINESS PROFILE

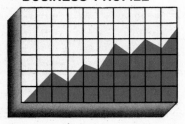

The AFL-CIO

Since 1955, the AFL-CIO has served as a general trade union organization for all the national and international unions affiliated with it on a voluntary basis. The purpose of the AFL-CIO is to promote the cause of unionism.

The organizational structure chart of the AFL-CIO (Exhibit 10–9) depicts its various functions. The AFL-CIO has state and central bodies in all states and Puerto Rico that promote and represent labor's statewide interests on legislative matters. Local chapters of different national and international unions make up local central bodies. They deal with civic, community, and other local matters of mutual interest.

The six Trade and Industrial Departments are separate organizations within the AFL-CIO. Their purpose is to promote the interests of specific groups of workers who are in different unions but have common interests.

The convention of delegates from national and international unions that meets every two years makes the policies. Between convention meetings, the Executive Council serves as the governing body for the AFL-CIO. The executive officers conduct the business of the federation. The president appoints standing committees to deal with specific subjects. The General Board considers policy questions referred to it by the officers or the Executive Council.

In 1952, George Meany was elected president of the AFL and served continuously until his retirement in 1979. Shortly before he died at age 85, Meany saw his close coworker and the Secretary-Treasurer of the AFL, Lane Kirkland, succeed him as president. Under Meany's leadership, the AFL developed into a unified political, economic, and social force when it and the CIO merged in 1955. Kirkland has indicated he will be guided by the principles and policies set down by George Meany. In 1981, the UAW was reaffiliated with the AFL-CIO.

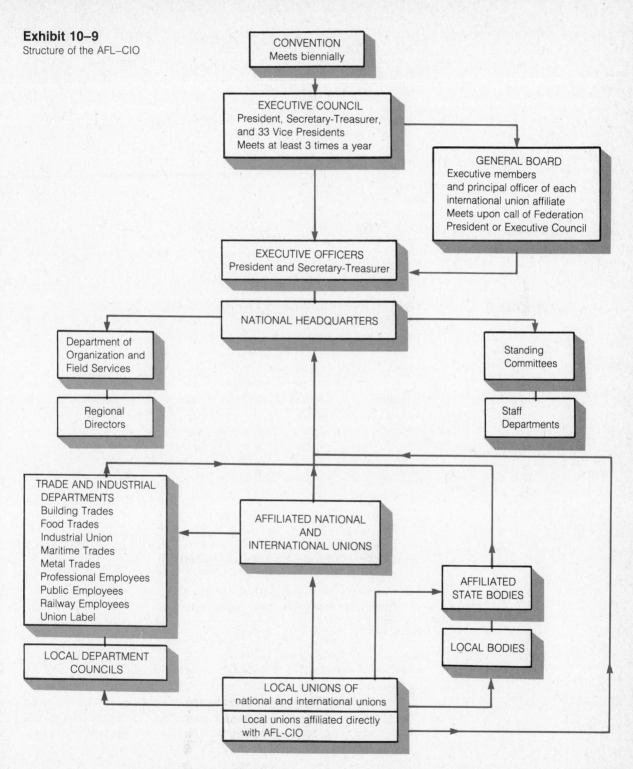

Exhibit 10–9
Structure of the AFL–CIO

CONVENTION
Meets biennially

EXECUTIVE COUNCIL
President, Secretary-Treasurer,
and 33 Vice Presidents
Meets at least 3 times a year

GENERAL BOARD
Executive members
and principal officer of each
international union affiliate
Meets upon call of Federation
President or Executive Council

EXECUTIVE OFFICERS
President and Secretary-Treasurer

NATIONAL HEADQUARTERS

Department of
Organization and
Field Services

Regional
Directors

Standing
Committees

Staff
Departments

TRADE AND INDUSTRIAL
DEPARTMENTS
Building Trades
Food Trades
Industrial Union
Maritime Trades
Metal Trades
Professional Employees
Public Employees
Railway Employees
Union Label

AFFILIATED NATIONAL
AND
INTERNATIONAL UNIONS

AFFILIATED
STATE BODIES

LOCAL BODIES

LOCAL DEPARTMENT
COUNCILS

LOCAL UNIONS OF
national and international unions

Local unions affiliated directly
with AFL-CIO

Human Resource Management and Labor Unions

Careers in human resource or personnel management and in labor unions afford many challenges. Selected career opportunities and their expected growth as well as some of the many opportunities available are listed below.

Occupation	Number Currently Employed	Number of Openings for Each Year to 1990
Personnel and labor relations workers	405,000	17,000
School counselors	45,000	1,700
Employment counselors	7,000	650
Rehabilitation counselors	19,000	2,100
College career planning and placement counselors	4,100	250

SOURCE: U.S. Department of Labor, *Occupational Outlook Handbook*, 1980–81.

HUMAN RESOURCE (PERSONNEL) MANAGER Plans and carries out company policies relating to all phases of personnel activities: recruitment, selection, training, negotiations with labor unions, and maintenance of personnel records of employees.

EMPLOYMENT MANAGER Supervises recruiting, interviewing, employing, and orienting new employees. May counsel employees.

INDUSTRIAL RELATIONS DIRECTOR Organizes, directs, and coordinates industrial relations activities of a firm, including collecting and analyzing data on problems of absenteeism, labor turnover, and employment of women and physically handicapped workers. Helps develop company policies on layoffs, employee evaluation, and manpower policies.

HUMAN RESOURCES (EMPLOYEE) RELATIONS TRAINING DIRECTOR Organizes, administers, and conducts training and educational programs for the purpose of employee development; organizes lectures, training manuals, visual aids, and other training techniques and aids. Coordinates training courses with programs offered in schools and universities.

SAFETY DIRECTOR Plans and administers safety programs. Activities include training programs in areas of safety procedure, such as accident prevention, fire prevention, and health habits.

EMPLOYMENT COUNSELOR Assists individuals in developing and planning career goals. Helps individuals recognize how to make progress in their chosen careers.

SALARY AND WAGE ADMINISTRATOR Establishes and administers wage-evaluation system in industrial organizations. Evaluates jobs in order to determine fair wages and salaries for employees. Studies government wage regulations and agreements with labor unions to establish fair wages and salaries.

PERSONNEL CLERK SUPERVISOR Supervises and coordinates activities of workers who compile and maintain personnel records.

JOB ANALYST Collects and analyzes detailed information on jobs, job qualifications, and worker characteristics in order to prepare job descriptions.

PERSONNEL RECRUITER Travels to colleges and other locations in search of promising job applicants. Interviews applicants and selects and recommends those who appear qualified to fill vacancies.

WAGE ADMINISTRATOR Establishes and maintains pay system.

TRAINING SPECIALIST Supervises or conducts training sessions, prepares manuals and other materials for training courses, and looks for new methods of training.

LABOR RELATIONS SPECIALIST Advises management on all aspects of union-management relations.

LABOR UNION CAREERS These positions involve managing functions of labor unions, such as relations of unions with employees, promoting membership of unions, placing union members in jobs, negotiating with management on hours, wages, and grievances.

Business Agent	Union Representative
Labor-Relations Agent	Executive Secretary
Union Organizer	Union Field Worker
Union-Labor Representative	

Matthew Sauer began working as a clerk and assistant manager in a 7-Eleven store on a part-time basis while in high school. After high school and after fulfilling his military obligation, he returned to work for his former manager at the 7-Eleven store, continuing his formal education through the University of Virginia's Extension Division. He says that his part-time work was very valuable in helping him make a smooth transition to full-time employment with 7-Eleven.

Matthew has advanced steadily in the Southland Corporation, the parent company of 7-Eleven. At the age of twenty-one, he became a store manager. He was soon promoted to auditor and shortly thereafter to store supervisor, overseeing nine stores. He was then promoted to division personnel manager, in charge of the personnel function for approximately 75 management, 100 office and clerical, and 2,000 store employees. Two years later, he advanced to the position of operations personnel manager.

Most recently, he has been promoted to the position of stores personnel manager. In this position, Matthew has the responsibility of personnel administration for Southland's 6,500 stores, the office and clerical staff, and all the managers necessary to supervise these stores. Four operations personnel managers report directly to Matthew.

The most gratifying aspect of Matthew's managerial position is helping people grow and become professional in their careers. He thinks that the toughest part of being a manager is delegating authority and giving people the freedom to make mistakes—a risk that is necessary if they are to learn and grow.

Matthew has set two career goals for himself: (1) to help develop great personnel managers, in order to keep up with Southland's needs, and (2) to always do the very best for the corporation by keeping an open, flexible mind and by learning new things each day from those he meets.

Karen Kraft began her career in management as a part-time retail clerk while attending college, which provided her with very valuable experience.

After graduation from Orange Coast College, she applied for an Executive Training Program with the May Company. As she stated, "It was a challenge to see if an eighteen-year-old junior college graduate could get a job normally requiring a B.A. and an older applicant (twenty-one or over)." She was hired and after three years with the May Company, she joined Petrie Stores as a store manager.

Karen recognizes many gratifying aspects of her job. Specifically, she states, "The real challenge can be in the people you deal with (employees, buyers, customers)."

Karen feels that her Introduction to Business course was very helpful. To her, it was the beginning of an "eye-opening" experience into the vast world of business—how it touches our lives and provides numerous opportunities for careers.

Karen's Introduction to Business instructor was Robert Mitchell of Orange Coast College.

The Marketing Environment

11

The Marketing Process and Physical Distribution

LEARNING GOALS

After reading this chapter, you will understand:

1. The meaning of the marketing process.

2. The marketing concept.

3. The eight functions of marketing.

4. The meaning of term *utility*.

5. The difference between market segmentation and marketing mix.

6. The four stages of the product life cycle.

7. Pricing policies and pricing strategies used by business firms.

8. The distinction between national and private brands of goods and services and what a generic product is.

9. The importance of physical distribution in our economy.

10. The four factors that managers should evaluate when selecting a physical distribution system.

KEY TERMS

Marketing process	Product life cycle	Manufacturer's brand
Marketing concept	Price	Distributor's brand
Marketing functions	Demand curve	Generic products
Physical distribution	Supply curve	Class rate
Marketing research	Equilibrium price	Commodity rate
Utility	Elastic demand	Common carrier
Market segment	Inelastic demand	Contract carrier
Marketing mix	Brand	Private carrier

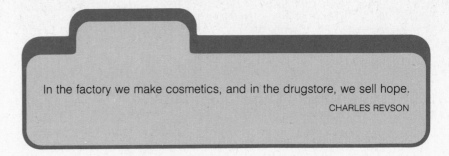

In the factory we make cosmetics, and in the drugstore, we sell hope.

CHARLES REVSON

Marketing managers are charged with the significant responsibility of making the management decisions that chart the direction of the firm's marketing strategy. Their functions are to plan the marketing strategy, to provide the guidance for implementing the strategy into action, and to evaluate the success of the strategy in such critical areas as satisfaction of customer wants and needs and earning a fair profit for the firm. There is no common understanding of the term *marketing*. For example, some use marketing to describe a specific marketplace, such as the stockmarket. However, marketing managers consider marketing as a process. For the marketing managers, the **marketing process** is the "performance of business activities that directs the flow of goods or services from producer to consumers or users"[1] to satisfy their wants and needs.

Goods are classed as either durable or nondurable. Durable goods last for a relatively long time, even though they may be used repeatedly. Examples are autos, furniture, and appliances. Nondurable goods are used up in one or a limited number of uses. Examples of nondurable goods are food, gasoline, and medical drugs. *Services* are activities that are offered for sale, such as the services provided by plumbers and electricians.

MARKETING CONCEPT

Marketing has evolved through three stages. The first stage, which lasted from the Industrial Revolution until the 1930s, was production oriented. Production managers and engineers set company plans. Mass production of goods at low per-unit costs was emphasized. At this stage, companies had sales departments, but usually all other marketing activities, such as advertising or market research, were set up as separate departments. Salespeople were hired to sell the output.

In the second stage, the sales stage, emphasis was placed on selling the output. In this stage, mass producing goods was not enough. Efforts had to be directed toward selling the goods. This stage, which placed marketing activities (research, advertising) in one department under a sales manager, extended from the 1930s into the 1950s.

In the third, or modern, stage, emphasis is focused on the marketing concept. The **marketing concept** states that a firm should have as its

---

[1]Committee on Definitions, *Marketing Definitions* (Chicago: American Marketing Association, 1960), p. 15.

"THOSE HONEST ADS OF OURS
DON'T EXACTLY HELP."

basic objective the satisfaction of consumer wants. In order to accomplish this objective, marketing managers try to identify what consumers want and then produce the goods that will satisfy these wants. Marketing managers then evaluate how successful the firm is in satisfying consumers while at the same time earning a fair profit for the firm.

In marketing goods and services, companies today emphasize their social responsibility role. That is, companies strive to fulfill the social responsibility obligation to society, not just to special interest groups.

MARKETING FUNCTIONS OF THE MARKETING PROCESS

For goods to move from producer to consumer, marketing managers must see that certain **marketing functions** are performed. Eight marketing functions that make up the generally accepted activities needed to complete the marketing process include:

1. Selling	5. Risk bearing
2. Buying	6. Standardization and grading
3. Physical distribution	7. Financing
4. Storage	8. Market information

Selling

The selling function is not solely concerned with making sales. Selling also involves locating and identifying buyers, making buyers aware of goods through advertising and sales promotion techniques, and offering advice and service to the purchasers. Chapter 12 discusses the selling function.

Buying

The buying function involves both the marketing manager and the customer. The marketing manager must have knowledge about customers so that their demands and buying patterns can be predicted. For the consumer, the buying function includes a consideration of price, quality, quantity, kind, and style of goods, as well as selection of the retail store from which to buy.

Physical Distribution

Goods are usually produced far from the marketplace. The physical distribution function fulfills the need to move goods from where they are produced to where they are sold. Physical distribution is discussed in more detail later in this chapter.

Storage

Manufacturers produce goods for consumers. Some products are produced only seasonally but are purchased by consumers throughout the year. The storage function is for the convenience of the consumer because it allows goods to be available when consumers want them.

Risk Bearing

Keeping large stocks of merchandise in inventory involves some risk. Demand for goods may decline because of a change in fashions; goods may be lost through fire or flood; or they may be stolen. Some customers may fail to pay for merchandise and put the seller in a financial squeeze to meet bills. A discussion of some of the methods for dealing with risk is presented in chapter 17.

Standardization and Grading

With thousands of products available today, the consumer could become hopelessly confused when attempting to compare them unless there was some basis for comparison. Thus, standardization and grading are essential marketing functions. Standardization establishes the specifications of a manufactured product, such as the size or quality of clothing. Goods that cannot be produced of a single size, weight, or color, such as fruit, grain, eggs, or cotton, are graded or sorted into classes on the basis of quality.

Financing

Financing plays an integral role in the distribution of goods and services. Buying on credit from suppliers enables a company to acquire merchandise for sale to its customers. Likewise, the company may extend credit to its customers as well, such as the thirty-day open charge accounts available to customers of a retail store. More is said about this in chapter 15.

Market Information

The marketing concept states that a major objective of the business firm is to produce goods and services that satisfy the wants and needs of society and thus earn a profit. Managers of firms must constantly seek data about their specific market: size, location, type of customers, shifts in consumer demands, knowledge of competitors, and general economic trends in the country. The gathering of this market information is marketing research. Managers analyze and interpret the findings of consumer research and attempt to make projections of future market conditions based on these data. Studying buying patterns and analyzing the trends in personal consumption expenditures can serve as a useful guide to future product planning (see Exhibit 11–1).

ECONOMIC UTILITY AND THE MARKETING PROCESS

In the economic sense, utility refers to the power that goods or services have to satisfy a human want. There are four types of utility: form, possession, place, and time. Form utility is produced when raw

Exhibit 11–1

How consumers spend $100 on average after savings and paying taxes.
(SOURCE: U.S. Bureau of Economic Analysis.)

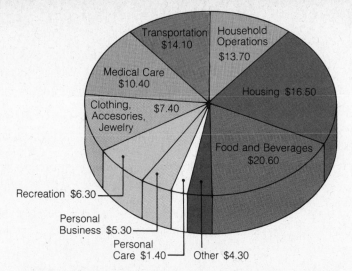

materials are extracted from nature and their structure or shape is changed so that they satisfy a human want. For example, wheat is ground into flour by the miller, and then the flour is converted into bread by a bakery. Form utility is a production utility. The other three types of utilities are included in the marketing process. If goods or services are to satisfy individuals, they must be in their possession (possession utility). For this to happen, goods and services must be moved from the place where they have limited usefulness to the location where they have maximum usefulness in fulfilling consumer wants (place utility). Furthermore, if goods (or services) are to be of value to the final consumers, they must be available when they are demanded (time utility). For example, an appliance dealer stocks more air-conditioning units during the spring and summer months, when demand is greatest.

MARKET SEGMENTATION AND MARKETING MIX

Marketing managers in large and small businesses must develop a marketing strategy to move goods from where they are produced to final consumers or users of goods. A marketing strategy consists of two parts. First, marketing managers must identify the **market segment** that is the target group of customers to whom the firm wishes to appeal. For example, the consumer market may be segmented on the basis of sex, age, race, income level, geography, level of education attained, or occupation. Second, a decision must be made regarding the **marketing mix**. The marketing mix, which consists of the marketing strategy that will be followed to satisfy the wants and desires of the customers identified in the market segment, involves decision making in four areas: product, price, distribution, and promotion.

Product

Marketing managers plan and develop the right products or services in terms of quality, packaging, branding, and design for the market segment. This planning includes determining the product line and the product mix of the firm. The product line is a broad group of products that are reasonably similar, such as wearing apparel. Product mix is the total list of products sold by the company.

Price

Marketing managers determine a competitive, fair price for goods. The price must earn a fair profit for the company.

Distribution

Marketing managers make their product or service available to customers by distributing goods through channels of distribution.

Promotion

Marketing managers inform customers about their product by means of such marketing functions as personal selling and advertising. Promotional strategy is discussed in chapter 13.

Marketing Strategy

When marketing managers plan the marketing strategy for their firms, they should give equal weight to each activity. Each of the factors is equally important, and they are also interdependent. The result of an effective marketing strategy will be customers whose needs and wants are satisfied and a fair profit earned by the firm.

PRODUCT LIFE CYCLE

Marketing managers must be aware that products have life cycles. This knowledge is significant for guiding marketing decisions in product planning. The **product life cycle** shown in Exhibit 11–2 has four stages:

1. Introduction—the product is brought into the market; sales are slow as demand is developed and the production is improved technically.
2. Growth—the product catches on; sales rise rapidly and the total market expands.
3. Maturity—growth in sales volume levels off; competitors enter the market; many sales are of the replacement type.
4. Decline—sales fall off as new products enter the market, consumers' tastes change, etc.[2]

At each stage of the product life cycle, a different element of the marketing mix may be stressed. For example, in the introductory stage, promotion (advertising or free samples) may be emphasized to attract customers. The growth stage may emphasize mass distribution to capture as large a share of the market as possible. In the maturity stage, some form of product differentiation may prove effective, such as a new package. Price cutting may be effective for halting or slowing down a sales decline.[3]

---

[2]Ben Enis, *Marketing Principles,* 3d ed. (Santa Monica, Calif.: Goodyear Publishing Company, 1980), p. 334.

[3]Ibid.

Exhibit 11–2

The product life cycle concept.

(SOURCE: From *Marketing Principles*, 3rd Edition by Ben M. Enis. Copyright © 1980 by Scott, Foresman and Company.)

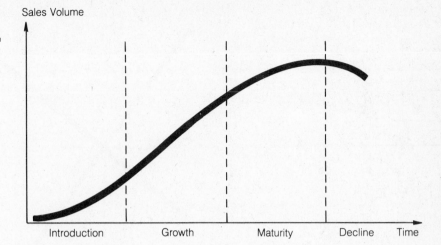

PRICING

One basic element of the marketing mix is pricing. A **price** for a product or service refers to the amount of money needed to acquire that product or service. In a competitive business environment, marketing managers strive to establish pricing policies for goods or services to meet several objectives: (1) to enable the firm to earn a fair profit based on a certain percentage of net sales or investment, (2) to meet or stay ahead of competition, (3) to maintain or increase the firm's share of the market, and (4) to stabilize its prices.

Economic theory assumes that a firm will set prices that will maximize profits. To achieve this goal, prices will be set where the quantity of a product demanded at a certain price is equal to the quantity that suppliers are willing to supply at that price. This demand and supply relationship is shown by demand and supply curves. The **demand curve** shows the amount of a product demanded at different prices. The **supply curve** shows the quantity of a good offered for sale at various prices. The point at which the quantity demanded is equal to the quantity supplied is called the **equilibrium price** (see Exhibit 11–3).

Demand for goods is described as **elastic** or **inelastic.** When purchasers will buy more of certain goods as prices decline, the demand for these products is said to be elastic. When increases or decreases in price bring about relatively little change in demand, demand is said to be inelastic. Enis describes elastic and inelastic prices as follows:

> Clearly, therefore, a marketing manager should determine, if possible, whether product demand is elastic or inelastic. In general, elasticity of demand increases as a function of three factors: product substitutes, product uses, and percentage of total purchasing power required to buy the product. The price elasticity of demand for a product with many substitutes—e.g., steel, wheat, television programming—will be greater than demand for a product such as gasoline or salt, which has few substitutes. Secondly, demand for products with many uses, e.g., wood, petroleum, plastics, will be

Exhibit 11–3

Supply and demand are in equilibrium at point *e*, where the price of a dozen apples is 46¢ and the quantity bought and sold is 365 thousand dozens.

(SOURCE: Richard T. Gill, *Economics,* 3d ed. Santa Monica, Calif.: Goodyear Publishing Company, 1978, p. 41.)

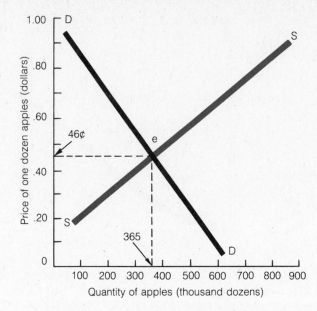

more elastic—sensitive to price changes—than will demand for products such as foodstuffs—which have one primary use. And demand for a product such as a major appliance or an automobile will be more elastic than demand for a product like cigarettes or chewing gum, since the price of the former products would represent a significantly greater proportion of the consumers' total budget.[4]

However, setting prices for the individual firm is a complex activity for marketing managers. They cannot always achieve profit maximization in establishing prices for the firm's goods and services. They have to consider competitors, consumers, economic conditions, and legislation. (Legislation is discussed in chapter 23.) In addition, the federal government may sometimes step in and set price ceilings to control prices. For example, in 1978, voluntary wage and price guidelines were proposed by President Carter to help control the rate of inflation.

Pricing Strategies

A number of pricing strategies may be used by marketing managers to achieve the objectives stated above. For example, when introducing a new product, two strategies might be considered: skim-the-cream pricing and penetration pricing.

Skim-the-Cream Pricing. This strategy sets prices at the highest level at which goods can be sold. It is used when a firm has a unique product that is promoted extensively when it is first introduced. This pricing policy may

---

[4]Ibid., pp. 336–367.

be extended indefinitely or lowered sometime later to capture sales from another market segment.

Penetration Pricing.   Low prices are set to reach a large market immediately. This strategy is effective when goods or services are sensitive to price changes or when the product faces strong competition after it is introduced. McDonald's used this strategy when they introduced their 15¢ hamburger. Their low price enabled them to build up a sales volume and made it difficult for competitors to use the same strategy.

Some other pricing strategies available to marketing managers are discussed below.

Odd Pricing or Psychological Pricing.   This is the practice of pricing goods at odd-ending prices, such as $1.98 or $44.95, rather than the even-ending prices of $2.00 or $45.00. Retailers may use psychological pricing because they believe that consumers may find the slightly lowered price more appealing. They believe consumers may feel the price of a $1.98 item is closer to $1.00 than to $2.00.

One-Price System or Variable-Price System.   In a one-price system, every customer who buys the item is charged the same price. Under a variable pricing system, prices charged for the same quantities may vary among different customers as a result of bargaining with the seller.

Price Lining.   A price-lining policy, commonly found in retailing, consists of choosing a limited number of prices at which merchandise will be sold, such as $9.95, $12.95, and $18.95. Then all related merchandise is marked at these prices. For example, one style of shirt may be sold for $10, another for $12.50, and another for $15.

Leader Pricing.   A policy of leader pricing results in advertising one or a few products at a price below cost to attract customers. The expectation is that consumers will purchase not only the below-cost item but also others. Below-cost items are called loss-leaders. If a loss-leader is going to attract an increased number of shoppers, it should be a product that is purchased frequently, is used by most people, has a regular price that is well known, and does not represent a large cost to the customer.

Follow-the-Market Pricing.   This policy finds prices being set that follow average or usual prices of other firms in the same line of business.

Cost-Plus Pricing.   Prices are set at a level where they will cover the costs of the merchandise plus a percentage to cover all selling costs and provide a profit for the firm. This percentage is called the *markup*. Markup on cost of goods is the amount added to the cost to determine the selling price. For example, if the cost of a product was $5.00 and a retailer

Gillette uses both family brands and individual brands to identify products.

wanted a markup of 30 percent, the markup amount would be $1.50 ($5.00 × 30 percent). The selling price would be $6.50 (cost of $5.00 plus markup amount of $1.50). The seller may figure 15 percent for selling costs, 10 percent for overhead costs, and 5 percent for profit.

PRODUCT IDENTIFICATION: BRANDING

Selling and buying goods and services is made easier by use of product brands. A **brand** is a "name, term, sign, symbol, or design, or a combination of them, which is intended to identify the goods or services of one seller or group of sellers and to differentiate them from those of competitors."[5]

There are basically two kinds of brands. One is the **manufacturer's** or "national brand." A manufacturer owns a national brand, and advertises and sells in all or nearly all sections of the country. Another is the **distributor's** or "private" brand. A distributor (a middleman or a retailer) owns a private brand. Usually, private brands are distributed on a more limited basis, such as locally or regionally. There are some exceptions, however; Sears' "Kenmore" brand is a private brand distributed nationally, as is the "Signature" brand of Montgomery Ward.

By using their own brands, distributors can better control their markets. They can sell products at prices below national brands and can advertise this difference in price comparisons.

Manufacturers of more than one product must decide whether to use the same brand name for all products (called a family brand) or use a different brand for each product (called an individual brand). Such compa-

---

[5]Committee on Definitions, *Marketing Definitions* (Chicago: American Marketing Association, 1960), pp. 9–10.

nies as Del Monte and Heinz use a family brand. When they introduce any new products, they have the advantage of being identified with an already well-known brand name. However, if the new product is a failure, all other products of the family brand might suffer because of brand-name association. Some companies, such as Lever Brothers, Colgate-Palmolive, and Procter & Gamble follow a policy of individual brands under which new products are introduced with their own brand names.

Generic Products

Consumers are increasingly concerned about the rising costs of consumer products. One method of countering rising prices is through the use of generic (or no-name) products. The products are sold without a brand name or fancy labeling and their primary appeal is a lower price than the national and distributor's brand-name products. In food items, these products are just as good nutritionally but have no frills, no promotion, and no advertising.

PHYSICAL DISTRIBUTION

A key reason for America's economic growth has been the development of modern physical distribution systems. Without modern forms of physical distribution, many of the products we enjoy or take for granted would not be available when we want them.

Business firms require efficient physical distribution systems to deliver raw materials to them and to distribute manufactured goods from where they are produced to where they are sold to middlemen or consumers. Thus, physical distribution fulfills both time and place utilities.

ECONOMIC JUSTIFICATION OF PHYSICAL DISTRIBUTION

Physical distribution systems offer two main advantages in the production and distribution of goods. Manufacturers can take advantage of specialization of labor and of geographical location.

Specialization of Labor

Large-scale operations allow manufacturers to use mass-production techniques. By producing in large quantities, manufacturers can use the talents of specialists in the various phases of the manufacturing process. Specialization of labor also helps manufacturers to realize substantial savings in production costs. Large-scale operations that permit specialization are feasible because of modern physical distribution systems. These systems allow manufacturers to expand distribution of goods from a local level to regional, national, and international markets.

Geographical Location

Some sections of the country enjoy particular advantages, such as suitable climate, availability of raw materials, good power supply, or adequate labor supply. As a result, they can grow a particular crop or manufacture a product more efficiently. Physical distribution provides the means by which these crops or goods, produced in one area, can be moved to locations where people can use and enjoy them. Hence, these areas can take advantage of their geographical location and specialize in producing a particular item.

Universal Product Code and the Computerized Checkout

The Universal Product Code (UPC) is an identification system required by the government for all types of packaged products. The UPC is the set of lines of various widths imprinted on everything from paper towels to nonprescription drugs. Each product has its own unique symbol identification, which contains information about the name, manufacturer, and size of the product, but not the price. The numbers printed below the bars identify the manufacturer and the manufacturer's product.

When a consumer buys a product with a UPC symbol, the clerk at the checkout counter merely slides the product over an optical scanner which uses a laser beam to read the UPC code. As many as 10 trillion individual machine-readable numbers can be generated from the UPC symbols. This information is sent immediately to the store's computer, which identifies the customer's purchase. The computer, which is programmed to reflect the current price, registers the price and prints a receipt with the item description and price. In some systems, the computer is programmed to "call out" the product prices by means of a voice computer. This process speeds up customer checkout

time, increases productivity of clerks by as much as 45 percent, and eliminates the need to manually stamp prices on each item on the shelf, thus lowering labor costs. The UPC can also be linked to the computer to function as an automated inventory control system, which will automatically reorder when stocks of UPC items get low.

Those favoring the use of UPC list these advantages:

1. Faster service can be provided at the checkout counter when computers are substituted for cash registers.
2. Consumers can be provided with a more informative receipt.
3. The system will largely eliminate the possibility of human error in price marking and in checking prices.
4. Stores can more efficiently control their inventory.
5. The labor force will not be reduced because new stores will be opened, older stores will be renovated, and some jobs will be upgraded.

However, there has been concern voiced by consumer groups and organized labor over the use of the UPC. Some of their reasons for opposing UPC are:

1. Doing away with item-pricing makes it difficult to compare prices.
2. The labor force of both wholesalers and retailers will be reduced.
3. There is no assurance that savings realized from the efficiencies of the system will be passed on to consumers in the form of lower prices.
4. If prices are not marked on individual items, the consumer may tend to buy too much.
5. If prices are marked only on the shelf, it may be easier for stores to raise food prices in the computer before or without changing them on the shelf labels.

In this example, the "0" indicates a grocery item. The numbers "51000" designate the manufacturer. In this case, it is the Campbell Soup Company. The last five digits, "01261," indicate that the item is a can of cream of mushroom soup. The electronic scanner reads the vertical bars.

FACTORS OF PHYSICAL DISTRIBUTION

Managers study the unique physical distribution requirements of their firm. Then they evaluate the suitability of each of the factors of physical distribution to satisfy their firm's specific distribution requirements. The factors of physical distribution include: (1) speed of delivery, (2) cost of delivery, (3) flexibility of delivery services, and (4) bulk delivery.

Speed of Delivery

In the highly competitive business world, managers often demand a physical distribution system that can provide rapid delivery of merchandise so that the maximum time utility can be added to the product. In some cases, such as with fashion goods or perishable merchandise, speed of delivery may be the most crucial factor in selecting a physical distribution system.

Cost of Delivery

you pay for delivery

Users of physical distribution systems carefully analyze the cost of each system and normally choose the service that meets their needs at the lowest rate. Physical distribution costs are an important consideration because they are included in the price at which goods are sold. Thus, if the physical distribution cost factor is ignored, a product can be priced out of the market.

Flexibility of Delivery Services

A physical distribution system must be flexible so that it can adapt to the special needs of individual shippers. Included among such services would be any special handling of merchandise or special delivery services. A physical distribution system that does not adjust to changing customer requirements fails in its service function. In our rapidly changing world, flexibility is an ever-important criterion for evaluating a physical distribution system.

Bulk Delivery

The ability of a physical distribution system to accommodate bulky cargo is a vital consideration. Where bulky items are being shipped, the user should choose the system designed to move bulky materials.

TYPES OF PHYSICAL DISTRIBUTION SYSTEMS

Let us examine the extent to which different physical distribution systems—waterways, rail, motor, air, and pipeline—satisfy each of the above factors. (See Exhibit 11–4.)

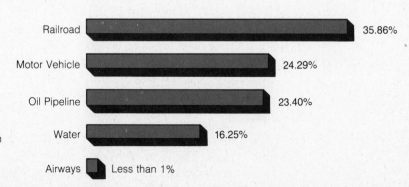

Exhibit 11–4
Percentage of freight moved by various types of physical distribution systems.

(SOURCE: Statistical Abstract of the United States, 1981.)

Railroad — 35.86%
Motor Vehicle — 24.29%
Oil Pipeline — 23.40%
Water — 16.25%
Airways — Less than 1%

Water

Physical distribution by water is the slowest of all the major modes of shipping. However, the cost of shipping freight by water is low. Freight rates for moving goods by water are less than freight rates for the other carriers. The volume of freight moved by water is measured in ton-miles. A ton-mile is the movement of one ton (2,000 pounds) of freight one mile.

Obviously, a major limitation of physical distribution by water is that an area cannot be served unless it has harbor and port facilities. However, this system has some flexibility. For example, the *fishyback system* allows water and motor distribution to be combined. Here, loaded trucks go to ports where they are loaded on barges or ships and delivered to the next port for delivery to their final destination. Another variation of fishyback combines water, truck, and rail transport. Loaded trailer vans drive onto rail flatcars, are delivered to ships, and then are moved to the next port where they are transferred back to railcars for shipment to the final destination. Water distribution is ideally suited for hauling bulky items such as petroleum, fertilizer, and iron ore.

Supertankers and Deepwater Ports.   Today, supertankers are responsible for hauling substantial amounts of oil. Supertankers, which can transport as much cargo as six smaller tankers, require deepwater ports of 100 feet or more depth. Deepwater ports are facilities located many miles offshore that have the single function of unloading crude oil from supertankers; this is pumped through pipes buried in the seabed into storage tanks on shore.

Rail

Physical distribution by rail offers the shipper faster speed of delivery than waterways. Large quantities of freight can be moved over long distances in a comparatively short time.

Low cost is a feature of rail transport. Shippers can take advantage of substantial savings in freight charges if they ship in carload lots (CL) instead of less-than-carload lots (LCL). Carload lots can usually be shipped for about one-half the cost of less-than-carload lots. A carload, one that fills a freight car, can be shipped cheaper because of the economics realized by shipping a full car rather than a partially filled car. Whether a product falls into a **class rate** or a **commodity rate** determines the cost of shipping.

Class Rates.   Class rates try to simplify the problem of determining shipping rates for over 10,000 manufactured items. Those products that are grouped into the same class are charged the same rate. The value of the product, similarity of size, weight, perishability, or special handling requirements determine a product's class.

Commodity Rates.   Shippers of bulky, low-value freight such as coal, cement, brick, steel, sand, gravel, and grain are charged commodity rates. These rates were devised so that a specific rate on a specific quantity could be charged. These charges usually pertain to shipments between certain points or over specific routes. Commodity rates often develop from negotiation between shippers and railroads. Consequently, there is a commodity rate for many bulky items shipped frequently in large volume.

Railroads have increased the flexibility of their services in order to remain competitive with other distribution systems. While most freight is hauled in box cars, special cars and services have been developed.

Rail systems provide for the economical movement of bulk items. Approximately as much freight is moved by rail as by all other carriers combined.

Motor

A chief advantage of truck lines is their capability to move goods rapidly across the country. Trucks account for almost all the deliveries of wholesale and retail goods within towns and cities.

Truck lines move goods at a relatively low cost. Over shorter distances, trucks can move goods more cheaply since they handle the complete hauling operation. Truck lines, like railroads, provide lower rates for truckload lots (TL) than for less-than-truckload lots (LTL). Truckload rates are up to 50 percent less than LTL rates.

Another distinct advantage of trucking service is its flexibility. Trucks are not restricted to waterways or railroad roadbeds but can travel and deliver almost anywhere. This flexibility also extends to special services trucklines can provide for shippers, such as various kinds of special trucks: tanker trucks, refrigerated trucks, and dump trucks.

In the *piggyback system,* trailers are loaded, sealed, and placed for shipment on railroad flat cars. When they reach their destination, they are removed from the flat cars, picked up by the tractor trucks, and delivered to their final destination. Trucks and water transport also coordinate their efforts in the fishyback operation.

A modification of the piggyback concept is a trailer with rubber tires and flanged wheels that runs on both the highway and the rails.

Containerization. This is a method that truck, rail, and water transport systems use to make their operations more efficient. *Containerization* means a number of smaller packages are placed inside larger containers, 20-foot to 40-foot containers weighing up to 40 tons, which are sealed at the shipping point and remain unopened until they reach the final destination. The piggyback operation is a special kind of containerization. This shipping method has reduced packing costs, damage and theft losses, and costs and time of loading and unloading. Nearly everything that can be placed in a container is shipped in this manner. Bulk cargo, liquid cargo in tanks, and temperature-controlled cargo, both refrigerated and heated, are shipped in specially designed containers.

Trucklines are also well suited for hauling bulky items. Heavy and bulky machinery, pipe, oil-field equipment, furniture, and building materials can be handled efficiently by trucklines.

Ocean shippers and railroads cooperate on the landbridge concept. Railroads serve as a link in the trade between Europe and the Orient. Containers are unloaded at one coast, loaded into trains, and shipped across the continent for loading on ships on the other coast.

Container shipping in Boston.

Air

MOST EXPENSIVE BUT FASTEST

Regularly scheduled cargo shipments by air began more than fifty years ago when Ford Motor Company used air transportation to supply parts for production lines. However, as carriers of freight, airlines carry less than 1 percent of all intercity freight. The primary advantage offered by air carriers is the speed with which delivery to distant markets can be made. Products can be delivered to another city the morning after a shipment is made. Air transportation includes air express and air freight. Air express is door-to-door shipment, which includes pickup and delivery services. Air freight refers to shipment from one air terminal to another.

Items suited to air transport are normally lightweight. Bulky items usually are not moved by air except when the situation demands it. Moving freight by air is more expensive than any of the modes of surface freight, and the major disadvantage of shipping by air is its high cost. At times, the high cost of delivery by air can be justified on the basis of need for fast delivery. For example, time-sensitive items such as auto parts, newspapers, magazines, cut flowers, and fresh fruit and vegetables are the main cargo hauled by airlines, but air cargo can accommodate live cargo, i.e., animals. Airlines are also active in the overnight delivery of packages weighing less than seventy pounds.

Specialized services are limited, since the volume of freight hauled is small. However, by working with other modes of transportation, air cargo carriers can serve areas without airport facilities by delivering an item to a major city and having the item picked up and rushed to the nearby town. Airlines have designed a special twenty-foot intermodal container to allow fast interchange of air cargo with trucks and ships.

Evaluation of Physical Distribution Systems

Physical distribution managers must evaluate the various types of distribution systems according to the importance of each factor discussed. Exhibit 11–5 summarizes the relative advantages of each of the four basic types of physical distribution systems according to these factors.

Pipelines

The volume of freight moved by pipeline has been increasing steadily. Some 24 percent of intercity freight is moved in over 200,000 miles of oil pipelines. Speed is not a primary consideration in pipeline physical distribution systems, and, obviously, once the lines are laid, they are inflexible. However, once the lines have been laid, it is possible to move liquid or gaseous products economically. One of the best known carriers of natural gas is the Big Inch pipeline, which extends 1,500 miles, carrying gas from Texas to New York. Pipelines now also move slurrified solids, such as coal. In the future, it is anticipated that dry, solid cargo will be moved through pipelines.

BASIC FORMS OF CARRIERS

Carriers use the following three legal classifications: (1) common carrier, (2) contract carrier, and (3) private carrier.

Common Carrier

The common carrier offers its services to the general public and is covered by various state and federal regulations. Familiar examples of common carriers are buslines, airlines, railroads, and freight trucklines. They must accept shipments from anyone who desires to use their services, charge the same standard rate to all customers, and maintain regularly scheduled service. Since they are highly regulated, they are limited in coping with specialized transportation needs of customers. They must usually have governmental approval to change rates, to offer a new service, or to stop service to a given area.

Contract Carrier

The contract carrier company offers its services to move an individual's goods, and thus has considerable flexibility in coping with individual situations. Contract carriers have fewer government regulations than common carriers. Hence, rates may vary widely depending on the special circumstances involved. Furthermore, contract carriers do not have to maintain

Exhibit 11–5

The relative advantages of physical distribution systems.

Factors of Physical Distribution	Water	Rail	Motor	Air
Speed of delivery	Poor	Fair	Good	Excellent
Cost of delivery services	Excellent	Good	Fair	Poor
Delivery flexibility	Poor	Good	Excellent	Fair
Bulk capabilities	Excellent	Good	Fair	Poor

regular schedules. Personalized service can be offered to a shipper by contract carriers. Examples of contract carriers are chartered airplanes, buses, and trucks.

Private Carrier

Companies using their own physical distribution systems to move their goods and make their deliveries are **private carriers.** For example, a bakery may operate its own fleet of trucks to deliver products to retail outlets. The private carrier is usually regulated only by local and state governments because its operations often are small and do not cross state boundary lines. This type of service is economical where there is a high degree of use of the physical distribution equipment or when very specialized distribution services are required.

SUMMARY OF KEY POINTS

1. The marketing process is the performance of business activities that directs the flow of goods or services from producer to consumer or user to satisfy their needs and wants.

2. The guiding principle of the marketing concept is that the basic objective of the firm is to satisfy consumer wants and needs.

3. The eight functions of marketing are selling, buying, physical distribution, storage, risk bearing, standardization and grading, financing, and market research.

4. *Utility* refers to the power of a good or service to satisfy a human want.

5. Marketing strategy consists of (1) identifying the market segment, and (2) determining the market mix, which includes product, price, distribution, and promotion.

6. The product life cycle consists of four stages: introduction, growth, maturity, and decline.

7. Firms employ different pricing strategies when marketing their products and services.

8. Product and service identification is aided by the use of brands. "Generic" products are products with no brand identification.

9. Physical distribution fulfills two main objectives: (1) specialization of labor and (2) geographical location.

10. The four factors of physical distribution are speed of delivery, cost of delivery, flexibility, and the ability to handle bulk merchandise.

11. Types of physical distribution systems are water, rail, motor, air, and pipeline.

12. Basic forms of carriers are common, contract, and private.

DISCUSSION QUESTIONS

1. How would a marketing manager explain the term *marketing?*
2. Explain the significance of the *marketing concept.*
3. Distinguish between market segmentation and marketing mix.
4. Identify the four stages of the product life cycle.
5. Explain the difference between elastic and inelastic demand for goods.
6. Suggest two pricing strategies particularly suited for introducing new products.
7. Distinguish between a national brand and a private brand and between an individual brand and a family brand.
8. What are the advantages of using physical distribution systems?
9. What factors should be analyzed by users of physical distribution systems before deciding on the appropriate system?
10. Under what conditions would a marketing manager use an airline service to move freight?

STUDENT PROJECTS

1. In a local supermarket, make a list of four national brands. Determine whether the store stocks any private brands. Are generic products stocked? If so, what type?
2. List three or four items that you would classify as products that have elastic demand and three or four that you would classify as having inelastic demand.
3. Prepare a short report on one physical distribution system that services your area. What are its characteristics, what are its uses, and what future changes are predicted for this system?

CASE A

Wal-Mart Stores

Wal-Mart currently operates a chain of over 300 discount retail stores in 11 southern and midwestern states. The firm has plans for adding some 400 outlets and expanding operations into four additional states. A typical store is stocked with over 30,000 items, and prices of brand-name merchandise are from 7 to 8 percent below prices charged by competitors. The ability to charge lower prices is related to a number of factors: Wal-Mart's philosophy of placing most of its stores in small towns where operating expenses are lower; high-volume buying from manufacturers; and a computer system that links individual stores to the firm's major warehouses.

   Wal-Mart uses its own fleet of trucks to transport merchandise and builds most of its own stores. Employees participate in a generous profit-sharing plan and clerks receive bonuses for progress they make in keeping down losses due to theft and damaged merchandise.

SOURCE: *U.S. News & World Report,* July 20, 1981, p. 73.

Questions

1. Discuss the marketing strategy of Wal-Mart.
2. Identify the market segment for Wal-Mart.
3. Explain how the marketing concept relates to Wal-Mart.
4. What type of carrier does the firm use to ship merchandise?

Rags to Riches

From its beginning four years ago, Rags to Riches has been a success. Rags to Riches is a unique ladies clothing store. In it, customers can find the finest merchandise at reasonable prices. The merchandise carried includes better and designer ladies' clothing, including dresses, sportswear, separate accessories, handbags, belts, and almost everything for the better-dressed woman. The store owners stock only high-quality, new merchandise at lower prices than other stores carrying the same merchandise. No second-quality merchandise is stocked.

The store owners go to New York where they select the merchandise that will ensure the quality they wish to sell in their store. Their purchases are made directly from New York manufacturers.

They also purchase merchandise later in the season, when manufacturers are willing to sell to them for less. They pass these savings on to the customers. Customers can save about one-third on all their purchases. As the store owners emphasize, they discount price, not quality.

Questions

1. Explain how the marketing concept applies to Rags to Riches.
2. What factors are they considering in their pricing policy?
3. What is their market segment?
4. How is the product life cycle related to the merchandise carried in Rags to Riches?

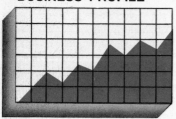

BUSINESS PROFILE

Levi Strauss & Co.

Levi Strauss came to America from Germany when he was fourteen years old. For a time he lived in Louisville, Kentucky, until stories of gold in California stirred his interest. Levi traveled to New York to consult with his brothers, Jonas and Louis, who ran a merchandise business. They encouraged Levi to go to California and set up a business selling supplies to miners.

Levi sailed to San Francisco, taking with him silk, broadcloth, fine dress goods, and canvas for Conestoga wagons and tents. By the time he reached San Francisco, he had sold all his supplies except the canvas. Levi soon met with a miner who told him he should have brought pants with him because "Pants don't wear worth a hoot up in the diggin's and you can't get a pair strong enough to last no time."

These turn of the century miners at the Last Chance Mine in the California Gold Country are wearing Levi's jeans, whose rugged dependability has become as much a part of Western lore as the men who wore them.

With this idea, Levi decided to make pants rather than tents from canvas. He hired a tailor to make the garments, and they became so popular for their strength that miners soon were asking for "those pants of Levi's."

Capitalizing on his success, Levi had more pants made, and in 1853 formed a partnership with his brothers to establish Levi Strauss & Company. Soon he switched from using canvas and began making Levi's from heavy-weight denim made to his specifications. A special indigo dye was developed for the fabric, which resulted in blue jeans.

A tailor, Jacob Davis, added copper rivets to the pockets of the miners' pants to keep them from tearing when bearing heavy tools. He later told Levi Strauss about his work. Levi thought that it was such a good idea that he started using it on his own pants. In 1873, he had the idea patented. Levi's pants have remained basically the same ever since.

Until 1946, Levi Strauss & Company operated primarily as a wholesaler and jeans manufacturer. At the end of World War II, three-fourths of its business was in wholesaling. At that time, the company changed directions: it dropped its wholesaling operations and began manufacturing pants under its own label. Today, Levi's products are manufactured in fifty-eight company-owned or controlled plants in the United States and in facilities in thirteen foreign countries. In 1946, Levi's had sales of just under $10 million. Today, Levi's products are sold in over fifty countries by more than 30,000 retailers, with sales of nearly $3 billion annually.

New markets for Levi's have opened in Communist countries. Executives from Levi's signed a licensing agreement with government officials in Hungary in 1977 to sell Levi's in their country. Other potential markets are Russia and China. In fact, Levi's jeans are so popular in Russia that they have been sold on the black market for as much as $140 a pair.

The company has also diversified its product lines. While Levi Strauss & Co. focuses its attention on pants, and is the world's largest maker of pants, it now produces jackets, skirts, shirts, and belts. The firm has over 20,000 employees. The divisions of Levi Strauss are Levi's Youthwear, Levi's Jeanswear, Levi's Womenswear, Levi's Sportswear (incorporating Activewear), and Levi Strauss International. The firm acquired Miller Belts, featuring leather and synthetic belts. The name of Miller Belts has been changed to Levi's Accessories. In 1964, the company introduced permanent press to men's wear, the Levi's Sta-Prest Slacks. They have also introduced Levi's for Feet, shoes and sandals in leather, denim, and suede. They are produced by Brown Shoe Company of St. Louis under a licensing agreement with Levi Strauss. The company has moved into the fashion jean market also. The newly created Activewear division eventually will produce such things as ski overalls, down parkas, vests, and outshirts. The firm plans to branch out into warm-up suits and jogging and tennis outfits. Some predict the firm will eventually diversify into producing sports equipment.

Levi's Market Planning Department conducts research to find out who buys pants and what are the per capita pants ownership and style preferences by regions in the country. Levi's continues to go after the youth market while keeping customers as they grow older.

12 Retailing and Wholesaling, Channels of Distribution, and Consumer Behavior

LEARNING GOALS

After reading this chapter, you will understand:

1. The differences between a retailer and a wholesaler and a retail sale and a wholesale sale.

2. The various kinds of instore and nonstore retailers.

3. The different ways of classifying retail ownership.

4. What a cooperative is.

5. The different kinds of wholesalers.

6. The channels of distribution for consumer and industrial goods.

7. The differences between the kinds of consumer goods.

8. The purchase decision process.

9. The reasons why consumers prefer shopping in one store instead of another.

KEY TERMS

Channel of distribution
Middleman
Retailer
Wholesaler
Scrambled
  merchandising
Chain store
Corporate chain
Voluntary chain

Cooperatives
Agents
Brokers
Consumer goods
Industrial goods
Consumer behavior
Demographic research
Motivation research

Convenience goods
Shopping goods
Specialty goods
Primary buying motives
Selective buying motives
Rational buying motives
Emotional buying motives
Patronage motives

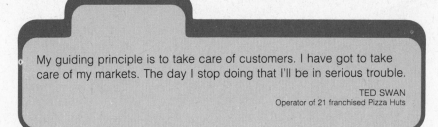

My guiding principle is to take care of customers. I have got to take care of my markets. The day I stop doing that I'll be in serious trouble.

TED SWAN
Operator of 21 franchised Pizza Huts

Only a small percentage of all goods and services is distributed directly to final users by manufacturers. Instead, the distribution of goods and services is facilitated by the marketing institutions of retailing and wholesaling. Retailers and wholesalers are middlemen who play an integral role in the marketing **channel of distribution** (the route that goods and services follow to the final user of the product or service). A **middleman** is the intermediate agent (individual or business firm) who performs the marketing functions in the channel of distribution between the manufacturer and ultimate consumer. A **retailer** is an intermediary who sells to the final consumer for personal or household consumption. A **wholesaler** is an intermediary who sells products and services to retailers, to other wholesalers, and to industrial and commercial users. We will discuss each of these marketing institutions in the following sections.

RETAILING

The street vendor selling fresh-cut flowers at a busy intersection, who has annual sales of a few hundred dollars, and Sears and Penney's, with sales of billions of dollars annually, represent the two ends of the broad spectrum of retailing. Although most consumers make their purchases in stores, there are some significant nonstore retailing methods. Various kinds of instore and nonstore retailing are highlighted in our discussion.

General Store

A general merchandise store usually stocks a limited selection of a wide range of merchandise, such as groceries, hardware, dry goods, and clothing. Today, general stores are few in number and are found in such places as rural communities or beach or mountain resort areas.

Single-Line Store

Single-line stores stock a wide variety of one line of related merchandise. Typical single-line establishments are furniture, sporting goods, and hardware stores.

Specialty Store

Specialty stores concentrate their offerings on a limited variety of merchandise but offer an extensive assortment of the goods that are stocked. Examples of specialty stores are tobacco shops, bakeries, and meat markets.

Department Store

A department store is a collection of specialty stores under one roof. In department stores, shoppers find large assortments of goods, and these stores offer numerous services to their customers. Some of the major department stores are Macy's, New York; Broadway, Los Angeles; Marshall Field, Chicago; and Bambergers, New Jersey.

Variety Store

Variety stores stock a wide range of relatively inexpensive goods for the household, such as small appliances, dry goods, stationery, and notions. Well-known national variety stores are S. H. Kress, F. W. Woolworth, and S. S. Kresge.

Supermarket

The present-day supermarket is a product of the depression of the 1930s in the United States. The supermarket was initially designed to appeal to people with limited incomes by offering limited services and low-priced merchandise to customers in an atmosphere with few comforts. An innovation of the supermarket was the concept of self-service. The basic philosophy of the earliest supermarket was to sell a high volume of fast-moving merchandise, primarily grocery items, at low prices. The first supermarkets were located in large warehouse buildings where merchandise was displayed on wooden crates and lighting and ventilation were often poor. The present-day supermarket bears little resemblance to its forerunner. Modern supermarkets are large, specially designed buildings, well-lighted and air-conditioned, with ample free customer parking on spacious lots. Although they primarily sell food items, supermarkets are adding an increasing number of nonfood lines, such as photo supplies and processing services, automotive supplies, garden supplies, paperback books, fresh plants and flowers, delicatessens, small appliances, clothing, and health and beauty aids, to increase sales volume and profit. This marketing strategy is called **scrambled merchandising**. Although self-service is still a feature of the supermarket, many customer services are now provided. Nationally known supermarkets include Safeway and Grand Union. (See Exhibit 12–1.)

Exhibit 12–1
Major supermarket chains, ranked by sales.
(SOURCE: *Progressive Grocer*, April, 1982, p. 94.)

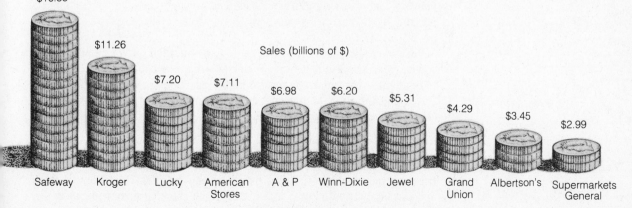

Sales (billions of $)

Safeway	Kroger	Lucky	American Stores	A & P	Winn-Dixie	Jewel	Grand Union	Albertson's	Supermarkets General
$16.58	$11.26	$7.20	$7.11	$6.98	$6.20	$5.31	$4.29	$3.45	$2.99

Supermarket Chain

Exhibit 12–2

Convenience stores in the United States.

Number of stores	37,800
Total sales	$22.8 billion
Share of total U.S. grocery sales	5.8%

SOURCE: *Progressive Grocer*, April 1982, p. 112.

Discount Store

Discount stores appeared on the retailing scene shortly after World War II. They feature self-service and lower prices. They stock a wide variety of hard and soft goods and health and beauty aids. Major discount stores are K mart and Woolco.

Convenience Store

Convenience stores are self-service retail outlets that are usually located away from major shopping centers. These stores are open long hours, usually from 7 A.M. to 11 P.M., every day of the year. Many are open 24 hours a day. These drive-in stores are small in comparison with supermarkets. They stock a limited range of basic grocery items as well as milk, soft drinks, ice, and beer. Their prices for comparable items are almost always higher than the prices found in the supermarket. Convenience stores generally stock only nationally known products and items that sell rapidly. The growth in sales and number of convenience stores is shown in Exhibit 12–2. Major convenience store chains are Southland (7-Eleven), Munford, Circle K, National Convenience Stores, and Utotem.

Warehouse and Catalog Showroom

Warehouse showrooms include in one building a large warehouse used for storage and a showroom where a sample of each piece of brand merchandise is displayed. By performing some of the retailer's functions, such as delivery and uncrating of merchandise, customers can save as much as 15 percent by taking the goods with them. This retailing operation is very popular in selling furniture.

Catalog showrooms use the same retail method as warehouse showrooms. Merchandise is displayed in a showroom. A catalog is also available to customers for orders by mail or phone. Catalog showrooms feature low prices and nationally known lines of merchandise. Best Products Company is a typical catalog showroom firm, and is also the nation's largest catalog showroom retailer.

Vending Machines

Vending machines represent a nonstore retail method that is used for distributing merchandise that has high demand and high frequency of sales and can be distributed on a mass scale, such as soft drinks and candy. An advantage of vending machines is that they can be placed in locations where customers have easy access to them.

Mail-Order (Catalog) and Telephone Selling

The beginning of rural free mail delivery was a major factor that contributed to the early success of Montgomery Ward and Sears, Roebuck in mail-order sales. Today, many firms use catalog and telephone sales to supplement instore sales. Mail-order selling is an important method of distribution used by growers to sell seeds, trees, or plants. Many small manufacturers use this as their chief method of selling their merchandise.

SHOPPING CENTERS

In the 1950s large segments of the population moved to the suburbs, downtown business districts became more congested, and the automobile became a part of the American way of life. These factors helped the growth of shopping centers. A shopping center is a group of different kinds of stores located in a single area. The stores of the center share a common parking lot for customers and may advertise as a group.

There are three basic types of shopping centers. The neighborhood shopping center is usually small, with from three to a dozen stores. This center might consist of a barber shop, drug store, beauty shop, bakery, dry-cleaning establishment, and appliance store, with a supermarket as the main store. Community shopping centers are larger, with from twelve to fifty stores. These centers usually have major stores, such as a supermarket, variety store, or small department store, and smaller stores sim-

Many modern shopping centers are enclosed malls for added customer convenience.

ilar to those in the neighborhood centers. Regional shopping centers consist of from fifty to one hundred or more stores. They ordinarily have several department stores, many kinds of single-line and specialty stores, and perhaps a variety store and a supermarket. Many modern shopping centers are enclosed malls for added customer convenience when shopping.

FORMS OF RETAIL OWNERSHIP

Retailers may be classified on the basis of the type of ownership: single-unit independent store, multi-unit store, or cooperative.

Single-unit Store

Retail stores that operate as single-unit, independent stores are the typical small businesses. Most are organized as sole proprietorships. The Census of Business reports that 84 percent of all retail firms are single units and account for some 55 percent of all retail sales.

Mutli-unit Stores

Only about 16 percent of all retail firms are multi-unit stores, but they account for some 45 percent of all retail sales. Chain, branch, and manufacturer-owned stores (discussed in the next section in channels of distribution) are types of multi-unit stores.

Chain Stores. A chain or **chain store** consists of two or more stores that are operated under the control of central ownership and stock. They distribute similar lines of goods, e.g., groceries, drugs, or variety items. A well-known grocery chain is Safeway; Woolworth's is a popular variety store chain; and Walgreen's is a well-known drug chain (see Exhibit 12–3).

Exhibit 12–3

The ten largest retailing companies, ranked by sales.

Company	Sales ($000)
Sears, Roebuck	27,357,400
Safeway Stores	16,580,318
K mart	16,527,012
J. C. Penney	11,860,169
Kroger	11,266,520
F. W. Woolworth	7,223,241
Lucky Stores	7,201,404
American Stores	7,096,590
Federated Department Stores	7,067,673
Great Atlantic & Pacific Tea	6,989,529

SOURCE: *Fortune*, July 12, 1982.

" I UNDERSTAND WE'RE WORTH MORE WHOLESALE
THAN OUR GRANDPARENTS WERE WORTH RETAIL."

Chains may be national in scope of operation; they may be limited to a particular geographic region; or they may be local, limiting their operation to only one city. Such stores can be corporate chains, voluntary chains, or cooperative chains. A **corporate chain** is centrally owned by a group of stockholders. In the corporate chain, professional managers operate all stores. Corporate chains have the advantages of large size and high turnover of merchandise, which permit them to purchase large volumes of merchandise at lower prices.

A **voluntary chain** is sponsored by a wholesaler. Groups of retail stores associate with a wholesaler to take advantage of volume purchases and lower prices. However, the retail stores remain independently owned and operated but may use a common name, storefront, and operating procedures. Examples include Western Auto in auto supplies, Ace in hardware, and IGA in groceries. **Cooperative chains** are formed by independent retailers. They set up their own wholesaling organization, which enables them to compete with chains.

Branch Stores.   Many central-city stores have opened branch stores in shopping centers to compete with other stores located there. These branch stores operate under the same policies, offer the same quality and line of goods, and provide the same services as the parent store.

Cooperatives

Cooperatives are unique retailing outlets. They are owned and operated by consumers who have voluntarily joined together to buy and sell merchandise to the members, who are also the stockholders. Since members own the consumer cooperative, any profits are returned to members in the form of patronage dividends in proportion to their purchases. Each member of the cooperative has only one vote in controlling the cooperative, regardless of the number of shares of stock owned. Furthermore, all sales are for cash, and goods are sold at the prevailing market price. Despite the apparent attractiveness of the cooperative, its effect on retailing in America has been minor.

WHOLESALING

Wholesalers are intermediaries who play a vital role in the mass distribution of goods and services. The distinction between a wholesale sale and a retail sale is the intention of the purchaser. Retail sales are made to consumers for their own or family use, while wholesale sales are purchases made for the purpose of resale or for further use in industrial or commercial operations. According to the Census of Business, nearly 383,000 wholesalers sell about $1,258 billion worth of goods annually in the United States. (See Exhibit 12–4.)

Many manufacturers are small and specialized, and they do not have the capital to maintain a sales force to contact small retailers throughout the country. Even some manufacturers whose capital is sufficient do not have a large enough output to justify a sales force. Most retailers are small. They buy in small quantities and have limited knowledge of sources of supply or markets. The wholesaler's role, then, is to pool the orders of many small retailers and provide a market for a small manufacturer and perform the buying function for the retailers. Wholesalers also supply other wholesalers with goods for resale, and they sell goods for industrial use.

Merchant Wholesalers

Merchant wholesalers are classified according to the range of merchandise they handle and the services they perform. They may be either full-service or limited-function wholesalers, and their functions are shown in Exhibit 12–5.

Exhibit 12–4

Major wholesalers in the United States, ranked by sales.

Company	Sales (millions of $)
Super Valu Stores	$4,204
The Fleming Cos. Inc.	2,817
Wakefern Food Corp.	1,858
Malone & Hyde Inc.	1,854
Wetterau Incorporated	1,503
Certified Grocers of Calif. Ltd.	1,495
Farm House Foods	1,400
Associated Wholesale Grocers Inc.	1,080
S. M. Flickinger Co.	1,061
Nash-Finch Co.	988

SOURCE: *Progressive Grocer*, April 1982, p. 110.

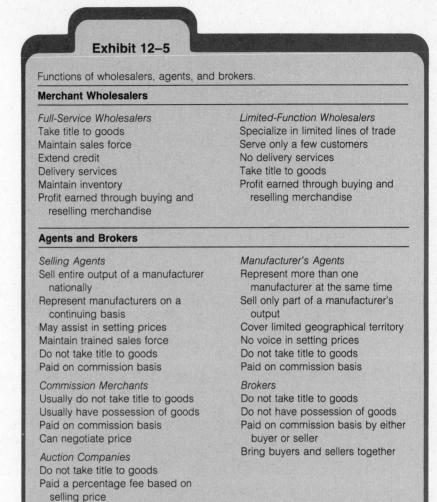

Exhibit 12–5

Functions of wholesalers, agents, and brokers.

Merchant Wholesalers

Full-Service Wholesalers	*Limited-Function Wholesalers*
Take title to goods	Specialize in limited lines of trade
Maintain sales force	Serve only a few customers
Extend credit	No delivery services
Delivery services	Take title to goods
Maintain inventory	Profit earned through buying and
Profit earned through buying and	reselling merchandise
reselling merchandise	

Agents and Brokers

Selling Agents	*Manufacturer's Agents*
Sell entire output of a manufacturer nationally	Represent more than one manufacturer at the same time
Represent manufacturers on a continuing basis	Sell only part of a manufacturer's output
May assist in setting prices	Cover limited geographical territory
Maintain trained sales force	No voice in setting prices
Do not take title to goods	Do not take title to goods
Paid on commission basis	Paid on commission basis
Commission Merchants	*Brokers*
Usually do not take title to goods	Do not take title to goods
Usually have possession of goods	Do not have possession of goods
Paid on commission basis	Paid on commission basis by either buyer or seller
Can negotiate price	Bring buyers and sellers together
Auction Companies	
Do not take title to goods	
Paid a percentage fee based on selling price	
Activities mainly centered in agriculture	

Agent and Brokers

Agents and **brokers** are wholesalers who do not take title to (do not purchase or otherwise own) goods in which they deal. Rather, they represent the seller of the goods, called the *principal*. They receive a commission on sales for their services. Several categories of agents and brokers are shown in Exhibit 12–5.

CHANNELS OF DISTRIBUTION

Marketing managers choose the proper channel of distribution for the thousands of goods and services offered for sale. Most firms use multiple channels of distribution in order to accomplish their goal of reaching the various segments of their market. Thus, goods and services may

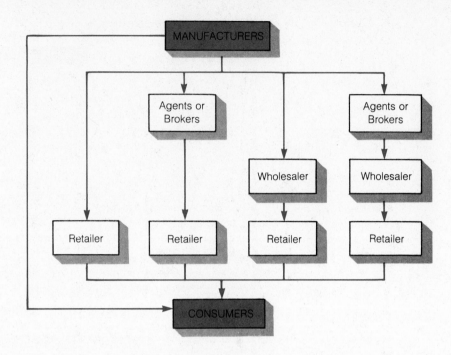

Exhibit 12–6
Channels of distribution of consumer goods.

pass through a combination of middlemen (retailers, wholesalers, agents, or brokers) before reaching final users.

Much of the blame for escalating costs of products and services has been placed on the middlemen. Some critics have suggested that if the middlemen were eliminated from the distribution process, the outcome would be lower prices. However, lower prices will result only if middlemen are performing the marketing functions inefficiently. Marketing functions performed by the middlemen cannot be eliminated. If middlemen are removed, the marketing functions must be executed by someone else in the distribution process.

Channels of Distribution for Consumer Goods

Consumer goods are products that are purchased and used by the ultimate consumer for personal or household use. In contrast, **industrial goods** are products that will be used in producing another product or used up in connection with carrying on a business activity. A tube of toothpaste purchased by the housewife for family use is a consumer good. However, crude petroleum extracted from underground and further processed for producing gas and oil is an industrial good. Exhibit 12–6 shows five channels of distribution for consumer goods.

Manufacturer to Ultimate Consumer. The simplest channel of distribution is one in which manufacturers sell directly to ultimate consumers, such as door-to-door selling of Avon Products. Manufacturers who operate their own retail outlets and sell directly to consumers also use this channel. For example, some shoe manufacturers employ this method for distributing their shoes. Although this channel is the simplest and most direct, it is not widely used because of the high cost to manufacturers.

Manufacturer to Retailer to Ultimate Consumer. Many manufacturers choose to sell their merchandise in large quantities to selected retailers who then sell to the final consumer. This channel assures manufacturers of widespread distribution for their merchandise. Department stores and discount stores are examples of the type of retailing outlets selected by manufacturers. To use this channel, the manufacturer must have its own sales force that contacts the retailers, promoting and selling the manufacturer's products.

Manufacturer to Agent or Broker to Retailer to Ultimate Consumer. Some manufacturers use agents or brokers to contact retailers and encourage them to stock and sell the manufacturer's goods to the consumer. The manufacturer pays a percentage commission of all its sales to the retailers rather than a salary. Thus, the manufacturer has a sales force, but is spared the expense of training and maintaining a sales force.

Manufacturer to Wholesaler to Retailer to Ultimate Consumer. This is the most commonly used channel for the distribution of such consumer goods as candy, cigarettes, and grocery items. Manufacturers of these types of consumer items usually produce only a limited line of goods but distribute them on a broad scale to thousands of retail outlets spread across the country, from the smallest town to the largest metropolitan area. It is not economically feasible for the manufacturer's sales personnel to contact all these retailers personally. Thus, the manufacturer's sales force centers its efforts around contacting and selling to wholesalers, who then provide services to the manufacturer. Most wholesalers not only buy and keep the manufacturer's products stocked in their storage facilities (such as a warehouse), but they also provide the added services of contacting and making deliveries of merchandise to retailers. Most wholesalers determine their profit from the difference between the cost of the goods to them and their price to retailers.

Manufacturer to Agent or Broker to Wholesaler to Retailer to Ultimate Consumer. Economically, manufacturers may not be able to justify maintaining their own sales force to contact wholesalers. These manufacturers usually have a small sales volume or produce goods that are in season only a short time. Such manufacturers may rely on the use of agents or brokers to contact the wholesalers. Wholesalers then contact retailers, who sell to the ultimate consumers. For their services, the agents or brokers receive a percentage commission of their sales.

Exhibit 12–7
Channels of distribution of industrial
goods.

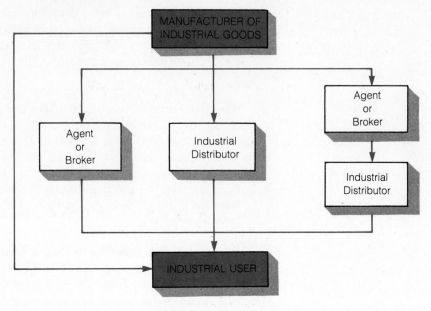

Channels of Distribution for Industrial Goods

Exhibit 12–7 presents the channels of distribution that may be followed in the distribution of industrial products from manufacturer to industrial or commercial users.

Manufacturer to Industrial User. The manufacturer may sell products directly to the industrial user without using any middlemen. This is a common practice because there are only a few likely users of many industrial goods, and the users are located in just a few market areas, not widely scattered as are consumer goods users. Also, industrial goods usually have a high sales price, and they often require factory-trained personnel to install and service them. Generators or locomotives are examples of equipment sold directly to industrial users.

Manufacturer to Agent or Broker to Industrial User. A manufacturer may often elect to employ agents or brokers to sell products to industrial users on a commission basis. Many times a manufacturer will maintain a sales force to sell certain lines of products or sell in certain areas of the market where many customers live, and let agents or brokers sell other lines of merchandise or sell in areas of the market where few customers live.

Manufacturer to Industrial Distributor to Industrial User. Manufacturers may sell to industrial distributors who in turn sell to industrial users. Industrial distributors in the industrial channel of distribution are the counterparts of the wholesalers in the consumer goods channels. They buy in large lots and sell in smaller lots. Industrial distributors often perform a valuable function since they are located near the industrial user, who may obtain a needed product rapidly. Air-conditioning equipment or construction equipment manufacturers use industrial distributors.

Manufacturer to Agent or Broker to Industrial Distributor to Industrial User. Manufacturers may use agents or brokers to sell their products to industrial distributors, who then sell to industrial users, when there are a large number of industrial distributors scattered over a large territory. Manufacturers find that it is too expensive to maintain their own sales force for so large a market. However, the agent or broker is able to service the industrial distributors because the agent or broker sells more than one company's products.

CONSUMER BEHAVIOR

Marketing managers are constantly seeking to analyze and understand consumer behavior. We have stated that the marketing concept emphasizes that firms should produce goods and provide services that will satisfy consumer wants. In order to fulfill the marketing concept, marketing managers look for answers to such questions as: What are the needs of consumers and why do people buy some items and not others? Consumer behavior is defined as the "actions of individuals in obtaining and using goods and services, including the decision process that precedes and determines these actions."[1]

Clearly, consumer purchasing habits are difficult to predict. Information on consumers is usually obtained from demographic data and motivation research. Demographic research deals with collecting statistical information about consumers, such as number, sex, income, age, marital status, and place of residence. The special interest feature presented in this chapter highlights some of the characteristics of the consumer market in the United States.

Motivation research, a technique designed to discover the underlying motives of consumer behavior, has been useful for collecting information about consumer purchasing patterns. Knowledge of what consumers want and need will enable companies to have goods or services available for sale when desired. Before discussing consumer behavior further, it is necessary to identify the types of consumer goods purchased.

TYPES OF CONSUMER GOODS

Consumer goods, those purchased by the ultimate consumer for his or her own or the family's use, may be separated broadly into three classes: convenience goods, shopping goods, and specialty goods. (See Exhibit 12–8.)

---

[1]James F. Engel, David T. Kollat, and Roger Blackwell, *Consumer Behavior* (New York: Holt, Rhinehart & Winston, 1968), p. 5.

Exhibit 12–8

Characteristics of consumer goods

Convenience Goods	Shopping Goods	Specialty Goods
Price per item is usually small	Price per item is substantial	Price per item may be be high or low
National advertising coverage	National advertising coverage	Scope of advertising coverage varies
Purchased frequently	Purchased rather infrequently	Frequency of purchase varies with nature of product
Sold through many outlets	Sold through fewer, selected outlets	Sold through restricted number of outlets
Little thought or deliberation given to purchase decision	Considerable thought and deliberation given to purchase decision	Extra effort expended to purchase this product
Product quality is standardized	Product quality varies	Product possesses special characteristics
Product brand name is important	Brand name of product less important than for convenience goods	Product may have a high degree of brand identification

Convenience Goods

Convenience goods are those that are convenient for the consumer to purchase. Their characteristics include general distribution through numerous retail outlets, sale at a low price per unit, and national advertisements. Consumers buy convenience goods frequently because they use them up quickly. Furthermore, the customer gives little thought to the decision to purchase a convenience item. Price and quality comparisons are not generally made, inasmuch as the cost of each item is low and the quality is standardized nationally. For example, a package of chewing gum is a convenience good, possessing all the characteristics of items in this category. People can buy chewing gum in many diverse outlets, such as grocery stores, service stations, restaurants, drug stores, and through vending machines. The price per package is low and uniform, and consumers buy gum often, since they literally chew up the product. The quality of each package of gum is standardized. Furthermore, the product is advertised on a national scale. The decisions required in making the purchase relate to the brand and the flavor of gum desired. Other examples of convenience goods are toothpaste, cigarettes, candy, magazines, newspapers, and most grocery items.

Shopping Goods

Household appliances, clothing, television sets, and furniture are some types of **shopping goods.** Price is an important factor when consumers begin to think about buying shopping goods. They make price as well as quality comparisons, since these goods usually involve a rather large expenditure and have a rather long life expectancy. Thus, consumers buy shopping goods infrequently. In addition, shoppers will usually visit several stores to compare other features, such as style and suitability, before making a final decision to purchase. Brand names are important in identifying shopping goods, but not as important as for convenience goods. Stores that handle shopping goods are usually located close to each other so that shoppers can compare products.

To illustrate, let us examine the purchase of a stereo. Consumers usually spend a great deal of time and effort in shopping at several different stores before deciding to buy a particular unit. They get comparisons on such features as number and size of speakers, price, and availability of a tape deck. They compare models with and without AM-FM radios and compare portable models against cabinet models. They also see the furniture styles (early American, modern) available in cabinet models. Shopping goods are found in fewer retail outlets (appliance stores, department stores, furniture stores) than are convenience goods. Marketing managers, therefore, concentrate on placing such goods at strategic locations.

Specialty Goods

Specialty goods possess some unique quality, characteristic, or high degree of brand identification that causes the consumer to try to buy them, even if he or she must go out of the way to do so. However, high prices are not necessarily characteristic of specialty goods. For example, a consumer prefers a special kind of pastry that costs only 25¢; and is sold only by a bakery located in an out-of-the-way section of town. In order to buy the product, the consumer has to make a special effort to go to the bakery, another characteristic of specialty goods. Also, the number of outlets for specialty goods is limited (in this case, to only one outlet). Fancy foods, certain brands of men's and women's clothing, and jewelry are types of specialty goods.

THE DYNAMIC NATURE OF CONSUMER GOODS

Classifying consumer goods as convenience, shopping, and specialty is somewhat artificial because the classifications are largely subjective. For example, a product classified as a shopping good by one person may be a specialty good to another. An attaché case that a woman purchases is considered a shopping good if she goes to several stores to compare brands, prices, styles, and quality. However, if she desires a special case or a particular brand that is sold exclusively by only one store, the attaché case would then be a specialty good.

Furthermore, the classification of consumer goods is not static but changes as consumer preferences change and with shifts in the standard of living. If the classification of goods changes, the channel of distribution will change. For example, an imported brand of cheese distributed only through a limited number of retail outlets that sells for a premium price is classified as a specialty good. However, with a rise in the standard of living, the consumer has more discretionary income (money available for items other than basic necessities of food, clothing, and shelter) to spend

No single formula exists to explain why consumers make the purchases they do.

on luxury items. If a large segment of consumers begin to purchase the imported cheese, it will be made available in many retail outlets to reach the maximum number of customers. This cheese, then, has moved from a specialty good to a convenience good and the channel of distribution has been modified so the product can be distributed through many outlets.

THE PSYCHOLOGY OF BUYING: THE PURCHASE-DECISION PROCESS

We have stressed that one of the chief concerns of marketing managers is to try to understand the psychology of consumer behavior. No single formula exists to explain why consumers make the purchases they do. For example, a shopper may purchase a radio for individual use, general family use, or as a gift. The complex issue is summed up concisely by Britt:

> What actually determines buying decisions? It may not be possible to obtain answers to such broad questions. The task is enormous. The answers are complex. Each of us has almost infinite likes and dislikes, and there are more likes and dislikes than there are people. And each individual's likes and motives are subject to change with different circumstances.[2]

Consumers are influenced by a wide variety of motives when making purchases. Sometimes consumers are unaware of their purchase motives

[2]S. A. Britt, *The Spenders* (New York: McGraw-Hill Book Co., Inc., 1960), p. 20.

or are unwilling to discuss them. Consumers have three levels of aware-ness with regard to purchases: conscious, subconscious, and unconscious. *Conscious motives* are those motives of which the consumer is aware and which the consumer is willing to talk about. *Subconscious motives* are the motives that a consumer may be aware of but not willing to talk about with others. If a consumer is unaware of what motivated a purchase, this is an *unconscious motive*. While these difficulties of understanding consumer be-havior do exist, the purchase-decision process discussed below provides some insight into the psychology of consumer behavior (see Exhibit 12–9).

Recognize a Need

In chapter 8, we learned that each of us has primary and secondary needs. Before we are motivated to make a purchase, we must be aware that we have an unfulfilled need that must be satisfied. For example, if we are hungry (a need), we will be motivated to buy some type of food to satisfy our hunger. The motives that prompt a consumer to purchase a particular kind of product to satisfy needs are **primary buying motives**. A con-sumer may recognize a need for a new TV to replace a worn-out set.

Exhibit 12–9
The purchase-decision process.

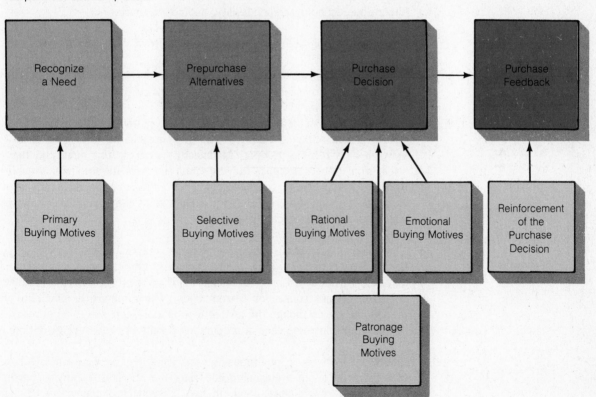

Prepurchase Alternatives

Once the consumer makes a decision to buy a new television set, he or she must consider a number of alternatives before making the purchase. One alternative is the brand (Zenith, G.E., RCA, Sony). Other alternatives include choices such as color vs. black-and-white, portable vs. cabinet model, screen size, furniture style for cabinet models, the manufacturer's guarantee, and the price. The motives that underlie the consumer's choice of which television set to buy are **selective buying motives.**

Purchase Decision

When the consumer decides to make the purchase, several other motives influence the kind of product he or she buys (rational or emotional) and where he or she makes the purchase (patronage).

Rational Motives. **Rational buying motives** involve conscious thought and deliberation by the consumer on the purchase decision. He or she tries to learn as much as possible about the product. In a rational buying decision, the individual seeks to justify to himself or herself the purchase of the merchandise. Common motivations that influence a rational decision to buy include economy, dependability, and convenience.

Economy. A consumer can achieve self-approval for a purchase on the basis of economy. For example, the purchase of a foreign- or American-made compact or subcompact auto is reinforced on the basis of the economy of higher gas mileage and lower maintenance costs.

Dependability. An important rational buying motive is dependability. A consumer can often be satisfied that the purchase is wise if he or she views it as a reliable product. Manufacturers stress this quality in their sales promotion campaigns. Maytag Company sells its automatic washer by showing the lonely appliance serviceman who never receives any service calls from customers. Such advertising helps the buyer believe he or she has made a sound purchase.

Convenience. A strong rational appeal that may influence a purchase is the convenience the product offers the user. For example, a consumer may select from a vast array of instant foods or beverages, such as instant potatoes, instant coffee, or frozen foods, which require a minimum of preparation. Even though the instant food is more expensive, its purchase is justified because the ease of preparation results in a real savings of time.

Emotional Motives. Sometimes the purchase may be done on impulse, meaning little or no preplanning goes into the decision to buy, as when purchasing a convenience good. In fact, an individual may not even be aware of the actual reasons prompting the purchase. Such buying motives are identified as **emotional buying motives.** A variety of the factors that influence an emotional purchase are discussed below.

Emulation.　Well-known personalities often give testimonials of their use of a particular product. Many people buy these items because they want to mirror the people who use the product.

Esteem.　Some individuals purchase a distinctive article in hopes that they will gain recognition from the people with whom they work or associate in social activities. A man may buy an expensive, high-quality suit or a woman may purchase an exclusive style of dress from a fashionable shop. The motivation behind each purchase may be to direct attention to themselves. Other examples include the purchase of the finest model of automobile with all accessories, the best appliances, or the most expensive furniture.

Pleasure.　People may decide they want a change in their daily routine. For example, a person who buys a boat can break away from the routine of a job and spend leisure time boating or skiing or fishing. The pleasure motive is also expressed by attendance at spectator events, such as professional sports or cultural activities. The increase in leisure time has increased the demand for all types of recreational equipment.

Social Acceptance.　The need to conform is the foundation for a powerful emotional buying motive. We buy items that conform to current styles. Hence, the products we buy are often those items that our friends value. Our purchases seldom run counter to the approved taste of those around us because we have a need to be accepted as part of a group.

Self-expression.　The desire to demonstrate our creative talents is a significant motivation for many purchases. Consumers purchase a variety of equipment and supplies that provide outlets for fulfilling their need for self-expression. Do-it-yourself kits and distinctive kinds of art and craft work help fulfill the need to be creative.

Patronage Motives.　The variety of factors that influence where customers will make their purchases are **patronage motives.** No one motive is more significant than any of the others. Instead, shoppers usually consider a combination of motives simultaneously when deciding just where and from whom to buy. Some of the important patronage motives that affect shoppers are suggested below.

Friendliness and Helpfulness of Sales Personnel.　In a retail store, the consumers' attitudes toward the store are shaped to a large extent by the

TO OUR CUSTOMERS:

    WE HAVE ENJOYED HAVING YOU AS A CUSTOMER AND YOUR COMMENTS ARE SINCERELY APPRECIATED. THANK YOU FOR TAKING TIME TO HELP US SERVE YOU BETTER.

PLEASE MAIL YOUR COMMENTS TO:

Office of the President
THE PIZZA INN, INC.
P. O. Box 22247
Dallas, Texas 75222

WE PATRONIZE THE PIZZA INN LOCATED AT:

STREET_____ DATE_____

CITY_____ TIME_____

STATE_____ HOW MANY IN PARTY?_____

NUMBER OF VISITS TO THIS PIZZA INN IN THE LAST MONTH [____]

PLEASE COMPARE THE SERVICE OF THE PIZZA INN TO THE SERVICE OF OTHER FOOD SERVICE ESTABLISHMENTS IN YOUR AREA:

CHECK ONE   [__]   [__]   [__]   [__]
         EXCELLENT GOOD AVERAGE POOR

PLEASE COMPARE THE ATMOSPHERE OF THE PIZZA INN TO THE ATMOSPHERE OF OTHER FOOD SERVICE ESTABLISHMENTS IN YOUR AREA:

CHECK ONE   [__]   [__]   [__]   [__]
         EXCELLENT GOOD AVERAGE POOR

PLEASE COMPARE THE QUALITY OF FOOD AT THE PIZZA INN TO THE FOOD OF OTHER FOOD SERVICE ESTABLISHMENTS IN YOUR AREA:

CHECK ONE   [__]   [__]   [__]   [__]
         EXCELLENT GOOD AVERAGE POOR

WHAT WERE YOU SERVED?

PIZZA [__]

SALAD [__]

SANDWICH [__]

SPAGHETTI [__]

ADDITIONAL REMARKS:

_____
_____
_____
_____
_____

NAME_____

ADDRESS_____

CITY_____

STATE_____

ZIP CODE_____

1869

Exhibit 12–10
Customers are invited to comment on Pizza Inn's food and service.

(SOURCE: Pizza Inn, Inc. Reprinted by permission.)

type of treatment they receive from the store's sales personnel. Consumers usually agree that sales personnel who are friendly, helpful, and courteous greatly influence their decision to return to a store for future purchases. On the other hand, salespersons who are indifferent or even discourteous toward shoppers will likely drive customers to competitors. Pizza Inn uses the questionnaire in Exhibit 12–10 to get customers to grade the service they received while dining.

Reputation of the Seller.   Many customers stress the seller's reputation as a factor that causes them to shop at a store. Likewise, retailers conscientiously strive to build a positive image in the consumer's eye. Sears, for example, has for years emphasized a policy of complete customer satisfaction on all purchases and stands solidly behind the products it sells in its effort to maintain a sound reputation. As a result, many people who shop at Sears say they do so because of its outstanding reputation for guaranteeing its merchandise and for good customer relations.

Convenience of Location.   Crowded downtown shopping areas have caused many customers to prefer the convenience of suburban shopping centers. To cope with this problem, many downtown merchants have joined forces to provide for free parking on private lots while other merchants have built their own parking lots near their stores. Location is one of the key factors in the success of retail stores.

Customer-Oriented Services.   Consumers say one reason they buy from a given store is the extra services that the store provides. These services are not directly related to the products sold but are oriented toward making shopping a more pleasant and convenient experience. Retail stores emphasize delivery services, welcome charge accounts from their customers, and provide complaint and adjustment departments.

Product-Related Services.   One reason for patronizing a store is that it not only sells well-known products but also provides excellent service after the sale of the product. Such services include free installation and free parts and labor for a specified period of time. Service after the sale has become an increasingly important factor to consumers as products have become more complex.

Variety of Merchandise Available.   Frequently, the consumer desires to find many products housed in one store, such as in a department store. Stores capitalize on this point by advertising that customers can complete all their shopping with one visit to the store.

Breadth of Assortment.   A wide selection of merchandise from which to choose is of keen interest to many shoppers. For example, when shopping for a new washing machine, a customer frequently patronizes the store that handles a wide assortment of brands and models. This allows the consumer to make comparisons easily before making the purchase.

Price.   Another of the many reasons expressed for preferring a store is the price factor. Customers patronize stores that emphasize a fair price for the quality of goods sold.

Ownership of Establishment.   For some shoppers, the type of ownership of the store plays an important role in deciding where to purchase. Some prefer large chain stores while others prefer the personal services that they can receive from the small business owner-manager.

Purchase Feedback

When consumers begin to use a product after its purchase, they form opinions about it. Frequently, they try to find ways of gaining approval or reinforcement for their purchase decision. They may seek approval from their friends or read literature that explains the merits of the product.

Consumer Demography: A Profile of the Consumer Market in the United States

The study of consumer demography is important to marketing managers. *Demography* is the statistical study of the population in reference to size, density, distribution, and vital statistics. The knowledge of the characteristics of the population and the consumer market enables marketing managers to more effectively develop the firm's marketing strategy. Shown below is a profile of demography of the consumer market and the general population as reported by the Census Bureau.

Population (in millions)

Number of persons	226.5
Number of households	77.3
Number of families	59.4

Age (in percentages)

Under 5	7.1
5-13	13.9
14-17	7.4
18-21	7.7
22-24	5.5
25-34	15.8
35-44	11.4
45-54	10.4
55-64	9.5
65 and over	11.2

Race (in percentages)

White	88.2
M 48.8	
F 51.2	
Black	11.8
M 47.5	
F 52.5	

Marital Status (in percentages)

	Male	Female
Single	29.9	23.0
Married	60.3	54.9
Widowed	2.5	12.3
Divorced	5.4	7.2
Separated	1.9	2.6

Age of Householder (in percentages)

Under 25	8.2
25-34	22.0
35-44	17.2
45-54	16.3
55-64	15.9
65 and over	20.4

Households by Number of Persons (in percentages)

1 person	22.2
2	30.9
3	17.3
4	15.9
5	8.0
6	3.3
7 or more	2.3

Households by Size of Families (in percentages)

2 persons	38.9
3	22.4
4	20.8
5	10.5
6	4.4
7 or more	2.9

Income Level of Families (in percentages)

	White	Black
Under $5,000	5.4	17.9
$5,000–9,999	12.3	22.5
10,000–14,999	15.4	17.5
15,000–24,999	30.2	22.5
25,000–34,999	20.1	12.5
35,000–49,999	10.9	5.4
50,000 and over	5.7	1.8

Educational Attainment (in percentages)

Elementary School	
0–4	2.7
5–7	5.6
8	8.7
High School	
1–3	13.3
4	37.6
College	
1–3	15.0
4 or more	17.2

SUMMARY OF KEY POINTS

1. A retail sale is one made to a final user for household or personal use.

2. A wholesale sale is one made to other wholesalers, retailers, or industrial users for the purpose of resale or business use.

3. Some types of retail stores are general merchandise, single line, specialty, department store, variety store, supermarket, discount store, convenience store, and warehouse and catalog showroom.

4. Types of nonstore retailing are vending machines and mail order (catalog) and telephone selling.

5. Three kinds of shopping centers are neighborhood, community, and regional.

6. Retail store ownership may be classified as single-unit, multi-unit, or cooperative.

7. Merchant wholesalers, agents, and brokers are types of wholesalers.

8. A channel of distribution is the route a good follows from manufacturer to final user.

9. There are a variety of channels of distribution that manufacturers can use to distribute consumer and industrial goods.

10. *Consumer behavior* refers to the actions people take in obtaining goods and services.

11. Types of consumer goods are convenience, shopping, and specialty goods.

12. The purchase decision process involves the consideration of rational, emotional, and patronage motives.

DISCUSSION QUESTIONS

1. Distinguish between a single-line store and a specialty store. Give an example of each.

2. What is scrambled merchandising?

3. What is a cooperative?

4. Distinguish between full-service and limited-function wholesalers.

5. What is an agent or a broker?

6. Why don't all manufacturers of consumer goods sell directly to final users and eliminate the middleman?

7. What is consumer behavior?

8. Explain the characteristics of convenience goods.

9. What are some examples of emotional buying motives?

10. Of all the factors listed as patronage motives, which would you consider most important and least important?

STUDENT PROJECTS

1. Visit a shopping center in your local area. List the stores in the shopping center and classify them according to kinds of retailing outlets. Also, classify the shopping center according to whether it is a neighborhood, community, or regional center.

2. Prepare lists of convenience, shopping, and specialty goods. Compare your lists with your classmates' to determine if there are differences in the classification of the various goods.

	Convenience	Shopping	Specialty
a.	_____	_____	_____
b.	_____	_____	_____
c.	_____	_____	_____
d.	_____	_____	_____
e.	_____	_____	_____

3. Prepare a report about a retail store in which you have shopped. Indicate what type of store it is (variety, department, specialty, single-line, etc.). Then evaluate the store in terms of the patronage motives listed below:

a. Friendliness and helpfulness of sales personnel
b. Reputation of seller
c. Convenience of location
d. Customer-oriented services
e. Variety of merchandise available
f. Breadth of assortment of merchandise
g. Price of merchandise
h. Ownership of establishment

General Industries, Incorporated

General Industries is a highly diversified corporation that manufactures and distributes a wide variety of products. Some products marketed by General Industries are as follows.

1. The Automotive Division manufactures oil filters, air filters, and spark plugs for automotive engines.

2. The Appliance Division has developed a new microwave cooking oven. It features digital time control, automatic temperature sensor to take the guesswork out of cooking, touch-sensitive controls, a see-through door, and has a memory that enables the user to program the oven for a two-stage operation, such as defrost and cook. It also has a special energy-saving feature.

3. The Heavy Equipment Division has manufactured a new front-end loader tractor.

4. The Book Publishing Division has published a new 26-volume encyclopedia.

5. The Consumer Division has developed a brand of sugarless chewing gum. Extensive tests have proven that its flavor lasts for twenty-four hours of consecutive chewing and that it helps prevent tooth decay.

6. The Home Service Division has developed a new detergent. It contains no phosphate and no enzymes and is biodegradable. It is a low-suds, highly concentrated detergent, and only a half cup is required per washload.

Questions

1. Specify whether each of the items is a consumer or industrial good.

2. Would you classify each of the consumer goods you have identified as a convenience, shopping, or specialty good?

3. Indicate an appropriate channel of distribution for each product.

4. If a retailer is included as part of the distribution process, indicate some types of retailers that should be used for each product.

Walt's Drug Store

Walt Perry recently graduated from pharmacy school and has just opened a drug store in a town of 50,000 population. It is a medium-sized drug store offering the usual merchandise that is found in drug stores: prescriptions, tobacco products, candy, cosmetics, perfume, health products, cameras, small radios, some small appliances, patent medicines, some gift items, etc.

Walt has two major competitors. One is an older drug store that has been in business for over twenty-five years. It looks somewhat run down, offers credit, does not deliver, and has prices equal to Walt's drug store. The other competitor is a discount house with a prescription department. The discount house does not offer credit nor make deliveries but has lower prices than Walt. Walt offers credit, delivers prescriptions, and feels he has the best location.

Questions

1. Name one product for each type of consumer good that Walt would carry and explain why it is that type.

2. Name one item Walt might carry that might involve the following buying motives:

Emotional Buying Motives	Rational Buying Motives
Emulation	Economy
Esteem	Dependability
Pleasure	Convenience
Social acceptance	
Self-expression	

3. What patronage motives should Walt stress?

Mary Kay Ash, founder and chairman of the board, Mary Kay Cosmetics, Inc. as photographed by Francesco Scavullo in 1981.

BUSINESS PROFILE

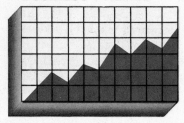

Mary Kay Cosmetics

Mary Kay Ash retired in 1963 after working in direct sales for twenty-five years with Stanley Home Products and later as national training director for World Gift. After one month, she realized she was not satisfied with retirement. Her original plan for retirement was to write a book showing women the techniques of how to sell based on her own direct-selling experience. As she wrote about the problems she had encountered, she began to think about the solutions to the problems. Out of this came the marketing plan used by Mary Kay Cosmetics today. She had a marketing plan without a product. Her goal was to find a product that women could identify with, something that would be easy to sell, and that any woman, even one who had no selling experience, could easily sell.

Her product turned out to be a private-label skin treatment she had been using herself for some years. Mary Kay bought the formulas from the maker. Armed with a marketing plan and a product, she founded a company that makes it possible for salespersons to be highly successful through direct selling of cosmetics to women.

She and her husband invested her $5,000 life savings in the Mary Kay Cosmetic business and recruited ten salespersons, or independent beauty consultants, as they are called. Shortly before the business started, her husband, who was to be her administrative partner, died. One son, Richard Rogers, then joined the firm to manage the financial and administrative part of the business; another son later joined the business to manage distribution.

Mary Kay's marketing program is implemented through direct selling. The sales program involves a beauty show that the consultant (salesperson) has in a hostess' home for no more than six people. The consultants present a do-it-yourself beauty care session. Guests at the make-up party apply the make-up on themselves. Mary Kay Cosmetics' channel of distribution involves one wholesale sale (from company to beauty consultant) and one retail sale (from beauty consultant to customer). Each consultant buys all cosmetics from Mary Kay and carries enough inventory to fill orders on the spot at the party. Sales commissions are generous. Consultants' earnings are usually 50 percent of what they sell. Top consultants, known as directors, earn an average of $25,000 annually while national sales directors (the very best consultants) earn an average of $150,000 annually. Active consultants can earn $600 to $800 monthly. Consultants also earn additional income by recruiting and training new consultants.

Mary Kay offers incentives to the consultants for their sales efforts, such as gifts of mink coats, diamond rings, watches, luggage, typewriters, and vacations. Another incentive is year-long use of pink Cadillacs or Buick Regals to sales directors whose sales volume is high enough. Pink is the official company color.

In its first year of operation, 1964, Mary Kay had sales of almost $200,000, and there were 318 consultants. Sales exceeded $800,000 the second year. The company went public with its stock in 1967, and today Mary Kay is listed on the New York Stock Exchange. In 1969, a large manufacturing facility was built in Dallas, the company headquarters, where the cosmetics are manufactured. In the early 1970s, four new distribution and training centers were opened in the United States, and the company expanded its operations into Canada and Australia. In 1977, the firm moved into a $5.7 million corporate headquarters building. Recognizing its continued growth, the company has recently purchased 177 acres for construction of a corporate "campus" facility.

Mary Kay has grown rapidly since 1964. Today, Mary Kay Cosmetics has net sales over $250 million and there are over 150,000 independent beauty consultants working for the firm. Her firm, along with Avon and Tupperware, is one of the few successful direct-selling companies in the United States.

13 Promotional Strategy

LEARNING GOALS

After reading this chapter, you will understand:

1. The factors that comprise the promotion mix of the firm.

2. The various types of advertising, their advantages and disadvantages, and what publicity is.

3. The role of an advertising agency.

4. What factors are important when selecting the advertising media.

5. The personal selling process.

6. The different types of personal selling.

7. The several plans for compensating the sales force.

8. What sales promotion is.

KEY TERMS

Promotion mix   Specialty advertising
Advertising   Personal selling
Media   Service selling
Publicity   Creative selling
Advertising agency   Supportive selling
Institutional advertising   Missionary salesperson
Milline rate   Detail men
Network advertising   Technical salesperson
Spot announcements   Sales promotion
Local advertising   Point-of-purchase display

Find a need, and fill it.

THEODORE LEVITT

If a firm designs and manufacturers a new product, improves an existing model, or develops a new service, there is no guarantee that the product or service will make the firm economically successful. Potential customers must be informed about the product or service and believe that the product or service will satisfy their needs before they purchase it. Promotional strategy is the process of communicating information about the firm or its products and services to its target market. Promotional strategy is designed to inform customers about products and services and to encourage them to respond by purchasing the product or service. Promotional strategy is such an influential and pervasive force in society that it is regulated by law to prevent deceptive business practices (see chapter 23).

PROMOTION MIX

Promotional strategy communicates the firm's message to its market segment. The **promotion mix** includes the four basic channels used by firms to reach their target market: advertising, publicity, personal selling, and sales promotion. Each firm places varying degrees of emphasis on each of the components of the promotion mix according to its specific needs. However, all firms must use promotional strategy to make consumers aware of their products and services. Each of the components of the promotion mix will be discussed in the remaining sections of this chapter.

ADVERTISING AND PUBLICITY

We experience a wide variety of advertisements daily. **Advertising** is "any paid form of nonpersonal presentation and promotion of ideas, goods, or services by an identified sponsor."[1] Advertising is a one-way communication between the marketer and the potential customer. Advertising messages may be conveyed by many methods, as we will see later in this chapter. A firm may deliver its messages through an advertising medium—a single source, or **media**—more than one source.

Publicity is a form of promotion that is different from advertising. The American Marketing Association defines publicity as:

---

[1]Committee on Definitions, *Marketing Definitions* (Chicago: American Marketing Association, 1960), pp. 9–10.

Advertising agencies plan and carry out the total advertising campaign for the firm.

Nonpersonal stimulation of demand for a product, service, or business unit by planting commercially significant news about it in a published medium or obtaining favorable presentation of it on radio, television, or stage that is not paid for by a sponsor.[2]

Thus, a news report in the media that a company donated $1 million to charitable organizations is publicity.

Advertising Agency

Some firms have an advertising manager to direct the planning of the firm's advertising program, including writing the advertising message, or copy. Other firms use the services of an **advertising agency**, which is an independent company that specializes in advertising. Advertising agencies plan and carry out the total advertising campaign for a firm.

Agencies are paid either a fee or a commission for their services. Usually, the commission method provides the agency an amount equal to 15 percent of the cost of the media space or time. The commission is paid by the media, who bill the agencies for the full amount, less 15 percent. The advertiser pays the total rate to the agency. If an agency prepares and places a radio advertisement worth $60,000, the medium bills the agency for $51,000 ($60,000 less 15 percent). The agency then bills the advertiser for $60,000. The $9,000 is for advertising agency services. Some of the largest ad agencies are Young & Rubicam; J. Walter Thompson Co.; Ogilvy & Mather; Foote, Cone, & Belding; Leo Burnette Co.; Ted Bates & Co.; and McCann-Erickson.

Choosing the Advertising Media

Marketing managers consider a number of factors in choosing the appropriate medium or media to convey the firm's promotion message. Four factors—purpose, cost, selection, and message requirements—are discussed below.

---

[2]Ibid., p. 19.

Purpose of the Advertisement.   The choice of advertising media is influenced by the purpose of the specific ad as well as the total advertising program. In planning advertising strategy, marketing managers set goals for the advertising campaign, such as the representative goals highlighted below.

1. One goal is to inform potential customers about products or services in order to increase sales and profits.

2. A second goal of advertising is to inform consumers about the superiority of the firm's products or services over competitors.

3. A third goal of advertising is to make a brand name so familiar that it becomes a household word. Sponsors can direct their ads to broad, national markets or to specific market segments (regional, local, age groups, or music lovers).

4. A fourth goal of advertising is to reemphasize the qualities of an established product or to introduce a new product.

5. A fifth goal of advertising is intended to build a favorable image of the company; this is called **institutional advertising.** For example, International Paper Company advertisements stress that, while they use the wood from their forests to make paper, they also use the forests for making the best possible home for wildlife. They also believe that forests should be used for human enjoyment and they have opened areas of the forests to hikers, campers, bike riders, and have built boat launching ramps, picnic sites, and nature trails.

Firms spend large amounts of money annually as they try to capture their share of the consumers' dollars. Exhibit 13–1 presents the top ten adver-

Exhibit 13–1

The ten leading advertisers in the United States.

Company	Advertising Expenditure (millions of $)
Procter & Gamble	$649.6
Sears	599.6
General Foods Corporation	410.0
Philip Morris, Inc.	364.6
K mart Corporation	319.3
General Motors Corporation	316.0
R. J. Reynolds	298.5
Ford Motor Company	280.0
American Telephone & Telegraph	259.2
Warner Lambert Company	235.2

SOURCE: *Advertising Age*, September 10, 1981, p. 1.

Exhibit 13–2

Distribution of the advertising dollar.

(SOURCE: Reprinted with permission from p. 48 of the September 14, 1981 issue of *Advertising Age*. Copyright 1981 by Crain Communications, Inc.)

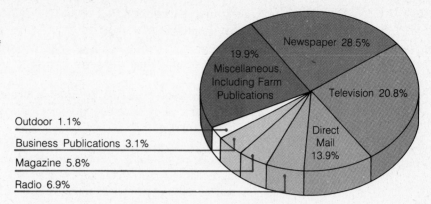

Outdoor 1.1%

Business Publications 3.1%

Magazine 5.8%

Radio 6.9%

tisers. Newspapers receive a greater share of each advertising dollar than any of the other media, as shown in Exhibit 13–2.

Cost of Advertising Media. Those charged with the responsibility for the advertising program of a company should compare the ad costs for the various media to the size of the audience reached. We are considering here comparative costs, not actual costs. Actual costs are available from the various media or such sources as the *Standard Rate and Data Service,* which is the main source of data on national and local rates in various media for those who buy advertising space.

One method of evaluating cost is based on how much it costs to reach each reader or viewer. This is determined by the cost of the advertisement divided by the size of the audience. For television and radio, this cost is based on cost per thousand, the cost of reaching a thousand viewers or listeners with a commercial of a certain length (ten-second, thirty-second, or sixty-second spot). Rates vary according to the time of day or night the ad is broadcast. Magazine rates are also measured in cost per thousand, the cost for a one-page ad for each thousand circulation. Each publisher has a rate card showing the cost for advertising space in the magazine.

Newspaper rates vary for each paper. Newspaper ads can be compared by the use of the **milline rate,** or what it would cost per agate line to reach one million circulation of a paper. An agate line is a unit of measurement of advertising space one column wide and one-fourteenth inch deep. The cost is determined by the actual circulation of the paper and its rate per line. Newspaper advertisers are not billed at the milline rate. Instead, they can use this figure to compare the relative cost of advertising in newspapers with different rates and circulation.

The milline rate is calculated on the following basis:

$$\frac{1,000,000 \times \text{rate per line}}{\text{quantity of circulation}} = \text{milline rate}$$

If a newspaper had a circulation of 250,000 and its rate per line was $1, the milline rate would be

$$\frac{1,000,000 \times \$1}{250,000} = \$4$$

Marketing managers evaluate costs and the size of the audiences and determine the relative effectiveness of the media for the company's advertising program.

Circulation of Media.   In order to maximize the return on each advertising dollar, marketing managers must select media with the capability of reaching the geographical market (local, national) where the firm desires to promote its goods or services. *Media circulation* means the actual number of readers, viewers, or listeners in a specific area or in a particular time period of the day or evening.

Advertising Message Requirements.   Media must be appropriate for presenting the firm's message to the specific market segment. The advertising message must be tastefully presented to the consumer in a clear and factual manner. Advertising copy should follow the "AIDCA" Principle to be effective. This principle includes a series of steps:

1. Attention—causes the consumer to stop and read the copy or listen and/or watch the ad.
2. Interest—arouses curiosity.
3. Desire—increases urge to acquire.
4. Conviction—substantiates that a decision to buy would be good judgment.
5. Action—actually moves the consumer to go out and buy.[3]

ADVERTISING MEDIA

Marketing managers may select the advertising medium from among newspapers, television, radio, magazines, direct mail, transportation, billboards, or specialty advertising. Normally, firms use a combination of media for their advertising campaigns.

Newspaper Advertising

Newspaper advertising's major advantage is that it covers a selected geographical market, and broad coverage can aid in selling a product in that specific area. As a result, the newspaper is the chief means of advertising on a local basis. Newspaper ads are also flexible and timely. Newspaper advertising messages can be changed daily, or even two or more times daily when there is more than one edition of a paper.

A major disadvantage of newspaper advertising is that the advertiser cannot select the specific target market for the promotional message since the paper is distributed to a mass audience.

[3]C. Winston Borgen, *Learning Experiences in Retailing* (Santa Monica, Calif.: Goodyear Publishing Company, 1976), pp. 258–59.

Television Advertising

Advertising expenditures are rising at the fastest rate in the medium of television. One of television's major advantages is that a product can be advertised, the advertising message can be delivered, and the product can be demonstrated simultaneously.

Television advertising may be classed as a network, spot, or local advertisement. **Network advertising** is directed toward large audiences covering a wide territory. Messages can go to a nationwide market at one time via network advertising, and the cost of each message per listener is low, since television reaches such a large potential audience.

Spot announcements, on the other hand, are a means by which an advertiser can broadcast a message over one or many stations at various times. Each station sends out its message separately. Specifically, spot announcements permit the advertiser to choose the station, audience, time, and program for the presentation.

Local advertising means that the advertising message is in the local area. Since one's goods or services are advertised over the television station in one's own city, the business person is able to judge the effectiveness of the advertisement by the effect it has on sales. Local advertising rates are also cheaper than either network or spot rates.

Some 45.1 percent of the dollars spent for television advertising went for network advertising, 28.7 percent for spot, and 26.2 percent for local. (See Exhibit 13–3.)

Measuring TV Viewing Habits. Advertisers who use television to project the merits of their products must know the types of people watching television programs in order to know if these viewers are the best prospects for buying their products. Advertisers also want to know how many people are watching TV, how long they watch, and at what times of the day. Such information helps advertisers to determine the prime times to advertise their products, thus getting the most coverage for each advertising dollar.

Market research firms, such as the A. C. Nielsen Company of Chicago, research and analyze television viewing habits of the public in order to tell advertisers the size of the viewing audience, what types of people view the programs (age, sex, education, and income level), how many switched channels to their program, and how many switched channels to another program. This information is valuable to television networks and

Exhibit 13–3
Distribution of advertising expenditures by medium, among local versus national advertisers.

(SOURCE: Reprinted with permission from the September 14, 1981 issue of *Advertising Age*. Copyright 1981 by Crain Communications, Inc.)

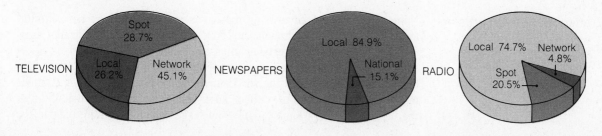

TELEVISION
Spot 28.7%
Local 26.2%
Network 45.1%

NEWSPAPERS
Local 84.9%
National 15.1%

RADIO
Local 74.7%
Network 4.8%
Spot 20.5%

local TV stations as well. Such data help them plan their programming and sell commercial time to advertisers.

In the future, television will be gaining in importance with the expansion of cable television and HBO.

Radio Advertising

Radio gives the advertiser the advantage of selecting the territory and audience to which he or she wishes to direct the message. The advertiser can direct messages to a national audience or to a smaller local market. In recent years, an increasing share of advertising expenditures have been directed toward local rather than national radio advertising. Approximately three-quarters of each dollar spent for radio advertising is spent for local advertising. The influence of television is one of the main reasons for the shift from national to local radio advertising. See Exhibit 13–3.

Magazine Advertising

A magazine advertisement has a longer life than a newspaper ad, which is normally read and discarded daily. Magazines are retained for longer periods of time and are usually read in a more leisurely manner. Another advantage is that magazines are sent to a selective audience (subscribers) and ads can be inserted that direct their message appeal toward customers in various geographical areas of the country. However, a disadvantage of magazine ads is that since the printing of a magazine is much more complex than that of a newspaper, most advertisements have to be placed well in advance (up to several months) of the time they finally reach the reader.

Direct-Mail Advertising

Every household has at one time or another received some type of direct-mail ad, such as a catalog, circular, letter, or free sample. There are two major advantages of direct-mail ads. First, the message can be directed to specific customers and thus it is selective; second, it can be spread over a wide territory. Both national companies and small, local firms effectively use direct-mail advertising.

A disadvantage of direct-mail advertising is that the message may be discarded without being read by the recipient. Furthermore, some people react negatively to some forms of direct-mail advertising because of its impersonal nature (for example, being addressed to current resident). One other disadvantage is that when names are used for the mailing list, there is a possibility that the list may not be accurate or current. Despite these disadvantages, millions of dollars are spent annually on direct-mail advertising.

Transportation Advertising

Numerous kinds of advertising messages are displayed on the different forms of public transportation (city buses, subways, suburban trains, taxicabs). This type of advertising message, commonly identified as a *car card*, is best suited to larger metropolitan areas where many people have the opportunity to notice the ad. Usually the advertising message contains more information than an outdoor advertisement (discussed below) since the individual sees it longer. These messages are often printed above the windows in the bus or subway, allowing a person to read them in some detail. Since the messages are usually above eye level, the advertiser's name usually appears at the bottom.

Firms that sell car-card advertising also sell other types of transportation advertising. Dash posters or traveler displays appear on the front, back, or sides of buses, and taxi posters are on the backs of taxicabs. Messages that appear on the sides of express trucks and posters that are placed in bus and train stations are forms of transportation advertising. Such advertising can be selective in the area covered and usually is relatively inexpensive.

Outdoor Advertising

Outdoor advertisements must be simple and to the point since a reader usually sees the message for only a matter of seconds. These messages are printed on billboards, painted signs, porta-trailers, or displayed on electric signs. Since the message must necessarily be short, the advertiser's trademark, a slogan, or a visualization of the package is usually presented. Outdoor advertising lends itself to products that are used frequently (such as daily), are well known, and whose message can be displayed quickly. An advantage of this type of advertisement is that the advertiser can select a specific geographical area.

Billboards, a familiar form of outdoor advertising, are posters containing advertisements pasted onto a panel. Painted signs, a second type, are painted by hand on surfaces, such as on the wall of a building. The third type of outdoor advertising is the electric spectacular. These are specially built frames that present the message with flashing electric or neon lights. They are costly and are erected at points where there is a possibility that many people will see the advertising message.

Porta-trailers are portable trailers that have a display board for an advertiser's message. They are flexible and selective. The message's location can be changed quickly and easily, since it is literally on wheels.

Specialty Advertising

Advertisers have their names and messages imprinted on a wide range of useful items, which are then given to the specific market segment chosen by the advertiser. This is **specialty advertising,** and some examples are ash trays, bumper stickers, calendars, pens and pencils, scratch pads, and T-shirts. The purpose of specialty advertising is to get the ad message to the individual and keep the message before the person so that it serves as a constant reminder to patronize the particular business. It can also be used to express appreciation for past business.

MEASURING THE EFFECTIVENESS OF ADVERTISING

Marketing managers would like to be able to measure the effectiveness of advertising in terms of how much sales are generated from each dollar spent for advertising. One measure of advertising effectiveness is how much sales and profits increase after a new advertising campaign is initiated. However, not all of the increase can be attributed to the new campaign, since many other factors influence sales and profits.

Some Perceptions of Advertising

A number of perceptions exist about advertising. One is that advertising confuses or misleads the public. Another perception is that advertising appeals to customer emotions rather than helping customers choose the best products for their needs. Some critics argue that firms with large amounts of money to spend for advertising can dominate the public's attention and smaller firms have less chance of attracting customers. Some argue that if advertising would be substantially reduced, people would save money because they would buy fewer products or services. However, fewer purchases mean that sales will drop and that there will be fewer jobs. One question frequently asked about advertising is: "Doesn't advertising make people buy things they can't afford or don't need?" Otto Kleppner addresses this question.

"No doubt it does in many ways. If it spurs a man to work harder to earn the money to buy those things, that is a good effect. Advertising seeks to show people what else is going on in the world; it seeks to point ways to 'health, wealth, and happiness.' Books do this. A TV travel program may do this. A visit with a friend may do it. All these influences may serve to make us restless in our desire to attain what we may consider a better standard of living. Under our system of government, every man has the responsibility of deciding for himself how he wants to spend what remains of his money after taxes, what things are necessary or important to him, and what he wants to work for. Would it be right to withhold information about products from those who can afford them, in an effort to avoid arousing those who might not be able to afford them today? Or who might have more important priorities for the use of their money?

"A great service is performed by the man who shows people how they can live better, enjoy better things in life, get better satisfaction by improving their way of living. This is not the exclusive province of advertising. But advertising not only tells about these things; it is forever telling how they may be attained more easily, more quickly, and at less cost—the favorite words of advertising headlines.

"The selfsame advertising that encourages people to want things they can't afford at the moment helps make the luxuries of today become available tomorrow at a price people can afford. The exposure to such ideas does not exempt a man from having a philosophy of life about what values are most important to him and to his family.

"This question is often linked to the one asking, 'Doesn't advertising make people buy things they do not need?' The basic needs of man are for food, clothing, and shelter. Even primitive man had his ideas of what his needs were, and sought to improve himself on these counts; the caves of primitive man still show the paintings on the walls. All 'needs' above the subsistence level are acquired tastes, which today we call the standard of living, and each man sets that for himself as best he can.

"Often, one man will pass judgment on another for buying things he does not 'need' within his apparent income level. But how would that man passing judgment react if he were told someone had said the same about him? If a man buys something that he later decides he does not need, that experience is a reflection on his judgment, and not on advertising."

SOURCE: Otto Kleppner, *Advertising Procedure*, 6th ed. (Englewood Cliffs, N.J.: Prentice-Hall, Inc., 1973.) Reprinted by permission.

No accurate measurements of advertising's effectiveness have been developed. Some indirect measures seek to determine the following types of information:

1. How many readers or viewers actually saw or heard the ad?
2. Can the advertising message be recalled?
3. Do customers recognize brand names or advertising slogans?

However, even if people can remember an ad message or a brand name, there is no assurance that they will purchase the product.

PERSONAL SELLING

A vital part of a firm's marketing strategy is **personal selling**. Personal selling is the means by which customers are reached on a face-to-face basis. To be effective, salespersons must have adequate knowledge of the products they sell and of the policies of the company they represent. They must also gather information about actual or potential customers.

The process of making a sale includes the following general steps: (1) preparation, (2) prospecting, (3) planning the sale, (4) sales presentation, and (5) follow-up after the sale. Every sale does not follow this exact sequence, but marketing managers generally agree that these are the basic steps to effective selling.

Preparation

Sales personnel must be adequately trained in order to be prepared to supply customers with information about the product. They must use proper selling techniques and be knowledgeable about the wants and desires of customers.

Prospecting

Prospecting involves the search for potential customers. There are a number of sources of potential customers. Salespersons may watch for birth or marriage announcements in the newspaper and contact the new parents or newly married couple. Or, old customers may refer new customers.

Planning the Sale

This step involves using the sales approach that will appeal to the potential customer. To do this, the salesperson must try to find out as much as possible about the customer and must try to match the customer's wants with the goods or services sold by the company. For example, the salesperson should know what the store policies are regarding merchandising, such as prices, quality, lines handled, and service policies and warranties, so they can be matched with consumer wants.

Sales Presentation

The sales presentation may use a process called AIDA—attention, interest, desire, and action.

Attention. The salesperson may use a variety of techniques to attract the customer's attention: a friendly greeting, a catchy slogan, a question, or a sales display may attract a customer's attention. The salesperson should show the customer how the product will satisfy his or her wants.

Interest. After attracting the customer's attention, the salesperson should try to arouse and increase the customer's interest in a specific product, service, or idea.

Desire. In the process of getting attention and arousing interest, the salesperson is building up to the sales presentation. In the presentation, the salesperson strives to develop the customer's desire to purchase an item. The salesperson must try to achieve the balance between not pushing too strongly, taking too long to make the sales pitch, and quitting too soon in the sales presentation. The salesperson must be keenly aware of this important problem. Some salespersons are very pushy; some just like to hear themselves talk; and others, by their overbearing nature, lose a sale. By contrast, a salesperson may fail to push the sale and give the appearance of being uninterested. Oftentimes, a demonstration of how a product operates is a useful technique to let the customer handle the goods. The salesperson should continue to emphasize how the product benefits the customer.

Action. The salesperson must be alert to the reactions of customers after demonstrating or explaining the product and should try to close the sale. The salesperson can use several techniques to help complete the sale: ask the customer if the item is satisfactory, if the item should be wrapped, which model the customer prefers, or if the item should be delivered. The salesperson should be prepared to handle objections during the trial close, such as that the price is too high or the consumer is not ready to make a purchase at this time.

Follow-Up After the Sale

The salesperson must empathize with the customers. The salesperson should stress the importance of customer satisfaction and the desire to continue to serve the customer after the sale. Customer satisfaction is very crucial. If customers are not satisfied with a product or service, they probably will not patronize the firm in the future. Thus, it is essential for salespersons to establish good relationships and to empathize with customers in order to best serve them.

TYPES OF PERSONAL SELLING

Personal selling encompasses many different kinds of situations—selling directly to wholesalers, retailers, industrial users, and ultimate consumers. Personal selling may be classified as service, creative, or supportive selling.

Service Selling

Service selling refers to that type of selling in which a salesperson assists a customer in buying. Where service selling is involved, the customer has usually decided to make a purchase and ordinarily has a general knowledge of the merchandise desired. For example, a woman decides to purchase a new dress. She has in mind the style of dress she wants, so she goes to her favorite clothing store. While there, she talks with the salesperson who regularly assists her. The role of the salesperson in service selling is to display the different styles, colors, fabrics, and prices available. The salesperson points out the basic features of each dress and its unique merits, discusses the various prices, and furnishes the customer with information relative to current styles and colors. The salesperson also assists the customer by writing up the sales ticket and making arrangements for receiving payment or charging the purchase to the customer's account.

Creative Selling

Creative selling requires greater effort and skill on the part of the salesperson than does service selling. Salespersons use creative selling techniques to find new business for a firm by trying to find new customers, creating customers' interest in and desire for a new product, service, or idea, or influencing them to change from one supplier to another. Creative selling techniques are applicable to selling situations in wholesaling, retailing, and manufacturing. Creative selling techniques require a salesperson to be knowledgeable about the products, services, or ideas being sold. The salesperson must explain the relative values and special features of the products, services, or ideas to potential customers in seeking to convince them to buy.

Supportive Selling

Supportive selling differs from service and creative selling in that supportive salespersons do not try to get orders. Instead, they try to create good will and provide specialized services. Two types of supportive salespersons are missionary salespersons and technical specialists.

Missionary Salespeople. Salespeople employed by manufacturers to work with middlemen and their customers are called **missionary salespeople.** They may assist in setting up promotional displays or training the sales force of dealers in better selling techniques. In the drug industry, the salespeople who call on doctors and other professionals and provide them with information about new products are called **detail men** and are considered a type of missionary salesperson.

Technical Salespeople. **Technical salespeople** usually have an engineering or scientific background. For example, if a computer firm sells a computerized record-keeping system to a bank, the technical specialists explain how the computerized system works, assist in providing the technical expertise in installing the equipment, and assist in adapting it to the special needs of the bank.

COMPENSATING THE SALES FORCE

The sales force may be compensated according to three basic plans: straight salary, straight commission, or a combination of both.

Straight Salary

Under this plan, the salesperson receives a fixed amount at regular intervals as payment for his or her service. This plan may be used when employees must spend considerable time in nonselling activities or when the work flow is unpredictable.

Straight Commission

The salesperson receives payment either on a fixed or sliding rate directly related to sales or profit volume. This method is probably used less than other plans because it is applicable only when a person's job is confined to sales and when products are of high unit value, such as autos or major appliances.

Combination Salary and Commission

This plan guarantees the salesperson a base salary and rewards extra selling effort by paying a commission either on sales above a specific amount or on a small percentage on all sales, such as 1 percent on all net sales. This plan is widely used in department stores.

SALES PROMOTION

In addition to advertising, publicity, and personal selling, sales promotion is another important means of creating an awareness of products. **Sales promotion** refers to "those marketing activities, other than personal selling, advertising, and publicity, that stimulate consumer purchasing and dealer effectiveness, such as displays, shows and exhibitions, demonstrations, and various nonrecurrent selling efforts not in the ordinary routine."[4]

Some types of sales promotion activities and devices are premiums, contests, trading stamps, coupons, demonstrations, and point-of-purchase displays. We will use the point-of-purchase display to illustrate the sales promotion technique.

Point-of-Purchase Displays

In a retail store, you can see many examples of point-of-purchase displays used to promote various products, especially convenience goods. Displays located near or where the product is sold are called **point-of-purchase displays**. These displays are effectively used when located near checkout counters, near store entrances, or in show windows. Point-of-purchase displays are used to promote customer awareness of products they had given no prior thought to purchasing and to stimulate impulse buying.

PRODUCT PROMOTION AT LEVI'S

A variety of media are used in national advertising to reach the public. The promotion techniques used by Levi's to promote its products are discussed below.[5] The company's promotional goals are twofold: to communicate a contemporary fashion image through national advertising and publicity, and to maintain its strength in the Western-wear market through regional media and special promotions. These goals are based on extensive market research and reflect the breadth of the product line.

Network TV

The greatest emphasis for menswear is in network television because of its ability to reach a broad audience that includes teenagers, mothers, and

---

[4]Committee on Definitions, *Marketing Definitions* (Chicago: American Marketing Association, 1960), p. 20.

[5]SOURCE: Levi Strauss & Co.

"And Mr. Fugazy here will be helping us on the aspirin account."

adult men. Furthermore, the combination of sight, sound, motion, and color is considered highly effective in presenting a fashion story.

Prime-time network programs are scheduled during peak selling seasons—spring, fall, and Christmas. Use of animation affords flexibility to imaginatively present a contemporary image of the company.

Radio

Radio is considered a primary vehicle for reaching teens. Schedules are run on contemporary music stations in some thirty major metropolitan areas.

Magazines

Magazine advertising is used as a primary vehicle for Levi's Womenswear, while other divisions use it more for supportive advertisement. Consumer magazines (e.g., *Sports Illustrated, Glamour, Mademoiselle,* etc.) have been used to reach respective audiences. Youth publications (e.g., *Rolling Stone* and other music-oriented publications) have been used to reach the teen and young-adult market. Specialized magazines have been used to reach selected markets such as military personnel and blacks.

Displays

Levi's provides a broad range of advertising materials for retailers to use in their own store promotions. These include plaques, counter cards, posters, window displays, and special Levi's bags.

Publicity

Publicity for Levi's has generally been fashion oriented. During two peak selling seasons—back-to-school and spring/summer—fashion editors at major newspapers are sent stories and fashion pictures that have been put together into "press kits" for use in the women's/family section.

In the competitive world of business, marketing managers develop a company's promotional strategy to present information about its products and services to consumers. Through advertising, personal selling, and sales promotion, consumers are provided with information that is designed to make them aware of goods and services available and to make them better informed about their purchases.

SUMMARY OF KEY POINTS

1. Promotion mix consists of the messages used by the firm to communicate information about the firm's products and services. The promotion mix is made up of advertising, publicity, personal selling, and sales promotion.

2. Advertising is any paid form of nonpersonal presentation and promotion of ideas, goods, or services by an identified sponsor.

3. Publicity is newsworthy information about a company reported in the media but not paid for by the firm.

4. An advertising agency is an independent firm that specializes in designing advertising campaigns for companies.

5. When choosing the advertising media, the purpose, cost, circulation, and message requirements must be evaluated.

6. Numerous types of media can be used by advertisers to disseminate their message: newspapers, radio, television, magazines, direct mail, transportation, outdoor, and specialty.

7. No method has been devised to accurately assess the effectiveness of advertising in increasing sales and profits.

8. The personal selling process includes preparation, prospecting, planning the sale, sales presentation, and follow-up after the sale.

9. Types of personal selling include service, creative, and supportive selling.

10. Three methods of compensating the sales force are straight salary, straight commission, and combination salary and commission.

11. Sales promotion refers to the activities other than personal selling, advertising, and publicity that stimulate consumer purchasing and dealer effectiveness.

12. Sales promotion techniques are displays, trade shows and exhibitions, and demonstrations.

DISCUSSION QUESTIONS

1. Explain the difference between advertising and publicity.
2. What does institutional advertising mean?
3. What purposes does an advertising agency serve?
4. What are some of the factors to be considered when choosing advertising media?

5. What is the "AIDCA" Principle?
6. What are some advantages of newspaper advertising?
7. Discuss the advantages of television advertising.
8. What are some disadvantages of direct-mail advertising?
9. Why is creative selling more demanding than service selling?
10. What is a missionary salesperson?
11. In the sales presentation, what is AIDA?
12. Discuss the three basic plans for compensating a sales force.

STUDENT PROJECTS

1. Listed below are some of the purposes of advertising. Select an advertisement from TV, radio, magazines, newspapers, or any other advertising medium. Prepare a brief written description of the advertisement to include the product advertised, the content of the advertising message, and the purpose or purposes of the ad as indicated in the following list.

   Purposes of Advertising
   a. Increased use of products or services. Advertising which stresses that consumers should increase the use of a product or service they are currently using.
   b. More frequent replacement of products. Advertising that is designed to foster the replacement of a used, older product with a new one, such as replacing an old television set with a new one.
   c. Enlarge the uses for products or services. Advertising that demonstrates how and why products and services may be used for new purposes.
   d. Appeal to the new (younger) generation. Products that are well known to one generation must be advertised to the next generation in an attempt to make them regular users of the products or services.
   e. Special merchandise offer. Advertising that offers extra value in special offers, such as a special two-for-the-price-of-one promotion.
   f. Institutional advertising. Advertising designed to inform the public about a company and the activities in which it is engaged.
   g. Public service message. Advertising directed toward a public cause, such as presenting the services provided by United Way or the Red Cross.

2. From your experiences as a consumer, describe the actions and characteristics of salespeople that you feel were examples of how salespeople should respond to customers.

3. From your experiences as a consumer, describe the actions and characteristics of salespeople that have annoyed you.

The Frame Place

Martha Davis has just opened The Frame Place, a picture-framing shop. In this shop, customers can make and frame their pictures themselves, or Martha and her staff of two employees will custom frame the picture for the customer. By making the frames themselves, customers can realize substantial savings.

The Frame Place, located in the southwest section of a city of 300,000, is housed in a new small shopping center. Other stores in the center are a variety store, a pizza restaurant, a gift shop, a grocery store, an ice cream parlor, a donut shop, and a dry-cleaning shop.

There are two other picture-framing businesses in this section of the city. However, they do only custom framing; customers cannot make their own frames at these shops.

Martha and her two employees offer a number of services to customers. These services include:

1. Suggestions to customers about the type of picture-frame molding to use.
2. A wide selection of moldings.
3. Assistance with the selection of picture moldings.
4. Cutting of moldings and mats for pictures if the customer desires help.
5. All materials necessary to complete the framing process, such as nails, drill, hammer, putty, mounting board, paper backing for the frame, screws and wire for hangers, and personalized stickers with customer's name.

Since the business has just opened and the shopping center is also new, Martha realizes that she must do some advertising in order to make customers aware of her business. However, she has a limited advertising budget and must be selective in spending her advertising dollars.

Questions

1. What would you recommend as appropriate advertising media for Martha to use?
2. What type of sales approach should Martha and her employees use when waiting on customers?

Ralph Harrison

Ralph Harrison graduated from college last May with a degree in General Business. While going to school, he worked part-time for a firm that manufactures prefabricated houses. The outside shell of the houses is built at the firm's place of business in the industrial section of town, then moved to the buyer's lot. The interior is finished after the house is located on the lot, and then it is turned over to the owner, ready for occupancy.

Mr. Andrews, the owner of the firm, assured Ralph that he would be taught the business by moving through the different operations and that when he graduated, he would have an opportunity to move into a managerial training position.

However, the job has not developed as Ralph thought it would. Ralph has spent most of his time in one operation, building wall frames. Only a few times has he worked in such areas as painting or carpentering.

Two months after his graduation, Ralph's position has not changed. He has not moved into a managerial training position, and he is still being paid an hourly rate of $4.50 instead of a salary. Ralph recently had dinner with three high-school friends, all of whom are in sales positions and are making good salaries. During dinner they discussed many of the good features of sales as a career.

Ralph was very interested because he has been offered a position as a salesperson for a building-products firm. Ralph would sell to home builders and apartment builders. He would sell on a straight commission basis. Roland Matthews, sales manager of the firm, believes Ralph could make $300 to $600 a week.

Ralph has a meeting with Martin Buman, the president, and Roland, the sales manager of the building products firm, next week. Ralph would like a small salary plus commission until he can build his sales volume.

Ralph's three high-school friends have encouraged him to take the job with the best money offer. Ralph hasn't yet decided what to do. After Ralph has talked with Mr. Buman and Mr. Matthews, he plans to talk to Mr. Andrews about his future in the present firm as well as what Mr. Andrews plans to offer Ralph in a management training program.

Questions

1. What kind of selling would Ralph be doing with the building-products firm?

2. What problems are there in selling on a commission basis only, especially in the beginning stages of a new job such as Ralph is considering?

3. Should Ralph tell Mr. Andrews that college graduates with BBA degrees earn starting salaries of $1,000 or more per month?

4. What would you do if you were Ralph?

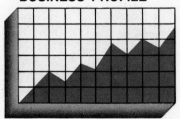

BUSINESS PROFILE

Procter & Gamble

Procter & Gamble was formed as a partnership in 1837 by William Procter, a candlemaker, and James Gamble, a soapmaker. Each partner put up half the original capital of $7,192.94. The firm was incorporated in 1890. In 1879, Ivory soap, a name familiar in millions of American homes even today, was first introduced. In 1882, the first advertisement for Ivory soap was used. This began the company's long tradition as a leading advertiser. The slogan, "It Floats," first appeared for Ivory soap in 1891, and this slogan is still used today.

Procter & Gamble extended its advertising to radio broadcasts in the 1920s. In 1932, P & G initiated daytime radio drama with "The Puddle Family," the first "soap opera." In the early 1950s, P & G began extensive television advertising. Today, the firm ranks as the top advertiser in the United States. Current expenditures amount to about $650 million annually. Procter & Gamble uses various media, including newspapers, magazines, spot radio, network television, and spot television for its advertising promotion. Approximately 95 percent of all P & G's advertising expenditures are allocated for television advertising.

Early ad for Procter & Gamble's Ivory soap.

Daytime television is still the most efficient means of selling soap and Pampers. P & G owns, produces, and sponsors six long-running television soap operas that get the attention of housewives. Products such as deodorants, which appeal to working men and women, are more efficiently advertised on evening television.

Procter & Gamble has consistently followed a policy of introducing and advertising new products under individual brand names. The individual brand names of the P & G line include those listed in Exhibit 13–4.

Exhibit 13–4

Established U.S. consumer brands (excludes test market brands).

Packaged Soap and Detergents

Heavy-Duty Products		*Light-Duty Products*
Bold	Era	Dreft
Cheer	Gain	Ivory Snow
Dash	Oxydol	
Duz	Tide	

Automatic Dishwashing Detergent	*Liquid Detergents*
Cascade	Dawn
	Ivory Liquid
	Joy

Bar Soap and Household Cleaning Products

Bar Soaps		*Household Cleaning Products*	
Camay	Lava	Comet	Spic and Span
Coast	Safeguard	Mr. Clean	Top Job
Ivory	Zest		

Fabric Softeners	*Laundry Presoak and Detergent Booster*
Bounce	Biz
Downy	

Food Products

Crisco (shortening)
Crisco Oil (salad & cooking oil)
Duncan Hines (prepared baking mixes)
Fluffo (shortening)
Jif (peanut butter)
Pringle's (potato chips)

Paper Products

Bounty (towels)
Charmin (bathroom tissue)
Pampers (disposable diapers)
Puffs (facial tissue)
White Cloud (bathroom tissue)

Toilet Goods

Crest (toothpaste)
Gleem (toothpaste)
Head & Shoulders (shampoo)
Prell (shampoo)
Scope (mouthwash)
Secret (deodorant/antiperspirant)

Coffee

Folger's vacuum packed
Instant Folger's Coffee Crystals
Folger's Flaked Coffee

Marketing, Advertising, Sales, and Physical Distribution

Career opportunities at both entry and higher levels in the many areas related to the field of marketing as well as expected demand in selected areas are shown below.

Occupation	Number Currently Employed	Number of Openings for Each Year to 1990
Sales and Marketing		
Auto salespersons	158,000	10,400
Real-estate salespersons, brokers	555,000	50,000
Retail-trade salespersons	2,851,000	226,000
Wholesale-trade salespersons	840,000	40,000
Manufacturers' salespersons	402,000	21,700
Travel agents	18,500	1,900
Buyers	115,000	7,400
Physical Distribution		
Air-traffic controllers	21,000	700
Aircraft mechanics	132,000	3,500
Airline flight attendants	48,000	4,800
Pilots and copilots	76,000	3,800
Airline reservation, ticket, passenger agents	56,000	2,200
Driving Occupations		
Intercity-bus drivers	23,500	500
Transit-bus drivers	77,000	3,100
Route drivers	195,000	3,600
Local truck drivers	1,720,000	64,000
Long-distance truck drivers	584,000	21,500

SOURCE: U.S. Department of Labor, Occupational Outlook Handbook, 1980–81.

ADVERTISING MANAGER Heads the advertising department of department stores, manufacturing companies, and other business organizations that use the services of advertising agencies; may place advertising directly in the media.

ACCOUNT EXECUTIVE Plans and directs the advertising program of individual advertisers of an advertising agency; determines medium to be used; submits to client for approval.

ADVERTISING COPYWRITER Collects data about products and the people who might use them, and writes descriptive copy to attract buyers for the products.

MEDIA DIRECTOR A specialist employed by advertisers or advertising agencies with ability to determine which advertising media will be most effective for the sale of the products.

RESEARCH DIRECTOR Processes and analyzes data collected by assistants in order to make the client's advertising campaigns successful.

PRODUCTION MANAGER Directs and works with assistants to convert the copywriter's text and artist's work into printed format.

ARTIST AND ADVERTISING LAYOUT PERSON Designs illustrations or uses the work of others to lay out the completed advertisement to represent the product.

RETAIL SALESPERSON Sells merchandise to ultimate consumers using knowledge of specific characteristics of the merchandise at the store or customer's home.

SALES ENGINEER Sells products, such as mechanical, chemical, or electronic supplies or services, which require professional engineering knowledge.

MARKET RESEARCHER Investigates market conditions in selected geographical areas to determine sales potential of products or services.

BRANCH MANAGER Responsible for supervising all activities of branch, plant, or territory operations of a business firm.

SALES MANAGER Directs sales department, coordinates sales distribution through setting up sales territories, and assigns sales territories.

STORE MANAGER Responsible for retail-store management. Involves all types of retail stores, such as food, clothing, variety, etc.

MERCHANDISE MANAGER Develops merchandising policies for the wholesale and retail establishments, such as prices, budget, and amount of merchandise to be stocked.

MANUFACTURER'S SALESPERSON Sales representative who displays, describes, or demonstrates products of a firm to wholesalers, retailers, business concerns, or individuals at their place of business or in their homes.

WHOLESALE SALESPERSON Sells to retailers and buyers for industrial and commercial institutions.

BUYER Purchases merchandise from manufacturers and wholesalers for retail firm. Buyers classed by the kinds they purchase: jewelry, clothing, etc.

OPERATIONS MANAGER Manages operations department of air, motor, railroad, or water transportation system. Activities include setting policies for providing efficient transportation services.

TRAFFIC-MANAGER Determines freight or passenger classifications and rates according to company policies and government regulations.

FREIGHT-TRAFFIC CONSULTANT Gives advice to firms relative to methods of preparing freight for shipment, rates, and mode of transportation to be used.

AIR-TRAFFIC CONTROLLER Gives instructions and information by radio to pilots to ensure safe movement of air traffic.

INDUSTRIAL TRAFFIC MANAGER Plans the movement of raw materials, equipment, and finished products to and from firms.

FLIGHT ATTENDANT Assists passengers on airline flights.

TRAFFIC AGENT AND CLERK Sells flight tickets, reserves seats, and supervises loading of planes.

AIRLINE DISPATCHER Coordinates airline flight schedules and makes sure all government and airline regulations are observed.

FLIGHT-SERVICE STATION SPECIALIST Provides pilots with weather and navigational information.

OPERATIONS AND STATION AGENT Supervises loading and unloading of aircraft.

TRAFFIC REPRESENTATIVE Contacts business customers to promote greater use of air freight and passenger service.

RAILROAD CLERK Handles paperwork necessary to keep track of company's cars and business with shippers.

DEMURRAGE CLERK Computes charges for use of railroad tracks and calculates weight of shipments or distance railroad cars have traveled.

CAREER PROFILES

Don Wilson attended Navarro Junior College and graduated from Texas Tech University. Don thinks that the college courses most helpful to him were management and economics. He got his initial job with 7-Eleven through interviews in the university's placement office.

Don advanced from a sales trainee to territory sales manager to branch wholesale sales manager to division merchandising manager. He then moved from sales and merchandising to the position of distribution systems analyst on The Southland Corporation's dairy staff.

Presently he is the distribution manager for the dairies group, and his functions include analyzing and developing individual distribution systems, dealing with government regulatory agencies, maintaining vehicle inventory records, conducting fleet energy conservation, and operating additional general "profit improvement projects."

There are several rewarding aspects of Don's job. One is the achievement of goals such as the success of a new distribution system or the successful incorporation of a new piece of hardware. Also, he derives personal gratification from helping people develop and observing them as they grow into new job skills. Other sources of satisfaction are the increasing importance of the work he is doing in the physical distribution department and the knowledge that his work is appreciated and recognized by upper management.

The most difficult part of Don's job is keeping abreast of the many regulatory agencies of the government in order to assure Southland's compliance with their many requirements.

Don's immediate goals at Southland are to plan, design, and manage a system of distribution that will be economically viable in the 1980s and 1990s.

Susan Davies graduated from the University of Oklahoma and began her career with an advertising agency. Shortly after her initial employment as a media secretary, she became a media buyer and was trained to become a radio and television-time buyer. She left that job and became media director for a small advertising agency. When that agency went out of business, Susan became a free-lance media buyer for the Stanford Agency, The Southland Corporation's advertising agency, buying television and some radio time for the 7-Eleven stores. Within six weeks, she accepted a full-time job as media buyer with the Stanford Agency. She became the agency's first female account executive, handling a division of the 7-Eleven stores headquartered in Dallas. Soon she was given responsibility for handling all advertising for three divisions, representing 1,200 7-Eleven stores.

Susan is now one of two account supervisors with the Stanford Agency. Reporting to her are three account executives who together are responsible for ten divisions. As account supervisor, Susan's responsibilities are to lend support to, advise, and train account executives in advertising skills. These include dealing with clients and merchandise managers for the 7-Eleven divisions, working with various media for local promotions, and making sure all point-of-sale displays are ordered and set up properly.

Susan feels that the most gratifying part of her job is watching account executive trainees mature into professional advertising experts, respected by their clients.

One frustration and difficulty of Susan's job is teaching the "how to" of the advertising business. This is difficult because so many advertising decisions are based on personal judgment that develops only after several years of experience.

Susan's advice for achieving promotion is to work very hard, learn from others, and have a good attitude about your work. She stresses the need to learn all you can from your professors at school—they can offer much assistance in preparing you for your career.

Financing the Business Firm

14

Money and the Banking System

LEARNING GOALS

After reading this chapter, you will understand:

1. The qualities money must have to function as a medium of exchange.

2. The functions money serves for our society.

3. How people are hurt by inflation, particularly those on fixed incomes.

4. The various types of money used in the United States.

5. How credit cards, certificates of deposit, money market funds, and interest-bearing checking accounts function.

6. The two types of banks and their importance in the monetary system.

7. How important it is to control the flow of money and credit and how they can be changed by government spending or actions of the Federal Reserve system.

8. How the Federal Reserve system can change the money supply.

9. Why the news media report changes in the prime interest rate at large banks and why they seem to consider it important.

10. The purpose and function of the Federal Deposit Insurance Corporation and the Federal Savings and Loan Insurance Corporation.

KEY TERMS

Money
Government-issued currency
Nongovernment-issued currency
Demand deposits
Time deposits
Certificates of deposit
Money market funds

Interest-bearing checking accounts
Banking system
Federal Reserve system
Inflation
Fiscal policy
Monetary policy
Reserve requirement

Open-market operations
Rediscount rate
Margin requirement
Prime interest rate
Federal Deposit Insurance Corporation
Federal Savings and Loan Insurance Corporation

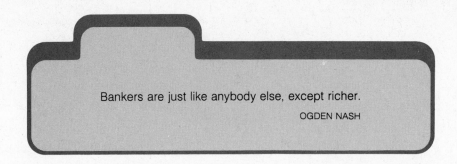

Bankers are just like anybody else, except richer.

OGDEN NASH

Business in a complex industrial society such as that of the United States could not function without acceptable money and a facilitating banking system.

Money, a medium of exchange, is the cornerstone of the industrial development of any society. Money is essential to industrial societies because it promotes specialization, makes possible the employment of large numbers of people in the economic system, and facilitates the exchange of products.

MONEY

Money must have certain qualities before it can serve its function as a medium of exchange. See Exhibit 14–1.

Qualities

To perform as a medium of exchange, money must be:

1. *Acceptable.* Money must be accepted as a medium of exchange in the society. The people must have faith in the issuing agency's ability to maintain the value of its currency.

Exhibit 14–1

Qualities and functions of money.

Qualities of Good Money	Functions of Money
Acceptable to the public	Medium of exchange
Stable in value	Eliminates the need for barter of goods
Divisible—Wide range of denominations	Serves as purchasing mechanism
	Basis for measuring or counting goods
Plentiful—Adequate supply for transactions	Yardstick for calculating wealth, income, and debts
Portable—Small in bulk, high in value	Store of value over periods of time
	Makes possible future or deferred payments
Durable—Resists wear	
Economical to produce	
Difficult to counterfeit	

2. *Stable in value.* Money must be relatively stable in value and be a means of storing value.

3. *Divisible.* Money must be divisible in order to allow transactions of any amount. People need a wide range of denominations of money to transact regular business.

4. *Plentiful.* An adequate supply of money must be in circulation at all times to meet the requirements of exchange in the economy. The supply of money should be elastic so that the amount in circulation can be regulated to meet the fluctuations of exchange in the economy.

5. *Portable.* To facilitate exchanges of various sizes, money must be portable. It must be small in bulk and large in value.

6. *Durable.* Money must maintain its appearance through large numbers of transactions.

7. *Economical.* Money should be economical to produce.

8. *Difficult to counterfeit.* In order for the issuing government to regulate its supply and maintain the faith of the public, money should be difficult to counterfeit.

Functions

The primary function of money is to serve as a medium of exchange. In order to achieve this function, money performs other services.

1. It eliminates the need for exchanging goods in a barter society.
2. It serves as a generalized purchasing mechanism.
3. It provides a basis by which goods and services can be measured.
4. It is a yardstick of value by which people calculate wealth, income, and debts.
5. It provides economic freedom over time by acting as a store of value.
6. It makes possible a system of future or deferred payments (such as credit sales).

TYPES OF UNITED STATES MONEY

Money may be classified into three broad categories: currency, demand deposits, and time deposits. See Exhibit 14–2.

Currency

The United States has used various types of government-issued and non-government-issued currency during its history.

Government-issued. There have been three basic types of government-issued currency:

1. *Full-bodied money* is the simplest type of money because its value as a commodity is equal to its value as currency. The United States circulated full-bodied money in the form of gold coins until 1933, when it withdrew them from circulation.

Inflation

Inflation causes problems for many people. The higher the rate of inflation, the more severe the problems and the greater the number of people affected. Particularly hurt by inflation are people on fixed incomes. Suppose George Browne retired ten years ago. The median family income at that time was $926 per month. To receive this amount at age 65, Mr. Browne would have had to pay annuity premiums of about $120 per month starting at the age of 25.

The U.S. Bureau of Labor Statistics calculates a measure of inflation called the Consumer Price Index (CPI). The CPI is a monthly and yearly statistical measure of the average change in prices of a "market basket" that affects the cost of living for a large percentage of the population of the United States. The "market basket" consists of thousands of goods and services normally purchased by people. Some of the major groups of items are food and beverages, apparel and upkeep, transportation, medical care, and entertainment.

Price data are collected by the Bureau from over 18,000 tenants and 24,000 retail establishments in ninety-five urban areas across the country. Ten years ago the index was at 125.3 (1967 = 100), the index today is 274.4. This means that because of inflation, the purchasing power of a dollar ten years ago has declined to forty-six cents today.

Because of the rate of inflation over the past ten years, Mr. Browne in our example would have to receive $2,028 today to maintain the same purchasing power he had ten years ago. Looking at it another way, the $926 per month has declined to $423 in purchasing power ten years later. Also, consider the fact that Mr. Browne was paying premiums when the purchasing power was much higher. The dollar amount may stay the same, but inflation can mean that it will buy much less in terms of goods and services. Even the working family finds it hard to keep up with inflation. A family making $11,000 per year ten years ago must make $24,089 today just to maintain the same standard of living. Mr. Browne would probably have two options: (1) learn to accept a reduced standard of living, or (2) return to the work force on at least a part-time basis.

The following shows how much inflation the United States experienced over the past ten years. If a person spent $1 on the following items ten years ago, that person would have to spend the following amounts to receive the same value today:

Food	$2.13
Rent	$1.72
Gas and electricity	$2.78
Apparel	$1.53
Transportation, private	$2.24
Medical care	$2.18
Entertainment	$1.75

Exhibit 14-2

Types and amounts of U.S. money (in billions of dollars).

Type of Money	Form	Amount
Currency		
Government Issued:		
Full-bodied money	Gold	0
Representative full-bodied money	U.S. gold certificates	0
Credit currency:		
Token coins*	1¢, 5¢, 10¢, 25¢, 50¢, $1	11.7
Representative token money*	U.S. silver certificates	.7
Promissory notes*	U.S. notes	.3
Nongovernment Issued*	Federal Reserve notes	108.2
Demand Deposits		236.6
Time Deposits†		1,101.9

*Currency in circulation today.
†Includes domestic banks, thrift institutions, U.S. Government, and money market mutual funds.
SOURCE: *Federal Reserve Bulletin*, 1981.

2. *Representative full-bodied money* serves as a claim that can be presented for payment in full-bodied coins or bullion. The United States Gold Certificate was a promise to pay the face value in gold or bullion until it was withdrawn from circulation in 1933.

3. *Credit currency* is circulated in the United States in three forms:
   a. *Token coins* contain an amount of metal that is considerably lower in value than the value of the coin as money. Token coins comprise the bulk of coins in circulation today. Inflation has caused problems with token coins. As the prices of silver and copper increased, the metal value in the coins became more than the value of the coins. The government was forced to change to "sandwich coins" to decrease the metal value and once again make them token coins.
   b. *Representative token money* is, in a sense, a warehouse receipt for coins or bullion held in storage by the government. However, more money is issued than is held in storage. The United States Silver Certificate was issued in an amount much larger than the value of the silver bullion the government stored to back it up. The government is now in the process of taking them out of circulation.
   c. *Promissory notes* are currency that the government promises to redeem in another form of money. Promissory notes have no backing in either metal or other commodities. The only promissory note issued by the United States in circulation today is the United States note.

"BILLY, I WANT TO INTEREST YOU IN OUR NEW KANDY KREDIT KARD."

Nongovernment-issued. The only **nongovernment-issued currency** in circulation today is the Federal Reserve note. It comprises about 90 percent of all circulating currency. The Federal Reserve promises to redeem the notes in United States currency (which can be other Federal Reserve notes).

Demand Deposits

Demand deposits (checking accounts) make up the largest amount of all exchange of money in the United States. Demand deposits are widely accepted for payment, although they may be refused and are not currency. They fulfill the function of money and are considered money in general terms. Approximately 80 percent of all money exchanges occur in the form of checks on demand deposits.

Time Deposits

Time deposits (savings accounts) are similar to demand deposits except that notice may be required for withdrawal and interest is paid on the time deposit balance at specified periods. Businesses do not accept time deposits as payment; however, they may be withdrawn with little delay to satisfy money transactions. In addition, time deposits are considered very liquid (i.e., easily converted into cash).

Time deposits are not usually included in calculating the money supply. Consequently, in one sense, they are not true money. However, because they are easily converted into cash, time deposits are usually included as a supplement to the money supply total.

MONETARY ACCOUNTS AND CREDIT CARDS

Credit cards, certificates of deposit, money market funds, and interest-bearing checking accounts are important factors in our money and banking system.

Credit Cards

Credit cards are not a form of true money since they are a form of personal debt. However, they are used extensively to purchase goods and services and are an important aspect of our exchange system. The primary bank-issued credit cards are Visa and MasterCard. The retail firm accepts them as payment and deposits them in its checking account as if they were cash. The bank then charges them (usually once a month) a percentage of all credit card deposits. This amount usually varies from 2 to 6 percent, depending on the average amount of each credit card charge slip and the volume of the slips deposited. The credit card holder is also charged a percentage of the average daily amount owed (currently 1½ percent per month). Department stores, oil companies, private financial institutions, and various retail stores also issue credit cards. They often do not charge interest on purchases if they are paid at the end of the month. Interest is added to any amounts carried over for more than one month.

Certificates of Deposit

Commercial banks and savings and loan associations offer their customers a special type of savings account that pays a higher interest rate than their regular savings accounts. These are **certificates of deposit** (CDs). The customer must deposit a minimum amount of funds and agree to leave them for a specific period of time. For example, a customer may deposit at least $100, leave it for 90 days, and receive about one-half percent more interest than the regular savings account. The customer may deposit at least $500, leave it for one year, and receive one-half percent more interest than the 90-day account and one percent more than the regular savings account. The longer the time the customer agrees to leave his or her money, the higher the interest rate. If the customer withdraws the funds from the CD before the specified time has elapsed, he or she will forfeit most of the interest earned.

The Federal Reserve dictates what interest rate can be paid on CDs of less than $100,000. On amounts over $100,000, financial institutions can set any rates they please as long as the CD time period is over 30 days.

"Money Market" CDs are also issued by banks and savings and loan associations. They usually require a $10,000 minimum and have interest rates that fluctuate weekly.

Money Market Funds

A money market fund exists when investors pool their funds to invest in high-yield, short-term debt securities. **Money market funds** sell shares, usually one dollar per share. They then take this money and invest it in debt securities (U.S. Treasury obligations, certificates of deposit, short-term business obligations, etc.) that have high interest rates and are short-term. Usually, they do not actually issue certificates of shares but, instead, send periodic statements showing deposits, withdrawals, and interest earned. There is usually a minimum amount that the investor must deposit to start his or her account. Withdrawals can usually be made on demand and without any penalty or charge. However, there often is some minimum amount, such as $100. Unlike certificates of deposit, money

market funds are not insured by the government (government insurance is discussed later in this chapter). A money market fund is, in one sense, like having a checking account on which a person or business earns interest.

Interest-Bearing Checking Accounts

On January 1, 1980, the government started allowing banks and savings and loan associations to offer interest-bearing checking accounts. The individual or business firm who has one of these accounts must maintain at least a minimum balance of some amount (most range between $500 and $2,000). If the balance stays above this amount, interest is paid on the average daily balance. If the account falls below this amount, no interest is paid and a service charge is deducted from the account.

In times of high interest rates, these **interest-bearing checking accounts** pay considerably less interest than the money market fund accounts. However, the checking accounts are insured up to $100,000 by the government while the money market funds are not.

BANKING SYSTEM

The United States banking system is extremely important in sustaining the nation's highly sophisticated industrial society. The **banking system** is vital to the nation in that it allows monetary exchange in the economic system; but, more importantly, it is able to change the total money supply through its day-to-day operations.

Federal Reserve System

The **Federal Reserve system** is the national agency that is responsible for controlling the nation's money supply. The Federal Reserve system is extremely important to the economic health of the United States because its actions in determining the size of the money supply have a major effect on the state of the economy. In fact, the Federal Reserve system has control over the money supply to such an extent that incorrect handling could cause severe depression or inflation.

The Federal Reserve Act was passed in 1913. Prior to this the banking system in the United States did not adequately control the money supply. It often overissued currency, causing inflation, or restricted the money supply, causing money panics. The Federal Reserve Act was an attempt to remedy this.

Twelve Federal Reserve cities were established and the country was divided into twelve Federal Reserve regions (see Exhibit 14–3). Two major organizations were established to control the Federal Reserve system: (1) a Board of Governors composed of seven members appointed for fourteen-year terms by the president of the United States, and (2) a Federal Open Market Committee composed of twelve members, including the seven governors and the presidents of five of the Federal Reserve banks. The Board of Governors supervises the operation of the system, and the Federal Open Market Committee determines changes in the system's portfolio of domestic securities and holdings of foreign currencies. (See Exhibit 14–3.)

Types of Banks

Banks in the United States may be chartered under either state or federal law. In the United States, there are 23,246 nationally-chartered banks and 27,626 state-chartered banks. A state charter is usually easier to obtain, and regulation is less stringent. Most of the larger banks are national banks.

Exhibit 14–3
The Federal Reserve system.

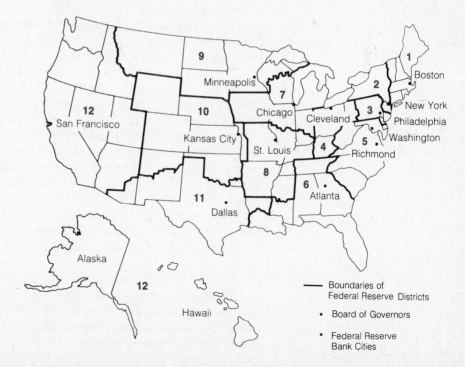

Nationally-chartered banks must be members of the Federal Reserve system, and state-chartered banks may elect to join the system. There are 29,102 member banks in the United States. Member banks must meet certain requirements. They must:

1. Purchase capital stock of the district reserve bank;
2. Maintain vault cash in their bank and deposits at the district reserve bank in the form of reserves (the amount is based on the bank's amount of demand deposits);
3. Remit at face value any checks drawn against them and presented for payment by any member bank.

Member banks gain a number of privileges through membership in the system. They may:

1. Obtain funds by discounting or borrowing from their district reserve bank;
2. Use the funds-transfer and check-collection services provided by the system;
3. Obtain expert advice and assistance;
4. Have a vote in electing six of the nine district bank directors;
5. Receive a 6 percent dividend on their federal reserve district bank stock.

CONTROL OF MONEY AND CREDIT

Our nation must have a flow of money and credit adequate to provide economic growth and a stable dollar. Efficient control of the money supply is indispensable to the steady development of the nation's resources and a rising standard of living. Controlling the flow of money and credit is extremely important.

If there is too little money and credit, the unemployment rate will rise rapidly because people will not have the money and credit to buy products, which, in turn, means that businesses will not have the money and credit to expand their production. We will use the housing industry as an example. If credit is not readily available, many people will not be able to buy homes. Because of the resulting reduction of homes built, many people in the industry will be unemployed: they will not have their paychecks with which to buy other products. This can result in unemployment in other industries.

On the other hand, if there is too much money and credit in circulation, it will lead to **inflation.** The same number of goods with more money and credit in circulation means prices are bid higher for these goods.

The trick is to balance the amount of money and credit in circulation to minimize both inflation and unemployment. It is not an easy task. There are two basic methods available for controlling the flow of money and credit: **fiscal policy** (government taxing and spending), and **monetary policy** (Federal Reserve actions).

Exhibit 14–4

Effects of government taxing and spending.

Government Budget	Change in the Flow of Money and Credit	Results of Excessive Change
Spending exceeds taxes (deficit)	Increase	Inflation
Taxes exceed spending (surplus)	Decrease	Unemployment

Government Spending (Fiscal Policy)

If the government engages in deficit spending (spending more than it taxes) the flow (velocity, not supply) of money and credit is increased. If it taxes more than it spends, the flow of money and credit is decreased. When there is excessive unemployment, the government can engage in deficit spending. When there is too much inflation, the government can tax more than it spends.

Government spending as a method of controlling the flow of money and credit has not been very effective. Congress must pass taxing and spending bills, and it takes too much time to change the balance of spending and taxing. In addition, political considerations often get in the way. Congress is much more likely to engage in deficit spending in times of high unemployment than to decrease spending or increase taxes in times of inflation. (See Exhibit 14–4.)

Federal Reserve Actions (Monetary Policy)

In practice, the Federal Reserve system has been the primary tool used to control the flow (supply) of money and credit. The Federal Reserve manipulates four instruments of control to achieve a healthy monetary environment: (1) the reserve requirement, (2) open-market operations, (3) the rediscount rate, and (4) the margin requirement. See Exhibit 14–5.

Reserve Requirement. The most powerful tool available to the Federal Reserve system for influencing the money supply is the **reserve requirement.** Member banks must maintain a certain percentage of their deposits in the form of reserves. By raising this percentage, the Federal Reserve is able to reduce the amount of money available for banks to lend for credit. By lowering the percentage, they are able to increase the amount of money available to lend as credit. Under current legislation, the Federal Reserve may set reserve requirements between the limits of 10 and 22 percent on demand deposits for large reserve banks and 7 to 14 percent on demand deposits for smaller banks. Reserve requirements on time deposits may range from 3 to 10 percent for all-size member banks.

Reserve requirements seldom change since even a small change in reserve requirements results in drastic changes in the money supply and availability of credit. A change of only 1 percent in the reserve require-

Exhibit 14–5

Major instruments of monetary control of the Federal Reserve system and their effects on the money supply.

Instruments of Monetary Control	Federal Reserve Action	Result of the Action on Supply of Money	Direction of the Prime Interest Rate
Reserve requirement	Raise the reserve requirement	→ Decreases	→ Higher
	Lower the reserve requirement	→ Increases	→ Lower
Open-market operations	Sell securities to banks	→ Decreases	→ Higher
	Purchase securities from banks	→ Increases	→ Lower
Rediscount rate	Raise the rate to banks	→ Decreases	→ Higher
	Lower the rate to banks	→ Increases	→ Lower

ment will result in a change of several billion dollars in the money supply. The availability of credit to business firms has a decided effect on business activity, so it is easy to understand why this drastic change in the availability of credit has such a pronounced effect on the economy.

Open-Market Operations. The Open Market Committee buys and sells bank securities—**open-market operations** of the Federal Reserve. Open-market operations serve two basic purposes: geographic equilibrium in the interest rate and control of the money supply. Federal Reserve banks in one section of the country may buy and sell eligible securities in other sections of the country. In this way, open-market operations transfer money from areas of plenty to areas of scarcity, which results in a national equilibrium of the interest rate.

Open-market operations alter the total money supply by purchasing or selling government securities to member banks. When the Federal Reserve purchases securities from member banks, they increase the supply of money by taking funds out of the reserve bank's supply and putting them into member banks. Then all money in excess of the reserve requirement is put into circulation. Open-market sales have the opposite effect: member banks sacrifice part of their cash balance to buy the securities, thereby decreasing money in circulation.

The Federal Reserve often uses open-market operations rather than changes in reserve requirements to control the total money supply, and thereby the availability of credit. Open-market operations allow the Federal Reserve to make small adjustments in the money supply that are not possible with the reserve requirement. In addition, changes in the total money supply in the process of daily operations by the Open Market Committee go unnoticed by the news media. This avoids the psychological effect that accompanies a dramatic change in the reserve requirement or the rediscount rate.

Rediscount Rate. When member banks need additional reserves (to meet the reserve requirement), they sell (discount) some of their paper (various types of securities—government obligations, business promissory notes, etc.—are commonly called "paper" in financial circles) to the Federal Reserve district bank. Each Federal Reserve district bank determines its own discount rate subject to approval by the Board of Governors of the Federal Reserve system.

Bankers resort to discounting commercial paper with the Federal Reserve when it is the cheapest and most advantageous of its alternatives. When the member bank's reserves fall below the reserve requirement, it may increase its reserves by selling securities to the Federal Reserve or by decreasing outstanding loans. If securities are discounted, the Federal Reserve credits the reserve account of the commercial bank, which allows the supply of money and credit to stay the same. However, if the bank decreases loans to balance its reserve account rather than discounting commercial paper, the total amount of money and credit outstanding is decreased. The amount of the **rediscount rate** then helps to determine the supply of money and credit by influencing the individual banker.

Use of the rediscount rate as a technique of controlling the money supply has consistently declined during the existence of the Federal Reserve system. Several advantages of the open-market operations over the rediscount rate for controlling the money supply have been mainly responsible for the declining use of the rediscount rate. The rediscount rate is now used by the Federal Reserve mainly to indicate policy to private bankers. An increase in the rediscount rate indicates that the Federal Reserve feels there is too much expansion of money and credit and expects member banks to assist in slowing it down by restricting credit. A decrease in the rate is used as encouragement to adopt policies that increase the expansion of credit.

Margin Requirement. The Board of Governors of the Federal Reserve system has authority to set the margin requirement for purchases of securities and member bank loans on securities. The **margin requirement** specifies the amount of down payment required on credit purchases of stock and other securities. For example, a margin requirement of 30 percent would require a person buying stock worth $100 to pay at least $30 in cash and would not allow that person to borrow more than $70 from a member bank on the purchase.

Legislation granted the Federal Reserve the power to set margin requirements in an attempt to stabilize the stock market. It is, in part, an attempt to avoid repetition of the 1929 stock market crash. Increases in the margin requirement are intended to reduce market demand during periods of excessively rapid increases in security prices. Decreases in the margin requirement are intended to prevent excessive stock dumping (selling) when the market is declining.

The margin requirement has little effect on the money supply, but it does provide stability to the stock market. Many people feel that a healthy, stable stock market is necessary to maintain a stable monetary system and a healthy economy.

Prime Interest Rate. In recent years, indications of changes in the money supply by the Federal Reserve have appeared more in the form of changes in the prime interest rate than in the rediscount rate. The **prime interest rate** is just what its name implies—the lowest interest rate available. It is the interest rate banks charge their best customers (usually large corporations) for short-term money. The news media report changes in the prime interest rate at the larger banks. For example, they may report that Chase Manhattan has dropped its prime interest rate from 14 percent to 13½ percent. This would probably mean that the Federal Reserve has increased the money supply and made more funds available. A series of drops in the prime interest rate usually shows that the Federal Reserve is attempting to stimulate the economy by increasing the money supply. A series of increases in the prime interest rate usually shows that the Federal Reserve is attempting to decrease inflation by restricting the money supply.

Federal Deposit Insurance Corporation

All members of the Federal Reserve system, both state- and nationally-chartered banks, must subscribe to the **Federal Deposit Insurance Corporation** (FDIC). Congress established the FDIC in 1933 to prevent large-scale bank failures and bank runs, such as occurred during the Great Depression. Nonmember banks also may subscribe to the FDIC if they desire. Fewer than 400 banks in the United States today are not insured by the FDIC. The FDIC is funded by having each member bank pay a premium that is based on a percentage of its deposits.

The FDIC will reimburse each depositor up to $100,000 if an insured bank fails or cannot pay its depositors. The FDIC makes loans when needed to keep insured banks from closing and to reopen closed banks that are insured by the FDIC. In addition, the FDIC performs an important function by establishing good banking practice guidelines that a bank must follow to be insured by the FDIC. Another important function the FDIC performs is examining all insured banks to ensure that they practice these safe banking policies. This is particularly important in controlling state-chartered banks that do not belong to the Federal Reserve system in states that have insufficient banking controls.

The **Federal Savings and Loan Insurance Corporation** (FSLIC) serves the same function for savings and loan associations as the FDIC does for commercial banks. It also insures deposits in savings and loan associations up to $100,000.

1. To perform as a medium of exchange, money must be acceptable, stable in value, divisible, plentiful, portable, durable, economical, and difficult to counterfeit.

2. The functions of money are: to serve as a medium of exchange; to eliminate the need for barter of goods; to serve as a purchasing mechanism; to be a basis for measuring or counting goods; to be a yardstick for calculating wealth, income, and debts; to be a store of value over periods of time; and to make possible future or deferred payments.

3. Money may be classified into three broad categories: currency, demand deposits, and time deposits. Currency may be either government-issued or nongovermnent-issued.

4. Currency in circulation today consists of token coins, representative token money (U.S. silver certificates), promissory notes (U.S. notes), and nongovernment-issued currency (Federal Reserve notes).

5. Credit cards are not a form of money but a form of credit. However, they are used extensively to pay for goods and services.

6. Certificates of deposit are a special form of time deposit. The customer agrees to leave a certain amount of money for a specified time and receives a higher rate of interest than he would for a savings account.

7. Money market funds sell shares and invest the money in high-yield, short-term debt. They are not insured by the federal government. Interest-bearing checking accounts pay interest on accounts that do not fall below a certain minimum balance. They are insured up to $100,000 by the government.

8. Banks may be federally- or state-chartered and both may belong to the Federal Reserve system.

9. The Federal Reserve system's primary mission is to maintain a supply of money to ensure a healthy and sound economy.

10. The reserve requirement is the amount of money banks must keep on deposit with the Federal Reserve or in their vaults. Changes in the reserve requirement have a drastic impact on the money supply.

11. The rediscount rate is the rate charged by the Federal Reserve to discount paper for the banks.

12. The margin requirement is the percentage of down payment that must be paid to purchase stock.

13. The prime interest rate is the amount of interest a bank or banks charge their best customers, usually large corporations.

DISCUSSION QUESTIONS

1. Examine each quality of "good money" and decide if you think the United States has "good money."
2. Evaluate United States money with regard to the functions of money.
3. Why do you think demand deposits are considered a part of the money supply?
4. List in order of probability the types of currency you might find if you looked in your pockets or purse. Which ones did you find?
5. Credit cards are used extensively to purchase goods and services. Do you think they should be considered money?
6. Would you rather have your money in regular savings accounts or in certificates of deposit? Explain your answer.
7. Should a person put his or her money in a money market fund or in an interest-bearing checking account? Explain your answer.
8. Do you think the Federal Reserve is important to the United States?
9. If you opened a bank, would you want it to be a nationally-chartered bank? Explain.
10. Explain what would happen if the Federal Reserve:
    a. Increased the reserve requirement;
    b. Bought more securities in their open market operations;
    c. Lowered the rediscount rate;
    d. Raised the margin requirement.
11. What would it mean if the larger banks in the nation dropped their prime interest rate several times over a period of a few weeks?
12. How does the Federal Deposit Insurance Corporation help guard against bank runs?

STUDENT PROJECTS

1. See how many of the following you can find to show the class:
   a. One token coin of each denomination in circulation;
   b. One silver certificate;
   c. One United States note;
   d. One Federal Reserve note;
   e. Any currency not currently in circulation.
2. Find the most recent issue of the *Federal Reserve Bulletin* in the library and determine the following:
   a. The latest prime interest rate charged by banks on short-term business loans.
   b. The Consumer Price Index for the current year. When was the base year?
   c. The latest margin requirement on stocks and convertible bonds.

The Business Expert at a Party

The host at a party introduces you as a person who knows a lot about business and economics. One guest explains that he is a native of a small nation with considerable tin reserves. His nation has received so much money for its tin that it has decided to invest some of it in the United States. He has been sent here to set up facilities to manufacture high-quality jewelry. While talking to him you learn:

1. He realizes high-quality jewelry sells better when the economy is good than when it is depressed.
2. He is concerned because he has found out that Federal Reserve notes are not backed by silver or gold.
3. The firm will have excess amounts of cash at various periods of time and he wants to know if he should put it in interest-bearing checking accounts, certificates of deposit, or money market funds.
4. He is concerned that the United States has suffered from high rates of inflation several times since World War II. He feels it might reach high levels and stay there because nothing can be done to control it.
5. He has read that the Federal Reserve has lowered the rediscount rate and the prime interest rate has dropped for six weeks in a row. He does not understand what this means.

Questions

1. Explain to him why the dollar is sound.
2. Explain what can be done to influence the rate of inflation.
3. Tell him the difference between interest-bearing checking accounts, certificates of deposit, and money market funds.
4. Explain to him the Federal Reserve actions and the drop of the prime interest rate.
5. Explain what the Federal Reserve actions mean to his business.

The Inheritance

A friend inherited a large sum of money and has $500,000 left after all taxes have been paid. He now has the money in a savings account.

He is worried because he just finished reading a book that said the economic situation in the United States during the past ten years has been much like that in the 1920s before the Depression. The book predicted the United States would have a period of runaway inflation and then a financial collapse. It pointed out that the dollar is just printed money and not backed by anything. It also predicted runs on banks to such an extent that they would all fail and all forms of United States money would be worthless. Your friend had been planning to invest some of his money in blue chip stocks and bonds and the rest in a business. After reading the book, he is considering putting his money into gold, diamonds, or land so he will have something of value if the dollar becomes worthless.

You feel the book is somewhat misleading and omits some important facts. Since you know a good deal about the United States monetary and banking system, you feel you must give him some additional facts before he reaches a final decision.

Questions

1. Tell him why you think United States money is "good" money in terms of the quality and functions of money.
2. Explain the circumstances under which he might lose buying power by keeping his money in a savings account.
3. Explain the various methods the government and Federal Reserve system can use to prevent runaway inflation.
4. Tell him why you feel there probably will not be any runs on banks.

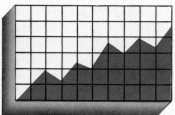

BUSINESS PROFILE

Wells Fargo and Company

Wells Fargo, a name that conjures up the colorful and daring in the rugged pioneer American West, actually had its beginnings in New York City. There, on March 18, 1852, Vermont-born Henry Wells and New Yorker William G. Fargo formally launched and gave their names to a banking and express business to serve gold rush California.

Wells Fargo & Co. opened its doors for business in July 1852 in San Francisco and rapidly expanded, with agencies located principally in the Mother Lode, California's main gold-producing region. In 1855 a financial panic caused a run on all the banking houses in San Francisco. Wells Fargo survived the crisis that removed from the scene most of the company's major rivals in the banking and express business in California.

Wells Fargo Bank is among the nation's largest financial institutions.

In 1866 Wells Fargo's stagecoach empire reached its peak, with the consolidation under its own name and ownership of the entire great overland mail route plus thousands of additional miles of stage lines west of the Missouri River.

In 1905 the banking and express portions of Wells Fargo went their separate ways, with the domestic express business consolidated with that of other companies under wartime regulations in 1918.

Meanwhile, in San Francisco the banking arm continued, and today's Wells Fargo Bank is a direct continuation of the banking business of the original Wells Fargo & Co. In 1969 the bank formed a one-bank holding company, taking as its name the legendary Wells Fargo & Company. With branches throughout California and extensive international operations, Wells Fargo Bank is among the nation's largest financial institutions.

15

Sources of Funds for Business

LEARNING GOALS

After reading this chapter, you will understand:

1. That the three basic sources of funds are retained earnings, debt capital, and equity capital.

2. That interest rates are set primarily by: (1) supply and demand of funds, and (2) risk involved.

3. The primary function and services of commercial banks.

4. The various sources of short-term funds and how they operate.

5. The various sources of long-term funds and how they operate.

KEY TERMS

Capital
Debt capital
Equity capital
Interest rates
Working capital
Commercial bank
Paper
Promissory note
Line of credit
Installment sales contracts
Factor
Accounts receivable

Sales finance companies
Floor planning
Vendor
Long-term loan
Savings and loan association
Insurance companies
Investment bank
Mutual fund
Pension funds
Trust companies
Small Business Administration

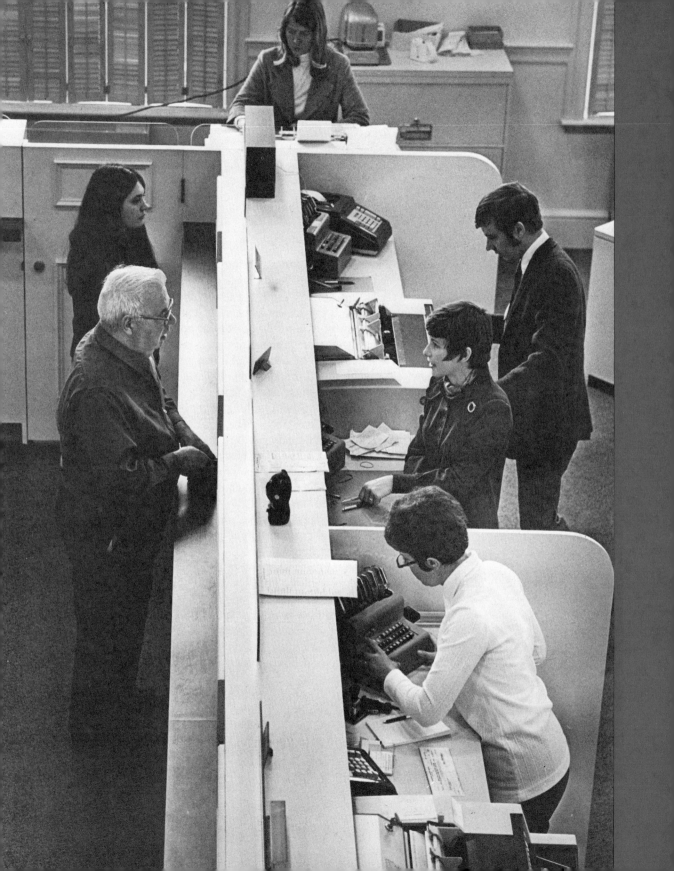

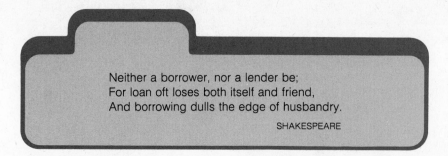

Neither a borrower, nor a lender be;
For loan oft loses both itself and friend,
And borrowing dulls the edge of husbandry.

SHAKESPEARE

Business firms must have money if they are to produce goods and services for the consuming public. Land, buildings, equipment, raw materials, customer credit, and payrolls are just a few of the items that require money. Finding sources to provide an adequate supply of money is a prime concern to management of both large and small business firms. Most business firms continually face the problem of raising money and rationing it among various uses. In fact, the success of a firm's operation often depends on how effectively the firm performs the acquisition and distribution of money. Management must always know the sources and cost of funds. **Capital** (money) needs must be satisfied at a reasonable cost and with a minimum risk to the firm. See Exhibit 15–1.

Increases in capital funds in a business may come from its own earnings or from sources outside the business. The source of least risk to a firm is the use of plowed-back earnings of the business; however, adequate growth financing usually requires additional funds. **Debt capital** (borrowed funds) and **equity capital** (ownership) are the most common sources of outside capital available for use to the business firm. (For a complete coverage of debt capital and equity capital, see chapter 3, "Capital-Accumulating Instruments.")

Debt capital is often described in the business world as being short-term or long-term, with the breaking point being either five or ten years. However, it is more accurate to divide debt capital into three categories—short-term, intermediate-term, and long-term: short-term is debt of less than one year; long-term is debt of more than ten years; and intermediate-term is debt of from one to ten years. Because the sources of short-term and intermediate-term debt are usually the same, we will group them both into the short-term category.

INTEREST RATES

Interest rates charged by the various sources of loans for business are determined primarily by two factors: supply and demand of money, and the amount of risk involved in loans.

Supply and Demand

When the Federal Reserve system causes changes in the money supply, a change occurs in the **interest rates** businesses must pay for loans. When the money supply increases, commercial banks have more money to lend and interest rates tend to drop. When the money supply decreases, commercial banks have less money to lend and interest rates tend to rise. Competition generally causes the interest rates of all lenders of money to rise and fall in response to changes in commercial bank interest rates. See Exhibit 15–2.

Demand for money and credit (often a result of the balance between government spending and taxing) has an effect on interest rates. For example, if the Federal Reserve were to hold the money supply constant, an increase in demand would result in higher interest rates. A decrease in demand would result in lower interest rates.

Risk

Interest rates vary according to the risk involved in loans. Higher-risk loans require higher interest rates. Lower-risk loans require lower interest rates. Commercial banks provide a good example. In a sense, the demand for loans from commercial banks always exceeds their supply of money. They supply their low-risk customers (for example, provide short-term loans to large corporations) before they give loans to anyone else. (This is why the "prime interest rate" discussed in the previous chapter is the lowest rate they give.) Then they supply each risk group in order of increasing risk until they have no more funds to lend. However, each increasing risk group must pay a higher interest rate. Some financial institutions specialize in high-risk loans in order to obtain high interest rates. These high interest rates must cover losses from defaulted loans, operating expenses, and profit. Lenders that specialize in low-risk loans lose less in terms of loan defaults and can charge a lower interest rate.

Interest rates also have an impact on the actions of borrowers. For example, a firm might consider borrowing money to build a plant to manufacture a new product. If they are able to borrow money at 10 percent interest, they may realize enough profit to justify the risk of the venture. However, if they have to pay 16 percent interest on the debt, the additional interest may reduce profit from the venture to the extent that it is not worth the risk.

Exhibit 15–1

Sources of capital for business firms.

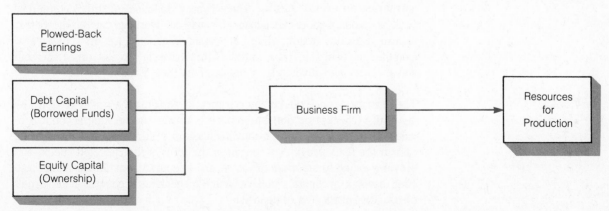

Exhibit 15–2
Changes in the money supply cause changes in interest rates.

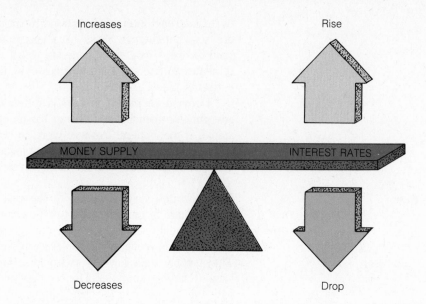

SHORT-TERM LOANS

Short-term funds are usually **working capital**—money used to carry on day-to-day operations of business for such purposes as financing payrolls, raw materials, merchandise, postage, utilities, travel, and office supplies. The operations of a business firm create many needs for working capital. A firm may need additional working capital when (1) there is a seasonal demand for its product or service; (2) money is needed to take advantage of trade or cash discounts; (3) extended periods of time are required to collect accounts outstanding; or (4) to take advantage of some unusual opportunity.

The most common sources from which to obtain short-term financing are commercial banks, factors, sales finance companies, friends, family, and vendors.

COMMERCIAL BANKS

The main financial institution that extends short-term commercial credit is the **commercial bank.** The primary function of the commercial bank is making short-term loans for use as working capital; however, it also provides many other important functions for its customers. Commercial banks in the United States have in excess of $1,253 billion in loans and investments outstanding. See Exhibit 15–3.

Services

The primary service offered by commercial banks is the privilege of drawing drafts (checks) on demand deposit accounts. A checking account provides customers with many conveniences: it reduces the risk of sending cash in the mail, provides a receipt in the form of the canceled check, and provides monthly statements for record keeping. Commercial banks also offer savings accounts, interest-bearing checking accounts, bank credit cards, and certificates of deposit.

Commercial banks also extend collection services to their depositors. All types of commercial paper (various forms of instruments representing debt) will be collected locally or through other banks for a relatively small fee.

Promissory Notes. Commercial banks extend credit primarily with the use of the promissory note. The promissory note is a legal contract in which the borrowing firm agrees to pay the bank the amount of the loan plus interest at the end of a specific period of time.

Business firms also receive promissory notes, often from their customers in return for purchases. A firm may hold a note until it matures,

Exhibit 15–3

The twenty-five largest commercial-banking companies (ranked by assets).

Rank '81	Rank '80	Company	Assets ($000)	Deposits ($000)	Rank	Loans ($000)	Rank
1	2	BankAmerica Corp. (San Francisco)	121,158,350	94,369,453	1	71,236,237	2
2	1	Citicorp (New York)	119,232,000	72,125,000	2	77,139,000	1
3	3	Chase Manhattan Corp. (New York)	77,839,338	55,299,670	3	50,459,433	3
4	4	Manufacturers Hanover Corp. (New York)	59,108,519	42,462,035	4	37,448,484	4
5	5	J.P. Morgan & Co. (New York)	53,522,000	36,024,000	5	28,220,000	6
6	6	Continental Illinois Corp. (Chicago)	46,971,755	29,594,005	6	31,463,328	5
7	7	Chemical New York Corp.	44,916,933	29,429,577	7	27,789,275	7
8	9	First Interstate Bancorp. (Los Angeles)	36,982,091	27,407,174	8	20,795,103	9
9	8	Bankers Trust New York Corp.	34,213,010	23,345,022	11	18,504,025	11
10	10	First Chicago Corp.	33,562,442	25,554,923	9	20,020,357	10
11	11	Security Pacific Corp. (Los Angeles)	32,999,142	23,446,393	10	21,521,100	8
12	12	Wells Fargo & Co. (San Francisco)	23,219,189	16,853,927	12	16,936,490	12
13	13	Crocker National Corp. (San Francisco)	22,494,462	16,494,955	13	24,003,786	13
14	15	Marine Midland Banks (Buffalo)	18,682,474	14,095,704	14	20,799,319	14
15	16	Mellon National Corp. (Pittsburgh)	18,447,860	11,837,780	17	9,793,649	17
16	14	Irving Bank Corp. (New York)	18,227,220	14,006,245	15	9,826,780	16
17	19	Interfirst Corp. (Dallas)	17,318,000	12,559,000	16	9,851,000	15
18	17	First National Boston Corp.	16,809,052	11,019,908	20	9,085,367	18
19	18	Northwest Bancorp. (Minneapolis)	15,141,380	11,386,218	18	8,639,829	19
20	20	First Bank System (Minneapolis)	14,911,285	11,022,734	19	7,842,799	20
21	22	Texas Commerce Bancshares (Houston)	14,511,591	10,528,654	22	7,682,156	22
22	21	Republic of Texas Corp. (Dallas)	14,441,096	10,086,276	23	7,781,972	21
23	23	First City Bancorp. of Texas (Houston)	14,291,097	10,859,113	21	7,347,617	23
24	24	NBD Bancorp (Detroit)	12,144,873	8,655,694	24	5,600,915	26
25	25	Bank of New York Co.	11,462,995	8,079,888	26	6,925,465	25

SOURCE: *Fortune*, July 12, 1982.

Cashless-Checkless Banking

For several years, experts have been predicting a "cashless-checkless" banking system. Computers will make it possible for all money transactions in the future to occur simply by debiting and crediting bank accounts. No currency or checks will need to change hands. The banking name for this type of system is electronic funds transfer systems (EFTS). Some forms of EFTS are already in existence in the United States.

Customers of one bank can dial the bank's computer. Using a plastic device that fits over the telephone's buttons, they can pay bills without writing a check. At income tax time, they can also obtain information on medical expenses and interest payments.

Another bank provides a plastic card to their customers which they use when making purchases from participating merchants. The card allows the transfer of funds from the customer's account to the merchant's account without the use of a check. Customers also get a 2 percent discount on these purchases.

One bank has installed computer terminals in major stores in their area. When customers use their credit cards to make purchases at these stores, funds are transferred without the store having to fill in the usual credit card form or the customer issuing a check.

Some bank clearing houses are using computers to credit employee bank accounts from company payrolls. The total payroll is deducted from the bank accounts of large companies and added to the balance of their employees' bank accounts without any checks being issued.

The massive volume of checks processed in the banking system today is time consuming and expensive. In the future, electronic funds transfer systems will make possible worldwide transfer of funds in a matter of seconds while greatly reducing the cost of transfer.

"BEFORE WE DISCUSS OUR SHORT-TERM INTEREST RATES, PERHAPS YOU COULD LET ME KNOW HOW MANY HOURS YOU'LL NEED THE MONEY FOR."

thereby financing its own credit extensions. The firm also has the option of discounting (selling) the note to a commercial bank and receiving immediate cash, which in effect transfers financing of the firm's credit to a commercial bank. The business firm discounts the note by endorsing it to the bank. The commercial bank then collects the note in one of two ways: they may notify the customer that the bank holds the note and that payment is to be made to the bank, or they may simply allow the customer to pay the firm, which in turn transfers the payment to the bank.

Line of Credit. A **line of credit** is an informal agreement between a commercial bank and one of its customers establishing the maximum amount of funds the customer may borrow without mortgaging specific assets. The commercial bank evaluates the credit of the customer and assigns the line of credit. A line of credit is particularly advantageous to a business firm because the firm can plan more effectively and also save time when it borrows money. The bank's board of directors usually must authorize a line of credit.

Finance Installment Sales. Commercial banks provide financing of credit sales for business firms by purchasing **installment sales contracts** their customers have signed in return for purchased merchandise. In this type of transaction, the business firm borrows the amount of the installment contract from the bank and puts up the contract as security for the loan. As the business receives payments from the customer, the business repays the loan to the bank. In this type of arrangement, the business must pay off the note even if the customer does not honor the note.

Exhibit 15–4
Function of factors.

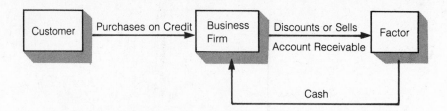

FACTORS

Probably the most pressing financial problem facing most businesses is the continued need for working capital. Accounts receivable often represent the largest dollar amount in the current asset section of the balance sheet and, consequently, are often the largest drain on working capital. One type of lender, a **factor,** may be an important source of working capital for business firms by converting accounts receivable into cash by either purchasing or discounting them. See Exhibit 15–4.

Purchasing Accounts Receivable

Financing of **accounts receivable** may be achieved by outright sale of the accounts to a factor. When the factor purchases accounts receivable, he assumes the credit risk and usually is responsible for collecting the accounts. Customers often make their payments directly to the factor. In exchange for relieving the business of the burden of supporting accounts receivable with large amounts of working capital, the factor buys the receivable at some amount less than the face value of the accounts. The fee is the difference between the face value, the price the factor pays for the accounts, and any interest the factor may collect on the accounts.

A factor who purchases accounts receivable must be extremely competent in judging their worth. The factor must offer the business a price high enough to motivate it to sell the accounts, yet be reasonably accurate in the estimation of how many he or she will be able to collect. If the factor fails to collect as many accounts as estimated, he or she may end up losing money on the transaction.

Discounting Accounts Receivable

When accounts receivable are discounted to a factor, the company retains ownership of the receivables and assumes all the credit risk. The factor simply lends an amount of money the accounts are estimated to be worth, and the business pledges the accounts receivable as security for the loan. In this type of arrangement, the business firm usually does not tell the customer that his account has been discounted, and the customer remits the payments directly to the business firm. The business firm pays the factor all monies received from customers until the loan from the factor, plus fees, is repaid. If the business doesn't collect enough money by the end of the loan period, it must make up the difference. Of course, if the business collects more money than it owes the factor, the business keeps the difference.

The factor usually charges a fee based on the average daily value of the accounts receivable. The factor will usually discount accounts receivable at a lower cost to the business than when he or she purchases them, since the factor does not assume as great a credit risk. In addition, factoring is usually more expensive than equal amounts of money obtained from direct commercial bank loans.

SALES FINANCE COMPANIES

Sales finance companies mainly purchase installment contracts from retailers who have obtained the contracts from customer purchases on the time-payment plan. **Sales finance companies** purchase installment contracts for their high interest rates and because the items mortgaged as the security of the contracts are usually very marketable. A wide market usually exists for items sold on installment contracts, such as automobiles and appliances. Retailers sell installment contracts to convert credit sales into cash sales and thus reduce their need for working capital.

Sales finance companies also offer financing to retailers of many kinds of consumer durable goods by **floor planning.** A trust receipt allows the retailer to keep the goods as inventory, with the sales finance company owning the merchandise. When the merchandise is sold, the retailer obtains an installment sales contract from the customer, gives the contract to the sales finance company, and receives money in excess of the value of the goods plus any service fee. Another method of floor planning is for the sales company to lend the retailer the price of the goods kept in inventory. When the merchandise is sold, the retailer gives the installment contract to the sales finance company and receives the purchase price less the original loan, interest on the loan, and any fees. The sales finance company usually checks on the inventory of the retailers periodically, since the retailer keeps the goods.

FRIENDS, FAMILY, AND VENDORS

Small companies sometimes use short-term loans from friends and family when they are unable to obtain funds from other sources. Two out of every three new businesses fail; consequently, the very type of business that is most likely to borrow from friends and family is the one most likely to fail. A very good way to lose friends or create ill will in a family is to lose their money in a business venture; therefore, it is not as attractive a source of money as it might first appear, even when it is interest-free money.

Almost all **vendors** provide credit terms, usually ranging from ten to ninety days, to businesses that purchase from them. Some vendors will also provide financing to customers other than the price of the goods they sell in order to create good will and continued patronage. Vendors are not as willing to extend credit to new businesses as to established ones and often set fairly low limits on credit they do extend.

LONG-TERM LOANS

Long-term loans are particularly important to the business firm, for they allow purchase of large amounts of high-value assets. Long-term loans are often used for such items as land, buildings, equipment, machinery, fixtures, customer installment financing, and vehicles. The following are sources of long-term loans:

1. Savings and loan associations
2. Insurance companies
3. Investment banks
4. Mutual funds
5. Pension funds
6. Trust companies
7. Small Business Administration
8. Private investors

SAVINGS AND LOAN ASSOCIATIONS

Savings and loan associations offer savings accounts, interest-bearing checking accounts, and certificates of deposit on which they pay interest to depositors. Savings and loan associations obtain their profit and operating expenses by lending a large part of the money deposited by customers at a higher interest rate than they pay depositors.

Savings and loan associations lend long-term funds to finance real estate purchases by both businesses and individuals.

Exhibit 15–5
Operations of an insurance company.

Savings and loan associations basically lend long-term funds to finance real estate purchases by both businesses and individuals. They are the primary source of loans used by individuals to purchase homes. Since the association lends the money to the home purchaser at an interest rate that is only a few percentage points higher than they are paying their depositors, they must make only low-risk loans.

Savings and loan associations make many types of business loans, such as property improvement loans, mortgage loans for construction of apartment buildings and shopping centers, and mortgage loans on other business property. The business loans must also be low-risk loans.

Savings and loan associations may hold either a state or federal charter. Both federal- and state-chartered savings and loan associations must have their accounts insured by the Federal Savings and Loan Insurance Corporation.

There are two basic types of savings and loan associations: mutuals, or corporations owned by stockholders. All federal- and most state-chartered associations are mutuals, that is, they are owned mutually by the people who have savings accounts with the association. State-chartered savings and loan associations in California, Texas, and Ohio have stockholders separate from the people who deposit funds.

Savings and loan associations in the United States hold in excess of $500 billion in mortgages. This large a sum of money shows how important they are to the money market.

INSURANCE COMPANIES   **Insurance companies** sell insurance and annuity protection. Policy holders paying insurance premiums provide the companies with vast sums to invest. The return on these investments provides the bulk of the insurance company's funds for administrative expenses and profit. Through the investment of these premium reserves, insurance companies make their principal contribution to long-term capital loans available to business firms.

Millions of people and businesses pay premiums, which allows insurance companies to accumulate billions of dollars in premium reserves available for investment. Insurance companies invest these billions of dollars in government securities, stocks and bonds, and business mortgage loans.

INVESTMENT BANKS

The **investment bank** is a middleman in the long-term security market. Its main function is to bridge the gap between suppliers and users of long-term capital funds. Investment banks act primarily as principals (buying and selling) and not as agents (go-betweens). They buy securities at specific prices, mark the prices up, and then resell in smaller lots at a profit. Investment banks mark up the price of the securities in order to cover expenses, risk, and profits.

The investment bank performs three important functions in the security market: investigation, risk bearing, and selling. The investment bank often advises the issuing corporation as to the types and terms of securities best suited for the company to sell at that time. In addition, the investment bank makes a detailed study of the corporation in order to determine the feasibility of selling its securities and to determine the price at which each security is expected to sell in the market. Their assessment of market price must be very close to the actual selling price, for it determines the price they will pay for the securities. A mistake in judgment on the market selling price may cost them vast sums of money.

The investment bank buys the entire security issue of the corporation, allowing the corporation to make use of the funds even before the securities are sold in the open market. The investment bank then sells the securities to independent brokerage houses or through its own retail outlets located in major cities. Generally, investment banks serve large corporations selling large issues of securities rather than small companies.

MUTUAL FUNDS

The general term *investment companies* describes firms that engage principally in the purchase of securities of other companies. A **mutual fund** is a company that combines the investment funds of many people and in turn invests their funds in a variety of securities. More specifically, mutual funds sell stock in their companies, generally to individual investors. They then take the money received from the sale of their stock and invest in the open securities market. They distribute profits realized from investing in the securities market as dividends to their stockholders, or reinvest in the securities market, thus increasing the value of the mutual fund stock.

Most mutual funds do not limit the sale of their own stock and stand ready at any time to redeem or buy back their own outstanding stock if presented by the investor. Mutual funds invest, generally, in common and preferred stock, and in bonds of corporations.

PENSION FUNDS

Business firms are large users of funds, but they sometimes play a significant part in providing long-term capital for other businesses. One of the most important ways they perform this service is through the large sums that are accumulated in their employee **pension funds,** which are invested in long-term securities of business and government. Unions also maintain pension funds that provide billions of dollars for the money market.

Investment policies of pension funds are less uniform and less well known than those of other financial institutions. In general, about 40 percent are in corporate stocks, 42 percent in corporate bonds, and the remainder in cash, government securities, mortgages, leases, and other investments. Pension funds are generally concentrated on acquiring high-grade securities.

TRUST COMPANIES

A trust is an agreement in which an individual transfers ownership of property to another person, a trustee, for the benefit of a third person, a beneficiary. The trustee in many types of trusts invests funds placed in his or her keeping for the benefit of the beneficiary. Income from the investment allows the trustee to be paid a fee and provides funds for transfer to the beneficiary. The combinations of types and conditions of trusts are virtually endless. Often trusts are placed with commercial banks; however, many other institutions may act as trustees.

Trust companies in the United States administer and control large funds and hold a significant amount of securities. In addition to administering trust funds, they provide complete records of all trust transactions, send monthly reports to customers, and provide investment counsel. By their investment in securities, trust funds provide extensive funds to the long-term capital market.

SMALL BUSINESS ADMINISTRATION

The only branch of the federal government that provides a significant amount of loans to business on a continuing basis is the **Small Business Administration** (SBA). They do make some direct loans; however, most of the help they provide small businesses in obtaining funds is through guarantee loans. They guarantee a percentage (often 90 percent) of a loan by a commercial bank. They do not compete with lending institutions—an applicant must have been turned down by one or two banks. They do have some specialized types of loans, such as disaster loans, but these are only a small part of the funding they provide for business.

PRIVATE INVESTORS

Friends, families, and other private investors are a source of small long-term loans to small businesses. Friends and families are often the only source of capital available to a new small business or to an existing small business that is in dire need of working capital. As pointed out earlier, these businesses are often very risky, and the business person is risking ill will when he or she persuades family and friends to invest in what may become a losing venture. Private investors, other than friends and family, sometimes lend capital to small businesses because of the higher interest rates they can charge.

SUMMARY OF KEY POINTS

1. Sources of business capital may come from retained profits, debt capital, and/or equity capital. Debt capital may be either long-term or short-term debt.

2. Interest rates charged to businesses are determined by: (1) the supply and demand of money, and (2) the amount of risk involved in the loan.

3. Short-term loans are usually used for working capital, which consists of funds necessary to carry on day-to-day operations.

4. The most common sources of short-term financing are: (1) commercial banks; (2) factors; (3) sales finance companies; and (4) friends, family, and vendors.

5. Commercial banks are the predominant short-term financial institutions and they offer a wide range of other services such as demand deposit accounts, collecting commercial paper, financing installment sales, and extending lines of credit.

6. Factors provide business financing by either purchasing or discounting the firm's accounts receivables, which increases available working capital.

7. Retailers reduce their need for capital to finance customer credit by selling installment sales contracts to finance companies.

8. Some sources of long-term loans for business are: (1) savings and loan associations; (2) insurance companies; (3) investment banks; (4) mutual funds; (5) pension funds; (6) trust companies; (7) the Small Business Administration; and (8) private investors.

9. Savings and loan associations pay depositors interest on their money deposited with them and loan it out at a higher interest rate.

10. Insurance companies collect premiums from policy holders and then invest the money in government securities, stocks and bonds, and business mortgage loans.

11. Investment banks buy large new issues of stocks and bonds from large corporations and then sell them in the market in smaller lots at a higher price.

12. Mutual funds sell shares and invest the money in the market. Money they earn is paid to their shareholders.

13. Pension funds are invested in government securities, mortgages, bonds, stocks, and other investments.

14. Trust companies manage trust funds. They take the money in the trust and invest it in various securities.

15. The Small Business Administration lends money and guarantees loans to small businesses.

DISCUSSION QUESTIONS

For the following questions, assume you own a retail store that sells radio and stereo equipment.

1. List in order the three basic sources of capital you would want to use if you were to expand your business. Explain your listing.
2. What would it cost you to borrow money from a commercial bank? Explain your answer.
3. Would you use short-term working capital in your business? Explain.
4. What services of a commercial bank would you use?
5. Would you sell or discount your accounts receivable to a factor? Explain.
6. How might you use a sales finance company?
7. Would you borrow money from family or friends to start the business? Explain.
8. List in order the sources of short-term funds you would use.
9. Would you borrow money from any of the following and for what?
   a. Savings and loan association
   b. Insurance company
   c. Mutual fund
   d. Small Business Administration

STUDENT PROJECTS

1. From the local telephone directory, see if you can find one name for each source of business funds listed in this chapter.
2. See how many services of commercial banks listed in this chapter a local commercial bank offers.
3. Visit a retail business and find out how many of the sources of business funds listed in this chapter they use.

Eric's Passion Punch

Ten years ago, Eric Brian, a chemist, was experimenting in his spare time with soft drink flavors. He developed what he considered an entirely new flavor of soft drink. Eric built a small bottling plant with a loan, guaranteed by the Small Business Administration, from the local commercial bank.

He sells his soft drink—Passion Punch—in a one-hundred-mile radius of the plant. His advertising has centered around the slogan, "Your passion will be our punch." The drink has been a big success. Two years ago he added several basic fruit flavors (orange, strawberry, etc.) to his line. They have sold well but have not achieved the success of the original drink.

Eric's cash position is very good. He now has $240,000 in excess of what he feels he needs for working capital. Eric is currently planning to expand his market by building a plant in a city 200 miles away. Preliminary estimates indicate that he will need the following items:

Land and building	$600,00
Bottling equipment	160,000
Other fixtures, equipment, and office furniture	110,000
Special promotional advertising	50,000
Working capital:	
Payroll and raw materials	100,000
Finance accounts receivable	80,000

In addition, he plans to have 200 special drink-cooling boxes with his brand name on them manufactured for him. As part of his advertising, he plans to sell these to stores that will buy them at his cost of $800. This means he must pay the manufacturer a total of $160,000 for the boxes as soon as the order is completed. He plans to offer a two-year payout plan to the retail stores.

Two months ago he heard from another businessman that the local commercial bank's prime interest rate was 13 percent. The Federal Reserve began tightening the money supply about twenty days ago. He wonders if he will be able to get a 13 percent interest rate on his loans.

Questions

1. Indicate where Eric might obtain funds for the various items he needs.

2. Do you think he will be able to obtain a 13 percent interest rate on his loans? Explain.

Cruise-Along Boat Company

The Cruise-Along Boat Company was opened in 1965 by John Stein and five of his associates on capital of $20,000 and property valued at $6,000. The company began its operations in one building, manufacturing a single model of motorboat. The public liked the boat, so the firm has enjoyed substantial growth. The firm now employs 700 people, and sales for the past year were $10 million, up 25 percent over the preceding year. The work force is comprised of production workers as well as technical (engineering, research) and managerial personnel.

The company forecasts a strong future demand for boats. Therefore, management officials have embarked upon a long-range program of expansion and diversification. They plan to build small boats (fifteen feet in length and under) and large boats (over fifteen feet). The company also intends to add sailboats to their product line. To implement these plans and also to provide for growth and expansion, the following proposals are under consideration:

1. Purchase data processing equipment to facilitate record keeping, payroll, production cost information.

2. Hire additional personnel in each of the following categories:
   a. Four trained personnel to operate new data processing equipment.
   b. An experienced methods and materials supervisor.
   c. Fifty new production workers to handle the additional work load of increased production of large boats and sailboats.

3. Replace the small air compressors located throughout the plant with the purchase of one large air compressor to serve the needs of the entire plant. This will improve the efficiency of production workers by allowing them to switch from hand tools to air tools.

4. Buy fifty new hand air tools consisting of ¼-inch drill motors and ⅜-inch drill motors, screwdrivers, and nut runners.

5. Erect a new building, 4,500 square feet in size, to be used by the engineering and customer service departments.

6. Establish a formal education plan by which the company will pay all costs for promising young employees who wish to continue their education at the university located in the city.

7. Construct a new 25,000-square-foot warehouse to be used as storage for boats not yet shipped.

The Chief Financial Officer is evaluating each of these proposals.

Questions

1. What type of funds does the business need for each type of expansion?
2. What are possible sources of funds for each proposal under consideration?

BUSINESS PROFILE

C.I.T. Financial Corporation

C.I.T. pioneered the sales finance field and is one of the leading sales finance organizations in the United States. The success and continuing growth of the company show the importance of consumer credit, as well as the need of businesses to have a source of converting consumer credit into working capital.

In 1908, Henry Ittleson was general manager of the May department store in St. Louis, Missouri. He had observed that many suppliers to the store were short of cash at the times they most needed it and were, therefore, forced to offer generous discounts for prompt payment. With $100,000 in borrowed capital. Mr. Ittleson started a business of lending companies money at an interest rate more favorable to them than the percentage discounts they were giving their customers. The new company made a profit its first year.

During its history, C.I.T. has been in the forefront of several innovative forms of financing. For example, C.I.T. was the first company to offer automobile financing, though this business was discontinued in 1968. Today the company is a leader in mobile home financing and home equity lending. Industrial financing and leasing, asset-based lending, factoring, and a range of insurance services are also principal parts of C.I.T.'s business. The company has $7.6 billion in financing receivables and $8.5 billion life insurance in force.

C.I.T. is one of the largest sales finance companies in the United States.

16

The Securities Exchange: Stocks and Bonds

LEARNING GOALS

After reading this chapter, you will understand:

1. The reasons people buy stocks.

2. The difference between investing and speculating.

3. The roles of the national, regional, and foreign stock exchanges.

4. The purpose of the over-the-counter market.

5. The steps in a typical stock transaction.

6. The role of the stockbroker (account executive).

7. How to read the financial pages for stock and bond quotations.

8. The financial services provided by Standard & Poor's Corporation and Moody's Investors Services.

9. What mutual funds are.

10. The laws that protect you and business firms in buying and selling securities.

KEY TERMS

Investors	Stockbrokers	Dow Jones Average
Stock market	Big Board	Blue chip stocks
Stock dividend	Amex	Bull market
Stock split	Over-the-counter market	Bear market
Speculators	Odd lot	Selling short
Penny stock	Round lot	Mutual fund
Stock exchange	Warrant	Prospectus
Brokerage firms	Price-earnings ratio	Commodity exchange

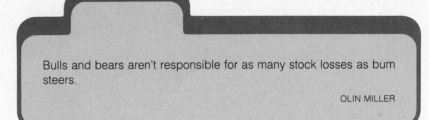

Bulls and bears aren't responsible for as many stock losses as bum steers.

OLIN MILLER

The volume of daily trading activity reported by the various news media on the number of shares bought and sold reflects in part the perception that people have of the outlook for an individual firm, an industry, or the entire economy. This helps to answer the question, "Why do stock prices fluctuate?" When investors are optimistic, demand for stocks generally is strong and stock prices usually increase. When investors are pessimistic about the future state of the economy, they often decide to sell their stocks. When large numbers of investors begin to sell their stock holdings, stock prices decline. Thus, attitudes of investors are important in determining stock prices. Other factors that may influence stock prices downward are reports that company earnings have gone down when they were expected to increase or that the company is losing a share of its market to competitors. A sharp increase in profits or an announcement of a new product or invention may cause stock prices to escalate. When a merger between two firms becomes known to the public, investors may increase their purchases of the stock thus causing the stock prices to rise. A merger occurs when one firm takes over control of another firm by purchasing assets and liabilities of that firm. Two of the largest mergers in America were the recent mergers of Dupont-Conoco and U.S. Steel-Marathon Oil. Thus, prices reflect—in a large measure—the level of investor confidence.

INVESTING AND SPECULATING

When managers of companies are optimistic about the economic outlook for their industry and the country, they will embark on a program to expand or modernize their facilities. Much of the capital to meet these objectives is obtained by issuing stocks and bonds. This action strengthens the economic health of the country, since new jobs are created and business activity rises to higher levels.

Investors

What do almost 30 million Americans have in common? They all own stock. Their motivation to buy stock can be categorized as either investment or speculation. Although we are considering mainly individual investors here, there are other large investors in stock, such as insurance companies and pension funds. Generally, **investors** (individuals who purchase shares of stock) buy shares of common stock on the **stock market**. Investors buy stock with the expectation of holding it for a relatively long period of time. They invest in anticipation of realizing a profit through the long-term appreciation in the value of their stock; they are usually less concerned about the short-term price fluctuations. However, there is always the element of risk, since stock prices may decline. To reduce risk, investors buy stock of companies that have strong performance records.

A second motivation for investing is that investors expect to receive income from their stock in the form of dividends. Dividends may be paid in the form of cash or stock. When a **stock dividend** is paid, the shareholder receives shares of stock from the surplus stock of the company instead of cash. By issuing a stock dividend, the company is able to retain its cash for such necessary operations as plant expansion or research and development.

An action that may be taken to broaden the company's ownership by making stocks available at lower prices is a **stock split.** A stock split divides the number of outstanding shares into a larger number, such as two for one. Each shareholder becomes the owner of twice as many shares, with each share's worth being half as much as the original one share. Since the price is lower, more small investors can buy the stock.

Speculators

Speculators mainly look for short-range price fluctuations in stock prices. The speculator's intention is to buy and sell stock within relatively short periods of time. While speculators and investors both assume risk, it is of different kinds and degrees. More risk is usually associated with speculation because of the shorter time in which the stock is traded, but the profits earned are usually greater than from investing. A type of highly speculative stock that sells at a low price is called a **penny stock.**

One type of speculation is in options. An *option* is a contract that gives the holder the right to buy or sell shares of stock within a specific time period. Two types of options are traded: calls and puts. A *call* is the right to buy, and a *put* is the right to sell a specific amount of a stock at a given price within a given period of time.

Although risk is involved, speculation differs considerably from gambling: whereas the gambler relies primarily on chance or hope, the speculator uses his or her knowledge about the country's economy and individual companies as a guide when buying or selling stock. Since a speculator can conceivably lose a large amount of money in a single day, he or she must have the nerve and the willingness to undertake such risk. In case of loss, the speculator must have adequate financial resources in reserve in order to speculate again.

STOCK EXCHANGES

The marketplace where stocks and bonds are traded is called the **stock exchange.** The two national stock exchanges—the New York Stock Exchange and the American Stock Exchange—as well as the regional stock exchanges and the foreign stock exchanges are discussed here.

Brokerage Firms

On all the organized stock exchanges, there are approximately 5,000 listed companies (companies whose stocks are traded on a stock exchange by exchange members). These stock exchange members are called **bro-kerage firms,** and they perform a number of important functions. They facilitate buying and selling of stocks and bonds for individual investors or speculators. In their role as investment bankers, brokerage firms underwrite and sell new securities issued by corporations and municipalities to raise new money for growth and expansion. (see chapter 15).

Stockbrokers (Account Executives)

Stockbrokers, or account executives, make the buy or sell transactions for investors and speculators. Through the services offered by their brokerage firms, stockbrokers provide various research services to clients, including booklets, financial reports on companies, and news bulletins that enable clients to evaluate and remain current on the status of certain securities.

New York Stock Exchange

The largest and most familiar stock exchange is the New York Stock Exchange (NYSE). Often referred to as the "**Big Board,**" the NYSE is located on Wall Street, New York, the hub of the financial market. In order to trade securities on this exchange, an individual broker or a brokerage firm must be a member. This membership is called a *seat* on the exchange and allows the brokerage firm to trade stocks. The number of seats on the NYSE is 1,366. To become a member, a prospective buyer must purchase the seat of a current member. The price paid for a seat can vary, depending on the condition of the nation's economy and the volume of trading activity on the exchange. Prices paid for seats on the NYSE have ranged from $625,000 in 1929 to $17,000 in 1942.[1] However, it is not enough to have the desire and money to buy a membership. Someone must be willing to sell their seat. Furthermore, approval of a prospective purchaser's character, reputation, and financial reliability by the Board of Governors of the exchange is required.

The financial section of the daily newspaper reports the price changes in the more than 1,500 stocks listed on the New York Stock Exchange. Included are the giants of industry, such as General Motors, IBM, EXXON, Ford Motor Company, and General Electric. The companies whose stocks are traded on the New York Stock Exchange hold more than one-third of all United States corporate assets, are responsible for approximately 40 percent of all United States sales, employ about 20 percent of all workers, and account for more than 75 percent of all United States corporate net income. In addition, more than 30 major corporations from foreign countries trade their stock on this exchange. Representative stocks are Sony Corporation of Japan, British Petroleum of Great Britain, and Northgate Exploration of Canada.

Listing Requirements.   To be listed on the New York Stock Exchange, a company must meet these principal requirements:

---

[1] *The Wall Street Journal,* August 4, 1967.

1. A minimum of 2,000 shareholders of 100 shares or more;
2. A minimum of 1 million common shares outstanding, which must be owned by the public, not by the company itself;
3. A market value for its publicly owned shares of at least $16 million;
4. Annual earnings of at least $2.5 million before taxes in the most recent year and at least $2 million in each of the two preceding years;
5. Net tangible assets of at least $16 million.[2]

"Delisting."   A firm must maintain the listing standards. If a firm fails to meet these standards, the exchange may consider "delisting" the stock of the firm. Delisting may be considered when: (1) the number of shares owned by the general public falls below 600,000; (2) the number of stockholders owning at least 100 shares declines to 1,200; (3) the market value of the shares publicly owned falls below $5 million; and (4) the value of net tangible assets falls below $8 million.[3]

American Stock Exchange

The second largest stock exchange is the American Stock Exchange, frequently referred to as the **Amex,** which operates in the same manner as the New York Stock Exchange. Called the New York Curb Exchange until 1953, the American Stock Exchange now has about 1,300 stocks listed for trading. Membership in the American Stock Exchange is limited to 650 seats. Many well-known companies are listed on the American Stock Exchange, including Lerner stores and Hormel Meat Packing Company.

Regional Stock Exchanges

Stock exchanges located outside New York City are known as *regional stock exchanges*. The Midwest Stock Exchange is the largest regional exchange and was formed when the Chicago Stock Exchange consolidated its activities with the Minneapolis-St. Paul, St. Louis, and Cleveland Exchanges. Other regional exchanges include the Pacific, Philadelphia, Boston, Cincinnati, and Spokane exchanges.

Regional exchanges were developed initially to trade stock and to meet the financial needs of small local companies that could not reach national investors. The New York and American Exchanges provided the national market for securities trading. When many of these local companies grew and expanded their operations, they withdrew from the regional exchanges in favor of listing on the Big Board. The regional exchanges have expanded their scope of operations, and today about half of all stocks traded on the New York Stock Exchange are also listed on the regional exchanges.

---

[2]Louis Engel and Peter Wycoff, *How to Buy Stocks,* 6th ed. (New York: Bantam Books, 1977), p. 57.

[3]Ibid., p. 58.

Foreign Stock Exchanges

Although we have centered our attention on securities trading in the United States, we should recognize that stock exchanges exist internationally. In Canada, there are the Toronto (the country's largest exchange), Montreal, Vancouver, and Calgary Stock Exchanges. Other exchanges around the world are found in Johannesburg, Stockholm, Madrid, Zurich, Milan, Frankfurt, Copenhagen, Paris, Vienna, Tokyo, Amsterdam, Hong Kong, Brussels/Luxembourg, and London.

OVER-THE-COUNTER MARKET

Only about 5,000 stocks are listed and traded on the New York, American, and regional exchanges. However, approximately 40,000 additional unlisted stocks are traded on the **over-the-counter market,** or OTC. The OTC is a way of trading in unlisted securities. Instead of bargaining face-to-face at a centralized location for stock, as floor brokers do on the New York Stock Exchange, over 5,000 OTC dealers are scattered throughout the United States and the world. They are in constant communication with each other, primarily by telephone, buying and selling stocks.

National Association of Securities Dealers

The National Association of Securities Dealers (NASD) uses a centralized computer system, called the National Association of Securities Dealers Automated Quotations (NASDAQ) to provide dealers with instant price quotations on securities traded over-the-counter. The computer system enables dealers to have price quotations for individual stocks instantly available on their computer terminals.

The types of securities traded on the over-the-counter market include numerous utility and industrial stocks, most insurance company stocks, most United States government securities, municipal bonds, and many foreign securities.

Principals and Agents

A dealer who handles OTC transactions may act as a principal for buyers of stock. To illustrate, an investor who wishes to purchase a stock sold over-the-counter places an order with the dealer. The dealer telephones one or several dealers in order to buy the stock at the best price and then sells the stock to the investor at a net price. In this transaction involving a net price, the dealer charges no commission but earns a profit from the difference between the price paid and the net selling price.

When an individual wants to sell stock, the dealer quotes a net price he or she is willing to pay. Again, no commission is charged, since a profit is earned by selling the stock at a higher price.

When acting as a customer's agent, the dealer performs the same brokerage functions for the customer as a broker does on the exchange floor. For these services, the agent receives a commission.

Prices of stocks traded OTC are reported as *bid prices* or *asked prices*. These do not reflect the actual prices paid for the stock. Rather, they represent the approximate price range for these stocks.

Modern communication systems and high-speed computers make rapid stock transactions possible.

STOCK TRANSACTION

Even though stocks are traded throughout the United States and the world, it takes only a few minutes at most to complete a transaction. The development of modern communication systems and high-speed computers make this possible.

Odd Lots and Round Lots

An individual may purchase any number of shares of stock as long as there is someone willing to sell. The purchase of from 1 to 99 shares (that is, less than 100) is called an **odd lot** transaction. Shares traded in lots of 100 are referred to as **round lots.** Stockbrokers handle stock transactions between buyers and sellers. For performing this service, the stockbroker receives a commission.

Stock Commission Rate

Prior to May 1, 1975, the commission rate was fixed and customers were charged the same commission on any stock transaction. However, the Securities and Exchange Commission stopped this practice, and now commission rates are competitive. The commission rate is a negotiated rate between stock purchaser and stockbroker. The commission rate will vary with the size of the dollar value of the transaction and with the brokerage firm.

If the investment is relatively small ($2,000 to $3,000), the commission will be approximately 2½ percent. A commission on a larger investment ($10,000 to $20,000) may be about 1½ percent. A larger investment of $100,000 or more may result in a commission cost that is a fraction of 1 percent.[4]

Some brokerage firms operate as discount brokerage firms. Brokers in these firms deal with experienced investors who require only broker services to execute the stock transaction. The commission rate charged for this service is much lower than for services provided by full-service brokerage firms.

---

[4]*How to Buy Stocks*, p. 63.

Exhibit 16–1

Ticker symbols of representative companies.

Company	Ticker Symbols
American Telephone and Telegraph	T
Del Monte Corporation	DEL
Ford	F
General Dynamics	GD
General Electric	GE
General Motors	GM
International Harvester	HR
Lucky Stores	LKS
Maytag	MYG
McDonald's Corporation	MCD
Parker Pen	PKR
Sears	S
U.S. Steel	X
Xerox	XRX

Ticker

The *ticker* refers to the electronic board that reports price and trading volume of stocks. Originally a paper "ticker tape," the modern ticker is a high-speed computerized system that makes stock trading information on individual stocks available worldwide within a few minutes after the trading activity.

Individual company stocks are identified by symbols. (See Exhibit 16–1.) A typical ticker would disclose the following for General Motors (GM), U.S. Steel (X), and Ford (F):

GM	X	F
36½	2s 24¾	1000s 18

The company identification symbol appears on the top line and the price and number of shares appear on the bottom line of the ticker. If the price appears alone, 100 shares were traded; if 200 shares were traded, then "2s" is shown before the price, and so on. When 1,000 shares are traded, the number is shown as "1000s."

A Typical Stock Transaction

The stock exchanges are open each business day, five days a week, during which time account executives buy and sell stocks for their customers. A stock transaction can be illustrated as follows. Suppose you have analyzed the potential earnings and growth for several companies and decided that an investment in 100 shares of XYZ Corporation stock listed on the NYSE appears promising for long-term growth.

You telephone your stockbroker and instruct him or her to buy 100 shares of XYZ stock at the market or at a specific price. An order to buy "at the market" (the best price available when the order reaches the trading floor of the exchange) is transmitted to the New York brokerage office. Your stock order is then sent to the floor broker (one of the stockbrokers on the floor of the exchange).

If you placed an order to buy at a specific price of $25 and the stock was selling for $26, the floor broker could not spend time waiting for the price to decline to the specified level. The floor broker would turn the order over to a stock specialist, who acts as the agent for the floor bro-

---

Exhibit 16–2

The sequence of activities in a stock transaction.

1

Account executive receives round-lot market order from investor by telephone.

2

Order goes to wire room of local office, where it is sent by teletype to New York headquarters . . .

3

. . . and simultaneously to the floor of the New York Stock Exchange . . .

4

. . . where it is given to the firm's floor broker . . .

5

. . . who executes it, bargaining for the best possible price, at the appropriate trading post.

6

Confirmation is teletyped to the local office . . .

7

. . . where it is received . . .

8

. . . and relayed to the account executive . . .

9

. . . so that he can notify the customer what price she paid—or received—for stock.

SOURCE: Merrill Lynch, Pierce, Fenner & Smith, Inc.

ker. The stock specialist is a broker who restricts his or her buying and selling to a limited number of stocks. The stock specialist centers his or her attention on these few stocks and places the order to buy when the price of $25 is reached. For these services, the stock specialist is paid a commission by the floor broker. There is no added cost to the investor for the services of the stock specialist.

You may instruct your broker to buy 100 shares of XYZ "at the market." At the same time, Ms. Jones calls her stockbroker and instructs her to sell 100 shares of XYZ stock at the current market price. This sell order is then transmitted to the New York office of the broker and given to the floor broker. The two floor brokers take this information and go to a trading post where XYZ is traded. A trading post is a center for trading specific stocks on the floor of the exchange. There are 23 of these trading posts, and about 75 stocks are traded at each post. At the trading post, the buyer's broker asks a quotation on the price of XYZ. Other brokers are present with orders to either buy or sell, and they buy and sell by calling aloud their bids.

Your broker realizes that 25⅞ is the lowest offer to sell and indicates that he has an order to buy for 25¾. Ms. Jones' broker recognizes that the highest bid up to this point is 25⅝. Thus, the two brokers agree on a compromise price of 25¾, the lowest offer to sell and the highest bid to buy.

Within minutes, this information is electronically transmitted to you, informing you of your purchase, and to Ms. Jones, informing her of the sale at 25¾. Both parties receive a printed confirmation of the stock transaction. Payment for the stock plus commission and any state tax must be made with five business days. Likewise, the seller must deliver the stock certificates to the broker within five business days. The account executive will deliver the stocks to you or hold them for you.

The account executive will hold stock certificates in an individual account, or custodian account, for investors who own a large number of shares. The account executive will hold the shares of the small investors in the street name. This means shares of small investors will be lumped together and held in the account executive's name. The account executive keeps a record of the individual investor's stock holdings.

THE FINANCIAL PAGE

Changes in stock prices and volume of trading are reported daily in *The Wall Street Journal,* the best known daily business newspaper, and in local newspapers and other media. *Barron's* and *The Commercial and Financial Chronicle* are two national weekly newspapers that report financial market activity. Understanding the financial page is easy when the reader knows what the numbers and symbols mean.

How to Read a Financial Page

A section of the daily NYSE-Composite Transaction is reproduced in Exhibit 16–3. This report indicates the volume of listed shares and warrants and the composite quotation of stocks traded on the New York, Ameri-

NYSE-Composite Transactions

Monday, April 12, 1982

Quotations include trades on the American, Midwest, Pacific, Philadelphia, Boston and Cincinnati stock exchanges and reported by the National Association of Securities Dealers and Instinet

Monday Volume
53,733,070 Shares; 134,400 Warrants

TRADING BY MARKETS

	Shares	Warrants
New York Exchange	46,520,000	133,500
American Exchange	....	....
Midwest Exchange	2,431,200	....
Pacific Exchange	2,062,700	....
Nat'l Assoc. of Securities Dealers	1,016,970	900
Philadelphia Exchange	1,084,700	....
Boston Exchange	302,500	....
Cincinnati Exchange	208,600	....
Instinet System	106,400	....

NYSE – Composite

Volume since Jan. 1:	1982	1981	1980
Total shares	4,153,612,853	3,766,959,893	3,593,571,467
Total warrants	11,551,000	11,467,200	20,072,200

New York Stock Exchange

Volume since Jan. 1:	1982	1981	1980
Total shares	3,577,763,773	3,297,927,693	3,180,589,547
Total warrants	11,531,900	11,446,300	20,068,900

MOST ACTIVE STOCKS

	Open	High	Low	Close	Chg.	Volume
Schlitz Brw	15¼	15⅝	15¼	15½	+ ⅛	934,700
Amer T&T	55⅜	55½	54⅝	54¾	− ½	626,400
Beat Food	19⅞	20⅛	19⅞	20	− ⅛	505,300
Exxon s	28⅝	28⅝	28¼	28½	.....	504,200
Am Airlin	15½	15½	15	15⅛	− ¼	487,000
Texaco Inc	29⅞	30	29¾	29⅞	.....	458,400
K mart	18¾	19⅜	18⅝	19⅛	+ ⅜	428,600
Plan Resrch	7¾	7¾	7⅛	7¼	− ¾	420,100
IBM	62¼	62½	62	62⅛	− ⅛	388,200
Citicorp	27⅝	27¾	27⅛	27¼	− ¼	386,400
Sterl Drug	25⅞	26½	25⅝	26⅛	+ ⅜	361,300
Datapnt	22⅛	22⅛	21	21⅝	− ½	354,100

52 Weeks High	52 Weeks Low	Stock	Div.	Yld %	P-E Ratio	Sales 100s	High	low	Close	Net Chg.
		– A–A–A –								
12⅜	6	AAR	.44	6.8	14	24	6¾	6½	6½	− ⅜
49½	31½	ACF	2.76	7.5	7	129	37	36¼	37	+1¼
28½	16⅝	AMF	1.36	7.6	10	852	18½	18	18	− ½
16	1⅛	AM Intl		..	..	738	1½	1¼	1⅜	+ ⅛
7¼	3¾	APL		..	..	2	4⅛	4⅛	4⅛	+ ⅛
37¼	23½	ARA	2	7.8	7	19	25⅞	25⅝	25¾	+ ⅛
56½	26¾	ASA	4a	12.	..	477	34½	33¾	33¾	− ¾
36⅝	11½	AVX	.32	1.7	..	56	19	18⅝	19	.....
32¼	23⅝	AbtLb s	.84	2.8	15	x2059	29⅝	29⅛	29⅝	+ ⅜
29½	17¼	AcmeC	1.40	6.4	8	16	22	21¾	21¾	− ¼
9⅝	7½	AcmeE	n.32b	4.1	7	10	7¾	7⅝	7¾	.....
6¾	4	AdmDg	.04	.8	6	9	5⅛	4⅞	5⅛	+ ⅛
15⅝	12¾	AdaEx	2.25e	16.	..	23	13⅞	13¾	13⅞	+ ⅛
8	4⅜	AdmMI	.20e	2.5	10	314	u 8⅛	7⅞	7⅞	− ⅛
31	14	AMD		..	36	804	24⅜	23½	24⅜	+ ⅜
48¼	33½	AetnLf	2.52	5.3	8	568	47¾	47⅛	47⅛	− ⅝
19½	9⅝	Ahmns	1.20	11.	..	118	10¾	10⅝	10¾	.....
4¼	2⅛	Aileen		..	..	28	2⅞	2¾	2¾	− ¼
46⅞	31	AirPrd	.80	2.3	8	314	35¼	34¾	34¾	− ⅝
16	7¾	AirbFrt	.60	6.0	15	33	10	10	10	+ ⅛
15¼	9¼	Akzona	.80	8.3	10	191	10	9½	9⅝	− ⅛
22½	15⅛	AlMoa n		..	..	382	18½	18⅛	18⅜	− ⅛
27¼	23¼	AlaP	pfA3.92	16.	..	9	25	24¾	24¾	− ¼
6⅞	5½	AlaP	dpf.87	15.	..	19	6	5⅞	6	+ ¼
61	53	AlaP	pf 9	16.	..	z390	56½	55½	56	.....
85⅝	75	AlaP	pf 11	14.	..	z50	78	78	78	+1⅜
65½	55	AlaP	pf 9.44	16.	..	z50	60	60	60	−1
55	46	AlaP	pf 8.16	16.	..	z100	52	52	52	+1¼
56¼	49½	AlaP	pf 8.28	16.	..	z1140	52½	51¼	52½	+ ¾
16	13⅛	Alagsco	1.60	11.	5	21	14⅛	14	14⅛	.....
33½	11⅛	AlskInt	.60	4.1	5	108	15	14⅝	14⅝	− ¼
37½	22⅝	Albany	1.20	4.9	6	11	24¼	23⅞	24¼	+ ⅝
16¼	9¾	Alberto	.50	3.6	8	16	13¾	13½	13¾	.....
29⅝	23	Albtsn	1	3.7	9	1072	27	26⅞	27	.....
37¾	17⅞	Alcan	1.80	10.	6	200	18⅜	18	18	− ⅛
21⅝	17¼	AlcoSt	s1.08	5.4	7	37	20⅛	19⅞	20	.....
30⅜	25¾	AlexAl	n1.94	6.6	10	252	29¾	29⅜	29½	− ⅛

Exhibit 16–3
A portion of the daily NYSE-Composite Transactions.
(SOURCE: *The Wall Street Journal*).

can, and participating regional stock exchanges, NASDAQ, and Instinet, a trading network used by financial institutions. A **warrant** is a certificate that gives the holder the right to purchase stocks at a stated price for a specified period of time or perpetually. A warrant may be offered with stocks as an incentive to buy the stock. The most active stocks traded on the NYSE for that business day are also shown.

The Stock Quotation

The individual stock quotations provide data informing the reader of the trading activity in each stock, its price range, and its rate of return. For example, the activity in K mart stock for one business day is shown in Exhibit 16–4. The figures in column 1 show the high and low prices of one share of stock sold in the preceding 52-week period. The name of the stock (column 2) appears next, followed by the current dividend (column 3) the corporation is paying per share (96 cents annually). In column 4 the percentage yield of the stock (5.0 percent) is shown. This figure is obtained by dividing the current dividend by the closing stock price for the day. The **price-earnings ratio** shown in column 5 is the market price of

Exhibit 16–4

K mart stock quotation.

(SOURCE: *The Wall Street Journal*, April 13, 1982.)

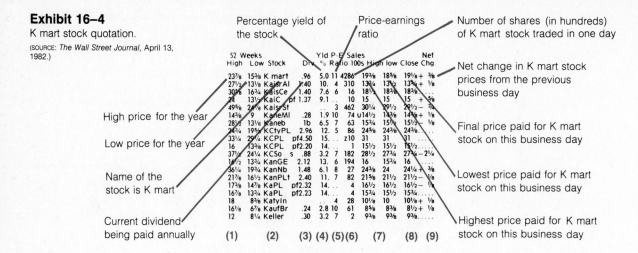

High price for the year

Low price for the year

Name of the stock is K mart

Current dividend being paid annually

Percentage yield of the stock

Price-earnings ratio

Number of shares (in hundreds) of K mart stock traded in one day

Net change in K mart stock prices from the previous business day

Final price paid for K mart stock on this business day

Lowest price paid for K mart stock on this business day

Highest price paid for K mart stock on this business day

(1) (2) (3) (4) (5) (6) (7) (8) (9)

the stock expressed as a multiple of the per share earnings. The P-E ratio of 11 is the market price of the stock divided by the annual earnings per share. The number of shares traded (in hundreds) of K mart stock on that day is reported in column 6. Trading volume is reported in round lots. The high and low prices of the stock this day are shown in column 7 and the closing price for the stock on this day is reported in column 8. The net change in column 9 reveals the change in price of the stock from the close of one business day to the next.

Active trading in a stock may be caused by increased interest following a favorable announcement by a company, such as the development of a new product or a major breakthrough on a long-standing problem by the company's research department. However, adverse news can also cause an increase in trading activity of a stock. Unfavorable news such as sales declines and lower profits may cause a sell-off of certain stocks.

STOCK AVERAGES

Each day business news analysts report the **Dow Jones Average.** This average is an index of stock prices, showing the condition of the market for the day and reflecting upward or downward movement of selected prices. The Dow Jones Average is actually composed of four different averages of stocks—an average of 30 industrial stocks, 20 transportation stocks, 15 utility stocks, and the overall average of these 65 stocks. The Dow Jones Average as reported on the financial page is shown in Exhibit 16–5. Of the four averages, the most familiar and most quoted is the industrial stock average.

Most of the stocks that comprise the Dow Jones Average are **blue chip stocks** (stocks of the largest and best-known companies in the United States) and are listed on the New York Stock Exchange. Prices of single stocks may move up while the industrial average moves down, or the opposite may be true. However, the real value of the Dow Jones Average is that it provides a capsule summary of daily stock market activity and movement.

Another well-known stock average is the Standard and Poor's 500 stock average. This 500 stock index is comprised of 425 industrials, 60 utilities, and 15 rails.

BEARS, BULLS, AND SHORT SELLING

Some unique terminology is associated with trading on the stock market. Two of these terms are *bulls* and *bears*. These two terms relate to a person's attitude toward the market.

A *bull* is a person who anticipates that the market is moving upward. Thus, a bull will buy stock today in anticipation that the price of the stock will go up. A **bull market** is one in which stock prices are advancing.

A *bear* is a person who expects the market to go down. Thus, a bear will sell stocks today with the expectation that they will fall. A **bear market** is a declining market.

Short Selling

Selling short is the opposite of the usual stock market transaction. Instead of buying the stock first and then selling it, the individual sells the stock and then buys it back at a later date. How is it possible to sell stock you do not own? Why is it done? The following example will aid in understanding how this can occur. As we have stated, a bear market is one in which stock prices are declining.

You may think that the market price of a stock is going to go down. Thus, you sell stock now at the higher price and then buy it back at a future time at a lower price. You go "short" on the stock because you do not own it. You sell stock that you do not own, which is borrowed from your stockbroker. Borrowing the stock is necessary so that delivery of the stock can be made to the buyer. The stockbroker lends stock that he or she has borrowed from his or her customers who have agreed to this arrangement. Or, if a stock a customer wants to sell short is not available from a customer, the broker may borrow stock from another stockbroker. The "short" seller must pay the broker for the use of the stock. If there is a high demand for the stock, the short seller may have to pay a premium to the broker. If the market price does decline, the short seller can repurchase it later at the lower price and return the borrowed stock to the

Exhibit 16–5

Dow Jones stock averages.

(SOURCE: Dow Jones & Company, Inc., 1982.)

Following are the Dow Jones Averages of INDUSTRIAL, TRANSPORTATION and UTILITY stocks, with the total sales of each group for the period indicated.

Date	Open	11	12	1	2	3	Close	Change	%	x-High	x-Low	Shares Sold
30 INDUSTRIALS:												
Apr. 12	842.56	840.37	840.18	842.18	841.99	841.32	841.32	− 1.62	− 0.19	847.32	836.38	4,158,100
Apr. 8	836.95	836.76	838.66	840.56	841.04	844.08	842.94	+ 6.09	+ 0.73	847.51	833.33	5,349,300
Apr. 7	839.33	836.76	838.76	839.33	839.92	839.99	836.85	− 2.48	− 0.30	845.03	832.48	6,184,100
Apr. 6	835.81	832.19	830.57	831.43	832.95	836.76	839.33	+ 4.00	+ 0.48	842.85	827.91	3,857,800
20 TRANSPORTATION COS.:												
Apr. 12	348.77	348.77	347.54	347.54	347.95	347.05	347.47	− 1.37	− 0.39	351.12	345.06	1,615,900
Apr. 8	344.85	345.95	346.71	347.19	348.02	349.05	348.84	+ 4.26	+ 1.24	351.67	343.75	2,100,300
Apr. 7	341.62	342.65	342.99	344.03	343.41	343.96	344.58	+ 3.31	+ 0.97	346.64	340.17	1,906,100
Apr. 6	338.73	338.86	337.49	338.86	339.14	340.58	341.27	+ 2.13	+ 0.63	343.41	335.90	1,458,800
15 UTILITIES:												
Apr. 12	110.52	110.56	110.65	110.69	110.81	110.77	110.93	+ 0.41	+ 0.37	111.54	110.20	1,286,100
Apr. 8	110.28	110.12	110.12	110.12	110.24	110.56	110.52	+ 0.04	+ 0.04	111.01	109.79	5,414,700
Apr. 7	110.24	110.44	110.40	110.32	110.40	110.48	110.48	+ 0.24	+ 0.22	111.05	109.75	1,061,000
Apr. 6	110.00	110.32	110.32	110.00	110.16	110.16	110.24	+ 0.08	+ 0.07	111.05	109.55	1,020,900
65 STOCKS COMPOSITE AVERAGE:												
Apr. 12	332.57	332.13	331.77	332.21	332.35	331.93	332.13	− 0.54	− 0.16	334.75	330.04	7,060,100
Apr. 8	330.14	330.34	330.96	331.49	331.89	332.99	332.67	+ 2.53	+ 0.77	334.69	328.82	12,864,300
Apr. 7	329.68	329.54	330.04	330.42	330.32	330.62	330.14	+ 0.56	+ 0.17	332.73	327.58	9,151,200
Apr. 6	327.98	327.42	326.68	327.10	327.58	328.80	329.58	+ 1.50	+ 0.46	331.33	325.28	6,337,500

Averages are compiled daily by using the following divisors: Industrials, 1.314; Transportation, 1.816; Utilities, 3.074; 65 Stocks. 6 255.

x-Averages of the highs and lows reached at any time during the day on the New York Stock Exchange by the individual stocks.

broker. This transaction is called "covering your short position." The profit is the difference between the selling and buying price less payments for borrowing the stock.

Should the market reverse itself and move up instead of down between the time the stock is sold and repurchased, the buyer obviously loses money. To illustrate, assume you sell 50 shares of stock at $30 a share. The stock declines to $25 a share and you buy it at this price to return to your broker. You have made $250. However, if you sold short at $30 and the price advances to $35, you must pay that price to return the borrowed stock. In the process, you have lost $250.

BOND QUOTATIONS

Bonds represent debt to the issuing corporation, as observed in chapter 3. The financial page reports daily bond trading activity in domestic corporation, foreign, and government bonds. A typical report for daily trading in corporation bonds is shown in Exhibit 16–6.

The quotation displays the name of the bond—American Telephone & Telegraph, the amount of interest paid (3⅞ percent semiannually), and the year the bond matures—1990. The current yield column shows 6.5 percent, which is more than the specified yield of 3⅞ percent. The reason for this is because bond prices are quoted at a face value of $1,000. If a bond is purchased at a "premium," the purchaser has to pay more for the bond than its face value. Bonds purchased at a "discount" are purchased at a lower price than the face value.

In this case, the bond is purchased at a discount, 59½, or $595.00, making the current yield higher than the rate of return specified on the bond. Other data reported are the volume—60 (how many bonds were traded that day), the high (59½) and low (58⅛) prices paid for the bond that business day, the closing (59½), and the net change over the preceding day's price (+ ½).

FINANCIAL RESEARCH SERVICES

Two of the largest firms offering financial research services are Standard & Poor's Corporation and Moody's Investors Service. Both Standard & Poor's *Corporation Records* and Moody's *Manuals* contain a brief

Exhibit 16–6
Daily quotation of prices and trading activity of New York Exchange Bonds.
(SOURCE: *The Wall Street Journal*, April 13, 1982.)

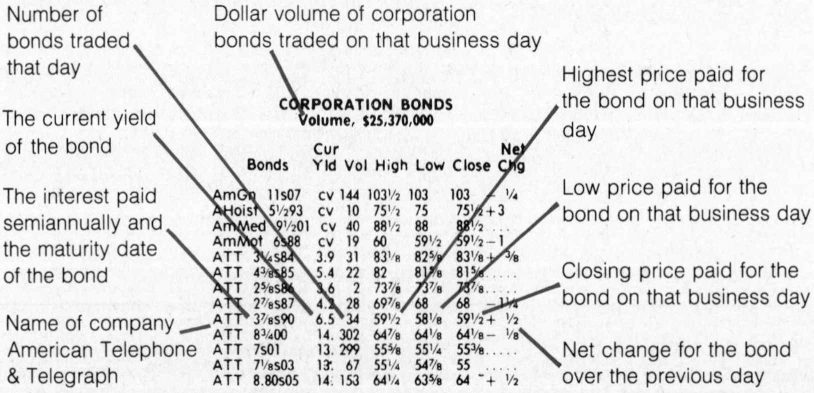
Number of bonds traded that day
Dollar volume of corporation bonds traded on that business day
Highest price paid for the bond on that business day
The current yield of the bond
Low price paid for the bond on that business day
The interest paid semiannually and the maturity date of the bond
Closing price paid for the bond on that business day
Name of company American Telephone & Telegraph
Net change for the bond over the previous day

CORPORATION BONDS
Volume, $25,370,000

Bonds		Cur Yld	Vol	High	Low	Close	Net Chg
AmGn	11s07	cv	144	103½	103	103	– ¼
AHoist	5½93	cv	10	75½	75	75½	+3
AmMed	9½01	cv	40	88½	88	88½	....
AmMot	6s88	cv	19	60	59½	59½	–1
ATT	3¼s84	3.9	31	83⅛	82⅝	83⅛	+ ⅜
ATT	4⅜s85	5.4	22	82	81⅝	81⅝	.....
ATT	2⅝s86	3.6	2	73⅞	73⅞	73⅞	.....
ATT	2⅞s87	4.2	28	69⅞	68	68	–1¼
ATT	3⅞s90	6.5	34	59½	58⅛	59½	+ ½
ATT	8¾00	14.	302	64⅞	64⅛	64⅛	– ⅛
ATT	7s01	13.	299	55⅝	55¼	55⅜	.....
ATT	7⅛s03	13.	67	55¼	54⅞	55	.....
ATT	8.80s05	14.	153	64¼	63⅝	64	+ ½

Exhibit 16–7

Rating	Standard & Poor's	Moody's
Highest grade, gilt-edge	AAA	Aaa
High grade	AA	Aa
Upper-medium grade	A	A
Medium grade	BBB	Baa
Lower-medium grade	BB	Ba
Speculative, interest not assured	B	B
Outright speculation, interest questionable or not paid	CCC/CC	Caa
Even more speculative, interest usually not paid	C	Ca

history of publicly owned firms as well as full financial data covering a number of years. Moody's and Standard & Poor's also assign quality ratings to new issues of bonds. These ratings are important since they affect the bonds' interest rates. The ratings given corporate bonds by Moody's and Standard & Poor's are shown in Exhibit 16–7.

MUTUAL FUNDS

Investors may buy shares in a mutual fund. A **mutual fund** is an investment company that specializes in investing and managing funds for a group of investors. One reason why mutual funds attract investors is that these companies employ full-time professional managers who have the time, training, and experience to decide which investments to make. Another advantage of mutual funds is that individual investors pool their funds with other investors. The result is that a larger sum of money is made available for investment purposes. Investment managers study the market and make investment decisions.

A third advantage of mutual funds is that investments are diversified. This means that the securities of a number of different companies are purchased. Thus, while there is the risk of the value of individual securities declining due to falling stock prices, the mutual fund seeks greater stability by making investments in a number of different companies.

Diversification of investment in the securities of a number of different firms is provided for by the Investment Company Act of 1940. This Act provides that a mutual fund may not have more than 5 percent of its assets in any one company or own more than 10 percent of the shares of any one company. Thus, a mutual fund must invest in the securities of at least twenty companies.

Mutual funds may be either "load" or "no-load." A load fund is one for which the investor pays a commission, or a loading charge. The Investment Company Act allows a maximum sales charge of 9 percent, but the charge is usually lower, between 8 and 8.5 percent. This charge is the

Ten Rules for Investors

Rule 1:
Own only bonds and stocks of leading companies in sound and essential industries.

Rule 2:
Own only stocks which are listed on a registered securities exchange, or which conform to exchange requirements.

Rule 3:
Own only stocks which can boast an earnings or a dividend record (or both) unbroken for at least ten years.

Rule 4:
Own stocks in at least five different industries.

Rule 5:
Own stocks in fairly equal amounts in at least eight or ten different companies.

Rule 6:
Own a few low-yield stocks as a means of building up capital and future income.

Rule 7:
Buy bonds below par (or but a little above) to reduce the likelihood of spending capital.

Rule 8:
Once a year sell at least one stock, choosing the weakest on the list with no consideration whatever for its original cost. Replace it by a more attractive stock.

Rule 9:
Do not be disturbed by losses on individual risks, but keep an eye out for a gain or loss on the aggregate.

Rule 10:
Subscribe to one high-grade financial publication and read it regularly and thoroughly.

SOURCE: Reprinted with permission of Barron's. © Dow Jones & Company, Inc., 1976. All rights reserved.

commission paid to the mutual fund for its selling effort. Most investors purchase this type of fund. Another type of fund is the "no-load." These firms employ no salespersons to call on investors and charge no commission.

REGULATION OF SALE OF SECURITIES

All states except Nevada have passed laws designed to protect buyers of securities. These are called "blue-sky" laws. This name comes from the fact that some stock promoters were selling stock in the "blue sky." These laws require the licensing or registration of dealers and salespeople and also the registration of securities before they can be sold within a state.

The Securities Act of 1933

The Securities Act of 1933 was passed in order to provide for investor protection by regulating the sale of stocks sold in interstate commerce. This law is called the "truth in securities law." The law requires issuers of primary (new) securities to disclose completely all information about themselves that affects the value of their securities. Stock issuers must file a registration statement with the Securities and Exchange Commission. This registration statement includes such data as the nature of the business, a list of company officers, and the articles of incorporation. Registration information that must be made public is contained in a booklet called the **prospectus** of the company. Information in the prospectus includes such items as corporate history, description of securities, the firm's investment objectives and policies, the regulatory bodies to which the company is subject, directors and officers, and other matters.

The Securities Act of 1934

The Securities Act of 1934 was passed to correct the limitations of the earlier act. Some of this act's major provisions were:

1. The Securities and Exchange Commission (SEC) was created and charged with the responsibility to regulate the securities markets.
2. Complete information about secondary issues (issues traded in secondary markets) is required. Secondary markets are any of the securities exchanges or over-the-counter markets. The earlier act only pertained to primary issues.
3. The SEC is given authority to require organized exchanges to register with SEC and agree to abide by the law, and adopt rules to control actions of members, and discipline or expel those who do not abide by rules.
4. The Federal Reserve Board is given authority to set margin requirements for buying stocks.

The Maloney Act

In 1938, the Maloney Act was passed. This act provides for setting up a self-regulating agency (National Association of Securities Dealers) by OTC dealers. The NASD establishes the regulations to protect buyers and sellers of OTC securities, and members agree to follow the rules.

As noted earlier, the Investment Company Act of 1940 governs mutual funds.

The Security Investors Protection Corporation

In 1979, the Security Investors Protection Corporation (SIPC) was established. The purpose of this corporation, similar to that of the FDIC, is to protect investors from failure by brokerage firms. If an investor leaves securities and cash with a brokerage firm and if the firm fails, the SIPC protects the investor from loss up to $500,000.

The Securities Act Amendment of 1964 gave the SEC additional power to oversee the markets. This amendment was strengthened with the passage of the Securities Reform Act of 1975, which allowed the SEC to increase its staff. This act enabled the SEC to better supervise the stock market and to enforce the rules and regulations more uniformly. These legislative acts have done much to uphold the integrity of the securities market.

COMMODITY EXCHANGES

Where the stock exchanges provide a market for stocks and bonds, the **Commodity Exchanges** are organized to provide a market for commodities (gold, silver, corn, soybeans) in the United States and in foreign countries. The largest commodity exchange is the Chicago Board of Trade. Specific rules govern commodity trading and it is regulated by the Commodity Futures Trading Commission.

1. Individuals who purchase stocks may be classed as investors or speculators.

2. Cash dividends or stock dividends are paid to stock owners.

3. A stock split occurs when the number of existing shares of stock of a company are increased, such as 2 for 1, and the value is decreased accordingly.

4. The stock exchange is the marketplace where securities are traded. The New York Stock Exchange and the American Stock Exchange are national exchanges, but there are regional exchanges as well. There are also foreign exchanges.

5. A company must meet specific requirements in order to be listed on the New York Stock Exchange.

6. The over-the-counter stock exchanges trade in unlisted stocks.

7. There are a series of steps involved in a typical stock transaction. High-speed computers facilitate stock trading.

8. The financial section appearing daily in your local paper or *The Wall Street Journal* reports changes in stock and bond prices.

9. By selling short, you can sell a stock you do not own (by borrowing from your stockbroker).

10. Financial services are provided by Standard & Poor's Corporation and Moody's Investors Services.

11. A mutual fund is an investment company that specializes in investing and managing funds for a group of investors.

12. The sale of securities is regulated by law.

DISCUSSION QUESTIONS

1. Explain the difference between a stock split and stock dividend.

2. Discuss the difference between a bear market and a bull market.

3. What are the requirements for a firm to be listed on the New York Stock Exchange?

4. What is the function of the over-the-counter market?

5. Select a stock from the financial page and explain what has been happening to this stock.

6. How can you sell a stock you do not own?

7. Explain the role of the stock specialist.

8. What is a mutual fund?

9. What are the main provisions of the Securities Act of 1934?

10. What is a prospectus?

11. What is the commodity exchange?

STUDENT PROJECTS

1. Assume that you have $10,000 that you plan to invest in common stocks. Using the financial page of the daily newspaper or the *Wall Street Journal,* select a stock or several stocks (up to $10,000, exclusive of any commissions) and invest the total amount. After a specified period of time designated by your instructor, sell your stock to determine your success in the stock market.

2. Visit a local stockbroker's office. Prepare a report (either written or oral) of the activities you observed.

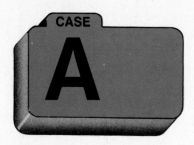

Rules for Investing

The following rules for investment were suggested by Joseph Goodman in 1935, as reported in the May 11, 1981 issue of *Forbes,* p. 341.

1. Never buy a stock that won't go up in a bull market. The smart money is out of it.

2. Never sell a stock that won't go down in a bear market. The smart money is into it.

3. Don't buy the sympathy stock. Don't buy a weak railroad because a strong one has started to move. Everybody does this, and it is rarely profitable. Buy the company that is going up.

4. When a bull market peaks, sell the stock that has gone up the most. It will fall back the fastest. Also, sell the stock that has gone up least. It didn't go up; therefore, it must go down.

5. When a bear market begins to bottom out, buy the stock that has gone down most. Also, buy the stock that has gone down least.

6. Never place a limit on your orders; make them at market. Many a profit became a loss by holding out for an eighth of a point.

7. Never sell a stock that has long been inactive just at the moment it begins to move ahead.

8. No man ever makes himself poor by taking a profit.

Question

Evaluate the appropriateness of these investment rules for the investor of the 1980s.

Shirley Edwards

Shirley Edwards inherited $8,000 from her uncle and feels she should invest the money in some type of security. She would like to invest in a security that is very safe but has the potential for spectacular growth. However, she is hesitant because she does not understand the securities market nor the different kinds of securities. Although she has seen the financial page in the local newspaper, she does not know how to interpret the stock market quotations. She has heard such terms as *calls* and *puts* and *bull* and *bear* but does not know what they mean.

The New York City headquarters of Merrill Lynch & Co., Inc.

Shirley has decided that she is going to go talk to an account executive on her lunch hour to get answers to her many questions. You are an account executive, and Shirley comes into your office and asks you the following questions.

Questions

1. Can you find a stock for me to invest in that it safe and also has the potential for spectacular growth?
2. Should I invest or speculate, and what is the difference?
3. What is meant by a "blue-chip stock?"
4. What is the difference between the over-the-counter market and an organized exchange?
5. What is the difference between an odd-lot and a round-lot purchase?
6. I have before me a copy of *The Wall Street Journal.* How do I interpret the quotation for IBM stock?
7. How can my money grow if I put the $8,000 in the stock market?
8. Would you recommend that I invest in a mutual fund?
9. Select a stock you would recommend to Shirley and explain why you think it is a good investment.

BUSINESS PROFILE

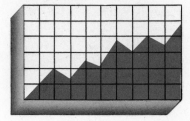

Merrill Lynch, Pierce, Fenner & Smith

A lone, lean, tough-looking bull is used by Merrill Lynch to project the image of the firm—a breed apart. The symbolism represents Merrill Lynch's objective to offer different financial investment alternatives for different economic conditions.

Merrill Lynch traces its beginnings to W.W. Gwathmey & Co., which was founded in Richmond, Virginia, in 1920. Gwathmey became a member of the New York Cotton Exchange in 1871 and, in the 1920s, merged with the firm that became known as W. A. Pierce & Co. In 1940, E. A. Pierce merged with Merrill Lynch, the firm Charles E. Merrill started in 1915. Then, in 1941, the newly merged company joined in the historic union with Fenner & Beane, which had started out in New Orleans in 1905 as a spot cotton and futures broker called Fenner & Solari. The firm was known as Merrill Lynch, Pierce, Fenner & Beane until 1957, when it became Merrill Lynch, Pierce, Fenner & Smith.

Since the days when founder Charles Merrill first propounded his philosophy of "bringing Wall Street to Main Street," the name Merrill Lynch has been associated with the individual investor. As one extension of this philosophy, Merrill Lynch devotes considerable efforts to investor education by publishing many booklets, producing educational films, and running informational seminars.

Merrill Lynch, Pierce, Fenner & Smith, the nation's largest securities company, is the flagship subsidiary of Merrill Lynch & Co., a leading financial services company with operations in securities, financing, insurance, and real estate. The brokerage subsidiary operates some 470 investment offices throughout the world, employs over 7,000 account executives, and serves customer accounts in every state of the union and 29 foreign countries. It is a leader in corporate and municipal investment banking and in commodity futures trading. Much of the success of the firm is attributed to management planning and a closely knit organization.

17

Insurance and Risk

LEARNING GOALS

After reading this chapter, you will understand:

1. The four basic methods of controlling the risks each business faces in day-to-day operations.

2. How business firms may avoid, reduce, assume, or shift the risk.

3. The five basic requirements that must be met for risks to be insurable.

4. The reasons for the existence of insurance as well as the difference between the three basic losses protected by insurance.

5. How the different types of insurance protect you or a business against a loss of earning power, loss of property, and legal liability.

6. The different types of insurance you will need when you begin your career.

7. How no-fault insurance functions.

KEY TERMS

Self-insurance	Term insurance	Accident policies
Hedging	Decreasing term insurance	Property loss insurance
Subcontracting	Endowment insurance	Fire insurance
Insurance	Whole life insurance	Theft insurance
Probability	Premiums	Surety insurance
Policies	Loan value	Liability insurance
Life insurance	Disability insurance	No-fault insurance

Individuals and businesses incur unavoidable risk on a daily basis. Individuals incur risk every time they drive an automobile, no matter how well they drive. A wide range of losses may be suffered as a result of driving an automobile; life may be lost, the car may be damaged, an accident may occur that obligates the individual for large sums of future income, or other losses may be sustained. A person may avoid this risk by not driving a car, but that is an unacceptable solution. Since people obviously cannot stop driving cars and thus avoid the risk, other actions must be taken to reduce risk and protect individuals from losses. The risk involved in driving can be reduced by:

1. Driving defensively and making a continued effort to avoid accidents;
2. Making sure the automobile is in safe driving condition by regularly having brakes, tires, and steering inspected.

Even after taking these steps, one may still be injured, disabled, or even lose life as the result of an accident. However, it is possible for individuals to protect themselves and their families from money losses resulting from accidents by purchasing:

1. Accident and life insurance on oneself;
2. Collision insurance to totally or partially pay for the repair or replacement of the automobile;
3. Liability insurance that will help pay any liability judgments obtained against one.

Business also sustains risks on a daily basis. Many of these risks are of such proportions that damages could force bankruptcy and closing of the business. An employee's negligence may result in large liability judgments. A fire may destroy the business. A tainted product may cause death, and the resulting publicity may result in a loss of nearly all customers. (One food company went out of business because cans of tainted soup caused some people to die.) Even theft may result in such a large loss that the business cannot survive.

Like good quarterbacking in a
football game, good management is
essential to risk reduction in
business.

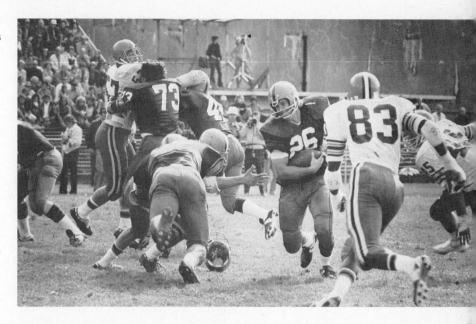

CONTROLLING RISKS

Just as the individual deals with risks by avoidance or insurance, businesses deal with risk by (1) avoiding the risk, (2) reducing the risk, (3) assuming the risk, and/or (4) shifting the risk. See Exhibit 17–1.

Avoiding the Risk

A business can avoid some risks that are too high in relation to the gain. Basically, business can avoid risk by substitution, screening, and elimination.

Substitution. A manufacturing company may be using a highly toxic and unstable chemical in its production process. If a suitable, nontoxic, stable

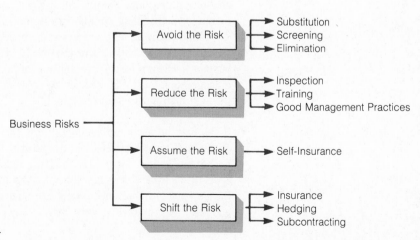

Exhibit 17–1
Methods of controlling business risks.

substitute is available, then a risk has been avoided. For example, the company using a toxic, flammable glue on its labels avoided some risk when it changed to a glue that was nontoxic and nonflammable.

Screening.   Inspection and testing of products and raw materials show how screening can help avoid a risk. For example, a manufacturing firm that produces compressed gas cylinders tests each cylinder produced to make sure it will withstand the required pressure in order to avoid the risk of explosion.

Elimination.   A trucking firm may avoid risk by refusing a contract to haul dynamite or other explosives. Another example is the chemical company that stopped production of a pesticide that was causing health problems for its workers.

There are many risks management can and should avoid; however, no business can avoid all risks. Risks are an inherent part of everyday business operations, and just as the individual must sustain risk if he or she drives a car, the business must sustain risk if it operates. In fact, a business may have less control over the risk than does an individual. Such a case would be that of the employee driving a company car on company business. The business is liable for the employee's driving, but management cannot be certain the employee will drive carefully. Since the business cannot avoid risk, management must seek other methods to deal effectively with it.

Reducing the Risk

Many unavoidable risks can be reduced. In fact, almost all risks that a business faces may be reduced by some form of management practice and policy. The risk of credit customers not paying their debts can be reduced by credit checks. Periodic inspection, preventive maintenance, and repair of machinery and equipment will reduce the risk of injury to employees and other persons. Safety training will also reduce the risk of injury to employees. Installing sprinkler systems reduces the risk of fire damage.

Good management practices are essential to risk reduction. Management has the potential to reduce more risk than does any other factor in business. Even if losses are shifted through insurance and other methods, management must still reduce the risk in order to avoid excessive costs through high insurance premiums.

Assuming the Risk

Risks may be assumed adequately by **self-insurance**. Funds may be set aside to cover certain risks in the future. For example, a sinking fund may be established to insure the building against fire and other losses. This type of insurance is generally not wise for one-plant companies because the amount of money necessary to replace the building must be set aside, and this may involve a very large sum relative to the size of the firm.

"NOW IF YOU'RE INTERESTED IN A
POLICY COVERING HIGH-RISK ACTIVITIES..."

However, for larger multiplant companies, the amount of money necessary to replace a single building may not be excessive. An amount that would replace a single building probably would be sufficient because the probability is slight that more than one plant would burn at the same time. The company would be doing the same thing an insurance company does, only on a smaller scale.

Shifting the Risk

A business may shift risk by several methods, among which are hedging, subcontracting, and insurance.

Hedging. Price changes in raw materials may be shifted to other persons by the use of **hedging** in the commodity market. By buying and selling futures in the commodity market, a business may insure a specific price for future purchases of raw materials.

For example, it might be important for a flour manufacturer to maintain a stable price on flour this year. The manufacturer may fear losing customers if the price changes as often as the price of the raw material used changes. To achieve a stable price, the manufacturer must be assured of paying the same price for wheat regardless of price fluctuations.

This can be accomplished by hedging in the commodity market. To illustrate:

On April 1, the flour manufacturer buys one million bushels of wheat on the market for $3.40 per bushel. At the same time, the manufacturer buys a futures contract through a local stock broker, promising to pay $3.60 per bushel for one million bushels of wheat in December.

On October 1, the manufacturer buys another one million bushels of wheat with which to manufacture flour and pays $4.00 per bushel. The manufacturer then sells a futures contract through the local stockbroker, agreeing to deliver one million bushels of wheat at $4.20 per bushel in December.

The two contracts are then canceled out, and the manufacturer does not buy or sell wheat. See Exhibit 17–2.

Speculators in the commodity market only buy and sell contracts. Real wheat is rarely exchanged in these contracts. Instead, they buy and sell contracts to cancel each other out.

Subcontracting. By subcontracting, a business firm may enter into a contract with another firm to perform certain high-risk activities. For example, a construction company may subcontract plumbing to another firm that agrees to provide all plumbing services for a fixed fee. The construction company is therefore unaffected by fluctuating prices of labor and materials. Also, the plumbing subcontractor is probably more able to perform the work correctly.

Insurance. The most common means of shifting business risk is insurance. An extremely large number of risks facing businesses may be shifted to insurance firms for a fee. In exchange for premiums, the insurance company agrees to sustain all or part of various losses. Each firm must analyze its risks and the cost of shifting the risks to insurance com-

Exhibit 17–2

Hedging in the commodity market.

Wheat Cost April 1	Futures Gain		Wheat Cost Oct. 1	
$3.40 per bushel	Oct. 1—Sell—	$4.20	$4.00	per bushel
	Apr. 1—Buy—	3.60	− .60	gain from futures
	Net gain	$ .60	$3.40	net cost per bushel

panies to decide what types of insurance coverage to buy and how much of the total loss to shift to the insurance companies.

PRINCIPLES OF INSURABLE RISKS

In order for risks to be insurable, they must meet five basic requirements:

1. The possible loss must be predictable;
2. The risk must be spread over large numbers;
3. The possible loss must be measurable;
4. The insured must also risk loss;
5. There must be a basis for selecting risks to insure.

Predictability

Insurance is based on **probability** (odds). The chance of certain events occurring is calculated for large groups and applied to the individual. For instance, accurate statistics are available showing how many people die within each age group each year. Insurance companies have found these statistics to be relatively constant over a period of time. Consequently, by using past statistical data, they can predict with extreme accuracy how many people will die in the next year and at what ages. Consider a simple illustration of an insurance company that plans to insure 1,000 persons, forty-nine years of age, on a one-year term policy. Suppose historical statistics show that .2 percent of fifty-year-old people die each year. The insurance company would then expect two people of their insured group to die next year, but they could not possibly know which two. As a result of this knowledge, if each person were insured for $10,000, then the insurance company should plan to pay out $20,000 the next year. The insurance company would then set premiums for all $10,000 term policies at a level that would return $20,000 plus operating costs. The company then would be able to invest the premiums during the year to provide profit.

The same principle is used in all types of insurance. Odds are calculated for the risk of large groups and applied to individual insurance. For instance, the type and number of houses that have burned in the past determines the premiums charged for fire insurance on homes.

Large Numbers

The above example illustrates why there must be a large number of risks for probability to be predictable. If the company were to insure only two persons for $10,000 each and both were to die the first year, the company would have to pay out $20,000 in exchange for a small amount of premiums. There would be no way for them to predict when the two insured persons would die. Generally, risks must also be spread over wide geographic areas. An insurance company that insured property in only one coastal city would be wiped out if a hurricane hit the town.

Measurability

The possible loss at risk must be measurable. In our example, each person's life was insured for $10,000. A building may be insured for the estimated market value. On the other hand, loss of a baby's bronzed shoes can be a real loss to the parents, but there is no way to measure the real sentimental value for insurance purposes.

Risk of Insured

The insured must also stand to lose something. For example, if insurance companies allowed people to insure homes and buildings for more than their value, the number of arsons would likely increase because the insured could profit from the destruction of their property. The individual must stand to lose something (time, money, effort, etc.) so he or she will not want a loss to happen.

Selection

The insurance company must have some basis for selecting risks they will cover. If the two persons in our example both had incurable cancer with less than a year to live, the insurance company would be assured a loss in issuing those persons insurance policies on their lives. The company must be able to select and eliminate risks that do not fit the probability basis for which their premiums are set. Automobile insurance companies could not insure a driver with a long history of accidents for the same premium they charge a driver with a good record.

The insurance company must also be able to exclude certain catastrophic risks. A nuclear explosion could conceivably destroy several cities with such destruction that no insurance company could possibly sustain the losses.

TYPES OF BUSINESS INSURANCE

Insurance protects business firms from losses in terms of (1) earning *power*, (2) property, and (3) liability. A business can buy insurance **policies** (contracts) to reimburse in full or in part a wide range of losses within these categories. See Exhibit 17–3.

Insurance for Loss of Earning Power

A business firm may have full coverage on the physical facilities of the business and be paid full value in the event of a fire. It would seem that the business has successfully shifted this particular risk to the insurance company; however, this may not be true. After a major fire, the company might be literally out of business for the period of time it would take to clear and rebuild its facilities. Loss of income for this period can often be a serious financial loss that may damage the firm. In addition, customers may establish patronage at other businesses and hesitate to change after the business is in operation again. A business may buy insurance to help sustain this loss of income.

Individuals may also suffer loss of income due to illness, injury, and unemployment. Insurance companies offer insurance to individuals to help shift this risk. In fact, governmental agencies aid many people when they

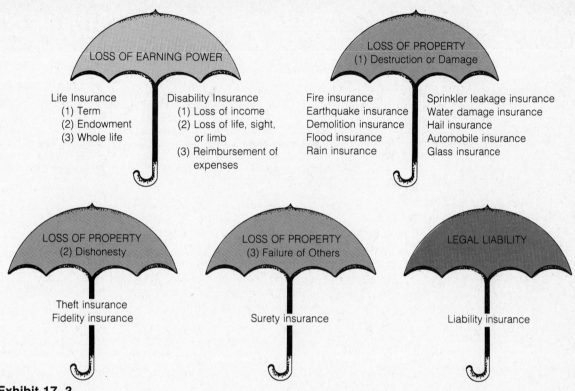

LOSS OF EARNING POWER

Life Insurance
(1) Term
(2) Endowment
(3) Whole life

Disability Insurance
(1) Loss of income
(2) Loss of life, sight, or limb
(3) Reimbursement of expenses

LOSS OF PROPERTY
(1) Destruction or Damage

Fire insurance
Earthquake insurance
Demolition insurance
Flood insurance
Rain insurance

Sprinkler leakage insurance
Water damage insurance
Hail insurance
Automobile insurance
Glass insurance

LOSS OF PROPERTY
(2) Dishonesty

Theft insurance
Fidelity insurance

LOSS OF PROPERTY
(3) Failure of Others

Surety insurance

LEGAL LIABILITY

Liability insurance

Exhibit 17–3
Reasons for buying specific types of insurance.

suffer injury and unemployment. Unemployment compensation and workmen's compensation are two types of governmental assistance programs intended to help shift the loss of income risk from the individual to society.

The basic types of insurance that insure against loss of earning power are (1) life insurance and (2) disability insurance.

Life Insurance

Life insurance is an asset to both individuals and businesses. Life insurance provides important shifts of loss and risk for the individual by making funds available for a person's family in the event of his or her death. Without life insurance, the burden of burial, care and education of children, and the maintenance of a relatively satisfactory income would be unreasonable for most families. Although not as critical, life insurance is often of considerable value to business firms. It is a fairly common practice for businesses to insure key personnel, because when these people die unexpectedly the business sustains disruption to some degree and also some extra costs.

The three basic types of life insurance available are term, endowment, and whole life.

Life Expectancy Tables

Expected years of life remaining at level of age.

Age (years)	Expected Years of Life Remaining	Age (years)	Expected Years of Life Remaining	Age (years)	Expected Years of Life Remaining
At birth	73.3	24	51.3	47	30.1
1	73.3	25	50.4	48	29.3
2	72.4	26	49.5	49	28.4
3	71.5	27	48.5	50	27.6
4	70.5	28	47.6	51	26.7
5	69.5	29	46.6	52	25.9
6	68.6	30	45.7	53	25.1
7	67.6	31	44.8	54	24.3
8	66.6	32	43.8	55	23.5
9	65.6	33	42.9	56	22.7
10	64.6	34	41.9	57	22.0
11	63.7	35	41.0	58	21.2
12	62.7	36	40.1	59	20.5
13	61.7	37	39.1	60	19.7
14	60.7	38	38.2	61	19.0
15	59.7	39	37.3	62	18.3
16	58.8	40	36.4	63	17.6
17	57.8	41	35.5	64	17.0
18	56.9	42	34.6	65	16.3
19	56.0	43	33.7	70	13.1
20	55.0	44	32.8	75	10.4
21	54.1	45	31.9	80	8.1
22	53.2	46	31.0	85 and over	6.4
23	52.2				

SOURCE: Statistical Abstract of the U.S., 1981.

Expectation of life (in years) at birth, by sex: 1900 to 1979.

Year	Both Sexes	Male	Female	Year	Both Sexes	Male	Female
1900	47.3	46.3	48.3	1945	65.9	63.6	67.9
1905	48.7	47.3	50.2	1950	68.2	65.6	71.1
1910	50.0	48.4	51.8	1955	69.6	66.7	72.8
1915	54.5	52.5	56.8	1960	69.7	66.6	73.1
1920	54.1	53.6	54.6	1965	70.2	66.8	73.7
1925	59.0	57.6	60.6	1970	70.9	67.1	74.8
1930	59.7	58.1	61.6	1975	72.5	68.7	76.5
1935	61.7	59.9	63.9	1978	73.3	69.5	77.2
1940	62.9	60.8	65.2	1979	73.8	69.9	77.8

SOURCE: Statistical Abstract of the U.S., 1981.

Term Insurance. A **term insurance** policy (contract) provides for the insurance company to pay the face amount of the policy to a beneficiary if the insured dies within the life of the policy. If the insured does not die within the life of the policy, it expires at the end of the period. Term insurance policies run only for a specific period of time, usually five, ten, or twenty years. Term insurance also has no cash value, and if the insured does not die during the policy life, one receives no monetary value for premiums, only insurance coverage against death.

As indicated earlier, the amount of risk involved determines the insurance premium. Historical data show that fewer people die at age twenty-five than at age sixty-five. As a consequence, insurance premiums for term insurance for persons twenty-five years old is many times cheaper than the insurance premiums for persons aged sixty-five. As a result, term insurance is more attractive at age twenty-five. Term insurance is particularly suitable for young married couples. They are just starting their work life, have accumulated little in the way of assets, and are usually at the bottom of their work life's pay scale. As a result, they need larger amounts of insurance but have fewer resources to purchase it. Term insurance provides maximum insurance at minimum cost for young people, thereby meeting the young family's needs. However, it should be remembered that as age advances, the premium costs of term insurance increase.

Decreasing Term Insurance. Another important type of insurance is **decreasing term insurance,** more popularly known as mortgage insurance. Many breadwinners desire a fully paid home in the event of their death so their families will not be burdened with large house payments. Decreasing term insurance provides this risk protection for relatively low premium amounts. A decreasing term policy is issued for the period of payout on the home, say for twenty-five years. In the event of death of the insured, the amount of money the insurance company will pay during the life of the policy is decreased each successive year of the policy.

Exhibit 17–4

Life insurance in force in the United States.

Year	Number of Policies (in millions)	Coverage per Family	Value (in billions)
1950	202	$ 4,600	$ 149
1960	282	10,200	586
1970	355	20,700	1,402
1980	402	41,500	3,541

SOURCE: Statistical Abstract of the United States, 1981.

Endowment Insurance.   Endowment insurance insures for a specific time period. The endowment policy promises to pay the face value of the policy to the beneficiary if the insured dies during the life of the policy; however, if the insured does not die during the life of the policy, the face value is paid to the insured at the expiration of the policy time period. In one sense, endowment insurance is a type of insured savings account. Endowment insurance premiums are relatively expensive, since they provide coverage in case of death and still assure payment of face value at the end of a specific period of time. Of course, the length of time and the risk of death (determined by age) decide the amount of the premium. As an example, a five-year endowment policy taken out at age sixty would require an exceedingly high premium payment. Endowment policies usually have a cash value if the insured cancels the policy before expiration.

Whole Life Insurance.   The whole life insurance policy provides coverage to the insured for his or her entire life. Face value of the policy is paid only at the death of the insured and only to the beneficiary. Whole life usually has a cash value of less than the face value if the policy is canceled before death, the amount being determined by the amount of premiums paid to the insurance company.

Premiums are calculated on the age of the insured at the time the policy originates, based on life expectancy tables, and may be paid in three ways: single premium, limited payment, and continuous premium. The single-premium method requires a relatively large payment at the issuance of the policy, and no other premiums are required. The limited-payment method requires the insured to pay premiums for a specific period of time (twenty years is a common time period), after which no further premiums are due, although the insured is covered for life. Of course, if death occurs before the insured pays all of the premium payments, the beneficiary receives the face value of the insurance and all premium payments stop. A continuous premium plan involves the insured paying a specified amount (all premiums are the same amount) as long as the policy is in force.

Another important feature usually incorporated in both endowment and whole life insurance is a loan value. Most policies in these categories allow the insured to borrow the amount of the cash value at any time. The amount of interest the insured must pay the insurance company on these borrowed funds is usually stated in the policy and is often a lower rate than that offered by other lending institutions. If the insured dies before the loan is repaid (interest must be paid each year), the amount of the loan is subtracted from the face value of the policy and the remainder is paid to the beneficiary.

Life insurance companies also offer a large number of special features in their insurance policies for increased premium payments. Waiver of premiums in case of disability and double or triple payments of the face value in case of accidents from certain causes are just two of the more common options available.

EXHIBIT 17–5

The twenty-five largest life insurance companies.

Rank	Company	Assets ($000)	Life Insurance in Force ($000)	Rank
1	Prudential (Newark)	62,498,540	456,174,632	1
2	Metropolitan (New York)	51,757,845	393,590,726	2
3	Equitable Life Assurance (New York)	36,758,160	223,874,676	3
4	Aetna Life (Hartford)	25,158,904	163,873,853	4
5	New York Life	21,041,380	137,456,394	6
6	John Hancock Mutual (Boston)	19,936,798	145,609,204	5
7	Connecticut General Life (Bloomfield)	15,103,332	90,809,773	9
8	Travelers (Hartford)	14,803,168	116,498,216	8
9	Northwestern Mutual (Milwaukee)	12,154,318	70,133,741	11
10	Teachers Insurance & Annuity (New York)	11,439,344	9,072,398	45
11	Massachusetts Mutual (Springfield)	10,022,231	55,978,807	13
12	Bankers Life (Des Moines)	8,765,096	42,680,898	17
13	Mutual of New York	8,388,961	42,827,888	16
14	New England Mutual (Boston)	7,273,819	34,991,635	19
15	Mutual Benefit (Newark)	6,619,044	46,732,485	14
16	Connecticut Mutual (Hartford)	5,818,322	29,553,555	24
17	Lincoln National Life (Fort Wayne, Ind.)	5,038,853	72,627,629	10
18	Penn Mutual (Philadelphia)	3,963,402	19,407,860	28
19	State Farm Life (Bloomington, Ill.)	3,759,829	58,479,552	12
20	Phoenix Mutual (Hartford)	3,352,372	33,513,245	20
21	Continental Assurance (Chicago)	3,323,163	28,804,867	26
22	Western & Southern (Cincinnati)	3,210,187	15,282,409	36
23	National Life & Accident (Nashville)	3,021,702	17,836,947	31
24	Pacific Mutual (Newport Beach, Calif.)	2,984,715	19,096,246	29
25	Nationwide Life (Columbus, Ohio)	2,766,057	14,913,866	38

SOURCE: *Fortune Magazine*, July 12, 1982.

Exhibit 17–6

Comparison of basic life insurance policies.

Type of Insurance	Period Premium Payment	Period of Coverage	Payment of Benefit (face value)	Cash or Loan Value	Premium Cost
Term life insurance	Life of policy specified in policy	Life of policy	Only if death occurs during life of policy	No	Lowest
Endowment life insurance	Period specified in policy	Until death	Payment at death or end of policy period	Yes	Highest
Whole life insurance	Until death	Until death	Payment at death	Yes	

Disability

Disability insurance provides coverage for three types of losses: income; life, sight, or limb; and expenses.

Loss of Income.   Insurance policies can protect against loss of income due to accident, sickness, or accident and sickness. If the insured becomes totally disabled, the policy will pay a specific amount for a specific time period. Many policies also include reduced payment for partial disability.

Loss of Life, Sight, or Limb.   **Accident policies** usually provide for a lump sum payment to the beneficiary in case of accidental death of the insured and payment of specific amounts to the insured in the event of accidental loss of sight or limb. These policies specify the amount of money to be paid for each accidental loss, such as a certain amount for loss of one arm and another amount for two arms.

Reimbursement of Expenses.   Disability insurance in the form of health insurance provides for reimbursement of all or part of expenses resulting from disability. Hospital and medical expenses in the traditional sickness insurance policy are paid as scheduled in the policy—that is, fixed amounts for operating room, drugs, nurses, doctors' fees, etc. Accident insurance, on the other hand, usually specifies payment of all costs of medical expenses up to a specified maximum.

LOSS OF PROPERTY

A business firm may suffer loss of property due to a wide range of causes. Most of these risks may be shifted to insurance companies in exchange for premiums. Property may be lost by (1) destruction or damage, (2) dishonesty, and (3) failure of others.

Destruction or Damage

Fire, wind, hail, lightning, water, riot, collision, and vandalism may destroy property. All these events may be covered by insurance, although under some circumstances the risk is so great that the premium is prohibitively expensive. For example, a business firm on the banks of a river with a history of flooding would not be able to obtain flood coverage from most insurance companies. The firm would be forced to obtain coverage from some company that accepts high risks, such as Lloyds of London (not actually a company but an association), and the cost of premiums would be so high as to make coverage unrealistic.

Destruction and/or damage of property may be covered by fire and other **property loss insurance.** Standard **fire insurance** policies reimburse in full or in part for losses due to fire and lightning. Fire insurance policies may cover buildings and/or their contents. Even businesses and individuals who rent may insure their property in rented buildings. Additional coverage may be obtained in the traditional fire insurance policy for an additional premium to insure against loss from windstorm, hail, explo-

Exhibit 17–7

Types of property loss insurance.

Insurance	Insures against Loss
Earthquake	Due to earthquakes.
Demolition	From changes in building codes and zoning; fire or other peril resulting from buildings being torn down.
Flood	Caused by flood damage.
Rain	Of income due to rain (such as cancelled baseball games) and expenses caused by rain damage.
Sprinkler leakage	Caused by automatic sprinkler system.
Water damage	Caused by plumbing system or roof leakage.
Hail insurance on crops	Caused by hail (from planting to harvest).
Automobile	From damage in accident, vandalism, fire, and glass breakage.
Glass	From glass breakage in businesses.

sion, riot, civil commotion, aircraft-caused damage, vehicle-caused damage, and smoke damage.

Insurance available to protect property loss is extensive. Some of these types are listed in Exhibit 17–7.

Dishonesty

Theft from business firms may be the act of employees or of persons outside the business. Employee theft has become a major problem in business today. Theft ranging from shoplifting to burglary by outsiders is also an extensive problem. The business can buy insurance to protect from such losses, although few firms carry insurance against shoplifting. Employee theft is usually covered only to the extent of bonding certain employees who handle large sums of money.

Business firms may insure against dishonesty by purchasing theft and/ or fidelity insurance.

Theft Insurance. Business firms may buy insurance against all types of theft. Some of the more common **theft insurance** policies are: mercantile safe burglary, mercantile robbery, paymaster, money and securities, storekeepers' burglary and robbery, office burglary and robbery, and valuable papers and records. Individuals may likewise obtain policies to protect themselves from all forms of personal theft.

"LET'S SEE NOW... THIS IS AN OAK TREE, AND YOUR POLICY COVERS ELM, WALNUT, MAGNOLIA, PINE..."

Fidelity Insurance. Businesses may also bond their employees, which protects the business from loss by theft or embezzlement by those bonded employees.

Failure of Others

A firm that enters into a contract with another party or business often stands to lose money if the contract is not fulfilled. For example, if a firm contracts for another company to construct a new building and the contractor does not complete the building, or fails to complete the building on time, the firm stands to lose money: it may have to renegotiate the contract at possibly a higher price, or, if the building is not completed on time, the firm will lose income by delaying opening of operations. Most firms will require contractors to be bonded (insured) to ensure compliance with the contract. That is, if the contractor does not complete the job or meet deadlines, the insurance company must reimburse the original firm for any incurred losses. This is called **surety insurance**.

LEGAL LIABILITY

A business may become liable for damages to other property or persons through its operations or through employees' actions while they are working. For instance, a firm's delivery person may cause an accident because of negligence, and the company may be liable for damages. If the accident causes a death, the courts may award the victim's estate a very large judgment against the firm. The heirs may then force property of the business to be sold to satisfy the debt.

Business firms and individuals can buy insurance to protect them from losses resulting from liability. Almost any amount of coverage is available for payment of premiums. However, just being covered by **liability insurance** does not fully shift the risk of liability judgments. The firm or individual with $50,000 of liability insurance on an automobile may be subject to a $100,000 judgment. In this case, the insurance company pays the full $50,000. The business firm that does not carry relatively large coverage in liability insurance is not acting in its best interests. Of course, insurance companies are not required to pay claims when fraud or criminal actions are involved.

Liability insurance includes protection against claims arising from accidents caused by: manufacturer and contractor operations, elevator operations, retail operations, druggists' mistakes, physicians' malpractice, taverns selling alcoholic beverages to intoxicated persons who cause injury, etc.

NO-FAULT INSURANCE

Some states have an automobile insurance law providing for what is called **no-fault insurance.** In a no-fault state, motorists are allowed to collect benefits from insurance companies regardless of who is at fault. Automobile no-fault insurance laws vary by state, but they generally have certain points in common.

1. Anyone injured in an automobile accident—driver, passenger, or pedestrian—may collect financial losses from their insurance company without regard to who is at fault. These financial losses usually include medical and hospital expenses and lost income.
2. Accident victims are limited in their right to sue. Generally, lawsuits are prohibited except when there is death, disfigurement, serious injury, or when medical expenses exceed a certain amount.
3. All drivers of private motor vehicles are required to carry insurance.

At least in part, no-fault insurance laws are an attempt to decrease paperwork, investigations, and the $1.5 billion spent each year on legal fees that result from automobile accidents. Supporters of no-fault insurance claim two benefits to automobile owners. One, that claims are paid more quickly. Two, that automobile insurance premiums are lower as a result of no-fault.

As states have adopted no-fault insurance, automobile insurance premiums have tended to drop on an average of about 20 percent.

Opponents of no-fault insurance have usually opposed it because they feel it limits the rights of the individual to legal recourse. They also contend that because of the no-fault provision, claims will increase after a period of time in both number and amounts. In the past, insurance companies have experienced an increase in the number of marginal claims, with larger amounts of money claimed during times of economic depression.

SUMMARY OF KEY POINTS

1. Business firms may deal with risk by: (1) avoiding the risk; (2) reducing the risk; (3) assuming the risk; and/or (4) shifting the risk.

2. Business risks may be avoided by substitution, screening, and elimination.

3. Some methods of reducing business risk are inspection, training, and good management practices.

4. Business risks may be assumed by the firm in the form of self-insurance, but this is not usually feasible except for large, multiple-facility firms.

5. Shifting business risks can be achieved by insurance, hedging, and subcontracting.

6. Insurance is based on probability—chances of certain occurrences are calculated on a statistical basis for large groups and applied to individuals.

7. There are five basic principles that determine insurable risks: (1) they must be predictable; (2) there must be large numbers of them; (3) they must be measurable; (4) the insured must risk something; and (5) the insurance company must be able to select which risks to insure.

8. Insurance may be used by business firms to protect them from losses in terms of earning power, property, and liability.

9. Protection from loss of earning power may be provided by life insurance and disability insurance.

10. The basic types of life insurance are term, endowment, and whole life.

11. Disability insurance provides coverage for three types of losses: (1) income; (2) life, sight, or limb; and (3) expenses.

12. Loss of property is covered by insurance that pays for: (1) destruction or damage (fire insurance, etc.); (2) dishonesty (fidelity and theft insurance); and (3) failure of others (surety insurance).

13. Legal liability protection is provided by liability insurance.

14. No-fault automobile insurance allows motorists to collect benefits from their insurance company regardless of who is at fault.

DISCUSSION QUESTIONS

1. Give an example for each of the following ways a business can:
   a. Avoid risk   c. Assume risk
   b. Reduce risk   d. Shift risk

2. If you headed an insurance company and were going to insure college students across the nation with life insurance, how would you go about determining their premiums?

3. What are some reasons for business firms' use of insurance?

4. What type of life insurance probably will be best for you when you begin your career?

5. Why might a person select endowment insurance as opposed to whole life?

6. If you owned a drugstore, what types of insurance would you purchase? Explain.

STUDENT PROJECTS

1. Visit an insurance agent in your community and find out what insurance coverage he or she feels you should obtain when you start to work at your chosen occupation.

2. Find out the estimated cost of this insurance.

3. Find out what insurance coverage a small business in your community carries and list any recommendations for changing the coverage that you feel would be beneficial to the small business.

4. Find out whether your state has no-fault insurance.

Morrow Grain Company

Oren Morrow recently bought the Beard Grain Company for $190,000. The inventory consists of the following: two concrete grain elevators for storage; one office building equipped with calculators, desks, chairs, safe, and other office equipment; one wooden tool shed containing conveyors, paint, rags, etc.; one truck; one automobile; and ten acres of fenced land.

    The Morrow Grain Company does not carry cash in the office except for a $25 petty cash fund in a locked drawer. All transactions are completed in checks received from customers and checks written by the bookkeeper and signed by Oren. The Beard Grain Company employed four people whom Morrow plans to retain: one truck driver, one bookkeeper, and two elevator workers. At the present time, the elevator is empty, but Morrow plans to buy two million bushels of wheat from the local farmers, store it for six months, and then sell it on the open market.

Morrow realizes he is subject to a number of varied risks, any one of which could mean the difference between success and failure. Consequently, he would like to shift or avoid as many risks as possible. He asks you for advice.

Questions

1. Point out ways Oren can (1) avoid risk, (2) reduce risk, (3) assume risk, and (4) shift risk.
2. Do you advise Oren to engage in hedging? Explain.
3. What types of insurance do you advise Oren to purchase?
4. What are some measures Oren himself can take to reduce and avoid risks in his business other than hedging and insurance?

The Insure-All Insurance Company

Joan Richards is a new insurance salesperson for the Insure-All Company. She is a recent college graduate and this is her first full-time job. She has just completed Insure-All's sixteen-week training program. As part of the training program she observed other salespeople's selling techniques. Today marks the first time that she is to go out on her own to begin selling. Her assignment is rather broad, since she will call on private individuals as well as owners and managers of business firms. Thus, she must have a wide knowledge about many different kinds of insurance plans suitable for the needs of all her clients—individuals and businesses.

Joan's first appointment is with Albert Smith, who has just moved to the city. Mr. Smith has bought and operates a small men's and women's clothing shop, and he has four full-time and two half-time employees.

Mr. Smith is married and has three children ages ten, eight, and six; he plans for them to attend college. The Smiths have purchased a home located on the lake. Mr. Smith likes to water ski, and he has his own boat. Mr. Smith is somewhat skeptical of insurance agents in general, because of some unfortunate incidents in the past. However, he has agreed to discuss his possible insurance needs with Joan. Therefore, Joan must be well prepared for this meeting, not only to possibly sell insurance to Mr. Smith but also to feel that she has succeeded on her first job.

As Joan begins her sales presentation, Mr. Smith immediately asks her some very pointed questions. What should Joan answer?

Questions

1. Why do I need insurance?
2. What are the possible means of dealing with risk?
3. What are my insurance needs as a businessman?
4. What types of insurance do I need as an individual?

John F. Dryden, founder of
Prudential Insurance Company.

BUSINESS PROFILE

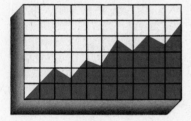

Prudential Insurance Company of America

The Prudential Insurance Company of America is the story of one man's dream that turned into the largest life insurance company in the United States.

John Dryden, an impoverished life insurance agent, had long dreamed of starting a company to sell insurance to low-income people. The average income of people in 1875 was so low that most could not afford the insurance offered at that time. John Dryden felt that insurance could be offered and collected weekly by an agent. He tried unsuccessfully to interest financial backers in his idea for many years. He finally met Dr. Ward of Newark, New Jersey, who knew first-hand the plight of low-income people and their need for insurance. He became the first to invest $1,000 and helped Dryden acquire other investors.

The Prudential Friendly Society was founded in 1875 with $30,000 in pledges, of which it had collected $5,900 in cash. One of the policies it offered in the beginning was an infant burial policy for which the company collected 3¢ per week in premiums. Prudential grew rapidly and became a mutual in 1915.

Today, Prudential has life insurance in force in the amount of $456 billion. It also serves another function in lending vast amounts of funds—$17 billion in mortgages and real estate investments, $21 billion in corporate and government bonds, and $4 billion in common stock.

Prudential has 62,817 employees, including subsidiaries, and assets worth $62 billion.

Banking, the Stock Market, and Insurance

Many careers at both entry and higher levels are available for those persons interested in the financial world of business. A sampling of these career opportunities follows.

Occupation	Number Currently Employed	Number of Openings Each Year to 1990
Banking		
Bank clerks	505,000	45,000
Bank officers, managers	330,000	28,000
Bank tellers	410,000	17,000
Credit managers	49,000	2,200
Stock market		
Securities salesworkers	109,000	5,500
Insurance		
Actuaries	9,000	500
Claims adjusters	155,000	7,000
Insurance agents and brokers	568,000	30,000

SOURCE: U.S. Department of Labor, *Occupational Outlook Handbook*, 1980–81.

VICE-PRESIDENT AND BRANCH MANAGER Responsible for the activities of a regional bank office, branch bank, or an administrative bank division or department.

ADMINISTRATIVE SECRETARY Carries out policies established by the bank president and other officials.

BANK TREASURER Responsible for directing the formal financial affairs of a bank.

CONTROLLER In charge and control of the financial affairs of a bank.

FINANCIAL INSTITUTION MANAGER Establishes and maintains relationships with customers, business, service, and civic organizations to promote goodwill and develop new business.

MORTGAGE LOAN OFFICER Examines applications for loans and analyzes potential loan markets.

LOAN OFFICER Approves cash loans.

CREDIT AND COLLECTION MANAGER Main responsibility is to investigate and evaluate the reputations and finances of those customers who are seeking credit.

RESERVE OFFICER Maintains and calculates the bank's reserve funds.

FOREIGN-EXCHANGE TRADER Responsible for banking transactions with foreign countries and exchanging credit with or extending credit to other nations.

BANK CASHIER Supervises the receipt, disbursement, expenditure, and custody of money for the bank.

OPERATIONS OFFICER In charge of seeing that standard procedural practices are carried out by the bank's employees.

SAFE DEPOSITS MANAGER Supervises the rental and maintenance of safe deposit boxes of the bank.

BANK TELLER Handles certain types of customer account transactions, such as receiving and paying out monies, recording customer transactions, cashing checks, and performing other banking duties. Specialized tellers include note tellers, savings tellers, payroll tellers, discount tellers, and securities tellers.

COMMODITY LOAN CLERK Keeps records of loans in foreign department, secured by commodities in warehouses.

ACCOUNT ANALYST Computes charges to be made against commercial accounts for services performed by bank.

RECONCILEMENT CLERK Reconciles bank statements received from other banks, such as branch banks and Federal Reserve banks.

STOCK TRANSFER CLERK Records security transfers and effects payment of interest and dividends for corporations.

MORTGAGE CLERK Types legal papers dealing with real estate on which money has been loaned.

ACCOUNT EXECUTIVE Employed by stock exchange member or securities firms to buy and sell stocks and bonds for customers on their instructions.

BROKER'S FLOOR REPRESENTATIVE Buys and sells securities on floor of stock exchange.

BROKERAGE CLERK Records purchase and sale of securities, such as stocks and bonds, in investment firm.

INSURANCE MANAGER Directs the insurance program for a company. Activities include directing study of company's assets, property, and operations to classify insurable risks; helps plan insurance coverage.

INSURANCE OFFICER MANAGER Supervises and coordinates activities of branch or district office personnel.

INSURANCE UNDERWRITER Reviews insurance applications to evaluate the degree of risk involved. The underwriter decides whether to reject or accept an application for insurance and determines the insurance rate applicable for each policy.

INSURANCE ADJUSTER Investigates claims to determine if damage is covered by insurance policy, estimates cost of repair or replacement of property, and helps work out a satisfactory settlement of the claim to all parties involved.

INSURANCE SALES AGENT AND BROKER Advises people on their insurance needs, and sells insurance policies in the three basic types of insurance: life, property and liability, and health.

ACTUARY Analyzes, studies, and predicts the likelihood of accidents or other types of events occurring and recommends the price that should be charged for insurance against these risks.

INSURANCE EXAMINER Evaluates policyholder complaints and conformity of insurance companies and agents.

CAREER PROFILE

Ronald Terry, a graduate of Memphis State University, began his career in banking in 1957 as a management trainee in the First National Bank of Memphis. Ronald's success in banking is noted by his advancement, having been promoted to executive vice-president by 1970.

In 1969, the First National Bank of Memphis formed the First Tennessee National Corporation, a bank holding company. In 1971, Ronald was appointed a director and also president of this corporation. By 1973, he was promoted to chairman and chief executive officer of the bank holding company, which has $2 billion in total assets, offices in seventeen states, and some 3,300 employees. Ronald is also vice-chairman and a director of the First National Bank.

Ronald's responsibilities include long-range planning, developing bank personnel, and maintaining contact with the groups that First Tennessee serves. He feels the most gratifying part of his job is the sense of accomplishment within the community and seeing the growth and development of the bank's personnel.

Ronald has the following suggestions for career planning: "Plan a career in about two-year increments. Any more than that allows personal goals to get fuzzy. Try to see yourself as others see you and recognize and respect the difference between you and your associates. You must get along with others to succeed, and this is more important as you go higher in a management hierarchy. The key word is empathy, the ability to put yourself in the other guy's shoes. If you can't do this, then you can't sell, you can't manage, you can't make it as a top executive.

"Do your homework. Never consider yourself too important to tend to the details of the job assigned to you. Learn to plan and make things happen. Remember that the gray area between being totally right and totally wrong is that area of risk in which great managers develop."

Deborah Jean Carufel has worked in the Arizona Bank since her graduation from Mesa Community College. She was a teller with the Arizona Bank, and was then promoted to an assistant operations supervisor. She worked in this position for eight months and was put into the bank's management training program, given her own branch bank, and has been an assistant manager/operations supervisor for the past two years. She currently supervises seven employees in all operations of the branch bank.

The most satisfying part of her job is helping to develop employees. Deborah states, "The biggest thrill of all is to see one of my employees advance and be promoted."

She feels that her Introduction to Business course was most helpful to her in channeling her interest toward management. She is looking forward to added responsibilities in a larger branch bank.

Deborah's Introduction to Business instructor was Louis Giallonardo of Mesa Community College.

Quantitative Aids of Business

SECTION SIX

18 Accounting Analysis and Budgeting

LEARNING GOALS

After reading this chapter, you will understand:

1. That accounting is one of management's most important tools and how it uses it to make decisions and control a business.

2. What records a business must keep for tax and other financial purposes.

3. What a balance sheet is and how it is used.

4. The items that make up an income statement and how it is used.

5. What financial ratios are and how they are used.

6. The importance of the budget to a business firm's success.

7. How a budget is prepared and how it functions to help management's decisions.

KEY TERMS

Accounting analysis
Balance sheet
Assets
Liabilities
Owner's equity
Income statement
Cost of goods sold
Cost of goods manufactured

Current ratio
Acid test ratio
Debt to net worth ratio
Rate of return on assets
Rate of return on owner's equity
Budget
FIFO
LIFO

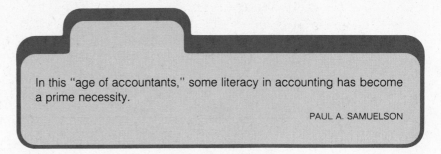

In this "age of accountants," some literacy in accounting has become a prime necessity.

PAUL A. SAMUELSON

Accounting is an area in which computers are widely used. They are used to keep all sorts of records—expenditures, sales, accounts receivable, accounts payable, etc. In addition, they provide accounting statements and many types of accounting analysis. The transfer of accounting information from branch plants or offices to the home office can be achieved by computer-to-computer linkup through telephone lines. Even small businesses can receive these services by using inexpensive microcomputers. All of the accounting records, statements, and analysis presented in this chapter can be retained and performed on many types and sizes of computers.

THE PURPOSE OF ACCOUNTING ANALYSIS

Management needs many analytical tools if it is to achieve efficiency in business. **Accounting analysis** is probably the most important information system available to management.

The efficient accounting system designed as an aid to management provides: (1) a system by which management can effectively control the organization, (2) information on which management can arrive at decisions, and (3) records to meet requirements of various governmental agencies and private groups.

Control

A business uses accounting information in an important process called *management control.* This is the function of ensuring that the business obtains and uses its resources effectively toward the accomplishment of the organization's goals.

The very basis of control of the business organization is the use of the management-by-exception principle. To control effectively by any other technique would be impossible. If managers were to try to check every detail that occurred in the business, a staff of managers at least as large as the employee work force would be necessary, greatly increasing costs. For example, how can the president of a company employing 1,000 people know that the person operating the third lathe in Department C is performing his job satisfactorily? The president cannot be sure by observation, since it is likely the worker will speed up when the president is in the department and slow down when he or she leaves. By the same token, the president cannot rely on the foreman for information because a bad report would make the foreman look bad and force the foreman to correct the situation. The foreman may prefer not to correct the situation because it may cause excessive trouble in the department. The only way the president will be ensured that the machine operator is performing satisfactorily is by the exception principle.

Business firms must establish standards of performance for all jobs by techniques that are best suited to the specific type of job. In the example above, the use of methods and time study techniques would probably be the best way to establish a standard performance for the job. By using job standards and existing wage rates, management constructs departmental and company budgets (discussed later in this chapter) as plans for future production. As long as the third lathe operator in Department C performs at existing quantity and quality standards for his position, all managers may assume that he is performing his job effectively. However, if he fails to meet either or both standards, management must determine the cause of failure and correct the situation. In this way management discovers a problem almost as soon as it happens. The exact location of the trouble is also identified by accounting information. Management can identify and treat causes and not just symptoms. In the example of the lathe operator, when the departmental supervisor contacts the foreman to determine the exact cause of below-standard output, he might find one of the following:

Symptom	Possible Basic Causal Factor
Inadequate performance of machine	Improper preventive maintenance
New worker not operating machine properly	Improper training by foreman or improper hiring procedures
Low morale resulting in improper motivation of worker	Inadequate human relations practices of foreman
Improper materials	Inadequate purchasing control

Aid to Making Management Decisions

Effective management decisions must be determined by a process that (1) recognizes that a problem exists, (2) identifies alternative solutions to the problem, (3) analyzes the consequences of each possible solution, and (4) compares the consequences of each possible solution to decide which solution is best. Accounting information is essential to this process in almost all instances.

Exhibit 18–1

Purpose and uses of accounting analysis.

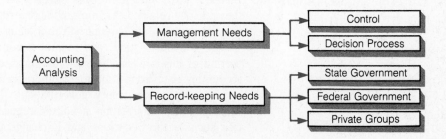

"WELL YOU SEE SIR, DOWN IN THE BOOKKEEPING DEPARTMENT I'M SWAMPED WITH WORK — PAPERS, LEDGERS, DIRECTORIES — AND, WELL, SIR, WHAT I REALLY COULD USE IS YOUR DESK."

Management must keep accounting records of past operations and present financial conditions to perform future planning and to evaluate the results of past planning. In choosing between alternative courses of action, management can express future consequences of various alternative actions in terms of net profit. For example, if a firm finds its raw material cost has increased because of a supplier's price increase, it must decide whether to pass on the increase to the consumer, absorb the increase, or enact some combination of the two alternatives. Sales forecasts in terms of dollars, and costs to produce the amount of forecasted sales in dollars at various selling prices, will be valuable to management in reaching its decision. In addition, management must measure the effect of the resulting change in profit for the year on other decisions—working capital needs, funds available for capital equipment, dividend rates, etc.

Although accounting analysis is probably the most important tool to management decision making, it is not the only one to be considered. Accounting information is seldom the only tool that should be used. For example, when receiving bids from suppliers on raw materials, management cannot automatically accept the lowest bid every time. Other factors, such as vendor dependability, cash discounts, transportation, order time, and credit, often enter into decisions.

Government and Other Record Requirements

Business firms must know what records are required by law and how long they must be retained. A sample of the records that must be kept by business and the period of their required retention are shown in Exhibit 18–2.

City, county, state, and federal governments require extensive reporting of financial data for various purposes. The government requires accounting data from firms for taxation purposes; this is particularly true of city, state, and county governments. The federal government may want additional information submitted regularly to a wide variety of agencies such as the Securities and Exchange Commission, Interstate Com-

Exhibit 18–2

Record retention requirements.

Record Item	Period of Retention
1. Bank statements	2 years
2. Cancelled payroll checks	2 years
3. Capital assets records (after disposal of asset)	3 years
4. Cash receipt books	3 years
5. Employee travel expense reports	3 years
6. Individual employee earnings records	6 years
7. Payroll registers	3 years
8. Time cards	2 years
9. Financial statements	Permanent
10. General books of accounts	Permanent

merce Commission, and Department of Labor. Records must also be retained for special purposes of investigations by other federal agencies. For example, when checking for possible violations of the Clayton Act (discussed in chapter 23), the Federal Trade Commission may ask a company for accounting justification of price differentials among different customers.

Business firms probably retain more records to satisfy requirements of the Internal Revenue Service than of any other agency. The problems a business will face if it has insufficient records to justify its income tax returns are common knowledge. However, almost every record required by any government agency can also be used internally in the control and decision-making process of the business.

Many other groups and individuals require financial records in their dealings with the business firm. Before lending funds to a business, bankers must know the firm's financial status. Investors must learn about the future profitability of the firm. Stockholders require financial information to arrive at a variety of decisions, such as the evaluation of present management.

ACCOUNTING STATEMENTS

The two primary accounting statements are the balance sheet and the income statement. Identified earlier as users of accounting information, bankers, government agencies, and investors are traditional users of these two accounting statements. In addition, they are two of the more important forms of accounting analysis used by management in its control and decision-making process.

Balance Sheet

The purpose of the **balance sheet** is to present the financial condition of a business at one moment in time. The balance sheet should be prepared in all businesses at least once a year, at the end of the fiscal period, and more often if required by the size or type of business.

The fiscal period is the accounting year of the firm, which may or may not coincide with the calendar year. For example, the fiscal period of the federal government is from July 1 to June 30.

The balance sheet is based on the following algebraic equation:

$$\text{Assets} = \text{Liabilities} + \text{Owner's equity}$$

Another way of expressing the equation would be:

$$\text{Assets} - \text{Liabilities} = \text{Owner's equity}$$

In other words, if you had $50 in cash and owed someone $20, you would be worth $30. Any time an amount is added to or subtracted from one side of the equation, there must be an opposite entry on the other side of the equation. The equation in the accounting process must always be in balance, or the bookkeeping has been incorrectly performed at some point. This is why modern accounting techniques are based on what is called *double-entry bookkeeping*. For example, in our simplified illustration, suppose you made an additional $20 by working and paid $10 on your debt. The original example and the two transactions would appear as follows:

	Assets	=	Liabilities	+	Owner's Equity
Original position	$50	=	$20	+	$30
(1) Received $20 for work	$70	=	$20	+	$50
(2) Paid $10 on debt	$60	=	$10	+	$50

As indicated by the equation, the balance sheet consists of a listing of all assets, liabilities, and owner's equity of the business. Exhibit 18–3 is an example of a balance sheet. Notice that the main sections of the balance sheet are the same as the items in the accounting equation: assets, liabilities, and owner's equity.

Assets. The asset section of the balance sheet is often divided further into current assets, plant and equipment, and intangible assets. Accountants do not always agree on what the subsections should be called. Four accounting authorities list the following categories, which differ considerably:

1. Current Assets
   Investments
   Property, Plant, and
   Equipment
   Intangible Assets
   Other Assets

2. Current Assets
   Fixed Assets
   Other Assets

3. Current Assets
   Investments and Funds
   Operational Assets—
   Tangible
   Operational Assets—
   Intangible
   Other Assets
   Deferred Charges

4. Current Assets
   Plant and Equipment

Exhibit 18–3

Balance sheet.

Eagle Heating Company
Balance Sheet, January 1, 1983

ASSETS

Current Assets

Cash		$ 15,000	
Accounts Receivable	$ 22,000		
Less Allowances for Bad Debts	1,000	21,000	
Inventory		12,000	
Total Current Assets			$ 48,000

Plant and Equipment

Building	$140,000		
Less Accumulated Depreciation	75,000	$ 65,000	
Equipment	95,000		
Less Accumulated Depreciation	55,000	40,000	
Trucks	33,000		
Less Accumulated Depreciation	11,000	22,000	
Land		100,000	
Total Plant Assets and Equipment			227,000

Intangible Assets

Patent		$100,000	
Goodwill		25,000	
Total Intangible Assets			125,000
TOTAL ASSETS			**$400,000**

LIABILITIES AND OWNER'S EQUITY

Current Liabilities

Accounts Payable	$ 22,000	
Income Tax Payable	2,000	
Total Current Liabilities		$ 24,000

Long-Term Liabilities

Mortgage on Land and Building	36,000

TOTAL LIABILITIES	**$ 60,000**

OWNER'S EQUITY

Bill Kramer, Net Worth	$340,000
TOTAL LIABILITIES AND OWNER'S EQUITY	**$400,000**

Current assets are relatively liquid (easily converted into cash); they include cash, accounts receivable, and inventory. Plant and equipment (sometimes called fixed assets) are not usually liquid assets and often include such items as land, buildings, equipment, tools, automobiles, trucks, and long-term notes receivable. Intangible assets are usually intangible items of value including goodwill, patents, and organizational costs.

Liabilities.　Liabilities are usually divided into current liabilities and long-term liabilities. Current liabilities are debts that come due within one year, such as accounts payable, current notes payable, and expenses payable. Long-term liabilities are debts that come due in excess of one year and commonly include such items as mortgages, long-term notes payable, and bonds payable.

Owner's Equity.　Owner's equity is the amount of funds invested by the owner(s) plus total accumulated earnings less total accumulated withdrawals.

$$\frac{\text{Owner's}}{\text{Equity}} = \frac{\text{Owner's}}{\text{Investment}} + \frac{\text{All Profit Ever}}{\text{Made by the Company}} - \frac{\text{All Withdrawals}}{\text{Made by Owner}}$$

Owner's equity is also equal to assets less liabilities on the balance sheet. Some accountants use "capital" or "net worth" in place of the term "owner's equity." The owner's equity section of the balance sheet will vary in appearance depending on the form of ownership of the business. The sole proprietorship and partnership balance sheets will usually present the name of the individual owner or partners and a statement of their share of ownership of the business (see Exhibit 18–3). A corporation balance sheet shows basically all outstanding stock at par value and retained earnings—which is all the profit (less losses) of the corporation minus all dividends paid over the entire life of the corporation.

$$\frac{\text{Corporation}}{\text{Owner's Equity}} = \frac{\text{Common \& Preferred}}{\text{Stock at Par}} + \frac{\text{All Profit of}}{\text{Corporation}} - \frac{\text{All Dividends}}{\text{Paid}}$$

Large corporations sometimes have more sophisticated entries in addition to outstanding stock and retained earnings; but they are basically details of the same categories, such as "Paid-In Capital (owner's equity) from Sale of Common Stock." See Exhibit 18–4.

Characteristics of the Balance Sheet.　The two basic characteristics of the balance sheet are that it is an estimate and a measure of one moment in time.

Exhibit 18–4

Owner's Equity		
10,000 shares of preferred stock, 6%, par $100,		
20,000 shares authorized, 10,000 issue		1,000,000
100,000 shares of common stock, par $1,		
1,000,000 shares authorized, 100,000 issued		$ 100,000
Retained earnings		1,800,000
Total owner's equity		$2,900,000

Exhibit 18–5

Eagle Heating Company balance sheet classified according to accuracy and estimate

Accurate Amounts	Estimated Amounts	
Cash	Allowance for Bad Debts	Land
Accounts Receivable	Raw Materials Inventory	Patent
Accounts Payable	Building	Goodwill
Mortgage on Land and Building	Equipment	Income Tax Payable
	Trucks	Bill Kramers, Net Worth

Estimate. The balance sheet is an estimate and not an accurate statement, which limits its use somewhat. The reason the balance sheet is not accurate is that many assets' true values can only be estimated. Many assets are carried on the books at what they cost to obtain. For example, land that cost a firm $100,000 is shown on the balance sheet at that value even though it may have increased in value many times that amount. A firm that purchases a building enters it on the books at cost and computes depreciation, which reduces the book value each year. Obviously, the amount of depreciation is an estimate. Even when assets are not depreciated, they are often estimates because fluctuating market prices deviate from cost prices carried on the books. The only way to measure the true value of most assets accurately is to sell them, and certainly a business would not sell just to provide an exact balance sheet. The appearance of any intangible assets on the balance sheet, such as patents and goodwill, must, by their very nature, be estimates. Even accounts receivable are estimates, since the firm cannot be sure of how much it will collect.

If any single asset item appears as an estimate on the balance sheet, then the total of the asset section is automatically an estimate. Liabilities are generally accurate, since the firm owes a specific amount of money to each lender. The owner's equity section is derived by subtracting liabilities (exact) from assets (estimated), and as a result is itself an estimate. It is important, particularly for investors, to understand that the balance sheet is an estimate. Techniques for estimating, particularly concerning depreciation and intangible assets, may vastly overstate or understate the worth of a company on its balance sheet.

Moment in Time. The values of assets and accruals continually change. A machine, for instance, sustains wear each minute it is in operation; it has less use remaining at the end of each day than it had when the day started, even though it may be a minute amount. Also, since interest is generally figured on a daily basis, interest to be paid or received is a little larger as each day passes. As a consequence, in order to construct a balance sheet, which is a measure of assets, liabilities, and owner's equity, it is necessary to measure the value of these items as of a moment in time. However, to be realistic, the balance sheet attempts to measure the value of a business as of the close of some business day, usually the first or last day of the company's fiscal period. For example, the balance sheet presented in Exhibit 18–3 measures the worth of the business firm at the close of business on January 1, 1983, and no other day.

Uses of the Balance Sheet. The balance sheet provides the business firm with an estimate of the value of the business at a specific time. Changes in the business are mirrored in changes in the balance sheet over a period of time. Assets relative to liabilities provide information as to the ability of the firm to meet both short- and long-term debts. The balance sheet shows the financial strength and value of the business. Ratios may be computed from the balance sheet to provide valuable analysis for both control and decision making (these will be discussed later).

Bankers, mortgage companies, private lenders, and other lenders need some means of evaluating the many companies applying for loans to determine which are the safest loans to grant. As a result, companies need to prepare balance sheets at regular intervals for submission to creditors and credit evaluating agencies.

Income Statement

The income statement is called many other names—profit and loss statement, expense and revenue summary, income and expense statement—but it remains the same accounting statement.

Characteristics of the Income Statement. The income statement has three basic characteristics: (1) it is a measure of income minus expenses, (2) it measures results of a period of time, and (3) it is an estimate.

Income Less Expenses. The income statement measures the profit of a firm for a specific period: that is, all expenses for the period are deducted from all income for the period. The income statement for the firm whose balance sheet is presented in Exhibit 18–3 is presented in Exhibit 18–6.

Period of Time. The income statement measures profitability of the firm over a specific period of time. Usually an income statement measures the amount of profit or loss of a business over the entire fiscal year; however, it may be constructed to measure any desired period—one day, one month, etc.

Estimate. The income statement is an estimate of profit. Uncollectible credit sales are estimated and written off as an expense. Depreciation is also an estimated expense that appears on the income statement. Even the methods of costing inventory used in production can differ. The two

Exhibit 18–6

Eagle Heating Company, income statement.

Eagle Heating Company
Income Statement, December 31, 1983

Revenue from Sales

Net Sales			$579,700

Cost of Goods Manufactured and Sold

Direct Labor	$ 93,500		
Raw Materials	101,500		
Factory Overhead	42,000		
Total Costs of Goods Manufactured and Sold			237,000

Gross Profits on Sales — **$342,700**

Selling Expenses

Sales Commissions	$140,000		
Advertising	25,000		
Entertainment and Dues	1,490		
Travel	3,000		
Total Selling Expenses		$169,490	

General & Administrative Expenses

Salaries and Wages	$ 45,000		
Depreciation Expense:			
Office Building	6,000		
Office Equipment	2,000		
Insurance	3,250		
Utilities	4,500		
Postage	485		
Telephone	2,800		
Payroll Tax	8,350		
Total General and Administrative Expenses		72,385	

Other Expenses

Loss from Bad Debts	$ 1,800		
Interest Expense	4,800		
Total Other Expenses		6,600	

Total Expenses — **248,475**

Net Profit — **$ 94,225**

Corporation Income Taxes — **24,615**

NET PROFIT AFTER TAXES — **$ 69,610**

Exhibit 18–7

Cost of goods sold as used by retailers and wholesalers.

Revenue from Sales		
Net Sales		$200,000
Cost of Goods Sold		
Beginning Inventory	$ 25,000	
Purchases	80,000	
Goods Available for Sale	$105,000	
Ending Inventory	30,000	
Total Costs of Goods Sold		75,000
Gross Profit from Sales		$125,000

basic methods of costing inventory are First-In-First-Out (**FIFO**) and Last-In-First-Out (**LIFO**). For example, suppose a firm bought a lot of 100 parts for $5 each and then the next 100 lot they bought had increased to $6. Then suppose they used 100 parts during the month in production. Under the FIFO method they would charge $500 to production. Under the LIFO method they would charge $600 to production. When any estimated item appears on the income statement, the income statement becomes an estimated measure of profit.

Expenses. Categories of expense items in the income statement vary by type of business. In the retail or wholesale firm, sales are reduced by Cost of Goods Sold to determine Gross Profit on Sales (also called *gross margin* and *gross profit*). All purchases made during the year are added to the Beginning Inventory, and the Ending Inventory is deducted to arrive at the **Cost of Goods Sold**. This section of the Income Statement of retailers or wholesalers would appear as presented in Exhibit 18–7.

In the manufacturing firm, **Cost of Goods Manufactured** is derived by adding the total amount spent for labor, raw materials, and factory overhead. Included in Exhibit 18–6 is the Cost of Goods Manufactured for a manufacturing firm.

In both retail/wholesale and manufacturing income statements, Selling Expenses, General and Administrative Expenses, and Other Expenses are deducted from Gross Profit on Sales to arrive at the Net Profit. Selling Expenses usually include all costs of selling the product, such as sales commissions or salaries, advertising, and entertainment of customers. General and Administrative Expenses usually include all expenses incurred as a result of office activity and general administration of the firm. Other Expenses usually carries all expense items that are not suited to the other two categories.

Uses of Income Statements. Business firms are subject to federal income taxes and would be unable to file their tax returns without yearly income statements. Many states also require businesses to submit income statements and pay income taxes.

The income statement as a record of a firm's earnings is of vital importance to the business in the determination of availability of funds for capital and other expenditures. Without the income statement, a growing firm would not be able to borrow funds and would not even know what funds would be needed for expansion.

RATIOS

Businesses use ratios developed from the balance sheet as guides to measure the financial operations and conditions of a company. By comparing ratios to established standards, a firm can see problem areas and make decisions to eliminate both present and future problems. In some instances, evaluation of a manager's actions is possible by comparing specific ratios to a standard.

Ratios for different industries are published by various groups such as industry associations, accounting service firms, and publishing companies. The individual business is then able to compare its ratios to the industry averages and obtain an indication of how well it is performing compared to other companies in the industry.

Some of the more important ratios used by management are the current ratio, acid test ratio, debt to net worth ratio, rate of return on assets, and rate of return on owner's equity. (All sample computations of ratios shown below are taken from the balance sheet and income statement of Eagle Heating Company, Exhibits 18–3 and 18–6.)

Current Ratio

The **current ratio** compares current assets to current liabilities and measures the ability of the firm to meet current debt.

$$\frac{\text{Current Assets}}{\text{Current Liabilities}} = \text{Current Ratio}$$
$$\frac{48,000}{24,000} = 2$$

Acid Test Ratio

Also called the *quick ratio,* the **acid test ratio** measures the extent to which cash and highly liquid assets insure payment of current debt. The basic difference between this ratio and the current ratio is that inventory is excluded from the acid test ratio.

$$\frac{\text{Cash} + \text{Accounts Receivable} + \text{Marketable Securities}}{\text{Current Liabilities}} = \text{Acid Test Ratio}$$
$$\frac{15,000 + 21,000 + 0}{24,000} = 1.5$$

Debt to Net Worth Ratio

The **debt to net worth ratio** shows the amount of money contributed by creditors relative to the amount of money contributed by owners. It is a measure of the amount of funds available for creditor and owner protection in the event of liquidation of the firm.

Showing a Loss While Profiting

Methods of depreciation can cause major changes in the balance sheet and income statement. To illustrate, suppose you own land and borrow a million dollars to build an apartment complex on it. If you use the accelerated method of depreciation accepted by the Internal Revenue Service (IRS) and estimate the life of the building to be fifteen years (shortest allowed by IRS), then your depreciation for the first year would be $116,667. On the other hand, if you use the straight-line method (also accepted by IRS) over a thirty-year period, your depreciation would be $33,334 for the first year. This represents a difference in profit shown of $83,333. The reverse would happen in later years, since only a total of $1 million can be depreciated.

Interest on the money borrowed to build the apartment complex, another expense item, is calculated on the unpaid balance and is much higher in the early years than in the later years. For example, if you borrowed the million dollars to build an apartment complex at 10 percent interest on a twenty-year note, your first twelve monthly payments would total $115,803. However, of the $115,803 total, only $15,935 would go to repay the principal, while $99,868 would go for interest. Of course, in the last years of payment this is reversed because the balance of the principal has declined and not as much interest is owed on it.

Adding the accelerated depreciation of $116,667 to the $99,868 interest gives a deduction from income of $216,535 from these two items alone. The only cash spent during the year to pay for the original cost of the apartments is the $115,803 in monthly payments.

It would be possible for you to show a loss on your income statement for several years while actually gaining in cash from the venture. Many owners of apartments and shopping centers keep them until they begin to show a sizable profit on their income statements (usually about five to seven years) and then sell them. They are then able to claim a capital gain on the profit from the sale, of which only 40 percent is taxed.

$$\frac{\text{Total Liabilities}}{\text{Tangible Net Worth}} = \text{Debt to Net Worth Ratio}$$

$$\frac{60,000}{215,000^*} = 0.28$$

Rate of Return on Assets

A measure of the effectiveness and profitability of the operations of the firm, the rate of return on assets indicates the relation of profit to the amount of investment in assets necessary to produce that level of profit.

$$\frac{\text{Profit}}{\text{Total Assets}} = \text{Rate of Return on Assets}$$

$$\frac{94,225}{400,000} = 0.24$$

Rate of Return on Owner's Equity

The rate of return on owner's equity ratio is also a measure of the effectiveness and profitability of the operations of the firm. It measures the profitability of the firm relative to the amount of ownership in the firm. Stated another way, it measures the amount of profit each dollar of ownership produces.

$$\frac{\text{Profit}}{\text{Net Worth (Capital)}} = \text{Rate of Return on Owner's Equity}$$

$$\frac{94,225}{340,000} = 0.28$$

THE BUDGET

The budget is a basic accounting device for control and decision making. In many instances the budget is the most important accounting tool management uses.

The budget has two characteristics that are important to management: (1) it is a projected income statement and (2) it is a standard against which to measure current performance.

A Projected Income Statement

The budget is in reality a projected income statement for some future period. While the budget is usually constructed for the coming year, it may represent some other time period. Exhibit 18–8 presents a sample budget that, when compared to the income statement in Exhibit 18–6, reveals that both statements contain basically the same categories. The income statement lists the year's (or other time period's) income less the year's expenses to arrive at profit (or loss) earned for the year. The budget estimates what income will be received in the coming year. Next it subtracts all estimated expenses from estimated income and arrives at an estimated amount of profit from next year's operations.

While expense items generally are the same both in income statements and budgets, expense categories differ between the two state-

---

*Owner's equity of $340,000 less the intangible assets of $125,000.

Exhibit 18–8

Eagle Heating Company budgeted income statement (all figures are estimates).

Eagle Heating Company Budget		
Expected Sales Revenue		**$650,000**
Deduct Estimated Cost of Goods Sold		
Direct Labor	$104,160	
Raw Materials	113,600	
Factor Overhead	44,100	261,860
Estimated Gross Margin		**$388,140**
Deduct Controllable Expenses		
Advertising	$ 27,000	
Entertainment and Dues	2,000	
Travel Expenses	3,200	
Sales Commissions	156,000	
Postage	500	
Telephone	2,800	
Miscellaneous	200	
Salaries and Wages	45,000	
Loss from Bad Debts Expense	1,900	238,600
Margin for Noncontrollable Expenses and Income		**$149,540**
Deduct Noncontrollable Expenses		
Interest Expense on Mortgage	$ 4,800	
Depreciation Expense	8,000	
Insurance Expense	3,500	
Utilities	6,500	
Payroll Tax	8,500	31,300
Estimated Net Income Before Federal Taxes		**$118,240**
Deduct Estimated Federal Income Taxes		**35,315**
ESTIMATED NET INCOME		**$82,925**

ments. Usually expenses are listed in the income statement under Selling Expenses, General and Administrative Expenses, and Other Expenses (see Exhibit 18–6). In the budget they are listed as Controllable Expenses and Noncontrollable Expenses. Noncontrollable expenses are those expenses the firm will incur just from being in business. They are expenses with little variance at different levels of production. Controllable expenses are just the opposite: the business can generally determine how much they want to spend for each item. Controllable expenses usually vary with amount of goods produced or sold.

Since the budget is next year's **estimated income** statement, its construction is part of the planning function of management. Sales must be forecast as the first step in constructing a budget. Plans must be developed for how much advertising, what size sales force, and what promotion activity will produce the forecast level of sales. Forecast sales are vital to the planning of almost all major activities in the organization. For instance, if a manufacturing firm forecasts sales of 10,000 units at $50 each, they can derive all manufacturing costs necessary to produce this level of output. If 10,000 chairs were to be produced, the firm would have established production procedures and processes. Wood would be introduced into the production process and proceed through the operations shown in Exhibit 18–9.

Each operation should have established standards of performance set by methods and time studies or other comparable methods. By applying the standards (the number of units that should be completed by each operation in a normal day's time) to the amount of pay for each operation, the firm can know the amount of direct labor necessary for production of the chair.

In addition, by determining the average amount of wood, stain, varnish, etc. required for each chair plus waste standards, management can compute raw material needs and costs to produce 10,000 chairs.

Indirect production costs or factory overhead may also be computed by using historical records and projections of indirect materials, supplies, supervisory salaries, utilities consumed in production, equipment depreciation, insurance on the factory building and equipment, etc.

By computing raw material cost, direct labor cost, and factory overhead cost, the firm can derive the cost of goods manufactured for 10,000 chairs and gross profit projected for the coming year. Other costs, such as salespeople's salaries, travel expenses, office salaries, etc., may also be computed with remarkable accuracy by comparing historical cost to projected needs.

In deriving the budget, management uses many factors that provide information for various other planning needs. For example, by projecting sales and production levels, needs for personnel in each phase of operations can be estimated for the coming year. The personnel department can

Exhibit 18–9

Deriving the cost of goods manufactured.

Work Station	Daily Pay per Worker	Standard Number of Items Produced per Worker per Day	Estimated per Unit Labor Cost
Sawing and Planing	$20	40	$ .50
Lathes	36	10	3.60
Sanding	24	24	1.00
Assembly	24	16	1.50
Finishing	32	5	6.40
Shipping	20	20	1.00
		Total	$14.00

plan for recruiting and hiring of personnel far in advance of the actual need. Needs for working capital and other funds are identified before the year starts, and financial planning makes it possible to obtain funds when interest rates are lowest for the period. The firm can negotiate contracts for specific amounts of raw materials and supplies for relatively long periods of time in order to obtain the lowest prices possible.

In addition, by projecting income, expenses, and profit for the next year, a business firm can learn how funds will be generated for dividends, investments, and other uses.

A Standard of Operation

Management uses the budget to measure results of the organization's operations. Management also uses the budget to compel the organization to conform to plans. Management sets up a budget and allocates money to various areas of the business to ensure that its plans will be realized in the future. Each division of the organization has a specific amount of money, personnel, and other resources to use and a specific amount of output to achieve. The divisions are not allowed to exceed allocations without approval from management. Management's review of excess expenditures of resources or of failure to meet expected achievements motivates each unit to conform to and realize plans.

By comparing actual performance to the budget, any division of the organization that deviates from the budget is immediately and automatically identified as a problem area. In addition, the budget narrows management's isolation of the problem by breaking resource allocation down into various items such as raw materials and direct labor. Management, by efficient use of the budget, can quickly see the cause of deviation and take corrective measures. Many times management is unable to hold performance to the budget level because of factors beyond its control, such as increases in the price of raw materials. Then it must decide (the budget is also an important source of information in reaching these decisions) what actions to take due to the price increase. Often, a new plan or adjustment in the budget emerges because of the uncontrollable deviation from management's original plans.

SUMMARY OF KEY POINTS

1. The accounting system aids management by providing: (1) information for management decisions; (2) a system with which management can control the organization; and (3) records for governmental agencies, investors, and creditors.

2. Accounting systems are vital if the organization is to be controlled by the management-by-exception principle. Management uses accounting information to perform future planning and to evaluate past planning.

3. The two primary accounting statements are the balance sheet and the income statement.

4. The balance sheet measures the financial condition of a business at one moment in time and is based on the equation: assets = liabilities + owner's equity.

5. The balance sheet contains some items that are estimated and therefore is an estimate itself.

6. The income statement is: (1) a measure of income minus expenses; (2) a measure of the results of operations over a specific period of time; and (3) an estimate itself, since some of the items are estimated.

7. Ratios developed from financial statements are used as guides to measure the financial operations and conditions of a business firm.

8. The current ratio is a measure of a firm's ability to meet current debt.

9. The acid test ratio is a measure of a firm's ability to meet day-to-day expenses.

10. The debt to net worth ratio measures the availability of funds for creditor and owner protection.

11. The rate of return on assets ratio measures the level of profit on investment in assets.

12. The rate of return on owner's equity is a measure of the effectiveness and profitability of the operations of the firm.

13. The budget is important to management as a projected income statement and as a standard for measuring performance. Management uses the budget to compel the organization to conform to their plans.

14. Expense items in the budget are divided into two categories, controllable and noncontrollable expenses.

DISCUSSION QUESTIONS

1. If you owned a business, would you use accounting? Explain how.
2. Explain the relationship between accounting and the management-by-exception principle.
3. What is the process by which management decisions should be determined if they are to be efficient?
4. How long would you keep accounting records in your business to meet government requirements?
5. What is the relationship between the accounting equation and the balance sheet?
6. What kind of capital section of the balance sheet would you use if your business were a sole proprietorship or partnership? A corporation?
7. If you were going to buy a business, would you pay the price shown on its balance sheet? Explain.
8. Can you tell with perfect accuracy how much money a business made by looking at the income statement?
9. If you went to the bank to borrow money for your business, which statements would the banker want to see and which one would be the most important to him or her?
10. Which of the accounting ratios listed in this chapter would you use if you owned a hardware retail store?
11. How does the budget function as a management control device?
12. What is the relationship between the budget and the income statement?
13. How does the budget function as a planning device for management? What happens if actual performance deviates from the budget?

STUDENT PROJECTS

1. Prepare a balance sheet for yourself listing all assets and liabilities, and determine your net worth.
2. Prepare a simple budget for the next week. Group expenses into general areas, such as food, entertainment, toiletry items, and gasoline.
3. At the end of the week, prepare a revenue and expense statement for the one-week period, listing all income and expenses. Compare it to the budget you prepared.
4. Prepare another balance sheet at the end of the week and compare it with the first one to determine what changes have taken place in your assets, liabilities, and net worth.

CASE

A

King Manufacturing

The King Manufacturing Company is a sole proprietorship started and owned by Arnold King. The company manufactures small electrical applicances that they sell directly to retailers. Mr. King is considering producing a small electrical heater. Competing brands of the same type of heater are sold to retailers for $20, and Mr. King knows he must meet or beat this price to be able to compete.

Mr. King estimates that his manufacturing costs for producing each heater will be as follows:

	Per Unit Cost
Labor	$7.50
Materials	4.00
Factory Overhead	2.00

Mr. King also estimates that he will have to mark up his Cost of Goods Manufactured by 40 percent to cover his operating and general expenses and have enough left over for a reasonable profit. Mr. King will have to borrow $80,000 with which to purchase new machinery. King Manufacturing's balance sheet and expense and revenue summary are as follows:

Balance Sheet			
ASSETS			
Current Assets			
Cash		$ 6,000	
Finished Goods Inventory		2,000	
Raw Materials Inventory		2,000	
Total Current Assets			$ 10,000
Fixed Assets			
Land		7,000	
Building	$40,000		
Less Depreciation	20,000	20,000	
Machinery	60,000		
Less Depreciation	45,000	15,000	
Total Fixed Assets			42,000
TOTAL ASSETS			**$ 52,000**
LIABILITIES			
Current Liabilities			
Accounts Payable (Due April 1)		10,000	
Long-term Liabilities			
Note Payable (Due 1983)		20,000	
Total Liabilities			30,000
Proprietorship			
Arnold King, Capital			22,000
TOTAL LIABILITIES AND PROPRIETORSHIP			**$ 52,000**

Income Statement		
Sales		**$130,000**
Cost of Goods Manufactured		**80,000**
Gross Profit on Sales		**50,000**
Operating Expenses		
Selling expenses:		
Sales Salary Expense	$ 11,000	
Advertising Expense	7,000	
Misc. Selling Expense	1,000	
Total Selling Expense		19,000
General expenses:		
Office Salary Expense	$ 8,000	
Depreciation Expense, Building	2,000	
Utilities Expense	1,000	
Total General Expenses		11,000
Total Operating Expenses		**30,000**
NET INCOME FROM OPERATIONS		**$ 20,000**

Questions

1. Can Mr. King's proposed electrical heater compete with the competition? Calculate the price for which he can offer his heater to the retailer.

2. Calculate current ratio, acid test ratio, debt to net worth ratio, rate of return on assets ratio, and rate of return on owner's equity ratio for Mr. King. Would you advise any action based on these ratios?

3. Do you think the bank would lend Mr. King the $80,000? Explain.

4. If Mr. King offered to sell you this business for $60,000, would you buy it if you had the money?

Harold's Hardware

Harold Green is the owner of Harold's Hardware, a sole proprietorship. Harold has one full-time employee in the store. Harold has just received his year-end balance sheet and income statement, which were prepared by James Loftus, an independent bookkeeper who maintains the accounting records for the hardware store. The financial statements are shown below. James Loftus included some additional information in this year's report on a number of business ratios. James told Harold that these are the ratios for hardware stores that have the highest total earnings.

These ratios are:

Current Assets to Current Liabilities = 6.00 to 1
Total Debt to Tangible Net Worth = 41%
Acid Test Ratio = 3.2 to 1
Rate of Return on Assets = 14.75%

Question

How does Harold's store compare to these ratios?

Harold's Hardware Balance Sheet December 31, 1982			
ASSETS			
Current Assets			
Cash		$ 4,520	
Accounts Receivable	$ 21,950		
Less Allowance for Bad Debts	1,875	20,075	
Inventory		19,160	
Total Current Assets			$ 43,755
Plant Assets			
Building		$ 20,000	
Land		6,000	
Equipment, Fixtures and Furniture		7,800	
Less Accumulated Depreciation on Equipment and Bldg.		11,000	
Total Plant Assets			22,800
Other Assets			
Good Will		500	
Patent		500	
Total Other Assets			1,000
TOTAL ASSETS			**$ 67,555**
LIABILITIES AND CAPITAL			
Current Liabilities			
Accounts Payable		$ 10,322	
Taxes Payable		3,600	
Total Current Liabilities			$ 13,922
Long-Term Liabilities			
Mortgage in Land and Building			3,500
TOTAL LIABILITIES			17,422
HAROLD GREEN, CAPITAL			50,133
TOTAL CAPITAL AND LIABILITIES			**$ 67,555**

Harold's Hardware Income Statement
December 31, 1982

NET SALES			$189,754
Cost of Goods Sold			
Beginning Inventory	$ 30,125		
Purchases	136,383		
Goods Available for Sale	$166,508		
Ending Inventory	19,160		
Total Cost of Goods Sold			147,348
Gross Profit from Sales			$ 42,406
Operating Expenses			
Advertising	$ 2,500		
Insurance	2,400		
Depreciation Expenses:			
Equipment, Fixtures, Furniture	750		
Building	2,000		
Salary Expense	6,000		
Total Operating Expenses		$ 13,650	
General Expenses			
Utilities	$ 1,800		
Postage	350		
Telephone	540		
Office Expense	3,600		
Accounting Service	600		
Repairs to Building	200		
Federal, State, and Local Taxes	2,375		
Store Supplies	200		
Total General Expenses		9,665	
Other Expenses			
Interest		1,400	
TOTAL EXPENSES			24,715
NET PROFIT			$ 17,691

BUSINESS PROFILE

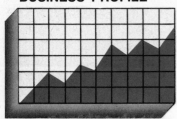

General Motors

David Dunbar Buick was born in Scotland in 1854 and came to the United States when he was two years old. He helped build a successful plumbing business in Detroit that developed a process for binding porcelain to iron, making the first white bathtubs possible. He sold his share of the business in 1900 for $100,000 and with this money and other backing formed the Buick Motor Company in May 1903. The company soon had financial difficulties and was purchased by the Flint Carriage Company and moved to Flint, Michigan. Flint was the center of a giant carriage manufacturing industry. The company borrowed heavily from Flint lending institutions and also had financial trouble. One of Flint's most prosperous wagon builders, William C. Durant, saw the future of the automobile, raised a half million dollars to save the Buick Motor Company, and took control in 1904. The first big success of the Buick company was the Model 10, introduced in 1907. Called the

White Streak, it had a four-cylinder engine with eighteen horsepower and sold for $850. Buick Motor Company built 8,829 in 1908 and 30,525 in 1910.

In 1908, Durant founded General Motors, with Buick Motor Company as the cornerstone. He used Buick profits to purchase several companies—Oldsmobile, Cadillac, Oakland (Pontiac), and other small automotive-related companies. Buick was the big profit maker for General Motors for many years. Buick Motors engaged in automobile racing, and the first Indianapolis Speedway race in 1909 was won by a Buick. That same year, Buick won 166 races, 90 percent of all races it entered. Two Buick race drivers were the Chevrolet brothers.

Today, General Motors is the largest industrial corporation in the United States with 1,138,000 stockholders, 741,000 employees worldwide in 1981, and annual sales of $62 billion in 1981. It operates 160 plants in the United States and Canada and has operations in thirty-five other countries. General Motors has twenty-nine operating divisions including such familiar names as Buick, Cadillac, Chevrolet, Oldsmobile, GMC Truck & Coach, Pontiac, AC Spark Plug, and Hydra-matic.

The major shift to front-wheel drive vehicles has created opportunities to incorporate new techniques and new technology, ranging from the design process through final assembly.

Exhibit 18–10
A portion of General Motors' income statement from the 1981 Annual Report.

Statement of Consolidated Income
For The Years Ended December 31, 1981, 1980, and 1979
(Dollars in Millions Except Per Share Amounts)

	1981	1980	1979
Net Sales	$62,698.5	$57,728.5	$66,311.2
Costs and Expenses			
Cost of sales and other operating charges, exclusive of items listed below	55,185.2	52,099.8	55,848.7
Selling, general and administrative expenses	2,715.0	2,636.7	2,475.5
Depreciation of real estate, plants and equipment	1,837.3	1,458.1	1,236.9
Amortization of special tools	2,568.9	2,719.6	1,950.4
Provision for the Bonus Plan	—	—	133.8
Total Costs and Expenses	62,306.4	58,914.2	61,645.3
Operating Income (Loss)	392.1	(1,185.7)	4,665.9
Other income less income deductions—net	367.7	348.7	560.3
Interest expense	(897.9)	(531.9)	(368.4)
Income (Loss) before Income Taxes	(138.1)	1,368.9	4,857.8
United States, foreign and other income taxes (credit)	(123.1)	(385.3)	2,183.4
Income (Loss) after Income Taxes	(15.0)	(983.6)	2,674.4
Equity in earnings of nonconsolidated subsidiaries and associates (dividends received amounted to $189.7 in 1981, $116.8 in 1980 and $112.8 in 1979)	348.4	221.1	218.3
Net Income (Loss)	333.4	(762.5)	2,892.7
Dividends on preferred stocks	12.9	12.9	12.9
Earnings (Loss) on Common Stock	$ 320.5	($ 775.4)	$ 2,879.8
Average number of shares of common stock outstanding (in millions)	299.1	292.4	286.8
Earnings (Loss) Per Share of Common Stock	$1.07	($2.65)	$10.04

19 Quantitative Methods in Business

LEARNING GOALS

After reading this chapter, you will understand:

1. The meaning of statistics.

2. The methods of collecting statistical data.

3. That quantitative data may be presented in various formats, such as tables, charts, or statistical maps.

4. The principal types of averages and their characteristics.

5. How managers use business forecasting as an aid to the decision-making process.

6. The components of time series analysis.

7. The steps involved in making a sales forecast.

8. The importance of index numbers to a manager.

9. How managers can use sampling techniques to facilitate decision making.

KEY TERMS

Statistics	Time series analysis	Depression
Descriptive statistics	Zero-based	Recovery
Inductive statistics	budgeting	Secular trend
Observation method	Forecasting	Erratic fluctuations
Interview method	Seasonal variation	Index numbers
Average	Cyclical variation	Sample
Arithmetic mean	Prosperity	Random sample
Median	Recession	Controlled sample
Mode		

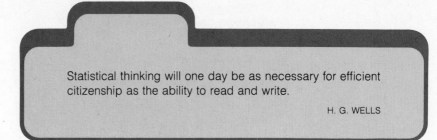

Statistical thinking will one day be as necessary for efficient citizenship as the ability to read and write.

H. G. WELLS

The increasing complexity of today's business environment requires that managers incorporate a great number of variables in their decision-making processes. If managers are to correctly identify, analyze, select, and implement the best alternatives when making decisions, they must utilize all the resources available to them. Modern managers rely extensively on **statistics** (quantitative data) to improve the effectiveness of their decisions.

THE MEANING OF STATISTICS

Each of us is exposed daily to large amounts of statistics in the newspaper, on the radio, and on television. There are a variety of meanings associated with the term *statistics*. First, statistics naturally deal with numerical data. Statistics may mean the number of births or marriages in a city, the batting average of a baseball player, or the average income per person in the United States. Such data are known as **descriptive statistics**. This means that a mass of information has been collected from a variety of possible sources, as discussed below. After it has been collected, statisticians organize the data into groups on some basis of similarity. These data are then summarized in tabular, graphic, or paragraph forms, and thus are more easily understood. Finally, statisticians analyze and interpret the data.

Another meaning currently applied to statistics is **inductive statistics.** Inductive statistics do not merely describe a particular characteristic; statisticians attempt to predict, forecast, and generalize about a large set of data based on information derived from a small set of data.

For our purposes, statistics are the various techniques used for collecting, organizing, summarizing, interpreting, and analyzing numerical data and making predictions and forecasts from the data. We shall emphasize quantitative information related to business situations.

METHODS OF COLLECTING STATISTICAL DATA

Statistical data needed for decision making may be obtained from sources within or outside the firm. A firm's own records and reports, such as sales or payroll information, are internal data, and managers ordinarily have ready access to such data. However, managers also require information on how the firm compares with competition in such areas as sales, profits, and share of the market. Collecting external

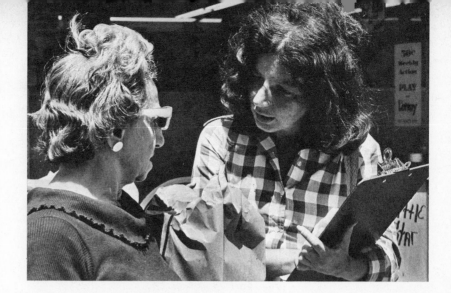

The interview method is the most frequently used method for collecting data.

data is a greater challenge and demands greater effort and planning. Two of the more common methods of collecting external information are observation and interviews.

Observation Method

Trained researchers collect and record valuable data by the **observation method.** Some common types of data collected by the observation method are auto or pedestrian traffic studies to aid in street planning and store location analysis, or observing what choices consumers make in their purchase decisions. A limitation of the observation method is that only a small amount of data can be observed.

Interview Method

The **interview method** is the most frequently used method for collecting data. Data may be collected by personal interview, telephone interview, and mail questionnaire. The chief advantage of the personal interview is that the person being interviewed will most likely answer the questions when approached directly. Its disadvantage is the high cost of data collection. Telephoning is cheaper, but often the kind of data needed cannot be obtained by phone, and many homes have no telephone. Mail surveys using questionnaires are also an inexpensive means of collecting data. However, the main drawback of this method is the very low percentage of people who complete and return the questionnaire.

PRIMARY AND SECONDARY SOURCES OF DATA

Managers also rely on published data to aid them in decision making—data taken from either primary or secondary sources. A *primary source* is an organization that collects data and publishes it. Some organizations report data collected and published by another source. This re-publication is called a *secondary source.* Data on wages paid to the labor force collected and published by the United States Department of Labor in its *Monthly Labor Review* is a primary source. However, if some other source, such as a business magazine or newspaper, takes the information from the *Monthly Labor Review* and republishes it, then this publication is a secondary source.

425

METHODS OF PRESENTING STATISTICAL DATA

Managers use statistical data as an aid to decision making. In order for this quantitative information to be most useful, it should be organized and presented in a clear and concise manner. The methods of organizing, summarizing, and presenting quantitative data to management include tables, charts, and statistical maps.

Tables

As seen in Exhibit 19–1, data can be organized and presented clearly in a table. The title of the table describes briefly what information the table contains. Within the main body, information can be arranged in rows or columns. The source from which the table is prepared is also indicated.

Charts

A graphic presentation can sometimes be useful in analyzing quantitative data. Charts provide the advantage of simple presentation, which makes it easy to compare data. Charts should contain the basic elements of title, the type of scale used in the chart, and the source. Types of charts include the bar chart, line chart, and pie chart.

Bar Charts. Bar charts are used to present all kinds of data. Examples of data commonly presented in bar chart form are data dealing with time periods, geographic divisions, and differences of kind (such as the dollar sales for each kind of product sold by a company). Exhibit 19–2 is an example of a bar chart.

Line Charts. If long time periods are covered by the data to be presented, the line chart may be more descriptive than the bar chart. To prepare a line chart, the time period is shown on the horizontal scale and the data being analyzed are shown on the vertical scale. Points are plotted on the chart and then connected with lines to complete the chart. Exhibit 19–3 is a line chart that shows the expected growth of the population to the year 2005.

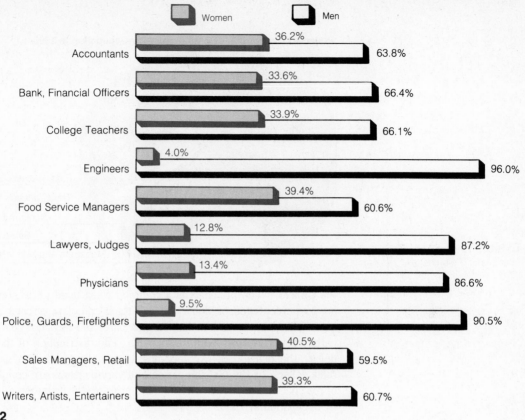

Exhibit 19–2
Sample bar chart.
(SOURCE: U.S. Department of Labor.)

Projected Population Growth in the United States, 1980–2005

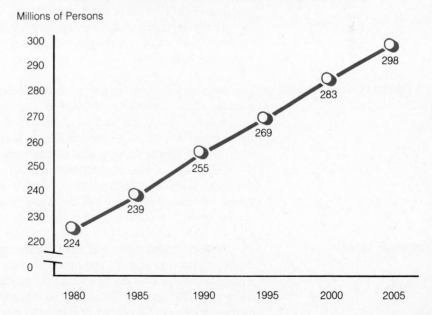

Exhibit 19–3
Sample line chart.
(SOURCE: U.S. Bureau of the Census.)

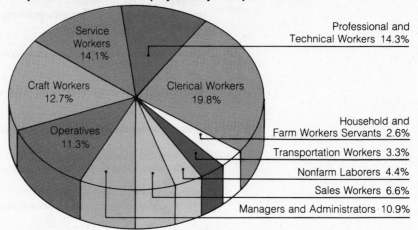

Projected Distribution of Employment by Occupation in 1990

Service Workers 14.1%

Professional and Technical Workers 14.3%

Craft Workers 12.7%

Clerical Workers 19.8%

Operatives 11.3%

Household and Farm Workers Servants 2.6%

Transportation Workers 3.3%

Nonfarm Laborers 4.4%

Sales Workers 6.6%

Managers and Administrators 10.9%

Exhibit 19–4
Example of a pie chart.
(SOURCE: Bureau of Labor Statistics.)

Pie Charts.   The pie chart is a common chart used to present data relating to percentages or dollar values. Each complete circular chart represents 100 percent and is divided into parts to show how each part compares proportionately with other parts. The distribution of the federal tax dollar, the division of a company's sales dollars, how consumers spend their dollars, or the division of costs of various items are common subjects of pie charts. Exhibit 19–4 shows the projected distribution of employment by occupation in 1990.

Statistical Maps.   An effective means of presenting data according to geographic divisions is the statistical map. The manager can see at a glance quantitative data for all of the United States, or for a specific region. Information may be recorded on the map by using symbols to represent numbers, with an accompanying explanation of what each symbol represents (see Exhibit 19–5).

STATISTICAL AVERAGES

The most widely used statistical measurement of numerical data is the average. The **average** is defined as the single, summary figure that is descriptive or typical of the characteristic measured when the individual items are all essentially different. If the average age of accountants in the finance department is nineteen, then nineteen should be the typical age of the accountants. For an average to be descriptive, the data should be "homogeneous," which means that differences between the individual items will be small. The three main types of averages are the arithmetic mean, the median, and the mode.

Arithmetic Mean

The most commonly used and most familiar of all averages is the **arithmetic mean,** or, simply, the mean. In fact, many people refer to the arithmetic mean as *the average,* using *the average* and *arithmetic mean* synonymously. The mean is the sum of all the individual values divided by the number of values. Expressed as a formula, the mean is:

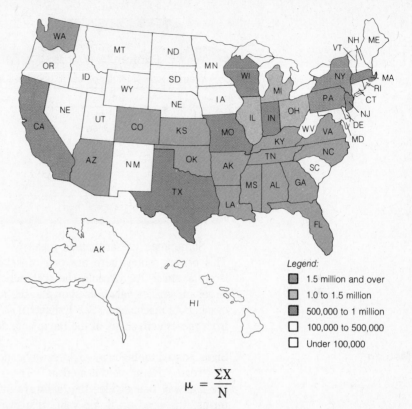

Exhibit 19–5

Sample statistical map
(SOURCE: U.S. Department of Labor.)

Legend:

- 1.5 million and over
- 1.0 to 1.5 million
- 500,000 to 1 million
- 100,000 to 500,000
- Under 100,000

$$\mu = \frac{\Sigma X}{N}$$

This formula uses the Greek letter mu, μ, to represent the arithmetic mean. The value for each item is indicated by X, and the number of items is represented by N. The Greek summation sign, Σ (sigma), stands for the total of the individual items, X. For example, to determine the arithmetic mean of hourly earnings of machinists in various areas of the United States, add the hourly rates paid in each area and divide the total of the hourly rates by the number of cities, as shown in Exhibit 19–6.

Exhibit 19–6

Average hourly earnings of machinists in selected cities.

City	Hourly Rate
San Francisco-Oakland	$9.57
Detroit	9.01
Houston	8.67
Chicago	8.39

$$\mu = \frac{X}{N} \qquad \mu = \frac{\$35.64}{4} = \$8.91$$

SOURCE: Bureau of Labor Statistics.

Exhibit 19–7

Average hourly earnings of machinists in selected cities.

City	Hourly Rate
Detroit	$9.01
Houston	8.67
Chicago	8.39
Boston	7.15

$$\mu = \frac{\$33.22}{4} = \$8.31$$

SOURCE: Bureau of Labor Statistics.

Sometimes the arithmetic mean will not be an accurate description. This occurs when there are one or several values that are either very large or small. As a result, the arithmetic mean will be biased toward the larger or smaller value, as shown in the following illustration of the hourly earnings of machinists. (See Exhibit 19–7.) This characteristic may detract from the effectiveness of the mean as a descriptive measure.

Median

Signs posted on highway expressways and super highways bear messages that read, "Keep off the median." The median is the land area between the highway that divides the highways into two equal parts. In numerical terms, the **median** is the value that divides a series of numbers so that half of the values are above and half are below the midpoint. To determine the median, the numbers must be arrayed in either ascending or descending order.

Exhibit 19–8 shows hourly rates, in order from highest to lowest, for tool and die makers in five cities. The middle value, $8.98, is the value for the median. This hourly rate divides the distribution of values in half. In this example, there is an odd number of values—five. Finding the median hourly rate for tool and die makers in six cities requires computation, as shown in Exhibit 19–9. When there is an even number of values, as in

Exhibit 19–8

Average hourly earnings of tool and die makers in five cities.

City	Hourly Rate	
San Francisco-Oakland	$10.53	
Detroit	9.31	
Chicago	8.98	← Median
Cleveland	8.77	
Baltimore	8.62	

SOURCE: Bureau of Labor Statistics.

Exhibit 19–9

Average hourly earnings of tool and die makers in six cities.

City	Hourly Rate	
San Francisco-Oakland	$10.53	
Detroit	9.31	
Chicago	8.98	$\dfrac{8.98 + 8.77}{2} = \$8.87$ (Median)
Cleveland	8.77	
Baltimore	8.62	
New York	7.36	

SOURCE: Bureau of Labor Statistics.

this example, the median is found by taking the arithmetic mean of the two middle values, $8.98 and $8.77, or $8.87. A characteristic of the median is that it is not affected by large or small values, as is the arithmetic mean.

Mode

The **mode** is a useful, but not widely used, statistical average. The mode is defined as the value that appears most frequently in a distribution. For example, the average weekly earnings of beginning computer programmers in selected cities are shown in Exhibit 19–10. The modal beginning salary is $260, since it appears more than any other weekly salary. If no number appears more than any other in a series, then there is no mode.

BUSINESS FORECASTING AND TIME SERIES ANALYSIS

Business firms must compete for customers. It is essential that managers recognize the changing conditions that affect competition. One method of measuring expected changes in business activity is to analyze variations that have occurred in the past and to expect that this trend will continue. The analysis of change over time uses the statistical technique known as **time series analysis,** which relies on his-

Exhibit 19–10

Average weekly earnings of computer programmers in selected cities.

City	Average Weekly Salary	
Detroit	$283	
Milwaukee	282	
Cleveland	260	Mode
Chicago	260	
Houston	257	

SOURCE: Bureau of Labor Statistics.

torical data to forecast the changes that will take place in business activity in the future. For example, in using this technique to forecast sales, it is assumed that events in the future will conform to what has happened in the past. The manager depends heavily on quantitative data to make these predictions. Suppose he or she evaluates sales records over a period of time and notices that they have been increasing at a rate of 5 percent per year. From this analysis of past performance, the manager will forecast that future sales should follow this trend and increase by 5 percent also.

During periods of economic uncertainty, a forecast that relies on historical analysis will be based on incorrect assumptions. A planning technique used by both government and private sector managers to cope with this situation is **zero-based budgeting.** Managers using this planning technique are required to evaluate all programs and activities each budgeting period instead of building on the performance of the preceding period. Planned budgetary expenditures must be rejustified by each department manager for each new budgeting cycle. Planned expenditures are also ranked so that high-priority items receive the greater share of the budgeted resources.

Business **forecasting** is of such importance that inaccurate forecasting can often mean disaster for many firms. Decisions that have the forecast as their base are often so important and costly to the firm that improper decisions can result in financial failure. Decisions related to production levels, financing, personnel needs, marketing expenditures, inventory levels, and capital expenditures are among the more common decisions based on the business forecast.

Steps to a Forecast

In forecasting sales for a business firm, five basic steps are necessary for an adequate prediction of sales volume. (See Exhibit 19–11.)

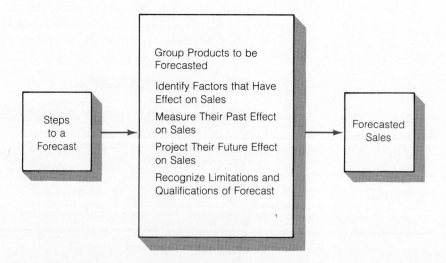

Exhibit 19–11
Steps used to forecast sales.

1. Select products to be analyzed. Management must decide whether all items sold are to be considered separately, considered in total as one, or considered in various natural groupings.
2. Select variables that affect the sales of the product. Such factors as Gross National Product, disposable personal income, population, and construction activity may determine sales level.
3. Measure how the selected variables have influenced sales volume in the past.
4. Analyze the selected variables for the present and the future to predict their effect on sales volume.
5. Recognize limiting factors that may arise to influence sales volume other than those selected. Also, recognize that sales forecasts cannot be expected to be perfect because they are predictions.

Components of Time Series Analysis

In making their business forecasts of what changes are expected to take place over a period of time, managers must include in their analysis the four types of fluctuations (or components) of time series analysis that affect business activity. These four fluctuations are seasonal variation, cyclical variation, secular trend, and erratic fluctuations.

Seasonal Variation.   **Seasonal variation** is a regular recurring fluctuation normally covering a one-year period. For example, the seasonal pattern of department store sales shows that sales increase sharply at the special seasons of the year, such as Easter, Thanksgiving, and especially Christmas. The custom of giving gifts during a holiday season causes the seasonal pattern to recur regularly year after year.

Cyclical Variation.   Seasonal variation covers a short period of time (one year), while **cyclical variation** usually extends over a longer period. The cyclical fluctuation does not exhibit a recurring pattern, as does seasonal variation. Instead, a business cycle may differ considerably from one cycle to the next, and one cycle may be more extreme than the other.

   The cyclical variations are completely beyond the control of individual firms, yet these same firms are affected by the variations in business activity. Hence, managers of individual firms must have knowledge of the general state of the economy. This information is reported in government reports, financial sections of newspapers, and data supplied by others in industry.

   There are four periods identifiable in a business cycle: prosperity, recession, depression, and recovery, which are illustrated in Exhibit 19–12. The peak of the business cycle is **prosperity.** During this period, the economy generally moves upward, funds are easy to borrow, wages are high, production of goods increases, and sales increase. During a **recession,** there is a downturn in activity in the economy. When this happens, prices decline as well as the volume of activity. If the recession continues

Horncastle, let someone else do that.

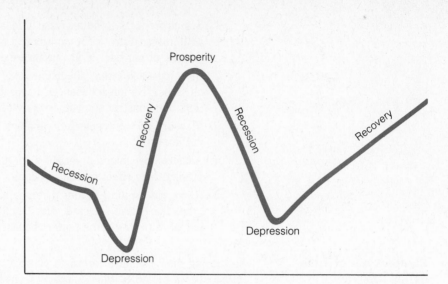

Exhibit 19–12
The four periods of the business cycle.

to the bottom of the trough, a depression exists. This is a time in which production slows greatly, sales drop, and the general economic outlook is pessimistic. During a **depression,** unemployment increases rapidly and wages drop sharply. When the economy begins to improve, the **recovery** state of the business cycle sets in. During recovery, conditions generally begin to improve: production increases, sales increase, wages move upward, unemployment drops, and an attitude of optimism prevails among business people and customers.

Secular Trend.   **Secular trend** reflects what is happening to a specific business (General Motors), an entire industry (the automobile industry), or a nation's economy over an extended period of time. For example, trend analysis may reveal long-term growth or decline for a particular industry.

Erratic Fluctuations.   **Erratic fluctuations** are defined as random components and are difficult to measure or predict because they are usually unexpected. They are of relatively short duration. Unanticipated fluctuations may be caused by such events as fire, labor strike, or storm.

INDEX NUMBERS

Index numbers are a widely used quantitative technique for measuring and analyzing changes in business and economic activity. Index numbers are defined as a ratio of two numbers expressed as a percentage. They reflect the relative changes that have occurred over a period of time, such as changes in the inflation rate in the economy of the nation or sales of a company.

For example, the Framesmith, a small picture framing business, reports current annual sales of $175,000. Sales last year were $160,000.

The Purchasing Power of the Dollar

Statistical data show changes in the purchasing power of the dollar. Taxpayer incomes continue to be eroded by the two forces of taxes and inflation. The following statistical data show the income required in 1975, 1981, and 1982 to equal the purchasing power of the 1970 dollar.

	$ 5,000	$10,000	$15,000	$25,000	$ 50,000
1970 PRETAX INCOME	**$ 5,000**	**$10,000**	**$15,000**	**$25,000**	**$ 50,000**
Less: Federal income tax	238	986	1,854	3,987	11,982
Less: Social security tax	240	374	374	374	374
Equals: Income after federal taxes	4,522	8,640	12,772	20,639	37,644
1975 NECESSARY PRETAX INCOME	**6,620**	**13,924**	**20,785**	**34,705**	**70,592**
Less: Federal income tax	110	1,411	2,667	5,935	18,797
Less: Social security tax	387	814	825	825	825
Less: Amount to cover inflation since 1970	1,601	3,059	4,521	7,306	13,326
Equals: Income after federal taxes, in 1970 dollars	4,522	8,640	12,772	20,639	37,644
1981 NECESSARY PRETAX INCOME	**10,856**	**22,477**	**34,402**	**59,012**	**119,098**
Less: Federal income tax	511	2,597	5,248	13,117	37,017
Less: Social security tax	722	1,495	1,975	1,975	1,975
Less: Amount to cover inflation since 1970	5,101	9,746	14,407	23,281	42,462
Equals: Income after federal taxes, in 1970 dollars	4,522	8,640	12,772	20,639	37,644
1982 NECESSARY PRETAX INCOME	**11,426**	**23,425**	**35,855**	**60,938**	**122,873**
Less: Federal income tax	522	2,484	5,047	12,491	36,298
Less: Social security tax	766	1,569	2,171	2,171	2,171
Less: Amount to cover inflation since 1970	5,616	10,732	15,865	25,637	46,760
Equals: Income after federal taxes, in 1970 dollars	4,522	8,640	12,772	20,639	37,644

Federal income and social security taxes are computed for a married couple, only one of whom works, with two children. No allowance is made for any other taxes. Calculations use the tax laws in effect each year. Deductible items are assumed to equal 17% of pretax income in 1970, 20% in other years. For calculating maximum tax and earned income credit, all income is assumed to be earned, personal service income. Inflation is calculated from the deflator for personal consumption spending, with a 7% rise assumed from 1981 to 1982.

SOURCE: The Conference Board, *The Two-Way Squeeze, 1982*, Economic Road Maps, Nos. 1924–1925, April, 1982.

Index numbers can be used to indicate to management the relative change in company sales. The period to which the comparison is being made is the base period and is normally assigned a value of 100 percent. To find the relative change in sales, current sales are compared to last year's sales.

$$\text{Index} = \frac{\text{Sales of current year}}{\text{Sales of earlier year}} \times 100$$

$$\text{Index} = \frac{\$175{,}000}{\$160{,}000} \times 100$$

$$\text{Index} = 109.4$$

The index indicates that this year's sales are 109.4 percent compared to 100 percent for the base period. Stated another way, Framesmith's sales are 9.4 percent greater than last year's sales.

The Framesmith earned a net profit of $14,000 this year, compared to $15,000 last year. What is the relative change in net profit for the current year as compared to the earlier period?

$$\text{Index} = \frac{\text{Profits (current year)}}{\text{Profits (earlier period)}} \times 100$$

$$\text{Index} = \frac{\$14{,}000}{\$15{,}000} \times 100$$

$$\text{Index} = 93.3$$

This index reveals that net profit is 93.3 percent, compared to 100 percent for the base year. In other words, profit has declined by 6.7 percent compared to last year. Management can use this information to try to analyze why sales increased while net profits decreased.

SAMPLING

One of the most important statistical techniques currently available to business for collecting data is sampling. A **sample** is a part of a whole, and a universe or population is considered to be the whole. All of the car owners in Florida could be considered a universe. If a selected number of Floridians were asked the kind of car they preferred, those people included in the survey would be the sample. The technique of sampling is valuable because it allows a manager to select only a small segment of a larger group in order to generalize, predict, or forecast about the general population. Furthermore, managers using sampling techniques can make great savings in money and time, since they are dealing with much smaller numbers. To illustrate, suppose a department store manager wants to find the average size of purchases made by the store's charge account customers. It is possible to take a sample of all charge accounts and determine the average size of the purchase of those included in the sample. From this the manager could make a prediction about the average size of purchase of all charge account customers. Another example of a practical use of sampling can be shown by a firm manufacturing automobile tires. Suppose this firm wishes to advertise that its tires are guaranteed to last a certain number of miles. The tire manufacturer must first find the average number of miles the tires will wear.

In order to accumulate this information, someone must test the tires by driving under normal road conditions. Literally, the tires must be destroyed to find their life expectancy (mileage). Clearly, if the manufacturer tested all the tires in this manner, there would be no merchandise remaining to sell. Thus, the manufacturer employs the technique of sampling and tests a sample number of tires. The mileage guarantee for the tires will be based on the results of this sample. If the test mileage is 30,000 miles, the manufacturer could use this figure as the mileage guarantee. When the product is actually used up, the sampling technique is called *destructive sampling.*

Today, the uses of sampling in business are increasing dramatically. For example, firms use sampling to check the quality of their manufactured products or to audit the internal accounting records of the firm.

Theory of Sampling

The theory of sampling is based upon the laws of probability, since some kind of random process is used to select those items in the sample. Probability is the likelihood of a particular event occurring, and a mathematical expectation is assigned to the occurrence of an event. Probabilities may be either *a priori* or *empirical.* If we refer to an a priori probability, we are talking about the likelihood of an event occurring that can be determined without experimentation. To illustrate, if we flip a coin, over an extended number of trials we would expect that heads would come up 50 percent of the time; this is the theoretical expectation. Likewise, if we roll a single die, the mathematical expectation of a two coming up is one-sixth, since there are six sides to the die and each side of the die has an equal chance of appearing on top (assuming we are dealing with a fair die). These expectations can be determined without experimentation.

On the other hand, in numerous cases it is not possible to determine in advance the probability of an event occurring. Therefore, a business must make a study—such as a sample or an experiment—to gain preliminary information on which to base the probability. This type of probability is termed an *empirical probability.* Examples of empirical probabilities are surveying a sample of voters to determine the candidates preferred or surveying a sample of shoppers to determine consumer acceptance of a new product (toothpaste, soap, deodorant, etc.).

Random Sample

The **random sample** is the most commonly used probability sample. A random or probability sample from a finite population means that each item in the universe being studied has an equal and known chance of being included in the sample.

To illustrate how a random sampling process works, let us assume that we have a universe composed of the ten letters at the left.

If we desire to select one letter at random, we could write each letter on an individual slip of paper, thoroughly mix the papers in a container so that each letter would have an equal chance of being selected, then draw

A B C
D E F
G H I
    J

one slip of paper as our sample. In this universe there are ten letters. Since one letter is to be selected, we know that each letter has one chance in ten of being picked. Stated another way, each letter has a $\frac{1}{10}$ probability of being chosen.

Controlled Sample

A **controlled sample** is a nonprobability sample. This sample does not provide every item in the universe with a known chance of being included in the survey. Instead, controlled samples are selected subjectively by the researcher. Types of controlled samples include convenience, judgment, and quota samples. A convenience sample is selected on the basis of speed and ease of contacting the respondent. In a judgment sample, the researcher chooses individual items that are judged to be the best samples for the study, such as selecting various economic experts to estimate the rate of inflation for the next year. Quota sampling is a more systematic approach than convenience or judgment sampling. Quota sampling involves identifying characteristics of the population that the researcher is interested in measuring, such as income levels by age groups. Then the sample is selected that reflects the same percentage of each characteristic as exists in the population. For example, if 20 percent of the population is over age sixty-five, then one-fifth of the sample should consist of this age group.

The survey in Exhibit 19–13 illustrates how statistical sampling techniques may be used to aid managers in decision making. A sample of 806 shoppers in North Little Rock, Arkansas, were interviewed to collect data concerning the factors consumers consider important when choosing a store. These data are useful to store managers for planning store operations.

Exhibit 19–13

What's important in choosing a store?

Reasons for Choosing a Store	Percentage of Shoppers
Lowest possible prices	78.9
Pleasant shopping experience/helpful personnel/good service	75.3
Do all shopping in one-stop store	72.1
Prices marked on individual packages	70.0
Store is located nearby	68.3
Selection or variety of store brands and lower-priced products	63.6
Finish shopping as fast as possible	54.4
Open late hours	43.5
Double coupons or other special incentives	41.7
Special departments such as deli or bakery	38.7

SOURCE: *Progressive Grocer*, November, 1981, p. 55.

SUMMARY OF KEY POINTS

1. Quantitative data (statistics) may be classed as either descriptive statistics or inductive statistics.
2. Two methods of collecting statistical data are the observation method and the interview method.
3. Tables, charts, and statistical maps are frequently used to present statistical data more clearly.
4. Types of charts include bar, line, and pie charts.
5. Three statistical averages are the arithmetic mean, median, and mode.
6. The components of time series analysis are seasonal variation, cyclical variation, secular trend, and random fluctuations.
7. Index numbers indicate the relative changes that have taken place over a period of time.
8. Sampling enables a manager to select a small number of a large group and make predictions and forecasts about the larger population.
9. A random sample is a probability sample; a controlled sample is a nonprobability sample.

DISCUSSION QUESTIONS

1. Discuss the two methods of collecting external data, and give examples of how and under what circumstances each could be used.
2. How does the arithmetic mean differ from the mode?
3. What are the four components of time series analysis?
4. What steps are involved in a sales forecast?
5. What are the four periods of the business cycle?
6. What is an index number? When should it be used?
7. What is a simple random sample? What is a controlled sample?

STUDENT PROJECTS

1. Auto workers' pay averages $20,520 annually. To keep up with inflation, an average income of $19,308 is needed. How have auto workers fared?
2. The average annual salary for retail salespersons is $7,368. To keep even or ahead of inflation, an average salary of $8,999 is needed. How have retail salespersons fared?
3. Given the following figures: 10, 5, 8, 5, 6, 4, 2
   a. Determine the arithmetic mean.   c. Determine the mode.
   b. Determine the median.

4. Given the following figures: 20, 30, 10, 20, 40, 50
   a. Determine the arithmetic mean.   c. Determine the mode.
   b. Determine the median.
5. What is the probability of a 4 appearing on top in one roll of a fair die?

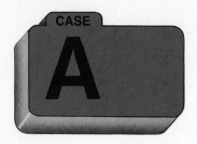

Borden Manufacturing Company

Borden Manufacturing Company is among the largest manufacturers of photo, printing, and industrial graphics products; roofing granules; office copiers; medical and surgical products; pharmaceuticals; and electronic calculators.

Records kept for current personnel include ages of employees. This information is important in planning for replacement of employees. The data for employees in one section of the electronic assembly for calculators show their ages to be 19, 22, 20, 24, 25, 19, 22, 19, 35, 38, and 50.

Records are also kept on hourly rates paid employees so that Borden is able to offer competitive wages to its employees. Competitive wages are important in helping to attract qualified employees as well as to keep current employees. The average hourly rates paid to electronic assembly workers in Borden's five electronics departments are:

Department 1	$8.65	Department 4	$8.25
Department 2	$9.00	Department 5	$7.75
Department 3	$7.50		

The arithmetic mean of hourly wages paid to employees in the same type of business is $8.15.

Borden's sales for the current fiscal year are $885 million, and its net profit is $47.3 million. Last year, sales were $795 million, and net profit was $35 million.

Questions

1. What are the median, mode, and arithmetic mean of ages of employees in the electronic assembly section?

2. Explain why there is a difference in these averages.

3. How does Borden compare to the overall industry average in wages paid to electronic assembly employees?

4. Five years ago, Borden's average hourly wage was $5.70 and the industry's average was $5.77. Which has had the greatest rate of increase?

5. Take a simple random sample of one department's average wage and compare that to the overall average of Borden. How close are they?

6. Of the wages reported, which is an example of internal data? External data?

7. In the financial data reported, what type of statistical measure should be used to compare relative changes in sales and relative changes in profits?

8. Compute the relative change in sales this year as compared to last year. Explain what this figure means.

9. Compute the relative change in profits this year compared to last year. Explain what this figure means.

Dick Edmundson's Washateria

Dick Edmundson is currently a student in your school and is looking for a way to help pay his way through four years of college. Dick is considering leasing a building one block from the campus on a four-year basis and converting it into a washateria. He can purchase twenty new washing machines and six dryers by putting up 10 percent of the purchase price. Dick has calculated his costs and discovered that if he could obtain 60 percent usage twelve hours a day on both the washing machines and dryers, he would be able to pay all expenses (including the monthly payments on the equipment) and still clear $500 per month. However, if he falls below 50 percent usage twelve hours a day, he will lose his investment. Dick is figuring his price at 75¢ per wash load and 25¢ per dryer load.

Dick must be sure of his market potential; otherwise, he will lose the money he invested and not be able to complete college. One of Dick's business professors has advised Dick that the only way to be reasonably sure of his market potential is to conduct a market survey. Since Dick knows very little about statistical techniques, he has offered you $300 to make the survey for him.

Questions

1. What information do you need? What will be your source of this information?
2. Will you use a random or controlled sample? Why?
3. Where might you use an average and which type—arithmetic mean, median, or mode?
4. Where might you use a time series analysis and which one?

BUSINESS PROFILE

A. C. Nielsen

From a company that opened its doors in 1923 and struggled through the depression in the late 1930s, the A. C. Nielsen Company has become one of the leading statistical research organizations in America. In 1939, the Nielsen organization expanded its business services to the United Kingdom. Today, Nielsen collects statistical data worldwide, with operations in twenty-four foreign countries and some 19,400 employees.

The Nielsen Company collects and analyzes statistical data for companies, such as how a company's products are selling or the size and characteristics of television audiences who watch programs on which a sponsor's products are advertised. Companies use such data to decide how to increase sales.

As an example of collecting statistical data, Nielsen uses a random sample of American households to gather data on their television-viewing habits. This information serves as the basis for predicting the number of people viewing certain programs. It also guides advertisers in deciding which programs should promote their products or services.

By using the sampling technique, Nielsen can assemble valuable information at a relatively small cost to users and enable them to base their decisions on more accurate information.

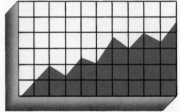

An A.C. Nielson field auditor conducting a market research study of a grocery store.

20 Computer Information Systems in Business

LEARNING GOALS

After reading this chapter, you will understand:

1. The impact that computers have on society and business.
2. The history of computer technology.
3. The functions that computers perform.
4. That the components of computers are input, processing, and output.
5. What a computer programming language is.
6. That there are different types of computers.
7. Some of the possible applications of the computer in business, as well as in other fields.
8. Some of the uses of the personal computer.
9. What a Management Information System is.
10. What a word processing system is.
11. Some of the potential problems of the computer.

KEY TERMS

Minicomputers	Analog computers	Management Information
Microcomputers	Digital computers	Systems
Microprocessors	Binary system	Batch processing
Hardware	Hybrid computer	Turnaround time
Time sharing	Software	Real-time processing
Access time	Linear programming	Word processing
Control unit	Computer simulation	Computer downtime
Flowchart		

> The computer revolution is one of the most advertised revolutions in world history. Yet one of the funny things about it is that we probably still underestimate its impact.
>
> HESH WEINER

Significant advances in technology have paved the way for the great scientific progress of the twentieth century, such as the exploration of outer space. Scientists agree that such accomplishments would not have been possible without high-speed electronic computers to process the mathematical data needed for these explorations.

In today's fast-paced business world, computer technology makes it possible for large quantities of data required by governmental agencies and parties-at-interest to the firm to be processed rapidly. Furthermore, the computer's processing capability gives managers access to greater quantity and quality of data on which to base decisions.

Companies, large and small, that are involved in the manufacture of computers and/or data processing equipment continue to introduce new advances in computer technology at a phenomenal rate. The largest computer firm is IBM. Other large computer firms are NCR, Control Data Corporation, Digital Equipment Corporation, Sperry Corporation, Burroughs, Honeywell, and Hewlett-Packard.

HISTORY OF COMPUTER SYSTEMS

While the development of electronic computer systems has occurred in the twentieth century, the concept of data processing obviously is not new. Managers have long used some type of devices to aid them in their calculations. History demonstrates that as far back as the 1600s there were attempts to develop machines to do laborious, monotonous calculations. In the 1830s, Charles Babbage designed a steam-driven analytical machine that incorporated the basic principles of modern-day computers.

First-Generation Computers

The history of computers in the twentieth century is often characterized as progressing through four generations. The first generation (1942–1959) included the development of the first real computer, called the Mark I. This was an electromechanical computer developed by Howard Aiken in 1944. In 1946, the first electronic computer, called ENIAC (Electronic Numerical Integrator and Calculator) was built by Eckert and Mauchly at the University of Pennsylvania. Remington Rand developed and sold UNIVAC (Universal Automatic Calculator) in 1954. These first-generation computers used the vacuum tube for data storage and were quite large. For example, ENIAC weighed some thirty tons, occupied 1,500 square feet of floor space, and had 19,000 vacuum tubes, which generated tremendous heat.

Second-Generation Computers

Second-generation computers (1959–1965) came about with the development of solid-state components (transistors and diodes), which replaced the vacuum tubes. Solid-state components ran cooler and were more powerful computers than those of the first generation. In addition, computer size was drastically reduced because the smaller solid-state components were used. The speed of processing was increased to a millionth of a second, and the computer memory was increased.

Third-Generation Computers

Third-generation computers (1965–1970), called **minicomputers,** were much smaller and more powerful than earlier computers. They used the integrated circuit—a complete electrical circuit on a small silicon chip—instead of transistors. Minicomputers are digital computers. They greatly increased the speed of processing data, and their cost was less than that of second-generation computers. Minicomputers are widely used today in schools (teaching-machine systems), manufacturing firms (control of production processes and quality control), insurance agencies (a system that allows personal statements of financial benefits to be sent to clients), and small businesses (systems that control various functions of the business, such as accounting and inventory control).

Fourth-Generation Computers

Fourth-generation computers (1970–?), called **microcomputers,** are small and inexpensive (but powerful) computer systems. A microcomputer is capable of input, processing, and output of data. Microcomputers are constructed of silicon chips. These chips are miniature integrated circuits referred to as **microprocessors;** a complete computer can be put on a chip smaller than a thumbnail. Sometimes such a computer is called a "computer on a chip."

Advances in computer technology are expanding the use of computers in communications by satellite around the world. Overall, microcomputers offer significant increases in input/output, storage, and processing capabilities at much lower cost than the earlier, larger computers.

Microcomputers are feasible for use by small business owners in their business operations. A complete business computer system, including keyboard terminal, videoscreen, data storage, programming instructions, and a printer, is available for less than $5,000.

Applications of Microcomputers. Countless possibilities exist for applications of microcomputers. Some uses include the following.

1. Auto manufacturers equip cars with microprocessors in the emission control systems that automatically control the fuel and air mixture for the most efficient fuel burning and thus minimize pollution.

2. "Robotics" are robots designed to replace people in hazardous job locations or in simple jobs. Robotics have skills beyond those of the robots used on assembly lines.

3. Home applicances with built-in microprocessors signal when malfunctions occur.

The Future—Fifth-Generation Computers

Futuristic computer experts predict the fifth-generation supercomputers will be radically different from today's models. These computers will have new hardware and software and will be more powerful and up to 1,000 times faster than today's computers. The outlook is that these supercomputers will be able to hear and talk in a natural human language, will have the capacity to think in human fashion, and will have knowledge and intelligence so that they can write their own computer programs and solve their own problems.[1]

COMPUTER FUNCTIONS

High-speed electronic computers are a valuable aid to business managers. Electronic data processing (EDP) can be most effectively used in situations where the work is repetitive, a large volume of data are to be processed, and speed and accuracy are required. Specifically, data processing done by high-speed electronic computers involves the following functions.

Recording

All business transactions are recorded, such as on sales slips, invoices, and in accounting records. These records are then converted into a form usable by the computer. Computer input is discussed later in this chapter.

Classifying

Data that are similar must be arranged in categories. Sales data may be grouped by sales territory or accounting data may be grouped on the basis of assets, liabilities, or proprietorship accounts. Often classifying is done by using a numeric, alphabetic, or alphanumeric coding system. For example, a numeric code may represent people classified by social security number. Alphabetic codes may be used to classify credit ratings of companies, such as AAA or BB. The alphanumeric code combines letters and numbers.

Sorting

After data are classified, they are arranged in sequence, usually alphabetically or numerically, to facilitate processing of data. For example, types of business may be listed alphabetically while personal checks are sorted numerically by banks in monthly statements to depositors.

Calculating

Calculating involves performing the arithmetic calculations (both simple and complex) of the data. One very common calculation is the weekly or monthly employee payroll for the firm.

---

[1]*The Wall Street Journal,* September 25, 1981.

Summarizing

Data are consolidated so that main points are made available to managers. For example, the total sales for individual stores, departments, or salespersons can be summarized and presented to managers who use the data as a basis for decision making.

Data Storage and Information Retrieval

Computers have made it possible for firms to store large quantities of records in the computer's memory bank and retrieve the information almost instantaneously.

Voice Response. Computers also talk their output by means of voice response terminals, which aid the information retrieval process. Data stored in the computer may be requested by use of a special coded message. The computer answers this request by using a prerecorded vocabulary to speak the answer into the receiver. For example, many companies use the voice-actuated response system that enables a salesperson to dial a special number to the computer on the telephone when a customer wishes to charge a purchase. The computer quickly scans a customer's credit record with the company. A voice authorizes the sale by telephone if the customer's credit standing is satisfactory.

Data Communication

After summaries of data are prepared, they are communicated to managers in the form of output. Data must be communicated clearly and promptly to managers so that they can use the information effectively. Various forms of computer output are discussed later in this chapter.

Thus, companies using computers realize the following advantages:

1. Increased quantities of records kept at lower cost;
2. Increased speed of processing data and retrieval;
3. Increased accuracy in data processing;
4. Reduction of labor requirements for routine clerical positions;
5. Creation of jobs of more responsibility.

COMPONENTS OF COMPUTERS

In a business computer system, hardware refers to the basic physical components of the computer: input, central processor, and output. Auxiliary hardware such as a key punch, which is operated independently and is detached from the main computer system, is called off-line equipment. Auxiliary hardware such as a printer directly connected to the computer is called on-line equipment. Time sharing allows a number of different users to participate in sharing computer time by means of "on-line" terminals located away from the central computer. Some advantages to a company in using time sharing are lower cost of processing data and more efficient use of the computer system. Since more users are using the system, the computer is not likely to be idle for long periods. Time sharing may be a feasible alternative for companies that cannot afford their own computer system yet need the processing capability of the computer.

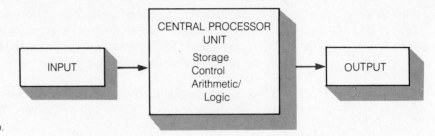

Exhibit 20–1
The basic components of a computer and their interrelationship.

Exhibit 20–1 illustrates the basic components of the computer and their relationship to each other. The arrows represent the direction of informational flow within the computer. Data flow from the input terminal into the processor unit. The processor unit includes the storage, control section, and arithmetic/logic section. Processed data are distributed as output and also returned to storage for future use.

Input

The computer is directed through its functions by a computer program. The computer program, written by a computer programmer, is a detailed series of instructions to the computer of the order and kind of operations necessary to process the data. These instructions are put into the computer by input devices. The program tells the computer to read input data, write output data, and rearrange data in storage and perform the arithmetic/logic function.

Input Devices.   Many kinds of input devices exist. Input devices include the punched card, which has a pattern of holes punched to represent data and is read by a card reader.

The 80-column punched card shown in Exhibit 20–2 was developed by Dr. Herman Hollerith but is frequently referred to as the *IBM punched card*. It has 80 vertical spaces, known as columns, which are numbered from left to right, from 1 to 80. One letter, digit, or character can be punched in each column, and 80 characters can be put on each card. If you desired to punch number 58047 in the card, five consecutive columns would be needed. *Five* would be punched in column one, *eight* in column two, *zero* in column three, *four* in column four, and *seven* in column five.

Other kinds of input devices include the following:

1. Diskettes, or floppy disks, are flexible, oxide-coated plastic disks, about the size of a 45 rpm record, on which data are stored by means of electronic impulse.

2. Magnetic tape has a magnetic surface on which data can be recorded in the form of polarized spots.

3. Magnetic ink character recognition (MICR) is a device that senses specially designed characters printed on paper with a special ink and converts these for input to the computer. This process is commonly used on checks and utility bills.

4. Disk storage units consist of a number of disks with magnetized recording surfaces mounted on a spindle.
5. Video-display screens (cathode ray tube—CRT) allow data to be entered on a keyboard terminal and displayed on the screen.
6. Optical character recognition (OCR) uses special character shapes and a device that picks up data from manually prepared forms.

Central Processor Unit

The central processor unit contains the storage, control, and arithmetic/logic sections of the computer.

Storage. Instructions and data go into the computer through the input terminal and are placed electronically in the computer's storage, called its memory. The data base, which contains all the information and knowledge used by the firm in decision making, is stored in the computer's memory for immediate availability. Data may be stored by a number of methods, such as on magnetic cores, on thin film, bubble memory, or floppy disks. These data are stored either temporarily or permanently until they are needed. An example of stored data is information used repeatedly in submitting regular reports, such as payroll data.

Access time is the interval of time it takes from the instant data are requested to when they are made available by the computer. Access times are measured in units of the metric system and include: millisecond (one thousandth of a second), microsecond (one millionth of a second), nanosecond (one billionth of a second), and, picosecond (one trillionth of a second).

Control. The **control unit** directs and controls the internal flow of information according to instructions contained in the program. The control unit provides the computer with the capability to interpret instructions and to establish and follow operating procedures.

The control unit directs and coordinates the entering and removing of data from storage. Furthermore, it directs the arithmetic calculations of the computer and controls both the input and output of data.

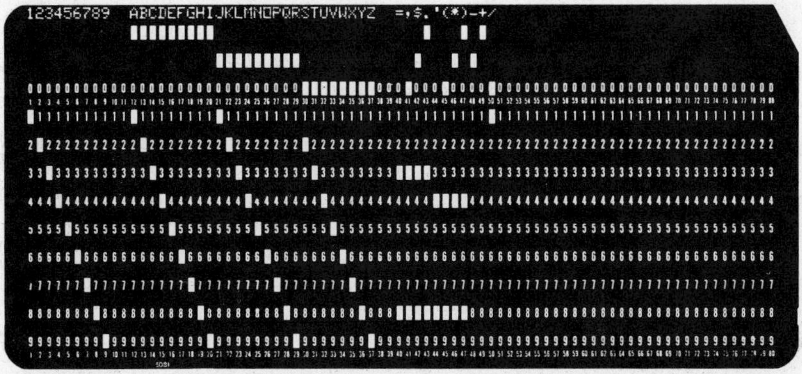

Exhibit 20–2
An 80-column punch card showing the digit-punching position for numbers, alphabetic characters, and symbols.

A control unit receives instructions one at a time from data in the memory. These instructions are then carried out in step-by-step procedures until the program has been completed. The instructions specify the functions that are to be performed as well as the location of data in storage.

Arithmetic/Logic Section.   The processor unit performs the arithmetic/logic function at fantastic speeds. The arithmetic section performs the functions of addition, subtraction, multiplication, division, comparison, rounding, moving, shifting, or storing data. The logic section performs the decision-making operations by examining data and comparing them. The logical decisions made by the computer include the ability to tell:

1. Whether two numbers or characters are equal or unequal;
2. Whether one number is greater or less than another;
3. Whether a quantity is positive, negative, or zero.[2]

Logic operations are performed in processing data using numeric, alphabetic, or alphanumeric quantities.

Output

Data that have been processed are referred to as *output*. This is the objective of data processing: to make requested information available in understandable form quickly, accurately, and completely. Output may be produced in many forms, including magnetic tape units, high-speed line printers, cathode ray tubes, data plotters, punched cards, punched paper tape, and remote output terminals.

FLOWCHARTS

Before a computer program is written, the problem to be solved and the relationship between the different parts of the problem must be analyzed. The computer programmer usually makes this analysis by developing a flowchart. A flowchart is a graphic representation of the operations and decisions that must be made as well as the order in which they must be made to arrive at a solution. In Exhibit 20–3, a system of symbols, arrows, and lines detailing the operations sequence necessary to get to school in the morning is presented.

TYPES OF COMPUTERS

The type of computer is determined by how it is designed to perform its internal operations and its purposes. The basic types of computers are analog, digital, and hybrid.

Analog Computers

Analog computers are primarily measuring devices, for measuring quantities on a continuous scale. Analog computers measure pressure, voltage, temperature, or speed. Since an analog computer's measurements

---

[2]Elias M. Awad. *Introduction to Computers in Business* (Englewood Cliffs, N.J.: Prentice-Hall, Inc., 1977), p. 118.

Exhibit 20–3

Detailed block diagram of "how to get to school in the morning."

(SOURCE: Elias M. Awad, *Business Data Processing*, 4th ed. Englewood Cliffs, N.J.: Prentice-Hall, Inc., 1975, p. 438. Reprinted by permission.)

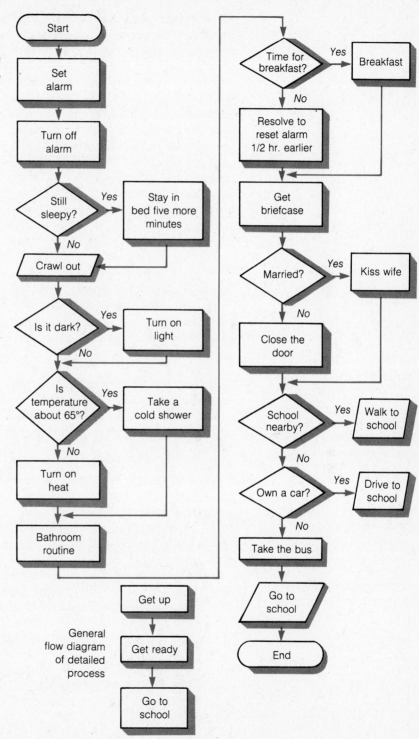

General flow diagram of detailed process

are on a continuous scale, the readings are approximate, not exact. For example, a temperature measurement of 150 degrees is an approximate reading, not an exact value. Temperature readings may be further refined by using more accurate measuring instruments.

Analog computers are particularly suited for controlling continuous manufacturing process operations, such as in oil refineries, paper mills, steel mills, and chemical plants. The analog computer can monitor a chemical mixing process by allowing or prohibiting chemicals to enter the process. Feedback from the chemical mixing process, obtained from continuous readings of the process, enables the computer to keep the process under control automatically.

Analog computers are not widely used in business, however. Most business data are first recorded in a form (usually on paper) that the analog computer cannot process, since it measures data directly from various kinds of measuring devices.

Digital Computers

Digital computers work directly with numbers, alphabetic symbols, and special characters and are the most widely used computers in business. They have the ability to count and deal with exact data, such as payroll information and merchandise in inventory. A digital computer can solve both simple and complex problems that require logical decisions.

General-Purpose and Special-Purpose Computers. General-purpose computers are digital computers that can be applied to a wide variety of problems, such as processing business-related data and complex mathematical information. Special-purpose computers are also digital computers, which are designed to perform a specific function, such as the monthly billing of customers.

Processing Data in the Digital Computer. Digital computers are made up of numerous electronic components. Data are represented in these components by electronic signals. There are only two possible states for these components: *on* or *off*. The *on* state means that the computer is open and can receive data in the form of electronic signals and process them; the *off* state means the system is closed to electronic signals. An example of this on-off state is a switch on an electrically driven machine. When the switch is on, the machine receives electric power, which permits it to operate. When the switch is off, the machine receives no power and does not function.

Instead of using the ten-digit, decimal number system that we ordinarily use to count, the digital computer uses a two-digit number system, called the **binary system.** This system uses only two digits, zero (0) and one (1), to represent various quantities. These two digits, called *bits* (contraction of BInary digiT), represent the data stored in the computer's memory.

In the binary system, the value that 1 represents depends upon its position in a binary system, reading from right to left. Also, digits increase in value by multiples of 2 as they are moved to the left. The 0 and the 1 can represent any value in the decimal system by their position. To illustrate:

Binary Number	Decimal Number
0000	0
0001	1
0010	2
0011	3
0100	4
0101	5
0110	6
0111	7
1000	8
1001	9

To represent 15, we would have 1111, which is read from right to left in binary as $1 + 2 + 4 + 8 = 15$.

Hybrid Computers

A computer that combines the best features of analog and digital computers is the **hybrid computer.** It combines the speed of analog computers and accuracy of digital computers. Hybrid computers are capable of receiving input data in the form of measurements, converting them into a digital format, and processing them into useful output. Applications of hybrid computers are found in manufacturing processes and production facilities as well as in science and engineering.

Although the computer is capable of producing a wealth of data, the data are of no value until they are used by a manager in decision making. The computer helps to remove some of the uncertainty in decision making because it makes possible a greater accumulation and summarization of data on which managers can base their analysis. The final authority for the decision to proceed or to explore other possible alternatives still resides with the manager, however, not with the computer.

COMPUTER LANGUAGES

Computer **software** refers to the programs and all documents (manuals, circuit diagrams) associated with a computer. Many firms specialize in computer software. These firms program computers and also sell or lease computer time to companies that do not require the computer full-time in their operation.

The computer progam provides the instructions for the computer as seen in the following developments in programming languages.[3]

1. Machine-oriented language, a set of coded symbols for use in first-generation computers. This language was found to be unsatisfactory for business problems, and a program written for one computer would not run on another.

---

[3]Ibid., pp. 293–95.

2. Symbolic-assembly language, a language in the form of symbolic codes that were used in second-generation computers. However, program writers used different symbolic notations, which made widespread application of this language difficult.

3. Higher-level languages, which offer better notation and are independent of the computer on which they are run, are in common use today. These programs are written and then translated into machine language by a special program, called the *compiler,* for processing.

Exhibit 20–4 shows the higher-level languages commonly used today: COBOL, FORTRAN, and PL/I, as well as other computer languages used for special applications.

USES OF COMPUTER INFORMATION SYSTEMS IN BUSINESS

The applications of computer information systems in business are almost limitless. New developments almost daily in computer technology are rapidly expanding these applications. The following situations rep-

Exhibit 20–4

Some computer languages.

Acronym	Language	Description
ALGOL	Algorithmic Language	Language suited to solving problems requiring numerical computations; similar to FORTRAN
APL	A Programming Language	Math-oriented language often used in time sharing
BASIC	Beginners All-Purpose Symbolic Instruction Code	Language used to solve numeric problems; best suited for programming with use of terminals
COBOL	Common Business Oriented Language	High-level symbolic language most suited for solving business problems
FORTRAN	Formula Translation	High-level symbolic language most suited for solving scientific or math problems
PL/I	Programming Language I	High-level symbolic language that combines the best features of FORTRAN and COBOL; can be used to solve both scientific and business problems
RPG	Report Program Generator	Language designed to generate management reports from existing data in the system

Faster service and more efficient inventory control are two results of substituting computers for conventional cash registers.

resent only a minute number of the vast uses of computer systems in business as well as other fields and illustrate the benefits provided by the computer.

Airlines

Travel agents and airline reservation personnel enter passenger requests for flights on a computerized airline reservation-and-ticket system. The computer processes the request by checking the flight, available seating, and confirming the reservation in a matter of seconds. Airlines also use computers to schedule plane maintenance, schedule flights, and make personnel assignments.

Retailers

Computers are used extensively in retail outlets. Electronic "wands" or computer terminals are directly linked to a computer system. When a sale is made, a record of the transaction is stored in the computer system and inventory records are updated to reflect the sale of the item. In inventory control, the computer can be programmed to keep continuous records of inventory receipts, shipments, costs, merchandise in stock, and automatic reordering when quantities drop to specified levels. Computers enable salespersons to validate credit card purchases and personal checks, permit salespersons to devote more time to the selling function, and provide better customer service.

Banks

Banks use computers to control financial data, to keep bank accounts of customers, as well as to send monthly statements to depositors. In addition, they use remote banking terminals located in shopping centers where customers can make withdrawals with "cash cards." Banks and savings and loan associations have installed automated cash machines on the premises so that customers can do their banking day or night.

Some banks have installed a signature validation system to make for better customer service and greater security in making withdrawals and cashing personal checks. The computer flashes a depositor's signature on a video-display screen for verification and banks now offer electronic transfer of funds (EFT) services.

Manufacturers

Computers aid in the manufacturing process for all types of manufacturers. One device that greatly aids the product design stage is the graphic display that allows designers to draw the item on the face of the display screen; the design can then be reproduced on paper by a plotter.

Process Control. In refineries, chemical plants, and other production lines, computers control the process. For example, a refinery engineer enters information on prices of petroleum products, as well as on chemical and physical properties of raw petroleum, in a computer. The computer is programmed to determine the most economical way to produce liquid petroleum gas and other oil products as well as to control the complex process of petroleum distillation to insure the most profitable production.

Production Scheduling. The computer is programmed to schedule employees, materials, and machines for the most efficient production. The computer determines the number of workers, quantity of materials needed, and productive capacity for each piece of machinery.

Railroads

Railroads maintain a constant computer check of where freight cars are located on their thousands of miles of track throughout the nation. For example, a railroad yardmaster can ask at any time for the latest information on any freight car. In the same railyard, a computer terminal automatically prints out a list and tells in sequence what cars are arriving in the yard. This makes it possible for cars to be switched for the fastest possible movement to their final destination.

Managers in all types of business situations use the computer in the following basic application areas to provide greater information and control: (1) accounts receivable, (2) accounts payable, (3) sales analysis and forecasting, (4) bill payments, (5) billing of customers, (6) recordkeeping, (7) payroll preparation, and (8) maintaining up-to-date information on company personnel.

Computer applications extend into many other areas. Library computer systems enable library personnel to maintain current information on the status of books at any time. In education, computer-assisted instruction (CAI) is used to aid the learning process. Terminals are connected to an on-line computer system and this enables students to receive information, give answers, and receive feedback.

COMPUTER TECHNIQUES FOR COMPLEX PROBLEMS

Computers are capable of generating data that will assist managers in more complex decision-making situations. Some of the more advanced computer techniques available to managers include linear programming and computer simulation.

Linear Programming

Linear programming is a quantitative approach that determines how to use limited resources to obtain the best solution—either to minimize cost or to maximize profit—for specific problems. For example, a manufacturer can use this approach to find the correct mixture for blending gasoline. Proper blending will minimize the cost of producing the gas and also ensure that the gasoline meets the manufacturer's specifications. Two additional uses of linear programming are (1) to schedule the optimum use of a limited number of a factory's machines used in producing more than one part or product, and (2) to determine a truck's minimum transportation costs from point of origin to final destination.

Computer Simulation

Computer simulation is a technique in which a model of a real system is designed in order to test a project or a management strategy prior to implementation of the project or strategy. Computer simulation models are valuable aids in planning and decision-making. For example, this technique enables managers to theoretically project results such as sales and profits of different management strategies for a number of years.

Business Game.   The business game is a computer-simulation decision-making technique. Teams of players (managers) represent the various management teams of hypothetical companies. These teams are required to make decisions of the type they would make in the real world, such as level of production and how to price the products. Teams compete to make the best (most profitable) choices. Team decisions are processed by the computer and the computer feedback is used to analyze the decision-making process and to improve decision-making skills.

MANAGEMENT INFORMATION SYSTEMS

"It's analyzed our situation thoroughly, and has concluded that our business doesn't need a computer."

The computer is an extremely valuable tool for today's managers. Rapid changes in computer technology are increasing the expectations of managers concerning the further applications of computers. One important area is the development of **Management Information Systems.** A Management Information System (MIS) is defined as a computer-based information system that is capable of providing managers at all organizational levels with the kinds of information they need for decision making. The computer-based MIS can supply managers with timely, accurate, relevant data that are as concise and complete as is economically feasible.

Some of the specific characteristics of MIS are:

1. On-line system with real-time capability, providing instant recording of and access to business transactions.
2. Regular evaluation and monitoring of the internal and external events and the elements that have a bearing on the existing data.
3. Man-machine interaction available for looking into possible relationships in the existing files.

4. The availability of periodic reports and special informational reports when needed.

5. A common data base to all subsystems, reducing data duplication and storage requirements and the cost of the total system.

6: Systems integration through sequential interdependence. Output from one system becomes the input for another. Data also may be shared by all subsystems.[4]

Batch Processing and Real-Time Processing

In MIS, two computer-based applications are available for providing information to managers: (1) batch processing and (2) real-time processing.

Batch processing is the traditional method of processing data. This method involves collecting similar records into batches and processing them all the same way. Batch processing is used in routine functions, such as payroll preparation, customer billing, accounts payable, and accounts receivable. **Turnaround time** refers to the time it takes to process data and produce the needed output.

A major advance in computer technology that has been a tremendous aid in speeding information retrieval and supplying data to managers has been the development of **real-time processing.** *Real time* refers to the processing of data or business transactions as they are received by the computer so they can be returned to decision makers in time for the processed data to be used in making the final decision. Thus, real-time processing makes it possible for the computer to provide almost immediate results relating to the data being fed into the computer. Applications of real-time processing are found in the airline industry, where ticket agents cannot complete a customer request for a ticket unless the computer verifies the availability of space on a particular flight. Retail stores use real-time processing to maintain sales data and inventory levels. Manufacturers have ongoing production information available to them by use of real-time processing.

WORD PROCESSING

There has been a dramatic increase in written communication within organizations and between organizations in recent years. One cause of the greater volume of paperwork has been the number of reports required by the various governmental regulatory agencies. Consequently, more efficient methods for handling the increased volume of communication have had to be designed.

Word processing systems have been developed to meet this challenge. "Word processing is a program to improve the efficiency and effectiveness of business communications. It is the combination of people, procedures, and equipment in the proper system design to meet the needs of an organization."[5]

---

[4]Ibid., p. 27.

[5]Robert B. LaDue, "Transition to the Office of the Future," *Word Processing* 5 (July/August, 1976): 3.

Personal Computers

The increasing popularity of the personal (or home) computer has been made possible by the technological developments of the microprocessor. Consequently, basic personal computer systems that are very easy to use and are flexible in their functions and applications are available to millions of households at an economical price and in a small size.

Personal computers were introduced in the latter part of the 1970s. Among the first companies to market personal computers were Apple Computer Company (Apple II), Commodore (Pet), and Radio Shack (TRS-80, Model I). Many firms have entered the field and now manufacture and market personal computers, including the industry leader in computers, IBM. These personal systems have a keyboard and video-display screen.

Most early sales of personal computers were to computer hobbyists for learning and experimentation with the computer. Since then, the role of the personal computer has been expanded so that they now have both hardware and software packages that enable them to perform a variety of tasks around the home.

Personal computers may be used for personal entertainment, such as games, or for learning through the use of educational games or learning drills. Another major use of home computers is in personal management, such as household recordkeeping, inventory of personal belongings, and computational functions. Personal computers enable the homeowner to monitor and control other equipment, such as appliances and security devices.

Personal computer users can hook up to a computerized information network that provides in-home stock quotations and newspaper and wire service reports. Predictions are that the electronic newspaper will someday replace the traditional newspaper. Other services include shopping information, home-study courses, and the ability to communicate electronically to order merchandise. Countless possibilities exist in the future for the applications of the personal computer.

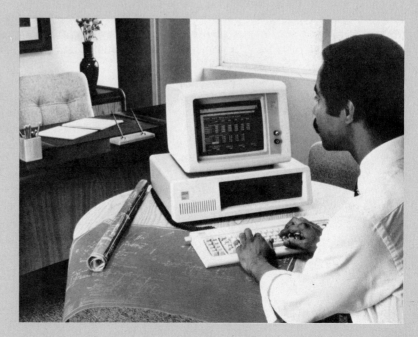

This IBM Personal Computer can generate and display charts, graphs, and numerical information.

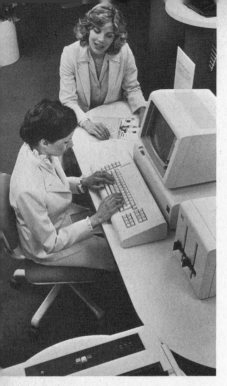

IBM's Displaywriter is a low-cost, easy-to-use word processing system that is modular, allowing users to tailor and expand it as their needs demand.

The computer is having a major impact in word processing since it can be programmed to assist in composing, editing, and reproducing business documents. Word processing equipment has greatly simplified the secretary's work. A word processor enables the operator to type information that appears on a video-display screen instead of on paper. Errors can be easily corrected and copy can be electronically edited on the screen before it is printed. The information goes from the video-display screen to the central processing unit, where it is recorded on disks (hard or floppy) for future reference. The information is then produced by the word processing system's printer.

Word processing systems make it possible to send "electronic mail." A memo can be prepared on a word processor terminal and routed to the terminal of the receiver. This system speeds the flow of communication since the message does not have to be written or mailed. The memo is stored electronically in the computer's memory until it is needed or, if it is not needed, it is deleted from the computer.

The trend toward office automation is certain. Predictions are that much of today's office equipment will be replaced by computers linked together in a communication network. The computer communication network may be a local network within one office or a broader network across the country and around the world. The advances in word processing equipment make it possible to have a truly "paperless" office system.

Advances in modern office technology have led to greater productivity and efficiency of clerical workers. If the electronic offices are to be truly efficient, however, managers and professional employees will have to adapt to the new technology as well.

The electronic office can bring about a substantial savings in the time needed to prepare communication, can result in higher quality work, and can speed up the communication process.

COMPUTERS IN BUSINESS—SOME PROBLEMS

No doubt computers have had a positive, profound effect on business operations. However, the management of a firm should be aware of some special problems before plunging headlong into computer acquisition. One issue is that the decision to install a computer may be based on an incomplete analysis of potential cost savings. Purchasing a computer may require large outlays of cash. Even if a firm leases a computer, the fixed rental fees may outweigh the savings. Not all firms can use computers efficiently.

For companies that use a central computer system, one of the main problems is computer downtime. **Computer downtime** refers to the time that the computer is not operational. With the smaller microcomputer, separate computer units can be placed in strategic work areas. Thus, if the computer is down, only the work in progress in the area served by that computer will be affected, and the entire system will not have to be shut down.

While computers are designed to aid managers, there are instances in which computer errors occur. Some examples include the following.

1. A customer received a $1,010 water bill when the actual bill should have been $7.38.

2. A person on social security received a check for $9,281.60 instead of the monthly benefit check of $202.60.

Other important concerns relate to protecting the right to privacy of individuals and preventing computer fraud and computer-related crime. For example, an employee in the Social Security Administration was able to manipulate the computer to pay herself and two accomplices over $100,000 in disability payments. Computer-related crimes are estimated to cause losses of $100 million to $300 million annually.

Another major problem area, but of a different nature, centers around the reaction of employees to the computer. Many companies have followed traditional business procedures developed over years of practice. In such companies, individuals may have developed the feeling that the work they are doing is their own creation. When a company makes the decision to install a computer, the computer assumes many jobs formerly done by employees. Unless the employees understand what the change in method of operation involves, there can be, and often is, negative reaction to the change, which may be expressed in a variety of ways. Employees may use unique methods to sabotage the new system, such as work slowdowns or an increase in the number of grievances. Employees may fear that the installation of the computer system will lead to large numbers of employees being replaced by machines. As a result, employees' anxiety about job security increases. However, instead of vast numbers of employees being thrown into the ranks of the unemployed, they have found that they are both retained and retrained for more responsible positions in the firm with an increase in salary. Thus, the computer system actually upgrades the status of the employee. Routine, monotonous, and boring tasks can be done with greater efficiency by the computer, leaving the worker to express himself or herself in a more creative manner on the job.

Problems of employee resistance to change are brought about primarily by the failure to understand what the change involves, why it is being made, and the possible advantages to be derived. In order to minimize the resistance to a proposed change as much as possible, management can and should take a number of positive steps prior to the introduction of a computer system. Among these steps are:

1. Lay the groundwork for the change thoroughly—explore all possible problems.

2. Communicate the plans for the change to employees.

3. Allow workers to participate in the change—encourage them to ask questions, seek their advice.

4. Listen to employee complaints about the proposed change and work cooperatively to solve them.

5. Stress the benefits of the new system to the worker as well as to the company.

"It can print information at the rate of 5,600 words per minute. Run a help wanted ad for someone who can read 5,600 words per minute."

SUMMARY OF KEY POINTS

1. Computer technology has passed through three generations and is now in the fourth generation, called *microcomputers*. Some experts are predicting the fifth generation computers in the not-too-distant future.

2. Computers perform these functions in processing data: recording, classifying, sorting, calculating, summarizing, data storage and information retrieval, and data communication.

3. The components of a computer system are input, central processor unit, and output.

4. The central processor unit contains storage, control, and arithmetic/logic sections.

5. A flowchart is a graphic representation of the operations and decisions that must be made and the order in which they must be accomplished in order to reach a decision.

6. Types of computers include analog, digital (general purpose and special purpose), and hybrid computers.

7. A computer programming language is the detailed series of instructions to the computer of the order and kind of operations necessary to process the data. COBOL is a language best suited for solving business problems.

8. Computers have broad applications in many types of business and nonbusiness situations.

9. Personal—or home—computers have many practical uses and are becoming increasingly popular.

10. A Management Information System is a computer-based information system capable of providing managers at all levels with the information they need for decision making.

11. Computer applications may be either basic or advanced. Advanced applications are linear programming and computer simulation.

12. Word processing is a system designed to improve the efficiency of the flow of communication within and external to an organization. The computer has greatly facilitated word processing systems.

13. Managers should be aware of some of the specific problems that have resulted from the use of computers.

DISCUSSION QUESTIONS

1. What is a computer-on-a-chip?
2. Identify the functions ordinarily performed by a computer.
3. Name and briefly explain each of the components of the computer.
4. What is a flowchart, and what is its purpose?
5. Explain the difference between an analog computer and a digital computer.
6. What is a computer programming language?
7. Explain what a Management Information System is.
8. Explain the difference between batch processing and real-time processing.
9. Explain the purpose of word processing.
10. What are some of the special problems management should be aware of when a computer is installed in a firm?

STUDENT PROJECTS

1. Develop the points for and against the following statement: "Computers are going to take over so much work that large numbers of people will be unemployed."
2. Read and summarize an article from a business magazine, such as *Business Week,* or a business newspaper, such as *The Wall Street Journal,* describing how computers are used in business.
3. Read and summarize an article that reports an incident pertaining to a computer error, computer fraud, or computer crime.

Iowa Nonsmokers' Life Insurance Company

Five years ago, Matt Laurel entered into a partnership with two friends to establish the Iowa Nonsmokers' Life Insurance Company. One of the partners owns 60 percent of the stock and is the President. Another partner owns 20 percent of the stock and is the Sales Manager. Matt owns 20 percent of the stock and is the Office Manager. Matt set up the office when the firm was organized, and it has been functioning effectively. Matt feels proud of his accomplishments; however, he has been reading about electronic data processing, and he wonders if it would improve his company's operations.

The company has 40,000 policies in force at this time and the number is increasing daily. In addition, the company now employs 300 people in its main office and 98 sales representatives.

Questions

1. Do you feel Matt's company could benefit from the use of a computer?
2. In what ways could the computer be used in the company?
3. What computer language might Matt's company use?
4. How would the computer aid the company's management?

Hometown National Bank

Hometown National Bank has been a family-owned bank for 100 years. The bank is located in a small town of 4,000 people. The economic base of the area is primarily agricultural, but also includes three brick-manufacturing plants.

The bank's operations were run much the same for the last 25 years. Bookkeeping and posting machines were operated manually by the bank's employees in the record-keeping section. The atmosphere in the bank was characterized as "one big happy family." The bank president's dress was casual, often blue jeans and western boots. Employees from the president down to the custodial staff were called by their first names. Employees have been with the bank for many years and know most people in the community by their first names also. Employee morale was high and customers were treated warmly.

Last year, the bank president died unexpectedly of a heart attack. The family has decided to sell the bank to a group of new owners from a large metropolitan area. The new owners plan to make many changes in the bank. Two major changes include:

1. Remodeling the entire physical structure of the bank inside and out, doing away with the image of an old-style bank with iron bars in the teller windows and redoing the bank in a more modern, open style.
2. Replacing the manual bookkeeping and posting machines and putting all accounts on a new computerized system. This would require some retraining of all employees.

Questions

1. What kind of analysis should be made before deciding to install a computer system?
2. Identify the functions that can be performed by the computer.
3. Are there any advantages to the bank and to the employees resulting from installing a computer?
4. If a computer system is installed, what class of computer should it be?
5. Develop a short statement that could be used to explain the components of the computer to the bank employees.
6. What are some of the applications that could be made of the computer in the bank?
7. What steps should be taken prior to introducing the change to the new system in order to gain the support of the clerical employees for the new computer system?

Thomas J. Watson, Sr.

BUSINESS PROFILE

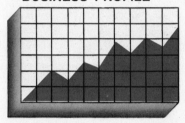

IBM

Thomas J. Watson took over the leadership of a small, financially troubled company that made scales, time recorders, and tabulating machines. He built a modern industrial company, a leader in the computer industry: International Business Machines Corporation.

IBM's initial success was in punch-card accounting machines. The company had a large number of sales, systems, and service people who contacted customers and installed and maintained the automated accounting systems. The concept of "service" has always been a major factor in the company's success.

In 1952, IBM placed its first commercial electronic computer on the market. With its initial success, IBM's management concentrated its efforts on the computer industry. In 1956, only a small percentage of its income was from computers. Now, the major share of IBM's gross income is from computer system sales.

IBM is a major multinational corporation. Over 50 percent of the firm's sales and profits come from its foreign operations. IBM has approximately 340,000 employees in its worldwide organization.

While IBM is recognized as the world leader in the computer industry, it is also a leader in office equipment, including information processors; electric, electronic, and magnetic media typewriters; dictation equipment; and office copying machines.

IBM's policy has been to use its own sales force to exclusively market its products. However, the company has embarked on a new policy of selling and servicing some of the lower-priced products, including the IBM Personal Computer, both by IBM sales representatives and through selected retailers, such as the Sears Business Systems Centers.

Accounting, Business Statistics, and Computer Information Systems

New demands in the business world have opened many career opportunities at various levels in the quantitative fields. Examples of such entry level and higher level careers as well as expected demand in selected occupations are listed below.

Occupation	Number Currently Employed	Number of Openings Each Year to 1990
Accounting		
Accountants	985,000	61,000
Bookkeepers	1,830,000	96,000
Statistics		
Statisticians	23,000	1,500
Statistical clerks	337,000	21,000
Computers		
Computer operators	666,000	12,500
Computer programmers	247,000	9,200
Computer systems analysts	182,000	7,900
Computer service technicians	63,000	5,400

SOURCE: U.S. Department of Labor, *Occupational Outlook Handbook*, 1980–81.

The major areas of employment in accounting are public, private, and governmental accounting. *Public accountants* work independently for a business or an individual and are paid a fee for their service. *Private accountants* are employed by firms and maintain their financial records. *Government accountants* keep the financial records of government agencies or audit the records of private companies. Accountants may specialize in certain phases of accounting, including those listed below.

BUDGET ACCOUNTANT Studies records of past and present operations, trends, and costs; helps develop, install, and maintain budgets; and estimates expected spending.

COST ACCOUNTANT Determines detailed cost data on products or services by analyzing cost records of items. Classifies and records all operating costs for use by management in controlling expenditures.

TAX ACCOUNTANT Prepares federal, state, and local tax returns of an individual, business, or corporation according to prescribed rates, laws, and regulations. Conducts research on the effects of taxes on firm's operations and recommends changes to reduce taxes. May specialize in one area of tax accounting such as income, property, corporation, or Social Security taxes.

AUDITOR Examines and determines accuracy and completeness of accounting records of a firm by inspecting items in accounting records.

SYSTEMS ACCOUNTANT Devises and sets up special accounting systems and related procedures for organizations unable to use a standardized accounting system. Organizes accounting procedures and machine methods for maintaining them.

MACHINE PROCESSING ACCOUNTANT Integrates machine accounting operations and works with management to adapt accounting systems to machine accounting processes.

ACCOUNTING CLERK Does a variety of routine activities—calculating, posting—to accomplish accounting.

CERTIFIED PUBLIC ACCOUNTANT An accountant who has met legal, education, and experience requirements of a particular state and has been certified by that state to practice public accounting.

GENERAL BOOKKEEPER Keeps financial transactions of an establishment, such as entering details of business transactions as they occur.

GENERAL LEDGER BOOKKEEPER Compiles and posts in general ledger information or summaries of various business transactions recorded in separate ledgers by other clerks.

BOOKKEEPER Keeps one set of financial records, such as accounts payable or accounts receivable.

BOOKKEEPING MACHINE OPERATOR Maintains complete set of records of financial transactions of a firm using bookkeeping machines.

PROPERTY ACCOUNTANT Identifies and keeps record of all company-owned or leased property and equipment.

JUNIOR ACCOUNTANT Verifies additions, checks audits and postings, analyzes accounts, and prepares statements, working under supervision.

ACCOUNTING CLERK Does a variety of routine activities—calculating, posting to accomplish accounting. Accounting clerks may be designated by function, such as payroll, accounts payable, accounts receivable, tax record clerk.

AUDIT CLERK Verifies accuracy of financial data relating to business transactions recorded by others.

BUSINESS AND ECONOMICS STATISTICIAN Plans and conducts surveys to gather data on business activities and economic needs, such as income, finance, prices, employment.

FINANCIAL STATISTICIAN Collects and evaluates data relevant to operations of financial institutions.

STATISTICAL CLERK Compiles and tabulates statistics for use in statistical studies. Various types of statistical clerks are listed below.

RECORDING CLERK Collects, records, and verifies accuracy of data.

SHIPPING CHECKER Ensures that merchandise is ready for shipment, is properly labeled, and contains desired number of items in wholesale and retail firms.

CODING CLERK Codes information for transfer to computer cards.

STATISTICAL ASSISTANT Calculates and computes numerical data for government and business research.

BUSINESS PROGRAMMER Writes in computer language the instructions that control the operations of the computer. Confers with department supervisors to solve questions about program purpose, output requirements, and sources of input data.

CHIEF BUSINESS PROGRAMMER Plans, schedules, and directs preparation of programs to process business data by electronic data processing equipment.

PROJECT DIRECTOR (Business Data Processing) Plans, directs, and reviews business data processing project, and works with department heads to establish the content and format of the proposed project.

DETAIL PROGRAMMER Usually works as understudy to business programmer.

SYSTEMS ANALYST Plans, schedules, and coordinates the activities necessary to develop systems to solve business problems by use of computer. Typical problems solved are accounting or inventory requirements.

KEYPUNCH OPERATOR Uses machines similar to typewriters that punch holes in cards to represent specific information.

CORPORATE DIRECTOR OF DATA PROCESSING OR MIS   The top executive for all computer processing.

MANAGER OF SYSTEMS ANALYSIS   Analyzes how data processing is applied to user problems.

SENIOR SYSTEMS ANALYST   Confers with users to define data processing projects; formulates problems; designs solutions.

MANAGER OF SYSTEMS PROGRAMMING   Plans and directs the operating system and assigns personnel to projects.

SYSTEMS PROGRAMMER   May specialize in support of one or a few operating system components or subsystems.

MANAGER OF COMPUTER OPERATIONS   Responsible for the operation of computers, including scheduling, assigning operators, and monitoring of efficiency.

COMPUTER OPERATOR   Assists in running the computers and may operate the central console in the absence of the senior operator.

WORD PROCESSING SUPERVISOR   Responsible for a staff that operates word processing equipment.

WORD PROCESSING OPERATOR   Operates intelligent typewriters, word processing systems, terminals for text editing word processing.

CAREER PROFILES

Joe Mann attended Marquette University and graduated from the University of Arizona with a business degree. His initial employment at The Southland Corporation was in the data processing department, where he was a systems analyst. After two years, he was transferred to the controller's department. Joe now serves as an intermediary between the controller's department and the data processing department. He is the liaison for Southland's accounting employees in the development of new computer systems and the enhancement of existing computer systems.

Joe thinks that one of the most gratifying aspects of his job is the challenge of working closely with the computer personnel and the accounting employees who use the computer systems.

The most taxing part of his job is working on the development of new computer systems that replace manual systems or out-of-date computer systems. The time span from beginning such a project to its completion is usually two to three years. Joe says that it is difficult for all the people involved in the project to keep their enthusiasm high for such a long time.

One of Joe's major goals is to get the computer users more directly and actively involved with the computer. He wants them to write some of their own computer programs. In this way, he thinks, these people will be able to eliminate many of their own boring, repetitive tasks, which the computer can easily perform for them.

Joe's advice to students is to get as much real-world experience as possible in their career fields while going to college. This will make their courses more meaningful and interesting.

John W. Hill, Jr., a graduate of the University of Maryland, is a staff accountant for the firm of Coopers & Lybrand, a public accounting firm. He started his career with Coopers & Lybrand as an intern and was given the responsibility of a beginning staff account. After only five months, he was given added responsibilities usually reserved for people who have been with the firm for two years. John notes that public accounting allows employees to assume as much responsibility as they can in the shortest time.

John's responsibilities include auditing accounting records in such fields as real estate, manufacturing, banking, and stock brokerage. The most gratifying part of his public accounting job is the ability to gain a wide range of experiences in very different types of businesses.

John says that his Introduction to Business course helped him to get a broad look at business and to see that business is a very complex and diverse field with many specialties.

John's Introduction to Business instructor was Alvin Schuster of the University of Maryland.

International,
Legal,
and Government
Environment

21

International Business

LEARNING GOALS

After reading this chapter, you will understand:

1. The importance of international trade and its relationship to standards of living.

2. The national advantages of trade—natural resources, labor, technology, and climate.

3. That there are three basic barriers to trade and the reasons for each of them.

4. The arguments for tariffs and the arguments against tariffs.

5. What the terms *balance of trade* and *balance of payments* mean.

6. The various ways countries cause problems in international trade.

7. The importance of multinational corporations and the problems they face.

KEY TERMS

Exporters
Importers
International trade
National advantage
Quota
Embargo
Tariff

Balance of trade
Balance of payments
Floating currency
International cartel
Product dumping
Multinational corporations

> The benefit of international trade—a more efficient employment of the productive forces of the world.
>
> JOHN STUART MILL

The United States is one of the world's largest **exporters** (selling goods to foreign countries) and **importers** (buying goods from foreign countries). Foreign trade is essential in maintaining what is one of the highest standards of living in the world. The nation must meet its needs by continuing to sell certain goods and buy vital raw materials. Many products would disappear from the nation's market without international trade. In addition, many factories would cease production and lay off large numbers of people if they were unable to obtain certain raw materials through international trade.

International trade is particularly important to consumers in all nations. Nations trading what they produce most efficiently in an atmosphere of competitive world trade results in increased standards of living for all people of the world. For a simplified example, imagine that both a Japanese citizen and a United States citizen have the equivalent of $10 to spend. They both want a fiberglass fishing rod and a transistor radio. Because of technological skills and wage rates, the following prices exist for these products:

	American-Produced	**Japanese-Produced**
Fishing rod	$ 5.00	$10.00
Radio	$10.00	$ 5.00

If the American buys only American products, he can own only the fishing rod and have $5 left over, or own only the radio. Roughly the same situation exists for the Japanese citizen, if he buys only Japanese products.

Exhibit 21–1

The ten highest nations in exporting and importing (shown in billions of dollars).

(SOURCE: Statistical Abstract of the United States, 1981).

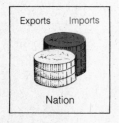

| Exports | Imports |
| Nation |

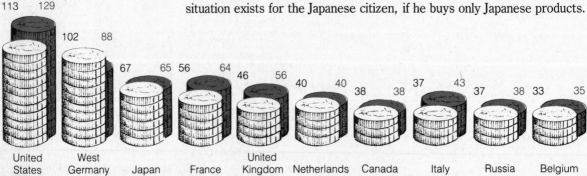

| 113 | 129 | 102 | 88 | 67 | 65 | 56 | 64 | 46 | 56 | 40 | 40 | 38 | 38 | 37 | 43 | 37 | 38 | 33 | 35 |

United States · West Germany · Japan · France · United Kingdom · Netherlands · Canada · Italy · Russia · Belgium

However, if they both buy American fishing rods and Japanese radios, they both can own two products for the $10, which results in higher standards of living.

In fact, international trade results not only in higher standards of living, but also in increased employment. In the United States, 4 million jobs are either directly or indirectly the result of exports.

NATIONAL ADVANTAGES IN TRADE

Nations will always have differences in their levels of efficiency in producing different products. All nations have factors that create a **national advantage** in trade for some products, such as (1) natural resources, (2) labor, (3) technology, and (4) climate.

Natural Resources

Any country that has an abundance of natural resources will have some advantage in international trade. Minerals, forests, agricultural land, fish, water resources, and other natural resources are not evenly distributed throughout the world. The United States and Canada would have an advantage over countries such as England and Japan in the production of wood products. By the same token, South Africa literally controls the world market in diamonds because they are found in greater amounts and extracted at less expense there than anywhere else in the world.

All industrial nations of the world must depend on other nations for many raw materials to sustain their industrially complex societies. Likewise, many underdeveloped, agrarian nations must rely on trading many of their natural resources to the industrial nations to obtain manufactured goods they are unable to produce. For example, the United States aircraft industry would be unable to exist without major importation of bauxite ore

Exhibit 21–2

Nations engaging in the most trade with the United States, in billions of dollars.

	Exports	Imports	Nation
United States	→	←	
	35.4	41.5	Canada
	20.7	30.2	Japan
	12.7	9.8	United Kingdom
	15.1	12.5	Mexico
	10.1	11.7	West Germany
	8.7	1.9	Netherlands
	7.5	5.2	France
	6.7	1.9	Belgium
	5.8	12.5	Saudi Arabia
	4.7	4.1	Korea
	4.6	5.3	Venezuela

SOURCE: Statistical Abstract of the United States, 1981.

"IT'S NOT SURPRISING. THE PRODUCTION DEPARTMENT IS IN SPAIN, THE WAREHOUSE IS IN KOREA, THE ACCOUNTING DIVISION IS IN BOLIVIA, THE BOARD OF DIRECTORS IS IN CANADA..."

by the aluminum industry. On the other hand, many of the nations that are major exporters of bauxite ore lack the trained labor, technology, or capital equipment necessary for the production of aluminum or airplanes. As a result, these nations must trade their ore and other natural resources for aluminum and airplanes.

Labor

Labor may be an advantage for a nation because of skills or low wage rates. Switzerland, for example, almost totally monopolized the watch-movement industry for many years because of its supply of highly skilled watch craftsmen. Highly trained and developed skills were passed down from generation to generation. The watch movement industry in Switzerland is also an excellent example of how a labor advantage can change. Electronic technology in the United States created the digital watch, which can be mass produced by automated processes. Skilled watch-movement craftsmen are rapidly becoming like the people who once made buggy whips before the development of the automobile.

Exhibit 21–3

United States exports and imports by commodity groups (by percent of total).

(SOURCE: Statistical Abstract of the United States, 1981.)

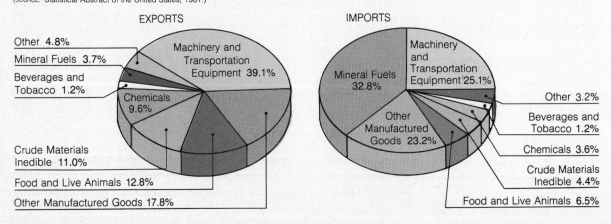

EXPORTS

Other 4.8%
Mineral Fuels 3.7%
Beverages and Tobacco 1.2%
Machinery and Transportation Equipment 39.1%
Chemicals 9.6%
Crude Materials Inedible 11.0%
Food and Live Animals 12.8%
Other Manufactured Goods 17.8%

IMPORTS

Machinery and Transportation Equipment 25.1%
Mineral Fuels 32.8%
Other Manufactured Goods 23.2%
Other 3.2%
Beverages and Tobacco 1.2%
Chemicals 3.6%
Crude Materials Inedible 4.4%
Food and Live Animals 6.5%

Low wage rates are a real national advantage in the production of some products that require little labor and are not easily shifted to mass production techniques. India, for example, has had lower wage rates than the United States for many years and has produced many items of handicraft, such as rugs, which could not be produced in the United States at the same price.

Technology

Technology is probably the most important advantage a nation can possess. Technology tends to breed technology, and the nation that has the most technology has the best chance of producing even greater levels of technology. Technology can overcome most other disadvantages of international trade.

The national advantage of technology is like the labor advantage in that it can rapidly disappear. Other nations borrow technology and a nation must continue to develop technology at a rapid pace if it is to continue the advantage.

Climate

The natural elements of rain, sunshine, snow, storms, and temperature may strongly influence not only the type of product produced but also the total productivity of a nation. Climatic conditions particularly have a decided effect on agricultural production.

Some nations with a favorable climate can trade large amounts of agricultural products for manufactured products of other nations. Brazil and other South American countries, because of climatic conditions, produce large amounts of coffee that they trade in the international market for products of other nations. For instance, they sell coffee to the United States and buy machinery and other manufactured products.

BARRIERS TO TRADE

It has been a long-standing joke that economists can never agree on anything, and this contains a grain of truth. However, the inherent advantage of free, competitive world trade is a concept that is accepted by present-day economists. Many also insist that competitive world trade reduces the chance of development of domestic monopolies and increases competition within nations. Three types of barriers to free world trade are quotas, embargoes, and tariffs.

Quotas

Quotas are quantitative restrictions on imports. By the use of quotas, the total number of goods to be imported is set. It can be directed at a nation or a specific product, usually a product. Quotas are particularly effective barriers to international trade because, no matter how low a foreign producer drops its price, its share of the domestic market is still limited.

Quotas have been used for many reasons, from protection of private industry in a nation to political pressures. Specific import quotas were legalized in the United States several years ago to protect cattle raisers from importation of beef cattle from nations such as Argentina, which have better climatic conditions for feeding beef cattle.

Embargoes

An **embargo** is an order of the government prohibiting goods from leaving or entering the country. Embargoes may be placed against nations or products. Embargoes may be enacted that prohibit any product produced in a specific country from entering the nation, prohibit a specific product no matter where it is produced, prohibit exports to a specific nation, or prohibit exporting specific products to one or more nations. Generally, embargoes are enacted in the United States for reasons of health, politics, and/or morality.

Governments may set embargoes against foreign products for health reasons. Usually they aim at specific offending products from specific countries. Some examples are toys containing toxic paint, fruit from countries with Mediterranean fruit-fly infestation, agricultural products contaminated with parasitic amoebae, and many types of drugs.

Political embargoes usually aim at specific countries. The United States has in the past enacted embargoes of arms and military supplies to many countries as a means of protecting our country and allies. Embargoes for political reasons most often prohibit both imports to and exports from a specific country. For instance, until a few years ago all trade with Red China was forbidden to American companies.

Embargoes for moral reasons are attempts to protect the public from imports that are considered immoral in nature. Embargoes for moral reasons are always restrictions against imports rather than exports and aim at a specific product and not a specific country. Although interpretation has become considerably freer in recent years, the United States has long had embargoes against pornographic material from any country.

Tariffs

The most common method of restricting international trade exists in the form of tariffs. Tariffs are aimed almost entirely at imports and are almost universally a method of protecting domestic industry from foreign competition. Tariffs on exports have existed but have had little effect.

Tariffs are almost always a tax placed on specific goods regardless of foreign origin. The tariff may tax the import at a specific amount per article or on a percentage of the dollar value of the import. For example, cham-

Exhibit 21–4
Major reasons for embargoes.

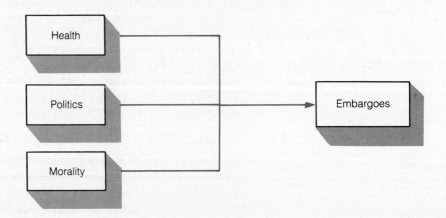

Exhibit 21–5
Barriers to trade.

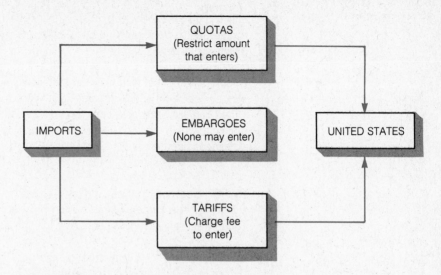

pagne could be taxed at two dollars a liter or 10 percent of the price the importer pays.

Supposedly, tariffs serve two functions: they produce revenue and provide protection. However, a closer examination will show that only about $4 billion a year is collected from tariffs. When the total value of all imports is considered, about 40 percent is duty free. The remainder is subject to tariffs. When $4 billion in tariff revenue is considered, relative to the size of the federal budget (without even considering the cost of collection), it would seem probable that if tax revenue were the only reason for tariffs, they would not exist today. The primary reason for tariffs is protection.

Various arguments have been offered over the years for the justification of tariffs: (1) the infant-industry argument, (2) the national-self-sufficiency argument, (3) the home-industry argument, and (4) the protect-our-high-wages-and-standard-of-living argument. Opposing viewpoints to these arguments have also been offered.

Infant-Industry Argument.   The infant-industry argument contends that new industries need protection from mature foreign industries in order to start and grow to a size that helps them compete effectively.

Counterargument.   It is virtually impossible today to find an industry in the United States that competes with mature foreign industries. There are infant industries in the United States, but if they compete against foreign industries, they compete against other infant industries.

National-Self-Sufficiency Argument.   This argument contains some validity. The constant flux of world tensions forces nations to desire to be as self-sufficient as possible. Military considerations motivate nations in international trade to some extent. For example, during World War II, the only supply of rubber this country had was cut off by the Japanese. This threatened to be a crippling blow until synthetic rubber was developed and produced in large quantities.

Counterargument. National self-sufficiency is impossible in today's complex societies. In addition, to even attempt to become totally self-sufficient would require such inefficient use of resources that the nation's standard of living would drop to a low point unacceptable to people. Often, economic considerations are so important to nations that they work out some of their problems and learn to live together.

Home-Industry Argument. This commonly used argument for tariffs contends that the United States should protect its own industry from foreign competition because if the industry cannot compete, jobs will be lost.

Counterargument. Competition is the very basis of our economic system because we believe that by competing, business will constantly become more efficient and as a result provide continually increasing standards of living. By protecting domestic industry from foreign competition, we may foster domestic monopolies and not derive maximum benefit from competition. Within the United States' economic system, inefficient producers are forced from the market by the market system. The home-industry argument sells United States technology short in saying that American firms cannot compete with foreign goods in the open market.

Protect-Our-High-Wages-and-Standard-of-Living Argument. This argument contends that other countries have lower wage rates and, if allowed to compete with United States industry, will force down wages in the United States and as a result lower the standard of living.

Counterargument. Wages are higher in the United States because of the higher productivity of the worker as a result of skills, technology, and capital equipment. Higher productivity always results in higher standards of living. By protecting inefficient industry, the United States would not be able to compete as effectively in foreign markets. Since imports and exports are somewhat dependent on each other, we should remember that United States export trade results in jobs for millions of citizens. Also, consumers would be forced to pay higher prices for the goods they buy and as a result would have a lower standard of living.

BALANCE OF TRADE/ PAYMENTS

Balance of trade refers to the difference between the total value of exports and the total value of imports. A country is said to have a favorable balance of trade when it exports more than it imports. For example, if the United States sells $5 million of goods to a nation and buys $4 million worth in return, the balance of trade would be called favorable. The $1 million difference would be paid in international trade credits. This would be called a favorable **balance of payments.**

A continued large favorable balance of trade will cause changes in currency exchange. This causes other nations to have economic problems and they will often adopt countermeasures, resulting in problems for the favorable balance-of-trade nation. A continued large unfavorable balance of payments is not desirable because it destroys confidence in a nation's currency in the international market.

PROBLEMS IN INTERNATIONAL TRADE

Free world trade has the potential of bringing many benefits to all the people of the world. Unfortunately, it has not always worked that way. Various self-interest actions of nations have been the biggest problem in free trade.

Currency Exchange

Gold has traditionally been the standard of payment in international trade. Nations established the value of their currency in terms of gold, and payment in international trade was based on the value of the currencies in terms of gold. The United States maintained a value of $35 per fine ounce of gold for many years.

Exhibit 21–6

Exchange rates of the United States dollar into selected currencies.

U.S. Dollar =		
1.09	Australia/Dollar	
16.59	Austria/Schilling	
41.14	Belgium/Franc	
1.21	Canada/Dollar	
7.80	Denmark/Krone	
4.51	Finland/Markka	
6.02	France/Franc	
2.37	Germany/Deutsche Mark	
9.21	India/Rupee	
1.49	Ireland/Pound	
1,263.20	Italy/Lira	
235.31	Japan/Yen	
2.37	Malaysia/Ringgit	
31.74	Mexico/Peso	
2.59	Netherlands/Guilder	
79.33	New Zealand/Dollar	
5.97	Norway/Krone	
69.07	Portugal/Escudo	
1.02	South Africa/Rand	
100.70	Spain/Peseta	
5.76	Sweden/Krona	
1.89	Switzerland/Franc	
1.85	United Kingdom/Pound	

SOURCE: Federal Reserve Bulletin, March, 1982.

Balance-of-payment problems caused the United States to devalue the dollar in 1973 to $42.22 per fine ounce. As the balance-of-payment problem continued and the price of gold on the private market rose, the United States was forced to allow the dollar to float on the international market. **Floating currency** means that the federal government, in effect, removes its relationship to gold and allows the international money market to set the price of the dollar to other currencies on the basis of supply and demand. For example, the price of the dollar relative to the Japanese yen dropped from 305 yen in 1975 to 235 yen in 1982.

It would appear that allowing the dollar to float relative to other currency should eliminate a deficit balance of payments. For example, suppose the dollar has a value of 300 yen, the price of an American computer is 1,800,000 yen ($6,000) in Japan, and the price of a Japanese automobile is $6,000 (1,800,000 yen) in the United States. If the value of the dollar falls to 200 yen because of a United States trade deficit with Japan, the price of the American computer in Japan falls to 1,200,000 yen ($6,000) and the price of the Japanese automobile in the United States increases to $9,000 (1,800,000 yen). This decrease in the value of the dollar should mean that more United States computers will sell in Japan because of the price decrease. At the same time, more people in the United States should buy American-made automobiles and fewer Japanese automobiles because of the price increase on Japanese automobiles. This should tend to eliminate the deficit balance of payments. Unfortunately, it does not always have this result. Nations often take actions they think give them an advantage in international trade.

Nontariff Penalties

Some nations have signed agreements to lower tariffs in exchange for the United States' lowering tariffs. Unfortunately, some of them adopt import penalties, such as import quotas, which allow roughly the same amount of goods to enter their country as before the tariff reduction.

International Cartels

Nations sometimes join together to create an **international cartel** (monopoly), which eliminates price competition and artificially sets the price on some economic good. The Organization of Petroleum Exporting Countries (OPEC) is one example. Oil is a vital product to industrialized nations, and they will use it in vast quantities, even with large price increases. By eliminating competition and artificially setting the price, OPEC is able to increase the price almost at will and cause a continuing deficit-balance-of-payments problem for many nations.

The OPEC cartel is also an example of nations' restricting competitive world trade at the expense of other nations. OPEC has effectively eliminated competition for their oil by setting an arbitrary price. For several years, much of the world's inflation has been the direct or indirect result of this inflated oil price. Their price-setting has brought them enormous amounts of money at the expense of other nations. Nations that can least

The 60th OPEC Summit, May 1981, in Geneva.

afford it, the nonindustrialized countries, have often been the hardest hit. Food production is dependent on oil and natural gas for energy and fertilizer.

A few people feel OPEC actions may be a blessing in disguise. They feel OPEC is forcing other nations to find an alternate source of energy before the world's supply of oil is depleted.

For others, it is difficult to accept that actions which have resulted in serious economic problems for many nations are a blessing in disguise. They contend that the billions of dollars in trade deficits between the United States and OPEC nations are being converted into foreign ownership of corporation stock and land. They feel OPEC nations will be able to influence decisions in the United States long after alternate sources of energy are found.

Product Dumping

Some nations mass-produce products to keep the prices low, which allows them to compete better in international trade. When world demand for their products falls (often due to changes in currency valuation), the nation's industry may engage in **product dumping**—selling the product in another nation at below-cost prices in order to achieve an overall lower per unit fixed cost.

For example, suppose a business firm produces 2 million tires a year with fixed costs (upkeep of the plant, etc.) of $24 million and variable costs (labor, materials, etc.) of $16 million. This means each tire would cost them $12 in fixed costs ($24 million ÷ 2 million tires) and $8 in variable costs ($16 million ÷ 2 million tires) for a total of $20 per tire. If the demand for their tire fell to 1 million a year, their total costs would decrease but their cost per tire would increase. They would have roughly the same fixed costs because they must still operate the plant. They would have fixed costs of $24 million and variable costs of $8 million. This would amount to $24 per tire fixed cost ($24 million ÷ 1 million tires) and $8 per tire variable cost ($8 million ÷ 1 million tires). Their total cost per tire is now $32. If they sold their 1 million tires for $30 each, they would now have a loss of $2 million. However, if they produce 2 million and sell 1 million in some nations for $30 and dump the other million in other nations for $18, they will have an average price of $24 per tire, resulting in a profit of $8 million.

While this may be an advantage in one nation, it tends to cause balance-of-payment problems in the nation where the tires are dumped. Some officials in the United States contend this has been a part of our problem of trade deficits with some nations.

Commodity Speculation

One person or company can have little impact on the price of commodities in the international market because of the vast amount of money involved. However, nations have vast sums of money at their disposal. They can speculate on the international market and exert influence on supply and demand. For example, several years ago Russia bought vast amounts of wheat from Canada and the United States, much more than they needed. By removing this much wheat from the market, they were able to drive the price up and later sell the excess for several times what they paid for it.

MULTINATIONAL CORPORATIONS

Worldwide commerce has given rise to more and more corporations that have billions of dollars in assets and produce and market goods over large parts of the world. These have appropriately been named **multinational corporations.** They have been welcomed in many nations because they bring technology, employment, and increased wealth for the nations. These large multinational corporations are the primary vehicle for international trade and all the benefits it produces.

The large multinationals engage in international trade for profit. Often their export sales are a significant part of their total sales. For example, the largest exporting multinational based in the United States is Boeing Aircraft. Boeing has total sales of $9.4 billion, of which over half, $5.5 billion, are sales outside the United States.

Multinational corporations face several difficult problems. Language is often a problem. A slight error in a word may result in an insult or a serious misunderstanding of what has been said or agreed upon. Nations have widely varying customs. For example, in several nations it is considered extremely rude to discuss business until a considerable amount of time has been spent in social exchanges. The foreign businessperson who does not know this custom will not be successful in business dealings in these countries.

"THAT'S WHAT COMES FROM BEING A MULTI NATIONAL — THE COMPANY PICNIC IS GOING TO BE IN TIERRA DEL FUEGO."

It is also difficult for a multinational firm to know what products will sell in different countries and how the product should be sold and advertised. If the firm operates manufacturing operations in other nations, it faces the problem of what type of management will best suit its needs. The customs of the nation often contribute to the type of management that will be accepted. The constant shift of currency exchanges in the international market often create serious problems that can result in large losses of money.

One of the more serious problems in many parts of the world is nationalization of the firm's assets. For example, some multinational corporations have gone into underdeveloped nations with the latest technology and equipment. Using their technology and equipment, they have undertaken expensive exploration and development of valuable natural resources of the host nation. Some of these nations have very unstable political situations that have sometimes resulted in the government seizing and taking over the assets of the multinational corporation in that country.

In spite of all the problems multinational corporations encounter, it is obvious that they have contributed much to the well-being of people all over the world as a result of their worldwide search for profits.

The Twenty-five Largest Industrial Corporations in the World.

Rank	Company	Headquarters	Sales ($000)	Net Income ($000)
1	Exxon	New York	108,107,688	5,567,481
2	Royal Dutch/Shell Group	The Hague/London	82,291,728	3,642,142
3	Mobil	New York	64,488,000	2,433,000
4	General Motors	Detroit	62,698,500	333,400
5	Texaco	Harrison, N.Y.	57,628,000	2,310,000
6	British Petroleum	London	52,199,976	2,063,272
7	Standard Oil of California	San Francisco	44,224,000	2,380,000
8	Ford Motor	Dearborn, Mich.	38,247,100	(1,060,100)
9	Standard Oil (Ind.)	Chicago	29,947,000	1,922,000
10	ENI	Rome	29,444,315	383,234
11	International Business Machines	Armonk, N.Y.	29,070,000	3,308,000
12	Gulf Oil	Pittsburgh	28,252,000*	1,231,000
13	Atlantic Richfield	Los Angeles	27,797,436	1,671,290
14	General Electric	Fairfield, Conn.	27,240,000	1,652,000
15	Unilever	London/Rotterdam	24,095,898	800,379
16	E.I. du Pont de Nemours	Wilmington, Del.	22,810,000	1,401,000
17	Française des Pétroles	Paris	22,784,032	175,807
18	Shell Oil	Houston	21,629,000	1,701,000
19	Kuwait Petroleum	Safat (Kuwait)	20,556,871*	1,690,312*
20	Elf-Aquitaine	Paris	19,666,141	682,316
21	Petróleos de Venezuela	Caracas	19,659,115	3,316,040
22	Fiat	Turin (Italy)	19,608,480	N.A.
23	Petrobrás (Petróleo Brasileiro)	Rio de Janeiro	18,946,056	831,215
24	Pemex (Petróleos Mexicanos)	Mexico City	18,804,190	40,790
25	International Telephone & Tel.	New York	17,306,189	676,804

SOURCE: *Fortune*, August 23, 1982.

The Twenty-five Largest Exporters in the United States.

Rank	Company	Products	Exports ($000)	Sales ($000)
1	Boeing (Seattle)	Aircraft	6,105,600	9,788,200
2	General Motors (Detroit)	Motor vehicles and parts, locomotives	5,731,100	62,698,500
3	General Electric (Fairfield, Conn.)	Generating equipment, aircraft engines	4,348,000	27,240,000
4	Ford Motor (Dearborn, Mich.)	Motor vehicles and parts	3,743,000	38,247,100
5	Caterpillar Tractor (Peoria, Ill.)	Construction equipment, engines	3,513,000	9,154,500
6	McDonnell Douglas (St. Louis)	Aircraft, space systems, missiles	2,769,100	7,384,900
7	E.I. du Pont de Nemours (Wilmington, Del.)	Chemicals, fibers, polymer products, petroleum, coal	2,646,000	22,810,000
8	United Technologies (Hartford)	Aircraft engines, helicopters	2,636,437	13,667,758
9	International Business Machines (Armonk, N.Y.)	Information-handling systems, equipment, and parts	1,857,000	29,070,000
10	Eastman Kodak (Rochester, N.Y.)	Photographic equipment and supplies	1,803,000	10,337,000
11	Westinghouse Electric (Pittsburgh)	Generating equipment, defense systems	1,311,450	9,367,500
12	Signal Companies (La Jolla, Calif.)	Trucks, engines, chemicals, audio-video systems	1,218,800	5,342,600
13	Raytheon (Lexington, Mass.)	Electronic equipment, aircraft	1,148,000	5,636,184
14	Union Carbide (Danbury, Conn.)	Chemicals, plastics	1,090,000	10,168,000
15	Monsanto (St. Louis)	Herbicides, industrial chemicals, textile fibers	1,042,000	6,947,700
16	International Harvester (Chicago)	Construction and farm equipment, trucks	1,008,000	7,327,165
17	Hewlett-Packard (Palo Alto, Calif.)	Electronic equipment	971,000	3,578,000
18	Weyerhaeuser (Tacoma, Wash.)	Pulp, logs, lumber, wood products, newsprint	946,000	4,501,512
19	Dow Chemical (Midland, Mich.)	Chemicals, plastics, magnesium metal	924,000	11,873,000
20	Archer-Daniels-Midland (Decatur, Ill.)	Soybean meal and oil, wheat, corn	899,836	3,647,491
21	Exxon (New York)	Petroleum and chemicals	896,000	108,107,688
22	Philip Morris (New York)	Tobacco products	833,500	8,306,600
23	Occidental Petroleum (Los Angeles)	Agricultural chemical products, coal	765,000	14,707,543
24	Ingersoll-Rand (Woodcliff Lake, N.J.)	Drills, compressors, pumps, bearings, tools	758,800	3,377,564
25	Northrop (Los Angeles)	Aircraft and related support services	716,400	1,990,700

SOURCE: *Fortune*, August 9, 1982.

SUMMARY OF KEY POINTS

1. International trade results in increased standards of living for all people of the world.

2. Every nation has factors (such as natural resources, labor, technology, or climate) that create a national advantage in trade for some products.

3. No nation in the world possesses all natural resources in sufficient abundance to support a complex industrial society.

4. Low wage rates create a distinct national advantage for some products but they are not permanent in nations that are rapidly developing into industrial nations.

5. Technology is the most important advantage a nation may possess and it can overcome many disadvantages of international trade.

6. The three types of barriers to free world trade are quotas, embargoes, and tariffs.

7. Quotas restrict the amount of a product that may be brought into a country.

8. Embargoes prohibit goods from entering a country and may exist for one or more reasons—health, political, and/or moral.

9. Tariffs are taxes placed on imports to protect domestic industry from foreign competition. There are several arguments both for and against tariffs.

10. Self-interest actions of nations have been the biggest problem in free trade.

11. Some nations use nontariff penalties (such as import quotas) after they agree to lower tariffs.

12. International cartels, such as OPEC, eliminate price competition and artificially set the price on some economic goods.

13. Some nations produce products and "dump" part of their production at below cost in selected countries.

14. Some nations have manipulated the price of commodities on the world market for their own gain.

15. Multinational corporations face several problems in their international operations, such as language, customs, marketing, management, currency exchange, and nationalization of assets.

DISCUSSION QUESTIONS

1. Should the United States engage in international trade? Explain.
2. What are some of the national advantages of the United States?
3. Should the United States engage in any of the three barriers to trade? Explain.
4. What is the difference between a favorable balance of trade and a favorable balance of payments? What is their relationship?
5. What do you think the United States should do about problems in international trade?

STUDENT PROJECTS

1. Go to a local shopping area and identify ten items that were imported for sale in this country.
2. Identify the country from which these items came.
3. Give the reasons why you think each item is able to compete in this country's marketplace.
4. Go to the library and find out the amount of the United States' current balance of payments.

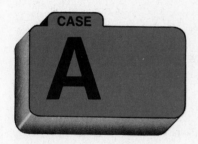

Senator James Backer

Senator James Backer has just made a speech at your college. The senator spoke at length on the topic of international trade. The major points of his speech were:

1. Imports into our country should be greatly reduced because they hurt our standard of living.
2. We should eliminate embargoes because they are of little use, but we do need quotas and tariffs.
3. We need tariffs to:
   a. Produce revenue;
   b. Protect our infant industry;
   c. Make people buy at home because it is patriotic;
   d. Keep us militarily strong;
   e. Protect American wages.
4. Other nations often take actions against free world trade.

Question

Evaluate each of the senator's statements.

Charles Rivers

Charles Rivers is a lobbyist who represents several major oil producers as well as a group of manufacturers who produce a wide range of products (including textiles, autos, and shoes). These firms are vitally concerned about protecting their markets at home. Hence, they would like to see Congress pass a stronger protectionist trade policy of restricting foreign imports. Currently, congressmen are discussing legislation that would increase the importation of these products into the United States. As a result, Charles Rivers is sent to Washington to lobby against the introduction of this new legislation. His first appointment is with Senator Hand, who is the coauthor of the legislative bill to allow increases in importation.

Questions

1. What arguments can Mr. Rivers use to convince Senator Hand not to introduce this legislation?
2. What are the arguments Senator Hand can use to counteract Mr. Rivers's points?

BUSINESS PROFILE

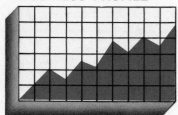

The Southland Corporation

The Southland Corporation, founded in Dallas, Texas, in 1927, is the world's largest operator and franchisor of convenience stores and the nation's 13th largest retailer.

Southland pioneered the convenience store concept during its first year of operation when its retail ice outlets sold milk, bread, and eggs as a convenience to customers.

Today, its 7,033 7-Eleven stores, located in neighborhoods across the nation and Canada, serve almost seven million customers every day. Each 7-Eleven store carries a product mix of more than 3,000 items, including groceries, dairy products, newspapers and magazines, tobacco, soft drinks, beer, housewares, and health and beauty aids. Other items like self-service gasoline, now in 2,517 7-Eleven stores, are constantly being added.

Southland's activities are grouped into three lines of business—a Stores Group, a Dairies Group, and a Special Operations Group—whose combined sales exceeded $5.73 billion in 1981.

The Stores Group operates and franchises 7,033 7-Eleven stores in 42 states, the District of Columbia, and five provinces of Canada. Other retail operations include 97 Gristede's and Charles & Co. food stores and sandwich shops in metropolitan New York, as well as outlets in other countries, such as Great Britain, Sweden, and Mexico.

The name "7-Eleven" originated in 1946 when the stores were open from 7 A.M. to 11 P.M. Now approximately 95 percent of the stores are open longer than the traditional hours, with 6,328 open 24 hours.

The neighborhood stores are operated by Southland under the decades-old but updated and modernized concept of the "Mom and Pop" stores. Forty percent of the stores are operated by franchisees; many are couples with children who also work in the store.

A modern 7-Eleven store in Japan.

Typical 7-Eleven stores are suburban drive-in stores with parking, but 7-Eleven also operates "city stores" in urban neighborhoods of New York City, Philadelphia, Boston, and San Francisco.

John P. Thompson, Southland's chairman of the board and chief executive officer, and Jere W. Thompson, president, are the sons of the late Joe C. Thompson, who as a young ice company executive started the convenience store idea.

Listed on the New York Stock Exchange in 1972, Southland has nearly 7,400 public shareholders and 23.7 million common shares outstanding. The company has established an excellent growth record with a 17.2 percent compound growth rate in revenues and a 20 percent compound growth rate in net earnings per share during the past five years.

22 Legal Environment of Business

LEARNING GOALS

After reading this chapter, you will understand:

1. The legal system of the United States as it applies to business.

2. The five types of law and their functions.

3. The difference between civil and criminal law and how each functions with respect to businesses.

4. The requirements for having a valid enforceable contract.

5. What the law will allow you to do when there is breach of contract.

6. The importance of the Uniform Commercial Code to business in the United States.

7. The relationship between principals, agents, and third parties, and the duties of each.

8. Negotiable instruments and how they are used.

KEY TERMS

Law	Recourse	Bond
United States Constitution	Uniform Commercial Code	Bill of exchange
State constitutions	Principal	Check
Common law	Agent	Money order
Civil law	Negotiable instrument	Letters of credit
Criminal law	Promissory note	Documents of title
Contracts	Bank note	Bill of lading
Mutual assent	Certificate of deposit	Warehouse receipts
Duress		Trust receipt
Undue influence		

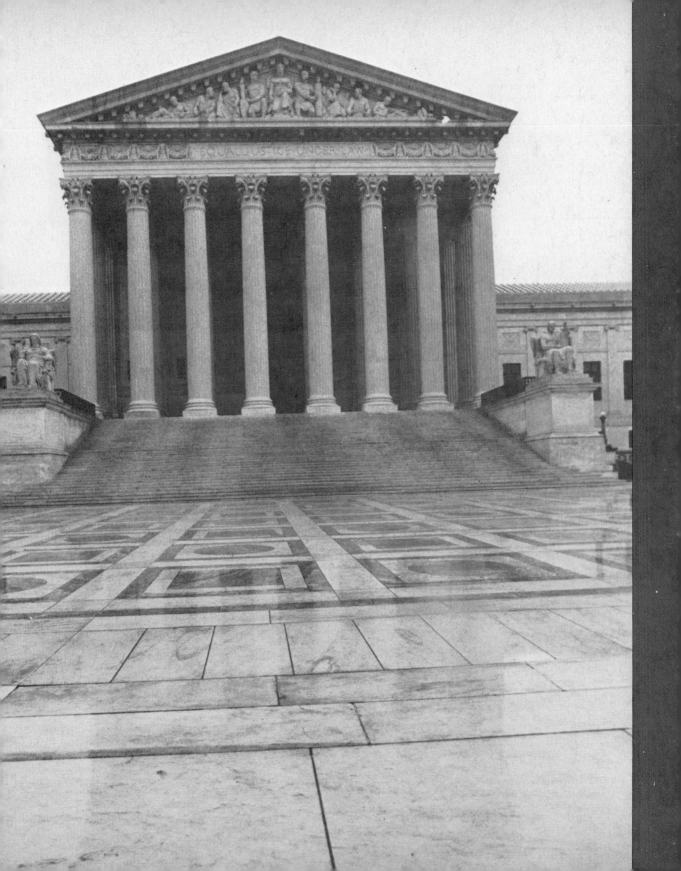

Law is a rule of action or conduct created by an organized political government. Law differs from morals, ethics, and custom in that it is prescribed and enforced by government. Law is not constant, but is continually being altered to meet the requirements of a changing society.

Law in the United States has several features that are vital to the operation of business enterprises as they exist in our society—rights of private property, the free-enterprise system, freedom of contract, and the inviolability of contract.

TYPES OF LAW

Business firms function within the confines of five basic types of law—United States constitution, federal statutes, state constitutions, state statutes, and common law. See Exhibit 22–1.

United States Constitution

The **United States Constitution** is the basic law of the United States to which all other law must conform. The United States Constitution performs three functions: it (1) prescribes the form and powers of government, (2) guarantees certain rights, and (3) sets the procedure for amendment.

Federal Statutes

The Congress of the United States enacts legislation within the limits fixed by the United States Constitution. These areas of legislation produce the following legal actions:

1. Raise money by taxation and duties;
2. Borrow money on credit;
3. Regulate commerce between states and foreign countries;
4. Establish uniform rules on naturalization;
5. Set bankruptcy laws;
6. Coin and control money—punish for counterfeiting;
7. Maintain standards of weights and measures;
8. Create post offices and post roads;
9. Establish copyright and patent laws;
10. Create federal courts;
11. Set punishment for violation of international law;
12. Declare war;

13. Raise and support armies;
14. Maintain a navy;
15. Govern the District of Columbia.

State Constitutions

All powers not delegated by the Constitution to the federal government are delegated to the states. The state constitutions establish the form and powers of the state governments.

Civil Law and Criminal Law

Another classification of types of law exists in the difference between civil and criminal law. Civil law refers to conflicts and differences between individuals such as legal actions involving recourse of contracts. Criminal law, on the other hand, exists to maintain law and order and refers to criminal acts such as murder, arson, and theft.

Common Law

Common law is also often accurately referred to as *unwritten law.* Judges establish these laws by interpreting federal and state constitutions and statutes and reaching decisions that set precedents. The basis of common law is the doctrine that forces judges to uphold former decisions as far as is reasonably possible.

State Statutes

The individual states may pass legislation within the confines of their state constitutions. There are considerable differences in law between the fifty states due to a wide range of state statutes. Although the state statutes must function within the constitution and federal statutes, there is considerable leeway for differences in state legislation–legalized gambling in Nevada is an excellent example.

AREAS OF LAW THAT RELATE TO BUSINESS

The section of law that applies to business transactions is generally known as business law or commercial law. In addition to contracts, business law deals with a wide range of topics of concern to business. Some of the more important laws relate to negotiable instruments, sales contracts, warranties, bailments, transportation agencies, trans-

Exhibit 22–1
The basic legal system of the United States.

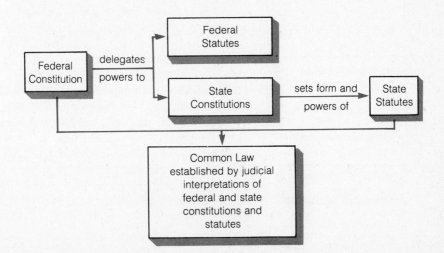

portation of goods, suretyship and guaranty, insurance, principal and agent, employer and employee, partnerships, corporations, government regulation of business, landlord and tenant, real property, personal property, mortgages, liens, debtor and creditor, and civil procedure.

CONTRACTS

Without **contracts,** businesses would be unable to enter into agreements with any assurance of their being completed. Considering all the written or verbal contracts a business person enters into, it is easy to understand why business would not be able to function in a complex society without legal contracts and different forms of recourse if contractual obligations are not fulfilled.

Requirement for Valid Contracts

In order for contracts to be valid under law, they must meet several requirements. These requirements are established by law in each state, but in general, contracts must be made by competent parties who give consideration for a legal purpose with mutual assent and they must be in a form that is legal. See Exhibit 22–2.

Competent Parties.   Both parties to the contract must be competent for the contract to be valid. Incompetent parties who may not enter into legal enforceable contracts are drunkards, insane persons, persons under the legal adult age (states determine legal age and eighteen is the most common age), and convicts. Persons under legal adult age are considered children but have the right to make contracts; however, while they may hold adults with whom they make contracts liable to the contract, they are not liable themselves. Common exceptions are contracts for necessities of life and misrepresentation of age by the child. In addition, under certain circumstances a person under legal adult age may appeal to the courts and be adjudged an adult in special circumstances.

One can say insane persons and drunkards are incompetent parties, but it is another matter to prove it in actual practice. An insane person must be declared insane under legal processes before being considered insane for legal purposes. By the same token, intoxication is not ordinarily a defense to a contract. A confirmed drunkard must be adjudged incompetent and a guardian appointed.

Consideration.   Both parties to the contract must give something of value for the contract to be valid and enforceable. Consideration may be in the form of money, property, services, or some sacrifice. In fact, if an uncle were to promise his nephew $100 to give up smoking for a year, then it would be a valid enforceable contract because the uncle promises $100 in consideration and the nephew, in giving up his right to smoke, makes a sacrifice. If only one party to a contract gives consideration, the contract is not valid or enforceable.

Exhibit 22–2
Requirements for a valid and enforceable contract.

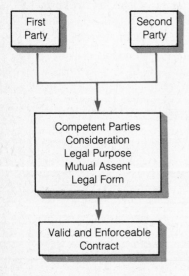

Legal Purpose. A contract is not enforceable by law if it provides for actions that are not acceptable by law. Any contract that calls for criminal or civil wrongs is not a valid contract. For example, a contract in which one person agrees to beat up another person in exchange for money is not a valid and enforceable contract because it calls for a criminal act. In addition, a contract between two businesses that provides for price fixing is not a valid enforceable contract because it requires action that is a civil wrong under law.

Mutual Assent. For a contract to be valid and enforceable, both parties must enter into it of their own free will. **Mutual assent** is not realized when there is fraud, mistake, duress, and undue influence.

Fraud. No legal contract exists when fraud is present. Fraud is intentional misrepresentation of material fact inducing one party to contract to his injury. An example of fraudulent misrepresentation would be a produce dealer selling a crate of supposedly high-quality tomatoes that has rotten tomatoes hidden underneath.

Mistake. If one party to a contract makes a mistake and the other party is aware of the mistake and enters into a contract based on the mistake, the contract is not valid. Our produce dealer might enter into a contract to sell twenty crates of tomatoes. If he made a mistake in the contract in multiplying the price and the buyer knew of the mistake, the contract would not be enforceable.

Duress. Action causing a person to perform an act against his will is **duress** and, if present in a contract, it voids the contract. As an illustration, if the produce dealer were to threaten to harm a person if he didn't buy tomatoes, the sale would be illegal.

Undue Influence. Undue influence exists when one person uses influence upon another, causing assent that is not voluntary, yet is not duress. It exists when one person in a professional or other superior position influences a person in a dependent or trusting position for his own gain rather than for the benefit of the dependent party. Some of the relationships where **undue influence** could occur would be guardian and ward, principal and agent, attorney and client, and physician and patient.

Legal Form. A contract need not take any specific form as long as it meets the requirements of the state law. Generally, contracts may be written or verbal; however, most states limit verbal contracts. It is quite common that transactions involving real property (defined as buildings, land, timber, crops, or anything affixed to land) must be in writing. In addition, many states require that contracts involving personal property

Simplified Legal Instruments

There is a considerable movement in the business world to simplify legal documents so that the layperson can understand them. A few examples are installment sales contracts, insurance policies, and promissory notes. Compare the two promissory notes shown here and decide which you prefer.

Form 136—2-76

INDIVIDUAL NOTE
(Straight Note)

No. _____ $ _____ _____, California _____, 19 ___

On demand, or if no demand, on _____, for value received, the undersigned ("Debtor" herein) promises to pay to

("Bank" herein), or order at its _____ office, the

sum of _____ Dollars ($ _____) with

interest from _____ at the annual rate of _____ percent payable _____

ACCELERATION OF MATURITY

On the occurrence of any of the following, Bank shall have the right to declare the entire balance of principal and interest immediately due and payable in full: If there is a failure to make any payment when due; or if Debtor or any guarantor hereof a) dies, b) becomes insolvent, c) defaults in payment of any debt to Bank, d) commits an act of bankruptcy, e) suffers a material adverse change of financial condition, f) defaults with respect to any order, judgment, injunction, decree, writ or demand of any court or other public authority, or g) if Bank in good faith believes that the prospect of payment is impaired. The entire balance of principal and interest shall be immediately due and payable in full; without demand, if Debtor or any guarantor hereof: a) makes an assignment for the benefit of creditors, b) is the subject of any voluntary or involuntary filing under any federal bankruptcy law, any receivership proceedings, or under any federal or state law for the relief of debtors, c) is the subject of any dissolution or liquidation proceedings, d) has issued against him or his property any writ of attachment, execution, or other legal process, or e) has filed or recorded against him or his property any notice of levy, notice to withhold, or other claim for taxes other than property taxes.

INTEREST AFTER MATURITY DATE

The total amount of principal and interest unpaid on the maturity date stated above shall thereafter bear interest at a rate per annum four percent (4%) per annum higher than the interest rate stated above, which Debtor agrees to pay.

RELEASE OF CREDIT INFORMATION

Debtor authorizes Bank to release information concerning Debtor's credit worthiness, record, and standing to other creditors and to credit bureaus, consumer reporting agencies, and other credit reporters.

ADDITIONAL AGREEMENTS OF DEBTOR

Debtor, without demand, shall pay all costs and expenses of collection, including attorneys' fees, incurred in the enforcement of this note. Debtor and any sureties, guarantors, and endorsers hereof hereby consent to renewals and extensions of time before, at, or after the maturity hereof, and waive diligence, presentment, demand, notice of nonpayment, protest, notice of protest, and notice of every kind, and waive the right to set up the defense of any statute of limitations to any debt or obligation hereunder. Such waiver of defenses shall be effective for the maximum period of time and to the full extent permissible by law. If this note is signed by more than one person the obligations of the signers shall be joint and several. Each spouse signing this note assents to the liability of his or her separate property for all debts and obligations hereunder. The term "Debtor" includes any successors in interest of Debtor. The term "Bank" includes any holder of this note.

_____ DEBTOR

_____ DEBTOR

Instalment Loan Agreement
Crocker National Bank

(Office) _____
(Address) _____

Dear Customer:
We're happy to make this loan to you. This is the agreement that covers it. If you agree to its terms please sign it in the lower right-hand corner.

Promise to pay.
You promise to pay us at one of our branches or by mail $ _____ in _____ instalments. Your instalments will be: _____ equal uninterrupted monthly instalments of $ _____ each on the _____ day of each month starting _____, 19 ___.

_____
_____
_____

Breakdown.
This is what you'll pay:

1. Amount of loan $ _____

2. Credit insurance premium

   a. Credit life $ _____

   b. Credit life and disability $ _____

3. Amount financed (1 + 2) $ _____

4. **Finance charge** (interest) $ _____

5. **Annual percentage rate** _____ %

6. Total of payments (3 + 4) $ _____

70-072 (10-75) **Unsecured Loan**

Late charge.
If you haven't paid an instalment within 10 days after it's due, you promise to pay a late charge of **5%** of the overdue instalment but no more than **$15** nor less than **$1.** You also promise to pay interest at the rate of **10%** a year on all instalments from their due date until paid.

Whole balance due.
If you have not paid an instalment within 10 days of the date it's due, we can without notice or demand declare the whole outstanding loan balance due and payable at once. If we do, you promise to pay all collection costs and reasonable lawyers' fees.

Your right to prepay loan.
You can prepay the whole outstanding loan balance anytime. If you do, we'll refund the unearned part of the FINANCE CHARGE figured by the "sum of the balances" method – a formula used for figuring refunds on instalment loans. But we won't return any refund less than **$1.** We'll also subtract whatever's necessary from your refund to make sure we've earned a total FINANCE CHARGE of at least **$20** on your loan. This is our minimum FINANCE CHARGE.

Our right to set-off.
Except as prohibited by law, we have the right to set-off amounts due or declared by us to be due on the loan against deposit balances (for example, savings and checking accounts) you have with us at the time such amounts become due. We can do this without prior notice or demand.

Loan not secured.
Subject to our right of set-off, this loan is not secured – no matter what any agreement you now have says.

Credit insurance not needed.
You don't have to take out credit life insurance or credit life and disability insurance to get this loan. Such insurance will not be provided in connection with the loan unless a charge for it is shown in item 2 above and the person to be insured signs a separate application for it.

Thank you for taking out this loan with us.

I've read this agreement and received a copy before signing. I agree to its terms and that my obligations under the agreement are joint and several.

Customer: _____
Address: _____

Customer: _____
Address: _____

Date: _____

(defined as anything that is not affixed to land, such as clothing, automobiles, and tools) in amounts over $500 must be written.

In actual practice, most contracts are verbal. For instance, when you read the menu in a restaurant and order the food, you enter into a verbal contract that requires you to pay the check. Normal daily transactions involving both businesses and individuals would be impossible without verbal contracts. However, contracts involving significant amounts of money should be made in writing although as verbal contracts they may be valid enforceable contracts under law. The matter of proof in courts of law is much simpler with written contracts and sometimes virtually impossible with verbal agreements.

Some types of written contracts must also be filed with the county clerk so that they become public records. One example is a land deed.

Recourse

When a valid enforceable contract under law is not fulfilled by one party (breach of contract), the other party to the contract has certain recourse under the law. **Recourse** includes discharge, performance, and damages.

Discharge. If one party to the contract fails to comply to the terms of the contract, the other party to the contract is under no obligation to proceed with the contract. For example, if a contract of sale requires a down payment, the seller does not have to deliver the goods if the down payment is not received.

Performance. The courts may require performance of the contract. For example, two persons enter into an option contract for the sale of land. A land owner signs a contract giving a buyer the right to buy a certain parcel of land within sixty days. The buyer gives the land owner $100 as consideration to be applied against the purchase price of the land if he buys it and to be forfeited to the land owner if the buyer does not exercise his option within sixty days. The buyer notifies the land owner within the time limit and with the method of notification specified in the option contract that he wishes to purchase the land. In the meantime, the owner has received an offer of more money for the land and refuses to transfer title of the land to the original buyer. The courts will force compliance and title will be transferred under the conditions of the option contract.

Damages. Parties to a valid contract are liable to each other for damages as a result of nonperformance of the contract. For example, an entertainer might contract to appear in a performance and negligently fail to appear. The owner of the establishment would be entitled to the amount of profit that was not received because of the entertainer's failure to appear. In addition, the owner, under certain circumstances, may collect additional damages for the loss of reputation of the business.

Exhibit 22–3
Recourse under law when breach of contract occurs.

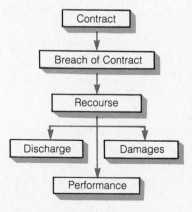

UNIFORM COMMERCIAL CODE

Until the Uniform Commercial Code, published in 1952, was adopted by the states, judges were faced with diverse commercial statutes, which often resulted in conflicting rulings.

The most important statute that has evolved in commercial law recently is the **Uniform Commercial Code.**

A very large percentage of business law results from state action. All fifty states are empowered separately to create laws encompassing a wide variety of commercial activities. As a result, during the early history of the United States, the different states evolved diverse statutes and conflicting judicial rulings. As commerce became larger in size and transactions became more complex, confusion and problems rapidly increased as a result of the nonconforming business laws of the various states. The enormous mass of statutes and judicial rulings that existed among the various states was virtually impenetrable by business firms that operated in multistate territories.

Since only the states could pass laws in these areas of commercial law, it became vital for these states to pass uniform statutes if the rapidly growing modern business world was to function properly. The National Conference of Commissioners on Uniform State Laws was established in 1890 to formulate uniform statutes to be recommended for adoption by the various states. Over the years this conference formulated more than sixty uniform statutes, most of which were adopted by many states.

The resulting Uniform Commercial Code was first published in 1952, and after much discussion was revised into its present form in 1958. Every state except Louisiana has adopted the Uniform Commercial Code, which has been of great value to both business and consumers.

The major areas of commercial law contained in the Uniform Commercial Code are as follows:

ARTICLE I   GENERAL PROVISIONS
ARTICLE II   SALES
ARTICLE III   COMMERCIAL PAPER
ARTICLE IV   BANK DEPOSITS AND COLLECTS
ARTICLE V   LETTERS OF CREDIT
ARTICLE VI   BULK TRANSFERS
ARTICLE VII   WAREHOUSE RECEIPTS, BILLS OF LADING, AND OTHER DOCUMENTS OF TITLE
ARTICLE VIII   INVESTMENT SECURITIES
ARTICLE IX   SECURED TRANSACTIONS, SALES OF ACCOUNTS, CONTRACT RIGHTS, AND CHATTEL PAPER
ARTICLE X   EFFECTIVE DATE AND REPEAL OF OTHER LAWS

THE LAW OF AGENCY

In very small businesses the owner performs almost all functions, and there is little need for a principal/agent relationship. However, in larger businesses it becomes impossible for the owner or owners to perform all functions, and they must depend on others to act for them in many situations. The law of agency is very important to these businesses because it controls the relationship between the **principal** (the person(s) being represented), the **agent** (the person(s) acting for the principal), and the third party.

Duties of Principal to Agent

The principal owes four primary duties and obligations to the agent:

1. To pay the agent for his or her services.
2. To reimburse the agent for any expenses incurred as a result of his or her services.
3. To pay the agent for any reasonable losses incurred due to his or her services, in order to shield the agent from normal risk.
4. To pay damages to the agent for any breach of contract by the principal.

Duties of Agent to Principal

The agent owes four primary duties and obligations to the principal.

1. To act with loyalty and good faith in the best interests of the principal.
2. To obey the instructions of the principal.
3. To perform his or her services with the necessary skill, care, and diligence demanded by the task.
4. To make a complete accounting of all money and property belonging to the principal.

Duties of Principal to Third Parties

The principal is liable to third parties for all legal contracts made by the agent. The principal has the same legal responsibilities and rights that would exist if the principal had made the contract personally.

NEGOTIABLE INSTRUMENTS

A **negotiable instrument** is a special type of contract that can pass freely from person to person in the form of a credit instrument or substitute for money. It is an instrument of value that can be assigned to another person by endorsement (signing one's name to the certificate and indicating passing of ownership) or sometimes just by delivery. See Exhibit 22–4.

The Uniform Commercial Code requires four conditions of a negotiable instrument:

1. It must be in writing and signed by the maker.
2. It must contain a promise to pay a certain sum of money.
3. It must be payable on demand or payable at a specified time.
4. It must be payable to a specific person or payable to the bearer.

Negotiable instruments are basically of two types: (1) promissory notes, and (2) bills of exchange. Another category, documents of title, are negotiable but are not considered pure negotiable instruments because they involve merchandise or goods. However, they are negotiable or semi-negotiable.

Promissory Notes

In a **promissory note** one person promises to pay another person a certain sum of money. Common types of promissory notes are bank notes, certificates of deposit, and bonds.

Exhibit 22–4

Types of negotiable instruments.

Promissory Notes
One person promises to pay another person a certain sum of money.
1. Bank Notes—Bank issued currency.
2. Certificates of Deposit—Certify money on deposit that can be transferred to another person.
3. Bonds—Debt instruments that collect interest and can be transferred to another person.

Bills of Exchange
Written order from one party to another party (usually a bank) to pay a third party a certain sum of money.
1. Checks—Negotiable instruments drawn against demand deposits in bank.
2. Money Orders—Purchased from post office or express office—seller pays third party certain sum of money.
3. Letters of Credit—Bank guarantees credit-granting holder will be paid.

Documents of Title
Certifies ownership of merchandise that can be transferred by endorsement.
1. Bills of Lading—Certify ownership of goods in transit.
2. Warehouse Receipts—Certify ownership of goods in storage.
3. Trust Receipts—Certify title of goods being held by creditor.

Bank Notes. A bank note is a note issued by a bank (a bank authorized to do so by the government) that is payable to the bearer on demand and is intended to circulate as money. The bearer of the note is assumed to be the owner of the note. The Federal Reserve note is a bank note.

Certificates of Deposit. A certificate of deposit is an instrument signed by a bank that states that a person has on deposit a certain sum of money payable to him or someone he designates at a time specified in the certificate.

Bonds. A bond is a certificate issued by a business corporation or a government (see chapter 3). It promises to pay the person to whom it is assigned a certain sum of money at a specified time. It also promises that interest will be paid at fixed intervals. The person to whom the bond is registered may transfer it by endorsement. A special type of bond, the bearer bond, is not registered and is payable to the person who presents it for payment.

Bills of Exchange

A bill of exchange contains a written order by one party to another party (usually a bank) to pay a third party a specified sum of money. Common types of bills of exchange are checks, money orders, and letters of credit.

Checks. Checks are negotiable instruments ordering a bank to pay someone a certain sum of money on demand. They are issued against demand deposits held by the bank for the person issuing the check. The person who receives the check may endorse it to someone else by simply signing his or her name to the back of the check. As indicated in chapter 14, demand deposits are considered money and account for over 50 percent of our money supply.

Money Orders. A money order is just like a check except that it is purchased at a post office, bank, or express office and is payable at a post office, bank, or express office. It is an order to pay a specific person a certain sum of money on demand. Only one endorsement is permitted on a money order.

Letters of Credit. A letter of credit is a written request that money be advanced or credit be given to a specific person. The bank issuing the letter of credit guarantees payment of the money. Letters of credit are usually used for out-of-town, state, or country transactions of business. The local bank is telling the business or bank that it knows the person and stands behind payment of the account.

Documents of Title

Documents of title are instruments that denote ownership of merchandise or goods which can be transferred by endorsement. Common types of documents of title are bills of lading, warehouse receipts, and trust receipts.

Bills of Lading. When merchandise is shipped by a carrier, a bill of lading is issued by the carrier. Usually bills of lading are not negotiable; however, a special type, called an "order bill of lading," is negotiable. The person named to receive the shipment may endorse it to another party, who then has the right to receive the shipment.

Warehouse Receipts. A warehouse receipt is a receipt issued by the warehouse when it receives goods for storage. This receipt can then be endorsed to another party. A common practice is for a person or business borrowing money to endorse the receipt to a financial institution as collateral against the loan. When the loan is paid, the receipt is endorsed back to the borrower.

Trust Receipts. A trust receipt is used when a person or business wishes to borrow money from a bank to purchase merchandise. The bank advances money to the customer to buy merchandise and takes the bill of lading for the goods in the bank's name. The goods are given to the purchaser, but the title remains with the bank. The money received from sale of the goods is given to the bank until the original purchase price plus interest is repaid.

SUMMARY OF KEY POINTS

1. Law differs from morals, ethics, and customs in that it is prescribed and enforced by government.

2. Business firms function within the confines of five types of law—the United States Constitution, federal statutes, state constitutions, state statutes, and common law.

3. The United States Constitution sets the powers of government, guarantees certain rights, and sets procedures for amendment.

4. Federal statutes are acts of legislation set within the limits fixed by the United States Constitution and generally deal with interstate matters.

5. State constitutions establish the form and powers of each state government. State statutes must be within the confines of the state's constitution and they vary from state to state.

6. Common law is unwritten law that is set by judges interpreting law. Civil law deals with conflict between individuals, while criminal law exists to maintain law and order.

7. Legal requirements for valid contracts are established by each state; however, generally, they must be made by competent parties who give consideration, for a legal purpose, with mutual assent, and in a form that is legal.

8. Generally, contracts must be written or verbal; however, most states impose certain limitations on verbal contracts.

9. When there is breach of contract, the law provides for remedies that include discharge of contract, performance of contract, and damages.

10. The most important statute evolved in commercial law recently is the Uniform Commercial Code, which provides conformity among the various states' commercial laws.

11. The law of agency establishes the duties of the principal, the agent, and the third party.

12. Negotiable instruments are basically of two types, promissory notes and bills of exchange. Documents of title are negotiable or seminegotiable, but they involve merchandise or goods.

13. The most common types of promissory notes are bank notes, certificates of deposit, and bonds.

14. The more common types of bills of exchange are checks, money orders, and letters of credit.

15. Some of the more common types of documents of title are bills of lading, warehouse receipts, and trust receipts.

DISCUSSION QUESTIONS

1. How does law differ from morals, ethics, and customs?
2. Explain how the five basic types of law relate to each other.
3. In general, with whom would you enter into a contract?
4. What type of consideration may be given in a contract? Must it be money?
5. Is an IOU for a gambling debt a valid enforceable contract in your state? Explain.
6. If you signed a contract with another person and he did not live up to his part of the contract, what could you do?
7. Give one example each of contracts that are invalid because of mistake, duress, fraud, and undue influence.
8. Do you feel your state should conform to the Uniform Commercial Code? Explain.
9. Identify a situation in which an agent might be used and point out how the principal-agent relation would function.
10. If you owned a retail clothing store, what types of negotiable instruments might you use and for what purpose?

STUDENT PROJECTS

1. Obtain a blank copy of some contract form (a promissory note or an installment sales contract) from some business in your community.
2. Fill in the contract with fictitious information and names.
3. Examine your contract to see if it would meet all the requirements of a valid contract.
4. Bring several forms of negotiable instruments to class to show.

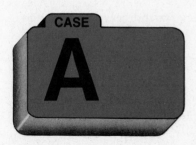

A Jupiter Dealership

The Jupiter Motor Company was recently organized for the purpose of manufacturing a line of sports cars. The plant is located in New Orleans, Louisiana, with the first car to come off the assembly line in just two months. The Jupiter automobile will be manufactured in three different styles. The Jupiter offers three motor choices: a 4-cylinder, 90-horsepower motor; a V6, 150-horsepower motor; and a V8, 210-horsepower motor. The 90-horsepower Jupiter weighs 2,000 pounds and gas mileage ranges from 26 to 34 miles per gallon, depending on the driving conditions and the driver. The V8 car will appeal to the speed-conscious motorist. It has a top speed of 150 miles per hour and reaches 60 miles per hour from a dead stop in six seconds. The V6 combines power with a reasonable gas mileage. All three Jupiters are built along the sports car concept with prices ranging from $6,000 to $7,000. The company expects to distribute the cars nationally to established dealers.

You have acquired an exclusive dealership in your area to market the Jupiter Sports Car. Construction of your showroom, service department, and body shop is presently under way. In order to sell the automobiles, you realize that you must finance them to the customers. Floor planning is available, but you have decided that if you can obtain financing, you would rather extend the credit in order to be able to receive the credit rate difference between what you borrow at and what you will charge.

A local investment agency has agreed to extend you a $550,000 line of credit at 14 percent interest. You plan to finance installment sales contracts at the prevailing interest rate of 18 percent from the line of credit.

However, to initiate the installment sales contracts, you must find out how to be certain that the contracts are binding and be aware of actions you may take if they are not fulfilled.

Questions

1. Investigate each requirement for a valid contract to determine if any potential problem might arise in the future.

2. What recourse could you follow if the conditions of the contract were violated?

3. If you filed suit against a customer for violation of contract, what kind of legal action would it be, criminal or civil?

4. Name several principal/agent relationships that would probably exist in the business. Select one and define the duties of the principal, agent, and third party in terms of the type of service the agent will perform.

5. What kind of negotiable instruments might you use in the dealership? Explain.

Henry Dallas

As part of the planning for his restaurant, Henry Dallas (see Case B, chapter 3) recognizes the need for legal advice before entering into any type of business agreement. He has read and heard of some of the unfortunate experiences others have encountered because they entered into business arrangements without first seeking legal advice. He recalls from his college days that his business law professor constantly stressed the importance of legal preparation before making any binding agreements. Henry hopes to have the following questions answered when he visits his lawyer tomorrow:

Questions

1. What is necessary for a contract to be binding to the parties involved?

2. If I sign a contract and fail to perform to its terms, what legal action could be taken against me?

3. Of what importance is the Uniform Commercial Code to me as a small-business owner?

BUSINESS PROFILE

American Telephone and Telegraph Company

The importance of the legal system is aptly illustrated by the early days of the American Telephone and Telegraph Company. What was then the Bell Telephone Company fought for protection of Alexander Graham Bell's invention through numerous court suits.

Alexander Graham Bell patented and spoke the first words through a telephone in 1876. Success for such an outstanding invention did not come automatically to Bell after he and several associates formed the Bell Telephone Company. Perhaps their greatest difficulty came in fighting against what they considered infringements on Bell's patent. The biggest battle was with the powerful Western Union Telegraph Company, which was trying to branch into the telephone business using equipment developed by other people.

It was a legal battle pitting a small, new company against an enormous, well-established, and well-financed company. The Bell Telephone Company tested the strength of the American legal system and won all its legal battles, including the one against Western Union.

From this embattled beginning, the American Telephone and Telegraph Company has grown to be one of the largest business organizations in the world. Today, AT&T has over 3 million stockholders, employs over one million people, maintains more than 145 million telephones, and earns more than $6 billion in yearly revenue. The American public and modern business cannot do without AT&T's service.

The maze of wires in Pratt, Kansas (1909) was only a hint of the coming impact of telephones in the Southwest.

23

Social Control
of Business

LEARNING GOALS

After reading this chapter, you will understand:

1. How competition plays a major role in our society and why it must be regulated by legislation.

2. Why natural monopolies must be controlled and why they cannot enter into competition.

3. The various legislative acts that provide social control of business and what agencies enforce them.

4. How the law protects patents, copyrights, and trademarks.

5. The various pieces of consumer legislation and how they are meant to protect the consumer.

6. That businesses have often joined together to provide self-regulation.

KEY TERMS

Competition
Natural monopolies
Social Control
Sherman Antitrust Act
Restraint of trade
Rule of reason
Pure Food and Drug Act
Clayton Act

Federal Trade Commission Act
Robinson-Patman Act
Truth in Lending Law
Fair Packaging and Labeling Act
Self-regulation
Copyright
Patent
Trademark

FLO
ERT
INN
AS VEGAS
NEVADA
FORUM
sted Nerve
TECHNICOLOR
KEN
GOOD TASTE
ORS
BEEFEATER
SNACK BAR
BOOKS
RESTAURANT

As we saw in chapter 1, **competition** is the basic motivator in a private enterprise system. Business people competing for profit provide maximum satisfaction of human wants and needs. Competition is necessary for our economic system to be efficient. Consequently, it is important that a competitive business environment be maintained in the United States.

COMPETITION

Competition in business is closely akin to competition in any other type of endeavor, for instance, sports. Imagine what the game of football would be like without rules, penalties, and referees. Suppose the team that crossed the other team's goal line the most times won the game and the trophy, and no rules were established. Without rules a team could bring baseball bats to the game and win easily until the other team was also forced to use some such lethal weapon. Soon the game of football would disappear because the resulting violence would not be worth the trophy to the players. If only rules were applied to the game, the results would be the same, because if a team were not penalized for violation of the rules, it would not pay any attention to them. If rules with penalties were applied without someone to administer them (the referees), then they would have no force and the same results would occur. However, with rules, penalties for violation of rules, and referees to enforce rules by administering penalties, the game of football becomes an organized and successful sport.

Competition in business is much the same as competition in football. It must have rules with penalties for violations (legislation) and referees (government agencies) to administer the rules and penalties. Without rules, penalties, and referees, business competition would become so violent and disruptive that society would not allow it to exist. If properly controlled, competition in business can provide a nation with highly efficient business firms.

Of course, governmental agencies are not perfect. Sometimes they establish rules and regulations and take actions that not only create excess red tape, but inhibit efficiency rather than promote it.

CONTROL OF NATURAL MONOPOLIES

Competition in business is not always possible or desirable. Some types of business have certain characteristics that preclude competition. The telephone industry, for example, operates more efficiently without competition. Consider the result if, in your hometown, there were two telephone companies competing for every customer. Wherever there is one telephone pole, there would have to be two, and double the amount of wire. In order to reach others, each home would have to have two telephones and two directories. Duplicate telephone services would greatly increase the cost of service that could not possibly be offset by any gains resulting from competition.

Generally, **natural monopolies** are industries that are high-fixed-cost industries. In addition to the telephone industry, utilities and railroads are also industries that are basically natural monopolies.

Natural monopolies must be controlled by government to ensure maximum benefits to society. If natural monopolies, such as the telephone industry, were allowed to exist as monopolies without control, they would be able to charge huge fees for their services and even decide who would receive telephones. Extensive harm could be done with this kind of power. Many business firms cannot compete without telephone communications; consequently, the telephone company could cause some companies to fail. Certainly, power such as this must be controlled by the people of our society through governmental control.

Governmental agencies at the federal, state, and local level perform control functions over natural monopolies. The Interstate Commerce Commission and Federal Communications Commission are two of the more important examples of governmental control agencies at the federal level.

LEGAL INSTRUMENTS OF CONTROL

Legislation in the United States has almost universally been enacted only after problems have arisen, and almost never as a preventative measure. Legislation providing for **social control** of business has certainly been no exception. The growth of industrial complexes containing big businesses produced a wide array of socially undesirable practices. Giant firms were able to eliminate their competition by financial means, rather than by efficiency of production. For example, one large trust in the 1800s was not only able by financial strength to force railroads to rebate part of the shipping fees on their shipment of oil, but received rebates on shipments by their competitors (their competitors were few in number and small in size). Numerous shady stock manipulations bilked the American public out of billions of dollars. Competition without rules and penalties produced excesses such as tainted food and false advertising.

Undesirable business practices became so numerous that Congress was forced to pass regulatory legislation in an attempt to outlaw business actions that were not in the best interest of society. Some of the more important legislation is discussed below.

Sherman Antitrust Act, 1890

The **Sherman Antitrust Act** attempted to prohibit agreements in **restraint of trade** (principally price fixing) and monopoly. Specifically, the main two sections of the act provide:[1]

Section 1. "Every contract, combination in the form of trust or otherwise, or conspiracy, in restraint of trade or commerce among the several states, or with foreign nations is hereby declared to be illegal. . . ."

Section 2. "Every person who shall monopolize, or attempt to monopolize, or combine or conspire with any other person or persons, to monopolize any part of the trade or commerce among the several states, or with foreign nations, shall be deemed guilty of a misdemeanor. . . ."

The United States Attorney General (Department of Justice) is directed by the Sherman Act to prosecute violations of the law through district courts. The Sherman Act is the only antitrust law that relies solely on the courts for its interpretation and enforcement. In addition, the Sherman Act provides that violations may be prosecuted in either criminal or civil suits or both. It also provides for private remedies by allowing persons sustaining injuries to their business or property by anything forbidden in the act to sue and recover three times the amount of damages sustained.

The courts interpret the Sherman Act and define what is a monopoly. In 1911, a suit was brought by the Department of Justice under the Sherman Act asking for dissolution of the monopolistic mergers of what was then the Standard Oil Company of New Jersey and the American Tobacco Company. The courts ruled in favor of the government; however, in reaching their decision, the court developed what is known as the **rule of reason.** The rule of reason provides for dissolution of mergers only when there is "alarming" and "ungentlemanly" conduct and an overwhelming percentage control of the industry. The Department of Justice brought action against United States Steel Corporation, which controlled about 75 percent of steel manufacturing in 1912. In 1920, the Supreme Court refused to order a dissolution because of lack of proof of "unworthy motives," predatory acts, and an overwhelming percentage control of the industry. The rule-of-reason interpretation by the courts generally destroyed the effectiveness of the monopoly section of the Sherman Act.

Pure Food and Drug Act, 1906

Congress rejected the first bill introduced in Congress to protect consumers against impurities in foods and drugs. Over 100 pieces of protective legislation were introduced in Congress during the next twenty-five years and every one was rejected by Congress. Not until 1906, following extensive publicity concerning food and drug impurities, was control legislation passed in the form of the **Pure Food and Drug Act.**

The Pure Food and Drug Act attempted to achieve two objectives: (1) to prohibit the sale of food and drugs unsafe for human consumption, and (2) to force manufacturers to tell the truth about their products. The Department of Agriculture was responsible for enforcing the law.

---

[1]United States Code, Title 15, Section 1–8.

Order of the Bird

Various federal agencies administer legislation that is related to business. It is not uncommon for business people to complain about many of the rules, regulations,and reports established by these governmental agencies. Some of these complaints are unfair, but some are justified.

One organization, the National Association of Professional Bureaucrats (NATAPROBU), was founded to poke fun at excessive red tape and bureaucracy in hopes of bringing about some changes. Tongue in cheek, NATAPROBU advises the bureaucrat: when in charge, ponder; when in trouble, delegate; when in doubt, mumble; and turn it over to a committee to study. Also tongue in cheek, the organization defends the right of the bureaucrat to achieve "creative nonresponsiveness."

NATAPROBU presents an award, "Order of the Bird," to government officials who exhibit bureaucratic excesses. One Order of the Bird went to an Internal Revenue official who wrote a rather lengthy memorandum about employee sideburns. Another official won one for writing a foreign policy paper on "the qualitative quantitative interface."

Another went to a Federal Aviation Administration official for taking steps to fine an individual for flying his home-made helicopter six inches off the ground even though it was tied to the ground. It seems he failed to get FAA clearance. The award so embarrassed the FAA that it dropped the case.

Federal agencies provide many vital services to our nation and the public, but occasionally some people in these agencies engage in bureaucratic excesses. It is refreshing to see humor being used to lessen some of these excesses.

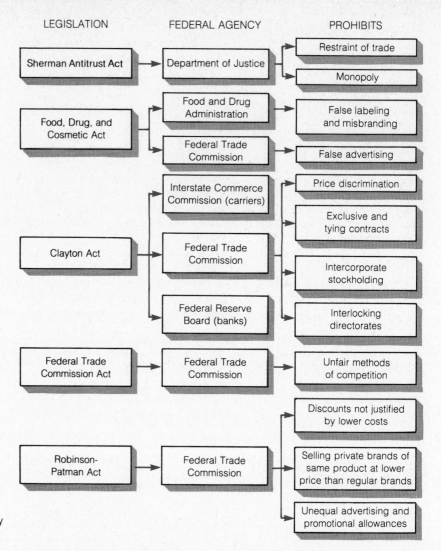

Exhibit 23–1

Major federal social control of business legislation administered by federal agencies.

The original act of 1906 was relatively weak and not sufficient to protect the public, but attempts to provide stronger legislation failed until 1937, when a drug manufacturer sold sulfanilamide contaminated with a poison that caused ninety-three deaths. The resulting publicity and public reaction was enough to cause passage of the Food, Drug, and Cosmetic Act of 1938. The new act was a considerable improvement over the original 1906 law in coverage, although it also basically prohibits adulteration and misbranding. Enforcement was removed from the Department of Agriculture. The Federal Trade Commission as a matter of practice has left false labeling and misbranding to the Food and Drug Administration (Department of Health, Education, and Welfare) while it handles false advertising, although it has the power to function in these areas.

Clayton Act, 1914

The inability of the Sherman Act to eliminate undesirable business practices led to the passage of the Clayton Act. The Clayton Act was intended to strengthen antitrust action by the government by providing more specific legislation. The Sherman Act suffered from the following three difficulties: (1) the act was punitive rather than preventative, (2) the courts interpreted the act inconsistently, and (3) businesses were finding new ways of avoiding the act.

The Clayton Act dealt basically with four main malpractices by business: price discrimination, exclusive and tying contracts, intercorporate stockholding, and interlocking directorates.

Price Discrimination. The Clayton Act prohibited any person engaging in commerce to discriminate in price between different purchasers when the effect of such discrimination substantially lessened competition or tended to create a monopoly, except when necessary to meet competition.

Exclusive and Tying Contracts. This section of the Clayton Act prohibits the following practices where there is injury to competition: (1) tie-in sales, such as the case of the manufacturer of mimeograph machines selling its machines on the condition that only its stencils, ink, and paper will be used with the machines; (2) exclusive dealerships, selling goods to a dealer only on the condition that the dealer will not buy the goods of competitors; (3) requirement contracts, the practice of selling goods to a customer only if he agrees to buy all future needs from the seller; and (4) full-time forcing, selling one line of goods only if the buyer agrees to purchase other lines of goods from the seller.

Intercorporate Stockholding. The Clayton Act provided that no corporation engaged in commerce could acquire stock in another corporation when the acquisition substantially lessened competition between them.

Interlocking Directorates in Competing Corporations. The Clayton Act provided that no person could serve as a director of two or more corporations (banks and common carriers excluded) if any of them had capital in excess of $1 million and were competitors. The ability of individuals to eliminate competition when serving as directors of competing companies is great and obvious.

The enforcement of the Clayton Act was assigned to the Interstate Commerce Commission for common carriers, the Federal Reserve Board for banks, and the Federal Trade Commission for other forms of commerce.

Federal Trade Commission Act, 1914

The courts, in interpreting the Sherman Antitrust Act, condemned the intent and purpose of cutthroat competition, but did not declare the acts unfair. Most business people, particularly the smaller ones, were concerned because of this and demanded action from Congress. In addition, businesses wanted advance opinions on acceptable and unacceptable prac-

"DOESN'T BOTHER ME — I'M ON THE BOARD OF 'BRAND'X', TOO."

tices. In response to public and business pressure, the **Federal Trade Commission Act** was passed by Congress and signed into law.

The principal provisions of the act are as follows:

1. The Federal Trade Commission is composed of five members appointed by the president for seven-year terms with not more than three from the same political party.

2. It declared as unlawful any unfair methods of competition.

3. It gave the Federal Trade Commission power to issue cease-and-desist orders that could be appealed to the courts.

4. It gave the Federal Trade Commission the power to collect information about business conduct and practices to be made available to Congress, the president, and the public.

Of course, the outstanding feature of the act was the section that declared unfair methods of competition unlawful.

The Federal Trade Commission also has been empowered to administer several other commerce acts:

1. The sections of the Clayton Act outlawing price discrimination, exclusive and tying contracts, intercorporate stockholding, and interlocking directorates.

2. The Export Trade Act of 1918 (Webb-Pomerene Act), which legalized export restraint of trade as long as it was not in restraint of trade within the United States. Export associations must file reports with the Federal Trade Commission of all their activities.

3. The Wool Products Labeling Act of 1939, which provides that all wool products except carpets, rugs, mats, and upholsteries disclose on their label the kind and percentage of fiber in the product.

4. Parts of the Lanham Trademark Act of 1946, which allows the Federal Trade Commission to apply to the Commissioner of Patents for cancellation of trademarks that are deceptive, are immoral, were obtained fraudulently, or are in violation of the Lanham Act.

5. The McCarran Insurance Act of 1948, which provides the Federal Trade Commission with certain power over the insurance business. These powers vary from state to state.

6. The Fur Products Labeling Act of 1951, which requires manufacturers to label all garments showing animal fur, country of origin, and certain processing information.

7. The Flammable Fabrics Act of 1953, which prohibits the sale of wearing apparel that is highly flammable.

The Federal Trade Commission closely examines business mergers and acquisitions to make sure they do not lessen competition. The Federal Trade Commission won a suit that required General Motors to sell its stock in DuPont because they use extremely large volumes of paint and the FTC felt it limited competition. However, it did not challenge the merger of Montgomery Ward and Container Corporation of America (and a later acquisition of the mergered companies by Mobil Oil) because they were in different types of businesses.

Robinson-Patman Act, 1936

The section of the Clayton Act prohibiting price discrimination was so destroyed by court interpretation that it was ineffective, and the Robinson-Patman Act was an attempt to correct the situation. The **Robinson-Patman Act** amended Section 2 of the Clayton Act by outlawing the following when they lessen competition: (1) discounts that are not justified by lower costs to the seller, (2) selling private brands of the same product at a lower price than regular brands, and (3) granting proportionally unequal advertising and promotional allowances to buyers. The act also sets the burden of proof in price discrimination cases on the seller. It also makes some types of price discrimination a criminal offense.

CONSUMER LEGISLATION

Consumer groups have been major factors in the creation of consumer-oriented legislation and regulations during the past twenty years. Some of the more important areas covered by federal law are:

Truth in Lending

The **Truth in Lending Law** requires that all business and financial institutions dealing in consumer credit must inform the borrower in writing of (1) the annual interest rate, (2) the total finance charge, (3) the cash price, (4) the down payment, and (5) the total amount charged. The law was intended to make consumers aware of the interest they are charged and allow them to compare credit costs.

Fair Packaging and Labeling

The **Fair Packaging and Labeling Act** includes the following provisions for consumer products:

1. The producer must show on the label the true net weight or volume of the contents.
2. Coupon offers and "cents-off" sales can only be shown on the label when the product is being sold below the regular retail price.
3. Products labeled "economy size" or with other like terms must be sold at a price at least 5 percent lower for equal amounts than all other sizes of the product.
4. For nonstandardized foods, the producer must list on the label all ingredients in decreasing order of amount. Prescription drugs are excluded.

Unordered Merchandise

Only free samples and items sent by charitable organizations can be mailed to a person without consent. Any other item is illegal unless the person has ordered it or agreed to receive it. If you receive an unsolicited item, you can do what you want with it; you do not have to pay for it, and the sender cannot send you a bill for it.

Credit Cards

Credit cards can be issued only to persons who request or apply for them. If a credit card is lost or stolen and used by an unauthorized person, the credit card holder is liable for no more than $50 if he notifies the company of the loss right away.

Holder in Due Course

Retailers often sell credit contracts (installment contracts) to financial institutions in order to receive their money before the buyer has made all the payments. The financial institution is then called a "holder in due course." Problems sometimes arose when a purchaser had problems with a product and the merchant had gone out of business or would not make good the purchase. The buyer would have to pay in full because the "holder in due course" had only purchased a credit contract.

Since 1976, a federal rule has required a notice on installment credit contracts which, in effect, makes the "holder in due course" responsible for all obligations of the retailer who sold the product.

Cooling-off Periods

Door-to-door salespeople selling items for more than $25 must give you a sales contract, an oral explanation of your rights to cancel the sale, and a form you can use to cancel the sale. You have three days in which to cancel the sale by written notification. The salesperson must return all money within ten business days and pay for all expenses of picking up the merchandise. If the merchandise is not picked up within twenty business days, you may keep it and not have to pay for it.

Cost of the Consumer Movement

Unfortunately, meeting the requirements of consumer legislation and regulations—such as notification and waiting periods—usually costs business firms money, and they have to pass it on in the price of the product (the average yearly profit before taxes of the 1,000 largest firms in the United States is usually around 4 to 5 percent of sales).

In addition, consumer groups usually act on what they think is in the consumer's best interests, which may not be what the consumer wants. For example, a consumer group might push for some automobile safety feature that is very expensive. If it is successful in getting a federal regulation requiring the feature, automobile manufacturers will be forced to pass on the price of the feature to the consumer. Each consumer will then be forced to pay for the new feature regardless of whether or not he or she wants it.

Business Self-Regulation

Almost all business firms recognize the importance of the consumer to their success. They pay close attention to customer complaints and try to avoid them. Several large firms rent toll-free telephone lines for their customers to contact them if they have problems.

Business firms have also joined together to provide **self-regulation**. One example is the National Association of Broadcasters, which has created a code of ethics for its members to follow. Another example is the Better Business Bureau. Sponsored by the business community, the BBB is located in more than forty cities around the United States. It can provide background information on local firms in your area, making it possible to check on a firm before you buy. One recent program offered by the BBB is a consumer arbitration program. It involves the following steps:

1. The customer attempts to get his or her complaint satisfied by the business. If the customer does not succeed, he or she then goes to the BBB.
2. The BBB will try to resolve the case informally by talking to the customer and the business. If unsuccessful, arbitration is offered both parties.
3. The parties sign an agreement to accept the results of arbitration.
4. An arbitrator acceptable to both parties is selected.
5. After investigation and hearing both parties, the arbitrator dictates the final decision.

Both small and large businesses have found the new program valuable as a low-cost means of reaching fair decisions with customers.

COPYRIGHTS, PATENTS, AND TRADEMARKS

The United States Constitution of 1787 provided authors and inventors exclusive rights to their writings and inventions. Congress has implemented this constitutional provision with additional acts in 1790, 1793, 1836, 1870, 1952, and 1976.

Copyrights

Copyrights provide authors with exclusive use of their musical and literary compositions for a specific period of time. The law that issued a copyright for twenty-eight years with a renewal of only twenty-eight years was changed in 1976 to the life of the author plus fifty years. Federal law has established fourteen categories of works that may be copyrighted.

1. Books
2. Periodicals
3. Lectures
4. Dramatic and dramatic-musical compositions
5. Musical compositions
6. Maps
7. Works of art
8. Reproductions of works of art
9. Technical drawings or models
10. Photographs
11. Prints, pictorial illustrations and labels
12. Motion picture photoplays
13. Motion pictures other than photoplays
14. Sound recordings

There are some exceptions that do not fit into the above categories which may be copyrighted. The copyright office requires a $10 fee for each copyright.

Patents

Currently, the law provides inventors with exclusive rights to make, use, and sell their inventions for a period of seventeen years. An invention must be a unique new idea to qualify for a **patent**. The prosecution of patent infringement must be brought by the owner of the patent and it must be upheld by the courts. If a person accused of infringing on a patent can prove to the court's satisfaction that it is not really a new and unique discovery, then he cannot be held liable and the patent is without force.

Trademarks

Trademarks, when registered in proper order, give the owner exclusive rights to the use of the trademark without consideration of any time limit. A **trademark** must be distinctive to be valid. Words in common use are not eligible for trademark protection. In fact, distinctive words may become ordinary through common use and cease to be valid trademarks. Some examples are *zipper, cellophane, linoleum,* and *aspirin.*

Exhibit 23–2

An early patent, a more recent patent, and a trademark.

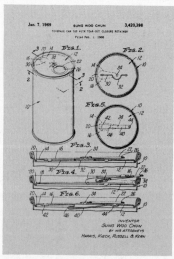

SUMMARY OF KEY POINTS

1. In order to have fair competition for maximum efficiency of business, there must be rules of the game, penalties for violation, and referees to ensure that the "game of competition" is played fairly.

2. Natural monopolies have certain characteristics that preclude competition; consequently, they must be regulated by government agencies.

3. Legislation was passed to regulate business because some practices that existed in business were not in the best interests of society.

4. The Sherman Antitrust Act prohibits agreements in restraint of trade and monopoly. The "rule of reason" developed by the courts made the monopoly section ineffective.

5. The Food, Drug, and Cosmetic Act prohibits false labeling, misbranding, and false advertising.

6. The Clayton Act prohibits price discrimination, exclusive and tying contracts, intercorporate stockholding, and interlocking directorates.

7. The Federal Trade Commission Act established the Federal Trade Commission and prohibited unfair methods of competition.

8. The Robinson-Patman Act is an amendment to the Clayton Act that prohibits price discounts not justified by lower costs, selling private brands of the same product at a lower price than regular brands, and unequal advertising and promotional allowances.

9. Some of the more important areas covered by consumer legislation are: (1) truth in lending, (2) fair packaging and labeling, (3) unordered merchandise, (4) credit cards, (5) holder in due course, and (6) cooling-off periods.

10. The cost of the consumer movement is eventually paid for in the price of products, and consumers may not want some of the things consumer groups want.

11. Business firms have often joined together to provide self-regulation. Most businesses pay close attention to customer complaints and try to avoid them.

12. Patents protect inventions of new ideas for 17 years.

13. Copyrights protect musical and literary compositions for the life of the author plus 50 years.

14. Trademarks give the owner exclusive right to the use of the trademark without consideration of any time limit.

15. Holders of patents, copyrights, and trademarks must prosecute for infringement since the government will not.

DISCUSSION QUESTIONS

1. Do you feel we should strive for competition in all businesses? Explain.
2. Are you in favor of social control of business? Explain.
3. Do you think the Sherman Antitrust Act is a good law? Explain.
4. Is the Sherman Antitrust Act effective today? Explain.
5. What are the main provisions of the Pure Food and Drug Act?
6. Why was the Clayton Act passed and what are its main provisions?
7. What are the main provisions of the Federal Trade Commission Act?
8. What are the main provisions of the Robinson-Patman Act?
9. If you wrote a song, would you want a patent, copyright, or trademark? What would it do for you?

STUDENT PROJECTS

1. Attempt to identify what you consider a violation of any legislation discussed in this chapter.
2. Attempt to find in a newspaper, magazine, or other source what you consider a false or misleading advertisement.
3. Identify a patent, a copyright, and a trademark.

CASE
A

Fleece Drug Company

Eric Brian has just been hired as president of the Fleece Drug Company and has discovered the following facts:

1. The company has an agreement with a competitor to charge the same price in order to avoid cutthroat competition.
2. One of the drugs the company produces will not relieve headaches to the extent or in the time claimed by the company's advertising.
3. The company has received several complaints that one of the company's drugs is causing considerable intestinal disorders, and quality control feels it may be the result of virus contamination.
4. The company charges retailers different prices without regard to the amount of purchase.
5. The chairman of the board of the company is also on the board of directors of the firm's main competition.
6. The company also produces the best X-ray unit available but will sell it only if the customer agrees to buy only Fleece X-ray supplies.
7. The company has recently cut prices below cost to drive a small competitor out of business and will raise the price when this has been accomplished.
8. The company is showing 25¢ off on their labels when in truth it is the regular retail price.
9. The company often sends their products to retailers who have never bought from Fleece Drug and then bills them if they don't send the product back.

Question

Evaluate each of the above practices to determine if they are legal. If any are illegal, specify the law or laws and identify the governmental agency or agencies that might bring action against the company.

Special Assistant to Congressman Powers

You are a special assistant to Congressman Powers and one of your main jobs is to answer letters from people in the congressman's district. Several complaints have arrived in the past two weeks and you must answer them.

1. One person complained that all the service stations in his small town meet once a month to agree on the price they will charge for gasoline.

2. One person complained about a product that was advertised as being able to grow hair on anyone in thirty days. He purchased several bottles that he used for two months and he is still bald.

3. An owner of a small business has complained that she pays more for a product than a large store in the same town.

4. Another owner of a small business writes that a large store sold products at below cost until it drove him out of business, and then raised the price above what he had charged.

5. Tom Strunk, a small store owner, complained that a large store in the same town receives an advertising allowance from the same manufacturer from whom Strunk receives none.

6. A businessman has complained about a local discount store selling drug items at 10 percent below the price he charges in his drugstore. He has a markup of 40 percent on all drug items.

7. A voter writes he has invented a new energy saving device and he is afraid someone will steal his invention.

Questions

1. In complaints 1 through 6, decide what you will tell the voter relative to:
   a. Is it a violation of the law?
   b. If it is a violation, what law does it violate and how does it violate the law?
   c. To what federal agency should the person complain?
2. What could you tell the voter in complaint number 7?

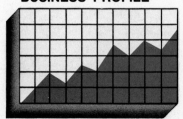

BUSINESS PROFILE

The Gillette Company

The Gillette Company is an example of a firm that was founded because an entirely new concept was created and patented.

King C. Gillette was a forty-year-old traveling salesman living in Brookline, Massachusetts, in 1895 when he created the world's first safety razor with disposable blades. Before, men shaved with a safety razor that was difficult to use and maintain. Needless to say, barber shops enjoyed a large volume of the shaving business.

King C. Gillette, and the first safety razor with disposable blades.

The Gillette Company was founded in 1901 and began production two years later. The first year Gillette sold 51 razors and 168 blades. The new product rapidly began to gain acceptance, and the United States government bought over three million razors in 1918 for the military services. Twenty-three years after the first razor was sold, the company had sold over 53 million razors.

Through the years The Gillette Company has diversified into nonshaving products through internal new product development, acquisitions, and product line expansion. Major acquisitions include the Toni Company in 1948 (women's grooming products), the Paper Mate Company in 1955 (writing instruments), and Braun AG, Germany, in 1967 (electric shavers, small appliances, and other products). The company acquired the French-based S. T. Dupont Company in 1971, makers of disposable and luxury lighters.

The Gillette Company employs over 34,000 people, approximately two-thirds of whom are based overseas, and sells more than 850 items in 200 nations and territories around the world. Net fixed assets total more than $1.5 billion and sales exceed $2 billion.

Government Employment and the Legal Profession

Government service, which is divided between federal, state, and local (county, city, town) agencies, is one of the largest fields of employment. Approximately 17 million employees, or 1 out of 6 employed persons, work for government agencies.

Through the 1980s, state and local government is expected to grow more rapidly than federal employment. However, thousands of jobs will be available in a variety of occupations in the succeeding years.

Government employees are found in the following three major categories:

White-collar workers	67%
Blue-collar workers	14%
Service workers	19%

Among the major white-collar occupational groups in federal civilian employment are:

1. Teachers.
2. Postal workers (postal clerks, mail handlers, rural carriers, postal supervisors, postmasters, motor vehicle operators, postal inspectors, protection forces).
3. Administrative and managerial occupations (typical trainees at this level are college graduates or have had responsible job experience). Typical positions are budget analysts, claims examiners, purchasing officers, administrative assistants, personnel officers, tax technicians, budget administrators, supply-management officers, purchasing officers, and inventory-management specialists.

4. Technicians, clerical, and aid-assistant entry-level jobs are filled by people who have high school education or equivalent. Persons with junior college or technical school training enter at higher levels. Typical jobs are engineering technicians, supply clerks, clerk-typists, office-machine operators, secretaries, stenographers, mail and file clerks, telephone operators.

In federal employment, the major service, craft, and manual occupations are policemen, firemen, repairmen, truck drivers, and skilled maintenance workers.

In state and local government, the largest fields of employment are educational services (public school and college teachers, other educational services); highway work (civil engineers, surveyors, machinery operators); police and fire protection.

Among the larger occupational groups engaged in state and local government occupations are bookkeepers, accountants, clerk-typists, stenographers, secretaries, and office managers.

Career opportunities for types of positions in government employment are listed below.

Occupation	Number Currently Employed	Number of Openings Each Year to 1990
Government		
Mail carriers	245,000	7,000
Postal clerks	260,000	2,000
Firefighters	220,000	7,500
Police officers	450,000	16,500
Government construction inspectors	20,000	2,200
Government regulatory inspectors	100,000	5,800
State police officers	47,000	1,800
Teaching		
College	673,000	11,000
Kindergarten, elementary school	1,322,000	86,000
Secondary school	1,087,000	7,200
School counselors	45,000	1,700
Teachers' aides	342,000	25,500
Librarians	142,000	8,000
Lawyers	487,000	37,000

SOURCE: U.S. Department of Labor, *Occupational Outlook Handbook*, 1980–81.

FEDERAL GOVERNMENT PAY SCHEDULES   Nearly half of all federal civilian employees are paid under the General Pay Schedule (GS). The GS rates are set by Congress and apply nationwide. They are reviewed annually in order to remain comparable with salaries in private industry. The General Schedule is for professional, administrative, technical, clerical, and other workers such as guards and messengers. The GS entrance salaries are shown below.

POSTAL SERVICE PAY SCHEDULE The pay schedule for postal employees at the entry level is shown below.

GS entrance salaries

GS Rating	Annual Salary
GS-1	$ 8,432
GS-2	9,381
GS-3	10,235
GS-4	11,490
GS-5	12,854
GS-6	14,328
GS-7	15,922
GS-8	17,634
GS-9	19,477
GS-10	21,449
GS-11	23,566
GS-12	28,245
GS-13	33,586
GS-14	39,689
GS-15	46,685
GS-16	54,755
GS-17	64,142
GS-18	75,177

SOURCE: Civil Service Commission.

Postal service salaries

Grade Level	Annual Salary
PS-1	$17,714
PS-2	18,143
PS-3	18,610
PS-4	19,115
PS-5	19,663
PS-6	20,251
PS-7	20,891
PS-8	21,577
PS-9	22,323
PS-10	23,112
PS-11	24,300

SOURCE: U.S. Postal Service.

LAWYERS Lawyers perform a variety of tasks related to interpreting the law. Law is a changing field, and lawyers must do research to remain current in order to represent their clients adequately.

Of the 396,000 practicing lawyers in the United States, almost three-fourths (or 280,000) are engaged in private practice. Of this number, about 40 percent are in practice for themselves and 60 percent (116,000) work in law firms. Of the 116,000, about one-third are employed by various business firms, one-fourth are employed by the federal government, and the remainder work in state and local government. At the state level, lawyers may work for the state attorney general. At the federal level, they may work in various regulatory agencies.

Lawyers engaged in private practice handle all kinds of legal work for their clients. For example, when representing a person who wants to buy property, they perform all steps necessary to assure that their client complies with the law.

Lawyers may specialize in a single branch of law, such as corporate, criminal, labor, patent, real estate, tax, or international law.

Within these branches there are further specializations; for example, there are lawyers who specialize in representing public utilities before various regulatory agencies.

Many people who have law degrees use their knowledge of law in other occupations, working as teachers, management consultants, financial analysts, insurance claim adjusters, tax collectors, or probation officers. Also, many public office holders have legal backgrounds. To practice law, a person must pass a state's bar exam. To qualify for a bar exam, an applicant must have completed three years of college and graduated from a law school approved by the American Bar Association or the proper state authorities. However, many states now require a bachelor's degree for admission to law school. While in college, students interested in specific areas of law should take related courses in their college curriculum that will benefit them. Graduates from a law school receive a JD degree, a "doctor of jurisprudence."

Career opportunities in law are expected to increase but competition will be keen for the salaried persons. Starting salary ranges are wide, with most being in the $15,000 to $18,000 range, according to figures reported by the Department of Labor. Lawyers with at least one year's experience in business firms earned about $18,000 a year; those with a few years' experience earned $30,000 or more annually. Federal government starting salaries range from $14,000 to $17,000, depending on qualifications.

CAREER PROFILE

Michael F. Spates holds a Master of Business Administration degree from the University of Maryland, with a concentration in quantitative methods. He learned of the opportunity with the U.S. Postal Service through his school's placement office. He selected the postal service because it offered him challenges and unlimited opportunities.

He has advanced rapidly, from an operations research analyst to a project manager in just over one year to his current position of operations research program manager.

Mike notes that his work is very demanding. Daily activities are far from routine and such problems as economic and operational analysis of major postal programs, labor matters, consumer and congressional inquiries, and interfacing with major postal customers are challenging.

Mike lists two goals that should be achieved in school and will enable a student to go a long way toward success in business:

1. Develop basic skills in the major areas of business (finance, management, transportation, etc.) with a quantitative emphasis, which crosses all disciplines.

2. Develop good human relations and communications skills.

Mike's Introduction to Business instructor was Rudolph P. Lamore of the University of Maryland.

APPENDIX A

Your First Job:
Four Steps to Success

Finding a job just doesn't happen. You have to make it happen.

Like it or not, the relative ease or difficulty you encounter will be influenced by where you fall on the supply/demand curve. If you majored in engineering or computer science or some other discipline that is highly sought after by employers, your task will be easier. In fact, you may receive a number of job offers. Even if you do, don't take the job search lightly. Sorting out a number of job offers requires time, effort, and research if you want to make a wise choice.

If, however, you majored in a discipline in which the number of graduates exceeds the jobs, you face a tougher task. That doesn't mean that there are no jobs for you. What it means is that you'll have to search for them yourself. You can't sit and wait for employers to come looking for you on campus. Even in the toughest of times, jobs are available. Somebody gets them. Why not you?

STUDYING YOURSELF

The purpose of the self-analysis is to set down and review all the components that have interacted to produce the kind of individual you are. What you discover will not only help your self-analysis, it will be invaluable later when you construct your resume and go for interviews. You will find the answers to many of the questions you'll be asked by prospective employers. This inventory acts as a memory jogger to insure that you don't omit important details later and it helps to organize your thinking.

Include your thoughts about how your values and personal characteristics will relate to the work situation you will soon enter:

—Do you like to work with people, data, things, or ideas? Almost every job has a combination of these, so emphasize your preferences.

—Do you have the ability to decide quickly and correctly?

—Are you patient?

—Do you work well under pressure?

—Do you mind close supervision or criticism?

—Are you a self-starter? Do you follow through on an assignment to its completion?

—How heavily do you weigh salary versus satisfaction?

—Do you like to assume responsibility, or do you prefer to work under somebody else's direction?

—Do you prefer a big city or a small city environment?

—Would you be happier in a large organization or a small one?

Traits on Which You Will Be Judged

1. **Personal Characteristics.** Do you have good grooming? Do you have good manners? Do you maintain good eye contact?

2. **Self-Expression.** Are you forceful or vague in expressing your ideas and when responding to the interviewer's questions?

3. **Maturity.** What about your overall sense of balance? Can you make value judgments and decisions?

4. **Personality.** What are you like? Outgoing? Shy? Overbearing? Quiet? Tactful? Enthusiastic? Warm? Do you have a good attitude?

5. **Experience.** What about your academic achievements? Involvement in extra-curricular activities? Job accomplishments? Job skills?

6. **Enthusiasm and Interest.** Are you really interested in the employer? The particular job? Industry? Perhaps you're simply getting interview experience?

7. **Career Goals.** What do you want to do in your professional life?

Adapted from *Guidelines to Job Interviewing* by Arthur R. Eckberg, Director, Career Planning and Placement, Roosevelt University. Reproduced by permission.

THE RESUME AND LETTERS

One of the focal points of the whole job search process is the interview. But there still is one more important piece of preparation before you reach the interview stage—development of a resume and, for those interviews you seek off campus, application letters to accompany your resume. Even if you have the opportunity to interview a number of employers on campus, you may still need to approach others through the mail. Written communications have to be well done, to the point, and written in a way that merges straight facts with a promotional approach. Not only do you have to introduce yourself to employers, you have to arrest their attention, arouse their interest, and persuade them that you are the person to interview, and (perhaps) ultimately hire.

Self-Evaluation Work Sheet

One important aspect of choosing a position is understanding yourself. Self-evaluation can help you analyze what is important to you in the kind of work you will do and the kind of organization in which you will work.

The following are some of the things you should consider in your own self-evaluation. Your answers should be honest. They are meant to help you and should not represent a "good" or "bad" value judgment.

1. What are the things you do best? Are they related to people, data, things?

   _____ related to _____
   _____ related to _____
   _____ related to _____

2. Do you express yourself well and easily?

   Orally: Yes _____ No _____ In writing: Yes _____ No _____

3. Do you see yourself as a leader of a group or team? Yes _____ No _____

   Do you see yourself as an active participant of a group or team? Yes _____ No _____

   Do you prefer to work on your own? Yes _____ No _____

   Do you like supervision? Yes _____ No _____

4. Do you work well under pressure? Yes _____ No _____

   Does pressure cause you anxiety; in fact, is it difficult for you to work well under pressure?
   Yes _____ No _____

5. Do you seek responsibility? Yes _____ No _____

   Do you prefer to follow directions? Yes _____ No _____

6. Do you enjoy new ideas and situations? Yes _____ No _____

   Are you more comfortable with known routines? Yes _____ No _____

7. In your future, which of the following things are most important to you:

   a. Working for a regular salary _____ b. Working for a commission _____
   c. Working for a combination of both _____

8. Do you want to work a regular schedule (e.g., 9 a.m. to 5 p.m.)? Yes _____ No _____

9. Are you willing to travel more than 50 percent of your working time? Yes _____ No _____

10. What kind of environment is important to you?

    a. Do you prefer to work indoors? Yes _____ No _____

    b. Do you prefer to work outdoors? Yes _____ No _____

    c. Do you prefer an urban environment (population over a million)? Yes _____ No _____
       Population between 100,000 to 900,000? Yes _____ No _____

    d. Do you prefer a rural setting? Yes _____ No _____

11. Do you prefer to work for a large organization? Yes _____ No _____

12. Are you free to move? Yes _____ No _____

    Are there important "others" to be considered? Yes _____ No _____

Remember the self-analysis you wrote when you were doing your self-evaluation? Dig it out and use it again. It will be invaluable in compiling the information you need for an effective application letter and resume.

The Application Letter

The application letter introduces you to the prospective employer. The content should not replicate the data in your resume, which will accompany the letter.

After you have gone through [this Appendix] and checked other sources of information in your career planning and placement office, write a rough draft of the application letter. (See page A-5 for guidelines.) Have another person read and react to your final draft. Written correspondence often can inadvertently sound impersonal, so you will want your finished letter to be warm, personalized, but businesslike in its approach to selling you.

Make the letter versatile enough so that small changes can be made to each employer who will receive it. *Never write a form letter to be duplicated and sent out.*

As noted previously, you cannot hope for a high response rate in your letters to prospective employers. So be realistic in your expectations. Your application may be one of hundreds, even thousands, received by the employer. If you receive some rejection letters, or no response at all, don't think that you've struck out and the game is over. You'll have other times at bat. It's imperative that you keep trying.

The Resume

Your resume should briefly outline your educational and employment experience, your interests, and—most importantly—your goals. In short, your resume should tell the employer:

—Who you are
—What you know
—What you have done
—What you would like to do
—What you can do for the employer.

There is no single prescribed resume format. If there were, everyone would appear stereotyped. And this is what you want to avoid. You want to come across as an individual with unique qualities who stands out above your competitors. Many credible books have been written on the resume, and your career office probably has several or more. Consult these, and also seek assistance from your career planning staff.

Everyone has their ideas on resume style. Some favor a chronological approach, others a functional approach. These approaches are outlined in the box on page A-7. [Two] sample resumes are [included here]. The purpose of these is merely to give some examples. They may not be the right style for you, for the approach you use should be dictated by your background—educational qualifications, work experiences, etc.

Guidelines for Application Letter

221 Poplar Street
Missoula, Montana 59801
September 18, 1980

Mr. John P. Johnson, Vice President
Ajax Accounting Company
555 Tamarack Drive
Billings, Montana 59801

Dear Mr. Johnson:

First Paragraph. In your initial paragraph, state the reason for the letter, the specific position or type of work for which you are applying and indicate from which resource (placement center, news media, friend, employment service) you learned of the opening.

Second Paragraph. Indicate why you are interested in the position, the company, its products or services -- above all, what you can do for the employer. If you are a recent graduate, explain how your academic background makes you a qualified candidate for the position. If you had some practical work experience, point out the specific achievements or unique qualifications. Try not to repeat the same information the reader will find in the resume.

Third Paragraph. Refer the reader to the enclosed resume or application blank which summarizes your qualifications, training, experiences, or whatever media you may be utilizing to present yourself.

Final Paragraph. In the closing paragraph, indicate your desire for a personal interview and your flexibility as to the time and place. Repeat your phone number in the letter and offer any assistance to help in a speedy response. Finally, close your letter with a statement or question which will encourage a response. For example, state that you will be in the city where the company is located on a certain date and would like to set up an interview. Or, state that you will call on a certain date to set up an interview. Or, ask if the company will be recruiting in your area, or if it desires additional information or references.

Sincerely yours,

Thomas L. Smith

Samples of Other Letters

Letter of Acknowledgement

```
Your Address

Inside Address
(If possible, use individual's name)

Dear _____ :

    Thank you for your letter of  (date)  suggesting a plant/office visit
at  (time)  on the following dates:  (list dates) .

    The most convenient date for me would be  (date) .  I will arrive at
your office at  (time) .

    Enclosed is a copy of my resume along with the application for employ-
ment.  (If necessary)

    I appreciate the opportunity to visit your plant/office.  I am very
interested and eager to learn more about possible employment opportunities
with  (organization name) .

                                        Sincerely,

                                        (Written signature)

                                        Your name typed
```

Letter of Acceptance

```
Your Address

Inside Address
(If possible, use individual's name)

Dear _____ :

    I am very pleased to accept your offer  (state offer)  as outlined in
your letter of  (date) .  (Include all details of offer---location, starting
salary, starting date.)

    (Mention enclosures---application, resume, employee forms, or other
information---and any related commentary.)

    I look forward to meeting the challenges of the job and I shall make
every attempt to fulfill your expectations.

                                        Sincerely,

                                        (Written signature)

                                        Your name typed
```

Guidelines for Developing an Effective Resume

Chronological

The chronological resume is the style most applicable for new graduates. As the name indicates, the format is a chronological summation in descending order, with the most recent events first.

Job Objective. Describe succinctly the type of job you want. Indicate how your abilities, skills, and background relate to your objective. If you are interested in a broad occupational field, state it as clearly and concisely as you can.

Education. Emphasize the positive aspects of your academic career and extracurricular activities. Describe any academic honors or financial awards you have received as well as any positions of leadership you have assumed.

Work Experience. Describe tasks related to the position you are seeking. Eliminate minor details. Emphasize major responsibilities. Indicate progressive increases in responsibility. Include civic projects, volunteer work, etc. Be specific and avoid vague generalities. Do not overlook periods of self-employment and include all employment experiences, summer or otherwise, if relevant.

Extra-Curricular Activities. Note your school activities and interests. This section should make you appear to be a whole person as opposed to a purely academic being.

Hobbies and Interests. As in the preceding section, you want to continue to fill out your character. The information is basically personal rather than professional.

Personal Data. Any information about sex, race, age, and marital status cannot be requested. Some counselors may suggest that you voluntarily include any data which could be to your advantage, but this is optional.

References. List faculty or previous employers who have knowledge of your abilities, goals, and interests. Some counselors advocate saying, "References furnished on request." Whether you list them or not, make sure you have permission from all references to use their names. You could be embarrassed if you don't.

Sample Resume

Chronological

NAME

Permanent Address

4922 Clover Ave.
Westburg, NY 32786
Tel. (422) 356-3245

Temporary Address

Room 312, Smith Hall
Alumni University
Sunnydale, NY 64234
Tel. (381) 879-3425

Professional Objective

Retail Sales Management.

Education

Alumni University, Sunnydale, NY, BA Marketing, 1982.
Special emphasis on retail sales and merchandising;
considerable work in consumer economics and accounting.

Experience

Summer 1981

Sales Clerk, Housewares Department. Arranged merchandise
displays, assisted buyer, handled consumer relations.
Also assisted department manager in training new sales
personnel, sold successfully on commission basis.

1978 to 1981

Sales Clerk. Worked part-time in specialty clothing
store. Assumed increased responsibility during time of
employment. Sold merchandise, arranged window displays,
assisted with inventory and ordering, assisted with advertising and copy layout.

Summer 1977 to 1978

Lifeguard. Performed general pool maintenance and
gave swimming instructions to children and young
adults.

Extracurricular Activities

Program Chairperson for American Marketing Association.
Planned programs, contacted speakers from area business
community, and coordinated programs.

Corresponding Secretary for National Sorority.
Handled all correspondence to national headquarters,
alumnae, and others. Maintained files and records for
group. Ordered materials.

References

Furnished upon request.

February, 1982

Sample Resume

Functional

```
                              NAME
                         STREET ADDRESS
                    CITY, STATE, ZIP CODE
                             PHONE


    JOB OBJECTIVE:  Entry-level management track position in personnel/staffing.


    EDUCATION

    College, Location (city, state)
    B.A.:  Psychology, minor in economics.  GPA   3.4 (A=4)
    June 1982


    SKILLS

    ADMINISTRATIVE AND MANAGEMENT SKILLS
        --Supervised staff, budgets, and facilities in business and nonprofit
            organizations.
        --Directed programs for university placement office, planned workshops,
            coordinated public relations, and evaluated effectiveness.
        --Attended to detail.  Challenged by making systems work.  Have gath-
            ered sophisticated information as research assistant.  Processed
            orders for meat company, and routed truck logistics (increasing
            efficiency by 20 percent).

    HUMAN RELATIONS AND COMMUNICATION SKILLS
        --Able to communicate verbally and in writing--clearly, concisely,
            and effectively.
        --Attentive listener, able to help people to "think out loud," re-
            flect on experiences, identify problems, and develop solutions.
        --Seasoned interviewer, skills developed as stringer for newspaper.
        --Able to develop rapport quickly and easily.
        --Actively committed to community service and university organizations.


    EXPERIENCE

    ASSISTANT MANAGER FOR INVENTORIES, Meat Wholesale Company, Place and Dates.
        Enjoyed industrial side of management by assisting in maintenance of
        inventories, processing of orders, and directing transportation
        strategies.

    SUPERVISOR OF TRAINING, Inner-City Counselors Program, City, Date.
        Recruited, trained, and supervised staff for program to educate high
        risk students about self-management skills.

    PLACEMENT ASSISTANT, University Placement Office, Date.
        Worked part-time for several years to present "Career Orientation"
        workshops to students.
```

JOURNALIST, City Newspaper, Place and Date.
    Worked as part-time "stringer," conducting interviews, gathering facts, writing news and features. Published 50 articles.

OTHER PART-TIME AND SUMMER EXPERIENCE INCLUDES student intern in psychology department; tutor in English, math, and other subjects; waiter; and camp counselor.

INTERESTS AND ACTIVITIES

Vice President of senior class.
Salutatorian in high school.
Active in Student Council, debate and swimming teams.
Spent year in Australia as exchange student (family head was personnel executive).

CREDENTIALS AVAILABLE UPON REQUEST

Quick Guide to Resume Writing

Who gets the job is not always the one who can do the job best BUT who knows best how to get the job! Hence, each detail of this process should have your meticulous attention since people are often screened OUT on the basis of a poor letter and resume.

People don't read resumes, they skim them. So think of your resume more as a piece of advertising than as a comprehensive data sheet. Use margins and good spacing which make it easily skimmed.

Don't use a lot of dates or numbers. That makes it hard to skim. Place dates at the END of a paragraph when describing experiences. Sure, they're important to you, but they are hard to read.

Use action verbs. Don't use the verb "to be." Instead of "I did . . . I was . . . I am . . ." use verbs like "initiated, created, developed, supervised, managed, instructed, counseled, negotiated, maintained, . . ." etc.

Emphasize skills, especially those which transfer from one situation to another. The fact that you coordinated a student organization leads one to suspect that you could coordinate other things as well.

Don't use negative words. Don't apologize for lack of experience or weaknesses. This is not the place to hang out your dirty laundry. Be positive, capitalize on strengths, and leave out the negative or neutral words. If your health is "excellent" then don't say "not bad." Avoid negative prefixes or suffixes.

Resumes should be one or two pages. Never more. Anything longer is an autobiography, not a resume. Don't overwhelm employers with information.

Expound on your relevant experiences, condense jobs or experiences which are not directly related. This means that you SLANT your resume to the type of job you are seeking. Hence, you will need more than one resume if you're applying for different types of jobs.

Example: If you are applying for a Child Care Counselor job, devote more space to your experience as a camp counselor. But if you're applying for a job as a Manager Trainee, condense that and emphasize your organizational and supervisory abilities.

Expect a phone call if they are interested. Most employers call to make an interview. Seldom will they write. Hence, make sure they have your phone number.

From *Zehring's Quick Guide to Resume Writing: How to Do It Effectively*. Copyright © 1978 by John William Zehring, Earlham College. Reproduced by permission.

Developing the Career Objective

The format for the career objective can be arranged to a person's unique background or wishes, and is of great help in organizing this difficult portion of the resume.

At the simplest level the career objective may be stated as a professional designation, followed by a specialty area in that field, e.g. Electrical Engineer—Research & Design, or Public Accountant—Auditing and Taxes, or Sales Representative—Industrial Hardgoods and Equipment.

The next level of sophistication in a career objective statement may simply state that an entry-level position is desired, followed by a comment on the functional area of work, e.g. Entry-level Bank Management Trainee—Loans, or Entry-level Store Management Trainee—Merchandising, or Social Service Trainee—Child Welfare.

After these simple formats, the matter becomes more difficult. There are a number of ways to organize career objectives.

The Short-Term/Long-Term Format

Immediate Objective:	Entry-level Accounting Trainee with an Industrial Firm.
Long-Term Objective:	Progression to Comptroller function, with responsibilities for a number of accounting systems and policy responsibility for fiscal affairs of a corporation.

The Functional Format

Functional Work Objective:	Position which includes responsibilities for systems analysis and creating data systems for maintenance of records, evaluation of programs, and projecting future sales trends.

The Skills Format

Skills Objective:	Position which requires knowledge of decision-making models, and application of models to marketing and production planning.

Functional/Industrial Format

Functional/Industrial Objective:	General Sales Representative with company that produces soap, toiletry, or food products.

Skills/Industrial Format

Skill/Industrial Objective:	Position which requires knowledge of COBOL, RPG II, and BASIC, and which requires sales/customer service abilities in the software industry.

When functional or skills types of objectives are used, the work experience section or the education section of the resume should reflect the abilities and wishes set forth in the objective statement.

Career objective statements should avoid terms such as: Opportunity for advancement; a challenging position; position dealing with people; a progressive company; position which requires creativity; a company that recognizes . . .; a chance to . . . .

While these terms may sound nice to the job applicant, they have little meaning to the person who will make a decision for an interview invitation, and in fact may indicate that the candidate has no idea about objectives. The candidate who applies vagueness will get a vague response in return.

By Warren D. Robb, Director of Counseling, Testing, and Career Placement, University of Texas at Arlington.

Correspondence Checklist

Letter of Application

1. Identify the position for which you are applying and how you learned of the firm and position.
2. Indicate why you are applying for this particular position.
3. Describe your main qualifications.
4. Refer the reader to the enclosed resume.
5. Request the next step in the employment process—personal interview, an answer to your letter, etc.
6. Be sure to sign the letter.

Letter of Acknowledgment

1. Acknowledge receipt of offer.
2. Express your appreciation for the offer.
3. Notify the company of the date you expect to make your decision.

Letter of Inquiry of Application Status

1. Request status of application.
2. Recap history of your application.
3. State why you need clarification of status of application.
4. Include thanks for cooperation.

Letter Declining Offers

1. Decline offer.
2. Express your appreciation for the offer and the company's interest in you.

Letter Seeking Additional Information

1. Indicate interest in the company and its offer.
2. Ask for the information you need. Be specific!
3. Express your appreciation for the cooperation you receive.

Letter of Acceptance

1. Accept the offer.
2. Refer to offer letter or document.
3. Tell your travel plans and anticipated arrival date.
4. Express your appreciation and your pleasure at joining the company.

Prepared by Prof. James W. Souther, Director, STC, University of Washington. Reprinted by permission.

The Interview: Some Points to Remember

Analyze Strengths and weaknesses. In preparing for interviews start by doing some solid, honest self-assessment. Analyze your strengths and weaknesses, your background, your academic performance, y. ur vocational interests, and your personal aspirations and values. In other words, begin to formulate, in your own mind, not only what you would like to do but also what you feel you are best prepared to do.

Read employer literature. Next, study your prospective employers. It is imperative that you have some knowledge about their policies, philosophies, products, and services. Failure to do your homework before an interview can be the kiss of death. Nothing turns recruiters off faster.

Dress in good taste. Although most employers are becoming more liberal in their standard of dress and appearance, let basic good taste be your guide. If a beard or "Alice-in-Wonderland" look is going to jeopardize your chances for a job, that's your decision. With some employers appearance could be the deciding factor. The question you have to ask yourself is, "How important is it?"

Be yourself. Your attitude is going to influence the interviewer's evaluation. Don't try to be something you aren't . . . just be yourself. Emphasize your strong points and remember that the recruiter is looking for inherent personal energy and enthusiasm. The interview is your opportunity to sell a product and that product is *you!*

Dwell on the positive. Try always to dwell on the positive. While past failures and shortcomings need not be volunteered, don't try to cover them up or side-step them. Should recruiters ask about them, try to explain the circumstances rather than give excuses or blame others. Remember, they're human too . . . and probably have made a few

Some Typical Questions Asked Candidates

1. How would you describe yourself as a person?
2. What two or three accomplishments have given you the most satisfaction? Why?
3. In what ways do you think you can make a contribution to our organization?
4. Why do you want to work for us?
5. Tell me about yourself.
6. What are your strengths and weaknesses?
7. How do you spend your spare time?
8. If you could construct your own job, within our organization, what factors would you include?
9. What are your short-term goals? Long-term?

Questions Regarding Education:

1. Do you think your grades are a good indication of your academic abilities? Explain.
2. Why did you major in _____?
3. Why did you attend this university? How do you assess your educational experience here?
4. What college courses did you like the most? Least?
5. What extra-curricular activities did you participate in?
6. What did you gain or learn from your part-time job experiences? Co-op? Internship?

From *Guidelines to Job Interviewing* by Arthur R. Eckberg, Director, Career Planning and Placement, Roosevelt University. Reproduced by permission.

mistakes. You'll create a better impression by being honest and candid.

Ask questions-when indicated. If appropriate, ask meaningful questions, particularly if you're not clear about the details of the job, the training program, or other job-related concerns. But, don't ask questions just because you think that's what is expected.

Follow up. Finally, follow up on the interview. Provide whatever credentials, references, or transcripts are requested by the prospective employer as soon as possible. Be sure to write down the name, title, and address of the recruiter. You may want to consider a brief typed letter of appreciation for the interviewing opportunity.

Use your career planning and placement office. These are, of course, only general suggestions and observations. For more detailed and personalized advice, take advantage of the services of your college's career planning and placement office.

Reprinted from the College Placement Council's pamphlet, "The Campus Interview."

How to Handle Questions About GPA

Frequently college graduates indicate that they feel their academic record does not tell the entire story of their achievements in college. Employers are not overly enthusiastic about hearing explanations of grade point averages if it appears that four years were spent just "getting by." So, don't tell an interviewer that you could do better if you had to do it over.

Employers are aware, however, that sometimes special circumstances affected grades, and they are receptive to legitimate explanations. For example, "My father died and I had to work 30 hours a week for one year instead of the usual 15 hours. My grades dropped that year, but since then they have continued to improve."

And, there's the case of the student who ". . . fooled around in college for two years, didn't know what my goals were, dropped out and went to work. When I came back I knew what I wanted to do and my grades the last two years show it."

These examples have become so common that some employers have space on the application blank for a listing of GPA averages for the first two years and the averages for the last two years.

Adapted from material prepared by Roland Swaim, former Director of Career Placement Services, University of Illinois at Chicago Circle. Reprinted by permission.

Additional career opportunities, with yearly job openings projected to 1990

Occupation	Number Currently Employed	Annual Openings Each Year to 1990	Occupation	Number Currently Employed	Annual Openings Each Year to 1990
Engineers			Geographers	10,000	500
Aerospace	60,000	1,800	Historians	23,000	700
Agricultural	12,000	6,000	Political scientists	14,000	500
Chemical	50,000	1,800	Psychologists	130,000	6,700
Civil	155,000	7,800	Sociologists	19,000	600
Electrical	300,000	10,500			
Industrial	185,000	8,000	*Technicians*		
Mechanical	200,000	7,500	Drafters	296,000	11,000
Metallurgical	17,000	900	Engineering, science		
Mining	6,000	600	technicians	600,000	23,400
Petroleum	17,000	900	Forestry technicians	13,700	700
			Soil conservationists	9,300	450
Scientists			Surveyors	62,000	2,300
Astronomers	2,000	40			
Biochemists	20,000	900	*Other Professions*		
Geologists	31,000	1,700	Actors	13,400	850
Chemists	143,000	6,100	Architects	54,000	4,000
Geophysicists	11,000	600	Commercial artists	67,000	3,600
Life scientists	205,000	11,200	Dancers	8,000	550
Meteorologists	7,300	300	Foresters	31,200	1,400
Oceanographers	3,600	150	Funeral directors,		
Physicists	44,000	100	embalmers	45,000	2,200
			Home economists	141,000	6,100
Merchant Marine			Industrial designers	13,000	550
Officers	13,500	700	Newspaper reporters	45,000	2,400
Sailors, deckhand	24,800	250	Radio, TV announcers	27,000	850
			Social workers	385,000	22,000
Health Service			Musicians, composers	127,000	8,900
Physicians, osteopaths	405,000	15,000	Photographers	93,000	3,800
Chiropractors	18,000	1,500			
Dentists	120,000	5,500	*Building Trades*		
Dental hygienists	35,000	6,000	Bricklayers	205,000	6,200
Dental assistants	150,000	11,000	Carpenters	1,253,000	58,000
Emergency medical			Cement masons	83,000	4,400
technicians	287,000	37,000	Construction electricians	290,000	12,900
Optometrists	21,000	1,600	Construction laborers	660,000	49,000
Podiatrists	8,000	600	Floor-covering installers	88,000	3,200
Registered nurses	1,060,000	85,000	Glaziers	19,000	1,000
Pharmacists	135,000	7,800	Ironworkers	78,000	4,100
Medical-lab workers	210,000	148,000	Painters	484,000	26,000
X-ray technologists	100,000	9,000	Operating engineers	581,000	36,000
Dietitians	35,000	3,300	Plasterers	28,000	1,100
Veterinarians	33,500	1,700	Plumbers and pipe fitters	428,000	20,000
Nurses' aides, orderlies	1,037,000	94,000	Roofers	114,000	4,500
Licensed practical nurses	578,000	60,000	Tile setters	33,000	1,800
			Paperhangers	20,000	1,500
Social Sciences			Sheet-metal workers	70,000	3,500
Anthropologists	7,000	350			
Economists	130,000	7,800			

SOURCE: U.S. Department of Labor *Occupational Outlook Handbook*, 1980–1981.

Occupation	Number Currently Employed	Annual Openings Each Year to 1990	Occupation	Number Currently Employed	Annual Openings Each Year to 1990
Services			Truck, bus mechanics	145,000	6,900
Auto-service advisors	25,000	1,100	Office-machine repairers	63,000	4,200
Barbers	121,000	9,700	Watch repairers	21,000	1,500
Bartenders	282,000	21,600			
Building custodians	2,251,000	176,000	*Printing*		
Hotel bellhops, captains	20,000	600	Bookbinders	69,000	2,600
Cooks, chefs	1,166,000	86,000	Composing-room		
Cosmetologists	542,000	28,500	occupations	181,000	3,900
Dishwashers, busboys	455,000	37,000	Electrotypers, stereotypers	8,000	150
Food-counter workers	463,000	34,000	Photoengravers,		
Gasoline-station attendants	340,000	5,200	lithographers	28,000	2,300
Guards	550,000	70,000	Printing pressmen	167,000	5,000
Homemakers and home,					
health aides	110,000	36,000	*Telephone Industry*		
Hotel housekeepers,			Central-office craft workers	135,000	1,000
assistants	20,000	2,000	Linemen, cable splicers	59,000	600
Jailers	110,000	13,900	Installers, repairers	115,000	3,000
Motion-picture			Operators	311,000	9,900
projectionists	11,000	750	*Other Crafts*		
Private-household workers	1,162,000	45,000	Boilermakers	37,000	3,100
Waiters, waitresses	1,383,000	70,000	Dispensing opticians	17,600	1,200
Social-service aides	134,000	7,500	Foremen	1,671,000	69,000
			Furniture upholsterers	29,300	1,100
Machine Occupations			Jewelers	19,000	1,300
Instrument makers	6,000	300	Locomotive engineers	34,000	2,000
Machine-tool operators	542,000	19,600	Maintenance electricians	300,000	15,900
Machinists	484,000	21,000	Shoe repairmen	22,000	1,600
Metal molders	21,000	500	Railroad conductors	37,000	1,700
Patternmakers	3,700	135			
Setup workers	6,500	3,000	*Other Operatives*		
Tool-and-die makers	170,000	10,400	Insulation workers	51,000	2,600
			Assemblers	1,164,000	77,000
Mechanics and Repairmen			Automobile painters	42,000	2,000
Air-conditioning, heating			Factory inspectors	771,000	35,000
mechanics	210,000	8,200	Meatcutters	204,000	5,200
Appliance repairers	145,000	6,900	Photo-lab occupations	51,000	2,700
Auto-body repairers	185,000	7,800	Production painters	133,000	5,200
Auto mechanics	860,000	37,000	Railroad shopworkers	76,000	2,100
Blacksmiths	11,000	300	Railroad signal workers	128,000	450
Diesel mechanics	100,000	5,000	Railroad track workers	59,000	1,400
Farm-equipment			Stationary engineers	175,000	7,700
mechanics	62,000	3,500	Waste-water-treatment		
Forge-shop occupations	77,000	2,000	workers	100,000	10,400
Industrial-machinery			Welders, arc cutters	679,000	108,000
repairers	655,000	58,000			
Millwrights	95,000	4,700	*Farm Workers*	2,798,000	108,000
TV, radio service					
technicians	131,000	6,100			

APPENDIX B
Glossary

Access time The speed with which data can be retrieved from storage in the computer.

Accident policy An insurance that covers losses or injury from accidents.

Accountability The obligation of employees to perform responsibilities assigned to them.

Account executive A stockbroker.

Accounting analysis The use of accounting information for control and decision making.

Accounts receivable Debts that others owe the firm due within a year's time.

ACE Active Corps of Executives, a volunteer group of active managers who advise small-business owners.

Acid test ratio Liquid assets (cash + accounts receivable + marketable securities) divided by current liabilities.

Actuating The management function that involves the direct supervision of employees.

Advertising Any sales presentation that is nonpersonal and paid for by a sponsor.

Advertising agency An independent business that specializes in planning and carrying out advertising ventures or campaigns for other business firms.

Aesthetic pollution Anything that detracts from the beauty of nature.

Agency shop A shop agreement in which both union and nonunion employees pay union dues but a worker does not have to join the union in order to remain employed.

Agents Persons authorized to represent and act for someone else.

Air pollution Gaseous elements or particles in the air.

American Federation of Labor A craft union whose members are skilled workers. Many local unions are affiliated with the AFL.

Amex The American Stock Exchange.

Analog computers Computers that are primarily measuring devices, measuring quantities on a continuous scale.

Application form A written summary of a job applicant's background—age, marital status, education, work experience.

Apprenticeship training Training to learn a skilled trade, involving formal classroom instruction in the principles and theory of a trade as well as on-the-job training.

Arbitration An impartial third party renders a decision that is binding on the parties to a labor-management dispute.

Arithmetic mean The sum of all items divided by the number of items.

Articles of copartnership A written agreement between partners that sets the relationship between the partners as to contribution, profit share, authority, etc.

Assets Items of value owned by a person or business; goods owned by others such as cash, plant, good will, etc.

Authority A manager's or employee's right to make decisions and take necessary actions to fulfill a responsibility.

Autocratic leadership One-person rule.

Average A number that is descriptive of a set of data.

Balance of payments The amount of money paid or received as a result of the difference between exports and imports.

Balance of trade The difference between the amount of goods a country exports and the amount it imports. A favorable balance of trade means a nation has exported more goods than it has imported.

Balance sheet An accounting statement that measures the assets, liabilities, and net worth of a business at a specific time.

Banking system The nation's system that provides for the exchange and control of money.

Bank note A note issued by a bank that is payable to the bearer on demand and is intended to circulate as money.

Barriers to trade Practices of nations that restrict the international exchange of goods—quotas, embargoes, and tariffs.

Batch processing Collecting similar records into batches and processing them all the same way, such as a company payroll.

Bearer bond A bond on which the owner's name is not registered and which is the property of whoever holds it at a specific time.

Bear market A market in which stock prices are moving upward.

Big Board A name for the New York Stock Exchange.

Bill of exchange A written order by one party to another party (usually a bank) to pay a third party a specified sum of money.

Bill of lading A document issued by a carrier to cover a shipment of merchandise.

Binary system A two-digit number system (0 and 1) used in the digital computer to represent various quantities.

Blue chip stock Stock of the largest and best-known companies in the United States.

Body language Signs, symbols, facial expressions, and gestures that convey information.

Bona fide occupational qualification (BFOQ) A requirement that is necessary in order for a person to perform a job.

Bonds Long-term debt instruments of corporations.

Bonus plan A payment system to provide an incentive for employees to produce more and thus earn more.

Boycott Encouragement by pressure groups not to buy products of a company that is being struck by a union or that may not be yielding to other measures for change.

Brand A name, term, symbol, sign, design, or combination of these that is intended to identify goods and services of one seller and to differentiate them from those of competitors.

Broker Brings a buyer and seller together, but does not take title to the goods. Receives a commission for services.

Brokerage firm Stock exchange members who facilitate buying and selling shares of stock and may underwrite and sell new issues of securities.

Budget A projection of future income, expenses, and profit. A standard against which to measure performance for management control.

Bull market A market in which stock prices are advancing.

Business game A computer-simulation decision-making technique.

Capital In common business usage, funds in a business. In economic usage, a labor-saving device, equipment, machinery, etc.

Capitalism An economic system in which almost all of the factors of production are privately owned.

Cease and desist orders Orders from the Federal Trade Commission that instruct a business to cease certain trade practices that limit competition.

Centralized authority Exists in government-ownership economic systems, where almost all business decisions are made at a central governmental level.

Certificate of deposit An instrument signed by a bank stating that a person has on deposit a certain sum of money payable to him or someone he designates.

Chain store A store under the control of central ownership that stocks and distributes lines of goods similar to those of other stores with the same owner.

Channel of distribution The route a product follows from a manufacturer to reach the final consumer.

Checks Negotiable instruments ordering a bank to pay someone a certain amount of money on demand.

Civil law Law that regulates and protects private rights.

Class rate Rate charged for shipping products grouped into the same class.

Clayton Act A federal law that controls various facets of food and drug sales.

Closed shop A business in which a worker must belong to a union in order to be employed.

Coalition of Labor Union Women (CLUW) An organization established to more aggressively organize women workers in labor unions.

Collective bargaining Workers, through a spokesperson, bargain as a group rather than individually for wages and other issues.

Collegial organization A philosophy of management that deemphasizes status and job titles and stresses self-discipline and teamwork, free-flow of communications, and a high degree of delegation of authority.

Commercial banks Sellers who do not take title to goods but have physical possession of merchandise and are paid on a commission basis.

Committee for Economic Development This committee provided a basic set of guidelines for classifying a business as "small."

Commodity exchange The marketplace where commodities are traded, such as gold.

Commodity rate Rate charged for shipping bulky items, such as coal or sand.

Common carrier A carrier offering its services to the general public, regulated by various state and federal agencies. The same rates must be charged to all customers.

Common law Law that is based on custom and usage and confirmed by the decisions of judges, as distinct from statute law.

Common stock A certificate of ownership of the corporation form of business ownership. The holder generally has full voting rights and shares the excess profits after other forms of debt and ownership have been paid.

Communication process The process of conveying information—consists of five elements: sender, message, channel, receiver, and feedback.

Communism An economic system in which virtually all of the factors of production are owned by the government.

Competition Business firms striving against each other to obtain the consumer's patronage.

Computer An electronic machine that either solves problems when given certain coded data, or otherwise processes that data.

Computer downtime The time a computer is not operational.

Computer language A language a computer can interpret, used to convey instructions for computer operations.

Computer program The detailed instructions that transmit the calculations a computer is to perform on a set of data.

Computer simulation A computer technique in which a model of a real system is designed in order to test a

project or a management strategy prior to implementation.

Conceptual skills The ability of a manager to see the overall picture.

Conciliation A third party, the conciliator, attempts to get labor and management together to discuss issues involved in their disagreement.

Congress of Industrial Organization (CIO) Provides union membership for industrial workers, such as in manufacturing and transportation.

Consumer behavior Actions of individuals involved in deciding which goods and services to purchase.

Consumer goods Goods purchased and used by the final consumer for personal or household use.

Consumer legislation Legislation intended to protect consumers from certain business practices.

Consumer movement The actions of consumer advocates to improve products and business practices.

Consumer demography Statistical study of the population in reference to size, density, distribution, and vital statistics.

Consumer Price Index A monthly statistical measure of the average change in prices of selected goods.

Contingency approach A leadership style that is adapted to the requirements of a specific situation.

Contract An agreement between two or more persons to do or not do certain things.

Contract carrier A carrier that offers its services to an individual person or firm. This carrier may charge different rates to customers served.

Control The management function of seeing that plans are carried out successfully in accordance with stated company objectives.

Controlled sample A nonprobability sample; for instance, a convenience, judgment, or quota sample.

Control unit The computer component that directs and controls the internal flow of information according to instructions contained in the computer program.

Convenience goods Goods sold through many retail outlets, at low per unit prices; they are nationally advertised and are purchased frequently, with little or no thought given to making the purchase. Also, the quality is standardized.

Cooperatives Retail outlets owned and operated by consumers who voluntarily join together to buy and sell merchandise to the members, who are also stockholders; any profits are returned to members as dividends.

Copyright The exclusive right to publish a certain book, dramatic or musical composition, photograph, picture, etc., granted by a government for a certain number of years.

Corporate chain A chain centrally owned by a group of stockholders.

Corporation An artificial entity that may legally own property, transact business, enter into contracts, sue and be sued, and engage in other business activity; a form of business ownership.

Cost of goods manufactured Direct labor plus raw materials cost plus factory overhead.

Cost of goods sold Beginning inventory plus all purchases less ending inventory.

Counseling Face-to-face interview between counselor and employee conducted in a private setting.

Craft union A union comprised mainly of skilled craft workers, such as carpenters.

Creative selling A selling technique that is designed to create customer interest in a product that the customer originally had no intention of buying.

Criminal law A branch of jurisprudence that relates to crimes—distinguished from civil law.

Critical Path Method (CPM) A technique developed by E.I. DuPont to schedule and control activities in building chemical plants. It determines the shortest and least expensive path to complete a project.

Cumulative preferred stock A type of stock that accumulates dividends even in years when dividends are not declared and not paid; when dividends are declared, holders of this stock must receive all accumulated dividends before holders of common stock can receive anything.

Current ratio Current assets divided by current liabilities.

Cybernetics The area of knowledge that compares the way electronic computers function to the way the human nervous system functions.

Cyclical variation A measure of the business cycle.

Debt The obligation incurred by a business to repay money that it has borrowed.

Debt capital Money that is borrowed by a business for use in the business.

Debt to net worth ratio Total liabilities divided by tangible net worth.

Decentralized authority Exists in a private-enterprise economic system where almost all business decisions are made at the business-firm level.

Decision-making skills The ability of a manager to choose the correct course of action to solve specific problems.

Decreasing term insurance A term insurance that decreases in coverage amount each year over the specified number of years.

Delegation The authority given to an individual to complete assigned responsibilities.

Demand curve A graph that shows the amount of a product that customers will buy at different price levels.

Demand deposits Checking accounts in commercial banks.

Demographic research Research methodology that involves collecting statistical information about consumers, such as age or income level.

Demotion Downward movement to a job of lesser responsibility and pay.

Depression A period in the business cycle when unemployment increases rapidly and the general economic outlook is pessimistic.

Descriptive statistics Quantitative data used to describe a particular characteristic, such as the number of autos sold.

Detail men Salespersons who call on doctors and other professionals.

Digital computers Computers that work directly with numbers, letters, and special characters.

Disability insurance An insurance that covers loss of life, sight, or limb.

Dispatching A production control function that consists of issuing instructions to various departments detailing the work with specific starting and finishing times.

Distributor's brand A private brand owned by a middleman and normally distributed on a regional basis.

Documents of title Instruments that denote ownership of merchandise or goods. Can be transferred by endorsement.

Dormant partner A partner who assumes no active role in a business and who is not known to the public.

Dow Jones Average Index of stock prices, composed of four different averages of stocks.

Economic indicators Various measures of business activity that are used to predict economic activity.

Elastic demand When changes in prices of goods or services bring about relatively large changes in the quantity demanded.

Electronic mail Messages sent electronically by means of computer.

Embargo Legislation that prevents goods from entering a nation. May be on a product or nation basis.

Emotional buying motive A decision to buy that involves little or no thought.

Employee safety Exists when a work environment provides personal protective equipment, control of exposure to air contaminants, and clean, orderly work areas.

Endowment insurance A form of life insurance in which premiums are paid for a specific period of time and the insured is covered during that time. If the insured is living at the end of the premium period, he or she collects the face value.

Entrepreneur A person who starts a business and takes the risk for profit.

Equilibrium price The price at which the quantity of goods demanded is equal to the quantity supplied.

Equity capital Funds obtained for a business by selling ownership.

Erratic fluctuations Changes of a short-term duration, difficult to measure and predict because of their unexpectedness.

Esteem needs Human needs for self-esteem and self-respect.

Exit interview An interview conducted with personnel leaving a firm to determine the cause of their leaving.

Expenses Items that represent a cost to the business.

Export A product shipped out of a nation for sale in another nation.

Exporters Companies that sell goods to foreign countries.

Factor A financial institution that buys or discounts accounts receivable.

Fair Packaging and Labeling Act Consumer legislation that requires producers to show on their labels true net weight or volume as well as ingredients, in decreasing order of amount; also includes regulations regarding package sizing.

Featherbedding A practice of paying workers for work not performed.

Federal constitution The fundamental principles of government of the United States.

Federal Deposit Insurance Corporation A federal agency that insures deposits in banks up to $100,000.

Federal Reserve system A United States national agency that is assigned the responsibility for controlling the nation's money supply.

Federal Savings and Loan Insurance Corporation A federal agency that insures deposits in savings and loan associations up to $100,000.

Federal Trade Commission Act A federal law that established the Federal Trade Commission and made all acts that limit competition illegal.

FIFO (First In, First Out) A method of costing inventory that assumes that the first raw materials purchased are the first used in producing a product.

Financing The business function of obtaining and using funds.

Fire insurance Insurance coverage for losses due to fire and lightning.

Fiscal policy The degree and balance of government taxing and spending.

Flextime The system of allowing employees, within limits, to develop a work schedule that fits their individual needs by providing for flexible starting and ending times to the workday.

Floating currency The federal government, in effect, removes its relationship to gold and allows the international money market to set the value of the dollar to other currencies on the basis of supply and demand.

Floor broker A stockbroker on the floor of the stock exchange.

Floor planning A trust receipt allows a retailer to keep goods as inventory and when the merchandise is sold an installment contract is given to the sales finance company, which reimburses the retailer.

Flowchart A graphic representation of the operations and decisions that must be made and the order in which they must be made to reach a solution to a problem.

Follow-up A production control function that consists of checking to make sure scheduled times are being met in the production operations.

Forecasting An estimation of a future period's activity, such as sales.

Formal organization The planned structure of a company, in which people from various departments work together as a team under authority and leadership toward common objectives that mutually benefit employees and the company.

Franchise agreement The basic agreement between franchiser and franchisee.

Franchisee A firm that receives a franchise.

Franchiser A parent company that grants firms the right to sell its products.

Franchising An arrangement in which one firm licenses another firm with exclusive rights to sell its products in a specified territory.

Free-form organization A type of organization structure that is appropriate for firms that must be flexible and able to respond to changing market demands, such as companies in high technology industries.

Free-rein leaders Leaders who emphasize "the less supervision the better."

Fringe benefits Indirect payments made to workers, such as Social Security, pension plans, paid vacations.

Functional organization An organization plan that uses specialized authority. This type of organization has characteristics of both line and staff.

General partner A partner who must maintain an active part in a business and who has unlimited liability.

Generic products Products that have no brand name.

Genetic engineering Technological manipulation of genes to produce certain desired characteristics.

Government-issued currency Coins and bills issued by the government to serve as money.

Grading A marketing function in which goods are sorted into classes on the basis of quality, such as color.

Grapevine The informal network of communications within a company.

Gross National Product The total of all goods and services produced by a nation.

Hardware The physical equipment comprising the basic components of the computer.

Hedging Buying and selling in the futures commodity market in order to shift the risk to speculators.

Human relations skills The ability of a manager to deal effectively with people.

Human resource orientation process The process of acquainting new employees with all aspects of the job.

Human resources The people of the firm—considered to be the most valuable asset of the firm.

Hybrid computer A special-purpose computer combining the features of analog and digital computers.

Import A product that is brought into a country from another country.

Importer A company that buys goods from foreign countries.

Income The amount of money that is received in a business.

Income statement An accounting statement that is a measure of income, expenses, and profit over a specific period of time.

Index number A ratio of two numbers expressed as a percentage.

Induction The orientation of the employee into the company.

Inductive statistics The making of predictions, forecasts, and generalizations about a large set of data, based on information derived from a smaller set of data.

Industrial goods Goods used in producing another product or expended in connection with carrying on a business operation.

Industrial union A union whose membership is determined by the nature of an industry, such as auto workers.

Inelastic demand When increases or decreases in price bring about relatively little change in demand.

Inflation Increases in prices that result in a reduction of the buying power of the dollar.

Informal organization The structure resulting from the interpersonal relationships of workers that exist within the framework of a formal organization.

Injunction A court order obtained to prohibit a person or organization from performing some act.

Input Putting into the computer data that are to be processed.

Installment sales contracts Contracts in which a customer agrees to pay for a purchase by paying a certain amount each month for a specific number of months.

Institutional advertising Advertising with the purpose of building a positive image for a company.

Insurance An insurance company promises to pay for certain losses in the future in exchange for regular payment of premiums.

Insurance companies Businesses that calculate the risk of any loss and insure against that loss, in return for the payment of premiums.

Intercorporate stockholding Exists when a corporation holds stock in other corporations—unlawful when it injures competition.

Interest-bearing checking accounts Checking accounts in banks and savings and loans that accrue interest, usually with the stipulation that a minimum balance be kept in the account.

Interest rate The amount of interest charged each year, as a percent of the amount borrowed.

Interlocking directorates An arrangement by which there are identical or overlapping boards of directors for competing firms.

International cartels Nations or international businesses that join together to set production and prices of a specific product.

International money market The supply and demand for money in the international market.

International trade Buying and selling products between nations.

International union An affiliation of local unions; a union with membership in Canada, Mexico, and Central America as well as in the United States.

Interviewing method Information-gathering technique, mainly using personal interviews, telephone interviews, and mail questionnaires.

Inventory control The process that strives to maintain adequate materials while minimizing inventory carrying costs.

Investment banks Financial institutions that purchase large blocks of stock from issuing companies and resell them in the market in small lots.

Investors Individuals who buy stocks and bonds with the expectation of holding them for a relatively long period of time.

Job analysis A systematic collection of all information about a job to determine its requirements.

Job description The description of the requirements of a job, such as the authority it entails, its location, and its major activities.

Job evaluation The systematic process of determining the correct rate of pay for a job in relation to other jobs.

Job performance How well a person carries out the functions of his or her job.

Job specification A detailed list of the personal qualifications needed for a job, such as education, experience, and abilities.

Joint venture Two or more people joining together in ownership for a specific limited purpose. A specialized form of a partnership.

Labor In the economic sense, it represents any human effort in the production process of economic goods and services. In usual business usage, it means employees or unions.

Land In economic terms, it represents any natural resource.

Law A rule of action or conduct created and enforced by government.

Leadership The relationship that exists between two or more people in which one tries to influence the other toward the accomplishment of organizational goals.

Letter of credit A written request that money be advanced or credit be given to a specific person.

Liabilities Debts of an individual or business firm.

Liability insurance Insurance that covers losses due to a person or business being responsible for damage to other property or persons.

Life insurance Insurance that pays when a person dies.

Limited partner A partner who may or may not be active in a business, but who has limited liability. May be a silent, secret, dormant, or nominal partner.

Line-and-staff organization An organization plan that adds specialists or staff personnel who give advice and make recommendations to line managers.

Linear programming A quantitative computer technique that determines how to use limited resources to determine the best solution for a specific problem.

Line of credit An amount of credit a bank determines it will lend without security being pledged.

Line organization The oldest and simplest form of organization plan, especially suited for small organizations. Line managers have general (overall), direct authority, and subordinates report to only one manager.

Loan value   The amount of cash that can be borrowed on a life insurance policy.

Local advertising   Advertising concentrated on the local market segment.

Local union   The primary organizational unit for labor groups.

Lockout   When employees are kept out of a firm until a settlement of a labor dispute is reached.

LIFO (Last In, First Out)   A method of inventory control in which the most recent inventory costs are assigned before earlier costs.

Long-term loans   Debt extending for more than ten years.

Management by objectives   A performance-appraisal plan in which each subordinate sets his or her own goals in conjunction with company goals as a basis for improving performance.

Management development   Training programs designed to provide managers with the opportunity to improve their managerial skills and to provide training for potential managers.

Management Information System   An information system designed to provide management with all information necessary for running a business.

Manufacturer's brand   A national brand owned by a manufacturer and normally distributed on a national scale.

Manufacturing firm   A company that converts raw materials into finished goods for resale.

Margin requirement   The percentage of down payment required by the Federal Reserve on stock and other securities.

Marketing concept   The concept that a firm should have as its basic objective the satisfaction of consumer wants.

Marketing functions   Activities that must be performed for goods and services to move from producer to consumer. Marketing functions include selling, buying, transportation, storage, risk bearing, standardization and grading, financing, and market information.

Marketing process   The performance of business activities that directs the flow of goods or services from producer to consumers to users to satisfy their wants and needs.

Marketing mix   The marketing plan to be followed to satisfy customer wants.

Market segment   The target group of customers to which a firm wishes to appeal.

Marketing research   Study of consumer buying patterns and other phases of business activity that affect the firm in order to gather information that will aid managers in making better decisions.

Matrix organization   An organization structure appropriate for firms that must respond quickly to changing market conditions and are engaged in research and development of new, unique products or projects. A product structure superimposed over a functional structure.

Media   The means by which advertising messages are conveyed.

Median   The value that divides an arrayed list of figures in half.

Mediation   The process of attempting to settle a labor-management dispute through the intervention of a neutral third party.

Merit raise   An incentive plan to reward good employee performance.

Microcomputer   A fourth-generation desk-top, limited storage computer.

Microprocessor   A miniature integrated circuit, sometimes referred to as a "computer on a chip."

Middleman   A business firm or individual that performs the marketing functions in the channel of distribution between the manufacturer and final consumer.

Milline rate   The cost per agate line to reach one million circulation of a newspaper.

Minicomputer   A third-generation digital computer.

Minority   A racial or religious group that is different from the majority group.

Minority Enterprise Program   A program to provide assistance in making business opportunities available to minority group members.

Missionary salesperson   Works with middlemen and their customers and assists in setting up promotional displays or training a sales force.

Mode   The value of greatest concentration in a group of figures.

Monetary policy   Actions of the Federal Reserve that influence the money supply.

Money   A medium of exchange.

Money market funds   Mutual funds that invest in high-yield, short-term debt securities.

Money order   A check purchased at a post office or express office, which is payable at another post office or express office.

Monopoly A type of industry in which there is only one supplier in the market and there is no significant competition from producers of substitutes.

Monopolistic competition A type of industry in which there are substantial numbers of sellers of identical or closely related products that are substitutable.

Morale The mental attitude of employees concerning their work environment.

Motivation The reasons people have for doing things. Most motivation is the result of reward or punishment.

Motivation research A technique designed to discover the underlying motives of consumer behavior.

Multinational corporations Corporations that trade in many countries.

Mutual funds Companies that sell their own stock to obtain money which they invest in the securities market.

National advantage A factor that gives one nation an advantage over others in producing a cheaper product.

Natural monopolies High-fixed-cost industries in which duplication is a waste or increases costs, such as utilities, railroads, telephone companies, etc.

Negotiable instruments Stocks, bonds, promissory notes, etc. that may have their ownership transferred from one party to another party.

Network advertising Messages beamed simultaneously to a large audience covering a wide territory.

No-fault insurance An automobile insurance law that allows motorists to collect benefits from insurance companies regardless of who is at fault in an accident.

Noise pollution High levels of sound that are harmful to humans.

Nominal partner A type of limited partner who actually does not have any ownership of the business but who lends his or her name to the business for a fee.

Nongovernment-issued currency Currency that has credit of the banking system as its basis.

Objectives The goals of a firm such as profit and service.

Observation method Direct observation technique used to gather statistical data, such as counting auto traffic on a certain street.

Occupational Health and Safety Act A federal law enacted in 1970 that is intended to protect the health and safety of workers.

Odd lot Trading in shares of stock in lots of less than one hundred.

Off-line equipment Auxiliary computer hardware, such as key punch, operated independently and detached from the main computer system.

Oligopoly A type of industry in which there are only a few suppliers of identical or closely substitutable products.

On-line equipment Auxiliary computer hardware, such as a printer, directly connected to the computer system.

On-the-job training Training in which trainees are shown how to do a job under actual working conditions.

Open-market operations Buying and selling of bank securities by the Federal Reserve to control the money supply.

Open shop Workers have the right to decide if they desire to become members of a union.

Organization chart The formal structural outline of the company.

Organizing The management function of arranging the people, tasks, and materials necessary for putting plans into operation to meet company objectives.

Output Data that have been processed by a computer.

Over-the-counter market A market for trading securities that does not have a centralized location. Dealers are spread throughout the country and transact their business by telephone.

Owner's equity Assets less liabilities; the amount the owner owns in the business.

Ownership Owning all or some part of a business.

Paper Various types of securities and instruments of debt and ownership.

Participating preferred stock A type of preferred stock that allows preferred stockholders to share in unusually high profits.

Participative leader A leader who attempts to get people actively involved in decisions affecting them.

Participative management program (PMP) A program developed by Motorola designed to enable employees to become involved in issues and problems that confront them and to recommend solutions.

Partnership A business ownership comprised of two or more owners who operate under a mutual agreement. It is not a legal entity form of ownership.

Party-at-interest A person or persons having a vested interest in a business firm.

Par value The stated value on stock. It is an arbitrary amount assigned to stock and has no relationship to either market value or book value. Exists for accounting purposes.

Patent A right to sole production of a product for seventeen years.

Patronage motives The motives that influence a person to return repeatedly to a store to make additional purchases.

Penny stock A highly speculative stock that sells at a low price.

Pension funds Funds set up by company and employee contributions to provide retirement benefits.

Performance appraisal Evaluation of a worker's job performance.

Perpetual inventory An inventory-control system that maintains a running account of materials on hand.

Personal selling The means by which customers are reached on a face-to-face basis.

PERT Program Evaluation and Review Technique, a management process used to plan, schedule, and control projects.

Philosophy of Management Establishes the primary, long-range objectives of a firm and provides the principles, practices, and ethical standards of a firm in its relationship with employees, customers, stockholders, and the community.

Physical distribution The marketing function of moving goods from the place where they are manufactured to where they are sold.

Physiological needs Needs of the body such as food, air, drink, clothing, and shelter.

Picketing The practice of workers marching at the entrance of a firm to protest some management practice.

Planning The management function of formulating in advance the direction a firm is to follow to reach its designated objectives.

Point-of-purchase display A sales promotion technique used especially for calling attention to convenience goods— usually located near checkout counters or near store entrances.

Policies Certificates issued by insurance companies that state the conditions of the insurance.

Preferred stock A certificate of ownership in a corporation that usually receives preferred payment but does not include voting rights.

Premium The amount of money that an insuree pays to an insurer in exchange for risk coverage.

Price The amount of money needed to acquire a good or service.

Price discrimination A vendor granting discounts that are not justified by cost.

Price-earnings ratio The market price of a stock divided by the annual earnings per share.

Primary buying motives The motives that influence the initial recognition of a need for a particular piece of merchandise.

Prime interest rate The rate of interest banks charge their best customers, usually large corporations.

Principal The person from whom an agent's authority derives.

Principles of organization Guides that managers follow to assist them in being more effective and efficient leaders.

Private carrier A carrier that moves its own goods by using its own transportation system.

Probability The chance or odds of something happening.

Processor unit The central processing unit of the computer, containing the storage, control, and arithmetic logic section.

Product dumping A nation's dumping a product in another nation at below-cost prices in order to achieve an overall lower per unit fixed cost.

Product life cycle The life of a product, from introduction through growth and maturity to decline.

Product safety Exists when products are free from contamination and pose no health hazards.

Production control A function that insures the orderly flow of work in manufacturing operations. It determines when, where, and how production of a job will occur.

Production management Management of manufacturing operations, which include inventory control, production control, purchasing, etc.

Production robots Computer-controlled machines that replace humans in the actual production process.

Profit The amount left to a business after all income is received and all expenses are paid. The prime motivator in a private-enterprise economic system.

Profit sharing plans A plan in which a percentage of a company's annual profits are shared with employees.

Promissory note A contract in which one party promises payment of funds borrowed, plus interest, to another party at some specific time.

Promotion Upward movement to a position of more authority, responsibility, and salary.

Promotion mix The four basic channels used by firms to reach their target market: advertising, publicity, personal selling, and sales promotion.

Prospectus A booklet containing all information about a company that would affect the value of new securities it wants to issue.

Property loss insurance Insurance coverage for destruction or damage, dishonesty, or failure of others.

Prosperity A period in the business cycle when the economy is moving upward and sales are increasing.

Publicity Any type of information about a company or a product that has apparent news value, is reported in the different media, and is not paid for by the firm.

Purchasing The process of acquiring materials and supplies.

Pure competition A type of industry in which there are many sellers and each is small relative to the market.

Pure Food and Drug Act A federal law that controls various facets of food and drug sales.

Quality control Inspecting and testing products to insure that only good products are sold to customers.

Quality control circle A small group of employees and managers who meet regularly to discuss production and other task-related problems and solutions.

Quality of work life An approach to management that is designed to improve the total workplace for employees, including the working conditions and opportunities for self-development.

Quota A restriction on the quantity of a product that can enter a nation.

Random sample Exists when every item from a finite universe has an equal and known chance of being selected for the sample.

Rate-of-return on assets Total profit divided by total assets.

Rate-of-return on owner's equity A measure of the amount of profit each dollar of ownership produces.

Rational buying motive A decision to buy that involves conscious thought and deliberation.

Real-time processing Processing data or business transactions as they actually occur, such as in production management.

Recession A period in the business cycle when there is a downturn in business activity.

Recognition needs Human needs to be accepted and recognized as a worthwhile individual by other people.

Recourse Actions available to a party to a contract when the other parties have not fulfilled their obligations.

Recovery A period in the business cycle when economic conditions begin to improve—production increases, sales rise, and unemployment drops.

Rediscount rate The rate at which the Federal Reserve will discount paper for commercial banks who are member banks.

Registered bond A bond on which the owner's name is registered and for which interest payments are automatically sent.

Reserve requirement The percentage of funds banks are required to maintain or deposit with the Federal Reserve system. It is the percentage of funds the banks are not allowed to loan.

Responsibility The duties (tasks) assigned an employee by a manager.

Restraint of trade Actions by business firms that tend to lessen or eliminate competition.

Retailer A firm that buys goods from suppliers and sells them to final users of the product.

Right-to-work laws Laws passed by individual states to permit workers the right to work without having to join a union.

Robinson-Patman Act A federal law that closed certain loopholes in the Clayton Act.

Round lot Trading in shares of stock in lots of 100.

Routing The production control process of identifying the correct order in which production operations must be performed.

Rule of reason A Supreme Court ruling that held that a monopoly was bad only if its conduct was bad.

Safety needs Human needs for safety of the individual and his or her loved ones.

Sales finance companies Financial companies that purchase installment contracts from retailers.

Sales promotion Marketing activities, other than personal selling, advertising, and publicity, that stimulate consumer purchasing and dealer effectiveness; for example, displays, shows, exhibits, and other nonrecurring selling efforts.

Sample A small part of a whole, intended to show the quality or style of the whole.

Savings and loan associations Financial institutions that pay interest to depositors on their deposits and lend that money on low-risk loans.

Scheduling Determining when operations will start and stop at each phase of the production process.

SCORE Service Corps of Retired Executives, a volunteer group of retired managers who advise small-business owners.

Scrambled merchandising A trend in supermarkets to handle increased lines of nonfood items in addition to food lines to increase sales volume and profit.

Seasonal variations Regular, recurring fluctuations within a one-year period.

Secret partner A partner who assumes an active role in a business but is not known to the public as a partner.

Secular trend Long-term growth or decay.

Selective buying motives The motives that enter into the final determination of the specific product purchased.

Self-insurance The retention of enough funds by a business to cover a specific loss.

Self-realization needs Human needs that exist when a concept or philosophy becomes more important than anything else to the individual.

Self-regulation Business firms' policing their own practices by their own initiative.

Selling short Selling a stock and then buying it back at a later date in order to make a profit.

Service Corps of Retired Executives (SCORE) Retired executives who volunteer their services to aid small business owners.

Service firms Businesses that supply intangible commodities, such as hotels, barber and beauty shops, and repair shops.

Service selling The type of selling in which a salesperson assists a consumer in completing a purchase that the consumer has already decided to make.

Sherman Antitrust Act A federal law that prohibits monopoly and price fixing.

Shopping good A good for which price and quality comparisons are usually made before purchase. The price is usually a sizable amount, purchases are made infrequently, and the good is widely advertised.

Silent partner A type of limited partner that does not take part in the management of the business but is known to the public.

Small business Is independently owned, is not dominant in its field of operations, meets specific size standards, and is operated for a profit.

Small Business Administration An agency of the federal government created to assist, encourage, and protect the interests of small businesses.

Social responsibility of business Actions that a business can take that enhance the good of the society in which it exists.

Socialism An economic system in which government owns the basic industries but wholesale, retail, and small manufacturing are owned privately.

Software The programs and all documents associated with a computer.

Sole proprietorship Ownership of a business by one person.

Solid waste pollution Trash and garbage that are not properly disposed of to avoid pollution.

Specialty advertising Sales promotion that involves distributing to customers items of small value, such as pencils or calendars, that contain advertising messages.

Specialty goods Goods that have some unique quality or characteristic, or a high degree of brand identification, which causes consumers to make a concerted effort to purchase them.

Speculators Those who engage in the quick purchase of stock, with the intent of making a profit in a short period of time. There is considerable risk in speculation.

Spot announcements Advertising messages that are broadcast over one or many stations at various times.

Staff personnel Employees with specialized knowledge and skills who advise and provide assistance to line managers.

Staffing The management function concerned with the human resources of the firm.

Stagflation A period of inflation with a decrease in business output and employment.

Standard of living A measure of the wealth of a nation: total production of the nation divided by total population.

State constitutions Documents of individual states that prescribe the form and power of state government within the limits set by the federal constitution.

Statistics The techniques used for collecting, organizing, summarizing, interpreting, and analyzing numerical data and making predictions and forecasts from the data.

Statutes Written laws enacted by legislative bodies.

Stock broker Acts as the middleman between buyers and sellers of stocks.

Stock dividend A payment to stockholders in the form of shares of stock instead of in cash.

Stock exchange The buying and selling of stock for the purpose of making money for the purchasers and sellers of the stock.

Stock market The marketplace where securities are traded.

Stock split Divides the number of shares of stock outstanding into a larger number, such as 4 for 1, in order to lower the price of individual shares of stock and make the stock more attractive to a broader number of investors.

Stockholders Owners of a corporation. Persons who own common or preferred stock of a corporation.

Storage unit The memory of a computer, where data are stored for future reference.

Strike Workers stay off the job, stopping work, to gain their demands. The most effective weapon of labor unions.

Subchapter S corporations Small corporations that are eligible for special tax treatment under Subchapter S of the tax code.

Subcontracting When a contractor enters into contract with another firm to perform part of the function he has contracted to perform.

Supply curve A graph that shows the quantity of a good suppliers will produce at various selling prices.

Supportive selling Selling efforts in which salespersons try to generate good will and provide specialized service rather than try to get orders.

Surety insurance Insures against loss in the event that one party to a contract fails to fulfill its obligation.

Systems approach The arrangement of interrelated parts of the firm to achieve objectives.

Tariff A tax placed on goods imported into a nation.

Team management A form of participative management in which a manager works with employees as a team rather than on a one-to-one basis.

Technical salesperson A specialist who provides technical expertise in installing and servicing equipment, such as computers.

Technical skills The ability of a manager to work with things (as distinguished from people).

Technology The branch of knowledge that deals with applied science and industrial arts. Knowledge in science or industry.

Term insurance A form of life insurance in which a person is insured for the life of the policy in exchange for premiums. If he does not die in that period, the policy ends.

Termination Permanent separation from a company.

Theft insurance Insurance coverage for losses due to stealing of property.

Theory X The part of McGregor's theory that assumes people do not like work and will try to avoid it.

Theory Y The part of McGregor's theory that assumes people do not inherently dislike work and do not try to avoid it.

Theory Z Holds that efficiency might be increased by a number of variables.

Time deposits Savings accounts in commercial banks or in savings and loan associations.

Time management The systematic analysis of how managers use their time.

Time series analysis A statistical technique that relies on historical data to forecast the changes that will take place in business activity in the future.

Time sharing A system that allows a number of users to share computer time by means of on-line terminals.

Trademark The legal right to sole use of a brand name.

Transfer Horizontal movement to a position that may or may not involve more money or responsibility.

Trust companies Companies that receive money and invest it for the benefit of a third party.

Trust receipt A title to goods that remain with a financial institution when it has lent a business money with which to purchase merchandise.

Truth in Lending Law Requires that all business and financial institutions dealing in consumer credit must inform the borrower in writing of (1) the annual interest rate, (2) the total finance charge, (3) the cash price, (4) the down payment, and (5) the total amount charged.

Turnaround time The time it takes to process data and produce the required output.

Tying contract An agreement that requires a customer to buy all future needs of a product from the seller as a condition of current purchasing.

Unfair methods of competition Acts that reduce competition.

Uniform Commercial Code A group of statutes that are recommended to provide some conformity between states' commercial laws.

Union shop A company in which a worker must join the labor union within a stipulated period of time after employment in order to continue working in that position.

United States Constitution The basic law of the United States to which all others must conform.

Unlimited liability A legal obligation of business ownership to use not only what the owner has invested in the business but also all the rest of the owner's assets in order to pay any accumulated debts of the business.

Utility The power of a good or service to satisfy a human want.

Value analysis Appraisal of regularly used items to determine whether the least expensive item that satisfies the purpose is being used in production.

Vendor Seller.

Vestibule training Training given in an area, away from the actual work area, in which a reproduction of the work area is set up.

Voluntary chain A group of retailers who voluntarily associate themselves with a wholesaler to take advantage of volume purchases and discounts.

Warehouse receipt Receipt for goods stored in a warehouse.

Warrant A certificate that gives the holder the right to purchase stocks at a stated price for a specified period of time or perpetually.

Water pollution Fouling of lakes, rivers, and ponds by agricultural runoff, storm sewer runoff, municipal sewage, and industrial plants.

Whole-life insurance A type of life insurance in which a person is insured as long as he or she pays premiums. Can be collected only upon death.

Wholesale firm A firm that buys and resells merchandise primarily to retailers and commercial and industrial users, and does not sell in significant amounts to final users.

Wholesaler The middleman between the producer and final consumer in the channel of distribution.

Word processing Use of computerized machines to improve the efficiency and effectiveness of business communication.

Working capital Funds used in the daily operations of a business for such purposes as payrolls, raw materials, and accounts receivable.

Yellow-dog contract The requirement by an employer that employees agree not to join a union as a condition of employment. This action currently is prohibited by labor legislation.

Zero-based budgeting A management planning technique that requires managers to evaluate all programs and activities each budgeting period instead of building on the performance of the preceding period.

Acknowledgments

COLOR SECTION

x–xi: top left: Charles Harbutt/Archive Pictures, Inc.; top right: Gregory K. Scott, 1979/Photo Researchers, Inc.; center left: John Running/Stock Boston, Inc.; center: Tom McHugh/Photo Researchers, Inc.; center right: Charles Harbutt/Archive Pictures, Inc.; bottom left: Jim Pickerell/Black Star; bottom right: Courtesy: Aluminum Company of America (ALCOA). xii: top: Charles Harbutt/Archive Pictures, Inc.; center: Owen Franken/Stock Boston, Inc.; bottom: Charles Harbutt/Archive Pictures, Inc. xiii: top: Farrell Grehan, 1979/Photo Researchers, Inc.; center: Courtesy of General Motors; bottom: Cary Wolinsky/Stock Boston, Inc. xiv: top: Stuart Cohen/Stock Boston, Inc.; bottom: Cary Wolinsky/Stock Boston, Inc. xv: top: National Football League Properties Inc., Courtesy of The Dallas Cowboy Football Club; center: Ann Hagen Griffiths/Omni-Photo Communications, Inc.; bottom: Ken Hawkins/Sygma. xvi: top: Sharon Beals/Photo Researchers, Inc.; center top: Mark Godfrey/Archive Pictures, Inc.; center bottom: Gerard Rancinan/Sygma; bottom page: Courtesy of Greyhound Lines, Inc. xvii: top: Peter Vandermark/Stock Boston, Inc.; center: John Coletti/Stock Boston, Inc.; bottom: Connie McCollum. xviii: top: Connie McCollum; center: Courtesy of IBM Corporation; bottom: Owen Franken/Stock Boston, Inc. xix: top: Erik Anderson/Stock Boston, Inc.; center: Stephan L. Feldman/Photo Researchers, Inc.; bottom: Mark Godfrey/Archive Pictures, Inc. xx: top: Courtesy of Greyhound Lines, Inc.; center top, center, bottom page: Courtesy of IBM Corporation. xxi: top: Harry Wilks/Stock Boston, Inc.; center: Charles Harbutt/Archive Pictures, Inc.; bottom: Dennis Stock/Magnum Photos, Inc. xxii–xxiii: top left: George Olsen for Levi Strauss, Courtesy Levi Strauss & Company; top center: Cary Wolinsky/Stock Boston, Inc.; top right: Courtesy IBM Corporation. center left: Gregg Mancuso/Stock Boston, Inc.; center right: Allen Green, 1976/Photo Researchers, Inc.; bottom left: John Lei/Stock Boston, Inc.; bottom center: Courtesy of Ideal Basic Industries; bottom right: J. P. Laffont/Sygma.

CHAPTER 1. 3: Charles Harbutt/Archive Pictures, Inc. 17: Gamma Liaison. 25: Courtesy The Dallas Cowboy Football Club.

CHAPTER 2. 27: Stuart Rosner/Stock Boston, Inc. 30: © 1982 by Sidney Harris. 35: Ray Ellis/Rapho Photo Researchers. 38: Ekm Nepenthe/Stock Boston, Inc. 45: Courtesy of the Goodyear Tire & Rubber Company.

CHAPTER 3. 47: Stuart Cohen/Stock Boston, Inc. 50: Paul Fusco/Magnum Photos, Inc. 51, 56: © 1982 Sidney Harris. 64: Courtesy of J.C. Penney Company, Inc.

CHAPTER 4. 67: Christopher Morrow/Stock Boston, Inc. 77: Will McIntyre/Photo Researchers, Inc. 81: © 1982 Sidney Harris. 86–87 (Case A): Reprinted by Permission from U.S. News & World Report, September 14, 1981. Copyright © 1981 by U.S. News & World Report, Inc. 89: Courtesy of Ralston Purina Company.

CHAPTER 5. 91: Charles Harbutt/Archive Pictures, Inc. 93: © 1982 by Sidney Harris. 96 (Exhibit 5–2): Reprinted with permission of Macmillan Publishing Co., Inc. from Human Relations in Business, Third Edition, by Fred J. Carvell. Copyright © 1980, Fred J. Cravell.

CHAPTER 6. 113: Courtesy of General Signal. 119: Courtesy Stockholder Relations Department, Ford Motor Company. 122: © 1982 by Sidney Harris. 125: Eiji Miyazawa/Black Star. 129: Courtesy Stockholder Relations Department, Ford Motor Company.

CHAPTER 7. 131: F. B. Grunzweig/Photo Researchers, Inc. 136: Susan McCartney/Photo Researchers, Inc. 144: © 1982 by Sidney Harris. 148: Courtesy of KFC Corporation.

CHAPTER 8. 155: Anne Hagen Griffiths/Omni Photo Communications, Inc. 161: Raymon Depardon/Magnum Photos, Inc. 167: © 1982 by Sidney Harris. 173: Courtesy The Lincoln Electric Company.

CHAPTER 9. 175: Connie McCollum. 177: © 1982 by Sidney Harris. 191, 199: Courtesy of Snelling & Snelling, Inc.

CHAPTER 10. 201: Burk Uzzle/Magnum Photos, Inc. 206: Bohdan Hrynewychi/Stock Boston, Inc. 216: Mark Godfrey/Archive Pictures, Inc. 217: © 1982 by Sidney Harris. 224: Robert Gumpert.

CHAPTER 11. 231: Mike Mazzaschi/Stock Boston, Inc. 233: © 1982 by Sidney Harris. 240: Courtesy The Gillette Company. 246: Peter Southwick/Stock Boston, Inc. 251: Courtesy of Levi Strauss & Company.

CHAPTER 12. 253: Gabor Demjen/Stock Boston, Inc. 255: From "Chains," Progressive Grocer, Vol. 61, No. 4, April 1982, p. 94. Copyright © Maclean Hunter Media Inc., 1982. 257: Peter Menzel/Stock Boston, Inc. 258: Chart entitled "The 50 Largest Retailing Companies (ranked by sales)," Fortune, July 12, 1982, Vol. 106, No. 1. © 1982 Time Inc. All rights reserved. 259: © 1982 by Sidney Harris. 260: From "Wholesalers," Progressive Grocer, Vol. 61, No. 4, April 1982, p. 110. Copyright © Maclean Hunter Media Inc. 1982. 268: S. Oristaglio, 1981/Photo Researchers, Inc. 278: Courtesy of Mary Kay Cosmetics, Inc.

CHAPTER 13. 281: Courtesy Dart & Kraft, Inc. 283: Charles Harbutt/Archive Pictures, Inc. 284: Reprinted with permission from the September 10, 1981 issue of Advertising Age. Copyright 1981 by Crain Communications., Inc. 290: Otto Kleppner, Advertising Procedure, 6th ed., © 1973, pp. 40–41. Reprinted by permission of Prentice-Hall, Inc., Englewood Cliffs, N.J. 300: Courtesy of the Procter & Gamble Company.

CHAPTER 14. 309: Henri Cartier Bresson/Magnum Photos, Inc. 314, 316: © 1982 by Sidney Harris. 326: Courtesy Wells Fargo Bank.

CHAPTER 15. 329: Ellis Herwig/Stock Boston, Inc. 333: Chart entitled "The 50 Largest Commercial-Banking Companies (ranked by assets)," Fortune, July 12, 1982, Vol. 106, No. 1. © Time Inc. All rights reserved. 335: © 1982 by Sidney Harris. 338: Larry Mulvehill/Photo Researchers, Inc. 345: Courtesy C.I.T. Financial Corporation.

CHAPTER 16. 347: James R. Holland/Stock Boston, Inc. 353: Richard Kalvar/Magnum Photos, Inc. 354: © 1982 by Sidney Harris. 367: Courtesy Merrill Lynch & Company, Inc.

CHAPTER 17. 369: Charles Harbutt/Archive Pictures, Inc. 371: Anestis Diakipoulos/Stock Boston, Inc. 373: © 1982 by Sidney Harris. 381: Chart entitled "The 50 Largest Life-Insurance Companies (ranked by assets)," Fortune, July 12, 1982, Vol. 106, No. 1. © 1982 Time Inc. All rights reserved. 384: © 1982 by Sidney Harris. 389: Courtesy of The Prudential Insurance Company of America.

CHAPTER 18. 397: Mark Godfrey/Archive Pictures, Inc. 400, 414: © 1982 by Sidney Harris. 421: Courtesy of General Motors Corporation.

CHAPTER 19. 423: Ellis Herwig/Stock Boston, Inc. 425: Esaias Baitel/Rapho Photo Researchers. 433: © Leo Cullum. 435: From the table entitled, "Pretax Income in 1975, 1981 and 1982 Necessary to Equal 1970 Aftertax Purchasing Power," in Economic Road Maps, April 1982. Published by The Conference Board. 438: From "Demographics: The Genes of Customer Format Selection," Progressive Grocer, Vol. 60, No. 11, November 1981, p. 55. Copyright © Maclean Hunter Media Inc., 1982. 441: Courtesy of the A. C. Nielsen Company.

CHAPTER 20. 443: Mark Godfrey/Archive Pictures, Inc. 445: Tyrone J. Hall/Stock Boston, Inc. 457: © 1982 by Sidney Harris. 459, 460: Courtesy of IBM Corporation. 461: © 1982 by Sidney Harris. 462: Courtesy of IBM Corporation.

CHAPTER 21. 473: Owen Franken/Stock Boston, Inc. 476: © 1982 by Sidney Harris. 483: Brucelle/Sygma. 485: © 1982 by Sidney Harris. 486: Chart entitled, "The 500 Largest Industrial Corporations Outside the U.S.," Fortune, August 23, 1982. © 1982 Time Inc. All rights reserved. 487: Chart entitled, "The 50 Leading Exporters," Fortune, August 23 1982. © 1982 Time Inc. All rights reserved. 491: Courtesy The Southland Corporation.

CHAPTER 22. 493: Mike Mazzaschi/Stock Boston, Inc. 500: Jerry Berndt/Stock Boston, Inc. 507: Courtesy of The American Telephone & Telegraph Company.

CHAPTER 23. 509: Jeff Albertson/Stock Boston, Inc. 516: © 1982 by Sidney Harris. 520 left, center: Courtesy of the Gillette Company. 520 right: Courtesy Levi Strauss & Company. 524: Courtesy The Gillette Company.

ENDPAPERS: Chart entitled "The 500 Largest Industrial Corporations (ranked by sales)," Fortune, May 3, 1982, Vol. 105, No. 9. © 1982 Time Inc. All rights reserved.

Index

THE 100 LARGEST INDUSTRIAL CORPORATIONS (ranked by sales)

RANK '81	'80	COMPANY	SALES ($000)	ASSETS ($000)	RANK	NET INCOME ($000)	RANK
1	1	**Exxon** (New York)	108,107,688	62,931,055	1	5,567,418	1
2	2	**Mobil** (New York)	64,488,000	34,776,000	3	2,433,000	3
3	3	**General Motors** (Detroit)	62,698,500	38,991,200	2	333,400	57
4	4	**Texaco** (Harrison, N.Y.)	57,628,000	27,489,000	5	2,310,000	5
5	5	**Standard Oil of California** (San Francisco)	44,224,000	23,680,000	7	2,380,000	4
6	6	**Ford Motor** (Dearborn, Mich.)	38,247,100	23,021,400	8	(1,060,100)	490
7	9	**Standard Oil (Indiana)** (Chicago)	29,947,000	22,916,000	9	1,922,000	7
8	8	**International Business Machines** (Armonk, N.Y.)	29,070,000	29,586,000	4	3,308,000	2
9	7	**Gulf Oil** (Pittsburgh)	28,252,000	20,429,000	11	1,231,000	14
10	11	**Atlantic Richfield** (Los Angeles)	27,797,436	19,732,539	13	1,671,290	9
11	10	**General Electric** (Fairfield, Conn.)	27,240,000	20,942,000	10	1,652,000	10
12	15	**E.I. du Pont De Nemours** (Wilmington, Del.)	22,810,000	23,829,000	6	1,401,000	12
13	12	**Shell Oil** (Houston)	21,629,000	20,118,000	12	1,701,000	8
14	13	**International Telephone & Telegraph** (New York)	17,306,189	15,052,377	16	676,804	24
15	16	**Phillips Petroleum** (Bartlesville, Okla.)	15,966,000	11,264,000	20	879,000	17
16	17	**Tenneco** (Houston)	15,462,000	16,808,000	14	813,000	19
17	18	**Sun** (Radnor, Pa.)	15,012,000	11,822,000	19	1,076,000	16
18	20	**Occidental Petroleum** (Los Angeles)	14,707,543	8,074,543	28	722,216	22
19	19	**U.S. Steel** (Pittsburgh)	13,940,500	13,316,100	17	1,077,200	15
20	21	**United Technologies** (Hartford)	13,667,758	7,555,103	32	457,686	37
21	23	**Standard Oil (Ohio)** (Cleveland)	13,457,091	15,743,296	15	1,946,898	6
22	22	**Western Electric** (New York)	13,008,000	8,338,300	25	711,300	23
23	26	**Getty Oil** (Los Angeles)	12,887,360	9,536,356	22	856,865	18
24	25	**Dow Chemical** (Midland, Mich.)	11,873,000	12,496,000	18	564,000	31
25	24	**Procter & Gamble** (Cincinnati)	11,416,000	6,961,000	35	593,000	29
26	32	**Chrysler** (Highland Park, Mich.)	10,821,600	6,270,000	38	(475,600)	489
27	28	**Union Oil of California** (Los Angeles)	10,745,900	7,592,800	31	791,400	20
28	29	**Eastman Kodak** (Rochester, N.Y.)	10,337,000	9,446,000	23	1,239,000	13
29	31	**Dart & Kraft** (Northbrook, Ill.)	10,211,000	5,053,800	56	347,500	53
30	27	**Union Carbide** (Danbury, Conn.)	10,168,000	10,423,000	21	649,000	27
31	30	**Boeing** (Seattle)	9,788,200	6,953,700	36	473,000	35
32	35	**R.J. Reynolds Industries** (Winston-Salem, N.C.)	9,765,700	8,096,000	27	767,800	21
33	43	**Amerada Hess** (New York)	9,396,219	6,321,581	37	212,591	92
34	34	**Westinghouse Electric** (Pittsburgh)	9,367,500	8,316,200	26	438,000	40
35	40	**Ashland Oil** (Russell, Ky.)	9,262,076	4,097,433	68	90,032	204
36	39	**Marathon Oil** (Findlay, Ohio)	9,219,991	5,993,623	41	343,059	55
37	33	**Caterpillar Tractor** (Peoria, Ill.)	9,154,500	7,284,900	33	578,900	30
38	36	**Goodyear Tire & Rubber** (Akron, Ohio)	9,152,905	5,354,259	50	260,295	73
39	44	**Cities Service** (Tulsa)	8,899,300	6,048,500	40	(49,200)	478
40	42	**LTV** (Dallas)	8,822,700	4,332,700	63	386,300	45
41	37	**Beatrice Foods** (Chicago)	8,772,804	4,236,555	65	304,211	65
42	38	**Xerox** (Stamford, Conn.)	8,691,000	7,674,400	30	598,200	28
43	45	**Philip Morris** (New York)	8,306,600	9,245,300	24	676,200	25
44	41	**RCA** (New York)	8,004,800	7,856,700	29	54,000	274
45	53	**McDonnell Douglas** (St. Louis)	7,384,900	4,364,200	62	176,600	109
46	49	**International Harvester** (Chicago)	7,327,165	5,346,122	51	(393,128)	487
47	47	**Bethlehem Steel** (Bethlehem, Pa.)	7,298,000	5,282,100	53	210,900	95
48	46	**Rockwell International** (Pittsburgh)	7,039,700	4,809,000	59	291,800	68
49	54	**PepsiCo** (Purchase, N.Y.)	7,027,443	4,057,061	69	333,456	56
50	48	**Monsanto** (St. Louis)	6,947,700	6,069,200	39	445,100	39